12⁹⁵

The Battle of the Books

Before the Title of the Battle.

The frontispiece to Swift's *Battle of the Books* (1710), reproduced by permission of Cornell University Libraries

Joseph M. Levine

THE BATTLE OF
THE BOOKS

*History and Literature in
the Augustan Age*

Cornell University Press

ITHACA AND LONDON

PUBLICATION OF THIS BOOK WAS ASSISTED BY A GRANT FROM
THE PUBLICATIONS PROGRAM OF THE NATIONAL ENDOWMENT
FOR THE HUMANITIES, AN INDEPENDENT FEDERAL AGENCY.

First published 1991 by Cornell University Press.
First printing, Cornell Paperbacks, 1994.

International Standard Book Number 0-8014-2537-9 (cloth)
International Standard Book Number 0-8014-8199-6 (paper)
Library of Congress Catalog Card Number 90-55735
Printed in the United States of America
*Librarians: Library of Congress cataloging information
appears on the last page of the book.*

⊗ The paper in this book meets the minimum requirements
of the American National Standard for Information Sciences—
Permanence of Paper for Printed Library Materials, ANSI Z39.48-1984.

Contents

vii

Illustrations

Acknowledgments

Parts of chapter 6 appeared in my article "The Battle of the Books and the Shield of Achilles," *Eighteenth-Century Life* 9 (1984): 33–61; and chapter 8 appeared as "Bentley's Milton: Philology and Criticism in Eighteenth-Century England," *Journal of the History of Ideas* 50 (1989): 549–68. I am grateful to the editors of both journals for allowing me to use them here. Readers may find echoes of two other pieces written long ago: "Ancients, Moderns, and History," in *Studies in Change and Revolution*, edited by Paul Korshin (Menston, Yorkshire: Scolar Press, 1972); and "Ancients and Moderns Reconsidered," *Eighteenth-Century Studies* 15 (1981): 72–89, where I first set forth some of the ideas in this book, and I am grateful to their editors as well for any reminiscences that may appear here. I am also much indebted to Syracuse University for time and support for a work that has been long in the making, and to the John Simon Guggenheim Foundation for a precious fellowship. In the later stages of writing and rewriting, I enjoyed the hospitality of two great institutions whose staffs and facilities were wonderfully helpful: the Center for Advanced Study in the Visual Arts, Washington, D.C., and the Institute for Advanced Study, Princeton. And I was able to use a part of my Guggenheim fellowship for a last revision. I owe a particular debt to Anthony Grafton, who read the manuscript and offered many valuable suggestions, and to many other friends who gave encouragement and criticism over the years, especially Donald Kelley and Michael Harris. My greatest debt, as always, is to my family: to my wife, DeeDee, and to my children, Peter and Caroline, who have read and criticized as well as lived with this work from the very beginning.
I hope I may follow it soon with another that will treat some of the other issues and separate events in the quarrel between the ancients and the moderns which I have been forced to omit here. But it may perhaps be better to keep in mind

the cautionary words of John Dryden. "The promises of authors that they will write again," he warned, "are, in effect, a threatening of their readers with some new impertinence: and they, who perform not what they promise, will have their pardon on easy terms."

JOSEPH M. LEVINE

Syracuse, New York

The Battle of the Books

Introduction

In the pages that follow, I shall retell a story that was once famous, although it is now largely forgotten or misunderstood. It began quietly in London in 1690 with an apparently innocuous event, the publication of a slight and rather commonplace essay by a retired English country gentleman, Sir William Temple. In a short time the air was filled with books and pamphlets, charges and countercharges, high principle and low invective. It was the beginning of one of the more raucous events in English intellectual history. It is what Jonathan Swift called the battle of the books.

The ground had been well-prepared. For centuries an argument had been drawing gradually to a head between the rival claims of the ancients and the moderns. Were the Greeks and Romans superior in all the ways of life and thought to everything that followed after? Or had the moderns in one field or another succeeded in equaling or surpassing them? Suddenly Temple's essay seemed to focus all attention on the problem. For a moment it looked almost as if the fate of Western civilization hung in the balance: whether to go forward to something new and better, an advancement of learning and a material culture beyond anything hitherto known, or whether to continue to hanker after a golden age in the past and to lament the decadence of the modern world. More practically, it seemed necessary to know whether to abide by the rules and examples of classical life and literature in coming to grips with the modern world or whether to be allowed to exercise some measure of freedom and invention. For decades the commotion continued unabated, as nearly every literate Englishman thought to offer his opinion and join the fray. Nor was the argument confined to England. Across the Channel an equally acrimonious and perhaps even noisier quarrel started up at much the same time. Then in the 1730s the storm subsided and a superficial calm succeeded. To all appearances the argument was over, although neither side had won an outright victory.

Indeed, the battle ended pretty much in a draw, whatever the combatants preferred to think, either then or now. Temple and Swift had claimed all the arts and sciences for antiquity, but long before the quarrel was over, the field was divided. All those activities that seemed to work by accumulation, such as the sciences and philosophy, were won for the moderns, while all those that seemed to depend upon imitation, such as literature and the arts, were left securely in the hands of the ancients. For a long time almost everyone was satisfied with this compromise, content to be half an ancient and half a modern, although the halves were not always equal.

Or so it appeared. On closer inspection, it seems that one area was not so easily amenable to this arrangement. As the quarrel developed, it became quickly apparent that one of the principal grounds of battle was history, and that no one was quite sure whether history belonged to the cumulative or to the imitative arts, to the ancients or to the moderns. Here was one difficulty that was not so easily resolved and that would not go away, a lasting and problematical legacy of the battle of the books. How had it happened?

The fact is that from the very beginning, Renaissance humanism and the revival of antiquity concealed a paradox. On the one hand, the humanists had resurrected the classics for immediate use and set about imitating them for the practical purposes of their own time and place. They valued them especially for their literary merit and soon renewed the techniques and methods of ancient rhetoric. On the other hand, the recovery of the ancient authors seemed to require, in order to make sense of them, the recovery of the whole world in which they lived and worked and wrote. As a result, Renaissance scholars invented many of the techniques and methods of modern philology. But the two purposes, which had started out in harmony, in the end proved incompatible. To the extent that the humanists had exalted ancient authority, they elevated the classics to a universal timeless status and made them modern, even while in their scholarship some of them began to chip away insidiously at the props that underlay that view of the ancient world. They began to perceive anomalies in the old authors, and something of their strangeness—and so set them at a distance. Thus the insistence on idealizing the ancients encountered—and to some extend arrested—the developing modernist sense of history. In time a fissure opened up between imitation and scholarship, rhetoric and philology, literature and history. There seemed to be no avoiding a choice, although some generous spirits tried to patch up the difficulty and reconcile the two sides. It is clear that the moment of self-consciousness in England, when all this latent antipathy came to a head, arose during the battle of the books.

In the following pages, I have chosen to retell this story and claim it for the history of ideas. It is curious that no one has done so before. Of course, the battle of the books is sometimes remembered by students of literature, if only from the works of Jonathan Swift. But Swift was himself a partisan, hostile to modernity and indifferent to the claims of history, and he wrote long before the quarrel was over. Nor have modern students done much better, content on the whole to see the quarrel as mere literary background, as a context perhaps for the works of Swift and Pope. In the one instance in which a real effort was made to rescue the quarrel for the history of ideas, the attempt was, I think, vitiated by an uncritical acceptance of the claims of modernity. The works of R. F. Jones once held the field but have finally outlived their usefulness. Jones was a pioneer in charting the relationship between literature and science and he was right to see the battle as one episode in the larger quarrel between the ancients and the moderns; but his perspective was one-sided and he misconstrued and sometimes ignored some of the more significant issues.[1] Nor did he ever read beyond the printed sources. No argument, I suppose, and very few propositions from the past can properly be understood in the absence of the questions addressed and the view from the other side; and in this case, there is a wealth of evidence beyond the published sources, in contemporary letters and documents, to illuminate the issues. It is one of the attractions of the subject that it can be described so closely, that the genesis and course of the argument can be calculated so exactly, and that its effects upon a contemporary audience can be so clearly charted. It is another that it is possible to retrieve the motives and personalities of many of the participants and so give some life to the occasion. I only hope that in my desire to recover the details and suggest the lasting significance of the quarrel, I have not altogether spoiled the fun and lost the contemporary amusement that so often attended it.

Intellectual history is not usually cast as narrative, but there are some undeniable advantages to telling a story, particularly when the subject is of combat. Swift was undoubtedly right to use a military metaphor, although he deliberately transformed his tale into a fiction. Needless to

---

[1] I have considered Jones's work and other pertinent matters in "Ancients and Moderns Reconsidered," *Eighteenth-Century Studies* 15 (1981): 72–89. Jones wrote about the subject in "The Background of the Battle of the Books," *Washington University Studies* 7 (1920): 99–162, partly reprinted in *The Seventeenth Century* (Stanford, 1951), pp. 10–40; and *Ancients and Moderns*, 2d ed. (St. Louis, 1961). In neither case did he devote much space to the battle itself. The account by Anne E. Burlingame is very slight, *The Battle of the Books in Its Historical Setting* (New York, 1920).

say, there is a sense in which every argument can be seen as a contest and all intellectual history as a struggle of competing ideas for victory on one battlefield or another. If that is the case, then what we should probably want to know first about past ideas is how they arose in response to immediate problems, what the alternative choices were, and to what extent they came into collision. To try to recover the answers without the questions and the propositions without their alternatives is almost certain to lead to anachronism.[2] And this, I fear, has been the particular misfortune of both the ancients and the moderns in the battle of the books. The "ancients," in their commitment to ancient authority, seem to have become largely inscrutable to the present, while the moderns turn out to be much less modern than they have been made out to be. But it is likely that a good deal of intellectual history has been too abstract—too remote from the battlefield—to permit us to grasp the meaning and the reality of past events. Still, the proof is in the pudding, and in what follows I shall try to use all the resources of narrative to tell the tale of this quarrel: to recount its several episodes in their temporal and causal succession; to describe the concrete relations between characters and events; to restore as far as possible the motives and intentions of the many participants; and finally, to set the precise scene and situation for each stage in the story.

I have chosen to begin deliberately *in medias res*. This device may disappoint the reader who would like to know more about the intellectual background—about that very long story of the quarrel between the ancients and the moderns which lies behind the climactic episodes of the battle of the books and the French *querelle*. Fortunately, there is now a good literature on the subject that allows us to trace some of the antecedents of the conflict back to antiquity itself and then forward through the Middle Ages (when there were several eruptions of the controversy) to the Italian Renaissance and beyond, when it became indigenous to Western Europe.[3] The most awkward problem, it seems to me, in furnishing

---

[2]This is controversial territory, I am aware. I have set out some further thoughts on the subject in "Method in the History of Ideas: More, Machiavelli, and Quentin Skinner," *Annals of Scholarship* 3 (1986): 37–60.

[3]See, for example, Hippolyte Rigault, *Histoire de la querelle des anciens et des modernes* (Paris, 1856); Henri d'Andeli, *The Battle of the Seven Arts*, ed. Joel Paetow (Berkeley, 1914); Albert Zimmermann, ed., *Antiqui und moderni* (Seiten, 1974); August Buck, "Aus der Vorgeschichte der Querelle des anciens et des modernes in Mittelalter und Renaissance," *Bibliothèque d'humanisme et Renaissance* 20 (1958): 527–41; Hans Baron, "The Querelle of the Ancients and the Moderns as a Problem for Renaissance Scholarship," *Journal of the History of Ideas* 20 (1959): 3–22; Robert Black, "Ancients and Moderns in the Renaissance: Rhetoric and History in Accolti's *Dialogue on the Preeminence of Men of His Own Time*," *Journal of the History of Ideas* 43 (1982): 3–32; Abraham C. Keller, "Ancients and Moderns in the Early Seventeenth Century," *Modern Language Quarterly* 11 (1950): 79–82; Hubert Gillot, *La Querelle des anciens et des modernes en France* (Paris, 1914); Giacinto Margiotta, *Le Origini italiane de la querelle des anciens et des modernes* (Rome, 1953); José Antonio Maravall, *Antiguos*

an appropriate background, is to explain the "ancients," and so make intelligible again the party that first endorsed the revival and imitation of antiquity and made it seem plausible to the ruling classes of Western Europe. What was the appeal of the Greek and Latin classics throughout the early modern period? How did they live on from place to place and from generation to generation? Why, finally, was the challenge so relatively ineffectual that modernism had to await its full victory only in our own time?

At least the contemporary answer was clear and forthright. From the Italian humanists to the English humanists and beyond, there was complete agreement that the classics were meant to instruct the young in all that was required to govern. From Thomas Elyot in the sixteenth century to William Pitt in the eighteenth, the justification does not seem to alter.[4] The best, the only political education, is a training in the classical authors. Latin and Greek are the keys to a treasure chest of wisdom and examples, unmatched by anything afterward. The student must model himself on his ancient predecessors for style and substance, in his speech and his behavior, and he is not likely to surpass them. Perfection can only be imitated. The goal is eloquence joined to moral and political wisdom. It is a renewal of the Ciceronian ideal of *humanitas* and the means are the classical humanities: grammar and rhetoric, poetry, history, and moral philosophy. Nor does it take long apparently for theory to be translated into practice at court and in the grammar schools. Already under Queen Elizabeth the curriculum is determined that will govern English education for two or three centuries. And it is deliberately restricted to the literature of classical Greece and Rome, with everything else set intentionally to one side. (Thus the seeds of modernity were left to germinate outside the schools in the new science and the grand old rivalry of the "two cultures.")[5] The best background to the battle of the books is therefore the history of education under the Tudors and Stuarts; and the first indication of modern resistance, as also its final triumph, appear invariably as challenges to the classical curriculum.

This, in brief, was the contemporary justification for the revival of antiquity, which can be illustrated from the curriculum itself, from a

---

y modernos (Madrid, 1966); Werner Krauss and Hans Kortum, eds., *Antike und Moderne in der Literaturdiskussion des 18. Jahrhunderts* (Berlin, 1966); Cesare Vasoli, "La Première Querelle des anciens et des modernes aux origines de la Renaissance," in *Classical Influences on European Culture*, ed. R. R. Bolgar (Cambridge, 1976), pp. 67–80.

[4]Sir Thomas Elyot, *The Boke Named the Governour* (London, 1531); William Pitt, *Letters Written by the Late Earl of Chatham to His Nephew Thomas Pitt* (London, 1804).

[5]See "Natural History and the New Philosophy: Bacon, Harvey, and the Two Cultures," in my *Humanism and History: The Origins of Modern English Historiography* (Ithaca, N.Y., 1987), pp. 123–54.

hundred manuals and textbooks, and from a chorus of comments by the statesmen and governors who enthusiastically endorsed (and paid for) the program of the ancients. If there was any dissent, it was generally halfhearted and occasional and to little effect. But does this explanation suffice? No doubt it requires a feat of imagination to recover the old conviction that it is the pedantic imitation of classical authors that is the only truly practical vocation, and that it is the natural sciences that are open to question as mere "curiosity." But so it appeared, to the ancients themselves (to Quintilian, for example, who drew up the first surviving syllabus of *ancienneté*), and now again to their early modern counterparts, the ancients of our story.[6] And it would be unwise to dismiss this defense of antiquity out of hand, because it no longer suits either our own practical sensibilities or our historical sense. No doubt it depended originally on an imagined affinity between the conditions of ancient political society and modern Europe; but it was not all illusion, for the affinity had its source in real life. It was real to the extent that the textures of political life in Augustan Rome and Augustan England were in fact similar (certainly more similar than anything in between) and required many of the same skills and abilities for success. In both instances, the education of eloquence provided just what the statesmen and ambassadors needed to perform their duties. But it was also imagined to the extent that the ancient world was idealized in the writings it left behind and in the way they were read in early modern Europe. What is beyond doubt is that when the eighteenth-century English gentleman read the letters of (say) Cicero or Pliny the Younger, he discovered in them a mirror image of himself and he naturally identified with his ancient Roman forebears. And in Pliny's case, he found not only the example of a Roman gentleman but of an ancient, already nostalgic for a golden age, and so ready (like the schoolmaster Quintilian) to teach him the meaning of *ancienneté*.[7] But it was a style of life and an outlook on culture, not a specific political posture, that gave the Greeks and Romans their general modern appeal. And so it is not possible, I think, to distinguish either the ancients or the moderns by their specific political allegiance; and we shall find Whigs and Tories, Protestants and Catholics, republicans and nonjurors, and nearly everyone else on both sides of the argument.

If this is right, then it was only when that delicate balance between a

[6]I shall borrow this expression for "ancientness" in the absence of a convenient English word. And I shall use the term ancients henceforth (without quotation marks) to apply both to the classical authors and to their modern counterparts in the hope that the context will make the different meanings clear.

[7]For Pliny, see the English translations by John Henley (1724), William Melmoth (1746), and the Earl of Orrery (1751), the latter two very popular; for Cicero see my article "*Et Tu Brute?* History and Forgery in Eighteenth-Century England," in *Fakes and Frauds*, ed. Robin Myers and Michael Harris (London, 1989), pp. 73–99.

real and imagined affinity of ancient and modern worlds disappeared, when the tension between the facts of political life and the classical ideal grew too great to bear, that the ancients lost their cause and finally gave way to modernity. We shall find, however, that this defeat did *not* occur during the battle of the books, or indeed for a long time afterward, although it was indeed just then that this new specter of modernity first began to haunt the quarrel and threaten its dissolution. Modern historical scholarship had developed by 1700 to the point where it was capable of calling into question the very foundations of *ancienneté*, but it was unwilling, as long as the classics still seemed to teach their practical lessons, to follow through and expose the gap between the ancient and modern worlds as finally unbridgeable. In the end, the moderns, those same scholarly innovators who fought in the battle of the books, were too much ancients at heart to give full play to their potentially revolutionary insights. What was required, I believe, was that both the real and the imagined affinity between ancients and moderns had to be dissolved together, as (sometime in the nineteenth century) the conditions of real political life and historical consciousness finally and irreparably altered. But that is to go beyond the limits of our story.

Here, then, is the battle of the books, the tale of one particular succession of events in the intellectual history of England between 1690 and about 1740. I have divided it for convenience into two parts. In the first, I have concentrated on the quarrel between literature and historical learning, beginning with Temple's little essay and William Wotton's large reply, and proceeding through the opening rounds of the controversy. I have gone on to describe the growing outcry when Richard Bentley took on the wits of Christ Church in what was probably the noisiest episode in the quarrel, the contest over the fraudulent epistles of Phalaris, during which Swift joined the fray and parodied the events. But the story cannot be left to end there; the quarrel between the men of learning and the men of taste continued for at least another generation, and I have tried to track its course in the arguments between Pope and his critics first over Homer, then over Shakespeare and Milton. In all this I have tried to attend to the many forgotten scholars who represented the moderns and the many minor wits who fought for the ancients, as well as to their more famous counterparts.

In the second part, I have reconsidered the argument from the vantage point of history, for whatever else then seemed to be in question, it was history—how to understand, reconstruct, and use the past—that was undoubtedly at the heart of the matter. Certainly both the ancients and the moderns had much to say about the subject; they had equally strong and antithetical ideas about the character, purpose, and method of historical writing, and they both wrote lots of history during the course of the battle. I have tried, therefore, to examine some part of that large literature to see how their views both reflected and advanced the issues in the quarrel and through it the historical consciousness of the entire period. I have begun with theory, with the opposing views of the two sides about the way history should be written and read. The ancients, as one might guess, advocated that modern history be written in imitation of the histories of Greece and Rome, according to the rules and examples of ancient rhetoric. (Needless to say, they saw no point in rewriting the classics.) They continued to believe that history was a branch of literature. To some extent the moderns agreed, though they were always more optimistic about the consequences. They accepted the continuing usefulness of historical narrative for practical life but thought that it might be possible to equal or surpass the ancients at it. At the same time, they offered a new and alternative way of arriving at knowledge of the past through the modern sciences of philology and antiquities, or what we might prefer to call classical scholarship and archaeology. By 1700 they were exultant at the opportunities afforded by these cumulative disciplines to go beyond anything that previous generations had known about the past, and they were prepared to challenge the ancients even on their own ground of ancient history, as well as everywhere else. As a consequence, both the ancients and the moderns undertook vast schemes for making their views good, and each succeeded in publishing some memorable works. I have taken advantage of the great wealth of documentary material that survives (much of it still in manuscript) to describe the making of these remarkable histories from conception to publication. The history of history has not often been given its due, and I have tried here and throughout this book to suggest some of the ways in which historical writing and thinking were bound up intimately with the general culture of the Augustans, both reflecting and contributing to its basic assumptions—and to ours.

For practical reasons, and to keep within the confines of an already large volume, it has seemed best to leave out some important matters. I have therefore skimped on the background and the ultimate destiny of the quarrel. I have also neglected much of what was going on contemporaneously both abroad and at home in that other parallel world of science and philosophy, except when it impinged directly on the conflict. Both sides drew immediately upon French sources, and I have made some effort to take that into account. But the great controversy over science and philosophy seems to have gone on quite independently of the battle of the books; it had, I believe, a separate origin, addressed different issues, and generally involved other combatants, although for one brief and distracting moment it converged on the battle. I have in any case written about that problem elsewhere and I hope to return to it on another occasion.[8] The advantage of concentrating all attention on the battle itself is that it throws into relief a single set of related issues—about the tension between literature and history and about the meaning and usefulness of the humanities—that seemed crucial then and still reverberate now. And it has the added virtue, I hope, of recovering an integral story, one that may prove, as the Augustans liked to say, both entertaining and instructive.

[8]See my *Dr. Woodward's Shield: History, Science, and Satire in Augustan England* (Berkeley, 1977).

PART ONE

LITERATURE

Chapter One

Wotton vs. Temple

I

Thomas Babington Macaulay was not really fair to William Temple. In his forthright and partisan way, he drew his character. He thought that Temple was cold and selfish, cautious to a fault, even cowardly. The great man, it appeared, had betrayed the Whig cause at its decisive moment. From 1680, he had preferred his library and his orchard to the risks of opposition. "While the nation groaned under oppression, or resounded with the tumult and with the din of arms," Temple, he wrote, had amused himself "by writing memoirs and tying up apricots." Yet beneath Macaulay's contempt there lay a skulking admiration. Even he could not deny the successes of Temple's earlier career or his distinguished literary retirement. In an age of almost universal political corruption, Temple alone had kept his integrity. Somehow he was a more complex and a more admirable man than Macaulay was willing to allow.[1]

In some ways he was typical of his generation. He had been born in 1628, the grandson of a secretary to Philip Sidney, the son of an Irish

[1]Thomas Babington Macaulay, "Sir William Temple" (1838), in *The Complete Works* (New York, 1898), 14:166–283. Several full-length studies of Temple have been published, beginning with Thomas P. Courtenay, *Memoirs of the Life, Works, and Correspondence of Sir William Temple*, 2 vols. (London, 1836), the occasion for Macaulay's essay. See also Clara Marburg, *Sir William Temple* (New Haven, 1932); Homer E. Woodbridge, *Sir William Temple: The Man and His Works* (New York, 1940); Pierre Marambaud, *Sir William Temple*, Publications de la faculté des lettres et sciences humaines de Nice 3 (Nice, 1968). There is a flattering contemporary account by Abel Boyer, *Memoirs of the Life and Writings of Sir William Temple* (London, 1714). Less helpful is the brief biography by Richard Faber, *The Brave Courtier: Sir William Temple* (London, 1983), and the brief literary survey by Robert C. Steensma, *Sir William Temple* (New York, 1970).

privy councillor and member of the Long Parliament. His education was characteristic: grammar school under one Mr. Leigh, "to whom he us'd to say he was beholding for all he knew of Latin and Greek"; Emmanuel College Cambridge under Dr. Cudworth, the famous Platonist; some time abroad learning French and Spanish; and at last, return to London for the life of a "young and idle man," as was then the fashion.[2] Of his Latin and Greek, his sister recalled, he had retained the first perfectly but "often regretted to have lost any part of the other." Of his university education there was perhaps less to say. Cudworth could have taught him "the harsh studies of logick and phylosophy," but his humor was too lively. He preferred entertainments, particularly tennis. His French and Spanish were more successful and while abroad he made his first tentative efforts to write. In those years, his sister remembered, he "read much and writt, both verses and some other short Essays upon severall subjects."[3]

Temple's early essays show a taste and a point of view that forecast his maturity. The young man was no scholar; his reading was wide, not deep; literary, not scientific. He was from the beginning a gentleman and man of taste. And from the first (1652), he displayed a contempt for the modern achievement. Contemporary learning he believed so corrupted and confused "that hee knowes most who knows as much as the ancients taught us."[4] Typically, however, he rebelled against Aristotle, still the authority at the university in philosophy and natural science. He preferred Plato to the "philosophicall Tyrant," and Epicurus to both. Among the moderns he enjoyed Montaigne. For a fleeting moment Temple seems to have considered the Baconian rebellion against authority, but he later recanted.[5] Meanwhile his own style was already forming, a style universally admired in its time. Macaulay thought it lucid and melifluous, rising sometimes into "Ciceronian magnificence."[6] At the Restoration, Temple began his political career modestly in the Irish Par-

---

[2]Lady Gifford, "Life and Character of Sir William Temple," in *The Early Essays and Romances of Sir William Temple*, ed. C. Moore Smith (Oxford, 1930), pp. 4–5. Leigh's school "was an excellent Nursery that supplied both Universities with great Numbers of Gentlemen, who proved eminent in Divinity, Law, and Physick, and some in matters of state": Sir Henry Chauncy, *The Historical Antiquities of Hertfordshire* (London, 1700), p. 169.

[3]Lady Gifford in *Early Essays*, pp. 6, 8. Temple remembered his college fondly in later years and faithfully sent it presentation copies of his various works; see Woodbridge, *Sir William Temple*, p. 11. Despite Temple's disclaimer, Cudworth's teaching seems to have left a strong impression on him, as we shall see.

[4]Temple, *Early Essays*, p. 144.

[5]See Woodbridge, *Sir William Temple*, p. 145.

[6]Macaulay, "Sir William Temple," p. 216. For other testimonies in favor of Temple's style, see Courtenay, *Memoirs*, 2:255–61; J. E. Spingarn, Introduction to *Sir William Temple's Essays* (Oxford, 1909), p. 4. And for a modern analysis, see Marambaud, *Sir William Temple*.

liament but did not let it interrupt his self-education. "He use to say he ow'd the greatest part of what he knew both of Phylosophy and Story, to the five years he pass'd then in Ireland."[7] At length, in 1665, he was chosen ambassador to Münster and after that to Brussels. His career as a diplomat was fairly launched; his preliminary education was complete.

Just how typical and how appropriate Temple's education was in the seventeenth century we shall have to see. But for the man of affairs it was the general conviction that the best formal education was an education in the classical authors. Although law and the modern languages were thought to be useful also, it was the literature of antiquity, the prose and poetry of the Greek and Latin classical authors, that was given preeminence in the training of the future statesman. This was the invariable theme of gentlemen's manuals, educational handbooks, and political treatises. Temple had met the ancients first in grammar school—no moderns were allowed there. And if his Greek failed him afterward, he continued to read and occasionally to translate and imitate the classical works in Latin and English for the rest of his days.[8] It is true that on occasion he read other things—his curiosity extended to such exotic cultures as ancient China and Peru—but his standards for life and for literature had been molded in his youth and borrowed from antiquity, from the Latin writers especially. If he was no scholar, his interest in the classics was as abiding as he thought it was immediately useful.

His diplomatic successes were swift and extraordinary. He helped to author the Triple Alliance in 1668, "the only good public thing," according to Pepys, "that hath been done since the King came into England." At a stroke he became famous.[9] Throughout the decade 1670–1680 he continued to foster the Dutch alliance and negotiated several treaties. With his remarkable wife, Dorothy Osborne, he assisted in the match between William of Orange and Princess Mary. He declined to become secretary of state on several occasions, devised a promising revision of the Privy Council, and in general played a useful and statesmanlike role in a trying period. Even Macaulay had to admit that he had occupied a high position in times of misgovernment without once being guilty of any disgraceful subservience or corruption. If only he had continued on that course!

[7]Lady Gifford, *Early Essays*, p. 8.

[8]See, for example, "Virgil's Last Eclogue translated or rather imitated at the desire of Lady Gifford (1666)," with some Horatian imitations and other poems, in Sir William Temple, *A Select Collection of Poems*, ed. J. Nichols (London, 1780), 2:33–87. Temple seems to have printed some of his poems privately in 1697: Courtenay, *Memoirs*, 2:106–8; Woodbridge, *Sir William Temple*, pp. 148–53.

[9]See J. de Witt to Temple, April 27, 1668, in Herbert Rowan, "John de Witt and the Triple Alliance," *Journal of Modern History* 26 (1954): 2. Rowan finds Temple's contemporary reputation overrated; but see now K. H. D. Haley, *An English Diplomat in the Low Countries: Sir William Temple and Jehan de Witt, 1665–1672* (Oxford, 1986).

Instead he retired abruptly in 1680. Despite his considerable achievement, the tide was against him; Charles II's interest was all French. By
1680 Temple was beaten and he knew it. "I have had, in twenty years
experience," he wrote, "enough of the uncertainty of Princes, the
caprices of fortune, the violence of factions, the unsteadiness of counsels,
and the infidelity of friends." He retired to the gardens of Moor Park in
Surrey. He had no regrets at leaving behind "those airy visions which
have so long busied my head about mending the world." He would
mend himself first; he had time now to read again and to write.[10] The
French traveler Muralt, who visited him, was all admiration for the
house and gardens, the air and the solitude, "free from Business," yet
with a "few Servants and some People of Sence to keep him
Company."[11]

Not that he had ever abandoned literature. For Temple, the man of
affairs and the man of letters were one. What drew them together, according to the traditional view, was the idea of eloquence, the classical
notion resumed by the Renaissance humanists. As Cicero, to choose the
most obvious example, had taught and exemplified, the best statesman
was the best orator; the most successful politician was the most persuasive speaker and writer. Temple admired Cicero, as did all his generation, moderns as well as ancients, and Temple owed his own successes in
large measure to his ability to write and to persuade. His first embassy to
Holland was a triumph, we are told, principally because of his ability to
converse with the bishop of Münster in Latin.[12] His early essays *Upon the
Present State of Ireland* and *The Original and Nature of Government*, his
Observations on the United Provinces, even his *Memoirs* were all written to
promote a political cause. And they helped undoubtedly to advance his
own career. But Temple was a complicated man; in 1680 he ended his
political life and withdrew into seclusion. The eloquence of politics was
succeeded by the peacefulness of contemplation. Yet Temple's ready pen
did not for a moment cease; like Cicero in old age, he fastened upon
moral philosophy and wrote some memorable pieces in an elegant and
captivating style.

The man, then, who sat down in later life to pen some thoughts on the
ancients and moderns was a man widely, if not deeply, versed in the
classical authors. He had assimilated them, at least the Latin writers, in
the natural manner of the seventeenth-century gentleman and man of
affairs. They had helped him to shape his style and to frame his manner

[10]*Memoirs*, in Temple's *Works*, 4 vols. (London, 1814), 2:567–68, 569.
[11]Béat-Louis de Muralt, *Letters Describing the Character and Customs of the English and
French Nations*, 2d ed. (London, 1726), pp. 86–87. The first French edition appeared in
1725.
[12]Temple, *Works*, 1:xii.

and they had been brought to bear on his politics and his diplomacy. Temple was neither a philosopher nor a scholar. He had no interest in speculation or theory of any kind, "airy daydreaming" to a practical and concrete intelligence. He was ready to consign all natural philosophy and science, both ancient and modern, to the dustbin.[13] Like Cicero, Temple was a skeptic, and only moral philosophy escaped his doubt. Nor had he the time and patience, much less the skills or interest, of a classical scholar. He was an ancient without a profound knowledge of antiquity, no more than a pale imitation of his beloved models, as he would have been the first to say. Among the ancients and the moderns he was assuredly neither the best informed nor the most able of the classicists. But he was not the less sincere for all that, or the less representative. Even in the superficial character of his learning, he was in fact the perfect example of his type.

2

Temple was provoked to his reflections by two works that had recently appeared, Thomas Burnet's *Sacred Theory of the Earth* and Pierre Fontenelle's *Digression sur les anciens et les modernes*. The two works are a reminder that the quarrel had been going on now for a long time both in England and in France and in the various realms of theology, natural philosophy, and literature. Perhaps we may spare the background for the moment and enter immediately upon the argument. Temple's "Essay upon Ancient and Modern Learning," like all his work, was noteworthy not for its ideas, which were thoroughly familiar, but for the grace of its style and the eminence of the author. It was thus the occasion for a grand renewal of hostilities, although the extent of the response must surely have startled the aging writer.[14]

Temple's essay begins with a restatement of the argument. He must, he thought, refute the two main challenges of the moderns, first, that "as to Knowledge, we must have more than the Ancients, because we have the Advantage both of theirs and our own"—a position, he noticed, that was commonly illustrated by the metaphor of a dwarf standing upon a

[13]Temple, "Upon the Gardens of Epicurus" (1685), in *Works*, 3:206, 208.

[14]The essay appears to have been written in 1689 and printed in 1690 as one of Temple's *Miscellanea, The Second Part*, along with essays on the gardens of Epicurus, heroic virtue, and poetry; it was reissued in 1691, revised in 1692, and reprinted in 1693, 1697, and 1705. It was translated into French in 1693. See Marburg, *Sir William Temple*, pp. 94–100. Temple's *Works* were printed in 1720, 1723, 1731, 1740, 1750, 1757, 1770, and 1814. Spingarn edited the essay (n. 6 above); and a useful bibliography along with several of the texts may be found in Jonathan Swift, *The Battle of the Books*, ed. A. C. Guthkelch (London, 1908).

giant's shoulders and seeing farther than he—and second, that "as to wit or Genius, that Nature being still the same, they must be much at a Rate in all Ages, at least in the same Clymates, as the Growth and Size of Plants and Animals commonly are."[15] Thus it seemed to Temple that the two central arguments concerned the possibility of progress in human knowledge and in human nature. To both he was clearly opposed and without reservation.

On the face of it, the first argument would seem to have been the more difficult. It was certainly hard, and more so with every passing year of the seventeenth century, to ignore the modern increments to knowledge, particularly in the new sciences. Yet Temple was willing to meet the problem head on. As he looked back over the whole course of civilization, he was confident of the Greek achievement here as elsewhere and the comparative pettiness and inconsequence of all modern speculation—despite the fact that most ancient learning had been lost forever through the neglect of centuries. In philosophy, he was certain, there had been nothing in fifteen hundred years to match the luster of Plato, Aristotle, Epicurus, and the rest, "unless DesCartes and Hobbs should pretend to it."[16] In astronomy, physics, and medicine, all he could find to rival the ancients were Copernicus, William Harvey, and Bishop Wilkins. Their ideas, he insisted (not altogether improbably), were neither as new nor as true as the moderns pretended, and, even more to the point, were of no practical value whatever. But Temple did not really have much interest in either the ancient or the modern scientific achievements, or for that matter very much knowledge about them; the Epicurean moralist was more concerned with human than with physical nature.[17]

If this was perilous ground in a contest that was bound to include the Royal Society, Temple was better off with the argument about human nature. It was surely harder to claim progress here, and indeed the moderns of this period were not quite ready for that assertion either. In fact, both sides agreed that human nature was pretty well constant.[18] But they drew different conclusions from this. For the moderns—for both Burnet and Fontenelle, for example—the constancy of human nature disposed of the superiority of the ancients; there were giants and dwarfs in every age.

[15]Sir William Temple, *Miscellanea, The Second Part* (London, 1690), pp. 5–6; *Works,* 3:446. For the notion of standing on the shoulders of giants, see Joseph M. Levine, "Ancients and Moderns Reconsidered," *Eighteenth-Century Studies* 14 (1981): 76n.

[16]Temple, *Works,* 3:468.

[17]For another contemporary dismissal of science and discovery, see Shaftesbury to Locke, Sept. 29, 1694, in *The Correspondence of John Locke,* ed. E. S. de Beer, 8 vols. (Oxford, 1976–1989), 5:150–54.

[18]See Temple's *Essay upon the Original and Nature of Government* (1680), ed. Robert Steensma, Augustan Reprint Society 109 (Los Angeles, 1964), pp. 45–46; Temple, *Works,* 1:29; and *Observations upon the United Province of the Netherlands,* in *Works,* 1:37.

Not so for Temple, for while human abilities might remain constant, circumstances did not. "May there not," he asked, "many circumstances concur to one production that do not to any other in one or many ages?" Just so it had happened in antiquity, especially for those abilities "which we call Wisdom or Prudence for the conduct of Publick Affairs or Private Life." Here the man of the world might well feel on comfortable ground. Temple knew the great modern wits and admired them: Boccaccio and Machiavelli, Sarpi and Montaigne; among the English: Sidney, Bacon and Selden. But the circumstances of learning in modern times explained to him their apparent failure to measure up to the ancients: religious controversy, civil conflict, weak patronage, and (not least) the pedantry of scholars. So too it was with poetry and the humanities in general. The "Gothick Swarms" of the Middle Ages might have been put to rout and the arts and sciences to some extent restored, but surely no one would seriously match the modern poets with Homer and Virgil. Only in drama—it is Temple's one exception—were the moderns, and especially the English, superior. But Temple did not mean to abandon his contemporaries altogether. New books could have their merits too, if only one did not claim too much for them, especially "those of Story or Relations of Matter of Fact." Their value obtained from their content, not their form, and they could be entertaining and instructive however they were told. But wherever "Wit, Learning, or Genius" was involved, the ancients were entirely superior and the moderns could only imitate. It was literature and moral philosophy (the Ciceronian *studia humanitatis*) that were the true concerns of Temple's *paideia* and that exalted the Latin and Greek classics above all their rivals.[19]

3

Since Temple was willing to allow some space for the moderns and for his own curiosity, it is not altogether surprising to find that in 1689 he was reading Burnet and Fontenelle. Not that it would have been easy to ignore them, for both works had burst upon the world in a blaze of controversy provoked by unorthodox ideas, cloaked in an agreeable, sometimes eloquent style. Modernity was ripe for a hearing and while neither Burnet nor Fontenelle persuaded many readers about their new ideas, both quickly found an enthusiastic audience. The subject matter was certainly intriguing, "one in English upon the Antediluvian World; the other in French upon the Plurality of Worlds, one writ by a Divine, the other by a gentleman." Burnet's large volume had appeared origi-

[19]Temple, *Miscellanea, The Second Part,* in *Works,* 3:463.

nally in two parts in Latin between 1680 and 1684 but was now made readily available in an updated English version as *The Sacred Theory of the Earth*. Fontenelle's smaller work, *Sur la pluralité des mondes*, with its appendix on the ancients and the moderns appeared about the same time and was also soon turned into English on no fewer than three separate occasions. Temple admired both of these tracts but he was very quickly irritated by Burnet, who "could not end his learned Treatise without a panegyric of modern learning and knowledge in comparison of the ancient," and by Fontenelle, who had added a small piece to his work in which he forthrightly preferred the new poetry to the old. Temple "could not read either of those strains without indignation."[20] Pride and ignorance seemed once again to have joined forces and Temple felt an urgent need to reply. Since this was the immediate occasion for his essay, and for the ensuing quarrel, it may be worth inquiring for a moment into this double-barreled modern provocation.

When Thomas Burnet wrote his Latin *Telluris theoria sacra*, he was already master of the Charterhouse School in London and seemed poised for high preferment.[21] Like Temple, he had studied at Cambridge under Cudworth; unlike Temple, who did not care a pin for speculation of any kind, Burnet seems to have drunk deeply in the new philosophy, particularly in Descartes, who was for a time all the fashion at Cambridge, but also in Pierre Gassendi, Marin Mersenne, and Francis Bacon. He had also studied with the Neoplatonists who surrounded Cudworth at Christ's College. These men accepted the ancient idea that theology was the principal of the sciences and they supposed that they could reconcile the claims of reason and faith. Burnet set out with them, but in his own independent fashion, to find out how far philosophy could decipher the meaning of the Christian universe. If his belief in reason seemed excessive and aroused the suspicion of contemporaries, so it had for almost all the other Neoplatonists. He nevertheless believed with them in the essential harmony of rational truth and Christian revelation and in the particular value of combining the two to arrive at a complete and fruitful knowledge. The *Telluris sacra* was therefore somewhat Janus-faced, both a philosophical treatise full of bold new speculation and a rather old-fashioned running commentary on Scripture, especially Genesis and Revelation.[22] It was also, and more precisely, a meditation on history, an

---

[20]Ibid., pp. 4–5.

[21]Brief biographies may be found in the *Biographia Britannica* (London, 1747) and prefixed to the 7th ed. of *Sacred Theory of the Earth* (London, 1759). See Mirella Pasini, *Thomas Burnet: Una storia del mondo tra religione, mito e rivelazione* (Florence, 1981).

[22]John Evelyn was captivated by the English translation, "finding in it severall things . . . omitted in the Latine (which I formerly read with delight) still new, still surprizing, and the whole hypothesis so ingenious and rational, that I both admire and believe it at once": Evelyn to Pepys, June 18, 1684, in *The Private Correspondence of Samuel Pepys*, ed. J. R. Tanner, 2 vols. (New York, 1926), 1:23–24.

attempt to divine the essential shape and ultimate meaning of the whole of the human past. Although the argument was posed hypothetically, Burnet nevertheless thought that he had discovered more than anyone before him about his grand subject. He did not claim to be a genius, merely a dwarf standing upon the shoulders of those who had gone before.

The *Theory of the Earth* envisions a "history of the world writ philosophically."[23] Burnet did not see much point to the ordinary view that history was the record of battles fought and the reigns of kings. "Such affairs are but the little under-plots in the tragi-comedy of the world; the main design is of another nature and of far greater extent and consequence." He wanted no less than an overall view of the past, "an account of the several states of mankind in several ages," not only as far as the present but even unto the millennium. He hoped to give "an account of the several states of mankind in several ages, and by what stages or degrees they came from this first rudeness or simplicity to that order of things, both intellectual and civil, which the world is advanced to at present."[24] In fact, the *Theory of the Earth* does not attempt to recount the whole of universal history but concentrates on the two points of greatest consequence, the beginning and the end, the creation of the world and its transformation by the Flood at the outset of the story, the fire and regeneration at the conclusion. (He provides a separate book for each.) Burnet examines the evidence of revelation and recorded history with the use of his reason, in the confidence that philosophy can discover in the hints and obscurities of each the outlines of the providential design. He was thus able to draw a picture of the earth upon its first creation, egg-shaped and smoothly perfect, and its transformation by the Flood into the awesome imperfection of the present globe, with its mountains, fissures, and seas; and to describe in vivid pages the conflagration that would consume everything in the end, in preparation for the last judgment and the return to paradise. "He has," applauded the *Spectator*, "according to the Lights of Reason and Revelation which seem'd to him clearest, traced the Steps of Omnipotence. He has, with a Caelestial Ambition, as far as it is consistent with Humility and Devotion, examined the Ways of Providence, from the Creation to the Dissolution of the

[23]Thomas Burnet, *Sacred Theory of the Earth*, 2 vols. (London, 1684–1690), 1:52. The first part of Burnet's work appeared in Latin as *Telluris theoria sacra* (London, 1681), enlarged and translated into English in 1684; the second part appeared in Latin in 1689, with a translation soon afterward. There were three Latin and eight English editions by 1759; see V. A. Eyles, "Bibliography and the History of Science," *Journal of the Society for the Bibliography of Science* 3 (1955): 64. The work drew warm praise and provoked immediate controversy; see Ernest Lee Tuveson, *Millennium and Utopia* (1949; rpt. New York, 1964), pp. 113–26; Marjorie Hope Nicolson, *Mountain Gloom and Mountain Glory* (1959; rpt. New York, 1963), pp. 184–224; Joseph M. Levine, *Dr. Woodward's Shield: History, Science, and Satire in Augustan England* (Berkeley, 1977), pp. 25–26.

[24]Burnet, *Sacred Theory*, p. 277.

visible World."[25] It was hard to know which to admire more, Burnet's grand philosophical vision or his style, which in Latin or English seemed to rise even to the majesty of his subject.

For Temple, however, who was looking on, and for most of Burnet's readers, the work was more entertaining than true, more philosophical romance than history. Burnet assumed that God had contrived to make and unmake the world entirely by natural means, and that these things could become fully intelligible to the rational mind. His deductive method reminded his readers (too much) of Descartes and seemed to take undue liberties with the evidence of both Scripture and nature. As a result, both the divines and the scientists attacked him profusely, equally skeptical of his conclusions, and in the end hardly anyone was satisfied. For Temple, the controversy was further proof, if any were needed, that all such speculation was doomed to failure, that all natural philosophy was inadequate to its subject, and that the best theology still lay in the past. He read the *Sacred Theory* with enjoyment because it was readable but he bridled at Burnet's all too explicit modernity.

Burnet was deliberately modern in two respects. In the first place, he was confident that his own philosophy was an improvement over all that had gone before. To clear the way, he saw that he must first dispose of the prevailing prejudice "against anything that looks like a novelty or innovation," and against that "superstitious Veneration for Antiquity" which prejudiced people against their own time.[26] (It was a familiar seventeenth-century complaint.) Though he tried to be diffident, he had no doubt that he knew more not only than Aristotle and Plato but more even than Descartes and the Neoplatonists. He knew more because he had the advantage of knowing their works and so could build upon, correct, and improve them. That was the way that natural philosophy and theology worked; and the future would know more and better even than Thomas Burnet—as indeed the Bible itself had forecast. He allowed but one qualification, accepting with Cudworth and the Neoplatonists that an ancient wisdom had been revealed to Moses and to Noah at the beginning of things and had been handed down through Eastern philosophy by oral tradition. But even here, he argued, the ancient wisdom had consisted only of conclusions without demonstrations and had been necessarily obscure.[27] In the fullness of time and with the use of reason all would become clear, as it had already grown clearer to him.

In the second place, Burnet believed that it was not only philosophy but almost every other human achievement that was progressive. The

[25]*Spectator*, no. 146, Aug. 11, 1711. I use the edition by Donald Bond, 5 vols. (Oxford, 1965), 2:76.

[26]Burnet, *Sacred Theory*, p. 566.

[27]Ibid., pp. 3, 379, 387–94, 537–40.

whole of civilization was thus a modern construction. But if the proponents of antiquity were thus bound to take offense, this view itself was paradoxically an ancient one, the view of Epicurus-Lucretius, dusted off now and elaborated—modernized, if you will—to meet the needs of the late seventeenth century. Burnet reaffirmed with his sources that human beings had lived first in primitive simplicity. Only afterward, when driven by necessity, had they begun to invent the tools, skills, and institutions that would improve their condition. "All the artificial and mechanical World," he concluded, "is in a manner new; and what you may call the civil world too." Even upon a superficial view, it seemed clear to him that the recent advances in navigation and printing, the discovery of the circulation of the blood, and a host of other insights and innovations marked off the modern age as having made "greater progress than all ages together since the beginning of the world. There is not a plough-boy now," he added, in a passage that must have infuriated Temple, "that would not have been a god, even to Jupiter himself, had he lived in his days with his present skill in husbandry. Had the mystery of printing been invented in antient time, Guttenburg of Mentz might have been a god of higher esteem throughout Germany than Mercury or Jupiter himself."[28] Temple remained dubious; the Alexandrian library had been larger than any collection of books after the invention of printing, and the ancient oral tradition, he was sure, transcended anything that had ever been written down.[29] Burnet's views on these matters may have been commonplace for a century but they were hardly conclusive yet.

Indeed, it was one of the weaknesses of Burnet's position with respect to the general progress of civilization that he had to admit a setback of immense proportions in the thousand years or so of the Middle Ages, a backward and barbarous period that, everyone agreed, had required both a renaissance and a reformation before the modern period could be born. God's ways, it seems, were not perhaps altogether intelligible and the march of progress not entirely consistent. Add to that qualification Burnet's concession (however modified) of the existence of an ancient philosophical wisdom and Temple might well hope for a victory yet and the conversion of the enemy. For the moment he read the *Sacred Theory of the Earth* with astonishment at its claims.

It required Fontenelle's little work, however, to provoke Temple to action. The *querelle* was already old hat in France when the young Breton descended on the capital and tossed off his little *feuilleton*. He had been

---

[28]Ibid., p. 576.

[29]Temple, *Miscellanea, The Second Part*, p. 38; for Burnet on the Alexandrian library, see *Sacred Theory*, p. 312.

trying, as a precocious youngster from the provinces, to establish himself with his poetry and his plays, but to little avail. In 1683, however, he began to find his true métier in prose with some *Dialogues of the Dead* that were well received and in which he displayed his modernist sympathies.[30] He sealed his fame, and his true vocation, however, with the work that Temple read, the popular *Entretiens sur la pluralité des mondes* (1686), in which he made Descartes available to the ladies, popularizing the new science, as Voltaire was to do a little later with Isaac Newton. If Fontenelle turned out to be no poet, he proved himself an immensely gifted and lucid expositor of the ideas of others. In 1686 he published his *History of Oracles*, borrowed largely from the ponderous Latin of the Dutchman Anthony van Dale, but simplified again and clarified, popular but also scandalous in its own way to the devout. And it was about that time too that he published the little *Digression on the Ancients and the Moderns*, which announced his definitive position in the *querelle*.[31]

The boldness and simplicity of Fontenelle's little work helped to focus an argument that had been going on in France for decades and it provoked an outcry that among other things barred him from the Academy for several years. It is hard to say how much Temple knew of the background or of the immediate occasion of the work in Fontenelle's rivalry with the ancient partisan Longepierre, though it was probably not a great deal.[32] What mattered to him was the frankness with which the author declared for the moderns in philosophy and science, like Burnet, but even more disturbingly in rhetoric and poetry. The *Digression* met the ancients frankly and directly. "They tell us," Fontenelle complained (in the words of his English translator, John Hughes), that "they are the sources of good Taste and Reason, and the Luminaries destin'd to give Light to all Mankind, that no body has Wit or Judgment, but in proportion to his Veneration for them; that Nature has exhausted herself in providing those great Originals."[33] Nonsense! Nature was the same in all ages; only climate and circumstance altered the forms of art and culture.

---

[30]See, for example, the dialogue between Socrates and Montaigue, in Bernard de Fontenelle, *Nouveaux dialogues des morts*, ed. Donald Schier, University of North Carolina Studies in Language and Literature 55 (Chapel Hill, 1965), pp. 63–72. John W. Cosentini is somehow able to read the dialogues as skeptical of both ancient and modern pretensions: *Fontenelle's Art of Dialogue* (New York, 1952), pp. 155–59.

[31]It was appended to a little volume of pastoral poetry, published in 1688 (and discussed in chap. 4). The text is given in Fontenelle's *Entretiens sur la pluralité des mondes*, ed. Robert Shackleton (Oxford, 1955), pp. 159–76. It was translated by John Hughes as an appendix to Fontenelle's *Conversations with a Lady on the Plurality of Worlds*, trans. Joseph Glanvill, 4th ed. (London, 1719), pp. 177–211.

[32]See Alain Niderst, *Fontenelle et la recherche de lui-même (1657–1702)* (Paris, 1972), pp. 366–99.

[33]Fontenelle, "A Discourse Concerning the Ancients and Moderns," in *Conversations with a Lady*, p. 180.

So far, we have seen, Temple agreed; but Fontenelle dismissed all such differences between ancients and moderns as insignificant, preferring instead a distinction of another sort—and more exasperating. It was time and experience alone that brought improvement, and that, Fontenelle insisted, was all to the advantage of the moderns. Like Francis Bacon long before and like many others since, he believed that in this sense, the moderns were the true ancients, for they had the benefit of the accumulated wisdom of the ages on which to base their claim to superiority.

Not that all subjects benefited equally from experience. Fontenelle accepted the traditional distinction between the sciences and the humanities, between natural philosophy on the one hand and rhetoric and poetic on the other. Natural philosophy, like say the astronomy of the *Plurality of Worlds*, needed both reason and experiment, and therefore a great deal of time, to ripen. Fortunately, Fontenelle believed, reason had been brought to perfection just lately by the greatest of the moderns, René Descartes. If his conclusions still needed adjustment, that was because natural philosophy required experiment as well as reason—and of experiment there could be no limit. Science (but also divinity, morality, and criticism) could thus be expected to go on improving indefinitely along Cartesian lines. It was otherwise with eloquence and poetry, the chief points now in dispute. Here Fontenelle wavered just a bit. "Tho' they are not in themselves of great Importance," he insisted (completely reversing the humanist view), "yet I think the Antients may have had the power to attain the Perfection of 'em."[34] Imagination, unlike reason, "has no need for a long Train of Experiences, nor of a great many Rules to form it to all the Perfection 'tis capable of." Even so, perfection could not be sought at the very beginning but had to be won through time. As a result, the Romans had improved upon the Greeks, and Fontenelle accepted unhesitatingly what the Romans themselves frequently doubted, that the Latin poets, orators, and historians (excepting only the tragedians) were superior to any that had gone before and that the age of Augustus Caesar was the most perfect yet in these respects. (It was, of course, modern in relation to the Greeks.) Like Burnet and everyone else in his generation, he allowed that the Middle Ages had seen only decline and barbarism and required a revival of antiquity before the modern age could be brought into being. But he was confident that the restoration of antique standards in the humanities had in fact brought new work into the world that was the equal of, and in a few instances superior to, anything that had been fashioned before. One should not forget that the ancients had had their

[34]Ibid., p. 190. See Hugh M. Davidson, "Fontenelle, Perrault, and the Realignment of the Arts," in *Literature and History in the Age of Ideas: Essays to George R. Havens*, ed. Charles G. S. Williams (Columbus, O., 1975), p. 5.

faults too, even here. "Let us," he concludes, "content ourselves to say, they cannot be excell'd; but let us not say, they cannot be equall'd." Indeed, for all one knew, the future might bring about an even greater perfection. "Heaven knows with what Scorn, in comparison of us, they will treat the great Wits and Genius's of their own time, who possibly may be Americans!"[35]

4

In taking on both Burnet and Fontenelle, Temple could not avoid defending the whole range of the ancient arts and sciences. Although his heart was with the humanities, with the rhetoric, poetic, and history of antiquity, he managed to cling also to a belief in the existence of an ancient wisdom in philosophy and science. So much had been lost during the long night of the Middle Ages that it was not always possible to tell how far the ancients had excelled the moderns; but even the few fragments that remained from the hundreds of thousands of volumes in the Alexandrian library were proof enough for him that the ancients had known more, as well as done better, than the moderns. Temple, it is true, was skeptical of the claims of all speculation, but he hewed to the line of his Neoplatonic teachers that insofar as philosophical wisdom was attainable on earth, it must have been held in earliest antiquity, beginning in the East and descending by word of mouth to classical times. "Science and arts have run their circles," Temple concluded, reaffirming the ancient view, "they are generally agreed to have held their course from East to West, to have begun in Chaldea and Egypt, to have been transplanted from thence from Greece to Rome, to have sunk there, and after many Ages, to have revived."[36] The modern age had thus capped a new cycle, though necessarily at a lower level than what had gone before. The Renaissance began, Temple supposed, in Italy with the revival of classical Greek and Latin, but being essentially imitative, it must necessarily have been less perfect than the original. Even the later restorers in the

[35]Fontenelle, "Discourse," pp. 198, 207. In a conversation with Abbé Trublet much later, Fontenelle denied being as modern as Charles Perrault (who followed after), which was why Abbé Bignon told him one day that he was the father of a sect to which he did not belong: Nicolas Trublet, *Mémoires pour servir à l'histoire de la vie et les ouvrages de M. de Fontenelle*, 2d ed. (Amsterdam, 1759), pp. 40–41. At the end of his long life Fontenelle was still proclaiming that Homer remained sublime and Virgil admirable, despite the undoubted progress of the new science; see Louis Maigron, *Fontenelle: L'Homme, l'oeuvre, l'influence* (Paris, 1906), pp. 194–95.

[36]Temple, *Miscellanea, The Second Part*, p. 36; *Works*, 3:463–64. See R. C. Cochrane, "Bishop Berkeley and the Progress of the Arts and Learning: Notes on a Literary Convention," *Huntington Library Quarterly* 17 (1953–54): 229–49.

North, Erasmus and Reuchlin, however admirable, could not measure up to their models.

Temple's allusions to an ancient wisdom, to a *prisca philosophia*, developed, therefore, out of the need to reply to Burnet. In passing, he invoked the Brahmans and the Chinese, recalled the debt of the Greek philosophers to the Chaldeans, Egyptians, and Phoenicians, and generally repeated what he maintained (correctly) was the prevailing view. But his main opponent was Fontenelle, who not only was more unequivocal than Burnet in his enthusiasm for modern science but had dared to exalt the achievement and possibilities of modern literature as well. It is true that there was some modest common ground between the opponents even here. Both Temple and Fontenelle agreed, for example, to praise the classical Augustan age, and both apparently took its prose and verse to be the model for their own.[37] But for Temple, the Augustans were already in the shadow of the Greeks as the moderns of their own time, imitators rather than originators, and so Virgil was necessarily beneath Homer, Cicero below Demosthenes, and so on, exactly reversing Fontenelle's judgments. Moreover, where for Fontenelle (as for Burnet) eloquence and poetry were merely ornamental, the products of a flippant imagination rather than reason, for Temple they stood at the very center of civilized culture, the only arts indispensable to politics and the practical life. The gap between the two cultures could hardly have been more pronounced.

Inevitably Temple adopted the strategy of the enemy, the coupling of ancients and moderns to test their superiority. And who can say that he had the worst of the argument? Were Hobbes and Descartes so evidently superior to Plato and Aristotle? Had not Copernicus and Harvey both looked intentionally backward to support their theories? And where was the practical value of all this new science? In the humanities the argument seemed even more secure. Among the poets, the orators, and the historians, where were the moderns to match the best of antiquity? Even Fontenelle had hesitated here. Although he had insisted upon their faults, even he had found it hard to imagine anyone superior to Cicero or to Livy, and he thought that the most beautiful verses that had yet been written were certainly those of Virgil—though they could have used some retouching and might yet be excelled! When, however, he went on to urge the general superiority of the poets, playwrights and historians of the age of Louis XIV, he went too far for Temple. "Are D'avila's and

---

[37]"The Height and Purity of the Roman Style, as it began toward the Time of Lucretius . . . so it ended about that of Tyberius . . . the Purity of the Greek lasted a great deal longer . . . till Trajan's Time when Plutarch wrote. . . . After this last, I know none that deserves the Name of Latin, in comparison of what went before them, especially with the Augustan Age": Temple, *Miscellanea, The Second Part*, pp. 62, 68; *Works*, 3:479.

Strada's Histories beyond those of Caesar? The Flights of Boileau above those of Virgil?" If this was to be allowed, "I must then yield Gondibert to have excelled Homer, as is pretended, and the modern French poetry, all that of the Ancients." One might as well argue "that the Plays in Moor-Fields are beyond the Olympick Games, A Welsh or Irish Harp excels that of Orpheus and Arion, the Pyramids in London those of Memphis, and the French Conquests in Flanders are greater than those of Alexander and Caesar, as their Operas and Panegyricks would make us believe!"[38]

So the argument was joined. But was it possible that no one, in an argument about literature—neither the ancients nor the moderns—thought to bring up Shakespeare or Dante or even John Milton? Apparently both sides in the quarrel shared more of their outlook than they realized. Indeed, it is clear that both sides implicitly accepted as timeless and universal very much the same set of literary and artistic standards that they were both sure had derived from antiquity. They disagreed only about how far they had in fact been restored or exceeded in the present—or how far they might yet be excelled in the future. It seems to have occurred to no one on either side to imagine that they might be altogether transformed. Modernity, it appears, had still a long, hard road to travel.

5

For the moment, the quarrel seemed suspended, though both sides continued to reconnoiter for advantage. In 1691 the skeptical deist Thomas Pope Blount published some essays "on several subjects," one of which was entitled "Of the Ancients: And the Respect that is due unto them," and which concludes "that we should not too much enslave our selves to their Opinions." It was a characteristic plea for modernity as it was then understood with respect to philosophy and science. Too strict an adherence to authority was an impediment (just as Bacon had said) to the advancement of learning, and Galileo's direct observation of nature was superior to anything in Ptolemy or Aristotle. In another essay Blount considered "whether the Men of this present Age are in any way inferior to those of former Ages," and agreed with Fontenelle that "humane Nature is much at the same standard as it was formerly." Blount's views were brief and conventional and do not seem to have been directly addressed to Temple, whom he praised elsewhere as "that Accomplish'd

[38]Temple, *Miscellanea, The Second Part*, p. 57; *Works*, 3:476.

Author."[39] A few months later the Protestant émigré Pierre Motteux tried to sum up the situation in his new literary periodical—the first of its kind in England—*The Gentleman's Journal; or, Monthly Magazine.*[40] Motteux was well placed to mediate in a quarrel between the France of Perrault and the England of Temple, and he reminded his readers how the battle had begun abroad with Perrault's poem on the age of Louis XIV, and how both sides had launched invectives until some "impartial" spirits had shown that there was something to be said on both sides. Motteux thought that when one descended to particulars, when one compared the actual achievements of ancients and moderns, it became clear "that the first were before us in several things, yet in many others the last did not yield to, but even surpassed them." More judicious spirits allowed that the ancients had excelled in rhetoric and poetry, which depended on "quickness of imagination" and could be easily perfected, while allowing the moderns to continue to advance in philosophy and the sciences, which depended on reason and needed the long term for improvement. He thus took up a position very like Fontenelle's, alleging that the Augustan Romans had brought the humanities to perfection or almost so, while the moderns had improved and would continue to improve in both the manner and the substance of reasoning. Motteux was not very optimistic about his conclusions, however; in such matters, most people tended to stick to their original notions. Just so, Temple had lately started up again for the ancients, and Thomas Pope Blount for the moderns.

Certainly the issues were in the air. In April 1691 the enterprising printer John Dunton brought some of his friends together to form an "Athenian Society" for the purpose of publishing a popular journal that was meant to raise and answer questions, drawing on such serious reviews as the *Acta eruditorum* and the *Journal des scavans*. The collaborators included a poet, Samuel Wesley; a mathematician, Richard Sault; and a theologian, the Platonist John Norris.[41] The very first supplement (1691) summarized at length the modernist arguments of Perrault; while among the many questions raised in early issues of the *Athenian Mercury* were such things as "Which do you esteem the greatest Artists in Painting, the Ancient or the Modern?"; "Whether the Ancients were as Skill'd in

[39]Thomas Pope Blount, *Essays on Several Subjects* (London, 1691), no. 4, pp. 77–89; no. 5, pp. 89–140; for the reference to Temple, p. 167.

[40]The two articles appeared in March 1692, pp. 17–22, 19–23.

[41]See the "Articles of Agreement," April 10, 1691, Bodleian MS. Rawl. D. 72, f. 118. "All the knotty points of Philosophy, Divinity, Mathematics, etc. . . . are form'd into Queries by the Inquisitive and answered with an Abundance of Reason by the Society": [Charles Gildon] *The History of the Athenian Society* (London, n.d.), p. 5. See Stephen Parks, *John Dunton and the English Book Trade* (New York, 1976), pp. 94–108.

Shipping and Navigation as the Moderns are?"; "Did all Learning come from the Jews and Eastern Nations?"; and "Whether the Queen of Sheba, if now living, might not receive as ample Satisfaction from our Modern Writers . . . as she did from Solomon?"[42] Eventually both Temple and Swift contributed, although Temple may have been a little disppointed by the answer to his question "Whether the Ancients knew the Mariners Compass? and who first invented it?" The Athenians believed that it had appeared only recently in the West, though the Chinese had known it (along with gunpowder and the printing press) long before.[43] In general, the society had much to say on both sides, leaving the reader to pick and choose among notions not entirely consistent. In one of the supplements, *The Young Student's Library*, a French philosopher declares his opinion that, "all things being considered, [he] was resolved to stick to the Ancients, and leave the Moderns to themselves." A few pages later, the Athenian reviewer of Robert Hooke's *Micrographia* forthrightly commends the modern inventions of telescope and microscope for their use to science. "They have discovered more Things in a few Years, than the Ancients have done with all their Reasons for the Course of many Ages. By this means all Nature has appeared new to us. For the Telescope has show'd us in the Firmament new Motions, new Stars, and new Meteors; and the Microscope hath discovered unto us, upon the Earth, a little World altogether new." As for the imitation of authors, the Athenians tried also to steer something of a middle way. "For as it wou'd be foolish to dispise these Admirable Monuments of Antiquity, so we ought on the other hand to avoid falling into over-respect to them, or approving of their over-sights."[44] The Athenian publications were very popular, but the quarrel did not advance much here.

What was needed was a good modern rejoinder, since neither Motteux nor Blount had really done very much to serve the modern cause. Unfortunately neither had the time or the learning to attend very properly to the issues. The opportunity was open, therefore, for a proper rebuttal, and it was taken by a younger and more able man. William Wotton was in his own way as good an example of seventeenth-century classicism as William Temple, although in spirit and temperament he

---

[42] *The Supplement to the First Volume of the Athenian Gazette* (London, 1691), pp. 8–10, using *Journal des Scavans* 18. The *Athenian Mercury* was born as the *Athenian Gazette* and was turned into the *Athenian Oracle*, which was reprinted in four volumes (London, 1703–1748). I quote from the latter, 1:188–89, 254, 326–27, 432–35.

[43] *Athenian Mercury* 5 (Dec. 22, 1691), q. 13; A. C. Elias, Jr., *Swift at Moor Park* (Philadelphia, 1982), p. 297 n. For Swift's "Ode to the Athenian Society" (written perhaps at Temple's suggestion), see *The Poems of Jonathan Swift*, ed. Harold Williams, 3 vols. (Oxford, 1958), 1:14–15; *The Correspondence of Jonathan Swift*, ed. Harold Williams, 5 vols. (Oxford, 1963–1965), 1:8; Gilbert D. McEwen, *Oracle of the Coffee-House* (San Marino, Calif., 1972), pp. 33–34.

[44] *The Young Student's Library* (London, 1692), pp. 187, 221–23, 466.

was a perfect contrast. Not only was he younger; he was very much more precocious. His education had been by any standard extraordinary; at the age of six he could read in three ancient languages; by the age of ten he was at the university. He had been trained by his father to become a scholar and he succeeded beyond expectation. The young Wotton became a celebrated *érudit* in an age of learned men—but he never touched upon the great world of events. If he was alert to nearly every activity in the world of scholarship and intellect, he knew almost nothing about the larger world of diplomacy and politics.

Wotton's father had been educated in the household of Meric Casaubon, the learned son of the greatest scholar of the age. His own achievement was slight but he early formed an ideal of learning which he turned to practical account in the education of his son. So proud was he of this accomplishment that he decided to commemorate it in a tract dedicated to Charles II; what he had achieved with young William might thus become an example for all England. Henry Wotton's essay on education, written about 1672 but printed only very much later, was accompanied by a "Narrative of what Knowledge, William, a child six years of Age, had attained unto, upon the Improvement of those Rudiments, in the Latin, Greek and Hebrew tongues."[45] It is a startling document—an anticipation almost of James and John Stuart Mill, except that Wotton's eye was fixed firmly and exclusively upon the past, upon the classical languages and authors and upon the humanist methods of instruction that had been introduced into England by Erasmus and his circle.

The elder Wotton was confident that more could be done with children than was usually accomplished in the grammar schools. It was a frequent complaint of humanists since the Renaissance—of John Milton, for example, whose little tractate on education had recently appeared.[46] The proof, he thought, lay in the education of his own son. William had shown promise and enthusiasm from the first, but his father was convinced that he had not been more exceptional than thousands in the kingdom. Wotton saw no reason why all these children could not complete an elementary education by the tenth instead of the sixteenth or seventeenth year. Nor would the content of the customary education need to be reduced or its intention altered. For Wotton, like most of his contemporaries, the basis of all learning was mastery of the ancient tongues, in this case Hebrew as well as Latin and Greek, "wherein both the Fountains of Learning," he wrote, "as well Philology as Philosophy, and the principal Streams and Rivers thereof, are to be had." Wotton

[45]Henry Wotton, *An Essay on the Education of Children* (London, 1753).
[46]See Milton, *Of Education*, ed. Oliver M. Ainsworth (New Haven, 1928), p. 53. The tractate was published first in 1644 and again in 1673. The more conventional view is given by Charles Hoole, *A New Discovery of the Old Art of Teaching School* (London, 1660).

knew the growing pride of his age; yet unless the moderns were "baptised with those Sentiments which former Ages have tried, examined and received," their achievements would come to nothing.[47] It was exactly his son's view some twenty years later.

Wotton's method was simple and not very original. It consisted essentially of introducing the child to the languages by having him read the classical authors rather than memorize the rules, by encouraging him to speak the new tongue as far as possible, and by regarding always the sensibilities of the student. The tutor was never to fatigue or compel the child and to mingle recreation with instruction. In all these respects, the advice was exactly Erasmian. And in just such a way was young Wotton actually taught, starting at the age of four years and six weeks. He began with the Bible in Latin, and in two months' time read through two chapters of the Gospel of John. Then the same text was employed to begin Greek lessons. By the age of five, according to his father, William could give "a competent Account of the Sense of the whole Gospel of St. John, both in Latin and Greek at first Sight," and "he began to be able to read any Greek Book."[48] In the fifth year, the daily routine was an English lesson the first thing in the morning, Latin at ten, Greek by two, and Hebrew between four and five o'clock. At the age of five and a half, Wotton was reading Homer and Virgil and conversing easily in Latin. In his sixth year, on May 24, 1672, one Mr. Oumbler, fellow of Corpus Christi College, Cambridge, examined the boy and attested to his competence. From that time on, the proud father kept a record of testimonials to his son's progress. By the time he was thirteen, according to one of them, he had extended his knowledge to fully a dozen languages.[49] And it was recalled later that "when he was very young he could remember the whole of almost any Discourse he heard, and has often surpriz'd a preacher with repeating his Sermon to him." Apparently this was how he won his first patronage.[50]

---

[47]Wotton, *Essay on Education*, pp. viii–ix.

[48]Ibid., p. 46.

[49]John Nichols, *Literary Anecdotes of the Eighteenth Century*, 9 vols. (London, 1812–1815), 4:253–59. Wotton collected more than two dozen testimonials from 1671 to 1681. The last was written in 1691. In 1672 one examiner certified that young Wotton, at the age of six, "read a Stanza in Spencer very distinctly, and pronounced it properly. As also some Verses in the first Eclogue of Virgil, which I properly chuse out, and also construed the same truly. Also some Verses in Homer, and the *Carmina Aurea* of Pythagoras, which he read well and construed. As he did the first Verse of the 4th chapter of Genesis, in Hebrew, which I purposely chose out": *The Letters of Sir Thomas Browne*, ed. Geoffrey Keynes (London, 1931), p. 423. Another testimonial by Sir Philip Skippon may be found in a letter to John Ray, Sept. 18, 1671, in *The Correspondence of John Ray*, ed. Edwin Lankester (London, 1848), pp. 87–88.

[50]See the life of Wotton (apparently by Wotton's son-in-law, William Clarke) in B. M. MS. Add. 4224, pp. 166–67. I owe this identification to Michael Hunter.

In 1676 Wotton was sent to Catherine Hall, Cambridge, not yet ten years old, and the master, John Eachard, noted in the register, "nec Hammondo nec Grotio secundus." Not long afterward, John Evelyn recorded Wotton's appearance in London.

> There was now brought up to London a Child . . . who read and perfectly understood Hebrew, Greek, Latin, Arabic, Syriac, and most of the Modern Languages; disputed in Divinity, Law, and the Sciences, was skillfull in Historie both Ecclesiastical and Prophane, in Politic, etc., in a word so universally and solidly learned at 11 years of age as he was looked on as a Miracle. Dr. Lloyd (one of the most deepe learned Divines of the Nation, in all sorts of literature) with Dr. Burnet who had severely Examin'd him, came away astonish'd and told me, they did not believe there had been the like appear'd in the world since Adam to this time. . . .[51]

They admired his judgment as well as his memory and declared him a universal genius even beyond Pico della Mirandola. For a youth of his attainments, there was, at the end of the seventeenth century, only one obvious career: the Church of England. Wotton took his several degrees in due course, including his B.D. He received his preferments as naturally, although they did not carry him beyond a respectable living. In 1687, at the age of twenty-one, he became a fellow of the Royal Society. A few years later, in 1694, he published his *Reflections upon Ancient and Modern Learning*.

No one, perhaps, was better prepared to defend the modern achievement against the strictures of Sir William Temple. The fellows of the Royal Society were the natural proponents of all the learning that Temple had so lightly dismissed, and they soon cast about for someone to reply. (They had, after all, been through all this before, even from the time of their foundation, when Bishop Thomas Sprat and Joseph Glanvill were called upon to answer the first critics of the new science.)[52] They felt, however, a certain reluctance to attack so great a man, so that when, late in 1690, Tancred Robinson solicited John Ray, the most eminent naturalist in the company, for the job, he was met with a rebuff, although Ray had very strong and deliberate opinions on the subject. In a letter to Robinson he anticipated most of the arguments of the moderns but declined the task of a formal reply.[53] What was more natural, then,

[51] *The Diary of John Evelyn*, ed. E. S. de Beer, 6 vols. (Oxford, 1953–1955), 4:172–73.
[52] See R. F. Jones, *Ancients and Moderns*, 2d ed. (St. Louis, 1961), pp. 183–267.
[53] "In summe the ancients excel the moderns in nothing but acuteness of wit and elegancy of language in all their writings, in their poetry and oratory. As for painting and sculpture, and music and architecture, some of the moderns I think do equal, if not excel,

than to turn to the young prodigy, a junior member of the society and a man eager to make his reputation? Robinson knew Wotton well, had great respect for his abilities, and seems likely to have proposed the task. But whatever it was that prompted him, Wotton made good use of his membership in the society, drawing freely upon the fellows for assistance, perhaps even reading over Ray's long letter on the subject.

The result is a good book, certainly a better book than Temple's. But Temple's was an essay; Wotton's is a volume. The man of taste was not well matched against the man of learning; for Wotton was no mere pedant but a wide-ranging intellect with a thorough command of learning, both ancient and modern. "The Field I chose was vast and uncultivated," he wrote to Evelyn, who had praised his book extravagantly, and he expected that there would be others to follow and improve upon his work. "I proposed but to outdoe Glanvile and to set Mons. Perrault and Sir Wm. Temple right."[54] (Glanvill's *Plus Ultra* had appeared in 1661; Perrault we shall discover picking up the mantle of Fontenelle in the several volumes of his *Paralèlle*, 1688–1697.) But Wotton was too modest; of all the works in the controversy that had yet appeared in English or French, his was easily the most complete and the most judicious. Where, for example, some had argued the case for the moderns by pressing their claims in all directions, Wotton made a deliberate effort to assess the whole question fairly and to sort out the possibilities on both sides. He was persuaded that the ancients, by exaggerating their claims, would discourage all chance of improvement—a chance he thought must at least be allowed. But he was equally convinced that should the moderns overstate their case, they too would in a short time cause the neglect of the old authors and, as a result, the eventual failure of all learning. The moderns must continue to draw from the ancient springs or all knowledge would dry up. Wotton proposed himself, therefore, as neither an

---

the best of them, not in the theory only, but also in the practice of those arts; neither do we give place to them in politics and morality, but in natural history and experimental philosophy we far transcend them. In the purely mathematical sciences . . . geometry and arithmetic we may vie with them, as also in history; but in astronomy, geography and chronology, we excel them much." Typically, the Baconian Ray was ready to dismiss oratory and poetry as frivolous because it was occupied with words only rather than things: Ray to Tancred Robinson, Dec. 15, 1690, in Ray, *Correspondence*, p. 229. Ray seems also to have written a note to Robinson, Aug. 3, 1691, a "curt attack Sir W. Temple," described by William Derham in Ray, *Further Correspondence*, ed. W. T. Gunther (London, 1928). p. 285. Ray wrote in favor of the "encrease of knowledge" and new discoveries in his enormously popular *Wisdom of God*. For more on Ray, see Charles E. Raven, *John Ray, Naturalist* (London, 1950); Levine, *Dr. Woodward's Shield*, pp. 24–30, and "Natural History and the History of the Scientific Revolution," *Clio* 13 (1983): 57–73.

[54]Wotton to Evelyn, Jan. 20, 1698, Christ Church MS. Evelyn Corr., no. 108; William Wotton, *Reflections upon Ancient and Modern Learning* (London, 1694), pp. 4–5.

ancient like Temple nor an unqualified modern like the Frenchmen Fontenelle and Perrault, but rather a mediator between the two.

The trouble was that Temple, whose opinions Wotton allowed were generally accepted, had confused the issue by confounding two questions: Who were the greatest men? and Who knew the most? Furthermore, Temple had for the most part rested with mere assertion rather than furnishing proof. What was required, Wotton thought, was a thorough and systematic comparison of the whole range of learning, something that had not yet really been attempted, despite the preliminary efforts of Glanvill and Perrault and before them of the Italian Alessandro Tassoni. Wotton began with the first and more awkward problem: Was change in human nature possible?

Like nearly everyone else, he thought not. But he drew a different conclusion than Temple. "Since Mankind varies little, if anything, any further than as Customs alter it, from one Age to another," Wotton believed that all peoples were able to draw "certain conclusions of External Truth."[55] If the ancients had excelled in some of these things—and Wotton, like Temple, believed that they had indeed set the standards and exhausted the possibilities of moral and political knowledge—he nevertheless thought that it was possible to rival their achievement. The fact that no one had yet done so did not mean that it might not still be done. What was needed—again the premise is the same but the conclusion is different—was the same kind of favorable circumstances that had operated in antiquity. Here Wotton was more optimistic than his rival. Thus the disagreement (so far) lay less in differing estimates of past and present or in contrasting evaluations of human nature than in disparate hopes for the future.

Wotton was not content, however, with the general argument. True to his claim, he set out to examine the various disciplines in detail, beginning with those that related to moral and political knowledge, the strongest territory of the ancients. Wotton allows that "all that is commonly meant by knowing the World, and understanding Mankind; all Things necessary to make Men wise in Counsel, dexterous in Business, and agreeable in Conversation" all this had been anticipated by the ancients.[56] In moral and political philosophy, the classical writers excelled. Yet even so, the moderns could share their insights, and the superiority of the ancients lay in their experience, not in any special genius. In eloquence and poetry Wotton allowed the ancients' superiority to be even more decisive. (Even the naturalist Ray had conceded as much.)

[55]Wotton, *Reflections*, p. 16.
[56]Ibid., pp. 12–13.

And the best of the moderns, Wotton was prepared to admit, were those who read the ancients carefully and drew the appropriate lessons. "The Masters of Writing, in all their several Ways, to this Day, appeal to the Ancients, as their Guides: and still fetch Rules for them, for the Art of Writing." If some among the moderns were able thereby to approach the classical standard, there was yet no denying the overwhelming literary superiority of the ancients. Here, at least, Temple had been right. Wotton supposes that he can explain the advantage of the ancients in the favorable circumstances of their language and their politics. The superiority of classical Greek (its natural "smoothness") and the priority of Latin to the modern languages ensured the preeminence of the classical poets. And the free political constitutions of the ancient world had fostered the development of eloquence. "When the Romans once lost their Liberty," Wotton explains, "their Eloquence soon fell." Modern public business, even the pulpit, was not so conducive to persuasion. Besides, few today were willing to rival the diligence and enthusiasm with which the ancients had studied the art of rhetoric. One had only to read Cicero and Quintilian to see the difference. "That former Ages made greater Orators and nobler Poets than these later Ages have done" seemed to Wotton, therefore, as it had to Temple, understandable and indisputable. But, with the same circumstances and advantages, it might yet be possible to produce again a new Demosthenes, Cicero, Horace, or Virgil.[57]

So too Wotton was prepared to concede the fine arts, although, following Perrault, he was more doubtful about architecture. But he felt otherwise about those truly cumulative disciplines, mathematics and the natural sciences. Here Wotton turned directly to the second of Temple's considerations, whether it was possible, irrespective of natural genius, to learn more than the ancients had known. As an active fellow of the Royal Society, an intimate of Boyle, Hooke, Newton, and the rest, Wotton could hardly think otherwise.[58] More than half his work was devoted to surveying the many disciplines that constituted seventeenth-century natural philosophy: chemistry, anatomy, physics, astronomy, mathematics, medicine, and so on. In several instances he acknowledged the help of his colleagues, and he drew deliberately on previous writing. In each case he found in favor of the moderns. Wotton understood the usefulness of modern inventions to the progress of modern learning: printing, engrav-

---

[57]Cf. "Of Ancient and Modern Eloquence and Poetry," in ibid., pp. 20–45.

[58]"The whole Book seems to be designed for a Vindication of that Sort of Learning which it is the intention of the Royal Society to promote, for which Reason probably he took no Notice that he had the Honour to be a Member of that Body": *Philosophical Transactions* 18 (1694): 275. Wotton was explicit about defending the society in his "Defense of the Reflections," appended to the 3d ed. of his *Reflections upon Ancient and Modern Learning* (London, 1705), p. 475.

ing, telescopes, microscopes, pendulum clocks, and the rest. Even in logic and metaphysics he was inclined to favor the moderns. Bacon, Descartes, and Locke had made some original contributions over and above anything that could be discovered in antiquity. Viewed from this perspective, the confidence of the moderns was understandable. Wotton's conclusion, however, was unfailingly judicious; the quarrel between the ancients and the moderns was for him, finally, something of a draw. One could not be sure in any case just what the future would bring. Wotton was certain of one thing only; contemporaries could best secure the future, "by joining Ancient and Modern Learning together . . . in those things wherein they severally do excel."[59] The Archbishop of Canterbury was not the only reader who found the work "to be very extraordinary both for the learning and judgment he hath shewn in it and for the manly and decent style." *The Works of the Learned* recommended it for every gentleman's closet.[60] John Evelyn was delighted, Samuel Pepys was positively ravished by it, and it continued to be read with approval for many years.[61]

6

The contest had begun; the battle of the books was launched. A torrent of pamphlets followed, and in the end both Temple and Wotton had second thoughts.

The temptation to join the fray was strong, especially for the friends of Sir William. Some of the fury was quite spontaneous, as when the young lawyer William Salkeld drew up some "reflections" against Wotton to show the weakness of his argument. "Who but Mr. Wotton ever question'd that nature it self is enfeebled by time and age and far short of the vigour of its first youth?" Among the errors Salkeld detected in Wotton's book was for it to treat the "smoothness" of the Greek lan-

---

[59]Wotton, *Reflections* (1694), p. 358.

[60]Tillotson to Burnet, June 28, 1694, in Thomas Birch, *Life of Dr. John Tillotson* (London, 1752), pp. 331–32; *Miscellaneous Letters, Giving an Account of the Works of the Learned* 1, no. 3 (Oct. 24–31, 1694), pp. 39–52.

[61]Wotton sent Evelyn a copy, which he read "with as much delight and satisfaction as an universally learned and indeede extraordinary Person is able to give the most refined tast[e]. This is he, whom I have sometimes mentioned to you for one of the Miracles of the Age, for his Early and vast Comprehension": Evelyn to Pepys, July 7, 1694, and Pepys to Evelyn, Aug. 10, 1694, in Pepys, *Letters and the Second Diary*, ed. R. G. Howarth (London, 1933), pp. 242–43, 247. See *The Diary of Dudley Ryder, 1715–16*, ed. William Matthews (London, 1939), pp. 263–64; and Joseph M. Levine, "Edward Gibbon and the Quarrel between the Ancients and the Moderns," in *Humanism and History* (Ithaca, N.Y., 1987), pp. 178–87.

guage as accidental, when it was due obviously to the superiority of
Greek culture; and to praise Strada as a good stylist, when Strada was
notorious for his bad Latin. Salkeld did not attempt a complete answer,
just enough "to show his deficiency the more defective than you imagined."[62] Whatever he intended, nothing further seems to have come of it.

As for Temple himself, he resisted replying for some time, though
obviously stung by Wotton's work. Apparently his friends rallied
around immediately and offered to reply for him, but he discouraged
them, arguing that his rival's book was "a thing onely of Ostentation or a
Discharge of the Author's Common-Place books." It was better to let it
die by itself than to dignify it by too much attention. Even so, an Oxford
friend, identified only as a Mr. H., seems to have drawn up a full-length
rebuttal and urged Temple to give him some further hints for it.[63] Temple declined but was finally persuaded to contribute and quickly sketched
out some further thoughts on the subject, an essay in six brief sections,
each apparently written out in a two-hour session. When, however, it
was proposed that the essay be added to Mr. H.'s book as an appendix,
Temple flatly refused. (He certainly had no wish to be publicly associated
with it.) As a consequence, the whole project collapsed, and it was only
after Temple's death that the essay was published by his secretary and
literary executor, young Jonathan Swift, in response to a new provocation. Perhaps it did not add a great deal to what had already been said,
but in one or two places it did develop and sharpen the issue. In the draft,
Temple (or his editor) included an attack ad hominem which contrasted
two antagonists, the one "brought up and long conversant with Persons
of the greatest Quality at home and abroad; in the Courts, in Parliament,
in Privy Councils, in Foreign Embassies," the other "a young Scholar
that confesses He owes all the Comforts of his Life to his Patron's Bounty, that knows no more of Men and Manners than he has learnt in his
Study."[64] Fortunately, perhaps, it was suppressed.

On the main point Temple was recalcitrant. The new attacks of the
moderns reminded him of the "young barbarous Goths or Vandals
breaking or defacing the admirable statues of those ancient heroes of
Greece or Rome."[65] He began his little tract with a review of the con-

---

[62]William Salkeld to Ralph Palmer, Sept. 3 [1694?], Osborn Collection MS., Yale
University. This was probably the man who became famous later as the author of some
well-known law reports.

[63]See the note headed "Fragment written upon the Subject of Ant. & Mod. Learning,"
which introduces Temple's manuscript "Hints Written at the Desire of Dr. F. and of His
Friend," Rothschild MS. 2253, now at Trinity College, Cambridge. The manuscript is
described in The Rothschild Library: A Catalogue, 2 vols. (Cambridge, 1954), pp. 609–10.

[64]Sir William Temple, "Some Thoughts upon receiving the Essay of Ancient and
Modern Learning," in Miscellanea, The Third Part (London, 1701); Works, 3:487–518.

[65]Temple, Works, 3:487.

troversy from its origins in the new philosophy to its resumption in the French Academy. According to Temple, the quarrel had begun about fifty or sixty years before, when the new science first began to take root in England. Before that time, no one had dared to challenge the ancients, excepting only Paracelsus and his followers, who for a while opposed Galen in a fracas that had long since subsided. Descartes was therefore the real villain for Temple, although he could not help wondering whether the Frenchman had really been sincere. The present quarrel broke out first in the Royal Society, then in the French Academy, where the controversy was taken up more broadly and in particular. Fontenelle and Perrault had extended the argument to literature and the arts. Indeed, Perrault had dared lately to match "the Bishop of Meaux against Pericles and Thucydides; the Bishop of Nimes against Isocrates; F. Bourdaloue against Nicias; Balzac against Cicero; Voiture against Pliny; Boileau against Horace; and Corneille against all the ancient and famous dramatic poets!" When, at last, Temple's reply had been translated into French, the ancients in the Academy, especially Boileau and Racine, had rallied and begun to pelt the moderns with their satires and epigrams, "and with bitter railleries in their discourses and conversations." Temple prints some of their verses here. He was satisfied that the battle was now going his way. He believed (incorrectly, as we shall see) that Perrault himself had recanted by translating Homer, and that Burnet too had shown a new respect for the ancient philosophers in his recent *Archaeologiae Philosophicae*. (In fact, although Burnet reaffirmed the Neoplatonic doctrine of the ancient wisdom and endorsed the idea of a kind of perpetual oscillation in human affairs, he nevertheless continued to support his own claims to have improved philosophy as well as the possibility of future progress.)[66] Anyway, since the moderns had generally conceded, however grudgingly, most of literature and the arts, Temple thought that all that was required now would be to review the rest. Unfortunately, at

[66]Burnet, like Temple, had been educated by Ralph Cudworth, the leading proponent in his time of the doctrine of the ancient wisdom; see Cudworth's *True Intellectual System of the Universe* (London, 1678). Burnet's *Archaeologiae Philosophicae* (London, 1692) reviews all the traditional sages—Moses, the Persian Magi, the Egyptians, the Cabala, Zoroaster, Hermes Trismegistus, and so on—and concludes that the ancients did indeed know the true system of the world, but that they obscured their knowledge either deliberately, by casting it into poetry or myth, or inadvertently, by lapse of time and the growth of sectarian controversy. In any case, the details of the system were wanting; the facts and demonstrations of physics and mathematics and the method of observation and experiment are therefore a true modern achievement. Burnet believed in further progress also; "Learning, like the Sun, began to take its Course from the East, then turned Westward, when we have long enjoyed its Light. Who knows whether leaving these Seats, it may not yet take a further Progress? Or . . . universally diffuse and enlighten all the World with its Rays": Thomas Burnet, *Doctrina antiqua de rerum originibus; or, An Inquiry into the Doctrines of Philosophers of All Nations Concerning the Origin of the World*, trans. Richard Mead and Thomas Foxton (London, 1736), p. 132.

this crucial juncture a gap appears in the essay (in the manuscript and in the printed version) and it is not clear whether Temple was defeated in his attempt to rescue the ancients for natural science and invention or whether he had left it all to Mr. H.[67]

Perhaps it does not matter; the ancients were not likely to win much advantage here, although it should not be forgotten that even Isaac Newton was wavering on this very same matter.[68] When Temple resumed his argument, he brought up a new subject altogether, one only lightly treated so far: the writing of history. And this proved to be an especially revealing ground, for it was as much about the nature of history as anything else that the ancients and the moderns were quarreling, and perhaps nowhere better can the two positions be so precisely differentiated.

In his original essay, Temple had barely alluded to history. But we have seen that in pairing off the ancients and the moderns under various categories, he compared the recent works of Enrico Davila and Famianus Strada with Herodotus and Livy, Johannes Sleidan with Caesar. The choice was not difficult. And although he was prepared to admit that all histories were useful, "how indifferently soever the Tale is told," he thought that the ancients alone had combined style with content to produce perfect works of instruction and entertainment. Their superiority was the result of their eloquence and their experience. Ancient histories should be read, therefore, he wrote in another place, because they furnished the sum of political wisdom and experience, the models for imitation of all government, institutions, laws, and events. The classical histories were thus the best possible instruction for modern statesmen, and the best modern histories were those that most closely imitated them.[69]

To all this, Wotton agreed, though with the usual reservations. He had, as we have seen, allowed the superiority of ancient eloquence, and under eloquence he had included "all their Stile." But if history was

[67]Temple, *Miscellanea, The Third Part*, p. 231; *Works*, 3:497. "Just where the Pinch of the Question lay," Wotton complained, "there the Copy fails": "Defense of the Reflections," pp. 517–18.

[68]Late in life, while in exile in France, Francis Atterbury read Fontenelle and Newton and discovered that Newton thought the ancients to have been "men of great genius and superior minds who had carried their discoveries (particularly in Astronomy and other parts of the Mathematicks) much farther than now appears from what remains of their writings." He added, "More of the ancients is lost than is preserved, and perhaps our new discoveries are not equal to those old losses": Atterbury to Thiriot, n.d., in Francis Atterbury, *Epistolary Correspondence*, 5 vols. (London, 1783–1790), 1:182. For Newton's *ancienneté*, see J. E. McGuire and P. M. Rattansi, "Newton and the 'Pipes of Pan,'" *Notes and Records of the Royal Society* 21 (1966): 108–43; Frank E. Manuel, *The Religion of Isaac Newton* (Oxford, 1974), pp. 44–49.

[69]Temple, *Miscellanea, The Second Part*, p. 57; *Works*, 3:479; "Of Heroic Virtue," in *Works*, 3:321–22.

joined naturally to rhetoric, it was not, as for Temple, wholly so. Wotton's own favorite among the ancients was Polybius, who had taken pains to neglect "all that Artful Eloquence which was before so much in fashion." And he was willing to match the Polybian virtues with at least two modern works, the *Memoirs* of Philippe de Comines and the *History of the Council of Trent* by Paolo Sarpi. Their merit lay in their matter, that is to say, in their impartiality and instruction. As for the other moderns, Davila and Strada, he was less sure; he would defend them more vigorously "if there was as much Reason to believe their Narratives, as there is to commend their Skill in writing."[70] As it was, he complimented them both but left the comparison with the ancients unspoken.

So much agreement is a little disconcerting, but there was at least one notion about history over which the two antagonists disputed profoundly. It was Wotton who raised the issue first in defending the claims of modern philology. He devoted an entire chapter of the *Reflections* to it, secure in the idea that here, at any rate, the moderns were unrivaled.[71] By philology Wotton meant a great deal more than the study of language, for it was his view that the Renaissance revival of the classical tongues had entailed the resuscitation of an entire civilization. It seemed to him that as a result modern scholars had come to know more about antiquity than even the ancients themselves! "To compare the Moderns to the Ancients may seem a Paradox," he was fully aware, "when the subject matter is entirely ancient," but there was no gainsaying the fact that such moderns as Joseph Scaliger, Isaac Casaubon, and John Selden (to name only a few) were without doubt superior in their knowledge of ancient things to the ancients themselves. How was it possible? Wotton did not mean that modern scholars knew Plato or Aristotle better than they had known themselves. But he did point out that the ancients had not all lived together at one time, though our great distance from them sometimes made it appear so, and as a consequence, they often knew less about their predecessors than a modern scholar with all the instruments of modern scholarship could attain. The invention of printing alone ensured their advantage, for the ancient books could now be compared, examined, and canvassed with an ease unknown to earlier times. Above all, however, it was the discipline of philology itself, barely known to past ages, that gave the moderns their advantage.

Clearly Wotton knew what he was talking about. Among his close friends (fatefully, as it turned out) was the greatest philologist of the age, Richard Bentley. Already in 1689 Wotton was doing manuscript colla-

---

[70]Wotton, *Reflections* (1694), pp. 23, 44, 318.
[71]Ibid., chap. 27, pp. 310–21.

tions for Bentley and referring to the example of Mabillon.[72] "To pore in old Manuscripts," he wrote now, "to compare various Readings; to turn over Glossaries, and old Scholia upon ancient Historians, Orators and Poets; to be minutely critical in all the little Fashions of the Greeks and Romans"—all this was new and fascinating, a triumph of modern ingenuity.[73] New too, and scarcely less important for history, was the modern invention of chronology and the modern competence in geography. Until John Greaves's recent work, there had been no fresh account of the pyramids since Herodotus, nor had there ever been an accurate one.[74] And all this—philology, chronology, antiquarian study of every kind— could recall the memory of things either quite unknown to antiquity or lost sometimes within fifty or a hundred years of its use. And if some of the wits were eager now to scoff at such inquiries, there was nothing they could really do to obscure the magnificent achievement of modern scholarship. It even seemed to Wotton that the thousands of corrections and annotations that had accumulated since the Renaissance had required "more Fineness of Thought and Happiness of Invention" than the originals themselves. After all, the young scholar wrote, "he that discerns another Man's Thoughts is therein greater than he who thinks!"[75]

Is it surprising that Temple bridled when he read these words? He chose the stronger and more obvious ground first. To place Sarpi and Comines next to Herodotus and Livy could only be a jest. He was doubtful that Sarpi's account of Trent could even be called a history, "the Subjects whereof are great Actions and Resolutions." Certainly all the ancient writers agreed that the first prerequisite of a true history was the choice of a "noble and great Subject." Comines, too, had written at best a memoir, truthful and simple in style but hardly a genuine history. As for the claims of modern philology, Temple was astonished. "I know not what to make of it; and less how it came into the number of the sciences." That it was once useful in editing, correcting, and translating old authors Temple was prepared to agree. But "he must be a Conjurer that can make these Moderns, with their Comments and Glossaries, and Annotations, more learned than the Authors themselves."[76] For all that

[72]Wotton to Bentley, May 14, 1689, in *The Correspondence of Richard Bentley*, ed. Christopher Wordsworth, 2 vols. (London, 1842), 1:1–5. Jean Mabillon's *De re diplomatica* appeared in 1681.

[73]Wotton, *Reflections*, p. 316.

[74]John Greaves (1602–1652) had been to Egypt to measure the pyramids; see his *Pyramidographia* (1646), printed among the *Miscellaneous Works* (London, 1737), with a life by Thomas Birch.

[75]Wotton, *Reflections*, p. 318. Naturally, the philologists were pleased, abroad as in England. See Gisbert Cuperus to Abbé Claude Nicaise, Dec. 1, 1695, in *Lettres critiques, d'histoire, de littérature, etc.* (Amsterdam, 1742), p. 440.

[76]Temple, *Miscellanea, The Third Part*, pp. 257–59; *Works*, 3:507.

he could see, modern scholarship was largely pedantry and generally dispensable. "To trouble themselves and the World with vain Niceties and captious cavils about Words and Syllables, in the Judgment of Style; about Hours and Days, in the Account of ancient Actions or Times; about antiquated Names of Persons or Places"—all this was ludicrous, so many trifles and beneath contempt. It was certainly not history, not in any way that the defender of the ancients could possibly recognize. Wotton might as well, he added in a passage that was later canceled, have made tautology into a science as his beloved philology.[77]

7

Temple died in 1699 and Wotton was able to have the last word. In a second version of the *Reflections* in 1697, he reminded his readers that he had meant to be impartial between the conflicting claims of ancients and moderns and willing to give some "Pre-eminence" to both sides, though Temple had not.[78] It was no use. In 1705, stung by the anonymous *Tale of a Tub*, Wotton published a third and final version. The second edition was notable for the contributions of Wotton's friends and especially for an essay appended by Bentley and entitled "A Dissertation upon the Epistles of Phalaris." The third included Wotton's reply to Temple's last thoughts.[79] Bentley attended to the attack on philology, Wotton to the criticism of his defense of modern historical narrative.

The latter problem was the simpler. Wotton at once corrected Temple's misapprehension that he had been exalting the eloquence of Comines and Sarpi. On the contrary, he had singled out Polybius among the ancients precisely "as an Instance that a History may be incomparable, that has not Rhetorical Ornaments to set it off." (That rhetoric might be more than merely decorative seems not to have occurred to Wotton; here, certainly, was another important difference between the two parties.) "The question between us was not," he continued, "whether the Modern Historians absolutely taken exceeded the Ancients"—presumably Wotton conceded the issue here—"but whether some Moderns have not, considering the Subjects they wrote upon, Composed as Instructing Histories as any of the Ancients." Wotton was convinced that they had, just as he was sure that the Council of Trent was a worthy

---

[77]Rothschild MS. 2253, Trinity College, Cambridge, ad fin.

[78]"It was not enough to tell the World I was of no Side, the contrary was taken for granted, since in so many Particulars I actually gave them the Pre-eminence, when Sir William Temple had given it them in nothing": Postscript (April 30, 1697), in *Reflections*, 3d ed. (1705), p. xxxi.

[79]Wotton, "Defense of the Reflections."

subject. In the afterglow of Reformation and Counter-Reformation, its importance was hard to deny. True, the work described no fighting, no burning of towns, "no knocking out of Mens Brains," all of which, Wotton agreed (somewhat ironically), were necessary for a great and noble subject. But surely there was a "Depth of Contrivance and such a Train of Refined Politics" in the modern event, and such insight into motive in the modern historian, that in his own way Sarpi stood alone.[80]

But there was available an even better example than Sarpi to serve the moderns. Wotton was delighted to discover, in a work that was appearing even as he wrote, a history superior to Sarpi's and Comines's, and better even than all but the very best of the ancients: the Earl of Clarendon's *History of the Rebellion and Civil Wars* (1702–1704). He believed that it was in every respect admirable and he was sure that Temple would have agreed. In fact, its virtues were exactly those that his rival, with all the conventional wisdom of Renaissance humanism, had assigned to the works of antiquity. The subject, Wotton declared, was as great, the events as surprising, and the conclusions as miraculous as any Temple could have desired. It offered fighting enough, and negotiations, examples of great virtue and fortitude, and characters of good and evil men vividly described. And all this was accomplished "with so much Strength of Stile, and such a rich Copia of Words," that posterity was bound to recognize it as the equal of the most celebrated classical histories both "for Matter and Elocution," a model for imitation in its own right.[81]

Would Temple have been persuaded? It seems doubtful, although the two men were actually not so far apart as it first appeared. The fact is that in this opening skirmish in the English battle of the books there had been revealed a large and surprising area of agreement between the ancients and the moderns, as well as a genuine difference. Thus the views of the two men about historical narrative showed their common respect for the literature of antiquity. Both thought that its function was to educate the statesman and citizen; both agreed that the most perfect examples of life and art lay in the ancient past and ought to be imitated, differing only about the possibility of success. And both believed that the moderns would have to be evaluated according to classical standards as to subject, style, and composition. If they disagreed somewhat in the emphasis they placed upon each of the special qualities of the ideal history and thus in their evaluations of specific works, there was still enough general agreement to identify them equally as part of a single common culture, the neoclassical culture that had been reborn in the Italian Renaissance and

[80]Ibid., pp. 495–99.
[81]Ibid., p. 500.

slowly but steadily taken root in England. If Clarendon was the best of the moderns—and it was hard to find an Englishman who did not then agree—it was precisely because he had deliberately and successfully emulated the classical virtues. Neither Temple nor Wotton took the slightest notice of anything medieval and therefore both deliberately overlooked the chronicle histories of their own time which still passed for standard but which owed their (unfortunate) style and form to the Middle Ages.

Philology was another matter. Here at last was a basic disagreement. If, for Temple, philology had once had some modest use in restoring the classical texts, the world had become quickly "surfeited" with it. It had, he insisted, exhausted its contribution on its first appearance. He denied that its continuing concern for minutiae could have any value and he failed to see how the discipline could achieve any cumulative advance. He condemned it, therefore, exactly as he had condemned natural science, for its uselessness and its futility, knowing and caring as little about the one as about the other.

Yet surely there was something of a paradox here, for philology had had its first impulse in that very desire for imitation which Temple so much admired. Both the ancients and the moderns accepted the Renaissance humanist view that culture had been reborn in Italy after a long period of barbarism and spread to northern Europe by Erasmus and his contemporaries. But it was beginning to be apparent that there was an ambiguity lodged at the heart of the movement that described itself as the "revival of Antiquity"; and that it seems to have arisen out of that very effort to restore classical culture, to renew an old ideal. The aim from the beginning had been to recover the *paideia* or *studia humanitatis* advocated by the ancient authors. But it was one thing to advocate imitation after Cicero or Quintilian; it was quite another to have to recover their whole teaching and their culture. The one entailed the mimicking of ancient models, the other the development of techniques of recovery— techniques made necessary by the lapse of more than a thousand years. The first meant restoring the rhetorical culture of the ancient world, the second inventing something altogether new, the historical disciplines that we know together as classical scholarship and that Wotton called philology. In impulse they may well have been the same but in practice they had early parted company and pursued rather different paths, always linked but increasingly uneasy; for the more the Renaissance learned of antiquity, of the complex and different cultures it embraced, the more difficult and pedantic did mere imitation begin to seem; yet the more the interest in imitation grew, the less desirable did it appear for the individual author to intrude the clumsy and nonclassical apparatus of modern scholarship into his work. For the man of taste, it was taste itself that seemed endangered by the new barbarities of textual glosses and marginalia, footnotes, appendices and indexes, minute quibbling over the meanings of words. For the man of affairs there was neither time nor use for such reading. For Wotton, however, philology was (like natural science) a true modern achievement, with hardly a precedent in antiquity and of a value inestimable. And it was justified not simply for its use to imitation but as an end in itself. Philology furnished the key to the understanding of the whole of classical life and literature; it was the historical discipline par excellence, the technique that allowed the moderns to know more about antiquity than even the people who had lived in it. And it did so progressively, cumulatively, adding little by little to the sum and precision of modern learning.

Thus,. even in this first episode of the quarrel, it is possible to define the main issue. In effect, the opening round of the battle of the books showed that Renaissance humanism, which had been the ultimate inspiration for both Temple and Wotton, had become divided against itself and that it was no longer possible easily to compose the difference. By 1700 it was becoming necessary to choose either one side or the other: either imitation or scholarship, either the standards of ancient rhetoric or the new techniques of modern criticism, either polished narrative or antiquarian compilation. It was not an easy choice and not everyone was prepared to concede the necessity. But the quarrel had only just begun and its full implications were only just beginning to become obvious.

Chapter Two

Bentley vs. Christ Church

Even before Temple's essay appeared to provoke hostilities, Wotton and Richard Bentley had become fast friends. They were drawn together by common associates such as John Evelyn, and common concerns not the least of which was their fascination with classical philology. It was therefore of the greatest interest to Wotton to discover one day that Bentley too had had some severe thoughts about Temple's essay. In particular, he was delighted to learn that his companion believed that Temple, in the course of his argument, had made a really ludicrous error in defending and extolling the spurious epistles of the ancient Greek tyrant Phalaris. Wotton immediately saw his opportunity and exacted a promise from Bentley to set out his thoughts on the matter for a new edition of the *Reflections*.[1] Here indeed would be proof of the capability of modern scholarship and a humiliating lesson to his adversary. In this fashion began the second episode in the battle of the books.

The moderns were on good solid ground. Early in 1693 Temple wrote a note to Joshua Barnes that betrayed his scholarly weakness. Barnes was an eccentric classicist, in a few years professor of Greek at Cambridge, who aspired also to a career in "polite" literature. He was naturally eager for the approbation of Temple and sent him a parcel containing several of his works, including a poem in Greek. When it arrived, the old man was grateful but embarrassed. The truth was, he complained to Barnes, that

[1]Richard Bentley to William Wotton, "A Dissertation upon the Epistles of Phalaris," appended to Wotton's *Reflections upon Ancient and Modern Learning*, 2d ed. (London, 1697), p. 6.

he had lost so much of the language that he could no longer read it without pain.[2] It was a telling admission for a connoisseur of ancient literature and a striking contrast to the next letter that Barnes received. This was a note from Richard Bentley, apparently in reply to an announcement by Barnes that he intended to edit the works of Euripides, pointing out that the letters of Euripides were forgeries. The authority of Bentley's scholarship was unmistakable and might have shaken a lesser spirit, but Barnes was not a bit perturbed. A year later he published his Euripides, with the letters, and suggested that anyone who doubted them was both ignorant and presumptuous. Moreover, he added gratuitously, the epistles of Phalaris were also genuine.[3]

He should have known better. Bentley's letter was only a sketch of an argument but it was a forecast of what might be done. He tried to explain to Barnes that forgeries had been the common practice of the Sophists in later Greek times and that the letters of Phalaris and Euripides, as well as those of Thucydides, Socrates, and so on, were characteristic examples of their type. "They searched a little into the history of the persons they designed to personate, and so adapted their letters to their circumstances. This was in great credit among them, to follow the character of the person well, and suit the affairs of the times; a man got a reputation by it, and it was owned at first by the true authors: but in time they forgot. . . ." After a while some of them were taken for real; yet the frauds were evident enough, if only one knew sufficient Greek to discern the inadequacy of the style and content. Unfortunately, such things were difficult to demonstrate when the sole evidence was the text alone. "As for arguments to prove them spurious, perhaps there are none that will convince any person that doth not discover it by himself. 'Tis always so, when there are no external proofs and testimonies to be had. . . . Then every man passeth his own judgment according to his genius and his proficiency." Temple might have the genius, he could hardly claim the proficiency; Barnes might have the proficiency, he certainly did not have the genius. "If a man cannot perceive by himself that they are the work of some Sophist, he may acquiesce perhaps in another man's judgment, but he cannot be convinced and understand that they are so."[4] So at least it appeared to Bentley at the beginning of 1693.

[2]William Temple to Joshua Barnes, Feb. 7, 1693, Bodleian MS. Rawl. Lett., 40, f. 37. Barnes is discussed in chap. 5.

[3]Richard Bentley, *Euripides quae extant omnia* (Cambridge, 1694), p. 523, and *Vita Euripidis*, para. 28. For these works and all things Bentleian, see James Henry Monk, *The Life of Richard Bentley*, 2d ed., 2 vols. (London, 1833), 1:52–54.

[4]Bentley to Barnes, Feb. 22, 1693, in Bentley, *Dissertations upon the Epistles of Phalaris*, ed. Wilhelm Wagner (London, 1883), pp. 582–85.

2

Temple's view of Phalaris was particularly revealing of the quality of his classicism. The passage in his essay that offended Bentley began with the flat assertion that the oldest books were invariably the best and that the most ancient works of prose were Aesop's *Fables* and the *Epistles of Phalaris*, both dating back to the time of Pythagoras and both deserving of the highest praise. The *Epistles*, he thought, had "more Race, more Spirit, more Force of Wit and Genius, than any others I have ever seen, either ancient or modern." Temple was aware that some people had questioned their authenticity; he knew that Politian (the fifteenth-century Italian humanist) and others had ascribed them to Lucian.

> But I think he must have little skill in Painting, that cannot find this to be an Original; such diversity of Passions and such variety of Actions and Passages of Life and Government, such Freedom of thought, such Boldness of Expression, such Bounty to his Friends, such Scorn of his Enemies, such Honour of Learned men, such esteem of Good, such Knowledge of Life, such Contempt of Death, with such Fierceness of Nature and Cruelty of Revenge, could never be represented but by him that possessed them.[5]

Outside of the letters not much was known about Phalaris, except for the famous story in Pindar about his burning men to death in a brazen bull. But it seemed to Temple that the *Epistles* were prima facie the work of one who must have been a great ruler and commander. No matter that Temple knew them only in translation, although Politian had read them in Greek. Having dismissed philology as menial, Temple could ignore its doubts and put all his faith in a purely literary evaluation. The letters had clearly struck a responsive chord in the politician's imagination.

With this advertisement, it was not surprising that a new edition of the *Epistles* was soon in preparation. The dean of Christ Church at Oxford was accustomed to having one of his undergraduates each year prepare a fresh version of a classical text. As Macaulay put it, "Aldrich, who knew very little Greek, took the word of Temple who knew none," and asked the young aristocrat Charles Boyle, the future earl of Orrery, to prepared an edition.[6] "The Dean probably thought that he could not have pitched

---

[5]William Temple, "Essay upon Ancient and Modern Learning," in his *Works*, 4 vols. (London, 1814), 3:478.

[6]Thomas Macaulay, "Francis Atterbury" (1853), in *Miscellaneous Writings* (London, 1860), 2:212. The epistles appeared as *Phalaridis Agrigentinorum Tyranni Epistolae* (1695) and contained a life, as well as the Greek text, a Latin translation, and a few pages of notes (largely paraphrase) at the end. Henry Aldrich wrote, among other things, a textbook for Boyle, the *Artis logicae compendium* (1691).

upon any antient Author more likely to inspire a young Man of Quality with Sentiments agreeable to his Birth and Fortune."[7] Being ill equipped for the job, however, and without proper guidance, Boyle did not distinguish himself. But he did worse; he deliberately insulted Bentley, then the royal librarian, over his alleged unwillingness to lend a manuscript for collation. The insult, an ironic remark about Bentley's "singular humanity," was duly enshrined in the preface to the new edition, which appeared in 1695. It made Wotton's invitation to say something about the matter doubly appealing to his friend.

Bentley was already a considerable scholar, well known abroad. He was also an irascible character, arrogant and contentious, though amiable enough in private life.[8] His "Dissertation upon the Epistles of Phalaris" was the first great quarrel of a long and stormy career but it was neither the last nor the least. No sooner had the work appeared than it was met with a reply, and the second and more violent episode in the battle of the books was on.

Bentley reveals the paradox in the quarrel between the ancients and the moderns most completely. He was par excellence the classicist-modern, equally versed in the new science and in humanist philology. When, in 1697, he turned his attention to Phalaris, he had already demonstrated his competence in both fields. He was not, perhaps, a prodigy like his contemporary Wotton, but it had not taken him long to master all the ancient tongues. At twenty-four he compiled a hexapla for the Bible, a six-column work in which all the Hebrew words of the Scripture were matched with their equivalents in the Chaldean, Syriac, Vulgate, Septuagint, and other versions. About that time, having passed through the usual grammar school and university education, he was employed by Edward Stillingfleet, bishop of Worcester, to tutor his son. He later became chaplain to the great man. This employment gave him leisure and access to one of the finest libraries in England. And it was here that he published his first work, an appendix to an edition of the obscure Byzantine chronographer John of Antioch, or Malelas (1692). Bentley's *Epistle to Mill*, as it is known, consists of nearly a hundred pages, correcting and illustrating the old author. Malelas had survived in a single Bodleian manuscript without beginning or end and purported to furnish

[7]Eustace Budgell, *Memoirs of the Life and Character of the Late Earl of Orrery* (London, 1732), p. 157. Some notes on Boyle's life by his son in B.M. MS. Add. 10,388 tell us that while at Christ Church, Boyle also wrote a life of Lysander under the tuition of Atterbury and John Freind.

[8]See Monk, *Life of Bentley*, 2:401–2, based on the recollections of his grandson, Richard Cumberland, *Memoirs of His Life* (London, 1806–7), pp. 7–14. See also "Bentley, Richard," in *Biographia Britannica*, 2d ed., ed. Andrew Kippis, 5 vols. (London, 1778–1793), 1:225n; and the letters to his future wife in *The Diary of Edward Rud*, ed. Henry R. Luard, Cambridge Antiquarian Society, Octavo Publications 5 (Cambridge, 1860), pp. 34–35.

a chronological record of history from creation. Bentley's notes have been described as less a commentary than a "set of dazzling dissertations pegged upon a random set of appalling howlers."[9] He corrects, emends, and rebukes his author on a great range of subjects, displaying a mastery of Greek learning and a critical sense that was at once acclaimed—especially abroad—although some readers had trouble with its characteristic bluntness and liveliness of style. "Well done little Johnny!" Bentley exclaims at one point, "you are the boy for seeing through a millstone!" One of his biographers thought he meant John Mill, but in fact he was addressing Malelas, or, as De Quincey (echoing Bentley) delights to call him, "the absurd old donkey of Antioch."[10] When Bentley corrected a fellow chaplain and editor, Humphrey Hody, on the spelling of Malelas, he was at once accused of arrogance and pedantry, charges that were to follow him for the rest of his long life. To be sure, Bentley made no effort at grace of style or tactfulness of manner; his overweening confidence arose from an honest notion of his own superiority in all matters of classical learning and criticism. But he was bound to give offense.

In 1692, through the offices of his good friend John Evelyn, he was appointed to give the first of the Boyle lectures. (It was an apt return for his seeing Evelyn's new work on ancient coins through the press.) The lectures were remarkable, among other things, for their employment of the latest scientific discoveries in biology, chemistry, and physics and for their first incorporation of Isaac Newton's views into a theological treatise. (Wotton had been able to play a small role as intermediary.)[11] Bentley's explication of his friend's ideas was among the first appreciations of the *Principia*, and Newton, who corresponded with him about it, was properly grateful. Evelyn thought the second lecture "one of the most noble, learned and Convincing discourses, that I had ever heard," and prevailed upon Bentley to publish it.[12] At the time of the Phalaris controversy, Bentley tried to bring his friends together in an informal meeting at his lodgings. "Wren, Locke, Newton, etc. (and I hope when

---

[9]G. P. Gould, Introduction to Richard Bentley, *Epistola ad Joannem Millium* (Toronto, 1962), p. 9. The *Epistola ad Millium* was appended to *Joannes Antiocheni cognomento Malelae Historia Cronica* (Oxford, 1691); Gould's edition is reprinted from the version in *The Works of Richard Bentley*, ed. Alexander Dyce, 3 vols. (London, 1836), 2:239–365.

[10]Thomas De Quincy, "Richard Bentley," in his *Works*, ed. David Masson (London, 1857), 7:52–53; Monk, *Life of Bentley*, 1:25–34.

[11]See James Craig to Wotton, June 24, 1691, in *The Correspondence of Isaac Newton*, ed. H. W. Turnbull et al., 7 vols. (Cambridge, 1959–1977), 3:150–51, conveying information about the Newtonian system for Bentley's use in the Boyle lectures.

[12]Evelyn to Bentley, April 4, 1692, in John Evelyn, *The Diary*, ed. E. S. de Beer, 6 vols. (Oxford, 1953–1955), 5:94. The lecture was printed as *Matter and Motion Cannot Think* (London, 1692), in Bentley, *Works*, 3:27–50. See *Correspondence of Newton*, pp. 321–35.

in Town Mr. Evelyn)," he wrote to the latter, "are to meet here once or twice a week in the Evening."[13] The first among the scholars of antiquity meant to play host to the greatest of the English moderns.

But Phalaris was waiting; the new edition of Wotton's *Reflections* was almost ready. Still smarting from Boyle's sarcasm and offered a convenient opportunity to respond, Bentley took the chance and put together a reply, which was appended to Wotton's tract in 1697. In January he was already at it, postponing for the moment the printing of a new set of Boyle lectures. News circulated fast. "Dr. Bentley is proving Phalaris, Aesop, etc. to be all Spurious poor pieces; how will Sir W. Temple and Mr. Boyle take it?"[14] Bentley had to work quickly to meet his friend's deadline, "while the Printer was employ'd about one leaf, the other was a-making."[15] In a few compact pages he showed the futility of Temple's estimation of Phalaris and the inaccuracy and incompetence of Boyle's edition. He also disposed of the claims of Aesop to antiquity and the braggadocio of Joshua Barnes. However, in joining together Temple and the Christ Church company (for he insisted annoyingly on their joint responsibility), Bentley obscured the fact that Boyle had not actually endorsed the *Epistles* of Phalaris as genuine. On the contrary, the young editor had scrupulously enumerated the arguments on both sides of the question, quoting the skeptics as well as Temple, and even adding some reservations of his own. He thus anticipated and in a few instances may even have stimulated Bentley's thinking on the subject.[16] For example, Bentley saw now that it *was* possible, after all, to marshal arguments against the letters, independent of their style, that might be conclusive for everyone. A further reading of the *Epistles* suggested to him that many errors in chronology—anachronisms and inconsistencies—made their early composition impossible. Boyle had seen something of this difficulty, though only partially and indecisively. For Bentley now it was another matter. "In a Disquisition of this nature," he argued, "an inconsistency in Time and Place is an argument that reaches every body. All will cry out, that Phalaris, etc., are spurious, when they see such breaches." In a way this was too bad, for Bentley remained convinced that he, and anyone with a sure grasp of Greek letters, could have spied the frauds of the Sophists, even if they had avoided such clumsy histor-

[13]Bentley to Evelyn, Oct. 21, 1697, in *The Correspondence of Richard Bentley*, ed. Christopher Wordsworth, 2 vols. (London, 1842), 1:152.

[14]Tancred Robinson to Edward Lhwyd, April 15, 1697, Bodleian MS. Eng. Hist. C 11, f. 82.

[15]Bentley to Evelyn, Mar. 27, 1693, in *Correspondence of Bentley*, pp. 74–75; Bentley to Evelyn, Jan. 12, 1697, in *The Carl Pforzheimer Library: English Literature, 1475–1700*, 3 vols. (New York, 1940), 3:1152–53; Bentley, *Dissertations*, ed. Wagner, p. 65

[16]Charles Boyle, *Phalaridis Agrigentinorum Tyranni Epistolae*, Preface; see R. C. Jebb, *Bentley* (London, 1878), pp. 56–57.

ical mistakes. "For as they were commonly men of small endowments . . . they did their business accordingly; and expressed rather themselves than those they acted."[17]

Indeed, Bentley was very harsh on the poor Sophist who had pretended to be Phalaris, thus damning the taste of both Boyle and Temple, as well as their learning. The *Epistles* were but a "fardle of commonplaces, without life or spirit." One had only to compare them with the letters of a real statesman—with Cicero, say—to see their futility. In Cicero, "what lively characters of men! what descriptions of place! what motifs of time, what particularity of circumstances! what multiplicity of designs and events!"[18] In Phalaris, only emptiness and deadness, silliness and impertinence, the work perhaps of some dreaming pedant, but hardly an ambitious tyrant. The *Epistles* were thus late and clumsy forgeries of no literary value, and in an incompetent edition. Bentley was ready in 1697 with the details to prove it. Wotton's argument was to be vindicated concretely; modern philology was to be shown to be indispensable to an understanding of the ancient world. Let all those who ignored its achievement beware; the indiscriminate worship of antiquity could only lead—had in fact brought Temple and Boyle—to error and frivolity.[19]

3

The scandal was immediate. Not only was Temple offended but the very honor of Christ Church was at stake. Bentley had ignored his young opponent and preferred to speak in plural of "the late learned editors." Henry Aldrich and Boyle's tutors, John Freind and Francis Atterbury, were at once implicated. But what was to be done? An answer was required, yet an answer to so formidable a critic would not be easy to arrange. "In truth," wrote Macaulay, "it would be as easy to persuade an educated Englishman that one of Johnson's Ramblers was the work of William Wallace as to persuade a man like Erasmus [who, like Politian, had suspected the epistles] that a pedantic exercise, composed in the trim and artificial Attic of the time of Julian, was a despatch written by a crafty and ferocious Dorian, who roasted people alive many

[17]Bentley, "Dissertation," pp. 122–23.
[18]Ibid., pp. 62–63.
[19]Evelyn thought that Bentley could not have chosen "a more apposite and just Occasion of not onely vindicating himselfe, but of chastising the petulence of those who returned his Civility with so ill grace, not to say ill manners. He has don himselfe right as he ought, and the whole University, as well as the rest of the Learned World, will be oblig'd for it": Evelyn to Wotton, June 26, 1697, Christ Church MS. Evelyn, Letter-Book (1699), f. 226.

years before there existed a volume of prose in the English language."[20]
But Macaulay underestimated both the ingenuity of the Christ Church
wits and the necessity of a reply.

In fact, Bentley had challenged a more formidable society than he
allowed. The Christ Church men—it is Macaulay again who describes
them—were "dominant at Oxford, powerful in the Inns of Court and
the College of Physicians, conspicuous in Parliament and in the literary
and fashionable circles of London." These were no mere scholars but in
every sense men of the world; and like gentlemen and men of taste in
their time, they were accomplished Latinists and convinced disciples of
antiquity. In this respect they much resembled Temple, the statesman
and diplomat who had composed speeches and diplomatic correspondence, and who wrote occasional essays that were enormously popular,
in contrast to Wotton and Bentley, who knew little of life outside the
academic cloister. To the men of Christ Church, real scholarship appeared mere pedantry. Unfortunately, the quarrel over Phalaris seemed
to require a range of classical, especially Greek, learning that was quite
beyond them. Nevertheless, they had in their favor style and wit
enough, a strong sense of cohesion, and sufficient Latin and Greek
among them to respond vigorously. And they were sure they had a cause
that was worth defending.

It was their common education that both equipped and handicapped
them for the fray. As it happened, Westminster School was closely connected with Christ Church in these years, and those who drew together to
reply had all been first to the one, where they had studied under the famous
Dr. Richard Busby, and then to the other, where they came under the
tutelage of Aldrich. Busby was the most famous and successful schoolmaster of his time, although he had gained a reputation for severity. "Dr.
Busby, a great Man!" writes Roger de Coverley, "he whipped my grandfather; a very great Man! I should have gone to him myself if I had not been
a Blockhead; a very great man!" It was said that when he was showing
Charles II about the school, he apologized for keeping his hat on, since it
would not do to let the boys believe that there was a more important man
in the world than he. He boasted of educating sixteen bishops to the bench,
exaggerating, it appears, only by a little. When he died in 1695, people
passing below reported that they saw flashes and sparks coming from his
window.[21] He ruled for fifty-seven years and it was Steele's opinion that

---

[20]Macaulay, "Francis Atterbury," p. 211.

[21]Sir Charles Lyttleton to Christopher Hatton, April 6, 1695, in *Correspondence of the
Family of Hatton*, ed. E. M. Thompson, 2 vols. (London, 1878), 2:216; *Spectator*, no. 329,
March 18, 1712. In general, see G. F. Russell Barker, *Memoirs of Richard Busby (1609–95)*
(London, 1895). And for Busby's notorious use of the rod, *A True Narrative of the Differ-
ences between Mr. Busby and Mr. Bagshaw, the First and Second Masters of Westminster-School*
(London, 1659), pp. 19–20; "The Diary of the Rev. John Tomlinson," in *Six North Country
Diaries*, ed. J. C. Hodgson, Surtees Society Publications 118 (Durham, 1910), p. 75.

"for education he had as great Effect upon the age he lived in, as that of any ancient Philosopher."[22]

Busby did not, apparently, record his educational views, although he supplied (with the assistance of his ushers) a steady flow of classical texts for his students. The curriculum at Westminster had been set earlier and there is no reason to doubt that it continued much as it had in young William Laud's day, when as a prebendary in the 1620s he recorded his weekly schedule.[23] All was Latin and Greek: some grammar, much reading of the classical authors, exercises in construing, memorizing, translating, and composing. When John Evelyn visited the school at the Restoration, he was startled by the adroitness of the classical compositions—in Latin, Greek, Hebrew, and Arabic—that he heard there, "such exercises in themes and extemporary Verses, as wonderfully astonish'd me, in such young striplings, with that readinesse and witt, some of them not above 12 or 13 years of age." Monitors were appointed to see that the students spoke only Latin, at the risk of penalty. A letter from Dryden to Busby complains that his son has been expelled for just such an infraction.[24]

In afteryears one of Busby's students, Henry Felton, wrote a tract that seems to reflect the master's views and in any case touches upon our controversy. His work was entitled *A Dissertation on Reading the Classics and Forming a Just Style*, and Felton aligns himself specifically with "Temple's party" in the quarrel between the ancients and the moderns. His work is a plea for the traditional classical education, freed from some of its more pedantic characteristics. He remembers that Busby "strictly forbade the Use of Notes, and for our Greek and Latin Authors we had nothing but the plain Text in a correct and chaste Edition." Felton, like the Christ Church wits (and apparently their teacher), resented the pedantry of modern philology. "Comments are generally an Art of making Authors difficult with Pretence of explaining them." There was no need for the "Heaps of Comments," he wrote, "which are piled so high upon Authors, that it is difficult sometimes to clear the Text from the Rubbish, and draw it out of the Ruins."[25] When Dean William Fell had begun in 1666 to require Christ Church students to edit ancient texts as New Year's exercises—a practice that Aldrich continued—he had subscribed

[22]Steele, *The Lover*, April 27, 1714; cf. Thomas Hearne, *Remarks and Collections*, ed. C. E. Doble et al., 11 vols. (Oxford, 1885–1921), 1:301–2, 2:307–8, 8:180.

[23]See Barker, *Memoirs of Busby*, pp. 77–81; Matthew Henry, *An Account of the Life and Death of Mr. Philip Henry* (London, 1712), pp. 5–10; "Locke at Westminster School," in *The Educational Writings of John Locke*, ed. James Axtell (Cambridge, 1968), pp. 21–27.

[24]Evelyn, *Diary*, May 13, 1661, 3:287; Dryden to Busby (1683), in John Nichols, *Illustrations of the Literary History of the Eighteenth Century*, 8 vols. (London, 1817–1858), 4:398. See James A. Winn, *John Dryden and His World* (New Haven, 1987), pp. 36–47.

[25]Henry Felton, *A Dissertation on Reading the Classics and Forming a Just Style*, 2d ed. (London, 1715), pp. 48–50. The work was written in 1709 and appeared first in 1713.

to Busby's views by dispensing with notes and commentary.[26] The edition of Phalaris, with its scanty scholarship, was thus a model of its kind, while the new version of Malelas must have seemed something of a monstrosity.

Felton's view of education is worth examining a little further, it is so perfectly representative of its type and so helpful in illuminating the culture of the "ancients." It was also very popular in its time.[27] Like Wotton's father, Felton hoped to teach the classical languages directly from the authors, with only a minimum of grammar. Unlike Henry Wotton, however, or Temple, he set Latin above Greek and neglected Hebrew altogether. He was not, after all, trying to educate a scholar; he meant rather to train the young man of affairs, in this case specifically the young nobleman John Lord Roos. For such an end, Latin culture was preeminent and the rest of negligible use. One studied Greek only because "the Latins have ransacked the Grecian Store," and therefore simply as an aid to the Latin. The Romans were "such happy Imitators that the Copies have proved more exact than the Originals; and Rome hath triumphed over Athens, as well in Wit, as Arms." A detailed comparison proves their superiority; "the divine Tully is all the Grecian Orators and Philosophers in one." The Roman poets, orators, and historians will yield "all that is admirable in Humane Composure."[28] Although the very same argument had been employed to serve the moderns (for if the Romans could excel the Greeks by imitation, then why should not the moderns excel the Romans?), Felton was certain that nothing new and nothing better could be composed than had already been said by the Latin writers. Perfection, after all, could hardly be improved.

Still the moderns could imitate, if not surpass, their predecessors, and this was the crux of the matter. For the gentlemen of the seventeenth century, reading the ancients was preliminary to imitating them; the study of the classical authors was immediately practical. Despite the earlier Renaissance enthusiasm for Greek, that language had never in fact succeeded as an instrument of fresh expression. The humanists wrote in Latin and they succeeded to a real extent in emulating classical style. But by the end of the seventeenth century, if not long before, Latin too as a literary language had begun to fail, although, to be sure, as the international language of science and erudition it still had some life. As a result, the only recourse for the humanist was to transfer his allegiance to the

[26]For the New Year's books (with a complete list), see E. G. W. Bill, *Education at Christ Church, Oxford, 1660–1800* (Oxford, 1988), pp. 255–63. The practice continued to 1715.

[27]See *Memoirs of Literature*, June 1713; and L. W. Bruggemann, *A View of the English Editions of Translations and Illustrations of Ancient Greek and Latin Authors* (Stettin, 1797), p. 816.

[28]Felton, *Dissertation*, p. 18.

new vernaculars and to inform them as far as possible with the classical virtues. English might thus imitate Latin as Latin had once imitated Greek—and with the same hope of success. Felton, who wrote long after the problem had become evident, was well aware of all this. In his long discussion of imitation, he remarks on the difficulty of imitating a dead language; nor was he hopeful that the "pedanticall Elucidators" (that is, the philologists) could furnish any help. The trouble was that when Horace wrote, the poet had distilled from the thousands of possibilities of Latin eloquence only just what he needed. We have Horace but we have lost thousands of alternative possibilities. We can therefore approach the poet successfully in the letter by imitation, but we cannot hope to restore the full extent and spirit of his expression. And if this means that we cannot rival the ancients in their own (dead) tongues, we can at least turn to our own living language. English, Felton believed, still offered unrealized possibilities. By joining its special virtues to a skill and mastery of Latin (still the most perfect language for Felton), we can best hope to express ourselves, although even so we must not expect to surpass the ancients.[29]

One studies Latin, then, as an inspiration to English style. To imitate is to write as a classical author would have written upon the same occasion. By saturating ourselves with the ancient authors, by habituating ourselves to their works from childhood, we may hope to recapture "the same Turn of Thought, the same Faculty of Expression, and in a word, the same Genius" as they had. In such a way Cicero had once taken profit from the Greek orators; and in such a way we may now take profit from Cicero. So important was style that the great Roman could write about moral philosophy, despite all the disadvantages of a pagan birth, even more brilliantly than the modern Christian with all the benefits of Revelation.[30] It is the divines not least that Felton thinks may profit from classical imitation.

Felton has some further remarks to add about historical writing. Like the other literary genres and at least as important, classical histories, he thinks, can contribute to the formation of a just style. But a perfect history is hard to find. To write well and to write truly is especially difficult; the historian, unlike the poet, is "confined to the Facts and Occurrences he relates." His subject is neither entertaining nor ornamental in itself and sometimes involves arid stretches where nothing much happens. Felton's notion of an appropriate subject is the traditional one; "the richest Fields of History are Scenes of Action and Commotion, where Nations are agitated by Wars abroad or Factions at Home." The

[29]Ibid., pp. 173–94.
[30]Ibid., p. 221.

historian's task is to penetrate the councils of states and princes, to evaluate the motives and springs of action, and to describe the characters of men. Apart from the choice of subject, the whole worth of the historian is in his power of expression, in his literary merit. Felton shows not the slightest concern with research. "History and Narration," he writes, "are nothing but just and lively Descriptions of remarkable Events and Accidents." The aim of the writer is to portray his scene so vividly that the reader seems to be present on the occasion; in this is the "Art and Perfection of a Historical Style."[31]

This, then, is the special virtue of the classical historians, whom Felton proceeds to evaluate. Herodotus and Thucydides, Sallust and Livy, each had an individual style, but all shared the same fundamental excellencies. Of these writers, Livy was perhaps the greatest, "if to the Perfection of his Style, we join the Compass of his Subject." Felton's praise is entirely for his expression, for "the Elegance and Purity, the Greatness and Nobleness of his Diction, his Happiness in Narration, and his wonderful Eloquence." Certainly there had been no modern to match him. To the extent that any of the moderns deserved praise, it was simply by virtue of their emulating "both the Height and Spirit of the Classic Diction." In particular, Felton singles out among the English historians Samuel Daniel, Francis Bacon, Lord Herbert of Cherbury, Walter Ralegh, and above all (Wotton's choice) the Earl of Clarendon, "the noblest and most impartial Historian this Nation hath produced." No other writer, he continues, can compare with him "in the Weight and Solemnity of his Style, in the Strength and Clearness of his Diction, in the Beauty and Majesty of his Expression, and that noble Negligence of Phrase, which maketh his Words wait everywhere upon his Subject, with a Readiness and Propriety, that Art and Study are almost Strangers to."[32] It was, after all, the opinion of the age, of the ancients and the moderns alike.

4

Apparently this, or something very like it, was what the Christ Church wits had learned in grammar school. Indeed, it was nothing more than the ordinary schoolboy view, familiar to everyone since the Italian Renaissance, and they would have had it reinforced at Christ Church under the two great deans, Dr. Fell and Dr. Aldrich.[33] It was during Aldrich's tenure that the bolt against Phalaris struck. How much

[31]Ibid., pp. 222–29.
[32]Ibid., pp. 249–50.
[33]See the commonplace book full of school exercises and Latin compositions by one Dr. Bridges of Christ Church, M.A. (1698) and Doctor (1711); in B.M. MS. Add. 64, 125.

he had to do with the reply is not clear; but several of his intimates and students, including two of his successors, Francis Atterbury and George Smalridge, were certainly involved.[34] The resulting work appeared under Boyle's name and was generally believed to be his, but if anything is certain, it is that he doubted that it was a good idea and had nothing to do with executing it. The real instigator was Atterbury, who called on his Christ Church colleagues to contribute: among them, Smalridge, Anthony Alsop, the brothers John and Robert Freind, and William King. All were Westminsters and all had had a thorough classical training, though hardly sufficient to overcome their redoubtable adversary.

Atterbury was in charge. Shortly after the appearance of the book, he wrote to Boyle that he had laid out its design, written more than half of it, reviewed the rest, and transcribed the whole. The task had taken half a year.[35] He was still a young man and very ambitious, destined eventually for high preferment and a stormy political career. He was also a brilliant controversialist, and "Boyle against Bentley" (as the tract became known) may well have been his masterpiece, although his later quarrels raised quite as much stir. He was especially close to Busby and Aldrich, and emerged from his education a fluent Latinist with a strong taste for letters. In afterlife he was intimate with many writers, including Swift and Pope—even with Addison, despite his politics. His first work, written while he was still a student, was a Latin translation of Dryden's *Absalom and Achitophel*. He wrote other Latin and English verse, translated some Virgil, edited Edmund Waller, and left a number of manuscripts on miscellaneous classical subjects.[36] But he had no taste for real

[34]For Aldrich's doubtful complicity, see W. G. Hiscock, *Henry Aldrich of Christ Church* (Oxford, 1960), pp. 50–56, although Hiscock admits that Aldrich did design the frontispiece engraving of Phalaris's bull. E. F. A. Settle insists, however, that he at least fostered the spirit of the enterprise: "Henry Aldrich, Dean of Christ Church," *Oxoniensia* 5 (1940): 124–25. Aldrich was a typical all-round virtuoso but not a real scholar; see the conversation between Arthur Charlett and Thomas Hearne in Hearne's *Remarks and Collections*, 6:47.

[35]See Atterbury's letter to Boyle in his *Epistolary Correspondence*, 5 vols. (London, 1783–1790), 2:21. Inside the flyleaf of a copy of the 3d ed. (Bodleian MS. Radcliffe E 100) is a note said to be copied from the poet Richard Duke, assigning Atterbury pp. 1–60, 90–112, 133–84, 215–30, and almost all the work dealing with Aesop. Duke was Atterbury's chaplain; see Colin J. Horne, "The Phalaris Controversy: King vs. Bentley," *Review of English Studies* 22 (1946): 290n. See also the testimony of Alexander Pope, quoted in a letter of William Warburton to William Hurd, Aug. 19, 1749, "that Freind, the Master of Westminster, and Atterbury wrote the body of the criticisms, and that Dr. King of the Commons wrote the droll argument to prove Dr. B was not the author of the Dissertation on Phalaris and the Index": William Warburton, *Letters from a late eminent Prelate to one of his Friends* (London, 1793), pp. 7–10; and Hearne, *Remarks and Collections*, 2:78.

[36]Biographies of Atterbury have been written by Folkestone Williams (1869), H. C. Beeching (1909), and G. V. Bennett (1975). Hearne thought the bishop "no ill Poet, in English and Latin": *Remarks and Collections*, 11:97. Contemporary praise for his prose style is collected in Atterbury, *Epistolary Correspondence*, 2:442–44. See also Thomas Stackhouse, *Memoirs of the Life, Character, Conduct and Writings of Dr. Francis Atterbury*, 2d ed. (London, 1727).

learning, for philology or antiquities, although according to Addison, when once he was compelled to search among the rolls and records, he actually began to enjoy the activity. If so, it was a belated taste and never resulted in any serious work.[37] Like the rest of the wits, he accepted the opposition between the classicist whose object was imitation and the classicist whose concern was scholarship. As his editor put it, to make oneself "master of the genius and spirit" of an ancient poet was a very different thing "from crowding together various readings, and mustering up quotations, according to the mode of modern critics." Scholars, he continued, "rather confound and puzzle the reader, and cast dark clouds over the brightest passages of an author, whilst they are making a parade of Greek and Latin learning, wild conjectures, and far-fetched interpretations, in order to lay claim to the title of learned men and critics." Despite all their efforts, "they could neither think nor write in the easy and elegant manner of the ancients."[38]

If Atterbury's classical learning was somewhat limited, he had the support of others. His friend Smalridge was at least as good a Latinist; a later critic judged his "purity of style and diction truly Roman."[39] Of the two brothers named Freind, the older, Robert, first became undermaster (1698), then headmaster (1711) of Westminster School, where he attracted and instructed the children of the aristocracy and wrote occasional Latin poetry. The younger brother, John, dabbled in politics and became one of the most successful physicians of the day, composing enough Latin prose to fill a posthumous *Opera omnia*. (When he died in 1728, Robert composed a long Latin epitaph of which Pope said that "one half will never be believed, the other never read.") And Anthony Alsop was a decent Latin poet who left many odes that were also published posthumously for which he was praised immoderately as "inferior only to his master, Horace."[40] The practical value of Boyle's exercise must have seemed apparent to everyone; by taking up the cudgels he could expect to win position through the good offices of Temple. Although there was also some danger, since Bentley was well thought of at court, Smalridge was optimistic that the "great lashes and Arrogance" of the

[37]*Spectator*, no. 447, Aug. 2, 1712; Hearne, *Remarks and Collections*, 3:108; see David Douglas, *English Scholars*, 2d ed. (London, 1951), pp. 203–6, and the amusing anecdote in "Diary of the Rev. John Tomlinson," p. 75.

[38]Atterbury, *Epistolary Correspondence*, 1:330–31. As Atterbury himself put it, apropos of his remarks on Virgil, "The text of great Authors well considered is the best Comment on itself, and affords the truest Lights towards entering into the Spirit and Sense of them." I quote from the manuscript "Observations upon the Design of Iapis in the Twelfth Book of Virgil's Aeneis," Bodleian MS. Eng. Poet. F 12, ff. 44–45. See Atterbury's *Antonius Musa's Character Represented by Virgil in the Person of Iapis* (London, 1740), reprinted in his *Epistolary Correspondence*, 1:329–66.

[39]The Rev. Edward Knyaston in Nichols, *Literary Illustrations*, 3:225n.

[40]See Leicester Bradner, "Some Notes on Anthony Alsop's *Odarum libri duo*," *Bodleian Library Record* 9 (1976): 231–34.

doctor would surely tell against him there, perhaps even at his own Cambridge. "This at least I am confident of, that all persons of Quality and good breading will declare against him, when it shall appear how clumsily and unlike either a gentleman or a scholar, he has treated Mr. Boyle and Sir William Temple, who have something at least of both."[41] In the event, it was not a bad prophecy.

The result of the coalition was formally entitled *Dr. Bentley's Dissertations on the Epistles of Phalaris and the Fables of Aesop Examin'd*. The Examiner began at once ad hominem with a nod at Temple and a slap at the doctor. Temple "had set the world a Pattern of mixing Wit with Reason, Sound Knowledge with Good Manners, and of making the one to serve to recommend and set off the other."[42] Bentley, by contrast, had been rude and unmannerly, dogmatic and opinionated. But the contrast was not limited to manners. At bottom there was a clash of cultural ideals. What bothered the Examiner most was the challenge that Bentley's classical scholarship seemed to pose to the very integrity and usefulness of the classical ideal. If Wotton and Bentley were right, a gentleman who needed the classics for practical life would have to submit to the discipline of lifelong scholarship or risk error. Moreover, the chief consequence of modern scholarship, whatever its declared intentions, seemed to be nothing more than to trivialize or call into question the very meaning and use of the ancients. Scholarly education seemed only effective in turning out uncouth pedants, not statesmen or men of the world, as Bentley's example showed only too plainly. What disturbed the Examiner, therefore, was not just the rudeness of the manner but the inappropriate nature of the matter. "Dr. Bentley's Appendix has all the Pomp and Show of Learning without the Reality." Who, after all, was better able to judge the authenticity of the *Epistles*—not to say their literary value—a man who had spent most of his life transacting affairs of state or an academic pedant? "He, Temple, had written to Kings and they to Him, and this has qualified him to judge how Kings should write, much better than all Dr. Bentley's Correspondence with Foreign Professors."[43]

[41]Smalridge to Walter Gough, Feb. 22, 1698, in Nichols, *Literary Illustrations*, 3:268–69. For Boyle's hopes for Temple's patronage, see ibid., pp. 270–71; and Boyle to Atterbury (1693), in Atterbury, *Epistolary Correspondence*, 1:19–20; Temple to Boyle, July 17, 1698, in A. C. Elias, Jr., *Swift at Moor Park: Problems in Biography and Criticism* (Philadelphia, 1982), p. 254.

[42]Charles Boyle, *Dr. Bentley's Dissertations on the Epistles of Phalaris and the Fables of Aesop Examin'd* (London, 1698), Preface.

[43]Ibid., pp. 25, 92. As Boyle's biographer put it later, "We see an absolute Monarch [i.e., Phalaris] scorning to palliate even his own Faults; and who, when he shews a fierce Contempt for the vulgar and common Herd of his Enemies, is ready to pay the utmost Tribute to uncommon Merit wherever he discovers it! If we form a Judgment from the Matter and Sentiments of these Epistles (which I must once more add is the best way of Judging of them) we have the strongest Reasons to believe they are genuine": Budgell, *Memoirs of Orrery*, pp. 189–90.

(Bentley had made the mistake of boasting about his foreign reputation.)
The Examiner was prepared to anatomize the doctor's pedantry ad nau-
seam, nicely obscuring the substantive issues. Among Bentley's many
foolish predilections, he singles out one especially, "to overrate the Price
of Knowledge, and to make a great ado about the true Rendering of a
Phrase, or Accounting of a Word as if in an Article of Faith." The
painstaking labor of the philologist meant nothing to the man of affairs.
He quotes the Frenchman, La Bruyère with relish against the pedants:
"They have a Vain, Dry, Insipid sort of Knowledge, that is Disagreeable
and Useless, can neither enliven Conversation, nor conduce to
Business."[44]

But it was necessary also to defend Boyle's edition of the *Epistles*.
According to the Examiner, his version of Phalaris had been intended
merely as an exercise of the pen to see whether he could catch the style
and sense of the original in another language (Greek into Latin). Boyle
had never meant "to set up for Exactness in that Dry Sort of Learning."
"To consult the several Editions, to collate the Manuscripts, to turn over
Dictionaries, nay, even to make 'em"—all this fussing appeared to the
Christ Church men but "Noise about Trifles." This sort of activity could
only harm true learning. Again the French were called upon for support.
This time Saint Evremond is invoked against the pedants for trivializing
the past. "In history, they know nothing of Men and Affairs, they turn
all to chronology. Cicero with them goes only for a Master of Orations,
Caesar for a writer of Commentaries; the Consul and General are lost to
'em." Put to the choice—for however much the reader would like to join
the alternatives, the Examiner will not allow it—the men of Christ
Church would rather be altogether ignorant of the Greek alphabet than
be like Bentley. "For as much as I value Learning, I value Good Sense,
and Common Civility more."[45]

Unfortunately, the wits could not rest content with personal abuse
and the disparagement of pedantry. Decry Bentley's methods they
might, there was no way they could evade the philological argument. It
was a tribute to the positive advance of scholarship that it was now
unavoidable. And so, pooling their large talents and limited Greek, they
attempted to meet the doctor point by point. The result was an ingenious
performance, well calculated to persuade the casual reader or the man
with little learning. One by one they tried to strike down Bentley's
arguments. They defended the Syracusan's odd choice of the Doric dialect and his awkward dates and the peculiar denominations of his coins.
They explained away anachronisms in names and places, as well as the

[44]Boyle, *Bentley's Dissertations*, pp. 94, 99.
[45]Ibid., pp. 202, 223, 225–28.

many phrases that Phalaris seemed to have borrowed from later writers. They even tried to make plausible the long disappearance of the letters from the world, neglected for a thousand years during antiquity, by finding some similar examples. They impugned Bentley's sources, emended texts to avoid inconvenient examples, and cited authors early and late that had been overlooked by their learned rival. And most ardently they defended the consistency and good sense that they found in the letters.

To the Greekless reader the rebuttal looked all too convincing. The Christ Church company had succeeded in clouding the scholarly issues for all but the most patient and knowledgeable of readers. But even more convincing, no doubt, was the satire that they then trained on Bentley's aggressive style and personal idiosyncrasies. A brilliant section, probably by William King, argued that Bentley's work, to judge by his own criteria, must itself look to future centuries like an evident forgery. Since the style of the "Dissertation" was "neither that of a Scholar nor an Englishman, neither Greek, Latin, nor English," and since the doctor was known to come of a good family, to have had a university education, "to have convers'd much in the City and at Court," it followed unmistakably that the work could not be his! King also seems to have added "A Short Account of Dr. Bentley by Way of Index" to assist the reader.[46] Here, arranged conveniently by page, was Dr. Bentley's "dogmatical air," his "modesty and clemency in contradicting great men" (many references), "his charges against the Sophists return'd upon himself," and so on.

It was a rhetorical tour de force; Macaulay was stunned when he read it. "I do not suppose," he wrote in his copy, "that there is in the whole history of letters a single instance of so good a fight made with such small a means—so fair a face put on so bad a cause." As Molière's miser said, it was one thing to make a fine show with plenty of money, but the proof of an artist was to make one without any.[47] Later he wrote of Atterbury:

That he was altogether in the wrong on the main question, and on all the collateral questions springing out of it, that his knowledge of the language, the literature, and the history of Greece was not equal to what many freshmen now bring up every year to Cambridge and

[46]See Warburton, *Letters from a late Prelate*, p. 11. The passage is in Boyle, *Bentley's Dissertations*, pp. 184–201. King had been present in the bookseller's shop when Bentley refused to extend his loan of Phalaris to Boyle; the Examiner cited his testimony in *Bentley's Dissertations* and again in *A Short Account of Dr. Bentley's Humanity and Justice in a Letter to the Honourable Charles Boyle* (London, 1699).

[47]See Jane Millgate, "Macaulay at Work: An Example of His Use of Sources," *Cambridge Bibliographical Society Transactions* 5 (1970): 96.

Oxford, and that many of his blunders seem rather to deserve a flog-
ging than a refutation is true, and therefore it is that his performance is,
in the highest degree, interesting and valuable to a judicious reader. It is
good by reason of its exceeding badness. It is the most extraordinary
instance that exists of the art of making much show with little
substance."[48]

It was a perfect example, he might have added, of ancient sophistic
rhetoric, of a certain kind of classical education assimilated and turned to
practical advantage.

But Macaulay's judgment is not altogether right. That a nineteenth-
century schoolboy trained in Greek could know more than the Christ
Church company combined might well be true; but so too could a
twentieth-century schoolboy claim to know more about physics than
Isaac Newton. It is not therefore either Atterbury's or Newton's competence that is at question. In each instance it is rather the cumulative
advance of the two disciplines that has made it possible now (as in
Macaulay's day) to see clearly and to know easily the solution to a
problem that was then still difficult. It is a case, as the moderns argued,
of dwarfs standing on the shoulders of giants. It is not too much to say
that Bentley was the Newton of classical philology and rather like his
friend could see the solution of the problem at once, although it was only
through his demonstrations that he could truly proclaim his genius and
the victory of his method. In either case, it is doubtful that anyone else in
Europe was as competent then to argue the matter; and it was to take a
good long time before Bentleian philology and Newtonian physics were
sufficiently assimilated so as to become everybody's property. Moreover, Bentley had yet to make his full demonstration when the Christ
Church men drew up their arguments; there was (we shall see) much
more to come.

Indeed, to contemporaries, the matter looked very different. For the
moment, nearly everyone agreed: Boyle and his friends had won a re-
sounding victory. In London, praise for them was universal. Young and
old (including the ninety-three-year-old mathematician John Wallis)
were reading the book with pleasure.[49] Oxford, of course, was particu-

[48]Macaulay, "Francis Atterbury," pp. 314–15. Macaulay read through the Phalaris
controversy twice on his arrival in India (1837) in preparation for an essay on Temple. Later
(1853) he reread "Boyle against Bentley" for his article on Atterbury. If anything, his
respect for the work grew. "It is really a masterpiece. . . . I never saw such an exhibition of
cleverness. Bentley's learning is not more wonderful than the show which Atterbury makes
of his ignorance": T. B. Macaulay, Letters, ed. Thomas Pinney, 3 vols. (Cambridge, 1976–
1981), 3:216–17, 317–18.

[49]"Dr. Wallis complained to me that the Women of his family allowed him but one Half
Hour in the first 48, and that by stealth; since then he has read it with equal Delight and
Satisfaction as he used to do a Discourse of Mathematicks": Arthur Charlett to Boyle, April

larly happy, but even at Cambridge the wits were making fun of the doctor. According to one account, "they drew his Picture in the Hands of Phalaris's Guards, who were putting him into their Master's Bull. And out of the Doctor's Mouth came a Label with these Words: I had rather be Roasted than Boyled."[50] Samuel Garth congratulated his old friends smugly:

> So Diamonds take a Lustre from their Foyle
> And to a Bentley 'tis, we owe a Boyle.[51]

Only Boyle himself hesitated. On the whole, society was relieved; the scholarly gentlemen had routed the uncouth pedant. But Dr. Bentley was biding his time.

5

The wits, of course, were delighted with the "Examination" and certain of the victory. "You and I and every Body," wrote Tom Brown (who, though he may not have loved Dr. Fell, was a loyal son of Christ Church), "have been charm'd with the Honourable Mr. Boyle's Answer to a stiff and haughty Grammarian. . . . Never did Wit and Learning Triumph so gloriously over Dullness and Pedantry as in that noble Book." "All the Polite Judges in Europe," he continued, "were pleased to see an Arrogant Pedant that has been crowding his Head twenty Years together with the Spoils of Lexicons and Dictionaries, worsted and foiled by a Young Gentleman, upon his own Dunghil, and by his own Criticisms."[52] To others the outcome was not so clear. "It is a hard matter to decide the controversy between Persons of this Study," complained one F. B., an M.A. of Cambridge, "for there is a great deal of subtlety and double-dealing in the ordinary managing of the Critick's Office; and it is an easy matter for a well-read man to thrust his Notions on the belief of the World, and to gain a good reception, tho' they have very little solidity at bottom."[53]

12, 1698, in *Orrery Papers*, ed. Countess of Cork and Orrery, 2 vols. (London, 1903), 1:19–20.

[50]Budgell, *Memoirs of Orrery*, p. 193. For the Oxford reception, see Smalridge to Gough, Mar. 22, 1698, in Nichols, *Literary Illustrations*, 3:269–70.

[51]Samuel Garth, *The Dispensary* (1699), canto 5, ll. 73–74, in *Poems on Affairs of State, 1697–1704*, ed. George Lord, 7 vols. (New Haven, 1970), 6:108.

[52]"Original Letters Lately Written by Mr. Brown," in *The Works of Monsieur Voiture* (London, 1705), pp. 133–34. Brown had been to Christ Church under William Fell in 1678; see B. Boyce, *Brown of Facetious Memory* (Cambridge, Mass., 1939).

[53]F. B., *A Free but Modest Censure on the Late Controversial Writings and Debates of the Late Lord Bishop of Winchester and Mr. Locke; Mr. Edwards and Mr. Locke; the Hon. Charles Boyle, Esq. and Dr. Bentley* (London, 1698), p. 16.

How to evaluate the learning? That was the problem. "Boyle against Bentley" was successful in large measure just because it diverted attention from the intellectual issue in order to concentrate upon the personal quarrel. That this was all to the Examiner's advantage was clear, since the ad hominem argument was more easily understood and more immediately interesting than the question of scholarship. Had Bentley been rude to Boyle by withholding the manuscript of Phalaris? Had Bentley been ruder still and unprovoked in his abrasive criticisms of Boyle and Temple in the "Dissertations"? Was Bentley's rough style and learned argument at all suited to the occasion? On the first point, Bentley tried to dispute the facts by recounting all the circumstances of the loan, although in the end it came down to his word against the bookseller who had tried to borrow the manuscript for Boyle.[54] For the rest, evasion was impossible; Bentley's sarcasm and his display of learning had been maliciously intended. John Evelyn at least welcomed Bentley's blast against those "supercilious and haughty pretenders." "Our learned friend," Evelyn wrote to Wotton, "could never have met a more apposite and just Occasion of not onely vindicating himselfe, but of chastising the petulence of those who returned his Civility with so ill grace, not to say ill manners. He had don himselfe right as he ought, and the whole University, as well as the rest of the Learned World, will be oblig'd for it."[55]

But Evelyn was a friend and Bentley's bite was not to everyone's taste. In Tancred Robinson's view, Bentley's appendix to Wotton was "too severe upon the University of Oxford and Sir W. Temple. The Dr. seems to be a great Critick in the Greek Affairs, but in my opinion he is too stiff, and overrun with Pedantry." Bentley had told him that he was preparing a Latin version, which Robinson feared would reflect on the university.[56] Even Pepys, who might otherwise have been expected to side with the moderns, believed that Bentley deserved rebuke. "I suspect Mr. Boyle is in the right," he confided to Evelyn, "for our Friend's Learning (which indeed I have great value for) wants a little fileing; and I doubt not, but a few such Stroakes on this of Mr. Boyl's will doe it and

---

[54]Monk's judicious account remains the best and generally exonerates Bentley: *Life of Bentley*, pp. 65–69; but Humfrey Wanley (librarian at this time to Robert Harley) describes how difficult the doctor could be: "I have at length got the Dr. in a perfect humor, and this day began to take a Specimen of the Alexandrian MS. The Dr. made me dine with him and treated me with great kindness; after dinner, I again mov'd to see the Library, having been put by 3 or 4 times before; which now he readily granted. The books lie in inexpressible disorder and confusion . . . ": Wanley to Charlett, May 30, 1698, Bodleian MS. Ballard 13, f. 41.

[55]Evelyn to Wotton, June 26, 1697, Christ Church MS. Evelyn, Letter-Book (1699), p. 226.

[56]Robinson to Lhwyd, June 26, 1697, Bodleian MS. Ashmole 1817a, f. 340; Mar. 5, 1698, ibid., f. 341; Sept. 28 and Aug. 23, 1698, Bodleian MS. Misc. Hist. C 11, ff. 85, 89v.

him good." The learned Thomas Gale seems also to have shared this view.[57]

Thus for many the quarrel was reduced to an exercise in decorum. In the lull that succeeded the "Examination," one T. R. took the field to measure the combatants and reinforce the point. *An Essay Concerning Critical and Curious Learning* (1698) was an attempt to review the controversy without prejudice; it succeeded only insofar as it avoided the intellectual issues. T. R., who was once thought to be Thomas Rymer but who has retreated again into anonymity, began by raising the question whether "critical and curious inquiries are really conducive to the advancement of solid and useful learning or not?" His answer was more than a little equivocal, for he dismissed almost all modern learning as being either too theoretical on the one hand or too minute on the other, allowing a place only for the new "experimental philosophy."[58] He conceded that chronology was a useful technical discipline as an accessory to history but dismissed its concern for accuracy with a sneer at its "small Punctilio's and Niceties; wherein perchance they are much concerned to discover whether Homer or Hesiod did really live first; to know what Day and Hour such a King or Consul dyed," and similar minutiae. Antiquities were likewise "but Uncertain and Conjectural, being drawn out of defaced Monuments, Coins, Inscriptions, Calendars, Traditions, Archives, Fragments, and scattered passages of lost Books." In a passage that recalls the now traditional satire on the virtuoso, he continued, "To discover the Year of a rusted Medal, or the date of a Moth-eaten Manuscript" was more important to the antiquary than "to be acquainted with the Life and Actions of that Emperour whose Image the Coin bears, or to understand the Style and Matter of the Book itself."[59] There was obviously not much hope here for the philological arguments of either Bentley or Wotton; nor was experimental philosophy likely to settle the issue. T. R. was left to consider the style and controversial manners of

[57]Pepys to Evelyn, Jan. 10, 1695, in John Evelyn, *Letters and Second Diary*, ed. R. G. Howarth (London, 1933), p. 255; Gale to Pepys, Mar. 18, 1699, in *The Private Correspondence of Samuel Pepys*, ed. J. R. Tanner, 2 vols. (New York, 1926), 1:169–70. Monk thought that Gale, who had once been Boyle's tutor, might even have contributed to the second edition of "Boyle against Bentley": *Life of Bentley*, 1:64.

[58]T. R., *An Essay Concerning Critical and Curious Learning in Which Are Contained Some Short Reflections on the Controversies betwixt Sir William Temple and Mr. Wotton and That betwixt Dr. Bentley and Mr. Boyl* (London, 1698), p. 10. Curt Zimansky, who edited the work for the Augustan Reprint Society (Los Angeles, 1965), dismissed Rymer's claims in his introduction; see also his edition of *The Critical Works of Thomas Rymer* (New Haven, 1956), pp. 287–88. Thomas Smith believed the work was Rymer's but found it "a very poor and mean Performance": Hearne, *Remarks and Collections*, 2:256–57.

[59]T. R., *Essay Concerning Critical and Curious Learning*, pp. 14–17. For satire on this theme, see my *Dr. Woodward's Shield: History, Science, and Satire in Augustan England* (Berkeley, 1977), chap. 7.

the contestants. These he found, with the one exception of Temple, equally unfortunate. He conceded that Wotton's position was probably the stronger but his style was bad and his manners worse. He had treated with "little Respect and Decency" one of the "most Gentlemanly Writers of our Age," quibbled needlessly over trifles, and repeated what was already common knowledge. Whatever the merits of his argument, Temple's essay, he concluded, "will always be read with more Pleasure than Mr. Wotton's *Reflections* with Profit." As for Bentley and Boyle, there was little to choose between them. If Bentley had written with insolence and pedantry, the "select Club" had replied with "schoolboy's Jests and little Witticisms."[60] Inevitably Christ Church was unhappy with the comparison, and T. R. found himself immediately challenged and forced to vindicate himself in a new exchange of pamphlets.[61]

Under the circumstances, then, it is not altogether surprising that even the moderns were divided and a bit uncertain. A few of them were confident enough in their cause and their champions. William Nicolson of Carlisle, a good Saxonist and a generally accomplished virtuoso, was enchanted by both editions of Wotton's *Reflections*. "I never in my whole life had more agreeable Conversation," he wrote to compliment the author upon receiving a copy. When Wotton replied that the opposition seemed dangerous, Nicolson reassured him: "I am less afraid of the storm you tell me of from the young men of Christ Church. I have not yet seen Mr. Boyle's book; but I can easily foretell what the poor gentleman's fate will be, that engages two such champions as Dr. Bentley and yourself, in such a field." He pledged his own support as well as that of two scholar friends, White Kennett and Thomas Tanner.[62] But when the "Examination" appeared, Nicolson's other friend and fellow Saxonist Edmund Gibson was able to report from London only that "Mr. Boyle's Answer is very much admir'd by all; even the Doctor's Friends cannot deny it to be such a fine mixture of wit, language, argument, and learning, as is hardly to be met with in any single Book. . . . The Dean of Canterbury and Mr. Pepys are perfectly ravisht with it." And Tancred

---

[60]T. R., *Essay Concerning Critical and Curious Learning*, pp. 46–47, 52, 62.

[61]*An Answer to a Late Pamphlet Called an Essay* (London, Aug. 6, 1698); T. R., *A Vindication of an Essay* (London, Aug. 23, 1698). A schoolmaster named John Milner attempted to discredit the new science of chronology in favor of the Bible alone in *A View of the Dissertation upon the Epistles of Phalaris . . . also of the Examiner* (London, 1698). Temple bought them all; see Irwin Ehrenpreis, *Swift: The Man, His Works, and the Age*, 3 vols. (Cambridge, Mass., 1962–1983), 1:286–87.

[62]Nicolson to Wotton, Sept. 11, 1697, and May 7, 1698, in *Letters to and from William Nicolson*, ed. J. Nichols, 2 vols. (London, 1809), 1:71–74, 106–8. Eventually Nicolson fought his own battle against Atterbury and Christ Church, in a war over Anglo-Saxon rather than Greek antiquity. See Douglas, *English Scholars*, pp. 203–21, and my essay "William Nicolson, Virtuoso," in *The London Diaries of William Nicolson*, ed. Clyve Jones and Geoffrey Holmes (Oxford, 1985), pp. 11–17.

Robinson was relieved to find that "Mr. Boyle has performed beyond my Expectation in his Examination of Dr. Bentley; surely all the wit of Oxford has flow'd in to assist him." It seemed to Bentley at one point that his friend John Evelyn was the only one who was willing to support him. "Among the cry of such as are concerned as a Party to run me down, You alone would stand up for me."[63]

Almost as puzzled and divided was the small group of Greek scholars who alone in Britain could really evaluate the battle. There were not many of them altogether, for although Greek was taught in the schools, it was very much a second language to Latin and a belated accomplishment in England. Yet at least a few had mastered it beyond question, and they naturally looked on the quarrel with great interest, if little enthusiasm. The trouble was that the personal issue, even for them, came to becloud the larger question. A good example is Dr. Edward Bernard, mathematician, professor of astronomy at Oxford, and fellow of the Royal Society. He applied himself also, we are told, "with the utmost attention and diligence, to the more useful studies of History, Philology, and Philosophy, particularly to Philology, which he had a very great inclination to, and of which he was infinitely fond." Anthony Wood thought him the finest scholar of the age. His career was largely unfulfilled, however, bad luck and an indecisive character combining to abort a large number of ventures, though he was recognized by everyone as a profound scholar with a good knowledge not only of Latin and Greek but of Hebrew, Syriac, Arabic, and Coptic. At Paris and Leyden he mixed with the learned, and he kept up a foreign correspondence until his death in 1696. His friend Thomas Smith, also a Greek scholar, who had actually lived in the East, wrote his biography and praised his learning. Withall, Smith noted, Bernard was "of a mild disposition, greatly averse to contests and quarrels."[64]

Bernard was certainly of another disposition than his friend Richard Bentley. When Bentley was working on Malelas, he appealed to the older man for help. Unfortunately, upon receiving it, he turned aside some of Bernard's suggestions in his usual brusque manner, which led the old scholar to complain to Smith of Bentley's continual "boastings." "You will find by two of his epistles, especially the latter, how arrogance grows upon him, yet, though I might easily make him appear a very

[63]Gibson to Charlett, Mar. 26, 1698, Bodleian MS. Ballard 5, f. 120; Tancred Robinson to Lhwyd, April 8, 1698, Bodleian MS. Ashmole 1817a, f. 342; Bentley to Evelyn, April 21, 1698, in *Correspondence of Bentley*, 1:167.

[64]Anthony Wood, *Athenae Oxoniensis*, ed. P. Bliss, 4 vols. (Oxford, 1813–1820), 4:705; Thomas Smith, *Vita Edwardi Bernardi*, appended to *Roberti Huntington: Epistolae* (London, 1704), p. 55; Kippis, *Biographia Britannica*, 2:263–67. Some of Bernard's correspondence with foreign scholars may be found in Bodleian MSS. Smith 5, 14, 16.

rashe and foolish Critic both, as to verse and prose, I choose the sweeter way and permit his mistakes to go to the public by himself without encreasing his stock from my conjectures."[65] When the *Epistle to Mill* appeared, he alone and his friend Thomas Smith were not impressed; he thought Bentley had committed several errors and was bound to do himself harm, especially when he dared to correct the text of St. Paul. In general, the two scholars disagreed profoundly over the relationship between the ancient Greek writers and Christian tradition, Bentley taking a markedly more skeptical line. Bernard was alarmed to discover that the younger scholar believed that a fragment criticizing polytheism, attributed by several church fathers to Sophocles, was actually a late forgery. Bentley also suspected the Orphic and Sybilline writings that had been used for the same apologetic purposes, most recently by the Cambridge Platonists (including Temple's teacher Ralph Cudworth).[66] And he continued to disagree with Bentley even over the Boyle lectures. When Bentley got his doctor's degree in 1696, Bernard was sure that he had "lost credit." "His verses are too poor for one that would put out Lucretius, Manilius, Callimachus and what not." (We shall hear that criticism again.) Nevertheless, Bernard had to concede, however grudgingly, Bentley's skill in Greek.[67]

Temple's defense of the ancients was another matter. Upon reading the *Miscellanies*, Bernard wrote to Smith that he had found Temple's essay a "mixture of learning and wisdom and ignorance." There was no denying Temple's "delicate parts and easy learning," but he was appalled by his many errors and facile judgments. Of these, making the epistles of Phalaris and the fables of Aesop the best Greek prose was one. It was hard to believe that Temple had also argued "that there is nothing new in Astronomy, for all Tycho, Kepler, Galileo, Hevelius, Cassini; nothing in medicine but from Harvey; nothing in Architecture, nothing in Gresham College . . . noe good Greeke after Marcus Aurelius (pray what mischiefe hath Herodian done to him, or S. Basil of Caesaria or S. Iohn Chrysostome that they must not be allowed baser Grecians), no demonstration in natural philosophy. . . ." Smith agreed entirely with Bernard; he had himself found a host of other mistakes and bad judgments, even to questioning Temple's skill in Latin. One had to admire the style, but "forty such like mistakes shew that tho' hee may be a very fine and

[65]Bernard to Smith, Bodleian MS. Smith 47, ff. 54, 82; see also ibid. 4, ff. 53, 161–62; *Correspondence of Bentley*, 1, pp. 10–41.

[66]See Anthony Grafton, *Defenders of the Text: Traditions of Scholarship in an Age of Science* (Cambridge, Mass., 1991), Introduction.

[67]Bernard to Smith, July 19, 1696, Bodleian MS. Smith 47, f. 206. Other letters in this correspondence throw light on Bernard's relations with Bentley, e.g., ff. 54, 81v, 82, 85, 101, 121. Hearne summarized Bernard's views sympathetically in *Remarks and Collections*, 3:76–77, 273.

ingenious gentleman, yet that hee is but a very superficial scholar."[68]
Nevertheless, when Wotton's reply appeared in 1694, Bernard was not
much impressed. "I have read Wotton's booke," he reported to Smith,
"and find him as much out as Sir Wm. and also fill'd like the french
books, with easy borrowed stuffe." He did not, however—perhaps
could not—find the same sort of error he had discovered in Temple and
was content with the general allegation. Almost at the same time, he
wrote to Joshua Barnes that "the Epistles ascribed to Phalaris are the
devise of a cunning schoole master of Constantinople."[69] He was therefore distressed with Boyle's edition of that "meane and frigid" author
when it appeared, and judged the Christ Church editors "very indifferent
Critics."[70]

Bernard died before the resumption of hostilities and was spared the
need to make a judgment on "Boyle against Bentley" or "Bentley against
Boyle." What he would have said is not hard to imagine; undoubtedly he
would have condemned the quarrel and said some uncomplimentary
things about both sides, exactly as did his friend Thomas Smith. "The
controversy between Mr. B. and Dr. B.," Smith admitted, "gives great
diversion to the public." However, "the wise and judicious and most
impartial Readers, whilst they commend and applaud Dr. B's great skill
in Critical Learning, are very angry with him for his . . . scurrilous way
of writing." As for himself, "I interest not myselfe in the quarrel: which I
am sorry has not been managed with that fairness and decency as it
ought."[71] It was impossible for some among the onlookers, however
much better they knew, not to wish that Dr. Bentley would be
humbled.[72]

6

Temple was not involved in "Boyle against Bentley" but he was
enormously pleased by it. (He hastened to buy each new book in the
controversy as it appeared.)[73] He himself had no mind "to enter the List,

[68]Bernard to Smith, Nov. 29 [1690], Bodleian MS. Smith 47, f. 150; Smith to Bernard,
Dec. 2, 1690, ibid. 130, f. 9.
[69]Bernard to Smith, Nov. 3, 1694, Bodleian MS. Smith 47, f. 147; Bernard to Barnes,
June 6, 1694, Bodleian MS. Rawl. Lett. 40, f. 152. Cf. Bernard to Smith, Jan. 29, 1695,
sending him "the vaine Epistles of the false Phalaris": Bodleian MS. Smith 47, f. 157.
[70]"They have said meanly upon an author more meane": Bernard to Smith, Jan. 8,
1695, Bodleian MS. Smith 47, f. 156.
[71]Smith to Dr. Crosthwaite, Mar. 14, 1699, Bodleian MS. Smith 59, f. 363; see also
Smith to the Earl of Clarendon, Mar. 1, 1699, ibid., ff. 155–60v.
[72]See Hearne to West, Sept. 14, 1731, B.M. MS. Lansdowne 777, n.f., still praising that
"excellent Defense against Dr. Bentley."
[73]Ehrenpreis, *Swift*, 1:286–87, lists the books purchased by Temple in 1698.

with such a Mean, Dull, Unmannerly Pedant," but he approved the work without reservation. "The Compass and Application of so much Learning, the Strength and Pertinence of the Arguments, the Candour of his Relations . . . the pleasant Turns of Wit, and the Easiness of Style, are, in my Opinion, extraordinary." When the Christ Church party delivered their next attack, *A Short Account of Dr. Bentley's Humanity*, early in 1699, they were pleased to print Temple's commendation but added nothing to the argument except a new charge of plagiarism and the testimony of the bookseller who had borrowed the manuscript for Boyle.[74] By now, however, Bentley's friends were alarmed and his cause began to seem hopeless against so determined a company. "I have heard it more than once," wrote one, "that they give out, they would write a Book against him once a Month as long as he liv'd."[75] Was the great scholar to spend the rest of his life trying to extricate himself from a futile controversy? Yet, in a way, to fail to answer was to admit defeat.

To be sure, Bentley was not intimidated. "To the surprize of the Town it was soon got abroad, that the Dr. did not yield; nay, that he did but Laugh at them, and would certainly give them an Answer." How was it possible? Boyle's book had made him, so Bentley's friend conceded, "the Jest and Sting of I know not how many thousand Periods, the Common Chat of Coffee-houses and Taverns."[76] To the world it appeared as though the attack was unanswerable.[77] "It is only Don Quixot's Knight Errantry, and Romantick Chivalry for a single Man to place his solitary self in Battel-array, to be so little concern'd for his own person and for the power of others, as to bid defence to and fight with Armies."[78] The Christ Church men might have their faults, wrote Edward Lhwyd, "but I should not care for the Office of being their Monitor."[79] So much the better, then. "I am content," Bentley wrote to Evelyn, "to have it pass for an unanswerable piece; for it will be the more surprising and glorious to confute it; which (if you'll take my word and

[74]*Short Account of Dr. Bentley's Humanity*, p. 140. Temple was still looking forward to meeting Boyle for the first time in July 1698; see Temple to Boyle, July 17, 1698, in *Orrery Papers*, 1:21.

[75]*An Answer to a late Book written against . . . Dr. Bentley* (London, 1699), sig. A4. The author seems from the advertisement to have been Solomon Whateley, who also translated the epistles in 1699; see Monk, *Life of Bentley*, 1:131.

[76]*Answer to a late Book*, sig. A2v–A3.

[77]"The answer to Dr. Bentley's Dissertation, which one would think would mortifie and humble him for his insolent way of writing, does, it seems but enrage him more. Hee will not, I heare bee long behind hand with the Christ Church men, for an answer, but those hornetts, which hee has provoked by his rude and unmannerly reflexions, will sting him to death": Smith to Dr. Crosthwaite, Mar. 26, 1698, Bodleian MS. Smith 59, f. 357.

[78]*A Letter to the Reverend Dr. Bentley upon the Controversie betwixt him and Mr. Boyle* (London, 1699), p. 11.

[79]Lhwyd to Richard Richardson, Mar. 28, 1698, B.M. MS. Sloane 4062, f. 279b.

keep my Counsel) I shall do with that clearness and fulness in every particular great and little, both points of Learning and points of Fact, that the Authors will be ashamed, if any shame can be expected in them, after this present Specimen."[80] Meanwhile, Wotton entered the fray to protect his friend, writing abroad to answer Boyle's criticisms and to defend Bentley's already considerable foreign reputation. He soon found ready support from the scholar and publicist Jean Le Clerc, who promised to air Bentley's views in several foreign journals, including the *Nouvelles de la république des lettres*.[81] Across the Channel, the personal issues and the high station of Boyle and Temple were bound to matter less than the scholarly arguments, and Wotton did not perhaps have to worry too much. The foreign philologists and antiquaries were not likely to depreciate either the importance of the quarrel or the strength of Bentley's proofs. Some of them, including the philosopher Leibniz, had even anticipated his conclusions.[82] It was only too bad the quarrel was in English rather than Latin.

It remained only for Bentley to frame his reply. This time he would not hurry; he intended now to exhaust the argument, to leave no point unanswered, to crush the enemy beneath the weight and fury of his scholarship. Here was a chance to vindicate not only himself but also that modern learning to which he had committed his life. If only a few scholars were likely to be immediately persuaded by his arguments, he was confident that "the rest of the world will by degrees follow their sentiment." He began with a long preface in which he tried to answer all the ad hominem arguments. Then he directed himself once again to Phalaris. He chose to reprint his original criticisms in large type and then to take up one by one the rejoinders of his opponents in small, answering each of them in turn. In this way, the structure of his argument could remain exactly the same, while the substance would be greatly enlarged. "I have first produc'd the Chronological proofs, that Phalaris is spurious; then I consider the Language, then the Matter of the Epistles; and I

[80]Bentley to Evelyn, April 24, 1698, in *Correspondence of Bentley*, 1:167. Warburton relays a conversation in which Bentley explained, "Indeed I am in no pain about the matter, for it is a maxim with me that no man was ever written out of reputation but by himself": note to Pope's *Imitations of Horace* (1749), 5:104; quoted in Monk, *Life of Bentley*, 1:11.

[81]The correspondence of Wotton and Jean Le Clerc is summarized in Annie Barnes, *Jean Le Clerc et la république des lettres* (Paris, 1938), pp. 220–23. Le Clerc's article on the quarrel appeared in the *Nouvelles de la république des lettres*, June 1699. See also Wotton to Le Clerc, June 16, 1698, in *De Joanne Clerico et Philippo a Limborch dissertationes duae* (Amsterdam, 1843), pp. 83–85; and Le Clerc to Locke, June 7/17, 1698, in *The Correspondence of John Locke*, ed. E. S. de Beer, 8 vols. (Oxford, 1976–1989), 6:422–24. Testimonies to Bentley's scholarship by Spanheim, Graevius, Fabricius, Wolfius, and others are assembled in Kippis, *Biographia Britannica*, 2:224.

[82]Leibniz to Claude Nicaise, May 28, 1697, in *Lettres inédites de Leibniz à l'abbé Nicaise*, ed. F. Z. Collombet (Lyon, 1850), pp. 44–51.

conclude all with the Argument of their late Appearance in the World."[83] He believed, in reply to the charge against him of obscurity, that his method was perfectly plain and logical.

The result is not easy reading, though it has some lively moments. With his ironic style and frequent sarcasm, Bentley was almost a match for his rivals. By now the work had turned into an imposing set of learned disquisitions on subjects as apparently diverse as the age of Pythagoras, the origin of tragedy, the coinage of Sicily, and so forth. To George Grote it seemed "full of acuteness and learning, though beyond measure excursive."[84] To his critics it seemed all pedantry. In a way, Bentley understood both criticisms. The Examiner had insisted that the authenticity of the letters was "a very inconsiderable point, which a wise man would grudge the throwing away a week's thought upon." One might well wonder whether such lavish erudition was appropriate to the occasion. "To undervalue the Dispute," Bentley replied, "because it does not suit to one's Studies, is to quarrel with a Circle, because it is not a Square. If the Question be not of Vulgar use, it was writ therefore for a Few." Bentley did not pretend that his philology was of immediate value to the man of taste or the man of affairs. But then such "scholars" had no business meddling in critical learning and claiming a knowledge beyond their competence. This said, not much could be done to advance the quarrel, since the two vantage points on antiquity were so basically irreconcilable. "To such men as these," Bentley allowed, "if the Dispute be out of their way, they have liberty to let it alone; it was not design'd for them, but for others, that know how to value it."[85] He at least had no doubt that the single point about Phalaris was worth making, though he thought that the other subjects he had been compelled to canvass would prove equally interesting, whatever their discursive character, to other scholars.

Thus the new work, in its effort to retrieve the past truly and exactly, was in effect a work of history with a method and a viewpoint all its own and without any reference to the classical doctrine of imitation and narrative that served as the usual justification for historical writing. Bentley's *Dissertations* had no ancient model and offered no assistance either in fashioning a correct and graceful style or in furnishing wisdom for the active life. It was not that Bentley looked down on the ancients; quite the reverse. What they had done well, he thought, they had done for all time; like Wotton, he was as confident of their literary excellence as any of

---

[83]Bentley, *Dissertations*, ed. Wagner, p. 72.

[84]George Grote, *History of Greece*, 12 vols., Everyman Library (London, 1907), 5:87n. Grote complained that the letters of Phalaris were still being quoted as authoritative in his day!

[85]Bentley, *Dissertations*, ed. Wagner, p. 66.

their admirers. Once his daughter regretted his wasting his time and talent on "criticism" instead of writing original works. He felt no remorse, however. "The wit and genius of those old heathens beguiled me," he told her, "and I despaired of raising myself up to their standard upon fair ground. I thought the only chance I had of looking over their heads was to get up on their shoulders."[86] The moderns were left to excel the ancients (apart from science) only with their scholarship.

The end of Bentley's works, therefore, was historical knowledge, not perhaps entirely for its own sake, though very much released from its dependence upon literature. He saw the classics as individual and variable pieces written in specific and differing circumstances and in need of historical explication. But he was interested in their information as much as in their literary merit and he was eager to use them, along with the nonliterary evidence of coins, inscriptions, and monuments, to restore the whole life of the ancient world. Moreover, as much as he admired the ancients, he was not afraid to criticize them, to admit their shortcomings as literature or as testimony. Thus he was not concerned with the literary merits of either Malelas or Phalaris—he was indeed quite sure that neither had any—but he was deeply interested in what they could reveal about the chronology of ancient Greece, and about its social life and literary forms, its geography and its coinage. These things were for him intrinsically valuable and needed no further justification. The result was neither criticism in the Christ Church sense, an aid to literature, nor history in the Christ Church sense, a well-told narrative meant to instruct in worldly affairs. The result was philology and antiquities, pure scholarship, to use the modern term—or pure pedantry, as the Christ Church men preferred, for to them it came to exactly the same thing.

Take, for example, Bentley's first line of argument, chronology. The dates of Phalaris's life were obviously crucial for determining whether the work contained any anachronisms that would show it to be a forgery. Unfortunately, the ancient accounts disagreed widely and seemed to leave the question obscure.[87] "The oldest Historians now extant," the Examiner noticed, "had but very Slender Memoirs of these times; and accordingly we find their Accounts so confus'd and contradictory that No-body but a Man of Dr. Bentley's Judgment would pretend to draw Demonstration from 'em."[88] It is true that Bentley had some definite ideas here, but he was willing for the sake of argument to accept any of the dates proposed by the old writers, since even the latest served his purpose of showing that it was impossible to synchronize the references

[86]*Memoirs of Richard Cumberland*, 2 vols. (London, 1806, 1807), 1:14–15.
[87]Bentley, *Dissertations*, ed. Wagner, p. 92.
[88]Boyle, *Bentley's Dissertations*, pp. 119–20.

in the *Epistles* to the times of Phalaris. Were the Sicilian's correspondents, such as the poet Stesichorus and the philosopher Pythagoras, really contemporary with him? Were the cities that were mentioned in the letters yet founded? Were the drinking cups named after Thericles, a Corinthian potter, already invented? Was either comedy or tragedy yet in existence so that Phalaris could refer to them? In each case, and there were others, Bentley found against the letters, enlarging his demonstration now to take account of all objections.

But, although the Examiner had tried hard to poke holes in Bentley's chronological arguments, it was part of his strategy to divert attention from them whenever he could. On the matter of Phalaris's dates, therefore, the Christ Church company was happy to discover that a neighbor, the universal scholar and chronologist Henry Dodwell, was writing a book that differed from Bentley's. "I hear the famous Mr. Dodwell (who surpasses Dr. Bentley in Learning as much as he does in Candour and Modesty) is now printing some Lectures at Oxford, in which he shews how very obscure and uncertain the Histories of those Ages are; and . . . that Phalaris must be brought much lower than even S. Hierome places him. This perhaps would cut off most of the Drs. Arguments at One Blow."[89] "Your book," Thomas Smith wrote to Dodwell from Oxford, "is here much expected in which we fully believe that you will shew Dr. Bentleyes great errors in the Grecian History and Chronology."[90] Dodwell was an old friend of Smith and Edward Bernard, and a useful ally, if once he could be induced to enter the fray. All three of them had been involved with Bentley's Malelas and been put off by his conduct in editing it.[91] But, although Smith now warned him off, Dodwell found it hard to extricate himself altogether.[92] "The Christ Church men do themselves design an Answer to Dr. Bentley who has indeed used that excellent Body (who, if any, have all advantages desirable for understanding the Greek tongue, as having their Education in the best School in England for it) too coarsely." His only interest, he maintained, was in Phalaris, whose date he had tried to establish for his own ambitious chronological tract, *De Cyclis*, then still in progress. "The Drs.

[89]Ibid., p. 120.

[90]Thomas Smith to Henry Dodwell, April 30, 1698, Bodleian MS. Smith 55, f. 71.

[91]"I remember his [Bernard's] letters against Bentley upon Malela were particularly pleasing to me": Dodwell to Smith, May 31, 1704, Bodleian MS. Smith 49, f. 171. For Dodwell's letters on Malelas and his help to Bentley (1687–1690), see Bodleian MSS. Cherry 1, ff. 201–2, and 29, ff. 196–208; Bodleian MS. Eng. Lett. 29, f. 106.

[92]"Your own prudence will forbid you to interest your selfe in a controversy in which you are no way concerned and which indeede is in it selfe very meane and altogether unworthy of you": Smith to Dodwell, Oct. 30, 1697, Bodl. MSS. Smith 49, f. 65; 60, f. 63; 55, f. 65.

boasts of demonstration in that matter made me a little inquisitive into his proofs."[93]

The curiosity was reciprocal. Bentley, upon reading Boyle, asked Dodwell whether he might see the appropriate passages in his book, even before it was published. "In Mr. Boyle's Examination . . . you are more than once cited and appealed to, as having proved the age of Phalaris to be recenter than Chronologers have yet thought of." Could he have a look? "If I am convinced of your reasons; I shall be very ready to own my mistake, and to give you thanks for the information. Or, if I be still so unhappy, as to differ from you in my opinion, I shall offer my reasons for it, with the diffidence and respect, that is justly due to your eminent Learning."[94] When Dodwell sent along the desired sheets, Bentley found that the learned man had indeed put Phalaris some sixty years later than the chronologers had generally believed and that he had declared in favor of the *Epistles*.[95] On both points Bentley disagreed and, although Dodwell felt less confident than the doctor at assigning dates for that early period, he did think his attributions for Phalaris and Pythagoras "much the surest of anything I know of that Age."[96] It was obviously necessary, therefore, for Bentley to correct Dodwell as well as the Examiner; and here he found a further justification for his labor. It was one thing to criticize a trifler whose scholarship was suspect; it was another to set right a disputed point for men as learned as Dodwell and John Selden, who, Bentley discovered, had earlier made the same mistake. The long essay in the *Dissertations* on the ages of Phalaris and Pythagoras was thus intended to have permanent value as a contribution to the history and chronology of early Greece.

Dodwell's late date for Phalaris did not materially affect Bentley's argument, since it was not nearly late enough to account for all the anachronisms. Why, then, did Dodwell cling to his belief in the false epistles? In part it was because he did not yet know the whole of Bentley's argument,[97] and in part because he had devised an ingenious way around the many objections. "If Phalaris's Epistles were translated

---

[93]Dodwell to Smith, Nov. 8, 1697, Bodleian MS. Smith 49, f. 153. Smith agreed with Dodwell about Bentley's "haughty way of writing which is certainly a great Blemish": Dec. 18, 1697, MS. Smith 60, f. 63.

[94]Bentley to Dodwell, May 10, 1698, in *Pforzheimer Library*, 3:1153–54.

[95]Bentley, *Dissertations*, ed. Wagner, p. 95.

[96]Dodwell to Bentley, May 14, 1698, Bodleian MS. Cherry 22, f. 58.

[97]"I have leave to say, this part of his Book was printed before my Dissertation was made, so that only Two of my Arguments, and not those neither in the manner that I urge them, are here consider'd by Mr. Dodwell. But we may expect that in an Appendix to that noble Work, he will pass a Judgment upon the whole controversie": Bentley, *Dissertations*, ed. Wagner, p. 95.

out of the Dorick into the vulgar Greek," he suggested to Bentley, that would account for their use of the wrong dialect (Attic), for their long disappearance, and for their anachronisms, especially if the translator "tooke the liberty of the paraphrast, which you know was not infrequent." "You know how many more Sicilian Monuments were extant in the Age of the Sophist, for which he might take his materials than we have now by which you can confute him."[98] The chief trouble with the explanation was that it was unnecessary; Bentley's was simpler and more to the point. It also left Temple and Boyle without much real support, since now they would have to defend a late and clumsy paraphraser rather than an original author. But Bentley chose to answer Dodwell by taking up his chronology point by point to see if it could be refuted in detail and to see what could be done to restore a reliable set of dates for the period. In this way, he hoped to turn the controversy to constructive account.

When, however, Dodwell read the new *Dissertations*, which Bentley sent him, he too was dissatisfied with the tone, though willing to accept Bentley's word against Boyle on the issue of his "humanity."[99] He agreed with Smith that it was "written in the same, unpleasing style as the Dissertation, or rather worse and more outrageous."[100] On the other issues he was more equivocal. He agreed that Bentley's method of "hypothesis of Synchronisms" was the best way to judge the case. But he passed over the question of the authenticity of the letters to concentrate on the chronological dispute and to defend his original dates, though even so, he had to concede that there were good "material objections to my hypothesis, and good usefull subjects for a review." In short, Dodwell intended to keep to his Pythagorean chronology, irrespective of its relation to Phalaris, while his silence about the *Epistles* seems to have been a tacit admission of error. He hoped only to patch up the personal quarrel as a "mediator." If such resentment could only be set aside, "the Literary Dispute may be continued with greater advantage for the publick interest of Learning, in the first and difficultest part of History."[101]

7

For Bentley, chronology was only one part of the argument, albeit a crucial one, and having answered Dodwell and the "nibbling" here of

[98]Dodwell to Bentley, May 14, 1698, Bodleian MS. Cherry 22, f. 56.

[99]Dodwell believed that Boyle's information was all at secondhand: Dodwell to Bentley, March 1699, Bodleian MS. Cherry 22, ff. 61v–62v; Dodwell to Smith, Mar. 13, 1699, MS. Smith 49, f. 163.

[100]Smith to Dodwell, Feb. 25, 1699, Bodleian MS. Smith 60, f. 83; Dodwell to Smith, Mar. 13, 1699, ibid. 49, f. 163.

[101]Dodwell to Boyle(?), n.d., Bodleian MS. Cherry 22, f. 63.

Boyle, he was ready to resume his arguments about the language, substance, and disappearance of the letters. "Had all other ways failed us of detecting this Impostor," he wrote in 1697, "yet his very Speech had betray'd him. For his Language is Attic, the beloved Dialect of the Sophists. . . . But he had forgot that the Scene of these Epistles was not Athens but Sicily where the Doric tongue was generally spoken and written."[102]

It was a mistaken dialect that had first stirred Bentley's skepticism; now it was necessary for him to develop his arguments more fully and take account of some new objections of the Examiner and Joshua Barnes, who seemed to find several exceptions—or what they thought were exceptions—in a variety of Dorians writing in Attic. So, for example, they proposed as a remarkable instance one Zaleucus, "King of the Locrians, a Doric Colony; the Preface to whose Laws is preserv'd in Stobaeus, an exact and faithful Copier of old Authors: and has nothing of the Doric Dialect in it"[103]—to which Bentley replied with a long argument that Zaleucus was neither king nor lawgiver and that his preface was probably as much an imposture as the *Epistles* of Phalaris.[104] For each example Bentley was ready with an explanation to show its irrelevance, while his description of the circumstances of the Sicilian tyrant left no reasonable chance that he would have wanted to stray from his native tongue.

But the most interesting and the most telling of Bentley's arguments against the language of Phalaris was his notion that even if the Sicilian had written in Attic ("since Tyrants will not be confin'd by Laws"), it would have been nothing like the Attic of the Sophists, who wrote centuries later. "Every living Language, like the perspiring Bodies of living Creatures, is in perpetual motion and alteration; some words go off, and become obsolete; others are taken in, and by degrees grow into common use; or the same word is inverted to a new sense and notion which in tract of time makes as observable a change in the air and features of a Language, as Age makes in the lines and mien of a Face." Everyone knew that this was true for their own language; was there an Englishman, for example, who was unaware of the changes of the past century? "Now there are as real and sensible differences in the several ages of Greek; were there as many that could discern them. But very few are so versed and practiced in that Language, as ever to arrive at that subtlety of Tast."[105] Exactly so! The Christ Church company showed the weakness

---

[102]Bentley, *Dissertations*, ed. Wagner, p. 325.

[103]Boyle, *Bentley's Dissertations*, p. 44.

[104]Bentley, *Dissertations*, ed. Wagner, pp. 344–80. Jebb notices that here both Warburton and Gibbon protested: *Bentley*, p. 76.

[105]Bentley, *Dissertations*, ed. Wagner, p. 51.

of their collective Greek by arguing that Bentley had confused the issue by confounding the languages. English had indeed changed dramatically from Chaucer to Cowley but Greek had not, " 'twas incomparably the more fix'd and enduring." To compare the Greek, "the most holding Tongue in the World with the English the most Fickle and Fleeting of any," was something that only someone without any sensitivity to the beauties and proprieties of either language could pretend.[106]

It was a nice point, but a point that only a philologist with his specifically modern equipment could hope to settle. Bentley's essay on the rise of Attic should no doubt have been persuasive if the philological argument was to be admitted at all, since no one in his time knew better how to wield it. For more than two hundred years, ever since the Italian Renaissance, humanists had been sharpening their grammatical techniques and their perceptions of the historicity of language. And they had been accumulating in their ponderous commentaries, dictionaries, grammars, and indexes, slowly and laboriously, a great body of knowledge about the ancient tongues. It might be argued that "taste in the Beauties and Proprieties of these Languages" was the exclusive prerogative of men of letters such as Temple and Boyle and Atterbury, who could demonstrate it by their own command of the felicities of English and even Latin style. But it had become obvious to others that knowledge of past usage could not depend on taste or instinct alone; it required the pedestrian labors of the humanist grammarians. The Greek language had altered decidedly in a thousand years and Bentley was able to prove it to those who were willing to attend to his arguments—no easy matter unless one were willing to take some of the same pains as he. The wits were not persuaded, not just because they were impatient and wanted to win the argument, but because they had a rather different view of the classical past and its uses. When they looked back upon ancient Greece or Rome, without being entirely conscious of doing so they selected only what they found immediately useful and intelligible and turned it into a timeless and universal standard, ignoring or misconceiving the rest. They tended, therefore, to see antiquity as a static whole and found reflected in it their own taste and judgment, even amending it where necessary, as in the case of Phalaris. They had thus, necessarily, to deny Bentley's argument, which they felt instinctively (and correctly) to be destructive of their basic stance. It is doubtful whether Bentley understood this very clearly and his aplomb might well have shaken if he had, for like Wotton and all the judicious moderns of his time, he shared a great part of the culture of his opponents. The paradox of Renaissance humanism was only beginning to make its implications clear.

[106]Boyle, *Bentley's Dissertations*, pp. 70–72.

Instead, Bentley forged on determinedly. He had much more to say about the linguistic failures of the Sophist. So, for example, even if one allowed Phalaris the use of Attic, the forger was surely undone by his incomprehension of ancient money. "In Sicily," Bentley reminded his opponents, "as in most other countries, the name and value of the coins, and their way of reckoning sums, were peculiar." The Sicilian talent that Phalaris had bestowed so liberally on his friends in the *Epistles* should never have been confused with the Attic talent of the Sophist—which was worth no less than two thousand times as much! The Attic talent Bentley reckoned at 180 English pounds, the Sicilian at no more than five groats. From the sums mentioned in the letters, it was clear that the old tyrant did not know the value of his own currency! It was also clear that if Bentley was right, Wotton's claim that it was possible for the modern scholar to learn more than the ancients had known about themselves was not really farfetched. Thus when the Christ Church men dared to question Bentley's figures, he was ready with another salvo, a complete dissertation on the Sicilian coinage, full of close and accurate learning, with even a chart for "clearer illustration," and all spiked with the usual vitriol.

It was a virtuoso performance and still commands the respect of modern experts.[107] Bentley, it appears, had, along with his other modern achievements, made himself master also of the new science of numismatics. Perhaps this interest was to be expected, since the study of coins, as Bentley's own discussion shows, had been linked to humanist philology ever since the Renaissance. (If one wanted fully to understand the ancient texts, one had, for example, to find modern equivalents for all the ancient measures.) Bentley had just finished assisting John Evelyn with a general treatise on the ancient medals, correcting it and seeing it through the press. He understood the value of the nonliterary evidence for an understanding of antiquity, and while he seems never to have been a collector of antiquities, like so many of his contemporaries, he took an enthusiastic interest in the monuments of the ancient world, several of which (besides the coins) he used in the *Dissertations*.[108] If he was not himself an antiquary—for he preferred to study the monuments in his library rather than in the field—like Wotton and the rest of the moderns, he understood the value of archaeology to classical scholarship. But alas,

[107]So Jebb, citing the numismatist, Barclay Head: *Bentley*, p. 67.

[108]E.g., the Apotheosis of Homer, with commentary by Gisbert Cuperus, and the Arundel Marbles, which Bentley characteristically amended: *Dissertations*, ed. Wagner, pp. 468, 104–6, 239–41. For these monuments, see Levine, *Dr. Woodward's Shield*, pp. 173 and passim. Bentley didn't think much of collectors of any kind; see his remarks of Feb. 6, 1703, in *The London Diaries of William Nicolson*, ed. Clyve Jones and Geoffrey Holmes (Oxford, 1985), p. 199.

the argument was no more likely to prove persuasive here than before, the rust of old coins being no more acceptable to the wits than the dust of old parchment.

Bentley had, finally, two last points to defend: the matter of the *Epistles* which he had found objectionable and their long disappearance in antiquity. The Examiner had not been able to do much about the last, except to try to confuse the issue by pointing to the long disappearance of other classical texts during the Middle Ages. (But Phalaris was claimed to be lost during the very height of ancient culture.)[109] On the first point, the problem remained largely one of anachronism, although there were a few inconsistencies also to attend. The Examiner had not distinguished himself here either. An example is the temples he found raised to Homer, which, he argued, must have been like the temples raised to the poet Stesichorus in the *Epistles*. It was not hard for Bentley to show that all of these temples had been built at least three hundred years after the time of Stesichorus or Phalaris. "If a custom obtained in this latter age," he asked triumphantly, "will he infer, that it was used too in the former?" But of course, this *was* exactly the desire of both the forger and his modern defenders. They wanted to read their history backward and so find the precedents for their own Augustan ages at the very beginning of classical culture. "Has not the Doctor seen the fragments of Augustus's letters to Horace, pressing and obliging that poet to write?"[110] But Phalaris and Stesichorus were not like Augustus and Horace, or Temple and Atterbury, and Bentley properly insisted upon the barbarity and ignorance of the tyrant, Phalaris being no more (he insisted) than "an illiterate Publican before he usurped the tyranny."[111]

Yet even as Bentley wrote these words, he must have known that they would not convince the *beau monde*, much less his opponents; no more could he hope to turn a circle into a square. Evelyn was, of course, delighted to receive a copy of the *Dissertations*, and to scribble some

---

[109]Bentley, *Dissertations*, ed. Wagner, pp. 481–82. Bentley had sarcastically supposed a way to explain their long disappearance: Phalaris, or some trusty servant, hid them! "And it was well they did so. For if the Agrigentines had met with them they certainly would have gone to pot." When the Examiner came back with the example of books hidden by Numa, Bentley had even more fun. "If Numa's Books could consist of Aegyptian Paper, and contain Praecepts of Pythagoras, so many Generations before Paper was made, or Pythagoras was born, what wonder is it, if the Epistles of Phalaris, which we now suppose to have been buried like Numa's, should have the names of several Towns and other things, that were not built nor heard of til long after the Tyrant's death?" Just so had the Italian Inghirami employed linen paper for his invented Etruscan antiquities: ibid., pp. 492–94.

[110]In the same way, the Examiner imagined Phalaris and Stesichorus as models for Caesar and Tully, even though Cicero did not like tyrants! Boyle, *Bentley's Dissertations*, pp. 112, 105.

[111]Jebb was able to find some additional anachronisms that Bentley missed: *Bentley*, p. 74.

appreciative verses inside the front cover.[112] And Elizabeth Berkeley pointed out to Locke that those who thought the book "too reflecting" might have tried to put themselves in the doctor's place as the injured party. But even some of the moderns were unmoved. Tancred Robinson could find in the *Dissertations* only "a heavy learned piece, not answerable to the Wit and Genius of his Adversaries."[113] And when the *Works of the Learned* attempted to summarize the dispute, it found the whole controversy "a dry and insipid Business." But the *Works*, like many other observers, had never thought the main issue worth much attention, "a meer Trifle." "For it signifies but little whether the *Epistles* commonly ascribed to Phalaris were penn'd by that Tyrant or no."[114]

Yet it would be too easy to ascribe the quarrel simply to personal animosity and leave it at that. The fact is that the wits had detected a danger to their *ancienneté* more serious than any that had so far appeared and they tried to expose it. The Examiner had begun his attack on Bentley by admitting that "Phalaris has always been a Favorite book with me: I had now and then some suspicions that 'twas not Genuine: but I loved him so much more than I suspected him, that I wou'd not suffer my self to dwell long upon 'em. To be sincere, the Opinion, or Mistake, if you will, was so pleasing, that I was somewhat afraid of being undeceiv'd." It was the fear of giving up the present value of the ancients that made the Christ Church wits so adamant. If one were to concede to scholarship and abandon Phalaris, who was to say where such criticism might lead? Already the moderns in France had begun to train their critical batteries on that very stronghold of *ancienneté*, on Homer himself, the prince of poets. What was there to protect the rest of antiquity from the slings and arrows of jealous modernity? Surely not philology, whatever the classical scholars might have thought. In short, it was becoming clear that too much learning might be a dangerous thing for the classics, and that more and better knowledge of antiquity might actually bring less appreciation for its achievement. The authors of "Boyle against Bentley" certainly did not foresee this outcome very clearly, any more than the allies of "Bentley against Boyle" intended it; but there is little doubt that they sensed the danger that the new scholarship posed to their neoclassical ideals, and they did their best to meet it with the best weapons they had at hand, the rhetorical weapons that they were only too happy to believe had originated in antiquity.

Nevertheless, in 1699 it was hard to see how the strenuous efforts of either side had advanced its cause very much—except perhaps to influ-

---

[112]B.M. copy, shelf-mark Eve. a 132.

[113]Elizabeth Berkeley to Locke, Feb. 28, 1699, in Locke, *Correspondence*, 6:575–76; Tancred Robinson to Lhwyd, Feb. 23, 1699, Bodleian MS. Eng. Hist. C 11, f. 96.

[114]*Miscellaneous Letters, Giving an Account of the Works of the Learned* 1 (1699): 157–67.

ence the moderns abroad.[115] In England, the world remained divided
after the dispute almost exactly as before. Like the first episode in the
battle of the books, the second ended in something of a draw. Still, each
side could take some satisfaction perhaps in the thought that it had displayed almost perfectly the merits of its special posture toward the past.
The Christ Church wits had shown the world the possibilities of their
classical paideia in a tour de force of rhetoric, while Bentley was able to
demonstrate equally well his own alternative in a tour de force of humanist scholarship. Thus the second round in the battle of the books was
really a tossup, whatever contemporary opinion (which generally preferred Boyle) might say, or whatever the judgment of posterity (which
on the whole has preferred Bentley).[116] Perhaps the combatants understood this better, and that may explain why in the long run Bentley and
Atterbury eventually became reconciled, though neither ever gave the
slightest ground in their quarrel.[117]

[115]See the review in the *Nouvelles de la république de lettres*, June 1699, pp. 657–69.

[116]"The best judges almost universally now [1747] . . . give it in that respect to Dr.
Bentley . . . [whereas] Mr. Boyle, throwing a great deal of life and spirit into the controversy . . . with abundance of wit and humor; is, upon the whole, reckoned much the
best book": *Biographia Britannica*, 7 vols. (London, 1747–1766), 2:736–37. See also Warburton to Hurd, Aug. 19, 1749, in *Letters from a late Prelate*, pp. 7–10. Phalaris was still being
defended by Thomas Franklin in his translation of *The Epistles of Phalaris* (London, 1749),
pp. ix–xvi.

[117]H. C. Beeching, *Francis Atterbury* (London, 1909), pp. 28–29. Smalridge too seems to
have been reconciled; see Atterbury to Bentley, upon receiving a copy of his Horace, April
19, 1712, in ibid., p. 29; and the note by Samuel Salter in his edition of the *Dissertations*
(London, 1777), p. 309n. Bishop Thomas Newton remembered the Westminster School
elections when all three sat together. "There was something august and aweful too . . . to
see three such great men presiding . . . by their wit and learning and liberal conversation
[they] whetted and sharpened one another": Beeching, *Francis Atterbury*, pp. 28–29. When
Robert Freind's niece married Bentley's son, Bentley decided that "Freind had more good
learning in him than ever he had imagined!": "Freind, Robert," in *Dictionary of National
Biography*.

Chapter Three

Stroke and Counterstroke

I

Everyone, it seems, was fascinated by the quarrel and everyone, apparently, had to have an opinion. The intensity of the argument, the personality and position of the disputants, above all the issues that the battle appeared to raise about the very meaning and purpose of classical culture—all were calculated to attract attention.[1] While many contributed their opinions publicly and everyone tried to keep informed, the battle went merrily on.

On March 17, 1699, the Scot Thomas Burnett of Kemney wrote to his friend John Locke. It seems that Bentley had been reading the preface of his *Dissertations* to Burnett and managed to persuade him momentarily of the justice of his conduct to Boyle. Now, however, Burnett had been able to look for himself at the published work—along with the latest Christ Church reply, *A Short Account of Dr. Bentley's Humanity*, which had also appeared in the meanwhile, "exploring his plagiary, ingratitude, and inhumanity." "I do profess," Burnett wrote to Locke, "upon second thoughts (which sometimes are best), I think, considering Dr. Bentley's magisterial and supercilious language to Mr. Bennet [the bookseller], and on the other hand, Mr. Bennet's manner of justifying himself, and representing the matter in a sober and far less passionate, but more natural, narration of everything, so that his story seemeth the more likely if not the more true, of the two; and although the Doctor may have both truth and learning on his side, he hath no ways shown the spirit of

[1]"The controversy . . . has been of late years the common argument and subject of discourse among Gentlemen and Scholars in their ordinary conversation and entertainment": Thomas Smith to the Earl of Clarendon, Mar. 1, 1699, Bodleian MS. Smith 59, ff. 155–60.

meekness in reproving."[2] In other words, and like nearly everyone else, Burnett thought that Bentley's manners were bad and that he deserved reproof.

On the other matter, the intellectual issue, Burnett was equally unpersuaded. Bentley told him that William Lloyd, the bishop of Lichfield and Coventry, meant to publish a work simultaneously with his own to support his views on Phalaris, and that he would also engage two eminent continental scholars, Ezechiel Spanheim and J. G. Graevius, on his side. It would be hard to deny so formidable a triumvirate. According to Bentley, Lloyd thought that "Mr. Dodwell's opinion was wholly overturned upon this occasion, who founded his hypothesis upon the authenticness and the supposed antiquity of the *Epistles* of Phalaris." Apparently Lloyd dissented from Bentley on some minor matters, but Bentley thought that that would be just as well, "since thereby was taken away all suspicion of combination." None of this impressed Burnett, who believed rather that "a great number will be of another sentiment who would not be thought of the unlearned tribe." And he was satisfied to tell Locke that he had more recently heard that Lloyd was going to suppress his book after all and thus leave Bentley undefended.

What Locke thought about all this is not clear; he certainly followed the quarrel as it unfolded. When Wotton's book appeared in 1694, he wrote to J. G. Graevius to tell him about the new work in which the learning of the moderns was compared with the ancients—"a task not to be borne by everyone's shoulders." He seems to have approved Wotton's general position, "because inclining to neither side, he has written temperately, and is judged to have written more equitably than Perrault."[3] Locke did not, as he says, "love controversies," and he certainly remained aloof from the quarrel, particularly after Bentley joined the fray and the battle heated up, although he was undoubtedly drawn to the modern side.[4] As early as 1664 he had spoken out roundly against what he believed to be the prevailing *ancienneté*,[5] and the dedication to the

[2]Thomas Burnett to John Locke, Mar. 17, 1699, in *The Correspondence of John Locke*, ed. E. S. de Beer, 8 vols. (Oxford, 1976–1989), 6:586–91; Lord King, *Life and Letters of John Locke*, 2 vols. (London, 1830), 1:400–402.

[3]Locke to J. G. Graevius, Nov. 5, 1694, in Locke, *Correspondence*, 5:182–84. Locke's logic is briefly praised by Wotton in his *Reflections upon Ancient and Modern Learning* (London, 1694), p. 156.

[4]Locke to William Molyneaux, April 26, 1695, in Locke, *Correspondence*, 5:352–53. Locke received Temple's reply to Wotton with the recommendation of Awnsham Churchill, but we do not have his opinion: Churchill to Locke, Oct. 25 and 31, 1701, in ibid., 7:477–78, 482. Bentley, meanwhile, was siding with Locke against Stillingfleet; see Burnett to Locke, March 24, 1697, in ibid., 6:60–62. Churchill also sent Locke an "answer to Bentley" (probably the *Short Account*), April 8, 1699, in ibid., pp. 590–91.

[5]"Admittedly, there are some who continually rattle off the praises of former times, for whom there is nothing excellent, nothing even moderately good, except what is called

Essay Concerning Human Understanding (1689) is a forthright plea for the claims of novelty.[6] Locke believed (as he wrote to Robert Boyle) that antiquity was a recommendation for neither things nor opinions.[7] As a philosopher, he typically distrusted the polite arts, especially rhetoric, although he allowed their necessity to civil life. He therefore downplayed the importance of the classical languages in education, though he retained some Latin and even wrote passably in it from time to time.

Meanwhile, Burnett had been keeping another philosophical friend, G. W. Leibniz, informed also. For a time he acted as the intermediary between the two touchy rivals, relaying the opinions of one to the other. Leibniz tended to approach all matters in a truly irenic spirit, including the quarrel between the ancients and the moderns and the rivalry between the "two cultures." Unlike Locke and the Cartesians, he was sympathetic to the claims of both science and philology, and he believed in both a *philosophia perennis*, extending backward to the remotest past, and a dramatic new advancement of learning.[8] He took a great interest in English intellectual and political life and found Burnett an invaluable informant; he even managed to read English, though not, apparently, with perfect ease. Once, at least, Burnett, Locke, and Bentley discussed together whether they could obtain an English benefice for Leibniz.[9]

ancient (men in whom you will perhaps find the whole of antiquity except its morals); as if our ancestors excelled us as much in happiness as they do in age. We are told there that there have been golden ages in the past, but which ones they were seem always to have been concealed in the same poetic minds in which they first originated. . . . Let old age admire the past and, while lamenting the present, enjoy the good things it has lost. . . . Is it surprizing, if to a man wearing spectacles everything at a distance looks more conspicuous and larger?": from Locke's validictory speech giving up the censorship of his college, in *Locke: Essays on the Law of Nature*, ed. W. Van Leyden (Oxford, 1954), p. 225.

[6]John Locke, *An Essay Concerning Human Understanding*, ed. Peter H. Niddich (Oxford, 1975), pp. 3–5. The *Essay* was praised immediately by William Molyneaux as above "all the Volumes of the Ancients": *Dioptrica nova* (London, 1692), p. iv. See James Buickerood, "The Natural History of the Understanding: Locke and the Rise of Facultative Logic in the Eighteenth Century," *History and Philosophy of Logic* 6 (1985): 181.

[7]Locke to Robert Boyle, Dec. 2/12, 1665, in Locke, *Correspondence*, 1:227–29. "He affected to despise poetry, and he depreciated the ancients, which circumstance, I am informed from undoubted authority, was the source of perpetual discontent and dispute betwixt him and his pupil, Lord Shaftesbury": Joseph Warton, *An Essay on the Genius and Writings of Pope*, 2d ed., 2 vols. (London, 1806), 2:271–72.

[8]For some expressions of this belief, see Leibniz, *Philosophical Letters and Papers*, ed. Leroy E. Loemker, 2d ed. (Dordrecht, 1969), pp. 93–104, 186–91, 462–71, 654–55; Charles Schmitt, "Perennial Philosophy from Agostino Steuco to Leibniz," *Journal of the History of Ideas* 27 (1966): 505–32; H. L. Vleeschauwer, *Perennis Quaedam Philosophia* (Pretoria, 1968).

[9]Burnett to Leibniz, July 23, 1697, from a manuscript letter in the Niedersachsische Landesbibliothek, Hanover (cited hereafter as N.L. MS.). See Nicholas Jolly, *Leibniz and Locke: A Study of the New Essays on Human Understanding* (Oxford, 1984), p. 38n. Eduard Bodemann describes nearly a hundred letters between the two men in *Die Briefswechsel des G. W. Leibniz* (Hanover, 1889), pp. 30–31. See also Raymond Klibansky, *Leibniz's Un-*

Already in 1695 Leibniz was receiving news of Wotton's *Reflections*,
which he had not yet read, and Temple's *Miscellanea*, which it appears he
had.[10] In 1697 Burnett summarized for him the new edition of the *Reflections* with Bentley's appendix, and the danger that it seemed to pose for
Temple's reputation.[11] Leibniz knew a lot about Bentley's work and
respected it. He had read the Boyle lectures in a Latin translation and was
ready to compare the author with the greatest of the *érudits*, men such as
Hugo Grotius and Pierre Gassendi, who had managed the altogether
exceptional combination of learning *and* solidity. He thought that
Bentley's proposed new edition of Callimachus would be a wonderful
contribution to an understanding of ancient theology and mythology. As
for the letters of Phalaris, "tho' I infinitely esteem the wit and judgment
of Sir William Temple, yet I think, he is not sufficiently acquainted with
the discoveries of our age. And as for the Ancients, he might have pitch'd
upon works that are incomparably better than the letters ascribed to
Phalaris. . . . In my opinion 'tis very certain that these letters have been
forged since his time and every understanding person acquainted with
those things will subscribe to Mr. Bentley's judgment."[12] To his friend
the abbé Claude Nicaise he reported the latest news, adding that
Bentley's conclusions were what he had always known. It was true; in a
youthful dissertation, he had long before argued against the *Epistles*.[13] A
few months later he asked Burnett to send his regards to Bentley and
encourage him "to continue to enrich the Publick with his own Productions, which have as much Solidity as Learning." He admitted that he
had still not seen Wotton's *Reflections*, but concluded, "If Mr. Bentley
pronounces in Favour of the Moderns (as I believe he will) the Advocates
for the Ancients can hold out no longer; for his great Knowledge of all
that is valuable in Antiquity, and his Candour, admit of no Exception,
nor of any Appeal from his Judgment."[14] Typically, he meant his letter
to be shown.

Leibniz was surprised to learn from Burnett that the battle continued

known Correspondence with English Men of Letters (London, 1941). Many of Leibniz's letters
are published in *Die philosophischen Schriften von Gottfried Wilhelm Leibniz*, ed. C. I.
Gerhardt, 3 vols. (Berlin, 1887), 3:151–329. I am grateful to the librarian in Hanover for
supplying me with photocopies.

[10]Leibniz to Burnett, Nov. 22, 1695, and Mar. 7/17, 1696, in Gerhardt, *Philosophischen
Schriften*, 3:164–71, 177–78.

[11]Burnett to Leibniz, May 3, 1697, N.L. MS. ff. 52–53.

[12]Leibniz to Bentley, May 8/18, 1697, in Gerhardt, *Philosophischen Schriften*, 3:200–208,
trans. by Sharpe in B.M. MS. Add. 5104, ff. 54–55.

[13]Leibniz to Nicaise, May 28, 1697, in Gerhardt, *Philosophischen Schriften*, 2:569–86; see
Leibniz, *Dissertatio de principui individui*, ed. G. G. Guhrauer (Berlin, 1837), pp. 51–52, 87.
The disputation goes back to 1663.

[14]Gerhardt, *Philosophischen Schriften*, 3:208–19, trans. in *A Defense of the Late Dr. Samuel
Clarke against . . . Louis-Philip Thummig* (London, 1744), pp. 110–59 (esp. 119–21, 151,
157).

anyway. He thought that anyone who tried to defend the spurious letters could only hurt himself. An affirmation might be pardonable in a minister of state, "distracted by a thousand affairs like Temple," but not in a learned member of the profession.[15] Of course, the Christ Church company carried on, and Burnett dutifully reported the events in 1698–99, including the popular support for Boyle.[16] But Leibniz was unmoved, astonished about the fuss and unhappy about the personal recriminations. He was confident that the entire learned world would rally to Bentley's support. Despite the ingenious arguments of Boyle (including now the *Short Account of Dr. Bentley's Humanity*), it was impossible to believe that the letters were really genuine. By 1700 Leibniz seems to have gotten around to reading Wotton for himself and found the *Reflections* full of good things.[17] Put to the choice, Leibniz came down squarely with the moderns, whatever qualifications he may have wanted to make for the ancient wisdom. As he wrote firmly to the electress Sophia in 1699, if the moderns would but continue to attend to nature and art, they would continue to make discoveries that would advance knowledge and improve the human condition. The achievement of the last century had already surpassed all that the ancients had done; the future would do better still.[18] In 1702 Wotton and Leibniz began a correspondence that lasted until Leibniz's death. "Would God," Leibniz wrote at the very end of his life (1715), applauding the Earl of Shaftesbury's *Characteristics*, "Would God that a way might be found to reconcile learning with the education of a gentleman!"[19]

2

Burnett had been right about one thing. Bishop William Lloyd was in fact ready to enter the lists on Bentley's side, although discreetly and not until after the *Dissertations* had appeared. Yet even this much support was

---

[15]Leibniz to Burnett, n.d., in Gerhardt, *Philosophischen Schriften*, 3:219–23.

[16]Boyle to Leibniz, June 28, Aug. 5, and Oct. 15, 1695, in N.L. MS., pp. 69–70, 73–76.

[17]Leibniz to Burnett, Jan. 20/30, 1699; n.d.; and Feb. 2/13, 1700, in Gerhardt, *Philosophischen Schriften*, 3:243–72; Burnett to Leibniz, Mar. 23, 1699, and Oct. 20, 1700, in N.L. MS., ff. 92–93, 102r.

[18]"Car les modernes ayant surpasse depuis un siècle tout ce que les anciens avoient fait, je crois que nous nous surpasserions nous-mêmes en peu de temps, et rendrions l'éstat du genre humain bien meilleur qu'il n'est, si nous voulions seulement, mais avec assez d'empressement, nous servir de la grâce de cièl, en faisant tous les efforts possibles pour faire des déscouvertes, dans la nature et dans les arts": Leibniz to the electrice Sophia, July 12, 1699, in *Correspondence de Leibniz avec Sophie de Brunswick-Lunebourg*, 3 vols. (Hanover, n.d.) 2:132–35. See also Fernand Brunner, *Etudes sur la signification historique de la philosophie de Leibniz* (Paris, 1950), pp. 47–77.

[19]Leibniz, *Philosophical Letters*, p. 632. The Wotton-Leibniz correspondence can be found in N.L. MS. 1016. It consists largely of exchanges of cultural news.

significant, for next to Henry Dodwell, Lloyd was undoubtedly one of the most capable chronologists and distinguished scholars in Europe. Like William Wotton, whom he afterward befriended, he had been a child prodigy, skilled in all the ancient languages. His fellow bishop Gilbert Burnet praised him as an "exact Historian and the most punctual in Chronology of all our Divines."[20] In fact, his reputation in the chronological science had gotten abroad and he became the confidant of many foreign scholars who sought out his advice on matters of erudition.[21] It was he who had persuaded the reluctant Bentley to make his contributions to Malelas and had been willing to pay for its publication, and it was he who had enlisted Dodwell's support.[22] According to Bishop Burnet, "He had read the most books and with the best judgment, and made the most copious abstracts out of them, of any of this age, so that [Bishop John] Wilkins used to say that he had the most learning in ready cash of any man he ever saw." He was for a long time intimate with Dodwell, with whom he shared many interests, until in 1689 politics bedeviled their friendship; a decade later, when the *Dissertations* appeared, they seemed poised uneasily upon a reconciliation. Understandably Lloyd hesitated, beseiged by both parties and with his own reputation to defend. When Thomas Smith, who knew them both, heard that Lloyd meant to support Bentley against Dodwell, he was startled and a little dismayed. While he was able to tell Dodwell that the archbishop of Canterbury had counseled Lloyd against publishing his work, he had heard also that Lloyd was only temporarily delaying it and would soon bring it out on its own.[23]

Smith was right and the little book slipped quietly into the world not long after the *Dissertations* with the title *A Chronological Account of the Life of Pythagoras and Other Famous Men His Contemporaries*. Bentley told Thomas Burnett that it was something that Lloyd had had by him for years, and it was certainly true that Lloyd had been working on the chronology of the ancient world for a long time. Unfortunately, ecclesiastical politics had long delayed his magnum opus, which had grown increasingly complicated by his consuming interest in biblical chronology and prophecy. When John Evelyn went to visit him early in 1699, Lloyd, he wrote, "entertained me with his old discourse concerning the Destruction of

[20]Gilbert Burnet, *History of His Own Time* (London, 1724), 1:190; "Lloyd, William," in *Biographia Britannica*, 2d ed., ed. Andrew Kippis, 5 vols. (London, 1778–1793). See also Louis Dufour to J. A. Turretini, Jan. 13, 1694, in *Lettres inédites addressées de 1687–1737 à Turretini*, ed. F. de Budé, 2 vols. (Paris, 1887), 2:235. For Lloyd's life, see A. Tindall Hart, *William Lloyd, 1627–1717* (London, 1952); and Margaret Crum, "The Commonplace Books of Bishop William Lloyd," *Bodleian Library Record* 9 (1977): 265–73.

[21]See the voluminous correspondence with the continental chronologists Antoine Pagi and Enrico Cardinal Noris, in the Bodleian Library, MSS. Cherry 1 and 29.

[22]Lloyd to Dodwell, Sept. 16, 1690, Bodleian MS. English Letters C 29, f. 106.

[23]Smith to Dodwell, Feb. 25, 1699, Bodleian MS. Smith 55, ff. 83–84.

Anti-christ, interpreting Daniel and the Revelation with full Confidence of the Papacys fall, France's Conversion, the final burning of Rome, which should certainly come to passe before the 36 yeare of the next Century."[24] Millenarian concerns were ebbing a little with the dying century, and as a result Lloyd's reputation for learning began to suffer even in his own day, as it has even more decidedly in ours. But one must remember that he shared his interest with many distinguished contemporaries—Thomas Burnet, for one, and Isaac Newton, for another—and that it could be a great stimulus as well as a real hazard to serious scholarship.[25]

A contemporary story may help to place him. William Whiston (who recalls it in his autobiography) was a disciple of Newton's, at least in those years, a mathematician and a speculative philosopher who had proposed one of the more interesting alternatives to Thomas Burnet's *Sacred Theory of the Earth*. He was also a biblical chronologist very much interested in prophecy. Whiston remembers that upon one occasion Bentley had become involved in these matters, only to quarrel with both Lloyd and Newton.[26] It was at the time when Bentley was giving the second series of Boyle lectures (1692) and the prophecies had come naturally into his purview. Knowing Lloyd's interest, he consulted with him about them, only to discover that "the Bishop understood a Day in the Prophecies to denote a Year in their Completion, as all Expositors had done before him." Bentley was disturbed by this assertion and later, presumably after he had discovered Newton's passion for the same subject, asked the great man what he thought about it. He was dismayed to find that Newton agreed with Lloyd and the traditional view. This was too much for Bentley, who promptly asked Newton whether he could "demonstrate" his view. "Sir Isaac Newton was so greatly offended at this, as invidiously alluding to his being a Mathematician; which science was not concerned in the matter; that he would not see him, as Dr. Bentley told me himself, for a twelve month afterward."[27]

[24]John Evelyn, *The Diary*, ed. E. S. de Beer, 6 vols. (Oxford, 1953–1955), 5:321–22. Lloyd expounded his prophetic views to Evelyn and Pepys, Aug. 15, 1690, in ibid., p. 32; and *The Private Correspondence of Samuel Pepys*, ed. J. R. Tanner, 2 vols. (New York, 1926), 1:33. See also *Correspondence of the Family of Hatton*, ed. E. M. Thompson, 2 vols. Camden Society (London, 1878), 2:82–86.

[25]See Margaret Jacob, "Millenarianism and Science in the Later Seventeenth Century," *Journal of the History of Ideas* 37 (1976): 335.

[26]For what follows, see *Memoirs of the Life and Writings of William Whiston*, 3 vols. (London, 1749–1750), 1:94–96, 106–7. Whiston showed his *New Theory of the Earth* (1696) to Newton, Bentley, and Christopher Wren for approval; see ibid, p. 43, and Joseph M. Levine, *Dr. Woodward's Shield: History, Science, and Satire in Augustan England* (Berkeley, 1977), p. 307n.

[27]Correspondence in the British Library (B.M. MS. Add. 6489, ff. 67–71) shows that Newton approved Lloyd's views on the ancient calendar. Lloyd tried to discourage Whiston's Arian views and discussed chronology with him; see ibid. 24197, esp. ff. 14–44v. For further correspondence on these matters, see Ernest H. Pearce, *Hartlebury Castle* (London,

Whiston himself was not much happier with Bentley's "skepticism."
("When Dr. Bentley was courting his Lady, who was a most excellent
Christian Woman, he had like to have lost her by starting to have an
Objection against the Book of Daniel. . . . Which made the good lady
weep.") According to Whiston, Bentley "also tried to run down the
Apocalypse as not written by the Apostle John."[28] Nor was Whiston
much more impressed by Bentley's classical learning. He dismissed the
dispute about Phalaris, "which then made a mighty Noise in the World,"
as a "useless and trifling Speculation," hardly worth the attention of a
serious clergyman. On that point, however, Lloyd clearly disagreed. It is
true that he too had made the biblical chronology his principal concern,
but he recognized, as earnest Christians had done for centuries, that the
only way to devise a biblical chronology was to work out a scheme for
the whole of human history, beginning with creation and encompassing
the pagan as well as biblical worlds in a single comprehensive system.[29]
For that task, immense ingenuity and learning were required and a scrupulous attention to detail.

For some reason, Lloyd never did carry out his chief ambition, although he never stopped trying. If most of the Augustans still believed in
a universal history, the new accumulation of learning was making it
harder all the time to accomplish it. When Dodwell gave the Camden
lectures in 1688, he showed how hard it was to establish any dates at all
for early Greek history.[30] Paradoxically, the critical learning of the moderns, with its effort to distinguish and criticize the original sources, was
leading to less and less certainty with every increment to knowledge.
Only a conviction of the authenticity of scriptural history still kept the
edifice intact, though one by one each of its details was becoming suspect, and across the Channel, at least, large questions were beginning to
arise. About 1690 Lloyd ran off some sheets of his universal chronology,
in which he concluded characteristically that "there is no antient Account
of which there is anything certain in these very antient times, except only
that which we find in Sacred History." This difficulty did not keep him
from trying, any more than it inhibited either Dodwell or Bentley.[31]

1926), pp. 197–98; and for a brief recent account, James E. Force, *William Whiston: Honest Newtonian* (Cambridge, 1985), pp. 114–16.

[28] *Memoirs of Whiston*, 1:108–9.

[29] See Lloyd to Pagi, June 1686, Bodleian MSS. Cherry 1, ff. 173–75, and 29, ff. 5–22.

[30] See Francis Brokesby, *The Life of Henry Dodwell* (London, 1715), pp. 182–83.

[31] Benjamin Marshall's *Chronological Tables* (Oxford, 1712–13) was based on Lloyd's work; see Canon William Stratford to Edward Harley, Aug. 8, 1713, in *Historical Manu-script Commission Reports: Manuscripts of the Duke of Portland*, vol. 7 (London, 1901), p. 162; Stratford to Coke, Jan. 25, 1714, in *Historical Manuscript Commission Reports: Manuscripts of Earl Cowper*, vol. 3 (London, 1889), p. 109; Marshall to Postlethwayte, Sept. 3, 1709, in Pearce, *Hartlebury Castle*, p. 204.

Lloyd's *Chronological Account of the Life of Pythagoras* was thus a by-product of his own general concern with ancient chronology. And if he avoided siding too directly with Bentley there, he nevertheless made clear his basic agreement with the doctor by assigning Phalaris to a date similar to Bentley's and ignoring the *Epistles* altogether. In addition, he prefixed to his work a letter to Bentley in which he respectfully deferred to the doctor's superior knowledge in these matters.[32] It was a clear blow in favor of the moderns. The work itself, which was briefer than the preface, attempted to fix the times for early Greek history as precisely as the available sources would allow. However, since none of these dates were secure (Lloyd having first taken pains "to show what credit they are, as to matter of History"), he was forced to confess that "there is not in all my Collection, any one certain year in which any thing happen'd to Pythagoras, or was done by him." It was a modest and sensible conclusion, and one that is not far from the modern view, but it is not hard to see why the ancients failed to be convinced by it.[33] Indeed, as a modern discipline, chronology, like classical scholarship in general, seemed to be showing itself fruitless of any real consequence—or perhaps fruitful of only destructive consequence—exactly as the ancients had all along suspected.[34] It was hard to see how, beneath so uncertain a conclusion, knowledge of a sort was nevertheless slowly and steadily advancing.

3

For Dodwell the problem remained acute and exasperating. It did not help that his old friend Lloyd had enlisted on the side of the enemy. He only wished that the bishop had given him a chance to see his arguments before he published them.[35] His instinct was to plead with both sides to reduce their personal invective, and at once he took upon himself (as we

[32]William Lloyd, *A Chronological Account of the Life of Pythagoras* (London, 1699), p. iii. The mathematician John Wallis assumed that the work had actually been published by Bentley; see Wallis to Lloyd, May 8, 1699, Bodleian MS. Ballard 24, ff. 6–7.

[33]Locke asked Nicolas Toinard's opinion of it but characteristically refrained from giving his own; see Toinard to Locke, March 30, 1700, in Locke, *Correspondence*, 7:35–38. Thomas Gale approved; see Gale to Pepys, May 27, 1699, in Tanner, *Private Correspondence of Pepys*, pp. 175–77.

[34]"As it has never succeeded with so many learned Men, that have spent their whole Time and Pains, to agree the Sacred with the Prophane Chronology (not to exempt Sir John Marsham's great Industry), so I never expect to see it done to any Purpose": William Temple, *Some Thoughts on Reviewing the Essay on Ancient and Modern Learning* (London, 1701), p. 236. See also John Milner, "Of the Uncertainty of the greatest part of Chronology," in *A Defense of Arch-Bishop Usher* (Cambridge, 1694), pp. 3–34. Milner was to write a review of the Phalaris controversy in 1698.

[35]Dodwell to Bentley, March 1699, Bodleian MS. Cherry 22, ff. 61v–62v.

have seen) the unlikely role of mediator. To Bentley, he wrote asking him to give up his personal resentment and even managed to get his permission to intervene.[36] To Boyle he wrote that Bentley's book, "however otherwise unexcusable, shews his averseness to any difference with you." Bentley, he reported, was only sorry that the affair had been managed by someone else.[37] Alas, it was too late; Bentley and Boyle might be willing to compose *their* differences but now the whole world had become involved. Dodwell hoped that, if only the personal animus could be set aside, the dispute might still be turned to account for the advancement of learning. But he missed the point. In fact, the dispute was hardly at all about a learned question; and the quarrel over personality was not entirely irrelevant to the issue.

Perhaps Dodwell missed the point because he was unwilling to allow that the learning of a gentleman and the learning of a scholar were incompatible. He had given some thought to the matter even before the quarrel about Phalaris renewed the issue. In 1694, for example, he was asked by a publisher to improve a standard text, Degory Wheare's *Method and Order of Reading Both Civil and Ecclesiastical Histories*. Wheare had written early in the century as the first incumbent of the Camden Chair and his work was a characteristic example of its type, the Renaissance *ars historia*. Since Dodwell himself had held the same chair for a time, from 1688 to 1691 (before being deprived of it for his refusal to take the oaths), it was natural enough for the publisher to turn to him. Upon reviewing the work, however, the old scholar could think of no useful improvements to make, although he was willing to add an introduction, which appeared eventually—and was reprinted in 1698—as "Mr. Dodwell's Invitation to Gentlemen to acquaint themselves with Antient History."[38]

Dodwell could think of no useful improvement because, as he explained, the work was meant simply as an "initiation" for young students in history. Had it been intended for more "accurately learned Persons," it would indeed have required large additions to bring it up to date. But since it was intended for young students only, or for gentlemen with limited knowledge, it could stand as it was. He was, however, willing to furnish the work with a new introduction.

Dodwell's principal argument in the "Invitation" turned on the use of ancient history for the young gentleman who hoped to play an active part in the world. He was eager to put back together what had somehow been set asunder: theory and practice, the active and the contemplative

[36]Dodwell to Bentley, May 14, 1698, Bodleian MS. Cherry 22, f. 56.

[37]Dodwell to Bentley, n.d., Bodleian MS. Cherry 22, ff. 63–63v.

[38]Wheare's *Methodus* was published first in 1625, revised and enlarged in 1635, and afterward reprinted; it was translated by Edmund Bohun in 1685 and reprinted with Dodwell's essay in 1694. My quotations are all from this edition.

lives. In such a way, he remembered, Plato had once called upon the gentlemen of Athens to join wisdom with power, philosophy with politics. Even the modern farmer could usefully join the theoretical knowledge of the ancient agricultural writers—Hesiod, Virgil, Cato, Columella, and the rest—to his own immediate experience. "The like may be said concerning the other Discourses of the Antients, their Books of Architecture, of Mechanicks, of Hawking, Hunting and Fishing, of cures of Beasts, nay even of Cookery." Unfortunately, he saw that the value of the ancient writers was too little known by the practical modern men of the world because they could not understand their languages; while the modern scholars who could read and enjoy them were ignorant of practical matters and therefore unable to understand the things about which the ancients wrote. It was only by joining the two together, words and things, the virtues of ancients and moderns, that progress was possible. Dodwell's view therefore was not unlike Wotton's when he wrote against Temple that very year. "It very much hinders the improvement of that kind of Knowledge that none are skilled in the antient and modern Notions, which would be requisite for supplying the Inventions of each, and superstructing on them both. Thus where modern Inventions have failed they might be supplied by the Antients, and in other things the Antients might be supplied by our modern Inventions."

So Dodwell was forced (however reluctantly) to concede that a rift had appeared to divide the scholars and the gentlemen of his time, a rift that the quarrel over Phalaris was soon to enlarge. He acknowledges the problem even more clearly when he turns at length to his main theme, the usefulness of the ancient histories. He begins by defining his subject more exactly. "The peculiar Employment of a Gentleman, who would be eminently serviceable to his Country in that Station, should be to accomplish himself in Politicks and the Art of War." Dodwell accepts the Ciceronian view, resumed during the Renaissance, that the gentleman was defined by his civic role and responsibilities.[39] And he outlines the possibilities for an Englishman in his time, in Parliament, the courts, the executive, and the army. He was convinced that the most useful preparation for all these practical affairs was history, though he saw that this could hardly make sense for the scholar who was satisfied with a retired life or who aimed at learning for its own sake. Dodwell employs the traditional contrast between the active and the contemplative lives to make his point. "History," he insists, "is much more fitted for the use of

[39]See also Dodwell's "Apology for the Philosophical Writings of Cicero," in Jeremy Collier, *Tully's Five Books De Finibus* (London, 1702). The Florentine tradition of civic humanism and its influence are best described in the several works of Hans Baron, e.g., *The Crisis of the Early Italian Renaissance*, rev. ed. (Princeton, 1966); and *In Search of Florentine Civic Humanism*, 2 vols. (Princeton, 1988).

an active than a studious Life, and therefore much more useful for Gentlemen than Scholars."[40] It was a familiar sentiment but a telling admission, though I am not sure how far Dodwell understood its implications. Historical descriptions, he continues, much conduce to the accomplishments "not of the Speculative but the Practical Reader, that is of such a one as for the future should be engaged in Civil or Military Affairs. . . . Rarely, if ever, do Histories take notice of the Theoretical, or Oeconomical, but the Political, Virtues. So useless must the greatest part, and the most judicious, of Histories be for those who know nothing of the present Affairs of Mankind beyond those Studies, or their Families."

For Dodwell, therefore, not only was practice the proper end and purpose of learning, it directly contributed to knowledge by accumulating relevant new experience. And it allowed the man of the world to distinguish what was valuable from what was fruitless or frivolous and thus to shorten his labors. "That very Prudence which is the natural result of Experience, will enable such a Person to avoid needless Circuits in acquiring Knowledge, which Speculators are very liable to, and will withall contribute to Judgment for improving the same Knowledge to better Purposes than can be expected from them who are altogether unacquainted with the Practice of it. Such a Person will more easily foresee what parts of Knowledge are perfectly useless in Practice."

Dodwell (as his other writings confirm) was thus all on the side of civic activity, contemptuous of medieval monks, for Martha and opposed to Mary. The commonplaces of the Florentine Renaissance all fell from his lips completely naturalized. The purely contemplative or studious life did not seem to this very contemplative and unworldly scholar justified, and too much study was clearly an obstacle to success in life. "Studious Persons," he agreed, "have been thought the most unfit of all for Politicks or Military Exercises." Inevitably, the best public life was the one that had been guided by the examples of the past, by the lessons of history, assimilated not at secondhand but directly from the originals. And of all these works, it seemed to him that the ancient histories had a special though not an exclusive value. As in other matters, he believed that it was only when the ancients and the moderns were joined together that the best results could be obtained, although in politics and war, Dodwell did not doubt that the ancients were superior. He did not deny that the statesman or general, living and acting in the modern world, had to have some knowledge of contemporary affairs; but modern politics

---

[40]See the earlier debate between the Scots advocate Sir George Mackenzie and John Evelyn. In 1665 Mackenzie wrote *A Moral Essay, preferring Solitude to Publick Employment*, which was reprinted in London in 1685 and 1693. In 1667 Evelyn replied with *Publick Employment and an Active Life*. In 1690 the two men dined together, "most fondly reconciled": Evelyn, *Diary*, 5:12.

and modern strategy should never be taken for "standards." The ancients had particularly excelled in those things, and "we improve only on the Inventions of those Barbarous Nations which overran the Roman Empire." In these two matters, anyway, the moderns were far from "superstructing" on the ancient achievement. So Dodwell's modernity, even more than Wotton's, was tempered by his admiration for the ancient achievement, and there are times when he sounds more like Temple than his adversary. He was quite convinced of the ancients' superiority even in warfare, though space did not permit a full discussion. "To give an Induction of all the Particulars wherein the Antient Politicks and Military Disciplines excelled those of later Ages would be a Subject too copious for my present Design." Dodwell was willing to point to a few examples and pass silently over the inconvenient modern advantage of gunpowder.[41]

Nevertheless, Dodwell was himself a scholar, and it does not look as though he ever so much as looked upon a battlefield. He was a man of genuine learning and knew the pedantry of modern erudition as few others in his time. Moreover, he understood that the excellences of ancient political and military life could be completely appreciated only through a close study of the ancient monuments, through the discoveries of modern philology and archaeology. "Circumstances of time and place," he wrote in another connection, were essential, "for understanding others and for deducing the History of Opinion." He devoted his inaugural lecture in the Camden Chair, therefore, to a particular defense of that most abstruse and difficult of modern subjects, scientific chronology; and he devoted his many subsequent lectures to a marvelously detailed elucidation of a single text, the *Historia Augusta*, that most troublesome and perplexing of the classical histories.[42]

How, then, did Dodwell reconcile his own retired scholarly existence with his civic sensibility? his own vast and weighty erudition (so like the "natural heaviness of a studious Life" that he had deplored in his "Invitation") with his idea of a gentleman? his *ancienneté* with his modernity? The answer, I think, lies in his notion of scholarly utility. He would not allow learning to exist for its own sake but was more than ready to

[41]Cf. John Hall in his translation of Longinus: "If we remember that the old Tacticks and Strategems are, by the Invention of Gunpowder made in effect useless in this age, yet the greatest Captaines have made considerable use of them, and from Histories of different Climes and Governments, Politicians [yet] draw no small advantage, so in this part of Oratory . . . we may consider that those old precepts may well conduct the sharpest wits": *The Height of Eloquence*, trans. J. H. (London, 1652), dedication.

[42]Henry Dodwell, *Praelectiones academicae*, delivered 1688 (Oxford, 1692). For the approving reception, see Anthony Wood, *Athenae Oxoniensis*, ed. Philip Bliss, 4 vols. (London, 1813–1820), 3:267; Brokesby, *Life of Dodwell*, pp. 181–214; Thomas Hearne, *Remarks and Collections*, ed. C. E. Doble et al., 11 vols. (Oxford, 1885–1921), 10:1.

justify it for its value to things that really did matter. So, for example, he thought that historical knowledge was of immense use to religion and to all those ecclesiastical causes that needed defense. In an early "Letter of Advice for Direction of a Young Student in Divinity" he had considered "what use Philological Learning is to that End," and he never left off instructing his generation in the application of biblical and patristic history to present controversy.[43]

Even more to the point, perhaps, Dodwell saw that the classical histories that he so much admired for their immediate use needed elucidation;[44] he understood what had escaped Temple and the Christ Church company, that the very meaning and validity of the classical authors depended on the mundane collaboration and progressive labor of authenticating texts, collating manuscripts, deciphering language, and dating the ancient works and events. For these great labors he had won the appreciation of his contemporaries, not least Wotton and Bentley, as "the very learned Mr. Dodwell."[45] In 1701 the aging scholar tried to interest the young Thomas Hearne in digesting his massive chronological treatise, De cyclis, for a popular audience. He advised him to write a preface for it, an enchiridion, "just to touch the usefullness of antient History to all sorts of ancient learning, and the necessity of Chronology to judg accurately concerning all antient History and for considering counterfeits. . . ." [46] Thus Dodwell never lost his conviction that learning was necessary to illuminate the narrative histories, that it could disentangle the true from the false, and that the erudition of the scholar could serve the wisdom of the gentleman without any contradiction.

Unfortunately, what Dodwell did not see was that his own learning had become so cumbersome and involute as to seem almost unintelligible to the ordinary gentleman. Even his admiring biographer Francis Brokesby had to conclude that "his retired life, and his Unacquaintedness with the World, his studying Books more than men," had led him to an obscure and digressive style. This was the prevailing opinion of his friends; his opponents found much harsher things to say.[47] Dodwell's effort to combine the virtues of the active and contemplative lives, learn-

---

[43]Henry Dodwell, *Two Letters of Advice* (Dublin, 1672), pp. 277–94. Examples of Dodwell's historical writing are described by Brokesby, *Life of Dodwell*, pp. 58, 114, 135, 141, 175, 180; for the importance of the primitive church as the standard, see Dodwell to Daniel Whitby, n.d., Bodleian MS. Cherry 23, ff. 259–61.

[44]Brokesby, *Life of Dodwell*, pp. 309–20.

[45]See Graevius to Dodwell, Bodleian MS. English Letters C 28, ff. 51–52; Bodleian MS. Cherry 23, ff. 39–40, 51–52; Graevius to Bernard, Bodleian MS. Smith 5, ff. 67–72.

[46]Dodwell to Hearne, April 30, 1701, Bodleian MS. Rawlinson Letters 25, f. 4.

[47]Brokesby, *Life of Dodwell*, p. 354. See also Bernard to Smith, Oct. 6, 1699, Bodleian MS. Smith 49, f. 55; Hearne, *Remarks and Collections*, 6:198. Leibniz wrote, "J'estime infinement l'erudition de M. Dodwell, mais son raisonnement est pitoyable": Leibniz to Burnett, Feb. 22, 1707, in Gerhardt, *Philosophischen Schriften*, 311–14.

ing and a practical vocation, was thus an undoubted failure. As a result, he was not in a good position to influence the quarrel, which to some extent he misunderstood. In urging the combatants to forget their personal antipathies,[48] he meant well enough, but he was overlooking a difficulty that he himself had half realized and never really learned how to surmount, that the massive new learning of Renaissance philology had turned into something quite different now and was not wholly compatible with that equally Renaissance pursuit, the education and training of a gentleman.

Nevertheless, Dodwell would not let the issue drop, at least the scholarly issue that had called into question his own learning. The *De cyclis*, we have seen, was already in the press, with its questionable dates for Phalaris and Pythagoras, when "Bentley against Boyle" appeared. It was, in a way, Dodwell's lifework, the capstone of his career. In 1700, however, it was still in press. "My Book *de Cyclis*," he wrote to Lloyd, "increases beyond expectation. It is already a 100 sheets and will take a good many more before it is finished."[49] He was still trying to settle the chronology of Thucydides, the dates from Xerxes through the events of the Peloponnesian War. "I have fixt the place of some Archontes in that time," he boasted, "I think better than Diodorus, and upon better Auctorityes than his." (Once again we hear the claim that the moderns could come to know more about antiquity than the ancients themselves.) "I have fixt the Archonship of Themistocles otherwise than Lydiat, and of Aristides not yet known, and have settled the times of Themistocles, Cimon, Aristides, Pericles, and Alcibiades, nearer than hitherto has been, that I know attempted."[50] But that was only one small part of a scheme that embraced almost the whole of antiquity. The astronomer Edmund Halley, who eventually published an epitome of the work, was so staggered by its erudition that he was almost discouraged from attempting an abridgement.[51] The learned world abroad was equally impressed.

Inevitably Dodwell had to reconsider the times of Phalaris and Pythagoras. Bentley had to be answered, if possible, not by satire and scurrility but on his own scholarly ground and with the good manners of

[48]"It is a great temptation to disingenuity both to your self and your Adversaryes, when both sides are more concerned for Reputation than Truth": Dodwell to Bentley, June 24, 1699, Bodleian MS. Cherry 23, f. 159.

[49]Dodwell to Lloyd, July 9, 1700, Hardwick Court MSS., Worcester Record Office, Box 74, f. 27. There is a long correspondence between the two men on chronological matters in Bodleian MS. English Letters 29.

[50]Dodwell to Graevius, Dec. 12, 1699, Bodleian MS. Cherry 23, f. 56.

[51]Edmund Halley, "An Account of Mr. Dodwell's Book *De Cyclis* in a letter to Robert Nelson," reprinted in Brokesby, *Life of Dodwell*, pp. 611–38. Dodwell's treatise appeared as *De veteribus Graecorum Romanorumque cyclis* (Oxford, 1701).

a learned gentleman. In such a way Dodwell could hope to show just how such a controversy should be managed. Typically, he would not allow Lloyd's tract to ruffle their reconciliation, and he was soon confiding his plans to his old friend. "I have an unfinished Discourse," he wrote, "concerning the time of Phalaris where I am forced to prove what Dr. Bentley has graunted, but inconsistently with most of his arguments. I have shown Telemachus to have been concerned in the founding of Gela, not of Agrigentum, and that he could therefore have no hand in the death of Phalaris. From Pindar and Thucydides, better Auctorityes than can usually be expected for things of that Age, I have shown that Agrigentum it self was not elder than the 50th OL[ympiad]. But my Book swells so that it can have no place here. My chronology of Pythagoras is very little concerned in what has been opposed by the Dr."[52] In other words, Dodwell meant to take up those points on which Bentley had erred and try to correct them, while conceding the rest. "I see not the least need . . . to mix opinions of Persons in such cases as these are where Morals are not concerned, with opinions of things."[53] Only in such a way could the knowledge of antiquity be made to advance.

Dodwell's reply was ready at last in 1704, the same year in which Jonathan Swift decided to join the fray with *A Tale of a Tub* and only a little before Wotton's last riposte against the ancients. Unfortunately, the *Exercitationes duae*, like all Dodwell's works, appeared as a laborious exercise in ponderous Latin on an abstruse subject. Bentley had chosen English to answer his opponents and leavened his heavy subject with a sharp wit and spicy invective. Dodwell deliberately chose to elevate the discussion and open it to a European audience, but in the process he lost many of his English readers and was hardly noticed in the quarrel.[54] It didn't help that on the main question he sidestepped. Not only did he avoid the personal issue; in the end he said nothing directly about the authenticity of the letters of Phalaris.

What Dodwell did attend to were the chronological problems, the dates of Phalaris and Pythagoras, and the correction of some of Bentley's minor errors. He repeated his view that all the early dates were conjectural and hard to establish. He then tried to show by his favorite method of synchronizing times and authorities that some of the chronological discrepancies that Bentley had thought to expose were not discrepancies

[52]Dodwell to Lloyd, July 9, 1700, Hardwick Court MSS., Box 74, f. 27. For an account of his vast ambitions, see also Dodwell to Graevius, Dec. 12, 1699, Bodleian MS. Cherry 23, f. 56.

[53]Dodwell to Bentley, May 14, 1698, Bodleian MS. Cherry 23, f. 56.

[54]See the complaint of Cuperus to Graevius, July 12/22, 1699, Bodleian MS. D'Orville 478, ff. 160–61.

after all, that (for example) Phalaris could have built Agrigentum and corresponded with Stisichoras. To do this, he suggested that Bentley's confidence in the scholiasts had been misplaced, since they had written too late to be reliable. He was particularly adamant against Bentley's view that Atossa, the daughter of Cyrus, was the first person to write a letter. He questioned the authority of the historian Hellanicus, who again wrote late and whose work was known only at secondhand, and he proposed instead the testimony of Homer and Scripture. Besides, he pointed out, Atossa had lived about the same time as Phalaris.

At this point, having removed some of the chronological difficulties in the way of accepting the fraudulent letters, Dodwell tactfully changed the subject to consider the even more recondite problems in the dates for Pythagoras. And here, too, he found reason to disagree with Lloyd and Bentley, allowing the possibility of a coincidence of times between Phalaris and Pythagoras. The result was in its own way and on its own ground an impressive if slightly exasperating performance. Long afterward, Bentley's biographer and apologist James Monk found the book still of real value, "the most elaborate attempt ever made to approximate the truth respecting the history and biography of that remote age."[55] The editor of the contemporary *Bibliothèque choisie* also found much to admire in it. "In general [even] the little digressions in which his matter engages him are full of uncommon erudition which makes his work commendable." But when the Dutch scholar Perizonius read it and praised its learning, he wanted to know what most readers must still have wondered: Was Phalaris the author of the letters? and what did Bentley think of these alternative dates?[56] Apparently Dodwell had held fast to his first conviction that the *Epistles* were indeed genuine, though the work of a late paraphrast.[57] But one could hardly reach this conclusion from the work itself, which remained discreetly silent. As Monk wrote, "it was a model of controversial candour and good manners." But as such, indeed because it was such, it was almost completely ignored by all sides in the quarrel.

[55]James Henry Monk, *The Life of Richard Bentley*, 2d ed., 2 vols. (London, 1833), 1:180. More qualified but still very respectful is Henry Fynes Clinton, *Fasti Hellenici* (Oxford, 1834), p. xxv and passim.

[56]Perizonius to Bentley, July 7, 1705, Bodleian MS. St. Edmund Hall 13, ff. 29–30; *Bibliothèque choisie* 10 (1706): 138. *Miscellaneous Letters, Giving an Account of the Works of the Learned* also noticed and praised "the Industry and Accuracy of our Learned Chronologist": 6:435–42.

[57]Perizonius thought that Dodwell's views about Phalaris were like his own about Moses' Pentateuch: we have the meaning that Moses intended but not the words, phrases, or style of the original, which had long been altered in the transmission. See Perizonius to Bentley, April 13, 1706, Bodleian MS. St. Edmund Hall 13, ff. 33–35; and Arnaldo Momigliano, "Perizonius, Niebuhr, and the Character of the Early Roman Tradition," *Journal of Roman Studies* 47 (1957): 104–14.

4

Meanwhile, true to their word, the Christ Church wits were resuming their assault on Bentley and the moderns. Not that they had ever really ceased. In 1697 Bentley had threatened to expose Aesop with as much asperity as he had Phalaris. ("Of all the Compositions of the Aesopic Fables, these we have now left us, are both the Last and the Worst.")[58] Unfortunately, Dean Aldrich had already turned to one of the young Westminsters in his college, Anthony Alsop, to bring out a new edition of the text as a kind of companion piece to Phalaris. Like the rest of his company, Alsop was a good Latinist and a facile writer. Nothing daunted, he disposed of Bentley in the preface to his Aesop with a characteristic sneer at his pedantry, *in volvendis lexicis satis diligentem* (diligent enough in turning over dictionaries) and in the last of his fables, the dog in the manger, by invoking the now infamous phrase *singularis humanitatis*.[59] The work was held up briefly by the vice chancellor, who feared that the government might be offended by the "gentle touch upon Dr. Bentley," and it appeared eventually (1698) without his imprimatur.[60] It was clear that satire was meant to be the chief weapon against Bentley and that the fund of the wits was likely to prove inexhaustible.

If Alsop's joke was too slight to notice, the next Christ Church shaft must have struck harder.[61] William King was undoubtedly the cleverest of a clever company and had probably contributed the most effective passage to "Boyle against Bentley." He had also crossed swords with the Doctor a second time by contributing to, perhaps even writing, *A Short Account*, for which he got called a liar.[62] King did not forgive the great man for the insult and continued for the rest of his life to badger him with his satire, invective, and parody. But whatever the depth of personal animosity, which no doubt was genuine enough, it is plain that there

[58]Richard Bentley, *Dissertations upon the Epistles of Phalaris*, ed. Wilhelm Wagner (London, 1883), pp. 569–70.

[59]Anthony Alsop, *Fabularum Aesopicarum Delectas* (Oxford, 1698), Preface, sig. a4 and p. 128.

[60]Smalridge to Gough, n.d., in John Nichols, *Illustrations of the Literary History of the Eighteenth Century*, 8 vols. (London, 1817–1858), 3:260–61.

[61]"I do not believe Aesop's dog will hurt Dr. Bentley. . . . I Must needs say, I think what the Preface speaks of him is Childish and doubt it will be understood by many": W. Hopkins to Arthur Charlett, Jan. 15, 1698, Bodleian MS. Ballard 13, f. 31v. Hopkins thought it might do Bentley some good to be humbled but doubted that the Christ Church wits, "who attempt no defense against his Charge," could do it.

[62]"Memoirs of Dr. King," in *The Original Works of Dr. William King*, ed. John Nichols, 3 vols. (London, 1776); Colin J. Horne, "The Phalaris Controversy: King vs. Bentley," *Review of English Studies* 22 (1946): 289–303.

was an intellectual issue besides, an antithetical view of the meaning and use of history and literature, the same that we have seen everywhere else in the argument.

King's new attack (1699) was delivered in the form of some brief *Dialogues of the Dead Relating to the Present Controversy Concerning the Epistles of Phalaris.* It was aimed directly at the "snarling critic Bentivoglio," who appears on every page as the object of abuse. According to King, everyone was saying that he is "a Heavy writer, and . . . further that he is too Bulky and Tedious, that he argues upon Trifles only with great Gravity, and manages Serious things with as much Lightness that he has pillag'd Authors to gain a Reputation." In the second dialogue, King has Phalaris dispute with a Sophist; the Sicilian tyrant accuses the writer of having stolen his work. "Could such a wretch as thou art," he asks (echoing the argument in Temple), "be able to express such things as I have done?" How could a mere Sophist ever convince the world that the *Epistles* were his? The Sophist replies:

> Look you, Sir, I am resolved to own them and however improbable the thing may be, I have a Doctor to stand by me. And then, Sir, I shall endeavour to pacifie you with Reasons, if that will do it; my Arguments are drawn from the uncertainty of the Time in which you liv'd, and consequently of such Persons who might be your Cotemporaries, because you know there could never have been two of the same Name. Another Argument I draw from the Names of Familiar Towns and Villages. . . . Then you, who are a Dorian, pretend to write Attick, which is as absurd as a Berwick-man should write English; and lastly, you have four Sayings and six Words, that were not us'd till several Ages after you were born, as I am credibly inform'd.[63]

It was not a bad summary of Bentley's arguments, though ridiculous enough in this setting. (Bentley, incidentally, tried to turn the tables by invoking the Christ Church use of "cotemporary" as a dangerous barbarism; it was, he insisted, "a word of his own *Coposition*, for which the Learned World will *cogratulate* him!")[64] Was that all, asks Phalaris? No, there was a final argument. "There is not," the Sophist points out triumphantly, "one word relating to the old Gentlewoman, your Mother, which a Man of your Benevolence and Affection to your Family, could hardly have omitted!" After noticing a few similar oversights, the So-

[63] William King, *Dialogues of the Dead Relating to the Present Controversy Concerning the Epistles of Phalaris* (London, 1699), p. 2; King, *Original Works*, 1:133–86.

[64] Bentley, *Dissertations*, p. 53.

phist is ready to conclude. "You say the *Epistles* are *your own*: I say they are *my own*, and that Bentivoglio has prov'd them to be so by Arguments that are *his own.*" Phalaris is left speechless.

In the dialogues that follow, King drives home his satirical point, for example, in the one entitled "Self-Love" between a thinly disguised Ricardo and Narcissus; or better still between the ancient lexicographer Hesychius and the modern Francis Gouldman.[65] Taking up a boast by Bentley that he would restore the text of the Greek compiler, King has Bentivoglio attempt to vindicate the value of all dictionaries. To the wits nothing seemed more contemptible in contrast to real literature than an alphabetical list of words. Hesychius brags of Bentivoglio, "He has read half of me and has made Honourable mention of me in all his Works, he has restor'd me in ten thousand places and Collated me with all the Manuscripts in the World but those in the King of Poland's Library." Gouldsman's reply is a nice summary of the objections of the wits to all such scholarship.

> I grant that all Wit, Arts, Genteel and Mannerly Conviction are con-tain'd in Dictionaries, just as they are in the Alphabet . . . but then the joyning them is the Art our Dictionaries will never teach a Man; for suppose I was to discourse in Politicks, my first word I find in your 119th Page, your second in the 204th, and the third perhaps, an 100 pages after. Now this is too much for mortal Man to carry in his Memory.

The impracticality of philological learning for the active life could hardly be better put, and the reply of Hesychius–Bentley (which echoes Wotton's claims for the subject) appears only the more ridiculous. "Does not more of Homer's Wit appear in his Eustathius and Didymus [two late Greek commentators] than in all his Iliads? And is not *Clavis Homerica* better than either?"

Naturally, chronology also comes in for its share of mockery, although King allows that "nothing can be of more use than the Periods they fix, both for the Illustration of History and the Service of Religion." But he cannot appreciate the need for precision which seems to him ludicrous, or the absorption with such details as Thericlean cups, or the origin of Sicilian cities, or the evolution of the language. Bentivoglio, he says, can tell not only when Athens was founded but who laid the first stone. "There is not a Potter in Athens, or a Brasier in Corinth, but he

---

[65]King, *Original Works*, 1:155–57. Francis Gouldman was the author of a Latin-English dictionary that went through several editions after 1664.

knows where he set up, and who took out a Statute of Bankrupt against him." Were such things ever noticed by the great chronologists of the past?

> Perhaps not, but we stand upon their Shoulders, and therefore see things with greater exactness, perhaps never Man came to the same pitch of Chronology as the much esteem'd Bentivoglio. He has got the true Standard by which to judge of the Grecian time. He knows the Age of any Greek Word unless it be in the Greek Testament and can tell you the Time a Man liv'd in by reading a page of his Book, as easily as I could have told an Oyster-Woman's Fortune when my hand was crost with a piece of Silver.

Admirable indeed! Why, it seemed that even words had their rise and fall, the very same as monarchies!

There was much more to the same effect. King found Bentley's parade of learning all foolish because all irrelevant, all trivial because nothing useful. Can he decipher an ancient inscription on a defaced marble? (Bentley had used the Parian inscription to date the age of tragedy.) Who cared? Indeed, the moderns preferred the very illegibility of the old monuments to anything easily decipherable. "It is not a Criticks business," King remarks ironically, "to read Marbles, but out of Broken pieces, to guess at 'em, and then positively restore 'em."

No wonder, then, that King allows Bentivoglio respite only long enough to take on William Wotton and the *Reflections on Modern Learning*.[66] Once admit his general argument about the uselessness and triviality of modern learning and all he had to do was to quote Wotton against himself. What is Moderno doing in a ditch? (He is hunting tadpoles in order to advance knowledge.) Nor was the undertaking the less admirable, to quote Wotton, "because all of it perhaps, cannot be made immediately useful to Humane Life." It just proved that it was not gain alone that moved men to the pursuit of knowledge! Indeed, scientists and antiquaries deserved only commendation, King quotes Wotton, "for their seemingly useless Labours, and the more, since they run the hazard of being laugh'd at by Men of Wit. For nothing wounds as much as Jest, and when Men once become Ridiculous, their Labours will be slighted, and they will find few Imitators." Thus the Christ Church men let the cat out of the bag and gave away their intentions. And well they might feel in 1699 that the tide was flowing in their direction. "Notwithstanding the Dissertations of Bentivoglio," King was able to report, "the Sophist

[66] King, *Original Works*, pp. 167–74.

imposes his spurious Epistles upon the World under his Name and the Examiner, who has undertaken his Defence, has met with a kind Reception from the World whilst none complain. . . ."

5

A battle in progress looks like only confusion to the combatants. Afterward it is easy perhaps to choose the victor and award the spoils, but in 1699 the quarrel between the ancients and the moderns hung still suspended and the issue lay yet in doubt.[67] Bentley's *Dissertations* had certainly unsettled the ancients and renewed their fury. King's salvo was only the first in a new barrage; inevitably the ringleader, Atterbury, took to the field once more.

His first opportunity was another edition of "Boyle against Bentley." The tract was a best-seller, and the *Dissertations* only improved its sale. When a third edition was required in 1699, Atterbury hurried into print with a brief "addition." Significantly, although he did respond to one point of fact—the existence of Zaleucus as a Pythagorean lawgiver—Atterbury reiterated the chief contention of the ancients that no *fact* could really affect the main argument. For even if Bentley could "by the help of Chronological Tables, and confronting one Author with another," find new authorities for such particulars, it would be to no avail; upon such details "the stress of the Cause does not depend." At best, Atterbury conceded, Bentley could show with his method that the Examiner was sometimes wrong, "but he will never prove that he's right."[68] As we have seen, Bentley himself suspected as much, doubting that he could ever square a circle. For Atterbury, prolonging the controversy on such grounds, "in that heavy Bentleian way," could only prove dry and fruitless.

Although Bentley now kept silent and left the last word to Atterbury, so brief an argument was hardly an adequate reply. So Atterbury took a little more time from his burgeoning career of ecclesiastical controversy to compose a more complete and deliberate answer. It was published anonymously in 1701 as *A Short Review of the Controversy between Mr. Boyle and Dr. Bentley with Suitable Reflections upon It*, and was clearly meant to end the quarrel with a definitive reply. The trouble was, as Atterbury freely admitted, that Bentley's assault on Christ Church kept

---

[67]"Dr Bentley I hear . . . is upon a ramble. What, I wonder, will the Oxonians do? Shall we rest quiet: for my part, I do not yet think I have sufficiently cause to stir and I hope I am better employed": Wotton to Evelyn, Aug. 8, 1699, Christ Church Evelyn Correspondence, MS. 12.

[68]Charles Boyle, *Bentley's Dissertations . . . Examin'd*, 3d ed. (London, 1699), p. 266.

coming up in conversation so that every member of the College was forced into a continual defense.[69] The new challenge would have to be met again.

Not that there was anything new to say: Atterbury contented himself with finding a new way to say it, to reiterating the basic opposition between the two parties. He would not pretend here to resume the argument over matter of fact. The wits had made it plain from the beginning that the question of the authenticity of the letters of Phalaris was of little importance. Had the quarrel been merely about that, then "no body I believe would be much concerned who had the better Argument." Indeed, Atterbury was now ready to retreat from a defense of Phalaris to the original view of his young protégé. "The only question so far as Mr. Boyle's concern'd in it is, whether the Dr. has demonstrated them to be spurious (as he pretends to have done) or whether they are only under some just suspicions of being forged (as Mr. Boyle alledged)."[70] To some this must have seemed a rather damaging admission—but perhaps only to those who really cared about the authenticity of the *Epistles*.

For Atterbury and the men of Christ Church, the issue lay elsewhere, and they were not entirely wrong. The fact is that one could remain an ancient and yet concede that the letters were a late, though still admirable, work of the classical world. Perhaps Temple had erred on a point of fact; what did it matter? Even if the letters were spurious, they had pleased "some of the nicest judges of this Age," and well deserved their popularity and a new edition.[71] The real issue for the wits was how to use antiquity—how, for example, to employ the *Epistles* of Phalaris, not how to edit or date or correct them. The real contrast between the combatants was thus in their manner, not their matter. Dr. Bentley had "managed a dry Subject which no body was concern'd for in a stiff confused manner." Mr. Boyle (taking the same unhappy subject) had written not for the learned only but to "afford a general and lasting

---

[69]*A Short Review of the Controversy between Mr. Boyle and Dr. Bentley with Suitable Reflections upon it. And the Dr's Advantageous Character of himself given at length. Recommended to the serious perusal of such as propose to be Considered for their Fairness, Modesty, and good temper in Writing* (London, 1701), p. 32.

[70]Ibid., p. 137.

[71]According to a later translator, John Savage, "Should any supercilious Critick assert that some few of this Collection are not Genuine, let him enjoy his Opinion. I shall never think a Dispute like that about Phalaris Epistles, tho' learnedly manag'd on both sides, worth the Heats and Pains . . . especially when . . . they [the letters] carry such an air of Antiquity, and are so built on the Customs, Manners, and History of those times that they might well pass for Originals, inasmuch as they contribute to our common end, of bringing the Reader acquainted with the Antients": *A Select Collection of Letters of the Antients* (London, 1703), sig. A2v–A3. The *Epistles* were still being translated and authenticated in 1749; see Thomas Francklin, *The Epistles of Phalaris* (London, 1749), pp. xiii–xvi.

entertainment to the world." Dr. Bentley may have been a scholar but he was a pedant; Mr. Boyle was a scholar but he was also a gentleman. Dr. Bentley, Atterbury admitted,

> has read abundance of old Greek and abundance of modern Latin: he has much of both in his Head, and much more in his Collections. But he tumbles it out as they do Stones out of a Cart to mend the ways with, here and there a bit falls right and stops a hole; but most of his learned stuff lies on heaps, and serves only to puzzle and confound such as have any occasion or curiosity to travel over his writings.

Mr. Boyle, on the other hand, had written so well that "we are convinc'd from that excellent Pattern of writing he has set us, that there is no sort of matter but what will take a polish and may be made to shine by a skillful hand."[72]

It was thus polish or politeness (the Roman *urbanitas*) that the Christ Church wits demanded and that was one principal value of the classics for them.[73] Controversy about a subject such as Phalaris was pointless in itself unless one could manage it as Boyle (or rather Atterbury) had done, so "as to teach us to write and reason well upon any Subject, to form right Judgments of the value and importance of Books, and of the Conduct and Characters of Writers."[74] In short, it was the rhetorical ideal of antiquity come to life again, literature as imitation and the guide to life. It was enough for scholars to make the ancient works available again in a simple and accessible form; the lavish erudition of a Bentley was, from this perspective, all beside the point, and in its denigration of such authors as Phalaris threatening as well. Who knew where such pedantry would lead? In any case, it was hard to see how it could possibly help a young man who wanted to learn how to live and govern himself in the world.

Since there was not much that Atterbury could think of adding to the argument, he continued to look about for any new device to make his point. Naturally, he found it again in satire. Bentley's notorious confidence played into his hands. Atterbury saw that all he had to do was to quote Bentley against himself, taking his works almost verbatim but rearranging and retouching them, and he could draw a sardonic portrait not completely unlike the original. Thus Bentley is made to brag, in a

---

[72]*Short Review*, pp. 1–2, 70–71.

[73]For some classical precedents, see Edwin S. Ramage, *Urbanitas: Roman Sophistication and Refinement* (Norman, Okla., 1973).

[74]*Short Review*, p. 4.

pastiche of quotations drawn from his *Dissertations* and exactly cited, "that Eusebius's Histories are all shuffled and interpolated; that Plutarch would never balk at a good story, though it did not exactly hit with Chronology; that Diodorus forgets himself; that Scaliger and Meursius made great slips; that Casaubon is often deceived. . . ." Obviously no authority was too august for Bentley's criticism; the moderns were shown to be arrogant and heedless in their claims to the advancement of learning. As for the doctor's special genius in restoring texts, Atterbury makes him boast again of "a particular Knack . . . at giving clear Emendations of faulty Passages in Authors where great Men have attempted in vain. Had it not been for my extraordinary skill in these matters honest Thericles might have been a Turner and not a Potter, Thespis a Harper and not a Tragick Poet. . . ." Such were the rich rewards of modern philology! "A great many absurd and dangerous Errors as these," Bentley is made to continue, "have been either introduced or confirmed by the ignorance of Grammarians and Emendators." But more ridiculous to the men of Christ Church was his conclusion: "Emendators and various readings are much more intoxicating than good sense and fine writing; Manners, Propriety and Wit raise you but one step above common Mortals, but Words, Phrases and Derivations give you a seat among the Stars!"

Once again the Christ Church message was clear. Manners, propriety, and wit were the goal, imitation of the classics the means. Nothing seemed so obvious to Atterbury and his friends than that Horace and Cicero stood infinitely above their commentators, Thomas Farnaby and Marius Nizolius, "that one who mended a point or a word in a Book did not deserve the same consideration as he that understood the spirit of the Author, and that he who only understood the sense and meaning of a good Writer was a degree below him that was able to Write as well." Yet William Wotton had dared to suggest the very opposite when he had exalted the modern philologist, and Bentley had seemed by his very assurance to agree. For the wits, the one great object was to reproduce the spirit of the classics, to have it live again in their own manners and expression; and all the works of modern scholarship were beginning to seem irrelevant at best, dangerous perhaps, and certainly more than a little absurd in their arrogance and pretension. Had not Temple written letters, the most perfect in English, according to Swift? What could Wotton or Bentley or any philologist show to match them?[75]

---

[75]"It is generally believed that the author [i.e., Temple] had advanced our English tongue to as great a perfection as it can bear": Publisher's Epistle (Jonathan Swift) in Temple's *Letters*, in William Temple, *Works*, 4 vols. (London, 1814), 1:226.

6

Yet still the ancients were not done. Even as Atterbury was writing, a young man so far unknown was considering further how to avenge his cause against the upstart moderns. Jonathan Swift, fresh out of Trinity College, Dublin, and thirsting with ambition, had entered the service of Sir William Temple in 1689. For most of the next decade and during the height of the controversy, he lived with the great man at Moor Park, beginning as a servant, becoming a valued (if sometimes neglected) secretary, and growing finally into a friend and collaborator. If it was not always the easiest relationship—for Temple had grown moody in old age and Swift was chafing and impatient—it was nevertheless marked by a genuine and increasing mutual respect. In these years and for a while after Temple's death, Swift transcribed, edited, and published all of his patron's work—including, in 1701, *Some Thoughts on Reviewing the Essay on Ancient and Modern Learning*. And when at last Temple was no more, Swift remembered him as "a Person of the greatest Wisdom, Justice, Liberality, Politeness, Eloquence, of his Age or Nation, the truest Lover of his Country." Certainly the older man seems to have exercised a powerful influence in shaping Swift's ideal of a landed gentleman who was both a Christian and a humanist.[76]

It is well to remember that even before entering Temple's service, while still at Trinity College, Swift had exhibited a repugnance for philosophical and scientific learning, "for which he had no great relish by nature," and turned instead to classical history and poetry. John Boyle, who afterward became his friend and wrote his life, recalled that "he held logic and metaphysics in the utmost contempt and he scarce considered mathematics and natural philosophy unless to turn them into ridicule. The studies which he followed were history and poetry."[77] In

[76]See Swift's note at Temple's death on the flyleaf of his Bible, quoted in George P. Mayhew, "Jonathan Swift's *On the Burning of Whitehall in 1697* Re-examined," *Harvard Library Bulletin* 19 (1971): 404n. See also Swift's *Ode to the Honourable Sir William Temple*, in Jonathan Swift, *Poems*, ed. Sir Harold Williams, 2d ed. 3 vols. (Oxford, 1958), 1:26–33. A. C. Elias, Jr., has challenged the traditionally favorable idea of this relationship in *Swift at Moor Park: Problems in Biography and Criticism* (Philadelphia, 1982), but the older view seems to me still to hold; see, for example, Emile Pons, *Swift: Les Années de jeunesse*, Publications de la Faculté des Lettres de l'Université de Strasbourg 26 (Strasbourg, 1925), bk. 2, chap. 2, p. 4; Ricardo Quintana, *The Mind and Art of Jonathan Swift* (London, 1936); Irvin Ehrenpreis, "Swift and Mr. John Temple," *Modern Language Notes* 62 (1947): 145–54, and *Swift: The Man, His Works, and His Age*, vol. 1 (Cambridge, Mass., 1962).

[77]John Boyle, fifth earl of Cork and Orrery, *Remarks on the Life and Writings of Jonathan Swift* (London, 1752), p. 7; cf. Gulliver on the learning of the Brobdignagians. "I have got up my Latin pretty well, and am getting up my Greek, but to enter upon causes of philosophy is what I protest I will rather die in a ditch than go about": Jonathan Swift to Thomas Swift, May 3, 1692, in *The Correspondence, of Jonathan Swift*, ed. Harold Williams, 5 vols. (Oxford, 1963–1965), 1:6–11.

1690 Temple recommended the young man by recalling that "he has lived in my house, read to mee, writ for mee, and kept all accounts as farr as my small occasions required. He has latine and greeke, some French, writes a very good and correct hand, is very honest and diligent." At Moor Park, Swift continued to read the classics and English history, was introduced into society, and pursued Sir William's affairs, not least the quarrel between the ancients and the moderns. As for himself, he remembered beginning to write some things then as "a young Gentleman much in the World and . . . to the Tast of those who were like himself."[78]

Swift was thus particularly well placed to take up the cause of the ancients and he seems to have set about it earnestly at the time of the contretemps over Phalaris, possibly with the help of his cousin Thomas Swift, another of Temple's young chaplains, and drawing upon French example.[79] But (as we have seen) his master, Temple, was of no mind to dignify his opponent with an answer, and it looks as though he must have discouraged Swift's work, as he certainly turned back Mr. H. of Oxford. At any rate, this would explain why Swift delayed publishing. In 1699 Temple died, leaving his young assistant as his literary executor. It was Swift who decided to publish Temple's reply to Wotton in 1701, despite the fact that it was unfinished. He must have been well aware of its imperfections, as he must also have been increasingly conscious of his own merits and of the unpublished work still in his drawer. Meanwhile,

[78]Temple to Sir Robert Southwell, May 29, 1690, in Swift, *Correspondence*, 1:1–2.

[79]According to Ehrenpreis, the *Tale* was probably begun late in 1696, the digressions in 1697–98: *Swift*, 1:187. According to Deane Swift, "It was at Moore-Park that Swift corrected the *Tale of a Tub*, and writ his famous *Digressions*, every section of which, one after another, he submitted to the judgment and correction of his learned friend": *An Essay on the Life and Writings of Swift* (London, 1755), p. 60. This account may be correct but we have no corroborating evidence. For Thomas Swift's possible complicity, see Robert M. Adams, "Jonathan Swift, Thomas Swift, and the Authorship of *A Tale of a Tub*," *Modern Philology* 64 (1967): 198–232, and "The Mood of the Church and *A Tale of a Tub*," in *England in the Restoration and Early Eighteenth Century*, ed. H. T. Swedenberg (Berkeley, 1972), pp. 79–80. The satires of François de Callières and Antoine Furetière have been suggested as models; both found English translations in these years. Callières's *Histoire poétique de la guerre nouvellement déclarée entre les anciens et les modernes* (Paris, 1688) was translated in 1725; Furetière's *Nouvelle Allégorique ou histoire des derniers troubles arrivés au royaume d'éloquence* (Paris, 1658) was translated as *The Rebellion; or, An Account of the Late Civil-Wars in the Kingdom of Eloquence* (London, 1704). The translator of the last ironically commends the author of *A Tale of a Tub* for his "good Breeding and Piety and Good-humour, and Christian Charity and Aversion to Satyr": sig. A3. Wotton accused Swift of plagiarism from Callières in his "Defense of the Reflections," appended to the 3d ed. of his *Reflections upon Ancient and Modern Learning* (London, 1705); Temple's biographer Abel Boyer accused him of plagiarizing from Purerière: *Memoirs of the Life and Writings of Sir William Temple* (London, 1714), pp. 405–7. Swift is defended by A. C. Guthkelch in "The *Tale of a Tub* Revers'd and *Characters and Criticism upon the Ancient and Modern Orators*," *The Library*, 3d ser., 4 (1913): 281–84; and in his edition of *A Tale of a Tub* (London, 1908), pp. xliv–xlv, liii–liv.

the quarrel would not abate, despite the best efforts of the men of Christ Church.

Perhaps it was this that caused Swift in 1704 to launch his own work on an unsuspecting London world and create a sensation. No one, it is safe to say, had ever seen anything quite like *A Tale of a Tub* with its curious little appendage, *The Battle of the Books*. Satire and invective there had been aplenty throughout the quarrel, but here they were raised to new heights by a curious kind of imaginative power so far unequaled in English literature. Atterbury and his friends, needless to say, were perfectly delighted by it, and Atterbury at least soon learned its author. (Wotton, on the other hand, thought for a while that it was by Temple.) When Atterbury was shown the book by Matthew Prior, he wrote at once to Robert Harley to commend Swift and express his pleasure; and he recommended it to his colleague Jonathan Trelawny, bishop of Winchester. "I beg your worship (if the book is come down to Exon) to read *The Tale of a Tub*; for bating the prophaneness of it, it is a book to be valued, being an original of its kind, full of wit, humour, good sense, and learning. . . . The Town is wonderfully pleased with it."[80]

A Tale of a Tub is fortunately too well known to need summary here, if indeed it can ever be satisfactorily epitomized. Swift described it aptly as a satire on the "Corruptions in Religion and Learning," with a short narrative about religion and a long series of digressions about learning. It was the religious matter that disturbed Atterbury and shocked many readers but it is the digressions that are our immediate concern. There Swift dealt with the pretensions of modern learning. However, it is clear that the very form—or formlessness—of the whole work, with its prefaces, introductions, excurses, appendix, footnotes, and so forth, was meant of itself to travesty the scholarly treatise. Atterbury had already singled out the digressive character of Bentley's *Dissertations* as their chief fault; Swift's parody underlines this complaint even to introducing a

---

[80]Atterbury to Trelawny, June 15, 1704, quoted in H. C. Beeching, *Francis Atterbury* (London, 1909), pp. 232–33. Two weeks later Atterbury reported that the *Tale* was generally believed at Oxford to be by "one Smith and one Philips, the first a student, the second a commoner of Christ Church." A few days later he pointed out that the real author remained obscure; "he hath reason to conceal himself because of the profane strokes in that piece, which would do his reputation and interest in the world more harm than the wit can do him good": ibid., p. 233. When he learned that Swift was the author, he was pleased but concerned that he would be easily discovered: Atterbury to Harley, in *Historical Manuscript Commission Reports: Manuscripts of the Duke of Portland*, vol. 4 (London, 1897), p. 155. King, who was immediately suspected, wanted no association with the work and attacked the anonymous author in *Some Remarks on the "Tale of a Tub"* (London, 1704). Wotton owned a copy of *A Tale of a Tub* which I have not seen in which he scribbled annotations that indicate a hardening suspicion that Temple was the author. See the note in Swift, *A Tale of a Tub*, ed. A. C. Guthkelch and D. Nichol Smith (Oxford, 1920), p. 312.

To front the Title.   B. Lens delin: J. Sturt sculp.

The frontispiece to *A Tale of a Tub* (1710), reproduced by permission of
Cornell University Libraries

digression in praise of digressions—which he finds an especially notable modern improvement.[81]

The first of Swift's digressions, "Concerning Critics," puts directly his objections to the modern "philologers." He pretends to write a treatise on the history of criticism, from its primitive state to its present condition, in order to refute the claims of those who insist upon celebrating it as a wholly modern invention. The form and style of the argument are here, as elsewhere, a parody of the learned disputation. Swift begins with some definitions of criticism, two of which have lapsed with time, though each originally made sense. Thus it was once thought that critics were those who pronounced judgments on the works of the learned, sometimes censuring and sometimes praising. And it was also believed that critics were "the restorers of ancient learning from the worms, and graves, and dust of manuscripts." However, the term had now come to be applied, according to Swift, simply to the discoverers and collectors of the faults of writers. The pedigree of these "true critics" was the most ancient, as their modern offspring were the most flourishing. From Momus and Hybris, who begat Zoilus, to Bentley and Wotton, who begat Etcetera, Swift finds the genealogy uninterrupted. Wotton's arguments are, with some wonderful syntactical invention, turned upside down, "that the first things delivered of old have been long since invented and brought to light by later pens; and that the noblest discoveries those ancients ever made, of art or of nature, have all been produced by the transcending genius of the present age!" The true modern critic is compared with a mechanic or tailor in one place and with a dog in another, "whose thoughts and stomach are wholly set upon what the guests fling away, and consequently is apt to snarl most when there are fewest bones."

A little later, in a "Digression in the Modern Kind," Swift resumes his criticism of philology and particularly of Bentley's *Dissertations*. He notices that the arguments of the moderns have been so effective that there is a "grave dispute whether there have been any ancients or not." (Was Swift reading Père Hardouin, who just then was seriously arriving at this somber conclusion? Or more likely simply reducing to absurdity Bentley's attack on Phalaris and Aesop?) Little by little, he unfolds a position exactly like Temple and the other ancients had done. The critical learning of the moderns—that is to say, philology—is once again shown to be largely destructive, barren of all practical consequence and above all trivial. Swift uses Homer as his principal example. With the aid of the

<hr>

[81]The most useful commentary for our purposes remains Miriam K. Starkman, *Swift's Satire on Learning in "A Tale of a Tub"* (Princeton, 1950). All quotations are from the 2d ed. by A. C. Guthkelch and D. Nichol Smith, *A Tale of a Tub* (Oxford, 1958).

moderns, he has been able to discover many gross errors in that most venerable of the ancients. "For whereas we are assured he designed his work for a complete body of all knowledge, human, divine, political, and mechanic, it is manifest he has wholly neglected some, and been very imperfect in the rest." Homer did not know the wisdom of the Cabala, he was ignorant of that most useful modern instrument, a "save-all," and most astonishing, he was entirely ignorant of the common laws of the realm and the doctrine and discipline of the Church of England, "a defect indeed, for which both he and the ancients stand most justly censured by my worthy and ingenious friend Mr. Wotton, Bachelor of Divinity, in his incomparable *Treatise of Ancient and Modern Learning*, a book never to be sufficiently valued, whether we consider the happy turns and flowings of the author's wit, the great usefulness of his sublime discoveries upon the subject of flies and spittle, or the laborious eloquence of his style." Swift allows Homer to be the inventor of the compass, gunpowder, and the circulation of the blood. "But I challenge any of his admirers to show me in all his writings a complete account of the spleen. Does he not leave us wholly to seek in the art of political wagering? What can be more defective and unsatisfactory than his long dissertation upon tea? And as to his method of salivation without mercury so much celebrated of late, it is, to my knowledge and experience, a thing very little to be relied on."[82]

Needless to say, there is very much more to *A Tale* than this, more certainly about religion, but also more about modern learning, including the "new schemes in philosophy" which dared to propose new systems "in things agreed on all hands impossible to be known." Swift had even less use for science, ancient and modern, than Temple. But even with its many references to Wotton and Bentley, the *Tale* was less explicit about the quarrel than its little companion piece. The *Battle of the Books* may have been a less remarkable invention and a less memorable piece of satire, but it was the true culmination of the ancients' defense of antiquity.

7

It must seem a little presumptuous to try to summarize *The Battle of the Books* here and certainly unnecessary for the reader who either has a copy of the little work nearby or a reasonable recollection of it. It will

<hr />

[82]For the origin of these examples in the real activities of the Royal Society, see R. C. Olson, "Swift's Use of the *Philosophical Transactions* in Section V of *A Tale of a Tub*," *Studies in Philology* 49 (1952): 459–67.

certainly lose most of its fun, which was the real intention of the piece and the reason for its great success. But for the student who has lived so long with his subject there is a great temptation to dwell upon its satire. Swift had watched the quarrel from the beginning, chosen sides early, and followed each incident with relish. If he had little to add to an argument that had early exhausted the issues, he nevertheless contributed much to its future course, if only because he was still read when the rest were forgotten. In *The Battle of the Books* Swift elected to give his version of the struggle, recasting it in the shape of mock history or epic.[83] He did not intend to add anything substantive to the quarrel; he was determined rather, like any prejudiced reporter, to assign his own meaning to the event, to award the palm to the ancients, and to leave posterity in no doubt whatever about the outcome. In this design he very nearly succeeded.

Swift's view of the quarrel appears even in the brief bookseller's note to the reader—no doubt by Swift himself. He assigns the work there to the year 1697 and describes the manuscript that he prints as defective. Despite his disclaimer that "we cannot [therefore] learn to which side the victory fell," there is no mistaking where his sympathies lay. The bookseller remembers that when Wotton and Bentley attacked the ancients, "the town highly resented to see a person of Sir William Temple's character and merits roughly used by the two reverend gentlemen aforesaid, and without any manner of provocation." Clearly Swift had no intention whatever of meeting the moderns on their own ground. The main charge of the Christ Church wits was to be resumed; Bentley and Wotton were to be attacked ad hominem and shown to be guilty of a breach of decorum. But if Phalaris was thus to be left without any real defense, the gentlemanly ideal of Sir William Temple was not to be forgotten.

Like Atterbury, then, Swift had to use all his ingenuity to lure his readers away from the immediate issues raised by the moderns, such as the authenticity of the *Epistles*, to what he believed were the true grounds of the argument. Several times, therefore, each from a different perspective, he reviewed the quarrel in order to reach the same conclusion: Wotton and Bentley were ridiculous not so much because they were wrong on any substantive issue or point of fact as because their facts were trivial and irrelevant to any larger matter and their posture was arrogant and pretentious.

[83]The most recent text, with an introduction, is Hermann Josef Real, *The Battle of the Books* (Berlin, 1978). It has been suggested that a chief source for Swift's parody of Wotton and Bentley was the episode of Nisus and Euryalus in the *Aeneid*, IX, ll. 176–223. See A. Sanford Limouze, "A Note on Vergil and the Battle of the Books," *Philological Quarterly* 27 (1948): 85–89.

Swift's method was thus appropriate to his task. By adopting the heroic devices of the epic for his narrative, he at once confounded the reader's expectations of great events with the petty career of the actual quarrel. A military metaphor was no doubt inevitable in any account of the argument, but to take a battle of the books as seriously as a real campaign was necessarily to make fun of it, especially at a time when war and its glorification in epic still served as the chief inspiration to heroic virtue. Swift began his story by reminding his readers that when the Greeks had fought to a standstill and could not determine the victor, they set up trophies and drew up partisan accounts of the battle. Now in modern times learned men drew on classical precedent to fight their own wars and paraded their disputes, arguments, rejoinders, considerations, answers, replies, remarks, reflections, objections, and confutations. No wonder then that when all these conflicting versions were brought together in a great library, war should break out again. And this was how, Swift tells us, the battle of the books began.

As in any true epic, the battle Swift describes is conducted simultaneously on two levels. It began, he tells us, with the gods on Mount Parnassus. Apparently that mountaintop had two peaks, the higher of which belonged to the ancients, the lower to the moderns. According to Swift, the struggle broke out when the moderns grew jealous of the favored position of their rivals. They complained "how the height of that part of Parnassus quite spoiled the prospect of theirs . . . and to avoid a war offered them the choice of this alternative, either that the ancients would please to remove themselves and their effects down to the lower summit . . . or else the said ancients will give leave to the moderns to come with their shovels and matlocks and level the said hill." The ancients were astonished by this purely destructive ultimatum from a colony "whom they had admitted out of their own free grace, to so near a neighborhood," and pointed to the advantages of shade and shelter that their height afforded, threatening that their impregnable position could only break their rivals' tools and hearts. They concluded by advising the moderns "rather to raise their own side of the hill than dream of pulling down that of the ancients," and offered to help as far as they could. When this offer was rejected, the battle began with an exchange of insults and whole rivulets of ink.

At the same time, on a more mundane level, Swift continues, the quarrel broke out in the king's library, provoked by the royal librarian, who was a person of great valor but chiefly "renowned for his humanity." This heroic character had taken up the modern cause and vowed to knock down two of the enemy chiefs who guarded a high rock, "but endeavouring to climb up, was cruelly obstructed by his own unhappy weight and tendency towards his centre." Forced thus to retreat to his library, he took out his vengeance on the ancients by banishing their books to the most remote corners and threatening to turn them out of doors. In the resulting confusion (otherwise compounded by the further blundering of the librarian), the books, each of which, according to Swift, preserved the spirit of a living author, began their own terrible quarrel between the ancients and the moderns.

Swift is about to pursue these two battles when he intrudes into his story a brief allegory that by itself epitomizes the whole quarrel. It seems that just as hostilities were about to begin, a spider and a bee entered the library and began to argue.[84] The spider boasted that his web was a large castle built with his own hands out of materials extracted entirely from his own person. He owed no indebtedness to anyone for his architecture or his mathematics. The bee, on the contrary, described his way of life as a search for riches through "all the flowers and blossoms of the field and garden." These materials he claimed to turn to account without the least injury to the originals. According to Swift, while the spider and the bee were disputing, the books looked on quietly, until Aesop, "of late most barbarously treated," with a title page torn, text defaced, and chained in among the moderns, piped up to interpret the quarrel. "For pray, Gentlemen, was ever anything so modern as the spider in his air, his turns, and his paradoxes?" He praised the argument of the bee, "an advocate retained to us by the ancients," and continued: "Erect your schemes with as much method and skill as you please; yet, if the materials be nothing but dirt, spun out of your own entrails (the guts of modern brains) the edifice will conclude at last in a cobweb." He can recall no original modern achievement worth noticing except wrangling and satire. As for the ancients, like bees, they fill their lives with honey and wax, "thus furnishing mankind with the two noblest of things, which are sweetness and light."

At last both sides resolve upon battle and choose their leaders. Now Swift resumes the contest between the best of the ancient and modern poets, philosophers, and historians, offering as chieftains almost the very same list of names as Temple and Wotton. Above, the gods too consult and offer support to their heroes. Momus, the patron of the moderns, calls upon a malignant deity named Criticism to support her side and finds her "extended in her den, upon the spoils of numberless volumes half devoured." At her right hand sits Ignorance; at her left, Pride and Opinion; and beyond them her many children, Noise and Impudence,

---

[84]For the origin of this image, see Ernest Tuveson, "Swift and the World-Makers," *Journal of the History of Ideas* 11 (1950): 65.

Dulness and Vanity, Positiveness, Pedantry, and Ill-Manners. Criticism delivers a soliloquy.

> It is I (said she) who give wisdom to infants and idiots; by me children grow wiser than their parents, by me beaux become politicians, and schoolboys judges of philosophy; by me sophisters debate and conclude upon the depths of knowledge. . . . It is I who have deposed wit and knowledge from their empire over poetry and advanced myself in their stead. And shall a few upstart ancients dare to oppose me?

It is her son William Wotton who leads the moderns, assisted by Dulness and Ill-Manners. But as the battle begins, it is the ancients, especially the poets, who lead the way triumphantly until the manuscript breaks off abruptly. At this point Swift interjects a final skirmish into his incomplete work, "The Episode of Bentley and Wotton."

Bentley is introduced in full regalia:

> the most deformed of all the moderns; tall, but without shape or comeliness; large, but without strength or proportion. His armour was patched up of a thousand incoherent pieces; and the sound of it, as he marched, was loud and dry, like that made by the fall of a sheet of lead, which an Etesian wind blows suddenly down from the roof of some steeple. His helmet was of old rusty iron, but the vizor was brass, which, tainted by his breath, corrupted into copperas, nor wanted gall from the same fountain; so that, whenever provoked by anger or labour, an atramentous quality, of most malignant nature, was seen to distill from his lips. In his right hand he grasped a flail, and . . . a vessel full of ordure in his left. Thus completely armed, he advanced with a slow and heavy pace. . . . The generals made use of him for his talent of railing. . . .

Bentley is castigated, with true Homeric extravagance, by the great Scaliger and retreats to pursue his own adventures accompanied by the faithful Wotton until they come upon two of the ancient heroes, none other than Phalaris and Aesop, fast asleep with their armor hung nearby. Fortunately, the gods protect the sleeping ancients, who were dreaming defenselessly: Phalaris of how "a most vile poetaster had lampooned him and how he had got him roaring in his bull"; Aesop of how a wild ass had broken loose, trampling and kicking dung in their faces.

Swift now follows Wotton for a last adventure and comes upon two new heroes: Temple, "general of the allies of the ancients," and his young friend Boyle. Wotton strikes at Temple with his lance but the ancient neither feels the weapon nor hears it fall. Boyle then turns upon the modern and pursues him, though he is briefly distracted by the appearance of Bentley carrying the shield and arms of Phalaris, which he had stolen from the sleeping ancient. Boyle hesitates no longer; with a single great stroke of his lance, he kills both modern heroes. Here the manuscript again breaks off, leaving the final issue still in doubt.

I have attempted this rather inadequate summary simply to fix Swift as precisely as possible in the quarrel. It should now be clear that beneath his banter there lay exactly the same attitude as that of Temple and the Christ Church wits. For all of them it mattered little just what dates and what credit to assign to the *Epistles of Phalaris* or to the fables of Aesop. What they did care about sincerely was the rivalry that we have everywhere observed between the two classical forms of paideia, the one rooted in classical rhetoric, the other in classical philology and science. Swift's literary skill in *A Tale* and *The Battle* exemplified the virtues of classical imitation, while in his argument he expressed an unreserved admiration for the ancient models and their immediate practical value.[85] As a result of the immense popularity of his work, he nearly managed to impress the world with his own version of the quarrel. Unfortunately, Swift was obscuring in his polemic whatever common ground there was between the ancients and the moderns; for even less than his Christ Church allies was he willing to allow that Wotton and Bentley had any respect at all for antiquity or for the imitation of the classics, or that their efforts to divide the field in two made any sense. He saw only—perhaps felt only—the danger that the new disciplines of modern learning seemed to pose for his beloved ancients and the gentlemanly ideal of Sir William Temple. And, despite his willful unfairness, there was indeed something to be said for his fears—as the sequel perhaps may show.

[85]For some of the vast literature on Swift's attachment to classical rhetoric, see Henry W. Sams, "Swift's Satire on the Second Person," *E.L.H.* 26 (1959): 36–64; Ronald Paulson, *Theme and Structure in Swift's Tale of a Tub* (New Haven, 1960); Charles A. Beaumont, *Swift's Classical Rhetoric* (Athens, Ga., 1961); John R. Clark, *Form and Frenzy in Swift's Tale of a Tub* (Ithaca, N.Y., 1970).

Chapter Four

The *Querelle*

I

The battle of the books had gone too far to be concluded by satire, however brilliant. As we have seen, beneath the clash of personalities and the attacks ad hominem some real issues had appeared, and if they would not easily be resolved, they would not readily go away. Atterbury and his friends had welcomed the anonymous *Tale of a Tub*, although they worried a bit about its shafts at religion. Wotton saw his chance and struck back at once with a new and final edition of the *Reflections* (1705), in which he ridiculed Swift's orthodoxy—and helped to provide a stumbling block to the cleric's advancement.[1] In turn, Swift waited awhile but eventually brought out another edition of the *Tale* (1710), this time embellished with notes drawn from Wotton's works in a last ironic effort to turn the opposition into burlesque support.[2] It was all part of the fun, no doubt, but hardly calculated to advance the argument; for that we must look elsewhere.

It would be misleading to suggest that the battle of the books proceeded in a more orderly or intelligible way than any military campaign. We have followed it enough to see that there was hardly a field of human endeavor that was untouched by the dispute, and indeed everywhere, from architecture to zoology, there was squabbling. At the risk of overlooking some of the skirmishing, we shall try to hew to the main line of combat, which remained centered on the humanities, principally on poetry and history. Even so, it may be hard to see the whole field at once, and so it will be necessary to do a little backing and filling, to divide up the battleground and see what was happening, often simultaneously, in several areas of combat.

For the moment, while Swift was printing *A Tale of a Tub* and while Wotton was looking to reply, there was a temporary lull in the battle, and the next major episode in the quarrel began slowly to develop around the activities of the precocious young poet Alexander Pope. Though it took him several years before he began to think of attempting a new translation of the greatest poem of antiquity—and thus to provoke the next major crux in the quarrel—it was apparent, even from the very beginning of his career, that he would have to take a stand on some of the issues and risk combat. We may resume our story, then, by seeing if we can determine just why and how it was that the poetry of Homer should become the next great concern of the two sides in the battle of the books and how it was that the young poet got involved.

2

The quarrel over Homer was an old and persistent one. Its antecedents, like those of the quarrel between the ancients and the moderns, lay in classical antiquity itself, where Homer's reputation had been alternately exalted and criticized. The *Iliad* and the *Odyssey* had furnished a kind of bible for the Greeks, but Plato had also banished them from his republic. Nor was it easy to forget Zoilus, the carping critic par excellence of antiquity, whose first and principal target had been Homer. And among the Hellenistic critics there were undoubted "ancients" and "moderns" with respect to the poet. During the Renaissance, with the restoration of Greek learning, Homer's reputation had risen again—and again been challenged.[3] In England it was often recalled that the formidable Julius Scaliger had been chief among the moderns to turn against the "Prince of Poets." "He inveighs against Homer with as much Bitterness, as if he had a personal Quarrel with him." It was equally recalled that Isaac Casaubon had hastened to his defense. Scaliger had preferred Virgil to the Greek poet, initiating, or rather resuming, a contrast that was to

---

[3]See Jean Pepin, *Mythe et allégorie* (Paris, 1958), pp. 168–72; Félix Buffière, *Les Mythes d'Homère et la pensée grecque* (Paris, 1956), pp. 9–31; for the Renaissance, Noémi Hepp, *Homère en France au XVIᵉ siècle*, Atti dell'Accademia delle scienze di Turino 96 (Turin, 1961–62), pp. 1–120; D. C. Allen, *Mysteriously Meant* (Baltimore, 1970), pp. 83–106; Philip Ford, "Conrad Gesner et le fabuleux manteau," *Bibliothèque d'Humanisme et Renaissance* 47 (1985): 305–20.

become commonplace in the seventeenth and eighteenth centuries.[4] The comparison of authors was a stock device of Renaissance criticism; it was the natural result of a dependence on classical models that had necessarily to be arranged in order of preference before they could be imitated, of the need to establish a canon. When, therefore, the critic René Rapin, a great favorite in England, published a series of works comparing the various classical authors in various genres, he was elaborating a method that went back at least as far as Quintilian. And if his conclusions about ancient epic were a little equivocal, they were no less representative for that. "Homer has more fancy, Virgil more discretion and judgement, and if I should choose rather to have been Homer than Virgil, I should also much rather wish it that I had read the *Aeneid* than the *Iliad* and the *Odyssey*."[5]

That Rapin should prefer the *Aeneid* was not very surprising. However successful the Greek revival, Europe remained essentially Latin after the Renaissance. Greek was read and taught in the schools but it was Latin that was widely written and imitated.[6] Besides, there was a closer affinity between the real conditions of life and culture, and therefore the true sensibilities of the English and the Roman Augustans, than there could possibly be with the more remote Greeks; it was after all the "Augustan," not the "Periclean"—much less the "Homeric"—age that began with Charles II and Louis XIV.[7] It was therefore natural to feel closer to the Roman poet. On the other hand, there was the nearly insurmountable reputation of Homer in the ancient world to conjure with, as well as an increasing number of savants who had mastered both languages and could make their own comparisons. Although the balance remained tilted toward Virgil, there was no lack of Homeric enthusiasts. Among the party of the ancients, Temple was one and Swift another. Many tried to straddle the fence, like William King, who, forgetting satire for once, projected "a Parallel between Homer and Virgil," in which the claims of both were evenly balanced.[8] Yet Henry Felton was probably more representative when he wrote in 1713, just as Pope was

---

[4]Joseph Trapp, *The Works of Virgil* (London, 1731), 1:xxvii; John Dryden, dedication to the *Third Miscellany* (London, 1693), in his *Works*, ed. Walter Scott, rev. George Saintsbury, 18 vols. (Edinburgh, 1882–1893), 13:56. Scaliger's views had been set out in the *Poetices libri septem* (1561).

[5]René Rapin, *Observations on the Poems of Homer and Virgil*, trans. John Davies (London, 1672), pp. 127–28, from the 3d ed., *Comparaison des poèmes d'Homère et de Virgile* (Paris, 1669), pp. 164–65.

[6]See M. L. Clarke, *Greek Studies in England, 1700–1830* (Cambridge, 1945), p. 15; for France, see Arthur Tilley, *The Decline of the Age of Louis XIV* (Cambridge, 1929), p. 343.

[7]For Charles II as Augustus, see John Ogilby, *The Kings Coronation: Being an Exact Account of the Cavalcade . . . with a Description of the Triumphal Arches and Speeches Prepared by the City of London . . . also the Narrative of His Majesties Coronation* (London, 1685).

[8]"Adversaria," in King's *Original Works*, ed. John Nichols, 3 vols. (London, 1776), 1:267–74.

seriously setting about his translation of the *Iliad*, that though the Romans had borrowed from the Greeks, "the Copies have proved more exact than the Originals and Rome hath triumphed over Athens as well in Wit, as Arms." As to epic, he was confident that "all the world acknowledges the *Aeneid* to be the most perfect of its Kind."[9]

The challenge to Homer arose thus, first from the advocates of Virgil. And since Virgil had followed after Homer, he could (somewhat paradoxically) be viewed as a modern who had improved upon his model. But Virgil was not the worst challenge to Homer. From the first, we have seen, the French *querelle* was more extravagant than the English battle of the books, and it was followed closely across the Channel. Thus when Charles Perrault drew up his elaborate series of parallels (1688–1692), he meant to denigrate the entire classical achievement in favor of the moderns. For Perrault, the age of Louis XIV was elevated above everything in the ancient world. Homer might indeed be a "vaste et puissant genie," but how much more correct and polished would he have been had he lived in the seventeenth century![10] Perrault believed that he could show the superiority of the moderns in the arts, in eloquence, and in the drama, but it was very hard to find a worthy modern epic to set above the *Iliad*. Nevertheless, Perrault remembered Virgil and some seventeenth-century French epics that, though not quite the equal of the ancients, yet surpassed them in particular ways. Under the circumstances, therefore, it seemed better to expose Homer's faults rather than to extol the moderns, to reduce his transcendent genius to ordinary human weakness. Unfortunately, but like many in his generation, Perrault was handicapped by having to read his Homer in translation.

In fact, Perrault had opened the quarrel even before he published his *Parallèle des anciens et des modernes*. In 1687 he read a poem before the French Academy on the recovery of the king and launched the battle. It was titled, *Le Siècle de Louis le Grand*, and could be read eventually in English translation.[11] Perrault's intention was to show that the age of Louis XIV had surpassed even the age of Augustus in everything. He begins with a typical modernist flourish,

> Antiquity 'tis owned, does well deserve
> Profound Respect, yet not to be adored.

[9]Henry Felton, *A Dissertation on Reading the Classics* (London, 1713), pp. 20, 24.

[10]The phrase is from a poem read to the French Academy, for which see below. In general, for the French *querelle*, see besides the works of Rigault, Gillot, and Tilley the wonderfully thorough study by Noémi Hepp, *Homère en France au XVIIᵉ siècle* (Paris, 1968).

[11]Charles Perrault, *Characters and Criticisms upon the Ancient and Modern Orators, Poets, etc. together with a Poem (in Blank Verse) intitled the Age of Lewis the Great* (London, 1725), pp. 181–211.

> The Ancients I with argent Knees behold,
> For they, tho' great, were Men as well as we.

With this brief prologue, Perrault is ready to enter into a comparison of ancient and modern science, quickly dismissing Plato and Aristotle in favor of the telescope. He then elaborates on his main theme of eloquence and poetry, turning especially to Homer. He concedes that the ancient Greek was the father of the arts and a mighty poet, but that he had nevertheless lacked the good fortune to live in the modern age. Had the gods postponed his birth until Louis's time, the flaws in his poetry could have been avoided. Unhappily, the *Iliad* had many obvious defects. Perrault was particularly disappointed by the behavior of Homer's heroes; it is clear to him that they would have been less brutal and capricious if they had lived in the seventeenth century. He was also disturbed that Homer should keep interrupting his narrative with irrelevancies; time and again he compels his heroes to pause, their arms aloft, while he intrudes his "irksome Prefaces, on the great Arts of the Heroic Race." Of these, without doubt the most annoying was the long and tedious description of the shield of Achilles. Perrault did not doubt for a moment that a modern would have created a more plausible weapon. He notices that Homer's shield was supposed to have engraved on it "The Heavens, Air, the Sea, the Land," cities, orators, "and an hundred things beside." It may have been Vulcan's masterpiece, still it passed belief. No artist, however skillful, could represent the sounds and movement suggested by the poet, or fit the whole world into the circumference of a warrior's shield.

> This famous Buckler in a nicer Age
> Had juster been, and less engraved.

Horace was clearly right to say that Homer sometimes nodded.

The idea was provocative, and even while Perrault was uttering these lines, the audience began to stir. The encomium to Louis was greeted with applause, but one among the listeners had been muttering throughout. The great Boileau was affronted. When the recital was over, he sprang to his feet and shouted that it was a disgrace to speak in such a way of the greatest men of antiquity. The bishop of Soissons, Pierre-Daniel Huet, a celebrated *érudit*, at once rejoined, urging the critic to be quiet. If it was a matter of taking the part of the ancients, he thought he could do it better; but they had come to listen, not to harangue.[12] Racine

---

[12]Sainte-Beuve agreed; see his *Causeries du lundi*, trans. E. J. Trechmann (London, n.d.), 1:134, 142–43. Huet (1630–1721) was, among other things, the author of the *Demonstratio evangelica* (1679), where he argues for the ancient wisdom, and the editor of the famous Delphin classics.

complimented Perrault ironically, finding the poem a clever exercise that must have been designed to conceal the author's real sentiments! Boileau swore he would reply; still others joined the fray. Perrault realized that he must write a prose piece with a more substantial argument if he would be understood and taken seriously.[13]

3

And so began the first episode in the celebrated *querelle*. From the beginning, Homer's description of the shield of Achilles took center stage. It is true that when the *Paralèlle* first appeared, Perrault had somehow overlooked it. It was the fourth dialogue of 1692 that took up the Homeric epics in particular, but Perrault only promised there to treat the shield at a later time. For the moment, he was prepared to enlarge on his general criticism of Homer.[14] Now he suggested that there were some critics who were ready to deny the very existence of "Homer," and to claim that the *Iliad* and the *Odyssey* were no more than many small pieces by various authors which someone had afterward assembled. When pressed, he suggested that the abbé d'Aubignac was going to publish a whole treatise on the subject. (It was true, though the work appeared only in 1715.)[15] Perrault not only found the composition of the works suspicious; he was eager to show the story deficient, the characters badly drawn, the manners of gods and heroes gross, and the similes inept. Despite traditional claims to the contrary, he also found Homer to be a bad astronomer, geometer, and naturalist. Only time could bring about politeness and good taste; here was the great advantage of the moderns. Perrault was so contemptuous of Homer that he even allowed one character in the dialogue to wonder which was the more miserable, Homer or his characters.[16]

[13]Charles Perrault, *Mémoires de ma vie*, ed. Paul Bonnefon (Paris, 1909), pp. 136–37. This account is confirmed by the hostile testimony of Antoine Furetière, *Recueil des factums*, ed. Charles Asselineau (Paris, 1859), 1:302–3. See Paul Bonnefon, "Charles Perrault, littérateur et académicien: L'Opposition à Boileau," *Revue d'histoire littéraire de la France* 12 (1905): 549–610 (esp. 563–70).

[14]Charles Perrault, *Parallèle des anciens et des modernes*, 2 vols. (Amsterdam, 1693), 1, Préface, sig. *5v. There is a facsimile version by H. R. Jauss (Munich, 1964). The first two dialogues (with the poem on Louis XIV) appeared in 1688; the third (with much of the criticism of Homer) in 1690; the fourth in 1692. A fifth dialogue appeared in 1697 with some further criticisms of the *Iliad*, but Perrault does not seem to have returned to the shield.

[15]François Hédelin, abbé d'Aubignac, *Conjectures académiques; ou, Dissertation sur l'Iliade* (Paris, 1715); Perrault, *Parallèle*, pp. 23–25. D'Aubignac did not know any more Greek than Perrault, however; see H. L. Lorimer, "Homer and the Art of Writing: A Sketch of Opinion between 1713–39," *American Journal of Archaeology* 52 (1948): 12n.

[16]Perrault, *Parallèle*, p. 52.

Inevitably Boileau replied. He reaffirmed the existence of Homer and the unity of the two epics. "Never were two Poems so regularly pursu'd and so happily connected, as the *Ilias* and the *Odysses*." How weak were Perrault's arguments, how obvious his ignorance of Greek! He could not be too much condemned "who not understanding Homer's Language, charges him too boldly with the Errors of his Translators." "'Tis as if a Man born Blind, shou'd run about the Streets crying, Gentlemen, I know the Sun that you see is very Beautiful, but I who never saw it declare to you that 'Tis very ugly."[17] Boileau made his own Greek very obvious. But he was unwilling to find a single flaw in Homer's manners and language, no weakness in his heroes or coarseness in his expression. In the end, after further acrimony, the two rivals were personally reconciled, but they kept pretty much to their separate opinions.

There were others who knew Greek and came to Homer's defense. Huet was one, Racine another.[18] So too was the able young scholar André Dacier. According to Boileau, Dacier was "not only a Man of very great Learning and a Nice Critick, but also very Polite, a Quality so much the more valuable by how much 'tis rarely to be found with great Erudition."[19] That this was indeed a rare combination we have seen, and it remains a little doubtful whether Dacier really succeeded in joining the two. (Richard Bentley was not entirely convinced.)[20] In any case, he made his scholarly reputation with a translation into French of Aristotle's *Poetics*, together with a learned commentary. The object was to show the relevance and immediacy of the ancient philosophical teaching to the present consideration of poetry. Since Aristotle had clearly had Homer often in mind, Dacier had necessarily to bring the two great epics into his

[17]Nicolas Boileau-Despréaux, *A Treatise of the Sublime from the Greek of Longinus with Critical Reflections*, trans. Pierre Desmaizeaux, in his *Works*, 2 vols. (London, 1712), 2:115; and see the comment by John Ozell in the life of Boileau, in ibid., 1:xcvi. Boileau's original appeared first in 1693. In general, see A. F. B. Clark, *Boileau and the French Classical Critics in England* (1925; rev. ed., New York, 1965).

[18]   How comes it Perrault, I would gladly know,
      That Authors of two thousand years ago,
      Whom in their Native dress all times revere,
      In your Translation should so flat appear?

Racine's lines (with more) appeared in translation in Abel Boyer's *Memoirs of the Life and Times of Sir William Temple* (London, 1714); they appeared first in French in Temple's *Thoughts upon Reviewing the Essay on Ancient and Modern Learning*, in his *Works*, 4 vols. (London, 1814), 3:490. "Some of the French Academy," Temple says, "took the care to send these, and other such pieces, into England and other Countries, to clear their Reputation from the slander drawn upon them by two or three of their body; and treated the reverence of the ancients as something sacred, and the want of it barbarous and profane."

[19]Boileau, *Of the Sublime*, 2:8. See Dacier's *éloge* in the *Mémoires de l'Académie des inscriptions* 5 (1729): 412–20, and the notice in Jean Pierre Niceron, *Mémoires pour servir à l'histoire des hommes illustres*, 43 vols. (Paris, 1727–1745), 3:145–63.

[20]James Henry Monk, *The Life of Richard Bentley*, 2d ed., 2 vols. (London, 1833), 1:311–12.

discussion and defend them against the modern critics. Like Boileau, he insisted that ignorance of Greek was responsible for much misunderstanding. If Homer seemed to know little astronomy because he wrongly described the constellation of the bear, his error was due simply to a misunderstanding of the text. As for Homer's indelicate language, Dacier thought that that could be referred largely to changed circumstances; anyway, there were enough parallels with Holy Scripture to reduce the force of that complaint. There was left only the attack upon Achilles' shield.[21]

Dacier believed that the eighteenth book was so far from being digressive that it was one of the most beautiful parts of the poem. It had excited the admiration of the centuries, of the polite *and* of the learned. Some recent critics had objected to the movements of the figures and the sounds that Homer described there. Dacier was astonished. It was as though in explaining a painting by Raphael or Poussin one could keep from animating the figures or do less than make them speak conformably to the design of the picture! The critics were confusing the shield with Homer's description of it. One need only read Pliny on the ancient artists to see the same expressions. Beyond that, Perrault had complained that Homer had described two cities in the shield speaking different languages and two orators pleading simultaneously. Here was yet another example of misunderstanding due to a faulty Latin translation, for there was nothing like this in the original Greek. As for the whole design of the *Iliad*, had Perrault but read the ancient commentators, or the Byzantine Greek Eustathius, for example, he would have applauded its marvelous composition.[22] To have represented in so small a compass, with so few figures, the whole universe and all that passed in war and peace was the work not only of a great poet but of a great philosopher as well. (This the critics called a trivial subject!) Finally, the comparison with Virgil could only work to Homer's advantage. Above all, the imitation by that poet of the shield of Achilles—for Virgil gives a similar weapon to his own hero—is the perfect acknowledgment of the genius of his model. The Roman shield in the eighth book of the *Aeneid* was also marvelously detailed, with a noble theme in the descendants of Troy creating the majesty of Rome. But if one were to set the two shields side by side, it could only be to exalt Homer. "L'un paroit l'ouvrage d'un Dieu, et l'autre l'ouvrage d'un homme."[23]

[21]André Dacier, *La Poétique d'Aristote* (Paris, 1692), trans. as *Aristotle's Art of Poetry . . . with Mr. Dacier's Notes* (London, 1705).

[22]For Eustathius (c. 1115–c. 1197), see N. G. Wilson, *Scholars of Byzantium* (Baltimore, 1983), pp. 196–204.

[23]Dacier, *Poétique d'Aristote*, p. 497.

4

Almost at once the quarrel attracted a mock historian who cried plague on both parties. François de Callières, diplomat and littérateur, elected to poke fun at both sides in a work entitled *Histoire poétique de la guerre récemment déclarée entre les anciens et les modernes*, a satire that we have seen may have inspired Swift's *Battle of the Books*.[24] Callières set the stage for his imaginary contest with a description of Perrault's poem; the quarrel that ensues is for the heights of Mount Parnassus. As in Swift's poem, the preliminaries are taken up by choosing leaders, and as in Swift, Callières has Homer appointed "Generalissimo of the Grecian Poets." In both works the moderns have trouble matching him. "In vain did Chapelain stretch his Lungs," according to Caillières, "in crying he was the French Homer." (Perrault had hinted at the possibility.) If they would but examine his *Pucelle*, he insists, they "wou'd find it just, according to the Rules of the Ancients." "The Ancients had not only pleas'd the Ages they liv'd in, but all the following; whereas he had pall'd his own, and justly drawn the Raillery of his Contemporary Criticks." It remained perhaps the greatest weakness of the moderns that they could find no one to match Homer, especially since they admitted freely that the "Epick Poems have always obtain'd the first Rank in the Kingdom of Poetry."

Callières's narrative proceeds merrily to describe the war itself. Homer chooses Eustathius (the twelfth-century Byzantine commentator) as captain of the guards, and together they review the Iliads and the Odysseys to see where the moderns intend to attack. Inevitably they discover the enemy about to assault the Iliads by way of Achilles' shield. "It will grieve me sensibly, to have so beautiful a Work defac'd," Homer cries, "therefore I conjure you, my dear Eustathius, take care to defend it against the Efforts of These Barbarians." His indignation is understandable, since the shield was "one of the most admired Pieces of Antiquity," and since he had lavished on it all the skill of Vulcan. Eventually, after much confusion and many battles, Apollo himself descends to adjudicate the quarrel. He calls at once upon Homer to forgive his adversaries. "If they had not pay'd you the Respect due to your Merit, 'twas because they did not understand you: but I am satisfied the greatest part of them have declared their Opinions without being acquainted with you." Homer reflects that these new Zoiluses might have remembered their

---

[24]François de Callières, *Histoire poétique de la guerre récemment déclarée entre les anciens et les modernes* (Paris, 1688), mistakenly attributed to Fénelon and translated by J. G. as *Characters and Criticisms upon the Ancient and Modern Orators, Poets, Painters, Musicians, Statuaries, and Other Arts and Sciences* (London, 1714).

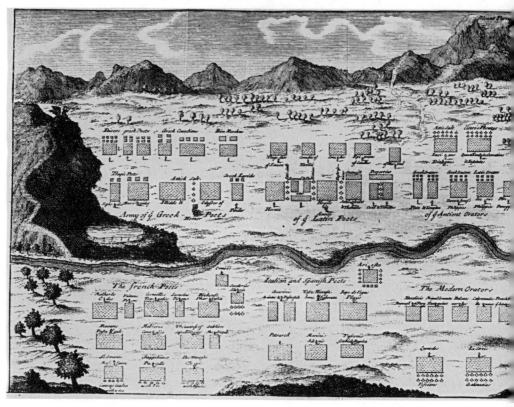

The frontispiece to the English translation of François de Callières's *Histoire poétique de la guerre nouvellement déclarée entre les anciens et les modernes* (1714)

namesake, who had been forever condemned to ridicule for his carping criticism. The dramatist Corneille, however, is allowed to speak for the moderns. Was there, he asks, not even a single line in Homer that could be laughed at? "Does he believe that Readers yawn at the Digressions he makes, when his Hero's are just ready to engage? Do the Moderns really do such injustice to Homer, in saying that he has put too much Work in so narrow a Space as that of Achilles's Buckler?" Finally, was not Perrault entirely correct to declare with Horace that Homer sometimes nodded?

At length Callières allows Homer to defend himself. The shield of Achilles, he claims, has always been especially admired. The size of the buckler was irrelevant to the ambition of its design. "There may be described in little what would have been greater in a large Space; 'tis sufficient each part of the piece is proportionable to the whole." The shield was like a map of the world, reducing immense detail to a confined space. As for the sounds and movements, of course the shield did not itself speak; it merely portrayed activities of speech and motion. Apollo finally offers his judgment. All modern poets hereafter are required to learn Latin and Greek; the place of the first modern epic is declared vacant; Homer and Virgil are chosen the two models for all time. The work concludes by drawing a judicious balance between the ancient literary claims and the modern scientific ones; Perrault's poem is both censured and praised.

It was a moderate and plausible conclusion and probably suited the majority. But there was more that could be said both for and against the two extremes. For all their ignorance of Greek, the moderns had glimpsed one point better than their adversaries. Homer, whoever he was, had written his epics in a world that had long ago vanished. For better or worse, the moderns saw that the manners and customs of the age of Louis XIV were not those of the age of the Greek heroes, and that it had different values, both moral and poetical. Needless to say, they did not hesitate to proclaim their own better; the moderns believed in the superiority but also the universality of their own convictions, and they did not hesitate to condemn anyone who failed to measure up. Unfortunately, they were at a loss to prove their point. They could not read the Greek originals; they could not find anyone to surpass Homer; and, most limiting, they were not yet ready to formulate any new, nonclassical critical standards. They were thus unwilling to propose Dante or Milton, much less Shakespeare, for the vacant modern throne. In the long run, knowledge was on their side; had they known Greek better, they might have seen even more clearly the disparity between ancient Greece and modern times and so bolstered their arguments.

As for the "ancients," they appreciated the ancient poetry keenly and often perceptively. But they ought to have seen the differences that set it apart from the poetry of their own time. This insight was obscured for them, however, by two conditions. In part, they did not want to see it; they had been taught to believe in the immediacy of the ancient authors, in the applicability of ancient poetry to modern life. In this too they had, of course, been preceded by ancient commentators who had themselves tried to assimilate Homer to their own time and thus already given to the world a "modernized" Homer. So, to an extent, the ancients deliberately looked past the awkward differences. Where this was hard to do, as with the pagan gods of the two poems, a clever allegorical exegesis could easily explain away or qualify the difficulty. Did not the Bible present many of the same problems? And here their ignorance helped also (their inability as well as their unwillingness to see differences), for the state of Greek learning—even modern Greek philology—was not yet sufficient to come to terms with the world of Homer. In France, as in England, the ancients were not at all the party of the learned. It is true that Boileau and Dacier knew their Greek and kept abreast of contemporary scholarship, but unlike Wotton and Bentley, they were agreed with the ancients on the importance of *politesse* and nearly as skeptical of the claims of minute scholarship. Like Swift, Boileau despised the pedant, and he was quite ready to agree with Perrault that too much learning was a dangerous thing.[25] Indeed, if the debate about Homer demonstrated anything, it was that neither the ancients nor the moderns in France really knew very much about the subject.

In short, as the battle over the *Iliad* heated up, two basic issues remained to divide the parties: the degree of reverence to be awarded the ancient authors and the appreciation due to the achievements of classical scholarship. That these issues could be incompatible we have already seen, for it was classical philology, more than anything else, that seemed to threaten the authority of the ancient authors. If this seems paradoxical, it is no less true that it is our knowledge of Homer today—of what we believe to be the forms and values of Homeric culture—that forbids us to imitate his poetry. We are struck too much by the differences that separate Homer's world from our own to try to attempt a heroic epic on the model of the master. But this was less easy to see in 1700, when Greek scholarship was feeble and the impulse to imitation was still overwhelming. As a result, some confusion divided the camps of both ancients and moderns. It was possible, for example, to revere Homer and despise philology, as Temple did; or to revere Homer and admire philology (though not without reservations), as Boileau did; or to criticize Homer (though not completely) and disparage philology, as Perrault did; or to admire Homer (though believing it possible to rival him someday) and admire philology, as Wotton did. Or, if one preferred, it was possible simply to have a good laugh at the whole thing, rather as François de Callières did! Although it may not have been the most thoughtful position, in 1700 undoubtedly it had much to recommend it.

5

For the time being, the quarrel between the ancients and the moderns sputtered on in France, until at last it died.[26] Nothing was resolved but much of the personal acrimony was repaired and a certain ennui began to

[25]Boileau, *Works*, 2:106–7.

[26]An anonymous English summary of the quarrel, taking the modern side, may be found in *Verdicts of the Learned concerning Virgil's and Homer's Heroic Poems* (London, 1697).

set in. Suddenly, in 1711, a lady resumed the contest. For many years the insults to Homer had rankled in her scholar's breast; and for a long time she had nursed a reply. She understood that what was most needed to stifle the moderns was a fresh and accurate translation of Homer from the original, with a commentary in the vulgar tongue. Only in a modern language could the poet hope to triumph over the otherwise invincible ignorance of his critics; only with a close reading of the text could the carpers be answered point by point. Anne Le Fèvre, Madame Dacier, had both the learning and the spirit for the job, as well as the infinite patience that was required.[27] Although only embers were left from the first quarrel when her version of the *Iliad* finally appeared, the new translation stirred them suddenly to life. The work was read at once in England in the original and in translation, and it was certainly known to Pope before he began his own version.

In the gap between the first and second episodes of the *querelle*, almost a whole generation had passed. In England it had been taken up with the battle of the books, but Homer had not somehow occupied much attention in the controversy. In part, this was because the combatants had been busy with other things—natural philosophy, for example. More obviously, the ancients and the moderns had not been so divided over the classical poets. Wotton and Bentley had too much Greek and too much respect for ancient literature to want to deride Homer. All they asked for was a recognition that the moderns might someday come to rival the achievement of the ancients. Madame Dacier had been a young woman when Perrault addressed the Academy. She had followed the quarrel eagerly, not less for having married one of the first contestants, the equally youthful André Dacier, friend of Boileau. The two were perfectly matched, with an education and sensibility almost exactly alike. Their union was celebrated throughout Europe as the perfect alliance of Latin and Greek, and few marriages then or later can have brought together so formidable a scholarship.[28] Together they spent their lives doing battle for the ancients.

Madame Dacier had had the good fortune to be educated by one of the best scholars of the previous generation, her own father, Tanneguy Le Fèvre. (He was, in the words of a contemporary, "un des plus hardie, mais en même tems un des plus capable Critiques de notre siècle.")[29] He

[27]For the following, see the *éloge* in the *Journal des scavans*, 1720, pp. 593–607; Niceron, *Mémoires*, 3:123–45; Charles-Augustin Sainte-Beuve, *Causeries du lundi*, vol. 9 (Paris, 1854), pp. 379–95; Enrica Malcovati, *Madame Dacier: Una gentildonna filologia del gran secolo* (Florence, 1952); Fern Farnham, *Madame Dacier: Scholar and Humanist* (Monterey, 1976).

[28]*Histoire des ouvrages des sciences* 1 (Rotterdam, 1721), p. 203; Malcovati, *Madame Dacier*, pp. 33–34.

[29]Adrien Baillet, *Jugemens des savans*, vol. 1 (Amsterdam, 1725), 249–50; see also Niceron, *Mémoires*, 3:102–23.

had been a professor of Greek and an editor of renown, turning out a long series of classical texts, along with miscellaneous works of erudition. In a small tract in French, *Les Poètes grecs* (1664), he dealt briefly with Homer. Le Fèvre was an independent spirit and he was more than a little suspicious of the biographical details concerning Homer, ancient and modern. He was equally doubtful about the authenticity of the minor works. What he admired most in the *Iliad* and the *Odyssey* was the style and the expression. Although the ancients had employed Homer to decide every kind of matter, Le Fèvre made no special claim for the poet's learning. Homer, he thought, stood above all the ancient Greeks for the purity and strength, the clarity and the simplicity of his language. Unfortunately, he concluded, there had never been a translation worthy of the originals and therefore there were many who had not been able to appreciate their beauty.

After the manner of his time, Le Fèvre had not intended much of an education for his daughter, preferring rather to lavish his attention on a younger son. But one day as the lesson proceeded, the little boy was puzzled by several of his father's difficult grammatical questions. His sister, who was sitting quietly by embroidering, offered to help out with an answer so complete and assured that her startled father at once resolved to afford her the same opportunity as his son. Thereafter, she quickly advanced in her knowledge of the two classical tongues. Le Fèvre had determined ideas about how the education of children should proceed, and he took the trouble to set them down in a small tract that eventually found an English translation.[30] He described it as "a plain and faithful History of the Method I observed in the Instructing one of my Sons," but it was of course exactly what he had offered also to his daughter. Like most of the great humanist teachers, Le Fèvre believed that reading books was more effective than studying grammar, and he claimed that before the age of fourteen his little boy had twice read through the *Iliad* in Greek, "and would give an exact Account of every Word, as well as any Greek Professor." Le Fèvre believed that Homer was especially suitable for beginners and noticed that the Greeks themselves had begun their education with the *Iliad*. Besides Homer, however, his children read many other classical authors in both languages. The boy died still young, but the daughter grew to maturity, a fine scholar and a modest and amiable woman. "Elle est fort modeste," Le Fèvre wrote to his friend Huet in 1671, "et ne veut pas qu'on sache qu'elle sait ny grec ni latin."[31]

[30]*A Compendious Way of Teaching the Learned Languages and some of the Liberal Sciences at the same time us'd formerly by Tanaquil Faber in teaching one of his Sons and the famous Madame Dacier* (London, 1721); cf. the *Journal des scavans*, 1720, p. 44.

[31]Léon-G. Pellesier, ed., "A travers les papiers de Huet," in *Documents annotis* (Paris, 1889), pp. 9–12.

It would be tedious to recount all the young woman's services to learning in the next years. Suffice it to say that she grew famous for her editions and translations of the classics, Latin but especially Greek. Queen Christina of Sweden singled her out (unsuccessfully) for her court; she was elected to the Academy of the Ricovrati at Padua, and won a royal pension. After her marriage to André Dacier, also a student of Le Fèvre's, she continued alone and jointly to make the ancient writers more readily accessible. Both Daciers contributed to the celebrated series of classical authors directed by the learned Huet which was dedicated to the Dauphin. Pierre Bayle thought that her several contributions surpassed all the rest; "voilà notre sexe hautement vaincu par cette illustre Savante!"[32] An edition of Callimachus (1675) brought her first to public attention; a translation of Anacreon and Sappho (1681) was even more successful, and others soon followed: Plautus, Aristophanes, Terence, Marcus Aurelius, and Plutarch (the last two accomplished with her husband). But fame did not disturb her modesty. When a German visitor called upon her to secure her autograph to add to his collection of the greatest savants in Europe, she demurred. When he pressed further, she quoted to him some Greek verses from Sophocles: "Le silence est l'ornament des femmes."[33]

In a way, it was all preparation for her great work. According to Ezechiel Spanheim, by 1701 she was hard at it, and despite terrible personal tragedy (the loss first of one child and then of another), she kept at the *Iliad* for many years. She had undertaken it in the heat of the *querelle*, and though it appeared only in 1711, when Perrault and Boileau were securely in their graves, it at once rekindled the sparks of that flickering controversy, carrying it now, through a further translation into English, across the Channel. "It has ever been my Ambition," she began, "ever since I have made Writing my Diversion . . . to present our Age with such a Translation of Homer, as, by preserving the main Beauties of that Noble Poet, might recover the greater Part of Mankind from the disadvantageous Prejudice infus'd into them by the monstrous Copies that have been made of him."[34]

A recent writer has preferred the preface to the translation.[35] That essay was certainly an impressive—and provocative—performance. Madame Dacier understood fully the difficulties of her undertaking; she had followed closely the many criticisms that had been leveled against

---

[32]*Journal des savants*, 1720, p. 596, quoting Pierre Bayle's *Nouvelles de la république des lettres*, Oct. 1684.

[33]Nicolas Trublet, *Mémoires pour l'histoire de la vie et des ouvrages de Fontenelle* (Amsterdam, 1759), pp. 108–9; Niceron, *Mémoires*, 3:135.

[34]Madame Dacier, *L'Iliade d'Homère traduite en français, avec des remarques*, 5 vols. (Paris, 1711), trans. by John Ozell as *The Iliad of Homer*, 5 vols. (London, 1712), 1:i.

[35]Malcovati, *Madame Dacier*, p. 61.

her subject. She saw that some of her readers would have difficulty accepting the heroic world of Homer. Popular romance had dulled the sensibilities of her age and left an audience accustomed only to the frivolities of a debased courtly love tradition. "What Hope is there, that our Age can be brought to relish those austere Poems, which, under the Veil of an ingenious Fable, contain profitable Instructions, and which do not present our Curiosity with any of those Adventures, commonly reckon'd moving and engaging, for no other Reason, but because they turn upon Love?" Madame Dacier understood Homer as the ancients had understood him, as the highest source of wisdom and inspiration, the Bible only excepted. One had to penetrate his allegories, it was true, and this was a second obstacle for the modern reader. But here also was the key to the problem of Homer's gods, for she supposed them to be entirely allegorical and believed that the poet had uttered nothing but what was agreeable to the soundest divinity. The Phoenix's speech to Achilles in the eleventh Book of the *Iliad* could thus be easily reconciled with the teaching of Solomon. The English translator, John Ozell, was easily persuaded, especially since that notion was already commonplace among his countrymen. "I shall not enter into the Debate whether Solomon wrote the Books that go under the Name of Homer," he wrote in the preface to the new work. But he was thoroughly persuaded by Madame Dacier, and by the English scholar James Duport, that the *Iliad* "was a kind of New Gospel to the Pagans, couch'd according to the Custom of those Times, under Fables, Parables, and Allegories, and everywhere carries a visible Conformity with Holy Scriptures both in Phrase and Sentiments."[36]

There were other difficulties. The customs and morality of the heroic age as Homer described them had also offended many readers, but here again Madame Dacier believed that it was a case of the effete sensibilities of the moderns, "so nice, so whining, and so polite," interfering with an appreciation of the noble simplicity of Homer's characters. The poet had imitated the manners of his day exactly as Aristotle (by way of Père Bossu and her husband) had thought that he should do.[37] That they were superior to those of the present no one could deny. "I am pleas'd to see Homer's Hermes doing the same the Patriarchs did who were greater than Kings and Hermes." How far had the moderns fallen! "The Gilding that defaces our Age, and which ought to be taken off, is its Luxury and Effeminacy, which most certainly beget a general corruption in our

---

[36]Dacier, *Iliad of Homer*, 1:xiv–xv. For the long tradition of Homer as allegorist, reaching back to antiquity, see Robert Lamberton, *Homer the Theologian* (Berkeley, 1986).

[37]René Le Bossu's *Traité du poème épique* (Paris, 1675) was translated by W. J. as *A Treatise of the Epick Poem* (London, 1695) and was very popular in both countries; see Clark, *Boileau*, pp. 243–61.

Souls."[38] This modest lady, devoted wife and mother and painstaking scholar, harbored a passion for heroic manners that was intended to put to shame her modernist contemporaries.

The greatest difficulty that she felt, however, was reproducing the style and the diction of the poem. "The more perfect an Original is in Grandeur and Sublimity, the more it loses in being copy'd." Of all writers, Homer must lose most in translation, "it being impossible to convey the Strength, the Harmony, the Loftiness, and the Majesty of his Expressions and to preserve the Soul which runs throughout his Poetry." It was enough to breed despair, even in this accomplished woman. "I own, in every Verse of Homer, I find a Beauty, a Force, a Harmony, a Grace, which it has been impossible for me to preserve." Why then persevere? First, because there was even greater merit to Homer's poetry than his style. (Here Madame Dacier seemed to depart a little from her father's teaching.) "The Loftiness of his Ideas, the Majesty of his Subject, that beautiful Nature which reigns throughout every Part of him, and the surprizing Variety of his Characters," all these helped make the *Iliad* matchless, even apart from the language. Besides, Madame Dacier wrote not to replace the original, which was impossible in any case, but only for those readers who were bereft of Greek and wished to form at least a correct idea of the matter, however much its manner must escape them. To this effect, she preferred to translate the work into prose rather than poetry. Though this meant sacrificing much, it was better than mocking the original with an inappropriate French verse—the only apparent alternative. This approach would still leave the *Iliad*, in its basic substance at least, perfectly intelligible. "I own it is not Homer alive and animated, but still it is Homer . . . and Homer much less alter'd than in the Translations that have been hitherto made, which have so strangely disfigur'd him, that he is no longer known."[39]

6

It *was* Homer, at least a Homer more recognizable than any yet. On this there was general agreement, then and now. While it made some concessions both to the taste of the time and to the sensibilities of Madame Dacier, it was much more faithful than any that had yet appeared. Indeed, for a very long time it was the only alternative for the reader who lacked Greek. In a short summary of her preface it is impossible to do justice either to the shrewdness with which she estimated many

[38]Dacier, *Iliad*, I:xxii; *L'Iliade*, I:xxxviii.
[39]Dacier, *Iliad*, I:xxviii, xxvii; *L'Iliade*, I:xxxvii–xxxviii.

of the difficulties of her translation or to the modesty with which she advanced her claims. But if the result was a translation that did make Homer accessible and recognizable, it was also, alas, a Homer in prose. And this, unfortunately, gave away too much to the opposition; the moderns were still being asked to accept on faith what they had denied out of ignorance, the merit of Homer as poetry. While that still left plenty of room for argument, since the moderns, at least as much as the ancients, preferred to consider Homer even more a philosopher and teacher than a poet, even so Madame Dacier was not successful. The trouble was that she had repeated the worst error of her predecessors: in all sincerity, she had yet claimed too much for her author. Pope, as we shall see, saw the dilemma clearly and tried to avoid it in his own work.

This was true not only for Madame Dacier's preface but for the life of Homer and the notes that accompanied her text. In the preface she re-called her father's skepticism about the sources and about the minor works, but she felt obliged anyway to repeat the outlines of that doubtful life which had anciently been ascribed to Herodotus. Perhaps (as her father thought) it was not really by the historian; yet it was certainly very old and Strabo had used it. Should we be more critical than that excellent writer? Take away that source and little enough remained: "the most celebrated of Men will for ever be the most unknown." To the Pseudo-Herodotus she added a few details. From Huet she took the ideas that Homer had learned much in Egypt, from her father (as against Leo Allatius) that he was an Aeolian. She placed the poet about 240 to 250 years after the taking of Troy, although in doing so she had to dispute the testimony of the *Marmora Arundeliana*.[40] Best of all, she knew the archae-ological evidence that supported Homer's reputation in antiquity and that was so useful for her attack on the moderns: the *Tabula Iliaca* of Fabretti, the *Apotheosis of Homer* by Gisbert Cuypers (Cuperus), and the curious medals struck at Chios, Smyrna, and Amastris. She was especial-ly pleased with the *Apotheosis*, which she had engraved as an illustration, along with a coin that claimed Homer for Amastris. For the most part she followed the explanation of Cuypers, except that she questioned his reading of the two mice in the *Batrachomyomachia*, preferring to believe (as Bernard de Montfaucon agreed afterward) that they were rats gnaw-ing away at Homer's reputation, "those vile Authors, who not being able to attain to any Reputation themselves, have endeavor'd to revenge that Contempt upon such Works as are in Greatest Esteem; and who whilst Time and the Whole Earth are crowning Homer, have made it their Business to cry him down."[41] Madame Dacier did not like mincing

---

[40]Dacier, *Iliad*, 1:19; *L'Iliade*, 1:28–29. For the Arundel Marbles, see below.
[41]Dacier, *Iliad*, 1:29; *L'Iliade*, 1:42.

words. Her life of Homer concluded with several pages of invective against those who had presumed to challenge the verdict of the ages, the new Zoiluses of her own time.

The notes carried the battle further. Madame Dacier had no intention of distracting her readers with either philology or antiquities; she deliberately avoided the typical classical commentary. Thus, despite her very real learning, she was a true 'ancient', in the sense that Temple and Swift and Boileau and her husband all approved. She offered few citations and little obvious erudition, although she knew most of what had been done. Instead, she concentrated on the defense of her poet, the vindication of Homer against his critics past and present. (Even the index was "poetical" only, confined to literary and philosophical matters.) In meticulous detail and point by point she could now elaborate the arguments of her preface: the perfection of the *Iliad* in form and style, the wisdom of Homer in all matters, the usefulness of the poem as a guide to life, its consistency with Holy Scripture. From time to time she explained a difficulty in the text or a strange custom from the heroic past, but more often she insisted on her main purpose: "to explain the principal Beauties of the Poem," so that her readers might come fully to appreciate them.[42] In this way she seems not to have wandered very far from her father, who, we are told, was particularly successful at kindling enthusiasm for his authors as he guided his students carefully through the text.

We may take as one example the characteristic note that introduces the "catalogue of ships" in Book II of the *Iliad*. Here was a problem for the poet, since any long enumeration was likely to prove irksome to the reader. How had Homer gotten around the difficulty? Madame Dacier shows us that he had "wonderfully vary'd it by ancient Histories, by Genealogies necessary for what follows, and by charming Descriptions which give a real Delight." Homer, we are assured, "was perhaps the only Poet that ever made a Muster-Roll which tired not." Inevitably she found a scriptural analogy, Moses in the book of Numbers, with a similar enumeration of families and tribes. She showed in detail how Homer's list had had the same authority in ancient Greece as Moses's had had among the Hebrews, and she noted briefly that the ancients had written several commentaries on it. The best of them was Strabo's, who showed, incidentally, that Homer "was no less excellent at Geography than Poetry." But this was not her theme; it was interesting, but it belonged more properly to the study of antiquities. "I shall not here," she concluded, "enter into the Particulars of his Remarks, but shall content myself to report what seems absolutely necessary for the Understanding of Homer; the rest tho' very curious and useful, will not, perhaps, give

---

[42] So she reminded her readers in the last note to the work: *Iliad*, 5:136; *L'Iliade*, 3:616.

any great Pleasure to my Readers; at present, we shall only seek in Homer, Moral and Political Instruction, the Wonders of Poetry, and the Charms of Fiction, and not Geographical Exactness."[43]

What, then, of the shield of Achilles? Madame Dacier could well remember how the critics had fastened upon that particular episode. "It was the fortune of those Arms of Achilles to occasion Quarrels and Debates," she reminded her readers. Even in recent times, she recalled, there had been great disputes on the matter; Scaliger had been "follow'd by other Authors who were as Ignorant as himself in the Nature of Epic Poetry." Madame Dacier was categorical in her own reply: the shield of Achilles had always been and would always be admired. It was nothing less than "the most beautiful Episode and the greatest Ornament Poetry ever employ'd." Fortunately, she could call upon various authorities to substantiate her claim. In antiquity there was one especially, a woman named Damo, daughter of Pythagoras, who had written a profound and copious commentary on it, unfortunately lost. Closer to hand, there was her own husband, André Dacier, who had so well defended the shield "that nothing further can be desir'd."[44] The translator was happy to refer her readers to his work, though to be sure, she now repeated most of his arguments in her notes. In either case there was fuel enough to begin the controversy anew.

7

But we must now abridge the quarrel that directly ensued; it has in any case been amply described elsewhere. It may be enough, perhaps, to single out the two moderns who answered Madame Dacier most boldly and who were both read in England on their appearance. They had one thing in common: an addiction to Cartesian rationalism, which through its very confidence in reason, had come to undermine both the history and the authority of the ancients. Although neither writer added much to the earlier criticism of Homer, both pursued their quarry more vigorously and confidently than ever before—not overlooking the shield of Achilles.

First in the field was a prolific writer who had recently won his place in the French Academy, Antoine Houdar de La Motte.[45] He was no scholar and hardly a poet but he possessed great facility and poured forth

[43]Dacier, Iliad, 1:91n.; L'Iliade, 1:359–61.

[44]Dacier, Iliad, 4:131n; L'Iliade, 3:476–78.

[45]See Trublet, Mémoires pour servir à l'histoire, pp. 330–414; Hepp, Homère en France au XVIIe siècle, pp. 661–88; and esp. Paul Dupont, Houdar de La Motte, 1672–1731 (Paris, 1898).

a flood of miscellaneous pieces that aspired to literature: odes, songs, operas, ballets, tragedies, comedies, fables, and the like, some of which were very successful in their time but few of which were noticed afterward. His reply to Madame Dacier consisted of an alternative French version of the *Iliad*, this time deliberately altered and modernized, abridged, rearranged, and versified. It was preceded by an ode in which the shade of Homer appeared to urge upon La Motte a new translation, pleading humbly that the *Iliad* be corrected and amended from its various faults! The ode was followed by a discourse that directly disputed with Madame Dacier and resumed most of the arguments of Perrault (who was only briefly mentioned, however) about the grossness of the gods and heroes, the *longueur* of the descriptions, the monotony of the battles, and so on.[46] La Motte defended the obligation of the translator to transform and correct the original, to embellish what he thought beautiful and bypass the rest. Ignorance of Greek was for him no embarassment; his touchstone was "reason," by which he seems to have meant some combination of Cartesian philosophy and the common-sense convictions of his time. He thus attempted to rid the *Iliad* of its tedious passages, to divest the gods and heroes of their bad manners, to abridge or suppress the endless speeches, to minimize the repetitions, and to cut out the marvelous and improbable. In this way Homer's twenty-four books became twelve and the *Iliad* was adjusted to modern taste. In the process the poetry vanished.

Needless to say, La Motte no more approved the shield of Achilles than he did the rest of the poem and he accorded it the very same treatment.[47] He thought it defective in just the way that Perrault had argued: too many scenes were crowded in upon it and the figures were given a movement quite impossible in a work of art. Homer had exaggerated the powers even of a god. There was but one obvious solution: reduce the variety of the scenes and substitute for them the static tableaux of neoclassical composition. La Motte settled upon three: the wedding of Thetis and Peleus, the judgment of Paris, and the abduction of Helen. It was an audacious—indeed (to the ancients), an outrageous—performance, but thoroughly consistent with La Motte's view that the original could and should be improved.

Yet even La Motte could be outdone. The abbé Jean Terrasson was willing to press the claims of reason against Homer even more fervently than his predecessor. Terrasson knew Greek but even less than La Motte did he appreciate poetry. Reason and geometry were for him almost

---

[46]Antoine Houdar de La Motte, "Discours sur Homère," *Les Paradoxes littéraires de La Motte*, ed. B. Jullien (Paris, 1859), pp. 181–268.

[47]Ibid., pp. 264–65.

identical; the method of Descartes was everything. "Les Grecs scavoient parler," he wrote in a philosophical work, "les Latins scavoient penser, et les François scavoient raisonner. Le progrès des tems a fait le second degré; le progres des tems et Descartes ont fait le troisième."[48] To bring about progress in literature it was as necessary to dethrone Homer as in philosophy it had been essential to defeat Aristotle.

In 1715, in the midst of the new controversy, Terrasson published a two-volume work that immediately won a partial English translation and eventually a complete one. It was entitled *Dissertation critique sur L'Iliade d'Homère ou . . . on cherche les règles d'une poétique fondée sur la raison.*[49] The arguments were once again nearly all familiar but the spirit was original. Terrasson's avowed aim was "to introduce the same Light of Reason and true Philosophy, by Help and Assistance of which there has of late been made such Great and Noble Discoveries in the Study and Knowledge of Nature, into all the several Arts of Speech also, such as Eloquence and Poetry, Criticism and Philology: in a word . . . *Belles Lettres.*" It was thus no argument for the Daciers to cite the applause of the ages or Homer's reputation in antiquity. The only true authority for Terasson was reason, which he proceeded to employ as thoroughly as possible on the *Iliad*. For the abbé, it was the philosopher, not the historian, who knew best how to read the past; it was the philosopher "who makes the true System of the Human Mind his principal Study and Application, [and who] knows how to transport himself into the remotest and earliest Ages of the World." He saw that the defenders of Homer had erred in making his virtues timeless and his qualities perfect. But then he applied his own set of values to the past, even more deliberately heedless of circumstance. In effect, Homer had failed because he did not know Descartes; he had lived in a barbarous age of darkness and ignorance. Should he not be excused, then, since he had done the best he could for his time? Terrasson would not allow it. Common sense, if not mathematical reasoning, was always available to the human mind. Homer could have done much better even within the limits of his age. "I have observed several Particulars," Terrasson argued, "in which it had been easy for Homer to have corrected the false Taste of his Age, by the easiest and simplest Dictates of Common Sense, and natural Morality." The poet had had "a confused and irregular Imagination; and in whatever Age he had liv'd, this Fault would have appear'd more or less."[50]

---

[48]Jean Terrasson, *La Philosophie applicable à tous les objets de l'esprit et de la raison* (Paris, 1754), p. 21; cf. Sainte-Beuve, *Causeries du lundi*, 9:402.

[49]Jean Terrasson, *A Discourse of Ancient and Modern Learning*, trans. Francis Brerewood (London, 1716), and *A Critical Dissertation on Homer's Iliad*, trans. Brerewood, 2 vols. (London, 1723, 1725).

[50]Terrasson, *Critical Dissertation*, 1:xxxiii, lxi.

Inevitably an instance was Achilles' shield. Terrasson at once objected to that "terrible Number and Multitude of Objects, in so narrow and limited a Compass, whatever Dimensions are given to the Buckler of Achilles." It was a fantastic, a "Gothic" notion. The interpretation of the Daciers, that Homer meant to represent the entire universe in one picture, was contrary to the rules of both perspective and painting. Using the rule of tangents, Terrasson easily showed that a spectator would have to be far above the highest mountains to obtain the perspective required to encompass the whole earth! Needless to say, the abbé was appalled by Homer's astronomy, especially his error regarding the constellation of the bear, and astonished by the movement of the figures. His objection to one of the scenes on the shield, "the extravagant Comparison of a circular Dance with the Swiftness of a Potter's Wheel," shows his method. He would not, he said, enlarge on the bad effect that that velocity would have upon the eyes of the spectators, or on the physical error of Madame Dacier in remarking that the weight of the matter diminished with the velocity. "I shall only observe, it is absolutely impossible, that without a successive Motion of the Figures, the Dance shou'd sometimes turn round like a Potter's Wheel, and sometimes open, to make so many Windings; for whenever it opens, the circular Motion must of Necessity stop. Nor can it happen that one Part should continually turn round while the other opens." The scene was impossible as described; thus it was easy to see that "Homer is destroy'd by Reason."[51]

Yet neither La Motte nor Terrasson proved very convincing. It is true that Terrasson's English translator was very much impressed by what he called (after a French journal) "the greatest and most commendable Performance in Critical Learning, that has ever appeared in the Commonwealth of Letters." It sold well enough and raised a great noise.[52] But the two Daciers at once responded vigorously to their critics, Madame Dacier to La Motte, Monsieur Dacier to Terrasson.[53] Others joined in as well, most notably the famous abbé Jean Hardouin, always grateful for a paradox. (Yet Hardouin was, on the whole, a defender of Homer, and of the shield of Achilles.)[54] The moderns, of course replied in their turn,

[51]Ibid., 2:259–60, 274–79.

[52]The translator, Brerewood, repeats the testimonies from the *Histoire critique de la république de lettres*, vols. 10–11, in ibid., 1:xxi–cxii.

[53]André Dacier, *Nouveau Manuel d'Epictète*, 2 vols. (Paris, 1715), 2: Préface; Madame Dacier, *Des causes de la corruption du goust* (Paris, 1715).

[54]Jean Hardouin, *Apologie d'Homère* (London, 1716), pp. 307–28. Hardouin did, however, attack the notion that Homer's theology agreed with Scripture and was answered by Madame Dacier in *Homère défendu contre l'Apologie du R. P. Hardouin* (Paris, 1716). The first part of Hardouin's work was translated into English as *An Apology for Homer* (London, 1717).

only to be met with still further rebukes.[55] Once again, as in the first
episode, satire had its day, this time in a work of Saint-Hyacinthe known
as *Le Chef d'oeuvre d'un inconnu*, where both ancients and moderns (but
especially the ancients) were pleasantly mocked.[56] It was all good fun,
although the bitterness of the ancients marred the humor somewhat.
Once again the episode ended in a reconcilation, this time between
Madame Dacier and La Motte, but it was as before only personal, and the
issues remained unresolved.

The whole affair was followed enthusiastically across the Channel, but
while each side had partisans in England, the temptation there was to
condemn both parties as too extreme. Thus the *Free-Thinker* arbitrated
the case between Madame Dacier and La Motte by suggesting that while
the lady had come out distinctly ahead, she might well have conceded a
few points instead of trying to defend everything. Madame Dacier had
the advantage in erudition, La Motte in reason; "the one is blind to the
Defects, the other to the Beauties of Homer." Madame Dacier was too
warm, while La Motte's good manners almost compensated for his lack
of Greek! Nevertheless, the *Free-Thinker* was confident that most readers, even those who did not know the original, favored the lady.[57] This
was pretty much the view also of Sir Richard Blackmore, a physician
with literary pretensions who had himself tried to write a modern epic,
as well as engaging briefly in the battle of the books.[58] Now in 1716 he
wrote an essay weighing up the two sides in the *querelle*. The ancients, he
thought, should concede that Homer had sometimes erred, particularly
in the "Deformity and Inequality in the Manners of his Heroes, who
often in their Actions, Speeches, and Passions, say and do many things
contrary or improper to their respective Characters." But the moderns,
too, should admit that no later poet had ever matched the two great
epics, and "that no future Author, that shall attempt a work of that kind,
is likely to succeed, if he deviates far from those Models, and much less if
he leaves them quite out of Sight."[59] And that, on the whole, was very

[55]See esp. La Motte's *Réflexions sur la critique* (Paris, 1716). For all these matters, see the
ever-dependable Hepp, *Homère en France an XVIIᵉ siècle*, pp. 688–708.

[56]Saint-Hyacinthe's *Chef d'oeuvre d'un inconnu* (Amsterdam, 1714) was accompanied by
a "Dissertation sur Homère et sur Chapelain," pp. 257–90.

[57]*Free-Thinker* 1 (1722): 119–26.

[58]Blackmore's *Prince Arthur, an Heroic poem in X Books* was published in 1695, with a 3d
ed. in 1714. In 1700 he published a *Satyr against Wit*, which provoked a collection of satirical
Commendatory Verses on the Author of the Two Arthurs and the Satyr against Wit, in which Tom
Brown had a large hand, and a retort by Blackmore, *Discommendatory Verses*. One of the
subjects of contention was Bentley's *Dissertations*. See Richard C. Boys, *Sir Richard Blackmore and the Wits*, University of Michigan Contributions in Modern Philology 13 (Ann
Arbor, 1949).

[59]Sir Richard Blackmore, *Essays upon Several Subjects*, 2 vols. (London, 1716, 1717),
1:156–85. Blackmore was no friend to the philologists, however. "The Accomplishments

much the view of Alexander Pope and his friend the Duke of Buckingham when they exchanged opinions about the matter a year or two
later.[60]

8

In all the excitement, one small work might easily have been overlooked, except for the fact that it made a most substantial contribution to
the argument. It was a defense of the *Iliad* against La Motte, with a
special essay on the shield of Vulcan, an *Apologie d'Homère et bouclier
d'Achille* (Paris, 1715). The author was Jean Boivin le Cadet, librarian to
the king of France, professor of Greek at the Collège de France, and
member of the Academy of Inscriptions and Belles Lettres.[61] Boivin had
received another of those remarkably precocious classical educations that
sometimes seems to have belonged to everyone in the later seventeenth
century, this time from an older brother named Louis. This young man
was a considerable scholar in his own right and, like the two fathers who
had instructed William Wotton and Madame Dacier, he eschewed the
customary exercises and set his young protégé at once to work on the
classical authors, beginning with Homer. He was, however, less kind
than they; he confined the little boy with his Greek text, a dictionary, and
a grammar, and would not release him until he had explicated in French
and Latin a set number of verses. Jean's only compensation seems to have
been to be allowed to accompany his brother on walks in the country,
where, however, he was compelled to continue to explicate as they
walked, Louis Boivin never failing to carry in his pocket a Greek or Latin
text. Whatever we may think of the method, it was successful; Jean
Boivin became a fine scholar, and as a result, so at least his biographer
assures us, he developed a characteristic sweetness of temper that was in
marked contrast to that of his preceptor.

---

of a meer Grammatical Critick, and a Commentator on the Classick Authors or the ancient
Philosophers, tho' perhaps they may in some sort be beneficial, yet must be contended with
the lowest Rank, because Mankind may be very happy without them": *The Lay-monk*, no.
8, Dec. 2, 1713. See also no. 2, Nov. 11, 1713.

[60]Alexander Pope, *Correspondence*, ed. George Sherburn, 5 vols. (Oxford, 1956), 1:485–
87. The exchange occurred in August–September 1718; Pope published Buckingham's
letter in his edition of *The Works of John Sheffield, Duke of Buckingham*, 2 vols. (London,
1723), 2:288–95.

[61]For the following, see the *éloges* in the *Mémoires de l'Academie des Inscriptions* 5 (1725):
433–42 and 6 (1726): 376–85; Christophe Allard, "Deux Normands membres de l'Académ-
ie des inscriptions . . . Louis et Jean Boivin," in *Précis analytique des travaux de l'Académie de
Rouen* (Rouen, 1890), pp. 219–58; and Hepp, *Homère en France au XVIIe siècle*, pp. 568–72.
Charles Rollin has a fine tribute to Boivin in *The Method of Teaching and Studying the Belles
Lettres*, 4 vols. (London, 1734), 4:177–78.

Boivin was well situated in the Royal Library to take advantage of its rare Greek books and manuscripts. It was one of these, an ancient copy of Longinus, that he brought to the attention of Boileau, thus joining company in that work with André Dacier. He began also to edit the fourteenth-century Byzantine history of Nicephorus Gregoras and to contribute to the meetings of the Academy of Inscriptions. At his installation he delivered a Latin address, "De boni grammatici graeci officio," and shortly afterward (1707) read a paper that described the quarrel over Homer and Virgil as it had been conducted through the centuries until the time of Rapin.[62] Boivin did not doubt that of the two ancient poets Homer was superior to his imitator; although Virgil had decided merits of his own, he could not match the true nobility and simplicity of the original. Boivin continued to publish papers about Homer, and several other manuscripts by him survive to show that he even contemplated editing the texts.[63]

Thus when La Motte's work appeared in 1714, Boivin could hardly sit idly by. He did not relish controversy but his lifelong devotion to Homer and his skill in Greek made him a natural partisan. Still he would not fight like Madame Dacier but chose rather to treat his opponent with tact and courtesy while showing him his errors. For this alone his work was admired, not least by La Motte himself, although there was more to recommend it than mere moderation. Especially original was his treatment of the shield. Boivin met La Motte's arguments first by showing how the description of the shield suited the design of the poem as a whole.[64] The episode was no mere digression but the capstone of the entire work. He then proceeded to meet the charge that had been raised first by Perrault and repeated endlessly afterward, that the design of the shield was impossible and that the number and variety of scenes on its face simply could not be made to fit. He did this in the most direct and persuasive manner possible, by showing exactly how in fact it could be done. He drew a diagram that laid out the surface of the shield in the form of a circumference with twelve compartments and a central boss. He then showed exactly how each scene described by Homer could be fitted into its appropriate place. Finally, lest any doubt remain, he engaged an artist, Nicolas Vleughels, to picture these scenes as they were described in the *Iliad*.[65] The resulting engraving provided the frontispiece

[62]Jean Boivin, "Querelle entre les partisans d'Homère et ceux de Virgile," *Mémoires de l'Académie des inscriptions et belles-lettres* 1 (1707): 176–79.

[63]The Bibliothèque Nationale has a small manuscript entitled "Projet pour une nouvelle édition d'Homère" and two other manuscripts described by Hepp, *Homère en France au XVIIᵉ siècle*, pp. 568–72.

[64]Jean Boivin, *Apologie d'Homère et bouclier d'Achille* (Paris, 1715), esp. pp. 234–41.

[65]On Vleugels, see Mlle Bataille in Louis Dimier, *Les Peintres français du XVIIIᵉ siècle* (Paris, 1928), 1:245–59; Pierre Clamorgan, "Un Directeur de l'Académie de France au XVIIIᵉ siècle," *Gazette des beaux-arts*, 4th ser., 13 (1917): 327–43.

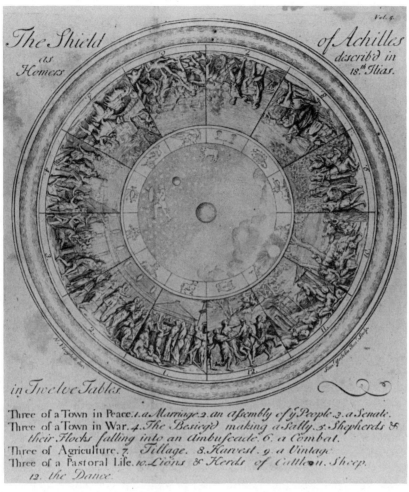

The shield of Achilles designed by Jean Boivin, drawn by Nicolas Vleughels, and reproduced in Alexander Pope's translation of the *Iliad*

to Boivin's work. It was a confirmation of the most persuasive kind of the reality of Homer's shield. Who now could doubt that the poet had had in mind an actual weapon, and not a fanciful one, an antiquity of the finest artistic merit? There was much more to Boivin's little work of sense and learning, all of which Pope absorbed gratefully, but this alone was enough to justify his performance.[66]

[66]Very solid and judicious was the consensus; see, for example, M. Fourmont, *Examen pacifique de la querelle de Madame Dacier et de Monsieur de La Motte sur Homère* (Paris, 1716), sig. A2v. Even La Motte found much in it to praise: *Réflexions*, pp. 269–70.

Chapter Five

Ancient Greece and Modern Scholarship

I

While the quarrel over Homer was going on abroad and the battle of
the books was in progress at home, the slow steady work of classical
scholarship proceeded quietly. Neither the ancients nor the moderns
could deny that year by year, ever since the "revival of antiquity" had
begun, a large and persistent collective endeavor had been growing to
resurrect every scrap of evidence for the lost world of the classical authors. And while the ancients might deplore its "excesses" and its pedantry and worry about its dangerous and distracting consequences, even
they were being forced by it to alter their perceptions of the ancient past,
or at least to align them more carefully with the evidence. As for the
moderns, they exulted, as we have seen, in the progress of the new
historical science, much as they did in the new science of nature, and
looked forward to a continuing accumulation of knowledge, heedless of
any difficulties it might present. Modern philology confirmed their suspicions that in fact the moderns knew more about the past than any of
their predecessors had known and that the present could certainly surpass
antiquity in both its manners and its morals. The future might do better
still.

But if these were the issues that were being proposed in the first stages
of the war between the ancients and the moderns, they had still to be
worked out in all their implications. And before we can take their measure fully—before we can appreciate what happened in the next episodes
of the battle of the books—it will be necessary to discover what the
classical scholars were up to at this time; to find out, in a word, just what
the state of Homeric scholarship was in 1700. Unfortunately, this is not
easy to do in a brief compass; but one thing should be clear anyway, that

the two separate branches of classical Greek scholarship, philology and antiquities, were both making deliberate if somewhat stammering progress throughout the period. In each case, the ultimate inspiration remained the same: the elucidation of the text, in this case the meaning of the Homeric poems. But sometimes the inquiry was more broadly intended; it was possible to develop an interest not only in Homer or the epic but in the entire Homeric world from which they had sprung. That poetry could yield information about history was becoming as obvious and to some as interesting as the reverse.[1] But whichever route the scholar took, from poetry to history or vice versa, the results were likely to seem pedantic enough and beyond either the grasp or the taste of the wits. Not that they were entirely ignorant of these matters. They could not afford to be, especially if they had presumed so much as to try to translate either the *Iliad* or the *Odyssey*.

The general condition of Homeric scholarship may be conveniently glimpsed in a small Latin work that appeared at the turn of the new century. Ludolf Kuster was a young German scholar with a taste for travel and a mastery of both the ancient tongues. When he left home it was to assume the characteristic humanist pursuit of old libraries and rare manuscripts and the company of learned men. While in Holland he contributed to the great compilations of Johann Graevius and Jakob Gronovius. Eventually he reached England, met Richard Bentley, and became a doctor at Cambridge University. He was soon off again, but not before he had published three great folio volumes of an edition of the Byzantine grammarian Suidas. This was the first of many important editorial labors that climaxed in the works of Aristophanes, for which Bentley contributed some of the notes. In the end Kuster became one of the best-known Greek scholars in Europe, important enough to provoke Gronovius and quarrel with Perizonius, to be pensioned by the king of France and made a member of the Academy of Inscriptions.[2]

His first work was entitled *Historia critica Homeri* (1696) and was dedicated to the illustrious Ezechiel Spanheim, who had earlier taken him under his wing. It was intended to bring together compactly all that was then known about Homer and his epic poems. Kuster began, therefore, by considering the problems of Homer's biography, and he assembled the evidence for the rival claims of several Greek cities and the various

[1]A good example is Everard Feithius, *Antiquitatum Homericarum libri IV* (Leiden, 1677), reprinted with similar works in Jakob Gronovius, *Thesaurus antiquitatum graecarum*, vol. 6 (Leiden, 1702). This interest, too, had ancient precedents; see Anthony Grafton and N. N. Swerdlow, "Greek Chronology in Roman Epic: The Calendrical Date for the Fall of Troy in the *Aeneid*," *Classical Quarterly* 36 (1986): 212–18. And the idea was already familiar during the Renaissance.

[2]See the *éloge* in *Mémoires de l'Académie des inscriptions* 3 (1723): xlviii–lvii; James Henry Monk, *The Life of Richard Bentley*, 2d ed., 2 vols. (London, 1833), 1:191–96, 402–4.

dates proposed for the poet's life. Besides the ancient writers, he noticed the work of the seventeenth-century Greek from Chios, Leon Allatius, who had taken up the career of the poet with a great show of erudition. Although the feeling was growing, as Pierre Bayle put it, that "there is more of Reading and Learning in his Productions than of Wit and Judgment," the work became standard and was reprinted by Gronovius and frequently cited.[3] If it proved anything, however, it was how very difficult it was to know anything certain about the life of Homer. In passing, Kuster also noticed the coins, in Spanheim and elsewhere, that could be used to place Homer, or indeed to show his portrait.

Kuster followed the life with many pages on Homer's reputation in antiquity, in which he assembled the evidence for his exalted stature. He did not, however, overlook the criticisms of Plato, of Zoilus, and of others in ancient times. And he quoted at some length a passage from a seventeenth-century writer describing the most important archaeological monument that had ever been raised to the poet, the marble known as the *Apotheosis of Homer*. Here Kuster was content to refer the reader to the learned treatises of modern antiquaries upon that subject, especially to the one by Gisbert Cuypers.[4] He meant to inform his readers of all the developments in modern Homeric scholarship, archaeological as well as philological.

Kuster's next topic was the writings themselves. The young scholar assembled the evidence for Homer's authorship succinctly, showing first the difficulties in assigning to him the minor works (the *Hymns*, *Epigrams*, etc.), then discussing the possibility of lost poetry, and finally reaffirming categorically against Perrault that Homer had written both the *Iliad* and the *Odyssey*. (The argument, which he drew from Boileau, was being popularized at the same time in England by Basil Kennett.)[5] He discussed the form of the poems, the *Iliad* resembling a tragedy, the *Odyssey* a comedy, and suggested that they should be read neither entirely literally nor allegorically, but as something between. Finally, and in greatest detail, he turned to the problem of the text.

Here indeed was the first concern of the philologist. Before one could know what Homer had meant, it was necessary to know what he had said. Kuster remembered the ancient tradition that the poem had been edited in antiquity, and he resumed the question raised by Perrault as to whether it was once only a string of separate "rhapsodies." He sided with Boileau, adding that the term "rhapsody" had altered its meaning in

[3]Pierre Bayle, *The Dictionary Historical and Critical*, ed. Pierre Desmaizeaux, 2d ed., 5 vols. (London, 1734–1738), 1:231–32; Noémi Hepp, *Homère en France au XVIIᵉ siècle* (Paris, 1968), pp. 86–92.

[4]Ludolf Kuster, *Historia critica Homeri* (Frankfort, 1696), p. 47.

[5]Basil Kennett, *The Lives and Characters of the Ancient Poets* (London, 1697), pp. 36–40.

antiquity after Homer's time, thus explaining away the late and apparently contradictory testimony of such as Aelian and Josephus. Along the way he noticed that it was the Alexandrian critic Aristarchus who had first divided the *Iliad* and the *Odyssey* into the books that we now know; and he recounts how the poems were first recited and dramatized.

For Kuster the most interesting problem was editing and emending the text. He takes some time to explain the accomplishments of ancient criticism before he considers the techniques of modern interpretation. He emphasizes the significance of early manuscripts, listing the most important that he knew. He discusses the scholia (those ancient glosses that sometimes accompanied the text), noticing particularly those ascribed without warrant to Didymus. And he discriminates among the various kinds of commentary, beginning with the Homeric lexica, of which the most important was Hesychius. He emphasizes, of course, the vast compilation of Eustathius, the indefatigable Byzantine commentator. And last, he enumerates the modern printed editions beginning with the first at Florence in 1488. Among the many he describes, he has particular praise for the Cambridge version of 1689, which added to the Greek a fresh Latin translation and rich annotation, including many variants and some of the old scholia. The last pages of his manual conclude with a list of recent works of scholarship. Here modern Homeric dictionaries and phrasebooks are commingled with treatises on special subjects. We are reminded of Cuypers and Allatius and of Rapin's comparison of Homer and Virgil. We hear also of the learned works of several Englishmen: the *Homeri Gnomologia duplici Parallelismo illustrata* of James Duport (1660), which had been encouraged by Dr. Busby; the *Comparatio Homeri cum scriptoribus sacris* of Zachary Bogan (1658); and the *De nupera Homeri editione* of Meric Casaubon (1659).

In a way, Kuster's work was impressive testimony to the steady concern for Homer among modern scholars. (His own tract, incidentally, was praised and employed in that monumental bibliography of all things Greek, the *Bibliotheca graeca* of Fabricius, where it gained a still wider circulation.)[6] Nor was his reading list improbable; at least one Englishman owned almost every title on it, including Kuster's tract and two sets of Fabricius.[7] But it was clear nevertheless how much more remained to be done. There were so many scholarly differences, so many unresolved problems. Despite all that had been accomplished, the text itself was so obviously uncertain. Indeed, the elder Casaubon and Kuster's contemporary Perizonius had both been impressed by the difficulties. Among

[6]Johann Albert Fabricius, *Bibliotheca graeca*, 3 vols. (Hamburg, 1705–1707), vol. 1, bk. 2, chaps. 1–7.

[7]Dr. John Woodward, the London virtuoso; see the *Catalogue of the Library, Antiquities, etc., of the Late Dr. Woodward* (London, 1728).

the manuscripts that had not yet been employed, Kuster mentioned one in Venice that was eventually to revolutionize Homeric scholarship. Doubtless he did not appreciate the significance of his brief description: "Venetiis in Bibl D. Marci servatur Ilias cum scholiis ab editis multum differentibus," and it was left to Villoison to discover the volume (1788), and to F. A. Wolf finally to employ it in his famous *Prolegomena ad Homerum* (1795).[8] But even Kuster's few words on the manuscripts were enough to remind scholars of that most fundamental level of research, the recovery and collation of the text. That the *Iliad* had survived in nearly two hundred early copies (only a few of which had been printed) was no mean obstacle, however, and enough to put off all but the most indefatigable.[9]

Fortunately there was one Englishman, anyway, who was ready to undertake the task. Somewhere about 1700, Joshua Barnes, poet, historian, now professor of Greek at Cambridge, pledged himself to a new edition of Homer. We have met him already in an awkward role as opponent to Richard Bentley. As the defender of the spurious letters of Euripides, he would not seem to be the most able candidate for the task.[10] But his credentials were not all bad. In particular, he had two qualifications that were helpful: a lifelong admiration for the poet and such fluency in Greek that he could both write and speak it with ease. From his youth he composed Homeric verse, much of it still in manuscript, and when the Greek archibishop of Philippolis visited Cambridge in 1701 and was awarded a degree, Barnes made an extraordinary ex tempore oration in the language of the visitor.[11] It was only his judgment that remained in doubt.

2

Barnes was writing Greek and Latin poetry of an extraordinarily miscellaneous kind even before he entered the university. He kept it up for the rest of his life. He also wrote English poetry, drama, and history; but

[8]See Charles Joret, *D'Ansse de Villoison* (Paris, 1910), pp. 184–85, 378–80; Mark Pattison, "F. A. Wolf," in *Essays*, 2 vols. (Oxford, 1889), 1:337–414; Anthony Grafton, "*Prolegomena* to Friedrich August Wolf," *Journal of the Warburg and Courtauld Institutes* 44 (1981): 101–29; R. C. Jebb, *Homer* (Glasgow, 1888), pp. 96–97.

[9]J. L. Myres, *Homer and His Critics* (London, 1958), p. 13.

[10]Nevertheless, his Euripides was praised at one dinner when the company included the dean of Lincoln, the dean of St. Paul's, and John Locke; see Mordecai Hunton to Joshua Barnes, April 30, 1697, Bodleian MS. Rawlinson Letters 40, no. 25. Edward Bernard also approved; ibid., no. 45.

[11]Charles H. Cooper, *The Annals of Cambridge*, vol. 4 (Cambridge, 1852), p. 46. See also the amusing account in a letter from W. Gill, Sept. 20, 1701, B.M. MS. Stowe 747, f. 147.

he preferred Greek, which he thought superior to his native tongue, and which, he explained, he had been familiar with from childhood. Eventually he went to Cambridge and became a fellow of Emmanuel College. In the next year (1679) he published a work with a Greek and Latin title that has been translated as *The Courtier's Looking Glass*, "or the Story of Esther paraphrased in Greek Verse, with a Latin translation in the opposite page and Greek Scholia or Notes, in which (to illustrate the sacred Text) besides many other particulars, the Antiquities and more remote customs of the Eastern Nations are explained. To which is added a parody in Homerics upon the same story and a copious Index of Things and Words."[12] In the tract, which was written when he was only twenty, Barnes identified King Ahasuerus, mentioned in the scriptural account of Esther, with the Persian Xerxes.[13] The likely inspiration for this idea was the Cambridge professor of Greek James Duport, whose *Gnomologia* (1660) was one of the landmarks of seventeenth-century Homeric study. Duport had brought together a large collection of sentences from the *Iliad* and *Odyssey*, which he illustrated by analogies drawn from the classical authors and especially from Holy Scripture. In the preface to his *Gnomologia*, he argued that there was a remarkable correspondence between Homer and the Bible, something that had been noticed before but that he now attempted to illustrate beyond question. (In later years he translated the Psalms of David into Homeric verse as though to prove the point, to the acclaim of both houses of convocation.)[14] Barnes adopted Duport's general viewpoint and it continued to govern his attitude toward Homer for the rest of his life.

In 1686 Barnes took his degree in divinity; two years later he published a large *Life of King Edward III*. Bishop William Nicolson found the digressions there interminable and the *Biographia Britannica* complained of the "long and tedious speeches which seem to be the result of his own imagination," in imitation perhaps of Thucydides.[15] Unfortunately, he dedicated it to James II and (with the Revolution) lost both his hopes of preferment and a good deal of money. The *Life* was not a popular success and cost Barnes several hundred pounds.[16] In 1694 he published his

[12]*Biographia Britannica*, 2d ed., ed. Andrew Kippis, 2 vols. (London, 1780), 2:490, quoting Barnes's preface to his Anacreon (1705).

[13]From an Emmanuel College manuscript.

[14]See James Henry Monk, "Memoir of Dr. James Duport," *Museum Criticum* 2 (1826): 672–98. See also Edmund Dickinson, *Delphi Phoenicizantes* (London, 1655), where Moses and Joshua are described as Bacchus and Hercules, and so on; William N. Blomberg, *An Account of the Life and Writing of Edmund Dickinson* (London, 1737), p. 9–60.

[15]William Nicolson, *English Historical Library* (London, 1736), p. 80; "Barnes, Joshua," in Kippis, *Biographia Britannica*.

[16]Barnes to Arthur Charlett, n.d., Bodleian MS. Ballard 17, f. 14; Barnes to John Hudson, Jan. 12, 1708, Bodleian MS. Rawlinson Letters 24, f. 10.

edition of Euripides, including the spurious letters, and in the following
year he was chosen Greek professor at Cambridge, a position to which
he had long aspired. He admired Sir Richard Blackmore's *Prince Arthur*
and planned a similar work of his own, though he seems never to have
finished it.[17] It may have been at this time that he first thought of attempting Homer. Despite his growing reputation, however, Barnes
lacked encouragement, particularly for so ambitious an undertaking. It
was providential then, that it should suddenly appear in the person of a
widow from St. Ives in Huntingtonshire, named Mrs. Mason. "The
story goes, that this lady, who was between forty and fifty, having for
some time been a great admirer of Mr. Barnes, came to Cambridge, and
desired leave to settle an hundred pounds a year upon him after her death
which he politely refused, unless she would condescend to make him
happy in her person, which was none of the most engaging. The lady
was too obliging to refuse any thing to *Joshua, for whom,* she said, *the sun
stood still*; and soon they were married."[18] Mrs. Barnes became at once
her husband's warmest supporter. For a time he worked at an edition of
Anacreon, while he began to collect notes for Homer and for Pindar.
When the Anacreon was finished (1705), he was at last ready to give full
attention to the great task. In that year he visited the Bodleian Library in
search of manuscripts and met Thomas Hearne.

The visit to Oxford was very successful. Barnes received a second
divinity degree while there and delighted his audience with some ex
tempore Greek verses. Hearne for one was very impressed and recorded
them in his journals, along with other miscellaneous English and Latin
pieces by the visitor.[19] Together the two men explored the Bodleian and
Hearne was pleased to show his Cambridge friend the famous Baroccian
library. This was the collection of Greek manuscripts that had been
brought from Venice to England in 1628 and presented to the Bodleian
by the third earl of Pembroke, "the most valuable parcel that ever came
into England," according to Humfrey Wanley.[20] Barnes was especially
interested in a manuscript on Oppian with scholia, which he told Hearne
he would use for a new edition; in a collection of Greek epigrams; and of
course in the manuscript of Homer. The two men became great friends
and when Barnes left began a regular correspondence. They had much in
common. Their politics were similar; both were now working at am-

---

[17]See Richard Blackmore to Barnes, Aug. 14 and Oct. 12, 1695, Bodleian MS. Rawlinson Letters 40, ff. 66, 72.

[18]Kippis, *Biographia Britannica*, 2:49.

[19]Thomas Hearne, *Remarks and Collections*, ed. C. E. Doble et al., 11 vols. (Oxford,
1885–1921), 1:269–74. The visit took place in July 1706.

[20]Humfrey Wanley to John Covell, Jan. 24, 1716, B.M. MS. Add 22911, ff. 185–86.

bitious editions of the classics—Hearne on Livy and Cicero. Both were more assiduous than critical. When Thomas Smith learned of their friendship, he wrote to Hearne that Barnes was a better Greek poet than critic. He thought him inferior even to Duport, for whom he was confident "judicious" scholars had little reverence.[21] But Barnes flattered Hearne with his attention and offered help for his Livy; and Hearne could hardly fail to respond to his appeals for assistance.[22]

The chief aid that seemed to be required was a transcript of the Baroccian manuscript of the *Iliad* which had not yet been printed; Hearne could also provide some rare editions and commentaries. Barnes was determined to produce as complete and exact an edition of Homer as was possible. When he turned to Hearne, he had already transcribed the whole of the *Iliad*, collated it with an old manuscript from Corpus Christi College, and employed Eustathius throughout. He hoped to obtain another old manuscript from the bishop of Ely besides the one from the Bodleian. He was willing, he said, to be entirely self-effacing, a role not very characteristic. "I value nothing like Truth and had rather have an exact Edition of Homer, tho' I had not one Word of my own in it."[23] All of his publications had somehow cost him money, but he was prepared to risk a great deal more for his favorite, Homer. Most important, he would take his time. "Don't you imagine me in too much hast," he insisted to Hearne, "I would not have a wrong Word."[24] On that score he was to find a most sympathetic collaborator.

Unfortunately Hearne was, for the moment anyway, busy with his Livy. He promised to do what he could, but "the Manuscripts require some months provided they be done accurately, as I think they ought to be." When finally Livy was accomplished, he set about earnestly to work. "You shall share in my success," Barnes had promised. He offered to pay Hearne, who politely declined.[25] Barnes was thankful for every help. "In short you have won my heart and Mrs. Barnes too for she is a good friend to Homer or els I could not venture at about a thousand pounds." Soon Hearne began to send along the collations, book by book, for the *Iliad*, beginning in March 1707 and continuing for more than two years. He had taken care, he wrote, "to be very exact in the

---

[21]Smith to Hearne, Aug. 3, 1706, in Hearne, *Remarks and Collections*, 1:280.

[22]Hearne to Barnes, Oct. 27, 1706, Bodleian MS. Rawlinson Letters 40, f. 77.

[23]Barnes to Hearne, Mar. 12, 1707, Bodleian MS. Rawlinson Letters 24, f. 349. Barnes first appealed for the Baroccian manuscript on April 10, 1707: Bodleian MS. Rawlinson C 146, f. 55.

[24]Barnes to Hearne, Jan. 12, 1708, Bodleian MS. Rawlinson Letters 24, no. 11. A draft of Barnes's proposals with a specimen is in ibid. 75, f. 181.

[25]Bodleian MS. Rawlinson Letters 35, no. 1, and 24, no. 9. Hearne replied, "'Tis enough for me that I can anyway serve Learning": June 26, 1708, ibid. 35, no. 17.

Collating MSS and so therefore have put down even the most minute lections that you may judge yourself."[26]

Inevitably Hearne reported Barnes's progress to his friends. He was worried about Barnes's lack of encouragement and feared that Homer might never appear. It was too bad, he wrote to Francis Cherry, for "no man is more able." As always, he consulted Dodwell for advice and passed it along to Barnes. The great man did not hesitate; if Barnes wished to improve the earlier editions, he should be reminded of the lives of Homer ascribed to Plutarch and Porphyry as well as various old scholia that he could enumerate. He thought it important also to print the minor works.[27] Unfortunately, Hearne could find no manuscripts of either Porphyry or Plutarch at Oxford, "and therefore Mr. Barnes cannot print them fuller than already." He could, however, supply a Baroccian text for Homer's *Batrachomyomachia*. When Barnes received it, he was ecstatic. Hearne had done his work with "incomparable Zeale, Paines and Fidelity." Barnes was confident he would "do Homer that justice that he has not had this 2000 years." Six weeks later he reported that he had told someone who thought the Elzevir edition was sufficient "that it was like a Wooden painted Cheese at Cheesemonger's Shops in London, for one that never Eat any as good, and most durable, than a true Cheese. But that for a Judge and learned man that would see Homer in his *puris Naturalibus* never any man in 1000 years has seen such a One as our Work . . . will certainly be."[28]

There was no question about Barnes's ambition. Only the finest materials would do for Homer, "the very carriage of the Paper will cost £10," while the frontispiece, which was to be done in Holland, would cost another £30. He was willing to venture all his reputation and his resources on the enterprise. He still received little encouragement and no bookseller would touch it, but he was able to scrape the money together somehow.[29] In 1710, with the work almost complete, he wrote to Hearne that he had paid off all but £56 out of the £500 that it had cost. "I have not yet touched Mrs. Barnes purse nor Mortgag'd a foot, nor sold, for fear of breaking her Heart, or els I had done better." Although he did not live to see it, Mrs. Barnes had eventually to assume his debts, and Hearne recalled gratefully that without her help "the World would have

[26]Bodleian MS. Rawlinson Letters 24, no. 8, and 35, nos. 9, 15.

[27]Hearne, *Remarks and Collections*, 2:104; Bodleian MS. Rawlinson Letters 35, no. 15.

[28]Bodleian MS. Rawlinson Letters 24, nos. 12, 19, 20.

[29]"Booksellers will cramp and spoyl by their baser spirit the best designed Author," Barnes wrote in 1707, "as Anacreon being confined to so small a volume was necessarily deprived of the Noble Indexes I had proposed. I therefore intend to print my self . . .": Emmanuel College MS. 174.

been depriv'd of the Benefit of his Writings particularly of his admirable Edition of Homer."[30]

The result was very impressive. Barnes's Homer appeared in 1711 in two stocky volumes and nearly 2,000 pages. One copy went to Kuster, who received it gratefully. At Cambridge they thought it "one of the most creditable performances that ever yet came from their press." Hearne never expected to see its equal. "The Book is admirably well done, is very correct, and will be a lasting monument."[31] Despite his pretensions, Barnes had been genuinely self-effacing. The temptation to enlarge upon his own interpretation of the poet had been very great. But he realized the danger of his unorthodox opinions; there was no sense in putting anyone off his edition unnecessarily. At least one subscriber hoped that he would not spoil his Homer as he had spoiled his Euripides! So, apart from a passing reference in the preface, he confined himself to giving the world Homer alone, a Homer that was "more himself than in these modern Ages ever before."[32]

It was just as well. Barnes's view of Homer was an amplification of the one suggested by Duport. "I have written a Poem," he confided to Hearne, "Greek Heroicks of about 200 Verses, to maintain a new Point," namely, that the wisdom of Homer's *Iliad* had all been appropriated from the teaching of Solomon. He was ready with large proofs to amplify the point. "Mrs. Barnes firmly believes Solomon in his wisdome might make so useful a jest." Hearne was less happy with the "paradox," although Barnes tempted him with some evidence about one of Hearne's own peccadilloes, the great antiquity of Oxford. "In my Disquisitions on Homer and Solomon (which some admire, others not comprehending . . . but at most pass only for a *Lusus Poeticus* till the Arguments are canvassed), I found that King Ebrank founded your University, near Solomon's time, that it had a Name at first Hebrew and next Brittish. . . ." Although he dared not say more for the moment, he promised the evidence in the future.[33] Unfortunately, in 1712 Barnes died unexpectedly and Hearne was left, if ever he felt the inclination, to puzzle his way back to Solomon by himself.

[30]Barnes to Hearne, Mar. 7, 1710, Bodleian MS. Rawlinson Letters 24, no. 16; Hearne to Mrs. Barnes, Aug. 14, 1712, in *Remarks and Collections*, 3:430–31. Barnes claimed that the work had cost him £1,000: Barnes to Robert Harley, Earl of Oxford, Oct. 16, 1711, B.M. MS. Add. 4253, ff. 47v–48v.

[31]Hearne, *Remarks and Collections*, 2:333, 4:72–73.

[32]Barnes to Hearne, June 12, 1708, in ibid., 2:113. The doubtful subscriber was Hilkiah Bedford: ibid., 3:68.

[33]Hearne to Barnes, May 19, 1708, Bodleian MS. Rawlinson Letters 35, no. 15; Barnes to Hearne, ibid. 24, no. 14; Hearne, *Remarks and Collections*, 2:113. The poem is in Emmanuel College MS. 147.

3

One of Barnes's practical problems was the dedication. It was not easy to find the right patron. For a time he hoped for the queen, but eventually he settled for that most appropriate of aristocrats, the virtuoso earl of Pembroke. The intermediary was the London polymath Dr. John Woodward. Hearne had solicited the doctor for a subscription and so brought the two men together. Woodward was not likely to miss a scholarly occasion; about this time he was helping Joseph Wasse with a remarkable new edition of Sallust. He offered Barnes every assistance, proposed him for the Royal Society, and found him a patron when all else seemed lost. He was especially enthusiastic about the new Homer. "I am truly in Expectation," he wrote to Barnes, "of an extraordinary Performance." Across the Channel at Deventer, Gisbert Cuper waited with the same impatience.[34]

Woodward was probably not disappointed. The work, after all, had been scrupulously done. Even Bentley's biographer, who was no great admirer of Barnes, was compelled to admit it. "In truth his edition of Homer . . . is a more useful one to the reader than any which had preceded it; nay more, there was no edition published for ninety years after it, which upon the whole deserves the preference of the scholar."[35] Barnes had systematically incorporated the whole of previous scholarship into his text. He knew all the printed editions from the Florentine to the most recent Dutch version; he listed sixteen earlier versions in his preface. He had employed besides several hitherto unpublished manuscripts: the Corpus Christi codex, which he attributed (incorrectly) to the seventh century; the bishop of Ely's *Iliad*, which he found especially helpful for its valuable grammatical gloss, and of course the Bodleian manuscripts, for which he now publicly thanked his humane and learned Oxford friend. Besides these, he knew and used all the secondary literature on the subject, the ancient and medieval commentators, Eustathius, Hesychius, Suidas, and the rest, and the modern writers, Duport, Zachary Bogan, Rapin, Cuypers, Ludolf Kuster, and a great many others. With all this learning to help him, he could confidently lay out his own

[34]Barnes to Hearne, Aug. 15, 1710, Bodleian MS. Rawlinson Letters 24, no. 24; Hearne, *Remarks and Collections*, 3:41; Woodward to Hearne, Aug. 19, 1710, Rawlinson Letters 12, f. 9 (and also ff. 94, 96), and April 5, 1710, Rawlinson Letters 40, f. 70; Cuypers to Barnes, Rawlinson Letters 75, f. 82. Woodward presented Wasse's work to the Royal Society, April 5, 1710: Royal Society Journal Book, 10:236.

[35]Monk, *Life of Bentley*, 1:296. There is a glowing contemporary appreciation in a letter of Thomas Rud to Barnes, Mar. 13, 1710, Bodleian MS. Rawlinson Letters 40, ff. 248–49. See also Edward Harwood, *A View of the Various Editions of the Greek and Roman Classics*, 4th ed. (London, 1790), pp. 2–3. For a modern criticism of Barnes's "very careless" collation of the Moore codex, see M. R. James, *The Western Manuscripts in the Library at Trinity College, Cambridge*, 4 vols. (Cambridge, 1900–1904), 2:399.

version of the Greek text, emended both from the manuscripts and by conjecture; and add a new Latin translation, many scholia, variants, and notes. He printed the minor and supposititious works along with the *Iliad* and *Odyssey* and did not neglect the early lives of Homer that Dodwell and Hearne had urged upon him. The indexes at the end of each poem ("heavy work to me," he had complained to Hearne) alone occupied more than two hundred pages. No alteration, he claimed, had been made without notice. The scholar had everything that was needed to read Homer once again as he had originally intended.[36]

But not everyone was satisfied. Barnes had suspected that some new Zoilus might arise to disturb his labor. Even before publication, Hearne reported that "some malicious Persons had raised prejudices against your Book when they saw the first subscription."[37] Did they suspect Barnes's critical abilities? Unfortunately, Barnes did not let sleeping dogs lie. In his preface to the *Odyssey* he wrote of one *Homo inimicus* who was impudent, arrogant, and malicious. There was only one shoe in England that would really fit; apparently Barnes believed that his old enemy Richard Bentley had (among other things) blocked his ambition to dedicate Homer to the queen.[38]

It was well that the charge remained vague. Bentley did not mind a good quarrel, and he knew better than anyone in England just what was wrong with Barnes's Homer. As it was, he was satisfied to warn his rival indirectly, by writing to a mutual friend, the Cambridge classicist Dr. John Davies, "I read over his dedications and prefaces, and there I found very opprobrious words against enemies in general and one *Homo inimicus* in particular." He had decided, however, not to apply the words to himself; after all, he had been an early subscriber to the work and would have been a "useful director to him, if he had followed good advice." He chose rather to show Barnes what might happen if he pressed his point, falling especially on several passages that exemplified the editor's weakness. For one interpolation alone Bentley thought Barnes "deserved to be burnt," while for another, where he had misunderstood the obvious meaning of a phrase, he ought "to be turned out of the Chair." Barnes had bragged of employing Pollux, Suidas, and the other Greek lexicographers and grammarians, but had apparently learned nothing from them. Even more to the point, Bentley poured scorn upon the editor's conjectural emendations. "The business is to correct the place neatly," he

[36]"Yours is the only one that has been made upon a collation of MSS and all the former editions": Thomas Rud to Barnes, Mar. 13, 1710, Bodleian MS. Rawlinson Letters 40, ff. 248–49.

[37]Barnes to Hearne, n.d., Bodleian MS. Rawlinson Letters 24, no. 30; Hearne to Barnes, Oct. 31, 1709, ibid. 40, no. 80.

[38]Monk, *Life of Bentley*, 1:291–92.

reminded Davies, "that is, truly as the author wrote it, which he has not done but has gone clumsily about it. I'll give him the true lections without altering half a letter." (It is worth noticing that Bentley's example was generally accepted and eventually confirmed by a manuscript.) Barnes had not only botched the words but sullied the sense. If he intended to push the matter further, "in one week's time, I can send him an hundred such remarks as these. . . ."[39] Indeed, anyone who recalled Phalaris was not likely to doubt it. But Bentley was willing to keep it all to himself—or almost so[40]—and not hinder the sale of the book, if only Barnes would mend his manners and say no more. In fact, the book was not a popular success, but this was not Bentley's fault, and Barnes remained circumspect in the brief time that was left to him before his death.[41]

Nevertheless, Homer continued to interest Bentley and eventually the new Aristarchus (his title to both friends and enemies) began to contemplate an edition of his own. What he would have accomplished is now impossible to say, for he died with his work incomplete. That it would have been very different from Barnes's, however, is perfectly clear. For one thing, Bentley had a radically different notion of the composition and meaning of the epics, nearer to Perrault and Abbé d'Aubignac than the controversial view of the Cambridge professor of Greek. True modern that he was, he did not share the exalted idea of Homer that ascribed to him, among other things, the whole basic wisdom of Western civilization. Nor indeed did he believe the original work was as we now have it. As early as 1713 he remarked, in the midst of a religious quarrel with Anthony Collins, that the *Iliad* did not display, as his opponent had claimed, "a universal Knowledge of things." "Take my word for it, poor Homer in those circumstances and early time had never such aspiring thoughts. He wrote a sequel of Songs and Rhapsodies, to be sung by himself for small earnings and good cheer, at Festivals and other days of Merriment; the *Ilias* he made for the men, the *Odyssies* for the other Sex. These loose songs were not connected together in the form of an epic poem, till Pisistratus' time about 500 years after." Unfortunately, Bentley did not amplify his view, although his brief comment suggested matter enough for two and a half centuries' debate.[42]

[39]Bentley to Davies, n.d., in *The Correspondence of Richard Bentley*, ed. Christopher Wordsworth, 2 vols. (London, 1842), 1:411–15.

[40]But see the *Acta eruditorum*, January 1711, pp. 1, 54, 308; "Barnes, Joshua," in Kippis, *Biographia Britannica*, vol. 2.

[41]The British Museum does attribute an anonymous criticism of Bentley's Horace to Barnes, I do not know on what authority: *Aristarchus ampullans in cura Horationis* (London, 1712), by Phylargyrius Cantab. (shelf mark 1087 i 14).

[42]Richard Bentley, *Remarks upon a Discourse of Free-Thinking* (London, 1713), p. 18. For Collins's work, see his *Discourse of Free-Thinking* (London, 1713), p. 9. In a tantalizing letter

Bentley saw two other major flaws in Barnes's edition. (He never addressed himself to Barnes's suppressed convictions about the role of Solomon, although there is not much doubt about what he would have thought of them.) In the first place, he saw that Barnes had not sufficiently consulted the manuscript tradition. It is not clear whether he knew Joseph Wasse's criticism of the editions of Homer which appeared in the *Bibliotheca literaria* (1722). If he did, and the two men were close friends with a great mutual respect, he would have discovered there a very able discussion of the manuscripts which Barnes had overlooked.[43] (It was not for nothing that Wasse had collated some eighty codices for his own editorial labor on Sallust!) On this basis alone, Wasse had declared that "Homer's text is not well settled," although he thought there was much else to do besides. For his own projected edition, Bentley had his nephew scour the Vatican, while the Earl of Oxford lent him eventually eleven different copies. He saw that there could not be too many manuscripts, however confusing they might first appear.[44] Still, this was probably not his greatest strength, and despite his diligence he might well have overlooked the all-important Venetian codex, which Wasse had not failed to mention.[45] Bentley's true genius lay in his skill at criticism and conjectural emendation. Barnes and Hearne had shown what could be done with the conventional editorial techniques, with the painstaking collation of printed and manuscript editions and the accummulation of detail from the commentaries. What they had overlooked was the critical judgment required in employing them. It was not enough to bring together the evidence, as though it were all equivalent. They had not asked, much less attempted to discover, the value of what they had found. When Conrad van Uffenbach visited Bentley in 1710, he heard Bentley complain about the early editions of the classics. He said that

to the boy Francis Godolphin, Aug. 7, 1690, John Evelyn makes fun of Homer as "an old Blind Squalid Ballad-Singer, who with a Bagpipe and his trull, roam'd about to the wakes and Faires of Greece. . . ." But it is hard to know how to take these flippant remarks. See Christ Church Evelyn MS. Letter-Book (1699), f. 139. For a contemporary reply that also anticipates some recent notions, that even if the poems did originate in oral fashion, they had to be put together eventually in a complete and consistent way by a single poet, see Henry Felton, *A Dissertation on Reading the Classics and Forming a Just Style*, 2d ed. (London, 1715), pp. 22–23.

[43]Joseph Wasse, "A Memorial Concerning the Desiderata in Learning," in *Bibliotheca literaria* 2 (1722): 25. According to Whiston, Bentley used to say "that when he himself should be dead, Wasse would be the most learned man in England": John Nichols, *Literary Anecdotes of the Eighteenth Century*, 9 vols. (London, 1812–1815), 1:263. Wasse called Bentley "vir in omni literarum genere maximus" in his preface to *Sallust* (Cambridge, 1710).

[44]See the letters of Thomas Bentley to Richard Bentley, in *Correspondence of Bentley*, pp. 668–73; and Bentley's *Remarks upon a Discourse*, pp. 63–77.

[45]Wasse, "Memorial Concerning the Desiderata," p. 25.

they served no real purpose (though he admitted some exceptions) "except to shew how the *errores* accumulated gradually in successive editions."[46] In fact, everything depended on how the books and codices were employed. To the extent that one considered the matter, it should have been clear that the value of the manuscripts depended in the end on how good their readings were, rather than the reverse. In the absence of autographs, no manuscript, however ancient, could claim authority. Several manuscripts were not necessarily better than one (since they might all be derivatives); nor was an older manuscript necessarily a better manuscript. There was no avoiding the responsibility of judgment. Every muddled passage had to be individually examined and established. "Conjectural criticism" was thus essential to the understanding of the classical authors, and even a mistaken guess was more useful—since it was likely to provoke criticism and refutation—than an unnoticed corruption.[47] What was clear (to Bentley, anyway) was that the simple accumulation of material did not by itself ensure that one was getting any closer to the original.

Thus the chief weakness that Bentley spied in Barnes's text was its lack of judgment. He had shown this easily in his letter to Davies. But even Barnes's epitaph at Cambridge raised the issue; he was "as remarkable for an unhappy judgment," so it ran, "as for a happy memory!" Bentley used to say that Barnes "understood as much Greek as a Greek cobbler."[48] What he meant was that Barnes, despite an obvious facility in the language, did not really know how to go about understanding his authors. Bentley's own genius was in the emendation of the ancient texts, and in many works (from the obscure Byzantine Malelas to the immensely popular Horace) he showed how the restoration of the meaning of an author could proceed. The editor must seek out the true meaning of the text, even though this might compel him to *depart* from the manuscript. If his conjectures were not always correct or convincing, they were always important. Bentley had nearly all the requisite qualities for *divinatio*, so often lacking in his (and our) contemporaries; the ability in the words of A. E. Housman, "to read attentively, think correctly, omit no relevant consideration, and repress self-will . . . [to have a] just literary perception, congenial intimacy with the author, experience

---

[46]In J. E. B. Mayor, ed., *Cambridge under Queen Anne* (Cambridge, 1911), pp. 135–37.

[47]See Paul Maas, *Textual Criticism* (Oxford, 1958), pp. 11–21. Maas calls Bentley's youthful essay on Malelas "the incunabulum of conjectural criticism" (p. 34). See also A. E. Housman in several works excerpted in his *Selected Prose*, ed. John Carter (Cambridge, 1961), pp. 44, 59–61, 87–88.

[48]*Memoirs of the Grub Street Journal*, no. 78 (London, 1737), p. 89; "Barnes, Joshua," in Kippis, *Biographia Britannica*, vol. 2. Both Cumberland in his recollections of Bentley and Jebb in his biography prefer Bentley to have compared him with a blacksmith rather than a cobbler; both cited in J. E. Sandys, *A History of Classical Scholarship* 2d ed., 3 vols. (Cambridge, 1906–1908), 2:357–58.

which must have been won by study, and mother wit."[49] Of these things, only self-repression was lacking, and that was indeed the cause of most of Bentley's misfortunes.

In the end, however, it is hard to account for Bentley's greatest contribution to Homeric study, his discovery of the digamma, unless we elevate mother wit to genius and leave it at that.[50] The problem lay in the pronunciation of ancient Greek, knowledge of which had been quite lost for two thousand years. Bentley was already considering the difficulty in 1713, although he did not reveal his thoughts about it for some years. The Alexandrian critics did not have to worry about the fact that the Homeric verses as written did not exactly match the metrical quantities as recited, since they had inherited a living tradition about how the poems should be read. When that tradition was lost and Greek was pronounced as it was written, with English values for the Greek letters, the verses appeared suddenly awkward, even barbarous. It was rather like the recovery of Chaucerian verse, which at first also seemed primitive and unskillful because the correct pronunciation had been forgotten. Here, then, were further grounds for complaint against Homer. Bentley saw somehow that most of these difficulties could be overcome if it were only supposed that the Greek language had in the course of time lost a consonant; a letter with a sound like the Latin *V* and a form something like an *F*; that is, the digamma. For the time being there was only the scantiest evidence for Bentley's hypothesis in the Greek grammarians and in some newly published inscriptions, although much more was to be discovered after his death. (Hearne had noticed one possibility already—though he did not see its significance—in the persistence of the digamma in the Latin language.)[51] Bentley's chief argument was the new sense that it gave to Homer's meters. At the same time, there was a more profound implication. "It was the first direct proof," according to a modern scholar, "that within the limits of literary tradition the Greek language had been undergoing change, and had in fact a historical perspective and it emphasized by material evidence the width of the gulf which separated the period at which the Homeric poems were composed from the classical civilization which inherited them."[52] But this was just the insight most lacking to the scholarly world in 1700, to the moderns as

[49]Housman, Preface to *Manilius* (1930), in *Selected Prose*, p. 51.

[50]For what follows, see Monk, *Life of Bentley*, 1:361–67; R. C. Jebb, *Bentley* (London, 1878), pp. 145–54; Myres, *Homer and His Critics*, pp. 49–53.

[51]Hearne, *Remarks and Collections*, 2:153–54; Hearne to Lloyd, Jan. 1, 1712, in ibid., 4:287.

[52]Myres, *Homer and His Critics*, p. 52. According to Samuel Blackwell, who visited him in 1735, Bentley said that Aristarchus, Demetrius, et al. "were all dunces who knew nothing of the Digamma which he himself restored the use of, after it had been lost 2000 years": "Reliquiae Galeanae," in J. Nichols, *Bibliotheca Topographica Britannica*, 10 vols. (London, 1780–1795), 3:175.

well as the ancients, and it took nearly a century before Bentley's discovery was really assimilated.

What Bentley might have accomplished had he given Homer his undivided attention is a fascinating speculation. What is clear is that no single individual, however talented, could anticipate the whole course of philological scholarship afterward, and Bentley would not have arrived at the nineteenth- or twentieth-century Homer by himself. (Indeed, he characteristically overstretched his hunch even about the digamma.)[53] What he did do, if only incompletely, was to demonstrate better than any of his contemporaries what Greek philology was capable of doing for an understanding of Homer if systematically applied, and how much yet remained to be done. Incidentally, he saw some things that no one else in his time (not even that extraordinary philologist from Naples, his contemporary Giambattista Vico) was able to discover in the works of the greatest of the ancients.[54]

4

But if philology suggested one pathway back to Homer and his world, Greek antiquities offered another. The first was difficult enough to pursue in 1700; the second was even harder. Yet progress had been slow and steady here too, and the monuments, such as they were, were beginning to be turned to account along with the manuscripts. They were few because Greek archaeology was young and the East was difficult to get to. The Earl of Arundel, it is true, had almost carried off an entire gate from the ancient wall of Constantinople, and he successfully brought back to England many valuable Greek antiquities, manuscripts and coins, marbles and inscriptions. Many of these treasures were scattered after his death, but some of the marbles, especially the busts, fell into the hands of the Earl of Pembroke, and one of the most famous, a portrait of the blind Homer, was eventually purchased by Dr. Richard Mead. Here indeed was a discovery for the student of the *Iliad*.[55] The rest of Arundel's collections were shamefully neglected, although some of the inscriptions finally found a home at Oxford, where, much defaced

[53]See Jebb, *Bentley*, pp. 151–53.

[54]See my forthcoming article "Vico and the Quarrel between the Ancients and the Moderns," in *Journal of The History of Ideas*.

[55]See Hearne, *Remarks and Collections*, 8:71; A. H. Smith, *A Catalogue of Sculpture in the Department of Greek and Roman Antiquities of the British Museum*, 3 vols. (London, 1892–1904), 3:3. For Arundel, see F. S. Hervey, *The Life and Collections of Thomas Howard* (Cambridge, 1921); Adolf Michaelis, *Ancient Marbles in Great Britain*, trans. C. A. M. Fennell (Cambridge, 1882), pp. 50–54; David Howarth, *Lord Arundel and His Circle* (New Haven, 1985).

and still neglected, they continued to fascinate the antiquaries. Chief among them was the famous Parian Chronicle (among the Marmora Arundeliana) that had so interested Dodwell and Bentley and that now offered the possibility of help with the Homeric chronology.[56] For a time Hearne considered reediting it with the rest of the series but was left envious when the work fell to Michael Maittaire, who republished it with the commentaries of John Selden, Humphrey Prideaux, John Marsham, and others.[57]

On the whole, however, scholars were forced to learn about the cultural and the material worlds of the Greeks largely from ancient literature. The standard work on Greek antiquities at this time was by a very young but very learned Oxford scholar, John Potter, who was just beginning a career that carried him eventually to the primacy of the English church. The *Archaeologiae Graecae* incorporated in two thick volumes information gleaned from every kind of literary source to describe the life and customs of the ancient Greeks. Gronovius thought it worthy of his *Thesaurus*, where it appeared enlarged, and it was reprinted again and again in Britain well into the nineteenth century.[58] It was very useful, although it had two obvious flaws. Like most such works in its time, it tended to jumble together the customs and implements of the various periods of ancient history by extracting information from the sources wherever they could be found and regardless of date. And, as I have said, it ignored the material evidence.

Thus, the reader with a special interest in the shield of Achilles might be mildly disappointed with the account here, although he could still learn something from it. Potter devoted most of his second volume to the military affairs of the Greeks, to their arms, armies, and tactics, and if his compilation was a little mechanical, at least he saw that he must distinguish the life and culture of the ancient world from those of his own time. He was thus a modern in respect to both his skills and his prejudices. "The ancient Greeks," he begins, "were an innocent and unpolish'd sort of Mortals, wholly unacquainted with the modern and more refin'd Arts of War and Peace." Like his modern contemporaries,

[56]See, for example, Louis Ellies Du Pin, *The Universal Library of Historians*, 2 vols. (London, 1709), 1:197–98. The first edition was published by John Selden in 1628. According to Henry Fynes Clinton, the Parian marble set the fall of Troy in 1709 B.C. and Homer 302 years later: *Fasti Hellenici*, 3 vols. (Oxford, 1824–1834), 1:127n, 132n, 147, 122n.

[57]Hearne, *Remarks and Collections*, 8:6, 9:72. Hearne was contemptuous of Maittaire for not attempting a retranscription of the stones: ibid., 11:112 and passim. But Maittaire's qualifications were praised in a letter from William Stratford to Edward Harley, in *Historical Manuscript Commission Reports: Manuscripts of the Duke of Portland*, vol. 7 (London, 1901), p. 439.

[58]John Potter, *Archaeologiae Graecae*, 2 vols. (London, 1698–1699). It was still thought worthy of reprinting at Edinburgh in 1832, when it appeared with a life of Potter and an encomium for the work. In England editions were published as late as 1813 and 1818.

he saw that neither the morality nor the aesthetics of Homer was exactly like his own. Achilles, he noticed, entered upon a long and dangerous war without any excuse for a quarrel with the Trojans except an obligation to Agamemnon. And although the exploits of Homer's heroes might seem "strange and incredible in our Days," they were, he was sure, "accommodated to the manners of the Times of which he wrote."[59] Homer's world was simply not the world of 1700.

What, then, of the arms of the heroes? Potter combed his classical authors for references to the various implements of war, including shields. He found all the passages in the *Iliad* where Homer had described how they were made. "Ajax's buckler," for example, "was compos'd of seven folds of Hide, and covered with a single Plate of Brass"; another had three folds more. He took the evidence of the epic and combined it with the evidence of other sources, the Homeric scholiasts and Eustathius, and the Roman poets Virgil and Martial, and he attempted to depict the design of the ancient Greek shield: its circumference, boss, leather thong, and so on. He noticed that the Greeks had apparently employed different kinds of weapons: one shield was large enough to cover the entire body; others were smaller and differently shaped, although these seemed to have been used only after the heroic age. Potter even supplied some illustrations for his text. Of the famous shield of Achilles, however, the reader could discover only that it was "a Lecture of Philosophy, and contains a description of almost all the work of Nature."[60]

It was not that Potter was unaware of change in the Greek world or of anachronisms in the ancient writers. In discussing the sieges of classical times, he noticed, for example, that military engines were altogether lacking in Homer but that the Roman writer Statius had credited them to the Trojan War. Statius had clearly forgotten the "rude and unskilfull Age of this Hero, and to have form'd his Description from the Practices of his own Times."[61] The trouble was that Potter's method was defective. It was all right to use the literary evidence, but what did that amount to for the age of Homer, apart from what Homer had said himself? Even so, when had Homer written? Was his description of the Trojan War reliable and meant to be taken literally? Of what use was a scholiast here, or Eustathius, much less Virgil or Martial? But to be persuaded of the difficulties of the literary evidence was to be left uncertain indeed, a prospect that few who cared about Homer were prepared to accept. Potter's sense of anachronism and his critical skills in general were thus dulled by the hopeless deficiency of his sources. Nor was anyone really prepared to do any better. The only monograph to deal

[59]Ibid., 1:1–2.
[60]Ibid., 2:25.
[61]Ibid., p. 100.

with the subject, the *Antiquitatum Homericarum* of Everard Feithius (1677), was, despite the praise of Thomas Hearne, if anything, even less ambitious than Potter's work.[62] At least the Englishman had much to offer of value when he came eventually to classical Greece and more plentiful sources.

It was no wonder, then, that the archaeological evidence, meager as it was, was eagerly examined when it came to light. Here again, however, the same difficulty appeared as with the literary sources, and it was avoided in much the same way. Like the manuscripts, the monuments were also late, too late indeed to tell much about the age of the heroes or the culture of the *Iliad*. But that was hardly noticed at first, particularly while the evidence was scanty. The appetite at least was there, the first condition of a Homeric archaeology, however thin the opportunities. The traveller to the East was expected to bring back what he could and the East was growing more accessible with every passing year. The English scholar could at last hope for access to the material remains of ancient Greek civilization.

Undoubtedly the voyage to the Levant by Jacob Spon and George Wheler in 1675 proved a particularly stimulating event, especially since both published accounts that were widely read.[63] Like Spon, Wheler took pains to describe the monuments and to transcribe the inscriptions. His *Journey into Greece* (1682) was well illustrated besides. One could see engraved there, for example, the Parthenon, "absolutely both for Matter and Art, the most beautiful piece of Antiquity remaining in the World"; Wheler also supplied its exact dimensions and a description of its sculptures.[64] In Athens especially the traveler found lots of inscriptions, many of which he printed, and when he returned to England he brought some marbles to add to the Arundel collection at Oxford. The few bas-reliefs that he retained he scrupulously described in his narrative.

Wheler's voyage was exceptional, however; tourists to the East were still unusual. But the commercial traveler was another thing. These were the years when the Levant Company reached its apogee, and the consuls and chaplains associated with that enterprise were invariably gentlemen with a classical education and time on their hands.[65] Time and again they

[62]Hearne, *Remarks and Collections*, 3:108. Hearne did not think much of Potter's work but he may have been influenced by his politics; see ibid., 9:243–44.

[63]Jacob Spon, *Voyage d'Italie, de Dalmatie, de Grèce et du Levant, fait aux années 1675 et 1676*, 2 vols. (Amsterdam, 1679); George Wheler, *A Journey into Greece* (London, 1882). For some earlier and contemporary accounts, see James M. Morton, *Chapters on Medieval and Renaissance Visitors to Greek Lands* (Princeton, 1951).

[64]Wheler, *Journey into Greece*, p. 360.

[65]For the following, see John B. Pearson, *A Biographical Sketch of the Chaplains of the Levant Company, 1611–1706* (Cambridge, 1883); Alfred C. Wood, *A History of the Levant Company* (Oxford, 1935), pp. 229–49; "The English Embassy at Constantinople, 1660–1762," *English Historical Review* 40 (1925): 533–62; G. Ambrose, "English Traders at Aleppo (1658–1756)," *Economic History Review* 3 (1931–32): 246–67.

put their leisure to an antiquarian purpose and collected and described
what they could of the ancient Greek past. It was for example, Consul
William Raye's collection of two thousand Greek coins that absorbed
Thomas Hearne when he first arrived at the Bodleian. And the master of
Christ's College, Cambridge, John Covel, had been among the first
chaplains to take advantage of the opportunity. Altogether he spent sev-
en years in the Mediterranean (1670–1677), collecting ancient Greek
coins and manuscripts, touring the monuments, and recording his observations in several notebooks. Like many others in the Royal Society, he
combined an interest in natural history with a passion for antiquities.
Covel apparently planned to publish his journal; he began to copy it out
for the press, and with its many drawings, inscriptions, and minute
observations, it would probably have been a great success.[66] Ludolf Kuster praised it in his edition of Suidas and Hearne's appetite was whetted
by the description that he read there of Covel's "Itinerary thro' Greece,
containing several curious matters relating to the Language, Antiquities,
Rites and Religion of that Country." The journal would no doubt have
been "of great Advantage to the Republick of Letters," but for some
reason it never appeared. Covel, however, was not the only chaplain to
keep a record of his voyages that remained in manuscript.[67]

In 1695 a flurry of excitement was created by the appearance of several
further reports from the East which were published together in the *Philosophical Transactions*. The readers of that journal were asked to forgive the
interruption, which indeed dominated several issues; but the news of the
Eastern antiquities seemed more than sufficient to warrant their inclusion. "The Philosophical thinker," the editor apologized, "is desired to
excuse our breaking in upon the Subject of these Tracts" (i.e., natural
science) "as also exceeding the Bounds of an Extract. But we hope the
Curiosity of the Subject, joyned to the Desires of the Royal Society may
make an easie Apology suffice."[68] The accounts consisted of several
narratives by merchants of the Levant Company who had set out deliberately in search of antiquities. Although only merchants, they were "gen-

[66]See John Covell to Lady Harvey, Aug. 1, 1699, B.M. MS. Add. 22910, f. 97. Covell's
journal is in ibid. 22912–14; Cambridge University MS. Mm VI 54. Part of it was published without the antiquarian portions in *Early Voyages and Travels to the Levant*, ed. J. T.
Bent (London: Hakluyt Society, 1893), pp. 101–287; and part of it with some antiquarian
materials by F. W. Hasluck in *Annual of the British School at Athens* 11 (1904–5): 50–62, and
17 (1910–11): 105–27. See also Mayor, *Cambridge under Queen Anne*, pp. 147–52, 470–77.
[67]Hearne, *Remarks and Collections*, 1:86. See F. W. Hasluck, "Notes on Manuscripts in
the British Museum Relating to the Levant Geography and Travel," *Annual of the British
School at Athens* 12 (1905–6): 211–12. One successful work with only modest antiquarian
interest was Henry Maundrell, *A Journey from Aleppo to Jerusalem in 1697* (Oxford, 1703).
[68]William Halifax, "A Relation of a Voyage from Aleppo to Palmyra," *Philosophical
Transactions* 19 (1695–97): 175. See also the letters of Halifax to Thomas Hyde, Dec. 7,
1694, and to Thomas Smith, Dec. 17, 1698, in Bodleian MSS. Smith 45, f. 49; 50, f. 13.

erally Men of more than ordinary Birth and Education," and thus "not wanting . . . to make Voyages of Curiosity, to visit the celebrated Remains of Antiquity in these Parts." The inscriptions that they transcribed aroused particular interest. Edmund Halley employed them soon afterward for an account of the ancient city of Palmyra which was also published in the *Transactions*. Cuypers found them especially notable and hoped that they would be translated into Latin; later two of Hearne's friends, Thomas Smith (another chaplain who had been to the East) and Abednego Seller, quarreled over the same inscriptions in separate and more ambitious treatises.[69] To reconstruct the history of an ancient city from archaeological evidence was an exciting prospect; it was possible to learn things there absolutely unaccounted for in ancient literature. Once again, the illustration in the *Philosophical Transactions*, in this case a handsome foldout engraving of the ruins of Palmyra, was bound to stimulate curiosity.

A more interesting event of the kind occurred only a few years later. A young Oxford man named Edmund Chishull was appointed chaplain to the factory of the Levant Company at Smyrna. There he resided from late in 1698 to February 1702. Like Covel, he kept a journal, and like Covel again, he found it difficult to publish either it or the collections he had accumulated in the East. But he was more fortunate than Covel in his friends, one of whom especially, Dr. Richard Mead, encouraged and assisted him, so that eventually, many years later, both inscriptions and journal did indeed see the light, the latter posthumously. Chishull used Wheler's *Journal into Greece* as well as the ancient topographers (especially Strabo and Pausanias) to guide him on his excursions. Once again he sought out the inscriptions and copied them into his notebooks and journal. The difficulties of exploration were real; in any case the traveler had little time to look about. Chishull was very impressed with Ephesus, which he visited in 1699, "but it is to be wished that some curious traveller might remain two or three days there; during which time by removing the weeds and clearing the confused ruins he might possibly discover many valuable inscriptions." The implication was clear: had there been but time and resources, serious Greek archaeology might well have begun. Meanwhile, Chishull visited, among other places, what he thought was the ground of old Troy; unfortunately he was confined to the boat, though the weather was serene, and for three days he fed his

[69]Cuypers to Graevius, Bodleian MS. D'Orville 478, ff. 84–85, 137–40. For an account of the quarrel, transcribed as though for publication by Hearne, see Bodleian MS. Smith 115. Smith's work was titled *Inscriptiones Graecae Palmyrenorum* (London, 1698); Seller's, *The Antiquities of Palmyra* (London, 1696). See also *Philosophical Transactions* 19 (1695–97): 160–75 (for Halley), 597–619 (for Smith), 358–60 (for Seller).

eyes "with an eager and boundless curiosity."[70] He used Strabo to define the area and tried to give what he believed was the first clear and distinct account of its modern appearance. He thought he could discern just where the walls and buildings of the ancient city were and where the Greeks had camped, exactly as Homer had described, although he was aware that even in Strabo's day all traces of the site had disappeared. Indeed, there was now "nothing but the rubbish of new Ilium, or of the city once attempted there by Constantine." It was a long time before a Schliemann could appear to test his thesis.

On his way home, Chishull toured the continent and visited the great European antiquaries. At Deventer he met Gisbert Cuypers, "who entertained me very obligingly, shewed me his library, coins, inscriptions, and other curiosities."[71] Like most of his contemporaries, Cuypers was fascinated by the East and sought out every avenue to discover its remains. Chishull also met Van Dale, Gronovius, Perizonius, and Le Clerc, but here his journal is disappointing in its brevity. When he returned to England he guarded his manuscripts while he sought and won preferment, becoming, among other things, chaplain to the queen. He quarreled with Mr. Dodwell over the immortality of the soul and was condemned forever for it in Hearne's journals as (among other things) a "Confident, Opinionative and little Writer," "a very furious, violent, hot-headed proud man." Twenty years later Hearne had still not forgiven him, although he did concede that Chishull was a good Greek scholar with an excellent memory, if "little Judgment."[72]

While Chishull was readying his inscriptions for the press, the new consul at Smyrna was making some even more remarkable discoveries, and these too came eventually into Chishull's hands. William Sherard was a noted botanist, a friend of John Ray, and an antiquary as well. He succeeded the consul William Raye, for whom he had once worked, and remained at Smyrna until 1716, collecting assiduously, traveling occasionally, and keeping up a learned correspondence with England and the continent. (It was not easy; a letter took many months, if it arrived at all.) His collections, he wrote, were his only diversion abroad, if one could call a diversion something that cost so much "anger, fatigue, and expense."[73] In 1705 he took an extended trip to Asia Minor, the first of several, and copied out many inscriptions, which he sent to Chishull for

[70]Edmund Chishull, *Travels in Turkey and Back to England* (London, 1747), pp. 28, 34–35. George Sandys had also located the Trojan plain (1615), relying on Strabo, but dared not leave the coast to visit; see Warner C. Rice, "Early English Travellers to Greece and the Levant," *University of Michigan Essays and Studies in English and Comparative Literature* 10 (1933): 230.

[71]Chishull, *Travels in Turkey*, p. 162.

[72]Hearne, *Remarks and Collections*, 1:290; 2:92, 105, 109; 4:358, 364; 12:212.

[73]B.M. MS. Sloane 4062, f. 289. "Where there is neither learning, books, nor news, 'tis hard to finish out a letter": Sherard to Charlett [1707], Bodleian MS. Ballard 27, ff. 10–11.

publication. His companions included a doctor named Antonio Picenini, who also kept a journal. When this man returned to England in 1708, he too brought inscriptions for Chishull and visited the antiquaries. In 1709 Sherard and Picenini again traveled, and this time they discovered the so-called Sigean inscription, the most famous of all their finds. It too was copied out and sent eventually to Chishull.[74]

On no account could Chishull be hurried, however. In 1711 Sherard wrote to his friend Dr. Hans Sloane, "I have sent above an hundred Greek inscriptions to Mr. Chishull by this convoy besides what he got before from Gyra and other places. He writes me he shall be ready for them at the return of the ships, having the rest in order for the press." Four years later he was still waiting for the publication of the "great number of Greek inscriptions" which he had sent along. Meanwhile he copied many of them for Gisbert Cuypers, who intended to use them, so he explained, to "illustrate the new editions of his works he is upon with the addition of some new tracts." Unfortunately, Sherard's collection of medals, the equal at least of his inscriptions, was drastically reduced by the theft of some six hundred coins shortly before he returned to England.[75]

When Chishull did finally publish, he began with the Sigean inscription, which he brought out separately, illustrated, transcribed, translated, and explicated.[76] Sherard had discovered the inscription on a pillar at Sigeum, near the Dardanelles, over seven feet high, and it fascinated antiquaries at once both for its great age and for its archaic alphabet. It was inscribed in the arrangement known as boustrophedon, with the writing from right to left and from left to right in alternate lines. Hearne thought that "it must be very ancient" when he heard its character described in 1718.[77] Bentley saw it before publication and attempted a hasty and paradoxical interpretation that convinced no one.[78] A rumor circulated that Pembroke was to get the original for Wilton; it was true, but he

[74]Picenini's journal, "Diarium itinere per Aseae Minoris" (1705), is in the British Library, MS. Add. 6269, ff. 36–48; extracts appear in Richard Chandler, *Travels in Asia Minor* (Oxford, 1775), pp. 113, 217, 227, 231, 239–40. For Sherard's description, see his letter to Charlett, Mar. 25, 1709, Bodleian MS. Ballard 27, ff. 10–11; and to Sloane, June 29, 1706, B.M. MS. Sloane 4040, ff. 187–88. For the Sigean inscription, see Sherard to Charlett, Jan. 31, 1716, Bodleian MS. Ballard 27, ff. 7–8; and Sherard to Richardson, same date, in John Nichols, *Illustrations of the Literary History of the Eighteenth Century*, 8 vols. (London, 1817–1858), 1:347.

[75]Sherard to Sloane, B.M. MSS. Sloane 4062, f. 289, and 4044, ff. 21–22.

[76]Edmund Chishull, *Inscriptio Sigea antiquissima* (London, 1721); see F. H. Marshall, *The Collection of Ancient Greek Historical Inscriptions in the British Museum* (Oxford, 1916), pt. IV, sec. ii, pp. 148–60; E. L. Hicks and G. F. Hill, *A Manual of Greek Historical Inscriptions* (Oxford, 1901), pp. 8–10.

[77]Hearne, *Remarks and Collections*, 6:160. See also Chishull to Dr. John Woodward, Mar. 3, 1721, Osborn Collection, Yale University.

[78]Monk, *Life of Bentley*, 2:156–61; Chishull responded with an appendix to his *Antiquitates Asiaticae*.

was disappointed and had to settle for a copy.[79] The stone contained, in fact, two old inscriptions, one in Ionic, the other in Attic. Antiquaries invariably sought it out on their subsequent visits to the East, but it became a seat for the neighboring indigent, who gradually wore it away, until Lord Elgin finally carried it off a hundred years later for its eventual destination in the British Museum. By then it had become quite defaced.

Chishull's next work was an appendix to Dr. Mead's Harveian oration. He thought that he had found on a series of medals from Smyrna evidence for an ancient Greek college of physicians, and this discovery made a nice compliment to his patron. Apart from Mead, however, not many were persuaded, and Thomas Hearne was particularly scornful.[80] Finally in 1728, after much prodding, Chishull at length produced his magnum opus, the *Antiquitates Asiaticae*. Even so, it was only half done, or a few sheets more, when his death interrupted its completion.[81] Still, even as it was, it recorded an impressive harvest of antiquities and stirred a lot of interest. It reproduced the Sigean inscription and commentary again, along with several hundred other inscriptions, most of them unknown before. Sherard, Picenini, the Frenchman Joseph de Tournefort, Chishull himself, all contributed. Not everyone was happy with the commentary, but the work was very stimulating. Richard Bentley was provoked to amend one of the inscriptions and to an exchange of letters with Chishull, and this time he was proved right (against the testimony of two original witnesses) when the stone itself was brought to England and reexamined. Every word of the inscription turned out to be exactly as Bentley had conjectured.[82] The *Antiquitates Asiaticae* was a real increment to the sum of Greek learning and a portent for the future. Unhappily, there was little in the whole collection that could help directly with Homer. Like the coins and the busts, the inscriptions, even the one from

[79]"My Lord mention'd to Dr. Sherard (when he went Consul to Smyrna) what Pausanias said of such a Manner of Writing, and told him he would be at any Expence if he would employ some Grecians there to find (if possible) such a one. It was six years before that was found, a Copy of which he sent my Lord. But, he himself having never seen it (his Business not permitting him), the Copy was only in Modern Greek. My Lord writ to him that he would bear further Expence to send the Grecians again that he might have the very same Lines, and Ducts of the Letters; which was by the next Ship, sent him": B.M. MS. Stowe 1018, f. 50. Further efforts to obtain the stone itself failed, although Pembroke does seem eventually to have obtained another written in boustrophedon.

[80]Hearne, *Remarks and Collections*, 8:286. For Chishull's "Dissertatio de nummis quibusdam in Smyrnaeis," in Richard Mead's *Oratio anniversaria Harveiana* (London, 1723), see Nichols, *Literary Anecdotes*, 1:277–82; M. Maty, *Authentic Memoirs of the Life of Richard Mead* (London, 1755), p. 37; John Nichols, *Biographical and Literary Anecdotes of William Bowyer* (London, 1782), pp. 34–44.

[81]Some of the printed copies have an additional twelve pages. The manuscript is in B.M. MS. Add. 5106; it was prepared by John Ward, ibid. 6269, ff. 52ff.

[82]John Taylor printed a facsimile of the inscription with Bentley's letter and Chishull's reply with his *Commentarius ad legem decemviralem de inope debitore in partes dissecando* (Cambridge, 1742), pp. 23–28; see Monk, *Life of Bentley*, 2:411–12.

Sigeum, were all too late and concerned largely with other matters. That they opened a promising pathway back to ancient Greece, however, there is no gainsaying, and, of course, there was no telling what the future might bring.

5

Despite the absence of any digging and the accidental character of much of the discovery, the material remains of ancient Greece were thus beginning to be examined. And if at first little of the archaic Greek world was to be found among them, and nothing at all earlier, at least two Homeric monuments did catch the interest of antiquaries. Both were engraved and explicated many times during this period, and one of them found its way eventually into Pope's *Iliad*.

The more elaborate of the two was a stone that had been unearthed near Rome and was published first by Raphael Fabretti as an appendix to his *De Columna Traiani Syntagma*.[83] It was an example of what became known as *tabulae Iliacae*, pictorial representations of the Trojan Wars, devised perhaps for the instruction of schoolboys. This one was quite small but very elaborate, with many scenes and a long inscription. It thus permitted Fabretti to celebrate the Greek military antiquities along with the Roman, the Trojan Wars next to the Dacian. The Italian antiquary supplied a Latin version of the inscription and much commentary, but his work was soon amplified still further by a German scholar, Laurentius Begerus. Begerus was a protégé of Spanheim's who had made a European reputation for himself by publishing the antiquities first of the elector Palatine, then of the king of Prussia, for each of whom he served as librarian and keeper of antiquities. He was an accomplished numismatist and skilled in the task of explicating antiquities by reference to classical literature. His work was eagerly examined in England.[84] In Begerus's treatise on the Iliac tablet (1699), he separately illustrated the various scenes, which he reorganized and enlarged, and he furnished a full explanation for each, drawing principally on Homer but also employing many other classical authors and parallels from coins, inscriptions, and gems. The life of Achilles could thus be portrayed from his birth until the fall of Troy. Indeed, two plates showed him receiving his new armor, for

[83]Raphael Fabretti, "Explicatio veteris tabellae," in *De Columna Traiani Syntagma* (Rome, 1683), pp. 315–84. See Otto Jahn, *Griechische Bildercroniken* (Bonn, 1873), pp. 1–4.

[84]See Woodward to Hearne, May 3, 1711, in Hearne, *Remarks and Collections*, 3:158. A month later, Hearne was reading it: ibid., p. 182. Cuypers was another who found stimulation in the work: Bodleian MS. D'Orville 478, ff. 75–76, 89–92. It was titled *Thesaurus Brandenburgicus selectus, sive Gemmarum et numismatum graecorum, in Cimeliarchio electorali brandenburgico*, 3 vols. (Cologne, 1696–1700).

which Begerus quoted the appropriate verses from Homer and Virgil,
adding, by the way, three appropriate illustrations taken from a marble,
a coin, and a gem. It was an exemplary performance, and a recent writer
(underestimating Fabretti) has nominated it as the beginning of modern
Homeric archaeology.[85]

A few years later the great French scholar Bernard de Montfaucon
chose to explicate it again in his monumental *Antiquité expliquée*. This
work attempted to summarize the modern achievements of antiquarian
scholarship, both Latin and Greek, in fifteen lavishly illustrated folio
volumes. (It too was a work well known in England in the original and
in translation.) For it Montfaucon drew heavily on his predecessors—on
Spon, Fabretti, Begerus, and others—but he tried also to examine most
of the objects himself. One work he especially admired was Boivin on
the shield of Achilles, which he summarized in his section on ancient
armor. He was impressed that Boivin had been able to represent everything in Homer's description on a plate no more than seven or eight
inches in diameter, proof indeed that Homer's critics were mistaken
about the implausibility of the shield.[86] In succeeding chapters Montfaucon traversed the whole subject of the ancient shields, Greek and
Roman—*scutum*, *parma*, and *clypeus*—reproducing several of them.
Montfaucon intended a systematic illustrated commentary that covered
the whole of classical life arranged by topic. His object was not to exhaust the materials, which he saw was impossible, but to classify them
with appropriate examples. Better than anyone else Montfaucon understood the special value that the material remains of the past could have
for an understanding of antiquity. "A Verbal Description," he argued in
his preface, "however exact and particular it may be, can never give us
such a clear Idea of some things, as the Image and Picture of those things
themselves, drawn from the Life." This had been the limitation of Potter
and all the others who relied simply on literary sources. Indeed, it often
happened that upon discovering a new antiquity, one found that "the real
Image surpasses vastly the Idea we form'd from the Description of the
Writer or Picture of the Designer who only drew them from Conjecture."[87] Joseph Addison had made the same observation on his trip to
Rome. "How much easier," Addison continued, "will anyone understand the ancient History when he sees with his Eyes the Forms of all
their Gods, their Temples, and Rites of Sacrifice, when he views the sure

[85]Lorenz Begerus, *Bellum et excidium Trojanum ex antiquitatum reliquiis tabula* (Berlin,
1699); see Myres, *Homer and His Critics*, p. 55. For Begerus, see Jean-Pierre Niceron,
Mémoires pour servir à l'histoire des hommes illustres, 45 vols. (Paris, 1729–1745), 4:81; Charles
Ancillon, *Mémoires concernant les vies et les ouvrages de plusiers modernes célèbres* (Amsterdam,
1709), pp. 432–68.
[86]Bernard de Montfaucon, *Antiquity Explained*, trans. D. Humphreys, 10 vols. plus
5-vol. supplement (London, 1721–25), 4: chap. 3, esp. pp. 28–30.
[87]Ibid., supplement 1: preface.

Habits of most of the known and ancient Nations, the Method and Order of their Eating and Entertaining, the Form of their Vases, Weights and Measures, and publick Buildings, the Ceremonies of their Marriages, their Baths, the Instruments of their Musick, their Arts of War, the Funerals."[88] Antiquities could teach many things that could not be found in any classical author and illustrate the rest.

The Iliac table was represented by a foldout plate as large as the original. Montfaucon offered little new explanation but summarized the work of Fabretti and Begerus. "This Table," he explained, "contains the History of the Trojan War, and very elegantly done indeed, together with Inscriptions in Greek Characters upon every particular Action." The inscriptions not only accounted for the picture on the relief, they could be used to date the tablet. Montfaucon had spent many years studying Greek paleography, which science indeed he could well claim to have founded, as Mabillon had recently done for Latin. The form of the letters, he thought, bore out Fabretti's contention that it had been made later than Virgil. Montfaucon placed it tentatively in the early Empire, comparing the writing on it with an inscription on a gem that could be confidently assigned to that period. Modern writers agree.[89] He then succinctly described the 119 small scenes that appeared on the relief, including the series that portrayed the forging of Achilles' shield. He also translated the inscription. Unfortunately, the relief was on too small a scale (42 by 25 centimeters) to be useful for details. Indeed, it was hard to see just what value it could have for illustrating Homer, since it was late, incomplete, and often unfaithful to the text, although a knowledge of the *Iliad* was obviously helpful in understanding it. "As to this Iliak Table," Montfaucon concluded, "I do not see there's any great Matter to be learnt from it, for the Figures in it are so very small, that one can neither distinguish well the Form of the Habits or of the Arms." (Thus even Begerus's amplification did not help with Achilles' shield.) Montfaucon thought that it would be much better to write a commentary on the *Iliad* than one on the table.

Still, the history of Troy was "very necessary to be known," and Montfaucon had some afterthoughts when he printed his supplement.[90] The Iliac tablet and the related antiquities that he appended could not tell

[88]Joseph Addison, *Remarks on Several Parts of Italy in the Years 1701, 1702, 1703* (London, 1705), in *Miscellaneous Works*, ed. A. C. Guthkelch, 2 vols. (London, 1914), 2:13–237; cf. Montfaucon, *Antiquity Explained*, 1: preface, and supplement, 1: preface.

[89]Besides Jahn, *Griechische Bildercroniken,* see Umberto Mancuso, "La tabula Iliaca del Museo Capitolino," *Atti dell'Accademia dei Lincei,* ser. 5, Memorie delle classe di scienze morali, storiche, e filologiche 14 (1909–1916): 662; Kurt Weitzmann, "A Tabula Odysseaca," *American Journal of Archaeology* 45 (1941): 161–81; A. H. Smith, *A Catalogue of Sculpture in the Department of Greek and Roman Antiquities of the British Museum,* 3 vols. (London, 1892), 3:254–55.

[90]Montfaucon, *Antiquity Explained*, supplement, 3:433–36.

much about Homer, but they could at least reveal what the ancients had *thought* about the Trojan War and the *Iliad*. Indirectly, they might thus yield something of value; in any case, the monument bore definitely on Homer's reputation and meaning in antiquity. Moreover, as a series of illustrations for the epic, it was clearly better than most of the (equally late) Homeric commentaries, and it gave a kind of reality to the *Iliad* that the turgid Eustathius, for example, was not likely to afford. If only it had been a more impressive work of art!

Here, at least, the other famous Homeric monument of this period had an advantage. It too was a relief that had been discovered in Italy in the seventeenth century and was entitled at once the *Apotheosis of Homer*. This is the piece noticed by Kuster and Barnes and Madame Dacier. From 1671 to 1714 and beyond, it was treated by a succession of writers, including Gisbert Cuypers, and illustrated many times. As with the Trojan table, the concern was to identify and explain the figures, and here again there was an inscription to help. But the game was made more interesting in this case because the help was only partial and several of the figures remained enigmatic.

There is no need to survey the whole literature that this famous monument produced. It was first described by Athanasius Kircher, the antiquarian polymath who is famous for his fanciful explications of Egyptian hieroglyphics, and who gave the details of its discovery and illustrated it.[91] It seems that it was unearthed in the mid–seventeenth century on the Appian Way near the ancient city of Bovillae, on the property of the Colonna family, whence it was removed to their Roman palace. (Eventually it too found its way to the British Museum.) Kircher noticed that the site had once belonged to the emperor Claudius, who had a special love for Greek letters and knew his Homer by heart, and so he thought it should be placed about that time. Modern writers agree that it belongs to an earlier period, however, and associate it rather with the Ptolemys, though no one has ever suggested any close connection with the age of Homer.[92] It was Cuypers who lavished the most careful attention on the identification and explanation of the figures, correcting Kircher and clarifying much. Cuypers was an avowed modern who applauded Wotton's defense of philology and carried on a vast correspondence with savants all over Europe. He left a few problems unresolved, and they continued to divide the antiquaries and to interest modern students, but he was able at least to establish the basic iconography of the stone beyond

[91]Athanasius Kircher, *Latium* (Amsterdam, 1671), pp. 81–87.
[92]See, for example, Smith, *Catalogue of Sculpture*, 3:244–54; Roger Hinks, *Myth and Allegory in Ancient Art* (London, 1939), pp. 99–101; Gisela Richter, *The Portraits of the Greeks*, 2 vols. (London, 1965), 1:54.

The Apotheosis of Homer, engraved in Gisbertus Cuperus, *Apotheosis vel Consecratio Homeri* (1683)

question.[93] Bayle could hardly praise his work enough for its usefulness and erudition.[94] Inevitably it became widely known and was sought out by knowledgeable visitors to Rome as one of the greatest of the ancient monuments.

One curious traveler who inquired for it at the turn of the century was the young Joseph Addison. His visit to Rome was the highlight of a tour that he made through Europe from 1701 to 1703. "A Man who is in Rome," he wrote later, "can scarce see an Object that does not call to Mind a Piece of a Latin Poet or Historian."[95] Addison was no antiquary—not, at least, in the full-fledged fashion of Cuypers or Montfaucon—but he was the perfect example of the gifted amateur, knowledgeable in the classics and modestly acquainted with the antiquarian literature. In Rome he had the services of a skilled Italian guide, Francesco de' Ficoroni, a writer on antiquities, who later claimed to have taught him all he knew.[96] Addison became particularly knowledgeable about Roman coins and afterward wrote a popular manual on the subject. With the help of Ficoroni and some reading in Graevius and elsewhere, he was ready to visit the sites of his beloved authors. The description of his tour at once became a popular success. In Rome he had sought out the monuments systematically, visiting all the great collections, public and private, and now he described them in the account of his journey. Among the bas-reliefs that he remembered, the best was the *Apotheosis of Homer*, "where the Thought is extremely noble."[97]

Addison's description was based essentially on Cuypers's explanation, though he does not mention any source. It consisted, he wrote, "of a Groupe of Figures cut in the same Block of Marble, and rising one above another by Four or Five different Ascents." At the top was Jupiter with a thunderbolt presiding over the ceremony. (Here Addison offered the appropriate Greek verses from Homer.) "Immediately beneath him are the Figures of the Nine Muses, suppos'd to be celebrating the Praises of

[93]Gisbertus Cuperus, *Apotheosis vel consecratio Homeri* (Amsterdam, 1683). Cuypers's progress on the work from 1672 may be followed in his letters to Graevius in Bodleian MS. Rawlinson Letters 75. In December 1695 he wrote to the abbé Nicaise to applaud Wotton's role in the battle of the books, although he insisted that (like Wotton) he opposed the "bigotry" of the dogmatic moderns as much as the ancients. See Cuperus to Nicaise, in *Letters de critique, d'histoire, de littérature, etc.* (Amsterdam, 1742), pp. 440–42.

[94]Pierre Bayle, *Nouvelles de la république des lettres*, March 1684, p. 83.

[95]Addison, *Remarks*, p. 140.

[96]See Joseph Spence, *Observations, Anecdotes, and Characters of Books and Men*, ed. James M. Osborn, 2 vols. (Oxford, 1966), 1:331. Of Ficoroni, Spence writes in 1732: "He is one of those people that we call antiquaries here. Their business is to go about Rome to shew strangers the Antiquities, Palaces, Pictures, and Statues that are there without number. . . . He is so old that he has been conductor to Mr. Addison when at Rome, and was to Ld. Middlesex at the time we stay'd there": B.M. MS. Egerton 2234, ff. 70–71; *Observations*, 2:501, 508, 510, 513. Le Président Charles de Brosses was less complimentary in his *Lettres familières sur l'Italie*, ed. Yvonne Bezard, 2 vols. (Paris, 1931), 1:94–95, 254.

[97]Addison, *Remarks*, p. 157.

the Poet. Homer himself is plac'd at one End of the lowest Row, sitting in a Chair of State, that is supported on each Side by a Figure of a kneeling Woman." It was Cuypers who had identified these figures, the one as the *Iliad* (the sword in her hand representing the actions of Achilles), the other as the *Odyssey* (an "Aplustre," as Addison explained, representing the voyage of Ulysses). "About the Poet's Feet are creeping a Couple of Mice as an Emblem of the *Batrachomyomachia*." There was some dispute over these matters—Madame Dacier and Montfoucon, for example, preferred to think that the mice were in fact rats who were, like Zoilus, gnawing away at Homer's reputation—but Cuypers's opinion seems to have carried the day. "Behind the Chair stands Time, and the Genius of the Earth." (These identifications were easier now, since the inscription furnished the labels.) The two figures were distinguished by what seemed to be their appropriate attributes and were putting a garland on the poet's head, "to imitate the mighty Reputation that he has gain'd in all Ages, and in all Nations of the World." Here was obvious fuel for the ancients in their quarrel with Homer's critics. "Before him," Addison continued, "stands an Altar with a Bull ready to be Sacrific'd to the new God, and behind the Victim a Train of the several Vertues that are represented in Homer's Works. . . ." (These figures were also helpfully labeled.) Unfortunately, at least two of them remained enigmatic, though Addison passed them by in silence, and not all of the detail was indisputable either. (Was the mountain, for example, Parnassus or Olympus? Did it have one or two peaks?) These were questions for the antiquaries, however, not for belles lettres, and indeed they soon inspired more learned treatises and conjectures: from Spanheim, Gronovius, Montfaucon, and others. In 1714, on the eve of Pope's *Iliad*, a good deal of this material was summarized for the general reader by J. C. Schott in his *Explanation nouvelle de l'Apothéose d'Homère* (1714). In any case, the collective labor of the antiquaries had clarified much about the monument and brought it public attention that few other antiquities enjoyed in the period.

If, then, these various monuments—the *Apotheosis* and the Iliac tablet, the Arundel Marbles, the Sigean inscription, and the bust of Homer—all helped to call attention to modern archaeology and its possibilities, it was nevertheless true, and more than a little disappointing, that they did not shed much new light on Homer, and that everything remained still to be done. Yet the monuments had begun at last to rival the manuscripts in the hopes that they inspired for the future. Both Addison and Montfaucon were unequivocal in their conviction that most antiquities still lay beneath the ground.[98] And those that had been so far unearthed could at

[98]Ibid., p. 152; Montfaucon, *Antiquity Explained*, 5:113. See also Cuper to Graevius, Bodleian MS. Rawlinson Letters 75, ff. 15–16.

least be employed to illustrate (if not to explain) the ancient poetry. It was of consuming interest at a time when the merits and even the identity of Homer were in question to be able to see him or his poetry portrayed as the ancients had envisioned them. Certainly the skills of the philologist and the antiquary had begun to look necessary to an understanding or appreciation of Homer's world and (thus) to the poetry of the *Iliad*. The famous shield of Achilles seemed a perfect case. Homer had described it, vividly and in detail, at the very climax of his poem, and it seemed to rank among the greatest of classical antiquities. As a result, its meaning and even its reality had come to absorb both the wits and the scholars, the ancients and the moderns, throughout the period. It remains to be seen just exactly what, with all their various skills, they made of it.

Chapter Six

Pope's *Iliad*

I

Alexander Pope's poetic vocation seems to have begun in childhood, despite a haphazard and irregular education. He taught himself to write, so he said, by imitating the ancients. Was there any other way? If his schooling left him at twelve years old scarcely able to construe Cicero's *De officiis* (so he remembered), he soon applied himself so diligently to the classical authors that he could translate into verse "many Passages of Homer, Virgil, Ovid, Statius and the most eminent Latin and Greek Poets." He also read the French critics for theory and even tried his hand at epic, "in Imitation of the Ancients." When that proved too ambitious, he turned instead to pastoral, recalling perhaps that his hero, Virgil, had done the very same thing.[1] Were all these early efforts only imitations? he was asked many years later. "Just that," replied Pope. By concentrating all attention on the Greek and Latin poets, he formed his own taste, which he insisted in 1743 "was very near as good as it is now."[2] In the quarrel between the ancients and the moderns, Pope had necessarily to find his place, and the ancients were, inevitably, his first recourse.

Pastoral poetry must seem an odd place for combat, but Pope's choice of the genre was bound to draw him into battle.[3] Pastoral was, of course, a specifically ancient affair, authorized by the works of Theocritus and

[1]From an account by Jonathan Richardson dictated by Pope (1730), in George Sherburn, "New Anecdotes about Alexander Pope," *Notes and Queries*, n.s. 5 (August 1958): 347; see also Joseph Spence, *Observations, Anecdotes, and Characters of Books and Men*, ed. James M. Osborn, 2 vols. (Oxford, 1966) 1:21.

[2]Spence, *Observations*, 1:11, 18. One of the moderns he read with appreciation was Sir William Temple (pp. 19, 170).

[3]See in general J. E. Congleton, "Theories of Pastoral Poetry in England, 1684–1717," *Studies in Philology* 41 (1944): 544–75.

Virgil, and revived and imitated during the Renaissance by Tasso and Spenser, among a host of others. Here as elsewhere, the familiar problem of the relationship of the author to his models, the basic concern of all *ancienneté*, had unavoidably arisen. It was the Frenchman Fontenelle who brought the issue to a head in his characteristically radical modern way. (We have seen how conservative Wotton was by contrast.) As a young man, Fontenelle had also tried his hand at pastoral, but modernized with characteristic abandon. When his contemporaries fell upon him for his transgressions, he was forced to defend himself and, as a consequence, modernity altogether. As Wotton saw, this was the real occasion for his *Digression sur les anciens et les modernes* and the provocation to Temple, and it was the immediate occasion for the French *querelle*.[4]

Young Pope had read Fontenelle and the quarrel over pastoral and was ready to take sides. He was only sixteen years old or so when he wrote his own poems, but he already understood the implications of his position; in the *Essay on Criticism*, a few years later, he laid them bare. During the years between, he continued to read voraciously the best poets and critics, both ancient and modern, in English, French, and Latin, assimilating easily their arguments and their styles. In the meanwhile he began circulating his pastorals among his friends and was flattered to be asked to publish them by the enterprising printer Jacob Tonson. In 1709 they made their first appearance in a motley collection of other works.[5] Pope's career as a poet—and as a controversialist—had begun.

Pope introduced the pastorals with a little prose piece setting out his views, but the preface was not published until 1717. He intended in it nothing less than a summary of the whole "substance of those numerous dissertations the Criticks have made on the subject."[6] His method was eclectic, to choose from among his predecessors the best ideas and put them together as a justification for his own prose work. He did not bother to cite his sources, but modern commentators have repaired the deficiency and we can now trace almost every thought in the piece. It is clear that in the dispute between the ancients and moderns on pastoral, the young poet had turned decisively to the ancients and thoroughly against Fontenelle.

Pope began by accepting the notion that pastoral started with the shepherds just after Creation, in that happy golden time when life was ideally simple, tranquil, and natural. Afterward the art was perfected by

[4]William Wotton, *Reflections upon Ancient and Modern Learning* (London, 1694), p. 4. See Alain Niderst, *Fontenelle et la recherche de lui-même (1657–1702)* (Paris, 1972), pp. 366–76.

[5]Jacob Tonson to Pope, Apr. 20, 1706, in Alexander Pope, *Correspondence*, ed. George Sherburn, 5 vols. (Oxford, 1956), 1:17. The pastorals appeared in *Poetical Miscellanies: The Sixth Part* (London, 1709), pp. 721–51.

[6]*The Poems of Alexander Pope*, ed. J. Butt et al., 10 vols. (New Haven, 1961–1967), *Poems*, 1:23.

Theocritus and Virgil, "the only undisputed Authors" of their kind. Pope was willing to admit a few minor defects in each—Theocritus was sometimes overlong in his descriptions and too rustic in his manners, Virgil not simple enough in style—but he believed that the two ancient poets had created unchallenged models for the rest of time. The best poets since were those who "have most endeavor'd to make these ancients their pattern." Spenser should therefore be compared with Theocritus, Pope with the ancients and with Spenser. If his own poetry had any merit, he concludes, "it is to be attributed to the good old authors, whose works as I had leisure to study, so I hope I have not wanted care to imitate." But it was Virgil who offered him the very best model, because it was Virgil who had shown him how to "refine upon an original."[7] Typically, the modern prefers to imitate an ancient imitating an ancient.

2

Pope's opinions were reinforced by his friends and patrons. In these years they were older men such as William Walsh and Sir William Trumbull, the playwright William Wycherley, and George Granville, Lord Lansdowne—wits and men of the world who dabbled in literature, very like Sir William Temple in social standing and outlook. Walsh had inherited money and aspired to position; he became a member of the House of Commons and a courtier and remained an outspoken Whig until the end of his days. He was well known for his fashionable dress and his amorous poetry, above all for his friendship with Dryden. "He was a Man of very good Understanding, in spight of his being a Beau."[8] In the 1690s he frequented Will's, the famous coffeehouse, where the great poet held forth, and he quickly won the old man's affection. In 1692 he published some pastorals of his own. Pope says that he first met Walsh when the older man learned of his poems and asked to see them; that was about 1704. They corresponded regularly thereafter, mostly about literary mat-

---

[7]Ibid., pp. 30–33. Pope's "Spring" has been characterized as "Virgil seen through Dryden," his "Summer" as Virgil seen through Spenser, and so on; see ibid., pp. 44–45, 47, 49ff. Joseph Warton says that the passages that imitated the classics and that were marked with the letter *P* in the *Poems* were by the printer William Bowyer at Pope's request: ibid., p. 6on. For Virgil as a "patchwork of Theocritan phrases and motives," see Henry W. Prescott, *The Development of Virgil's Art* (Chicago, 1927), p. 94; and for Pope imitating Virgil imitating Theocritus, see Charles Segal, "Virgil's Caelatum Opus: An Interpretation of the Third Eclogue," *American Journal of Philology* 88 (1967): 277–308. For the special importance of Virgil on the young Pope, see David B. Morris, "Virgilian Attitudes in Pope's *Windsor-Forest*," *Texas Studies in Literature and Language* 15 (1973): 231–50.

[8]So John Dennis in his attack on Pope, *Reflections Critical and Satyrical upon a late Rhapsody, call'd an Essay on Criticism* (1711), quoted in Sherburn, "New Anecdotes," p. 81.

ters. Pope visited his friend at his country estate; Walsh died just before Pope's pastoral poems appeared in print.[9]

In many ways, Walsh's relations with Dryden anticipated his friendship with Pope; his letters show how much the older man admired him and why he should have appealed to Pope. On reading some of Walsh's little squibs, Dryden wrote, "I knew before this discovery that you were ingenious, but not that you were a Poet, and one of the best that these times produce or that succeeding times can expect!"[10] Dryden approved his friend's prose style also, comparing it favorably with those of Cicero and Fontenelle. (Walsh preferred the judgment of his critics, that it resembled Dryden's.) Dryden calls Walsh "Padron," and this may account for the obvious flattery that marked their friendship, but there was more to it than that. In one exchange they agreed about the merit of Martial's epigrams and Boileau's epistolary imitations, and Dryden publicly pronounced Walsh the "best Critic of our nation." He may really have meant it, although Samuel Johnson was skeptical, but Walsh did take a serious interest in criticism.[11] He meant to write a large treatise on the subject and outlined it for Dryden in 1693. It looks as though he intended to defend Dryden's alleged modernity against the dogmatic *ancienneté* of Thomas Rymer. He meant to champion all those who were willing "to defy the Chorus of the Ancients." Dryden was pleased; not only present poets, "but all who are to come in England, will thanke you for freeing them from the too servile imitation of the Ancients."[12]

The treatise never got written, so we cannot be altogether sure what Walsh would have said. Rymer was an ancient in a very special and dogmatic sense, and Dryden protests here (as elsewhere) not against using the ancients as models but against a "too servile imitation."[13] It was an old problem, anticipated even in antiquity and renewed with Erasmus's famous dialogue, the *Ciceronianus*, which incidentally was reprinted at Oxford in 1693. Erasmus, like Dryden, wanted freedom for the writer, not from imitation but from servility, so he too may be said

[9]For Pope and Walsh (and most other Popean matters), see Maynard Mack, *Alexander Pope: A Life* (New Haven, 1985), pp. 110–17.

[10]Dryden to William Walsh, n.d., in *The Letters of John Dryden*, ed. Charles E. Ward (Durham, 1942), pp. 30–31. See Phyllis Freeman, "William Walsh and Dryden: Recently Recovered Letters," *Review of English Studies* 24 (1984): 195–202.

[11]Dryden, Postscript to the *Aeneid* (1697), in John Dryden, *Essays*, ed. W. P. Ker, 2 vols. (Oxford, 1926), 2:244; Samuel Johnson, *Lives of the Poets*, ed. George Birkbeck Hill, 3 vols. (London, 1905), 1:328–30.

[12]Dryden to Walsh, May 9 or 10 and Dec. 12, 1693, in *Letters of Dryden*, pp. 52–55, 61–64; see also Dryden, dedication to the *Third Miscellany*, in his *Works*, ed. Walter Scott, rev. George Saintsbury, 18 vols. (Edinburgh, 1882–1893), 13:60.

[13]Pope was more appreciative of Rymer. "He is generally right, though rather too severe in his opinions . . . on the whole one of the best critics we ever had"; Spence, *Observations*, 1:205.

to have argued for the modern side. Indeed, most critical discussion throughout the early modern period was concerned primarily with the nature and extent of classical imitation. And if there was no one in England who was eager to defend an abject servility, there was apparently no one yet ready to defend a complete originality without reference to the past. On these matters there was rather a long gradation of opinion, and Walsh seems to have agreed completely with Dryden. Nor did either show the slightest sympathy with the critical claims of the new philology.[14]

Pope's friendship was with Walsh, not Dryden, although he remembered seeing the great man once at Will's coffeehouse.[15] Like everyone else, however, he read Dryden and was profoundly affected by him as a poet, critic, and translator. In 1697 Dryden had turned Virgil into English and written once again about poetry, reiterating the views of a lifetime. There he repeated the commonplace notion that epic was "the greatest work which the soul of man is capable to perform," and that Homer and Virgil were the two principal models, indeed the two greatest poets of all time. "By reading Homer," Dryden wrote, "Virgil was taught to imitate his invention, that is, to imitate like him. . . . And thus I might imitate Virgil, if I were capable of writing an heroic poem and yet the invention be my own: but I should avoid servile copying. I would not give the same story under other names, with the same characters in the same order, and with the same sequel."[16]

Dryden's Virgil was particularly important for the young Pope and a chief inspiration for his Homer. It was not only Dryden's verse and criticism that attracted his attention, however (including, in the preface, a mild rebuke of Fontenelle), but the contributions of several others that accompanied it. For example, the work included an anonymous essay on pastoral that introduced the *Eclogues*, and was widely attributed to Walsh. In fact, it was by another friend of Dryden's, Kneightly Chetwood, and Pope certainly read it with enthusiasm and pillaged it for ideas.[17] Chetwood held strong opinions. Writing in the midst of the bat-

[14]"Not to follow the Dutch commentators always, may be forgiven to a man who thinks them, in the general, heavy dull-witted fellows, fit only to gloss on their own dull poets. But I leave a further satire on their wit, till I have a better opportunity . . .": Dryden, "Examen poeticum" (1693), in *Of Dramatic Poesy and Other Critical Essays*, ed. George Watson, 2 vols. (London, 1962), 2:164.

[15]See Sherburn, "New Anecdotes," p. 347; and Pope to Wycherley, Dec. 26, 1704, in Pope, *Correspondence*, 1:1–2.

[16]Dryden, Preface to *The Works of Virgil* (London, 1697), in *Of Dramatic Poesy*, 2:223–57.

[17]For the authorship, see Dryden to Jacob Tonson, Dec. 1697, in *The Letters of John Dryden*, pp. 98–100; for Chetwood, see *Dictionary of National Biography* and Helen M. Hooker, "Dryden's *Georgics* and English Predecessors," *Huntington Library Quarterly* 9 (1945–46): 298–300.

books, he was provoked by the moderns, particularly Fontenelle. The Frenchman had prefaced his own pastorals with a review of his predecessors and found them all, ancients and moderns alike, wanting. In place of classical precedent, Fontenelle hoped to substitute reason, "the Rules and true Idea of Things." So he argued against the example of Theocritus that the pastoral world should not be realistic and against Virgil that it should not be utterly fanciful. Shepherds should be portrayed neither as real shepherds nor as inhabitants of a mythical Golden Age. For Fontenelle and the moderns, history began with a primitive age and only later grew more polite. For the modern poet, pastoral should be modernized to mirror or idealize the modern age, and Fontenelle tried to describe the appropriate thought and garb, "the Pitch of Wit which Shepherds ought to have, and the Style they should use." He realizes that his barbs at the ancient poets will sting. "I have spoken here," he concludes, "with a great deal of Freedom of Theocritus and Virgil, not withstanding they are Ancients; and I do not doubt but that I shall be esteem'd one of the Profane by those Pedants who profess a kind of Religion which consists in worshipping the Ancients." Nevertheless, even Fontenelle did not dare to deny the merits of the ancients altogether, or their use. "I have partly approv'd and partly censur'd them, as if they had been some living Authors whom I saw every day. And therein lies the Sacrilege!"[18] "He is shy in declaring his mind," Wotton complained, "at least in arraigning the Ancients, whose Reputations were already established; though it is plain he would be well understood to give the Moderns the Preference in Poetry and Oratory, as well as in Philology and Mathematicks."[19]

Nevertheless, Chetwood felt the offense. His preface to Dryden's *Pastorals* was coupled with "a short Defence of Virgil against some of the Reflections of Monsieur Fontenelle." It is a pungent restatement of the position of the "ancients" and must surely have appealed to Temple and the men of Christ Church. According to Chetwood, poetry preceded prose in the history of literature, and pastoral is the oldest kind of verse. It should therefore reflect the simplicity and innocence of the first people on earth, in contrast to the fanciful refinement of the moderns. The ancients had invented all the useful arts: agriculture, mathematics, literature, music, natural science, "whilst the Moderns, like Extravagant Heirs, made rich by their Industry, ingratefully deride the good Old Gentlemen, who left them their Estate." As a result, pastoral in particular had fallen on hard times, not helped either by the neglect of the critics both ancient and modern. Presumably it could not occur to Chetwood

---

[18]See Fontenelle, "Of Pastorals," in René Le Bossu, *Epick Poetry*, trans. Pierre Motteux (London, 1695), pp. 294–95.
[19]Wotton, *Reflections*, p. 4.

(consistently) that Aristotle had overlooked pastoral in the *Poetics* because there was no pastoral yet. But why he failed to mention the French critic René Rapin is less clear, unless to conceal his own principal source. All Chetwood says is that even Boileau (the best of the moderns, "because he never loses the Ancients out of his Sight") had neglected the subject.[20] But Rapin had very consciously set out to repair Aristotle's omission in a Latin tract of 1659 which was turned into English by Dryden's friend Thomas Creech and used as the preface to his version of Theocritus in 1684.[21] Here the ancient rules were abstracted from the practice of the two "fathers" and exemplars of pastoral poetry, Theocritus and Virgil, and proposed as guides to the modern poet. Fontenelle, no doubt, had Rapin particularly in mind when he complained of the pedants who had made a religion of antiquity, and Chetwood must surely have had him in mind when he decided to answer Fontenelle.

In any case, Chetwood decided that it was necessary to refute Fontenelle's criticism of Virgil point by point. When, for example, Fontenelle criticized the Roman poet for making his shepherds speak above their station about such philosophical matters as the creation of the world, Chetwood reminds us (drawing upon "the fragments of the Phoenician Antiquity" that had been assembled by the learned Huet)[22] that it was a Chaldean shepherd who had taught the Egyptians and Greeks about these things. Nor was Virgil's shepherd quoting Epicurus; he had kept exactly to the ancient Mosaic physics, just like that ingenious modern writer Thomas Burnet, "who will by no means allow Mountains to be coeval with the World." Like Rapin, Chetwood believed that the ancients had invented the rules that governed good poetry. It was up to the modern author, therefore, to observe the rules and imitate the examples, as Virgil had done and Fontenelle had not. All poetry was imitation; good poetry was an imitation of nature, created both by direct observation and indirectly by the example of good imitators. Virgil was not only "faithful to the Character of Antiquity but copies after Nature herself." The young poet who read these words could not have agreed more.

Yet Chetwood thought that even a scrupulous adherence to the rules and precedents could not make up for the advantages that the ancients had in their languages, so superior to anything since. "Latin is but a corrupt dialect of Greek; and the French, Spanish, and Italian, a corruption of the Latine, and therefore a Man might as well go about to per-

---

[20]Kneightly Chetwood, "Preface to the Pastorals," in *The Works of Virgil*, trans. John Dryden (London, 1697), n.p.

[21]René Rapin, "Dissertatio de carmine pastorali," *Eclogae sacrae* (1659), trans. Thomas Creech, in Theocritus, *Idylliums* (London, 1684); see James E. Congleton, *Theories of Pastoral Poetry in England, 1684–1798* (Gainesville, Fla., 1952), pp. 53–71.

[22]This is a reference to Huet's famous *Demonstratio evangelica* (1679).

suade one that Vinegar is a Nobler Liquor than Wine, as that the modern Composition can be as graceful and harmonious as the Latine it self." One bad consequence was the introduction of rhyme, unknown to classical usage. Every modern suffered the same irreparable disadvantage, so that there were hardly ten lines in Cicero or Demosthenes, or even in the catalogue of ships in Homer's *Iliad*, which are "not more harmonious, more truly Rhythmical, than most of the French or English Sonnets; and therefore they lose, at least, one half of their native Beauty by Translation." (Here Chetwood was far more pessimistic than Dryden.) To put the modern French above the ancient Greeks or Romans, as Fontenelle and Perrault had done, was thus ridiculous. To think that any modern piece could be valued ten or twelve ages hence, as the ancients were now, seemed to Chetwood, as it did to Temple, inconceivable.

Although Chetwood's essay appears to have had Dryden's sanction, it did not perfectly reflect his ideas, or even those of Walsh, who was just then setting his hand to pastoral. Both poets accepted the necessity of imitation and the importance of comparison with the ancients, but each was distinctly more optimistic about the results. The gap between the ancients and moderns on this point was not very wide, however. Walsh was certainly deferential to the ancients in the little preface that he affixed to his own collection of poems in 1692 and that won Dryden's praise. He begins there with an evaluation of ancient and modern love poetry that is all in favor of the classical Romans. He finds their passion more realistic and moving than anything in Petrarch or the moderns. "It grieves me," he writes gallantly, "that the Ancients, who could never have handsomer Women than we have, should nevertheless be so much more in love than we are!" But he holds out some hope anyway that the ancients might be rivaled. Of the three kinds of love poetry, pastoral, elegy, and lyric, he thinks that pastoral is the lowest and (therefore) the most suitable for love, since that passion has the chief effect of humbling. "The Design ought to be the representing the Life of a Shepherd, not only by talking of Sheep and Fields, but by shewing us the Truth, Sincerity and Innocence that accompanies that sort of Life." Walsh's models remain Theocritus and Virgil, but he recognizes that they have faults, though once again the margin of difference seems small. "For though I know our Masters, Theocritus and Virgil, have not always conform'd in this Point of Innocence; Theocritus in his Daphnis, having made his Love too wanton, and Virgil in his Alexis, plac'd his Passion upon a Boy." He would have preferred Daphnis to be more modest and Alexis to have chosen a woman, "if we may be allow'd to censure those whom we must always reverence."[23]

---

[23]William Walsh, *Letters and Poems, Amorous and Gallant* (London, 1692), Preface, sig. [A5–A6].

Even if we allow for some irony here, it is clear that Walsh was still a good distance from Fontenelle in the sliding scale that separates the two opposite poles in the battle of the books. Walsh shared the underlying proposition of all the moderns (including Wotton and Fontenelle) that human nature is the same in all ages but that circumstances alter cases and that some periods are more favorable to learning than others. "And if they had not as Famous Men now, it was because they have not the same Advantages they had then."[24] On the other hand, he seems to have been willing to allow the actual superiority of the ancient poets—at least so far—and here he is closer to Wotton than to Fontenelle. But Walsh's essay is too slight to bear much critical weight, as indeed most people have found of his poetry. He may have been the "best critic" of his time, but if so, it was his conversation, not his publication, that must have made him so.

Still, for Pope in 1705, Walsh was a great man who had been praised by a greater one. When Walsh asked to see his pastorals, he was flattered and grateful to receive his criticism. "The Preface," Walsh wrote, "is very judicious and very learned; and the Verses tender and easy. The Author . . . has taken very freely from the Ancients, but what he has mixt of his own with theirs, is no way inferior to what he has taken from them. 'Tis no flattery at all to say, that Virgil had written nothing so good at his Age!"[25] Walsh's praise of Pope's classical imitation was very welcome, but it raised again the perennial problem of the practicing poet, "How far the liberty of Borrowing may extend?" Pope's view was not far from Dryden's. "I have defended it sometimes by saying, that it seems not so much the Perfection of Sense, to say things that have never been said before, as to express those best that have been said oftenest; and that Writers in the case of borrowing from others, are like Trees which of themselves wou'd produce only one sort of Fruit, but by being grafted upon others, may yield variety."[26] Had he perhaps taken too much license in the *Pastorals*? Walsh replied at once with a classical precedent. "'Tis very evident the best Latin Poets have extended this very far; and none so far as Virgil who is the best of them. As for the Greek Poets, if we cannot trace them so plainly, 'tis because we have none before them. 'Tis evident that most of them borrow'd freely from Homer, and Homer has been accus'd of borrowing from those that wrote before him." And he concluded categorically with the commonplace notion that "the best of the modern Poets in all Languages, are those that have the nearest copied the Ancients."[27] Since the usual subjects of poetry had all been

[24]William Walsh, *A Dialogue Concerning Women, Being a Defense of the Sex* (London, 1691), p. 100.

[25]Walsh to Wycherley, Apr. 20, 1705, in Pope, *Correspondence*, 1:7.

[26]Pope to Walsh, July 2, 1706, in ibid., pp. 18–20.

[27]Walsh to Pope, July 20, 1706, in ibid., pp. 20–21.

explored already, it was plain that whoever chose to write upon them now could only repeat what had been said before. This certainly was Pope's view in his *Essay on Criticism* only a few years later, and again when he republished his *Pastorals* in 1717.[28]

And so Pope continued to write and Walsh to offer advice. The older man took a consistent line: imitate the ancients but without pedantry. "Correctness" was very important; but neither servile imitation nor following mere "mechanical Rules" was tolerable. The guidance was certainly commonplace, but Pope assured Walsh that he was "glad to corroborate them by some great Authorities which I have met in Tully and Quintilian."[29] The young poet was working his way backward to the sources of the humanist tradition. Walsh himself noted that even the moderns were likely to admit the superiority of the ancient poets, however unwittingly. "I have seen some of these that would hardly allow any one good Ode in Horace, who cry Virgil wants fancy, and that Homer is very incorrect," and yet "they are great admirers of Ovid and Lucian."[30] Moreover, their own faults were only too obvious in their own verses. (Walsh was probably thinking of Fontenelle and Perrault.) To all of this Pope clearly gave assent, and he seems honestly to have meant the flattering lines in his *Essay on Criticism*:

> Such late was Walsh, the Muses Judge and Friend,
> Who justly knew to blame or to command.

As for pastoral, the battle between new and old continued for a time but without resolution.[31]

---

[28]Maynard Mack writes of Pope's *Essay on Criticism* (1711), "Here a young author's enthusiasm for Homer, Virgil, Horace, and some others has propelled him into a veneration altogether too undiscriminating, not to say servile": *Alexander Pope*, p. 176. He is thinking particularly of such lines as 119–80.

[29]Pope to Walsh, Oct. 22, 1706, in Pope, *Correspondence*, 1:22–25; and Pope's recollections, recorded by Spence and quoted in George Sherburn, *The Early Career of Alexander Pope* (Oxford, 1934), p. 56. See too the manuscript "Alterations to the Pastoralls (the Solutions of the Queries were written by Mr. Walsh)," in Pope, *Poems*, 1:477–82. For Quintilian as a favorite author, see Spence, *Observations*, 1:20, 231; Pope, *Essay on Criticism*, in *Poems*, 1: ll. 669–70; p. 315n.

[30]Walsh to Pope, Sept. 9, 1706, in Pope, *Correspondence*, 1:21–22.

[31]For Pope and Gay vs. Ambrose Philips (Pope in the *Guardian*, no. 40; Gay in *The Shepherd's Week*, etc.), see Congleton, *Theories of Pastoral Poetry*, pp. 80–87; Sherburn, *Early Career*, pp. 117ff.; Hoyt Trowbridge, "Pope, Gay, and the *Shepherd's Week*," *Modern Language Quarterly* 5 (1944): 79–88; and the commentary of John Gay, *Poetry and Prose*, ed. V. A. Dearing and Charles Beckwith, 2 vols. (Oxford 1974), 1:90–126, 511–40; Ambrose Philips, *The Poems*, ed. M. G. Segar (Oxford, 1937), pp. xix–xxiii. For a spirited "modern" defense, see Edward Howard, *An Essay on Pastoral* (London, 1695), Proem.

3

Pope was just twenty-five in the autumn of 1713 when he first announced his intention of translating the *Iliad*.[32] To his pastoral poetry he
had added some more verse and prose, including an anonymous *Essay on·
Criticism* and *The Rape of the Lock*. He was off to a promising start and
already on familiar terms with many of the wits, including Addison and
Steele. He had contributed to both the *Spectator* and the *Guardian* and had
had a public quarrel or two. What was it that prompted him, at this point
in his career, a young man who had just discovered his own genius for
poetry, who despised pedantic learning and was eager for reputation, to
spend the next six or seven years translating a familiar poem in a language with which he was not at ease and with an erudition he found
tedious and demeaning?

In part, it was sheer infatuation with Homer. Homer, he recalled,
"was the first author that made me catch the itch of poetry, when I read
him in childhood."[33] When he was about twelve, he wrote a play based
on the *Iliad*, which some of his schoolfellows produced, and there are
other early indications of his devotion to the poet. Among these early
efforts was a version of the Sarpedon incident in the poem, which was
first published in Tonson's *Miscellanies* (1709) and which Pope later used
for his complete work. His older friend Sir William Trumbull ("who
loved very much to read and talk of the classics in his retirement")
approved it heartily and urged on him the whole poem.[34] On the other
hand, Trumbull's nephew Ralph Bridges was less impressed and pointed
out several inaccuracies.[35] Pope blamed his predecessors George Chap-

---

[32]No copy of the proposals seems to have survived, but they were issued in October
and summarized in the advertisement to the *Rape of the Lock*, 2d ed. (1714). For this and
what follows, see vols. 7 and 8 of the Twickenham edition of Pope's *Poems*, with its
voluminous introductory matter by Maynard Mack et al. Among the many studies I have
found especially useful are Reginald H. Griffith, *Alexander Pope as Critic and Humanist*,
Princeton Studies in English 1 (Princeton, 1929); Sherburn, *Early Career*; Douglas Knight,
Pope and the Heroic Tradition: A Critical Study of the Iliad (New Haven, 1951); Maynard
Mack, ed., *Essential Articles for the Study of Alexander Pope* (Hamden, Conn., 1964); Hans-
Joachim Zimmermann, *Alexander Popes noten zu Homer* (Heidelberg, 1966).

[33]Pope, *Correspondence*, 1:297–98; Spence, *Observations*, 1:12, 2:13–14; Mack, *Alexander
Pope*, pp. 45–47. See too Pope's recollections of his childhood to Jonathan Richardson, in
Sherburn, "New Anecdotes," pp. 346–47.

[34]Spence, *Observations*, 1:31; Pope, *Correspondence*, 1:45. The text is in Pope, *Poems*,
1:99, 447–62. Trumbull has been characterized as Pope's tutor in the classics and compared
with Sir William Temple: Pope, *Correspondence*, 1:10n.

[35]For the correspondence between Trumbull and Bridges relating to Pope, see Sherburn, "New Anecdotes," see p. 344. The originals are in Bodleian MS. English Letters D
59; some specimens of Bridges's criticism are at ff. 90–93. Others are now in the British
Library, Trumbull Papers, Add. 136, along with the correspondence between Trumbull
and Pope, Add. 139, published by George Sherburn in "Letters of Alexander Pope, Chiefly

man and Thomas Hobbes, whose authority he was forced to use because of his own "imperfectness in the Language." Apparently he knew little Greek and less of Greek scholarship. If this was a disappointing admission for a prospective translator, it did not deter Pope, who told Bridges that he preferred "the Authority of one true Poet above that of twenty Critics or Commentatours." But he did promise to repair something of his ignorance by reading "all I can procure, to make up that way, for my own want of Critical understanding in the original Beauties of Homer." Trumbull promised him a copy of Barnes's edition of the *Iliad*, if he would only continue his translation.[36]

Meanwhile, Pope persisted in his *ancienneté*. The battle of the books had by no means been forgotten when news of the *querelle* rekindled the issues, as we can see from a contemporary diary by the young Dudley Ryder. (Ryder preferred Madame Dacier and Boileau to Perrault, but he liked Wotton best of all for steering a middle way).[37] With the pastorals Pope had set himself deliberately against Fontenelle and modernity. Now, in an anonymous contribution to the *Guardian*, he declared himself forthrightly, echoing Boileau. "Nature being still the same, it is impossible for any modern Writer to paint her otherwise than the Ancients have done." A little later that year, Addison backed him up in the *Spectator*.[38] But the *Guardian* followed up with a series of essays in 1715, probably by Thomas Tickell, that considered again how far one "may lawfully deviate from the Ancients," and that restored Fontenelle's idea of a "modern" (in this case English) pastoral.[39] Pope was not put off. In the preface to his poems (1717) he repeated the now familiar idea. "All that is left to us," he wrote, "is to recommend our productions by the imitation of the Ancients: and it will be found true, that in every Age, the highest character for sense and learning has been obtain'd by those who have been most indebted to them. For to say truth, whatever is very good sense must have been common sense at all times; and what we call learning, is but

to Sir William Trumbull," *Review of English Studies* 33 (1958): 388–406. The manuscript of Pope's *Iliad* translation also records an interchange between the two men: B.M. MS. Add. 4807, ff. 194ff. It was printed for the first time in the *European Magazine and London Review*, June 1787, pp. 389–92, where the remarks, which appear without signatures in the original, are labeled. See also Mack, *Alexander Pope*, pp. 104–9.

[36]Pope to Bridges, Apr. 5, 1708, in Pope, *Correspondence*, 1:43–45; Trumbull to Bridges, Oct. 18, 1708, Bodleian MS. English Letters D 59, f. 56.

[37]*The Diary of Dudley Ryder, 1715–16*, ed. William Matthews (London, 1739), pp. 30–1, 263–64. Ryder was "mightily pleased with the wit and extravagant humour" of *A Tale of a Tub* but typically worried about its irreligion (p. 114).

[38]"On False Criticks," *Guardian*, no. 12, Mar. 25, 1713; *Prose Works of Alexander Pope*, ed. Norman Ault (Oxford, 1936), 1:88–92; Addison, in *Spectator*, no. 253, Dec. 11, 1711, reviewing Pope's *Essay on Criticism*.

[39]*Guardian*, nos. 22–23, and also 28, 30, 32 (1715); see Congleton, *Theories of Pastoral Poetry*, p. 568. Another argument for Fontenelle and modern pastoral appears in Thomas Purney, *A Full Enquiry into the True Nature of Pastoral* (1717), ed. Earl Wasserman (London: Augustan Reprint Society, 1948).

the knowledge of our predecessors." A modern writer, a poet in English like himself, could hope to be read only "in one Island, and to be thrown aside at the end of one Age."[40] It was, of course, a sentiment that would surely have pleased Sir William Temple, as it clearly did Pope's new friends Jonathan Swift and Francis Atterbury.

But fidelity to the ancients and a genuine love for Homer were not Pope's only motives; there were practical considerations as well. As we have seen, public interest in the poet was growing, fanned by the contest between the ancients and the moderns. At the very end of his life, Dryden himself had begun to translate the *Iliad*.[41] From a publisher's point of view, the time could not have been better chosen for a new translation. It is true that several English versions had already been issued, but by 1713 they all seemed seriously out of date. Meanwhile, Joshua Barnes had supplied a Greek and Latin text to whet the appetite of the public and to serve the needs of the translator. And best of all, the *querelle* had heated up in France with Homer at the center once again, and every thrust was followed eagerly in England, either directly in French or in English translation.[42]

Among the first to take advantage of the situation and help to impel Pope was the young divine Richard Fiddes. When he learned (through Swift) that Pope was beginning to work on Homer, he began to waver in his own intentions and decided to throw his notes together into a brief tract that would consider the problems of translation and (incidentally) help to advertise Pope's proposals. While he was composing his thoughts, the translation of La Motte appeared like an electric shock. Fiddes was unmoved by its arguments against Homer, although he did acknowlege that there were "a great many beautiful Remarks in it," especially about the poet's morality.[43] When at last Fiddes's own little tract appeared, Hearne found it a "mean and trivial performance," but it did have the effect certainly of reinforcing Pope's design.[44] Like the young poet, Fiddes had only contempt for the learned critics with their

[40]Pope, *Poems*, 1:6–7; cf. *Essay on Criticism*, ll. 476–78, in ibid., 1:292–93. Later Pope argued the same point with Bolingbroke, *Correspondence*, 2:219–20, 226–29; and in the *Essay on Man*, ll. 169–99.

[41]We must not overlook Dryden's influence here too. Dryden accepted the current view that epic was "certainly the greatest work of human nature," and the *Iliad* "the best and most elaborate Heroic Poem ever written": *Essays*, 2:43. Pope knew Dryden's comparison of Homer and Virgil in the preface to his *Aeneid* and his translation of the first book of the *Iliad*. In the end, Dryden preferred Homer to Virgil; see Dryden to Montague, Oct. 1699, in *Letters of Dryden*, pp. 120–21.

[42]When the abbé Prévost visited England in 1728, he found almost everyone he met could speak French; see Emile Audrà, *L'Influence française dans l'oeuvre de Pope* (Paris, 1931), p. 119.

[43]Richard Fiddes to Robert Harley, Earl of Oxford, July 6, 1714, B.M. MS. Birch 4253, f. 66.

[44]Thomas Hearne, *Remarks and Collections*, ed. C. E. Doble et al., 11 vols. (Oxford 1885–1931) 4:367, 8:396–97.

"grammatical Niceties." They were never more out of place, he insisted, "than upon an Author wherein all things are great, entertaining and instructive." He thought that the translator should concentrate rather on making the beauties of the poem accessible, without trying, like Madame Dacier, to justify everything.[45] This was certainly Pope's intention, and he probably approved Fiddes's strictures against Scaliger and against Barnes's connection of the *Iliad* with Solomon. At the least, the little tract was good advertisement for his new translation.

It was another matter with Thomas Tickell, who also began a translation about this time. Whatever his motives, which remain obscure, it looks as though his effort was a response to Pope's project, rather than a cause of it.[46] And since Addison seemed to be involved, it signaled the end of Pope's friendship with the Whigs, the beginning of enmity, and a new association with the "Scriblerians," that little group of comic satirists who loved to poke fun at ponderous learning. In the end, Tickell stopped with only the first book, and Pope's translation won a clear victory. But the rivalry undoubtedly added to the peculiar public interest that surrounded Homer at this time.

In short, everything seemed to conspire in 1713–14 to promote the cause of a new English *Iliad*. Suffice it to say that the terms offered to Pope, the money and the reputation, were inducements at least as powerful as a disinterested admiration for the poet. In the end Pope made a small fortune from the *Iliad*, and the list of subscribers, with seventeen dukes, three marquises, forty-nine earls, seven duchesses, and assorted other celebrities, more than assured his reputation. Indeed, success led Pope eventually to an *Odyssey* as well as an *Iliad* and to undisputed recognition as England's greatest living poet.

4

Pope signed a contract for the *Iliad* with the publisher, Bernard Lintot, on March 23, 1714, and immediately set to work. Six volumes and as many years later, the work was done. However, much more was required now than a mere translation; no one touching Homer in 1714 could avoid the *querelle* or fail to take a stand. Pope must declare himself. Like Madame Dacier, his model thoughout, he chose therefore to buttress his work with all the armory of critical learning: with preface, life of Homer, extended notes, even poetical indexes. As Addison suggested to

[45]Richard Fiddes, *A Prefatory Epistle Concerning some Remarks to be Publish'd on Homer's Iliad* (London, 1714), p. 75.

[46]See Richard Eustace Tickell, *Thomas Tickell* (London, 1931), pp. 38–48; Sherburn, *Early Career*, pp. 129–30; Norman Ault, "Pope and Addison," *Review of English Studies* 17 (1941): 428–51.

him (while they were still friends), "the Prose will require as much care as the Poetry."[47] It was true; and the finished *Iliad* contained at least as much criticism as translation, as much prose as poetry. Everyone agreed on the necessity, especially perhaps Pope's fellow Scriblerians. Unfailingly they either contributed to the translator's erudition or they applauded it. Swift even seems to have thought that Pope's learned notes and essays were more successful than his translation, while Dr. Arbuthnot argued that it was Pope's scholarship that set him above his rival, Thomas Tickell.[48] Apparently, and without a semblance of embarrassment, they condemned the learning of the scholars Bentley, Barnes, and Dodwell, only to insist on something that looked very much like it in the activities of their friend.

But, of course, Pope's erudition was illusory. Like Dr. Arbuthnot, Pope thought that he could employ the learning of others (to the extent that it was necessary) without impairing his own artistic integrity. There is scholarship in the *Iliad* but it is not Pope's; moreover, it is a scholarship much less impressive than first appears, since it (deliberately) avoided the more abstruse and difficult achievements of Homeric philology and antiquities. Yet when all is said and done, it remains that Pope was compelled to attend to problems and disciplines that he publicly condemned and privately despised. He was a victim of the same paradox that seems to have plagued all the ancients: to have detested pedantry and yet be compelled to rely on it.

Pope's main difficulty was that his Greek remained uncertain and that his scholarship was nonexistent. It is, of course, hard to know exactly how competent he was in classical Greek. How does one measure ability in a dead language? Joshua Barnes, it is true, could compose fresh poetry in classical Greek, and it is almost certain that Pope could not. Richard Bentley could recover a lost consonant in the Greek language, and it is perfectly certain that Pope could not. His critics argued that he knew no Greek at all, but that is hardly likely either. He naturally proclaimed his own competence when he could, but he never directly answered these charges. He could recite some of Homer by heart[49] and his notes are sprinkled with Greek phrases and comments about Homer's meters. Yet there is little sign that he read any of the other Greek writers, and one of his collaborators once accused him of being unable to comprehend even

---

[47]Addison to Pope, Nov. 2, 1713, in Pope, *Correspondence*, 1:196. Dr. Johnson suggested that without the additions, the result would have amounted to mere pamphlets and thus failed to satisfy the subscribers; see *Lives of the Poets*, 3:115, 240. Pope seems to have developed his ideas about the commentary after he began his translation: Pope, *Correspondence*, 1:246–47.

[48]Swift to Pope, June 28, 1715, in Pope, *Correspondence*, 1:246–47; Arbuthnot to Pope, July 9, 1715, in ibid., p. 305.

[49]So said Dr. Hugh Blair, according to James Boswell, *Life of Samuel Johnson*, ed. George Birkbeck Hill, rev. L. F. Powell, 6 vols. (Oxford, 1934–1964), 3:403.

ten lines of Eustathius.[50] Since Pope used Latin, French, and English translations of the *Iliad* for his own, as well as the services of friends, we can never know for sure. We must be satisfied with Dr. Johnson's opinion: Pope had some knowledge of the language, but "with an irregular education and a course of life of which much seems to have passed in conversation, it is not likely that he overflowed with Greek."[51]

As for Pope's deficiency in Greek scholarship, we can be more certain; he was in any case less embarrassed to admit it. He had promised his friend Bridges that he would read the commentaries, but there is no sign that he ever tried. Yet the knowledge they supplied was essential. "Homer," he wrote afterward, "seems to have taken upon him the character of an Historian, Antiquary, Divine and Professor of Arts and Science, as well as a Poet. . . . All these ought to be preserv'd by a faithful Translator, who in some measure takes the place of Homer. . . ."[52] There were subtler problems also, since Pope saw that the precise meaning of the poet's language depended on an intimate knowledge of Homer's world. Yet the importance of scholarship only gradually dawned on him. At first (early in 1714) he wrote boastfully to Addison: "There are indeed, a sort of underlying auxiliars to the difficulty of a work call'd Commentators and Criticks who wou'd frighten many people by their number and bulk and perplex our progress under pretence of fortifying their author." Not Pope, however. "I think there may be found a method of coming at the main work by a more speedy and gallant way than mining under ground, that is, by using the Poetical Engines, Wings, and flying over their heads."[53] But try as he would, he could not avoid their learning, especially when he elected, later that year, to enlarge his notes. His one recourse was to turn to a more accomplished friend, his fellow Scriblerian Thomas Parnell. "You are a Generous Author," he pleaded with him, "I a Hackney Scribler, You are a Grecian and bred at the University, I a poor Englishman of my own Educating. . . ." Parnell alone could turn to account those awesome volumes of Homeric commentary; without his help, he was lost. When his assistant suddenly vanished into Ireland, Pope's despair was genuine, although he hid it characteristically beneath a bantering letter. "The Minute I lost you, Eustathius with nine hundred pages and nine thousand Contractions of the Greek Character Arose to my view, Spondanus with all his Auxilliaries in Number a thousand pages (value three shillings) and Dacier's

[50]William Broome to Elijah Fenton, June 15, 1728, in Pope, *Correspondence*, 2:499–500.

[51]Johnson, *Lives of the Poets*, 3:113. This view is endorsed by Norman Callan in Pope, *Works*, 7:lxxxiii; and by Douglas Knight, *Pope and the Heroic Tradition* (New Haven, 1951), pp. 111–13.

[52]Pope's postscript to the *Odyssey*, in *Poems*, 1:390.

[53]Pope to Addison, Jan. 30, 1714, in Pope, *Correspondence*, 1:208–9. The original letter seems to have been addressed to John Caryll, May 1, but was revised for publication and readdressed to Addison.

three Volumes, Barnes's two, Valterie's three, Cuperus half in Greek, Leo Allatius three parts in Greek, Scaliger, Macrobius and (worse then 'em all) Aulus Gellius: All these Push'd upon my Soul at once and over-whelm'd me under a Fitt of the Head Ache. I curs'd them all Religiously, Damn'd my best friends among the rest, and even blasphem'd Homer himself."[54]

No matter; when Parnell was away, there were others to help. There was William Broome, one of the trio who had already translated Madame Dacier's Homer into English. He was a capable Greek scholar in comfortable circumstances, and he offered his services freely.[55] Pope asked him to read Eustathius and make extracts for him. "Be so kind to take this method: translate such notes only as concern the beauties or art of the author—none geographical, historical or grammatical—unless some occur very important to the sense. . . ." Pope would not concede to the purely antiquarian impulse. He asked Broome specifically to note the pages.[56] Later there were others to help, though none besides Broome and Parnell were ever acknowledged. One of them was a young Cambridge scholar, John Jortin, afterward well known for a life of Eras-mus and some other works. He was recommended to Pope's publisher by his tutor and only reluctantly took up the work of extracting from Eustathius. He completed several books, however, and noticed one pas-sage along the way where Pope had made a mistake. "When that part of Pope's Homer came out in which I was concerned, I was eager, as it may be supposed, to see how things stood, and much pleased to find that he had not only used almost all my notes, but had hardly made any altera-tion in the expressions. I observed also, that in a subsequent edition, he corrected the place to which I had made objections."[57] Jortin hoped that Pope might inquire after his anonymous helper, but the poet unhappily took not the slightest interest in him and they never met.

5

The first volume of the *Iliad* appeared on June 6, 1715.[58] In a way it was the most ambitious of the lot for it included both a life of Homer and a lengthy preface. "I wrote most of the *Iliad* fast," Pope recalled after-

[54]Pope to Thomas Parnell, May 25 or June 1, 1714, in Pope, *Correspondence*, 1:225–26.
[55]See the distich by Orator Henley in Johnson, *Lives of the Poets*, 1:81:

> Pope came off clean with Homer; but they say
> Broome went before, and kindly swept the way.

[56]Pope to Broome, Nov. 29, 1714, in Pope, *Correspondence*, 1:225–26.
[57]John Nichols, *Literary Anecdotes of the Eighteenth Century*, 9 vols. (London, 1812–1815), 2:556–57n.
[58]The second volume was ready on Mar. 22, 1716; the third on June 3, 1717; the fourth on June 28, 1718; the fifth and sixth in May 1720. Pope wrote in his Greek Homer that he completed his translation Feb. 1720; see Spence, *Observations*, 1:45–46n.

ward, "a great deal of it on journeys, from the little pocket Homer on that shelf there, and often 40 or 50 verses on a morning in bed."[59] His usual method was to write swiftly from memory while inspired, then to correct each book using the original and various translations, and finally to polish it for the versification only. His manuscripts and proof sheets still exhibit his careful revision. This time his friend Bridges was satisfied; he was amazed that Homer could sound so like himself in the English language.[60] But it was not easy work; the prose especially tormented him. "I am wrapt up in dull Critical Learning," he complained to Parnell, "and have the Headache every Evening." He remembered afterward wishing a hundred times someone would hang him to release him from his work. "It sat so heavily on my mind at first that I often used to dream of it, and do sometimes still." He dreamed that he was on a long journey, confused about how to go and fearful that he should ever complete it.[61]

His efforts are still visible in the heavily scored manuscript of his preface.[62] Like Madame Dacier, Pope saw that he must make explicit the method of his work and his posture toward Homer. So he opened with a flourish in praise of his author, whose invention, he declared, had never been surpassed. And since invention was the very foundation of all poetry, it was no wonder that Homer had always been acknowledged the greatest of poets. In this fashion Pope continued for several pages to extol his author for his fictions, allegories, characters, speeches, sentiments (with a nod to Duport), descriptions, images, similes, diction, and versification. In each of these respects Homer excelled everyone, including (inevitably) his imitator Virgil. But at last Pope hesitated; he hoped not to be misunderstood. Unlike Madame Dacier, he would not defend Homer in everything. No poet, no writer could surpass everyone in everything. If Homer excelled in invention, Virgil must be credited with superiority in judgment. Echoing Rapin (whose name, however, was canceled in the manuscript and does not appear in the printed version),[63]

---

[59]Spence, *Observations*, 1:45; Pope to Gay, Sept. 23, 1714, in Pope, *Correspondence*, 1:254–55.

[60]Bridges to Pope, July 2, 1715, in Pope, *Correspondence*, 1:303. For Pope's way of working, see Spence, *Observations*, 1:86; Sherburn, "New Anecdotes," p. 347; Pope to Gay, Sept. 23, 1714, in Pope, *Correspondence*, 1:254–55. Pope's drafts are in B.M. MS. Add. 4807–8. For a newly discovered copy of the proof sheets of the *Iliad*, corrected carefully by Pope, see the articles by R. M. Schmitz and Norman Callan in Mack, *Essential Articles*, pp. 593–94, 626–29.

[61]Pope, *Correspondence*, 1:253; Spence, *Observations*, 1:83–85.

[62]B.M. MS. Add. 4807, ff. 2–15; reproduced in Pope, *Poems*, 10:409–44. My own references are to the manuscript. See also Douglas Knight, "The Development of Pope's *Iliad* Preface: A Study of the Manuscript," *Modern Language Quarterly* 16 (1955): 237–46; rpt. in Mack, *Essential Articles*, pp. 611–25.

[63]B.M. MS. Add. 4807, f. 9v.

he matched the two. "Homer was the greatest Genius, Virgil the better Artist. In one we admire the Man, in the other the Work." Homer's impetuosity was rivaled by Virgil's majesty, his generous profusion by the Roman's careful magnificence, and so on. Pope would have liked to avoid taking sides; in no case did he want to be thought to denigrate Virgil. But Homer remained for him the prince of poets and Virgil his imitator; the notes make plain that Pope invariably preferred the Greek to the Roman. In this respect the preface was just a trifle disingenuous in its attempt to appear fair-minded.[64]

What then was Pope's posture in the *querelle*? While he chose to concede that Homer did have faults, at the same time he insisted that they were the inevitable result of his virtues. The only plausible criticisms that had been alleged against Homer, he thought, were really due to the same invention that was his principal accomplishment. "The chief Objections against him," Pope argues, can be seen "to proceed from so noble a Cause as the Excess of this Faculty." This was certainly the case with those marvelous fictions and extravagant similes that had sometimes disturbed Homer's readers. On the other hand, some of his critics accused Homer of narrowness of genius, rather than an excess; they attacked particularly the manners of his gods and heroes. "Those seeming Defects will be found upon Examination to proceed wholly from the Nature of the Times he liv'd in."[65] As the notes make plain, Pope believed that the manners of gods and heroes in the *Iliad* were indeed sometimes course or immoral, but they were not therefore to be taken as Homer's. His job as a poet was to represent his characters as they were in fact, or might have been, and upon occasion Homer even condemns them himself. But Pope was not willing to endorse Madame Dacier's opinion either, "that those Times and Manners are so much the more excellent, as they are the more contrary to ours."[66] Pope was almost as sure of the superiority of his own Augustan world over the primitive age as was La Motte. Yet he would not be "so delicate" as to be shocked, the way some moderns pretended to be.[67] Madame Dacier was right (though she is not credited for it) to admire the simplicity at least of those ancient times. Anyway, "when we read Homer, we ought to reflect that we are reading the most ancient Author in the Heathen World; and those who consider him in this Light will double their Pleasure in the Perusal of him. Let them think that they are growing acquainted with Nations and Peoples that are now no more; that they are stepping almost three thou-

---

[64]A passage at the beginning of the manuscript explicitly answers Scaliger.

[65]Pope, *Poems*, 6:13.

[66]Madame Dacier, *The Iliad of Homer*, trans. John Ozell, 5 vols. (London, 1712), 1:xxv.

[67]In the manuscript, B.M. MS. Add. 4807, f. 8v, we are not left in doubt that Pope meant La Motte.

sand Years backward into the remotest Antiquity, and entertaining themselves with a clear and surprizing Vision of things no where else to be found, the only authentic Picture of that ancient World." As for any other criticisms of Homer (here at last Pope enumerates Scaliger, Rapin, Perrault, and La Motte), Pope discounted them as due to the aimless and invidious comparisons with Virgil which were, he thought, unworthy of reply.[68]

In the manuscript, apart from some revision (usually from the specific to the general), there are some wholly canceled passages of interest. For example, Pope thought to remove a short account of the previous translations that had been attempted, in Latin and the modern languages. Chief among the former was the edition of Spondanus, the Cambridge version of 1689, the Dutch version of 1707, and especially Joshua Barnes, whose work deserved praise, he thought, as "the most perfect Text and most Literal Version extant." Among the modern *Iliads* in French, he criticized the translation of La Valtérie (1681) for its inaccuracy, and praised Madame Dacier for her "most careful and elegant interpretation of the true sense of Homer." "I have sometimes dissented from it," he continued, "(the Reasons will be given in the Notes) but must confess to have received a great advantage from her Translation which has lost little besides the Numbers. Her Preface is admirable." It was simple justice for Pope to write these lines; it is only suspicious that he was unwilling to print them here, though to be fair, he did repeat them in the first note to the *Iliad*. He continued in the canceled passage to analyze Madame Dacier's notes, criticizing her for not sufficiently crediting Eustathius and Duport but ending again in a justified (if somewhat qualified) praise. "What renders her Notes the most valuable is that she has made a further attempt than the rest to discover the beauties of the Poetical Parts tho' often we have only general Praises and Exclamations instead of Reasons."[69] Here in a word was notice both of Pope's dependence on Madame Dacier and of his own intention to go beyond her in describing *specifically* the beauties of his poet.

Another canceled passage immediately afterward enumerates some of the ancient Homeric effigies that were still extant.[70] It is interesting because the published *Iliad* was illustrated and several of these pictures appear there. The list is obviously incomplete and limited entirely to coins, but Pope mentions an impressive number of authorities, including Spanheim, Cuper, Spon, Leo Allatius, and Gronovius. Did he draw it up himself? This is almost the only indication of Pope's interest in the mate-

[68]Cf. Dryden on Scaliger and Perrault in his dedication to the *Third Miscellany* (1693), in his *Works*, 13:56, 59.
[69]B.M. MS. Add. 4807, f. 14.
[70]B.M. MS. Add. 4807.

rial remains of Homeric culture. But he took care to reproduce several
other illustrations in his text, including the *Apotheosis*, which, like
Madame Dacier's, appears to have lost its muses, and two famous busts
of Homer, one from the Farnese palace (as the frontispiece), the other
belonging to Dr. Mead. Through his friend the painter Charles Jervas,
Pope had access to an impressive collection of prints and drawings of
ancient monuments, and he came in time to acquire some of his own.[71]
Yet even so, Pope does not appear to have been either very much concerned or very well informed about Homeric antiquities. As he later
advised his readers, they could well spare themselves the trouble of
reading most books about Greek antiquities (Feithius, for example),
since all they had generally done was first to quote Homer in verse and
then to rephrase him in prose.[72]

The rest of the preface was devoted to describing Pope's method of
translation. He insisted on the need for accuracy, but he argued that
neither a literal translation nor a "rash paraphrase" (that is, neither
Madame Dacier nor La Motte) could really capture the spirit of the
original. "It is the first grand duty of an interpreter to give his author
entire and unmaim'd; and for the rest, the diction and versification only
are his proper province." He was aware of the dangers of anachronism.
The use of "modern Terms of War and Government such as Platoon,
Campaign, Junto, and the like," employed by previous translators,
would not do.[73] Here he criticized his predecessors Chapman, Hobbes,
Ogilby, even Dryden, whom he otherwise revered but whose version of
the first book of the *Iliad* he thought had been done in haste and "in some
Places not truly interpreted the Sense, or preserved the Antiquities."
Once again Pope intended to steer a middle way; "a meer Modern Wit
can like nothing that is not Modern and a Pedant nothing that is not
Greek." But it was impossible to avoid the paradox that was latent in the
the attempt. On the one hand, the translator was bound "neither to omit
or confound any Rites or Customs of Antiquity"; on the other, "to study
this Author rather from his own Text than from any Commentaries how
learned soever."[74] Just how Pope expected to accomplish the one without reference to the other he did not attempt to explain. Nor did he
indicate the slightest interest in the critical problem of just what in this
case *was* the author's own text or how it could be retrieved. Had he
stopped to consider that awkward problem, however, he might never
have continued his work.

[71]See Pope, *Poems*, 2:237n.
[72]Ibid., 7:209n.
[73]Ibid., p. 19.
[74]Ibid., p. 23.

6

In the last note to the *Iliad* Pope thanked Broome and Parnell for their scholarly assistance, Broome for his extracts from Eustathius and "several excellent observations," Parnell for the "Essay on Homer," written "upon such Memoirs as I had collected." The essay was the most ambitious display of erudition in the work; it followed immediately upon Pope's preface and treated the writings and learning of Homer as well as his life. But there is no other sign that Pope furnished the materials for Parnell; it looks rather as though he received a manuscript from his friend which he thought defective in its form and style (too "stiff" even after rewriting) and tried to polish it accordingly.[75] Pope's contribution, as usual, was to the beauty of the work, not to its learning. But he took the responsibility and indeed the credit for it all upon himself.

It is hard to say how well equipped even Parnell was for the job. Oliver Goldsmith, who wrote his life, recalled some "surprising stories" of his childhood, including one "of his getting the third book of the *Iliad* in one night's time, which was given him in order to confine him for some days." He was an Irishman, a clergyman educated at Trinity College, Dublin, and a poet. He was moody and unpredictable but apparently talented and likable.[76] In 1712 he had become intimate with a fellow Irishman in London, Jonathan Swift, and was soon drawn into the Scriblerian circle. He contributed "some ideas" to the *Memoirs of Martinus Scriblerus*, but his work on Homer, begun with Pope that same spring of 1714, probably interfered.[77] Goldsmith tells how one day the Scriblerians set out for a walk in the country to spend the night, Swift forging on quickly ahead, as was his wont. Parnell suspected that he would get the best lodging and so took horse and, arriving first, got their host to send out a servant to warn Swift that there was smallpox in the house. The dean ate a cold supper by himself and was relieved from his plight to join the company only when he promised to reform his manners.[78] On another occasion Parnell spied Pope's *Rape of the Lock* in manuscript and committing it to his extraordinary memory, translated it into Latin verse, whereupon he confronted the astonished author and accused him of stealing his version from an old monkish manuscript! Unfortunately

[75]Spence, *Observations*, 1:83–84.

[76]See Oliver Goldsmith, *Collected Works*, ed. Arthur Friedman, 5 vols. (Oxford, 1966), 3:407. The life of Parnell was originally published in 1770. For Pope's character of Parnell, see Spence, *Observations*, 1:210.

[77]See *The Memoirs of Martinus Scriblerus*, ed. Charles Kirby-Miller (New York, 1966), pp. 57–59. According to Pope, Parnell was the author of the chapter on the origin of the sciences, though Spence was uncertain; see Spence, Observations, 1:210.

[78]Pope, *Poems*, 3:421–22.

there is not much more that we can say with any conviction about Parnell's contribution to the Scriblerians.

The essay is a substantial work, however. As Pope feared, it was not very well constructed or elegant, but it was a pretty full survey of the literature on the subject, ancient and modern.[79] When Parnell wrote there were many precedents for a treatise on Homer, as we have seen, and it is not easy to know exactly what Parnell read. It is tempting to think, for example, that he knew a previous English life that had appeared not too many years before and covered much of the same ground. This is the work included by Basil Kennett in his *Lives and Characters of the Ancient Grecian Poets* (1697). Kennett wrote in the midst of the first Homeric controversy and borrowed much from André Dacier and Père Bossu against Perrault, while exercising his own independent judgment. He chose a posture not unlike Pope's afterward, that Homer was largely but not entirely defensible, that he sometimes nodded, but that he was the greatest of the ancient poets. He also reviewed the possibilities for the person, place, and time of Homer, on the whole shrewdly and skeptically. If Parnell read the life, he would have had a useful start, but he would have had to add a great deal of his own.

The new life began helpfully by surveying the sources for Homer's career. Parnell saw that there was no certainty anywhere, merely "Tradition, Opinion, or Collection of Authors." Of the tales that were told, some (such as those in Eustathius) resulted from too extravagant an admiration for Homer; others from envy; still others from "trifling Curiosity." Like Kennett, Parnell was suspicious of the Pseudo-Herodotus, for example, pointing out at least one inconsistency in the dates for Homer between that work and the genuine history. He understood correctly that invention was the inevitable result of scarcity of information. "They find no Remains but his Name and Works and resolve to torture these upon the Rack of Invention." Nevertheless (like Kennett again), Parnell was tempted a little himself and offered a few conjectures of his own, although not dogmatically.[80] For example, he preferred the majority opinion based on the Arundel Marble that Homer wrote about three hundred years after the fall of Troy. He passed over Homer's birthplace, "a point so little essential" that it made the elaborate work of Leo Allatius appear ludicrous. He thought it likely that Homer became blind only later in life and was certain that he had traveled widely, especially in Egypt. (The catalogue of ships alone proved his geographical knowl-

[79]The essay appears in Pope's *Poems*, 7:1–43.
[80]Ibid., p. 39; cf. Basil Kennett, *Lives and Characters of the Ancient Grecian Poets* (London, 1687), p. 2.

edge.) Perhaps, Parnell suggested, Homer drew his own portrait in Nestor, but it was hard to tell anything much about him from his poetry.

If the literary sources were disappointing, antiquities were hardly better. Parnell was familiar with some of them, largely in their published versions. As we have seen, a number of them were printed by Pope, possibly upon Parnell's recommendation. Here in the essay he identifies them, beginning with the frontispiece, the bust of Homer from the Farnese Palace. He also noticed the coins from Chios, Smyrna, and Amastris, particularly the latter, "carefully copied from an Original belonging to the Earl of Pembroke." It was the very same coin that Gronovius, Cuypers, and Dacier had reproduced, "but very incorrectly performed." Finally he explicated once again the *Apotheosis Homeri*, "that which of all the Remains has been of late the chief Amusement of the Learned." On the whole, however, Parnell was doubtful of the usefulness of any of the portraits (which he thought "purely notional"), and it is hard to see what value the busts, medals, or marbles possessed for him.[81] The sum of their information about Homer was so small (a short curled beard perhaps and a certain largeness of head) that their description was probably meant simply to exhibit his (and hence Pope's) grasp of the antiquarian science. Even on that score, however, it is not very impressive.[82]

Parnell seems to have felt it necessary to enter also into the recondite world of Homeric philology. At least he thought to give an account of the way in which the poems were recorded and edited in antiquity. He brings together, therefore, the classical evidence for a series of Homeric recensions, beginning with Lycurgus and Pisistratus and climaxing in the Alexandrian critics Zenodotus and Aristarchus. (In a brief digression he compares the latter with Zoilus to show the two contrary sorts of criticism, the one proceeding from good nature, the other from ill will.)[83] Unfortunately, Parnell steps blithely across the Middle Ages to the revival of antiquity without the slightest concern for the transmission of the Homeric text to modern times. All he says is that "Ancient learning resum'd its dignity, and Homer obtain'd his proper place in the esteem of mankind." So much for the pedantic learning of modern textual criticism!

The final section of the essay appears at first sight more promising. Here Parnell thought to place Homer in the context of his times, to define the state of society and learning in his day, the better to estimate

---

[81]Pope, *Poems*, 7:54–55.

[82]Thus the nineteenth-century verdict; see John Mitford, *The Poetical Works of Thomas Parnell* (London, n.d.), pp. 67–69.

[83]Pope, *Poems*, 7:61.

his achievement.[84] We learn now something of poetry, theology, politics, morality, history, geography, rhetoric, natural philosophy, medicine, and statuary, both of Homer and of Homer's time. It seems not to have occurred to Parnell—or Pope—that to use Homer as a literal and reliable description of the world in which he wrote was to beg the main question. (To be fair, the antiquaries had done only a little better.) The result was to show Homer as the inventor but not the master of almost all the arts and sciences. Parnell warns his readers not to be surprised if they find less of learning in his work than his encomiasts had declared. The whole condition of society and all the arts and sciences had since improved—more or less. Homer's world was both primitive and pagan and thus essentially defective. Homer should be considered principally as a poet, describing a world that had passed and only incidentally bringing in the learning of his times. One might try to allegorize the *Iliad* to discover Homer's science; it was better to admit that "the age was not arriv'd in which it flourished."

It was not an unreasonable conclusion. In effect, Parnell and Pope were claiming for Homer a precedence in poetry alone, while relinquishing the rest. They were trying (not always consistently) to claim a perfection for the *Iliad* in its quality as epic, in its "sublime" character, and in its faithfulness to the world in which it had been made, independent of all those other possibilities that had been anciently credited to it. They were trying to walk the ground between the moderns, who could not see its beauties, and the ancients, who were not satisfied with them alone. In this respect they were closer than they probably suspected to the English moderns, to William Wotton and Dr. Bentley, than to the French ancients, Monsieur and Madame Dacier.

7

The very existence of Pope's notes should have embarrassed him. Ever since Swift had ridiculed the forms of modern learning in *A Tale of a Tub*, the learned commentary had come to look more and more ludicrous to the wits. Footnotes epitomized their concern that the grace and elegance of polite literature were likely to be buried beneath the erudition of the drones. Yet here upon every page of the *Iliad* they were, with every so often a learned essay and sometimes a map or diagram besides, to intrude upon the rapid flow of Homer's narrative.

No doubt Pope was uneasy at his work. Yet he meant to do more than

[84]Ibid., pp. 65–67.

simply satisfy his subscribers; the commentary allowed him to defend his
efforts at each stage of the way. Every translation is of course an interpretation, and Pope saw that the very act of committing Homer to English
compelled him to decide on a host of issues that had been raised by the
critics. Nor did he doubt that those same busy triflers who had
challenged his predecessors lay waiting for him as well; the examples of
La Motte and Madame Dacier were constantly before him as he roughed
out his daily fifty lines. How better to defend himself, then, than to
anticipate at every point the cavils of the critics and to make plain the
reasons for his every choice? And there was a further advantage as well;
there was the satisfaction of becoming the arbiter between the ancients
and the moderns and of playing the judge and critic as well as the poet, all
at the same time.

Of course, the best way to avoid the embarrassment of a learned
commentary was to omit the learning. Pope's notes, like Madame
Dacier's, were intended exclusively to show the merits of the *Iliad* as
poetry. "It is something strange," Pope began, "that of all the commentators upon Homer there is hardly one whose principal design is to
illustrate the poetical beauties of the author." This was to be Pope's own
task. The commentators, he continued, "are voluminous in explaining
those sciences which Homer made but subservient to his Poetry." They
were like Martinus Scriblerus, "men who had more reading than taste,
and were fonder of shewing their variety of learning in all kinds than this
single understanding in poetry. Hence it comes to pass that their remarks
are rather philosophical, historical, geographical, allegorical, or in short
any thing than critical and poetical." Even the grammarians (that is, the
philologists) had erred accordingly. "Tho' their whole business and use
be only to render the words of an author intelligible," they seemed intent
simply "to increase the number of various lections," or to add new and
obscure meanings to the obvious, often by dreaming up imaginary allegories. Pope could see no use for the work of such scholars as Hearne and
Barnes, or even Dr. Bentley, "for men of a right understanding generally
see at once all that one author can reasonably mean, but others are apt to
fancy two meanings for want of knowing one." Indeed, there was a vast
difference "between the learning of a Critick and the puzzling of a Grammarian."[85] It was not easy to make anything out of the labors of the
pedants, but Pope concluded his introductory note by promising to try.
He would read through Eustathius to see what could be gleaned from
that copious writer that might be of use to the poetry; and he would rely
on Madame Dacier, who had done the best so far. (He does not, however, say how much he depended on Broome and the rest for even

[85]Ibid., pp. 82–83.

this.)[86] The chief design of the notes, Pope repeated, was to comment on Homer as a poet.

And so it appeared. The bulk of the notes attempted to explain to the reader just how Homer had achieved his efforts, how he had wrought a narrative full of fire and invention, an imagery bold and vivid, a story gripping and faithful, a characterization consistent and truthful, a language musical and appropriate. He defended Homer's similes, speeches, and repetitions against his critics, especially the integrity of the poem; he insisted that Homer had composed his work as a whole and calculated every effect, erring only on occasion by an excess of imagination. "The plan of this poem," Pope announced, "is form'd upon anger and its ill effects," and he never failed to show that it had but one true subject, the wrath of Achilles.[87] Nor did he doubt that it had been composed like any other epic poem, like the works of Virgil or Milton or Tasso, who constantly entered into his notes by way of comparison. Homer had taken a theme from history, from the real events of the Trojan War as transmitted by records and traditions, and turned it to poetic account. In many ways, he appeared to be a poet writing for an audience not unlike the translator's own. "One may naturally believe," Pope suggested, that Homer took every occasion "of paying a Compliment to many great Men and Families of his Patrons, both in Greece and Asia," rather as Pope paid his respects to Halifax, Pembroke, and the rest at the end of his preface.[88] His Homer was a far cry in any case from Dr. Bentley's careless rhapsodist.

Pope tried to imagine Homer concretely at his task. The poet wrote long after the event; Madame Dacier had suggested about 250 years. It followed therefore that he must have seen the difference between his own

---

[86]"I have had the flowery walks of imagination to expatiate in," he wrote to Broome at the conclusion of his work, Mar. 24, 1720, "while you have drudged in only removing loads and clearing rubbish heaped together by the negligence no less than by the industry of past pedants": *Correspondence*, 2:40–41, 499–500. One of Pope's many later critics put it thus:

> For what are you in love with Homer? Speak
> And own the Wit is English, and not Greek.
> If Greek t'had been, I should have look'd about
> To know how P—— or you cou'd find it out.
> A hundred Comments are on Homer writ,
> A hundred Versions which those Comments fit,
> And he who such an Author can command,
> Must neither Greek nor English understand.

Gulliveriana (London, 1728), pp. 289–90, apparently from the *Daily Journal*, April 6, 1728. Pope owned a copy and assigned it to James Moore; it is in the British Library, shelf mark BMC 116 b3.

[87]Pope, *Poems*, 8:486.

[88]"Otherwise these particular Descriptions of Genealogies and other minute Circumstances would have been an Affectation extremely needless and unreasonable": ibid., 7:271.

time and the earlier period. Pope believed with Père Bossu that the epic writer remained faithful to the past that supplied his materials and only arranged it differently from the historian. "I think it plain," he declared in a note, that Homer had "composed his Poem from some Records of Tradition of the Actions of the Times preceding, and complied with the Truth of History." There were a thousand proofs of his "exact Knowledge in Geography and Antiquities."[89] He was confident that the poet had tried to avoid anachronism, that he had scrupulously avoided confusing the life of his own day with that of the Greeks and Trojans two and a half centuries earlier. "We may infer," he suggested of the poet's description of the shouts of the opposing armies, "that Homer was particularly careful not to confound the Manners of the Times he wrote of, with those of the Times he liv'd in."[90] It was a very useful notion for Pope, for it allowed him to accept the criticism that had been so often leveled against the morals of the Homeric gods and heroes, while at the same time relieving Homer of the opprobrium. The poet was the faithful recorder of a primitive and earlier time; in this matter Pope accepted the prevailing opinion.[91] It did not follow that he approved everything that he described. But it was not easy, indeed it was quite impossible, for Pope to prove this interpretation. Since Homer was his only source, how could he show that the poet had respected the difference in periods? It is true that on occasion he tried the antiquaries' trick and drew on the testimony of other ancient writers, of Pausanius and Strabo and Dictys, but he did not see that they too were largely dependent on Homer (at best) for their information and so could hardly corroborate him. In the end, it was his poetic conviction, not his classical learning, that settled the point.

Nor was Pope entirely consistent about the morality of the *Iliad*. It was not easy to stake out a firm position halfway between La Motte and Dacier, though his attempt was ingenious enough. If Homer was not the author of the morality of his poem, then he was innocent of it, and Pope could accept the criticisms that La Motte had leveled against it. This he did to a large extent, although he agreed with Madame Dacier that there was much to admire anyway in the simplicity and nobility of Homer's

[89]Ibid., 7:98, 6:111, 7:118. The index has an entry for "history preserv'd by Homer." All this was perfectly commonplace; see, for example, "Of Homer consider'd as a Poet and Historian," in Louis Ellies Du Pin, *The Universal Library of Historians*, 2 vols. (London, 1709), 1:197–98.

[90]Pope, *Poems*, 7:236, 389–90.

[91]According to Pope's friend Temple Stanyan, Homer "knew he might vary from the Truth as to Particulars, tho' not as to the main Subject; that he might adorn his Poem with probable Falsities but that his principal Action ought always to have some real Foundation in History": *The Grecian History*, 2 vols. (London, 1701), 1:35. See also Du Pin, *Universal Library*, 1:206–7.

heroes. On the other hand, the faithful description of immorality would seem to undermine the authority of the epic that everyone had always claimed derived its force from its moral conviction. "If the Reader does not observe the Morality of the *Ilias*," Pope wrote, "he loses half, and the nobler part of its Beauty: He reads it as a common Romance, and mistakes the chief Aim of it, which is to instruct."[92] The only way around the problem was to insist on the morality of the whole: The *Iliad* is about the evil consequences that resulted from the (immoral) wrath of Achilles. Yet even so, Pope was left with several unpleasant incidents, some contradictory characterizations, and some obvious breaches of decorum. These he had to admit as faults in Homer. What he did hold onto without equivocation, along with almost everyone else in his generation, was the moral standard of his own Augustan age, which, despite an occasional exception, he thought of as essentially true and timeless. "Wit and Sense," as Basil Kennett put it, "are the same in all ages," whatever the discrepancies in manners or customs.[93] It was thus possible to find Homer consistent with Augustan values (as Madame Dacier did), or inconsistent with them (as La Motte did), or half-consistent with them (as Pope did); but none of them doubted that these were the universal standards by which the past—and its poetry—had to be judged.

In other respects also Pope kept up a continuous commentary on the *querelle*. For the most part he sided with the ancients, with Boileau, Bossu, Monsieur Dacier, and Boivin (all of whom he quoted copiously), and against Scaliger, Rapin, Perrault,[94] La Motte, and especially Terrasson. With Madame Dacier it was harder to be sure, and not only on the issue of Homer's morality. Perhaps because of his very dependence on her, he thought it necessary to dissociate himself from her work and opinions whenever possible. So at times he criticized her translation, especially when he found it too refined for Homer's frank and even course expression. Yet he used her consistently and on occasion tried also to make his work more decorous than the original. He did not hesitate to accuse her of plagiarism from Eustathius. Yet he often borrowed from her work without acknowledgment. And he criticized her continuously for her overapologetic stance. He did not approve of her elaborate effects to justify Homer when he had obviously nodded, either in his morality or in his composition. Neither did he accept her insistence (following Eustathius) on allegory where the plain sense would do. Finally, despite a considerable respect for Homer's learning, he did not think, any more

---

[92]Pope, *Poems*, 8:557–58.

[93]Kennett, *Lives and Characters*, p. 26.

[94]Much later Pope added some lines (after l. 124) to the *Essay on Criticism* in favor of Homer and against Perrault's ambition to confine to modern rules and customs the poet "who for all Ages writ and all Mankind": *Poems*, 1:252–53.

than Parnell in his essay, that the *Iliad* was an anticipation of all modern knowledge, or that Homer was a Christian poet. He accepted many of Madame Dacier's scriptural parallels but by no means all. "In comparing Passages of the sacred Books with our Author we ought to use a great deal of Caution and Respect." If Scripture occasionally represented God with motives that sounded human, there were infinitely more passages to show his divine perfection, justice, and beneficence; whereas Homer's Jupiter was invariably subject to passion, inequality, and imperfection. The Daciers had been too zealous to defend Homer on every occasion, in theology as in all other respects.[95]

8

So far, Pope was able to attend to the poetic beauties of the *Iliad* with only an occasional lapse into philology or antiquities. But in other matters it was harder to avoid them. There were apparently simple things, such as the meaning of a Greek word, that forced him to consult the scholia in the critical editions, as well as his own poetic instinct. There was the problem of spurious verses, where however Pope invariably followed Barnes's lead. He was aware (if only from Barnes again) that the text had gone through many manuscript copies and variations.[96] At times he seemed to glimpse the value of the different readings. But he tried as far as possible to avoid such complications, no doubt because of a genuine contempt for such critical niceties. And it is likely also that Pope was simply not skillful enough in Greek to employ or to appreciate them.

With respect to antiquities, however, Pope felt more compelled to attend to the pedants. Once again it was a problem of meaning. Unless one understood the conditions of Homeric culture, it was impossible to translate the text correctly. Take, for example, the lines that his predecessors (including Madame Dacier) had invariably translated as "she fell on her knees." Pope was sure that this was a mistake, "an Oversight occasion'd by the want of a competent knowledge in Antiquities (without which no Man can tolerably understand this Author)." It ought to have been "how at his knee she begg'd," "for the custom of praying on the Knees was unknown to the Greeks and in use only among the Hebrews." (He was fond enough of this discovery to repeat it at least once.)[97] But this was only one of a whole class of such instances in which

[95]Pope, *Poems*, 7:402 and 112.

[96]Ibid., 8:530. See also 7:463 and 8:132. On occasion he was willing to condemn verses apparently on his own authority, when he thought them "so very gross as to be unworthy of Homer": ibid., 6:464.

[97]Ibid., 7:289, 465.

knowledge of the details of classical custom or belief was essential to the meaning of the text and therefore to the translator. It was necessary to know the methods of mowing and plowing in those days; how the dead were buried and what the ancients thought about the afterlife; the numbers of the contending forces; the forms of political life (did the Greeks have absolute monarchy?); the way time and money were measured; something about their sacrifices; and much more about their military affairs, their tactics (did they use cavalry?), their fortifications, and of course their armor. He quotes at length from Temple Stanyan's account of the ancient oracles in his *Grecian History*.[98] Again and again Pope introduced the antiquarian material, even forgetting at times to relate it to his text. (On one occasion, after noting that Homer correctly omitted a story about Aeneas which would have distracted the reader from the main plot, Pope tells it anyway in a footnote.)[99] A long section of the index was required simply to enumerate these materials. Once in a while he seems to have felt the anomaly. "I cannot pass over a Matter of such Importance as a Lady's Dress without endeavoring to explain what sort of Heads were worn about three thousand Year ago." When he was done, he adds, ironically, "the Ladies cannot but be pleas'd to see so much Learning and Greek [which he borrowed from Eustathius] upon this important subject."[100] On another occasion he tried a different tack. In what season did the events of the *Iliad* occur? "A Critick *might* take Occasion," Pope suggested, on translating these lines, "to speak of the exact time of the Year in which the Actions of the *Iliad* are suppos'd to have happen'd. And (according to the grave manner of a learned dissertation) begin by informing us. . . ." Whereupon, like any competent antiquary, Pope in fact proceeded to show that *if* one were to examine the matter, one would have to conclude that the event took place during the summer. And upon accomplishing this demonstration, "the learned Enquirer might hug himself with the Discovery, and conclude with Triumph."[101] The conditional clause only barely conceals Pope's uneasiness.

But Pope reserved his most ambitious scholarly display for the occasional essays he affixed to his translation. Press of time forced him to abandon two of them before publication, one on the theology and morality of Homer and the other on the oratory of Homer and Virgil, but he included disquisitions enough.[102] Like Madame Dacier, he thought it necessary to defend Homer's catalogue of ships, but he did so more

---

[98]Ibid., 8:250–51.

[99]Ibid., pp. 408–10.

[100]Ibid., pp. 250–51. The entry "Antiquities" in the index was subdivided into agriculture, armor, etc. In the published work all such subjects were subsumed under "Arts and Sciences." Cf. B.M. MS. Add. 4808, ff. 207, with *Poems*, 8:609–16.

[101]Pope, *Poems*, 8:154.

[102]Gone also were four "laborious and uncommon sorts of Indexes" that were once intended; see Pope to Digby, May 1, 1720, in Pipe, *Correspondence*, 2:43–44.

ambitiously than the lady, with a dozen pages of discourse in which he insisted on Homer's reliability as a historian and geographer. He included an elaborate map and cited his classical authorities throughout.[103] Since most of the *Iliad* was concerned with warfare, he thought it necessary a little later to compose an "Essay on Homer's Battels," which he appended to the fourth book. "I shall first endeavour to shew the Conduct of the Poet herein," he began, meaning to illustrate the work's poetic merit, "and next collect some Antiquities, that tend to a more distinct understanding of those Descriptions which make so large a Part of the Poem." The second half of the essay was devoted, therefore, to "a short View of the Scene of War . . . with the proper Field of each Battel."[104] Once again Pope included a careful map to accompany the text. His topographical interest did not extend far, if one compares him with the Levantine travelers we have noticed before (and whom he seems not to have known), but he did at least read George Sandys's *Relation of a Journey* for a recent account of the Troad. He cited it with pleasure in a later note.[105] Here he goes on to describe some of the instruments of combat, the chariots and swords especially, and, in a separate section, "some Customs of Antiquity relating to the Arms and Art Military of those Times which are proper to be known in order to form a right Notion of our Author's Description of War." Although this was less an antiquarian exercise than it sounds (since Pope remained more concerned with poetry than with history), it nevertheless made his point that Homer was a scrupulous historian of an earlier time. Moreover, Pope discussed such matters as the possibility of cavalry at the siege of Troy, a subject he takes up several times in the notes. He does not have time here, however, for the armor of the heroes. For that one must turn to the eighteenth book and Pope's account of the shield of Achilles.[106]

9

After what has been said, it will come as no surprise that Pope took the shield seriously, that he thought that the eighteenth book was integral to the poem, and that he believed that the shield was, or at least

---

[103]Pope, *Poems*, 8:173–85.

[104]Ibid., 7:252–62.

[105]Ibid., 8:463. See George Sandys, *The Relation of a Journey* (London, 1615). At least seven editions had been issued by 1673.

[106]Even so, some readers found Pope's antiquarian discussion dry and tedious, defensible only through "the Bigotry of a Succession of unpoetical Commentators, Men of Learning without Genius": Aaron Hill and William Bond, *The Plain-Dealer, being Select Essays on Several Curious Subjects*, 2d ed. (London, 1734). Others found it too shallow; see Robert Wood, *An Essay on the Original Genius and Writings of Homer* (London, 1775).

could have been, genuine. The *querelle* had forced the episode upon everyone's attention. Pope's response was an essay that he entitled "Observations on the Shield of Achilles."[107] It was the most ambitious piece of prose in the work; to compose it, he drew directly on many of the works of controversy that had recently appeared.

We must remember that Pope was free to choose among these various works as he set about translating the book. He had accepted some of the modern criticisms and agreed that Homer had sometimes nodded. But there was no mistaking his purpose now. The ancient poet had used all his talent for his description of the shield, and the result had been almost universal praise. "It is indeed astonishing how . . . the Arrogance of some Moderns could unfortunately chuse the noblest Part of the noblest Poet for the Object of their blind censures. Their criticisms, however just enough upon other points, yet, when employ'd on this buckler, are to the utmost weak and impotent." Pope saw that they must be answered, and so he turned first to André Dacier to reply to the critics, then to Boivin to show what the shield must have looked like. To their arguments he added one of his own, something not yet proposed: he would consider the description of the shield as a painting, and prove it in all respects "conformable to . . . that Art."

There is not much point in repeating Pope's summary of Dacier and Boivin, whom he almost literally translated here.[108] Pope took the chief objection to the shield to be the argument that its design was impossible. Fortunately, Boivin had "put an end to this cavil," as any reader could see simply by looking at the engraving that Pope appropriated from that author and affixed to his essay. (In his manuscript Pope drew a sketch that shows how seriously he took the matter.)[109] Some simple calculations were enough to show that there was indeed plenty of room on its face to contain all that Homer had described there. It remained only to consider the work as "a complete Idea of Painting, and a Sketch for what one may call an universal Picture." This was to be Pope's own contribution.

But here was a problem. Homer had described the shield both as a piece of sculpture and as a painting; the outlines were engraved, but the rest was inlaid, according to the poet's description, with various colored metals. Unfortunately Pliny, who was the best ancient authority on such

[107]Pope, *Poems*, 8:358–70. There is a brief essay on the subject by Fern Farnham, "Achilles' Shield: Some Observations on Pope's *Iliad*," *Publications of the Modern Language Association* 84 (1969): 1571–81.

[108]Pope had employed Boivin already in the sixth book, citing him only as "an ingenious French writer": *Poems*, 7:360. He translated André Dacier at length (ibid., 8:342) and quoted him elsewhere.

[109]B.M. MS. Add. 4808, f. 81v. He also drew a diagram to show how the buckler was fastened to the arm by three rings.

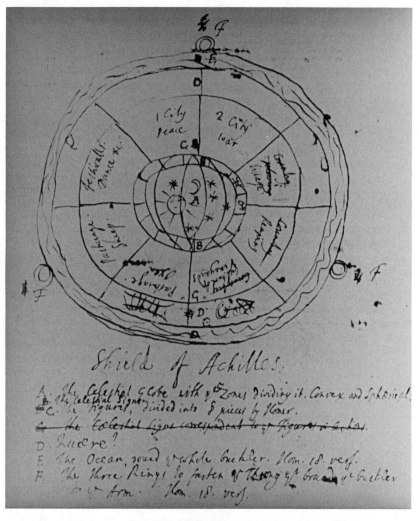

Alexander Pope's design for the shield of Achilles, reproduced by permission of
the Trustees of the British Library

matters, was quite sure that painting was in a very primitive condition in
Homeric times. Pope was unconvinced. Homer had described many
statues, carvings, tapestries, and ornaments of every kind in a way to
persuade the reader of their beauty, their relief, "and their Emulation of
Life itself. If we consider how much it is his constant Practice to confine
himself to the Custom of the Times wherof he writ, it will be hard to
doubt but that Painting and Sculpture must have been then in great

Charles Jervas's engraving of the bust of Homer for Pope's *Iliad*

Practice and Repute." He would (once again) use Homer to prove that
Homer had been a faithful reporter. Yet when that romantic antiquary
Heinrich Schliemann uncovered the first of the shaft graves at Mycenae
two and a half centuries later, it was revealed that Pope was right—or at
least as right as the abbé Claude-François Fraguier, from whom he had
expressly borrowed his observation![110]

Was Homer describing the real shield, then? Pope remained noncom-
mittal. It *need* not have been, since Homer attributed the work to a god,
and "he might excuse himself from a strict Confinement to what was
known and practiced in the Time of the Trojan War." But knowing
Homer's method as an epic poet, one might reasonably assume that he
had designed a shield that was probable. Moreover, Pope understood
Homer's descriptive powers to be those of a great draftsman, a natural
painter-poet. Indeed, he subscribed generally to the ancient doctrine that
poetry was a speaking picture.[111] What was certain, then, was that Homer had designed a shield that in every way accorded with what Pope
believed to be a true idea of the art of painting. Whether the shield had
been real or not was relatively unimportant; Pope was certain that it
represented the highest aspiration of pictorial art, and he intended to
demonstrate as much in detail by examining its invention, composition,
expression, and so on. Pope had not wasted his time studying painting
with his friend Charles Jervas in 1713. (The artist was responsible for the
frontispiece to Pope's *Iliad*, the bust of Homer.)[112] And he had been
careful, he assures his readers, to secure the advice of the best painters
and connoisseurs for his arguments here—particularly his friend Sir
Godfrey Kneller, who had entirely approved them.[113] With this support
he was able confidently to compare the shield to a Raphael cartoon, to
praise its "aerial perspective," and to demonstrate the futility of the abbé
Terrasson's objections. There can be no doubt that as Pope warmed to
his work and entered upon his exact description of the shield, it became
tangible in his imagination as few concrete objects had ever done. And
was this not, after all, the highest goal of all art: to create imperishable
images of reality, vivid, plausible, true beyond the fleeting existence of
material substance? If so, then Homer had accomplished his task to per-

[110]Claude-François Fraguier, "De l'ancienneté de la peinture," in *Histoire de l'Académie
Royale*, vol. 1 (Paris, 1717), pp. 83–84.

[111]Pope, *Poems*, 1:408; 2:32, 246, 423. The "Poetical Index" includes a very full account
of the "descriptions or images" of the *Iliad*, as well as another on "painting, sculpture, etc."
In general, see Jean H. Hagstrum, *The Sister Arts* (Chicago, 1958), pp. 229–33; Reuben
Brower, *Alexander Pope: The Poetry of Allusion* (Oxford, 1959), pp. 131–32.

[112]Charles Jervas to Pope, Aug. 20, 1714, in Pope, *Correspondence*, 1:244. Pope used
Jervas to become a historical painter, to reproduce scenes from ancient history; see ibid.,
1:376–77; Spence, *Observations*, 1:46; and in general, Norman Ault, *New Light on Pope*
(London, 1949), pp. 68–100.

[113]Pope, *Poems*, 7:212–13.

fection and the shield of Achilles would live forever in the minds of all who followed, more vivid than the antiquarian discoveries of all time; and the poet Pope would have shown once again the superiority of his sympathetic criticism to the pedantry of empty learning.[114]

[114]For the subsequent history of the shield, see Joseph M. Levine, "The Battle of the Books and the Shield of Achilles," *Eighteenth-Century Life* 9 (1984): 51–55.

Chapter Seven

Pope and the Quarrel between
the Ancients and the Moderns

I

Zoilus lay waiting; the new Homer could no more escape criticism than the original. Even before it appeared, however, the carpers had begun their venomous work, casting suspicions on the enterprise and aspersions on the enterpriser from behind the safety of their pseudonyms: *The High German Doctor*, *Aesop at the Bear-Garden*, *The Grumbler*, Nichydemus Ninnyhammer (*Homer in a Nut Shell*) and most wicked of all, Sir Iliad Doggrel in his *Homerides*.[1] Pope, they insinuated, had been won to Homer by greed; Pope was a papist; Pope knew no Greek; the *Iliad* was a fraud. "To prevent any farther Imposition on the Publick," they threatened, "there is now preparing for the Press by several Hands, *Homer defended: Being a Detection of the many Errors committed by Mr. Pope in the Pretended Translation of Homer*." It would be shown that the translator had sometimes misunderstood his author, sometimes falsified him deliberately.[2] But the boast proved idle and the work never appeared. It was left to Pope's old enemy John Dennis to carry out the threat. In *Some Remarks upon Mr. Pope's Translation of Homer* (1717), Dennis argued that although it was impossible for anyone to translate the *Iliad* successfully, Pope's failure was due entirely to want of skill and genius. He had "undertaken to translate Homer from Greek of which he does not know

---

[1]See J. V. Guerinot, *Pamphlet Attacks on Alexander Pope: A Bibliography* (New York, 1969); Norman Ault, "Pope and Addison," *Review of English Studies* 17 (1941): 428–51. For the conspirators behind the *Homerides*, see *The Letters of Thomas Burnet to George Duckett*, ed. David Nichol Smith (Oxford, 1914). Pope kept his own list; see the *Dunciad Variorum* (London, 1729), app. 2, "A List of Books, Papers, and Verses, in which our Author was abused, Printed before the *Dunciad*; with the Names of the Authors."

[2]From the *Flying Post*, quoted in George Sherburn, *The Early Career of Alexander Pope* (Oxford, 1934), p. 174.

one Word, into English, which he understands almost as little." It was one thing to admit that Homer sometimes nodded, "yet 'tis hard if he snores so like a Sot."[3] To this effect, Dennis proceeded to expose Pope's weakness in Greek, although he weakened his argument with his invective.

Pope, of course, was not unprepared for his critics; with his friend Thomas Parnell he at once conspired at an answer. The result was a new piece that appeared in 1717, an ingenious effort to forestall criticism by illustrating its dangers in advance. Parnell had been working at a translation of the *Batrachomyomachia* (the *Battle of the Frogs and Mice*, he called it). He was determined to issue it with a preface and a life of Zoilus which together would rebut the enemy. Pope saw the work through the press and it is clear that he had a hand in it from the beginning, but it was Parnell who wrote it and took the credit.[4] The preface consists of a dialogue between Parnell and the translator of the *Iliad* in which the translator defends his methods. He prefers rhyme to blank verse, he says, and an "air" that is neither modernized nor antiquated; an accuracy that is true to the spirit of the original, rather than perfectly literal. But what, Parnell asks, had the translator meant to do, "with all those Editions and Comments I observed in his Room?" The reply is characteristically Scriblerian. "If any one who had a mind to find Fault . . . wou'd but stay 'till it was entirely finish'd, he shou'd have a very cheap Bargain of them." Neither Pope nor Parnell would defend their learning, however earnestly they took their literary pretensions.

Nevertheless, and in all apparent seriousness, there followed at once Parnell's scholarly life of Zoilus. Here was the nub of the work, a criticism of the critics, an attempt to show the errors of the Homeric detractors in advance by setting forth the life and works and final retribution of the most famous of Homer's opponents. It was appropriate for the occasion, for the Scriblerians saw that their first enemies were, like Zoilus, more likely to be moved by envy than by any disinterested love of truth or beauty. Parnell drew, therefore, on a host of ancient sources to recount the life of his antihero, including his death by fire in disgrace and the lasting condemnation of the ages. It was astonishing only that there were some people who continued to follow his example. If they did not

[3]John Dennis, *Some Remarks upon Mr. Pope's Translation of Homer* (London, 1717), p. 12. Pope owned a copy, which survives with his annotations in the British Library (shelf mark C 116 bl), bound up with several other attacks; see John Dennis, *The Critical Works*, ed. Edward N. Hooker, 2 vols. (Baltimore, 1939, 1943), 2:115–58; and Hooker, "Pope and Dennis," *ELH* 7 (1940): 188–98.

[4]Pope to Parnell, March 1716, in "Some Unpublished Letters of Pope and Gay," *Review of English Studies* n.s. 10 (1959): 376–78; Alexander Pope, *Correspondence*, ed. George Sherburn, 5 vols. (Oxford, 1956), 1:284–85, 333. The work appeared as *Homer's Battle of the Frogs and Mice with the Remarks of Zoilus* (London, 1717).

meet the same fate, "they shall nevertheless meet a Proportion of it in the inward Trouble they give themselves and the outward Contempt others fling at them: A Punishment which everyone has hitherto felt, who has really deserv'd to be call'd a Zoilus."[5]

If the cavilers might thus be forestalled—though it is hardly necessary to say that they continued unabashed—what was Pope to do with the more serious complainants? What, for example, was to be done about Madame Dacier? That stubborn lady had naturally been offended by Pope's translation when it was called to her attention. Fortunately, she seems to have known only the preface and that only in translation. Yet even so she found enough there to arouse her ire, especially where Pope seemed to equivocate about Homer's merits. Consequently, she appended to the last edition of her *Odyssey* (1719) a characteristically vigorous reply. (Pope's enemies soon turned it into a brief English tract.) Her chief objection was to the opening lines, where Pope had allowed that Homer's beauty was of a special kind compared with Virgil's. "Our author's work is a wild paradise," he had written, "where if we cannot see all the beauties so distinctly as in an order'd Garden, it is only because the number of them is infinitely greater. 'Tis like a copious nursery which contains the seeds and first productions of every kind. . . . If some things are too luxurient, it is owning to the richness of the soil. . . ." "What!" she exclaimed. "Is Homer's Order of Symmetry, a Plot whereon nothing but Seeds, nor nothing perfect or formed is to be found?" The *Iliad* was "the most perfect Model in all kinds of Poetry." Moreover, she stood by her own judgment that modern times were inferior to the age of the heroes. Perhaps Homer's characters were not altogether faultless; did Pope prefer the corruptions of modern luxury to the natural simplicity of those ancient times? Finally (and most annoyingly) she noticed that Pope had borrowed without acknowledgment from her own remarks—much less, however, than she was aware! She concluded with a fine sarcasm; so bright a man should not confine himself to poetry; he should try politics. "A Man capable to correct Homer will be able to form the Manners of Men."[6]

Pope was disappointed; Madame Dacier had ignored the bulk of his observations to fasten only upon a few minor points. He elected to answer her, therefore, in a postscript to his own *Odyssey*—too late, however, for her to see it. In the event, he chose to be as respectful as possible. He had fought, he recalled, under Madame Dacier's own ban-

[5]"Life of Zoilus," appended to *Homer's Battle*, in Thomas Parnell, *Poems on Several Occasions* (London, 1737), app., pp. 38–39.

[6]*Madame Dacier's Remarks upon Mr. Pope's Account of Homer Made English from the French* (London, 1724), p. 17, translated from Madame Dacier's *Odyssey*, 2d ed., 3 vols., vol. 3 (Paris, 1719).

ner and defended Homer "against all the Hereticks of the age." Now he
stood accused by Madame Dacier herself of betraying the common
cause. It was necessary to reassure the world against that great critic's
authority, to show that her charges were unjust. But this was not hard to
do. Unfortunately, Madame Dacier had fallen into the same error as her
opponents; she had relied on a bad translation instead of the original.
"She knew less of my true sense from that faulty translation of part of my
Preface, than those blind censurers might have known of Homer's even
from the translation of La Valterie which preceded her own."[7] In his
manuscript Pope worked very hard to show exactly how the French
translation had departed from the sense of his original and caused her
confusion. In the published version he remained content with a more
general allegation. Anyone reading his original words would see that he
was as orthodox as Madame Dacier herself, although he was tentative
where she was doctrinaire and he was satisfied that Homer was the
greatest of human poets, whereas she must have him perfect and exalted
above humanity.

On one question, however, Pope was ready to admit a difference.
Madame Dacier had said that the manners of Homer's times were so
much the better the less they were like those of modern times. Pope
believed this judgment needed qualification. "I confest that in my own
opinion the world was mended in some points, such as the custom
of putting whole nations to the sword, condemning Kings and their families to perpetual slavery, and a few others." On the matter of heroic
simplicity, however, they quite agreed, although it was here that
Madame Dacier had charged Pope with plagiarism—unfairly, he
thought, since the idea had belonged originally to Eustathius and thus
been borrowed by them both. "I cannot really tell what to say to this
whole Remark," he concluded, "only that in the first part of it Madame
Dacier is displeased that I don't agree with her, and in the last that I do.
But this is a temper which every polite man should over-look in a
Lady."[8]

But Madame Dacier was in her grave when these words were written,
past further recrimination. What she would have made of them is not
hard to say and it was probably lucky for Pope that she could not reply.
Could she have read his translation next to her own, or could she have
run through his observations on the twenty-four books, she would have

---

[7] *The Poems of Alexander Pope*, ed. J. Butt et al., 10 vols. (New Haven, 1961–1967),
10:392–97. The manuscript version (B.M. Add. 4807, ff. 236–339v) is reproduced in ibid.,
app. B, pp. 445–46. Perrault's name is expressly written in the manuscript (f. 236v) but was
later canceled. See Pope to Buckley, Feb. 12, 1723, in Pope, *Correspondence*, 2:157; Sherburn, *Early Career*, p. 231.

[8] Pope, *Poems*, 10:392–97.

found more than enough for a new polemic. Pope was vulnerable, more vulnerable indeed than he probably knew.

2

No one saw Pope's difficulty better than Dr. Bentley. There is a famous story that tells how the two men once met at Dr. Mead's. Pope asked the redoubtable scholar what he thought of his translation. Bentley appeared not to hear but was pressed for his judgment. "Tis a pretty poem Mr Pope," he replied at last, "but it is not Homer."[9] When Pope struck back in later years, Bentley's nephew replied for him.

> You are grown very angry, it seems, at Dr. Bentley of late. Is it because he said (to your Face, I have been told) that your Homer was miserable stuff? That it might be called *Homer modernized* or something to that effect; but that there were little or no Vestiges at all of the old Grecian? Dr. Bentley said right. Hundreds have said the same behind your Back. For Homer translated, first in English, secondly in Rhyme, thirdly not from the Original, but fourthly from a French Translation and that in Prose by a Woman too, how the Devil should it be Homer? As for the Greek Language, everybody that knows it and has compared your Version with the Original, as I have done in many Places, must know too that you know nothing of it. I my self am satisfied . . . that you can barely construe Latin.[10]

Pope's weakness as a scholar was never put more forthrightly to him. Of course, by then he had more than earned the great man's censure. The Scriblerians had found Bentley's work hilarious from the time that Swift first assaulted it in *A Tale of a Tub*. His emendations and corrections on ancient writers were further ridiculed in a chapter set apart especially for them in the *Memoirs of Martinus Scriblerus*, and as the years passed, the members of the club returned to them again and again as a favorite theme.[11] This is not the place to recount that story, but it was Bentley who was the target of the *Virgilius Restauratus* (almost certainly by Dr. Arbuthnot), a burlesque on his critical methods as they might be applied

---

[9]Ibid., 4:346. The story may well be apochryphal; there are variant versions in the *Gentleman's Magazine*, October 1773, p. 449; and Joseph Warton, *An Essay on the Genius and Writings of Pope*, 4th ed., 2 vols. (London, 1782), 2:234.

[10]Thomas Bentley, *A Letter to Mr. Pope Occasioned by Sober Advice from Horace* (London, 1735), p. 14. Pope's *Sober Advice* appears in *Works*, 4:71–89. Pope denied authorship and tried to escape Bentley's censure; see Pope to John Caryll, Feb. 18 and May 12, 1735, in *Correspondence*, 3:451, 455.

[11]"How Martin became a Great Critic," in *The Memoirs of Martinus Scriblerus*, ed. Charles Kerby-Miller (New Haven, 1950), p. 129.

to the *Aeneid*; of *An Account of the State of Learning in the Empire of Lilliput together with the History and Character of Bullum the Emperor's Library Keeper* (probably also by Arbuthnot); and eventually of Pope's own *Dunciad Variorum*.[12] Bentley had come to represent all that the Scriblerians pretended to despise in the pedantic learning and dogmatic opinion of classical scholarship. But surely Pope's bitterness, unprovoked apparently by any personal consideration, was more than merely philosophical. Whatever the truth about the famous story of their meeting, it is clear enough that Pope understood that the new *Iliad* was unlikely to satisfy the Greek scholar. Pope knew his own weaknesses, however modern writers may equivocate about their extent, and it is hardly likely that he welcomed the idea of the most formidable critic of his or any other generation turning the pages of his translation alongside the Greek text and learned commentaries.

Fortunately, Dr. Bentley had other things to do; his hands were full enough defending his own editions of the classics, and of Milton and the New Testament also, to care very much about an English translation of Homer. Had he wanted to, he could easily have accomplished what later critics attempted and showed in detail, how Pope's translation was not up to the Greek.[13] Had he not already demonstrated to Barnes what he could do if he wished? At least he saw what some others had forgotten, that Pope's Homer *was* a pretty thing, that is to say, a fine poem in its own right. For the scholar, all translations are necessarily imperfect; interest lies almost wholly in the original. When Boswell mentioned the common opinion that Pope's Homer was not up to the original, Dr. Johnson told him flatly, "It is the greatest work of the kind that has ever been produced." (So too Gibbon: "It is the most splendid poetical version that any language has produced.")[14] But Johnson allowed elsewhere the basic correctness of the criticism. "Pope's version of Homer is not Homerical," he wrote, "it wants his awful simplicity, his artless grandeur, his unaffected majesty." And perhaps Richard Bentley would have approved his final judgment. "The purpose of a writer is to be read. . . . Pope wrote for his own age and his own nation."[15] Certainly no one could dispute that the new Homer was read and read again in its own

---

[12]See also *Critical Remarks on Capt. Gulliver's Travels*, by "Dr. Bantley," also printed among John Arbuthnot's *Miscellaneous Works*, 2 vols. (Glasgow, 1751), 1:115–40. Pope's lines in the *Dunciad* appeared only in the 1735 and 1742 editions, however.

[13]For some miscellaneous suggestions, see Gilbert Wakefield in his edition of Pope's *Iliad*, 6 vols. (London, 1796); Richard Hussey in *Notes and Queries*, 1944, pp. 231, 278; 1945, pp. 10–11, 24–28, 49–52, 74–76; Richard Lattimore, "Practical Notes on Translating Greek Poetry," in *On Translation*, ed. Reuben Brower (Cambridge, Mass., 1959), p. 54.

[14]James Boswell, *Life of Samuel Johnson*, rev. L. F. Powell, 6 vols. (Oxford, 1934–1964), 3:256; Edward Gibbon, *Miscellaneous Works*, 5 vols. (London, 1814), 5:583.

[15]Samuel Johnson, *Lives of the Poets*, ed. George Birnbeck Hill, 3 vols. (London, 1905), 3:238.

time and for a long time afterward as it passed through innumerable editions.

Yet the problem of Pope's fidelity should not lightly be dismissed. To the extent that a translator undertakes to reproduce his original exactly, he must necessarily assume the office of historian. This was Hearne's view, and this was why the old scholia and every other device of scholarship were necessary, "tho' undervalu'd by others who look upon them as trifles."[16] When Pope began the *Iliad*, he was not so far from the despised antiquaries as he thought, or as his struggle with the commentators suggests. But the translator at any time, and especially in Pope's day, was under a serious constraint. Not only must he be accurate, he must also be contemporary, that is to say, he must transpose the original into a language and an experience that is immediately intelligible to his readers. "Make him speak good English," Sir William Trumbull had instructed the young poet, "dress his admirable characters in your proper, significant, and expressive conceptions, and make him useful and instructive to this degenerate age."[17] If he does not make him contemporary, he will not be read, or if he is read anyway, he will not be useful. For it must be remembered that epic poetry (like all serious literature) was meant in Pope's time for more than mere amusement; it was meant to teach, like history, by example.[18] If the reader overlooks the morality of the *Iliad*, he reads it, says Pope, "as a common Romance, and mistakes the chief Aim of it, which is to instruct."[19] That was what had caused so much controversy. But if the manners and customs of the poem appeared to be too unlike those of the present, then it must lose its point, which of course it would do even more obviously if its language remained remote or obscure. The translator therefore faced a special dilemma that the antiquary could to some extent avoid. He had to try to accomplish what we now thnk unlikely, to be faithful to both past and present at one and the same time. To the extent that the Augustans believed in the fundamental likeness of antiquity with their present, this seemed possible. But

[16]Thomas Hearne, *Remarks and Collections*, ed. C. E. Doble et al., 11 vols. (Oxford, 1885–1921), 6:234.

[17]Trumbull to Pope, April 9, 1908, quoted by Reuben Brower, *Alexander Pope: The Poetry of Allusion* (Oxford, 1959), p. 85.

[18]"The *Odyssey* is a moral and political work, instructive to all degrees of men, and filled with images, examples and precepts of civil and domestic life": Pope's postscript to the *Odyssey*, in *Poems*, 10:382. William Pitt repeats the commonplace to his nephew, recommending Homer and Virgil; not only are they "the two greatest poets but they contain the finest lessons for your age to imbibe, lessons of honour, courage, disinterestedness, love of truth, command of temper, gentleness of behaviour, humanity, and in one word, virtue": *Correspondence of William Pitt, Earl of Chatham*, 4 vols. (London, 1838–1840), 1:62. For other testimony, see H. T. Swedenberg, *The Theory of the Epic in England, 1650–1800*, University of California Publications in English 15 (Berkeley, 1944), pp. 193–213.

[19]Pope, *Poems*, 7:557–58.

it was the antiquaries and the scholars—that is, the moderns—who had begun to erode that very confidence. It was Bentley who saw Homer as a careless rhapsodist, singing for a living in a primitive society long passed; it was Pope who imagined him a poet like Virgil or Milton (or like himself), composing an epic according to the rules of Aristotle for a patron in a society different, though not unrecognizably so, from his own. If he did not go so far as Madame Dacier to blur the distinction between past and present, he nevertheless accepted, like her, a fundamental continuity of culture and value between the classical world and his own time. (Such differences as he admitted were only accidental and remediable.)[20] It was left to the moderns to deny this identity and to emphasize the differences between the Homeric past and modern times, either from the perspective of Reason and Sensibility, like La Motte and Terrasson, or from the subtler vantage point of history and scholarship, like Bentley and Vico.[21]

For the commentator or antiquary, therefore, the problem was simpler than for the translator; the past could be approached for its own sake. But this of course was the very reason for the charges of pedantry leveled against them. What was the *use* of such activity? Who cared about the meaning of each phrase in a poem, or of each detail in the past? "When Curiosity or a desire of Knowledge *only* engages us in our Studies," remarked the *Censor*, "we are in a fair way of being Pedants, useless Criticks, Editors, Commentators, or Virtuoso's. . . ." Who cared, wrote Pope's colleague Broome, to "trouble the world with vain niceties about a Letter, or a Syllable, or the transposition of a Phrase?" "I have been very often disappointed of late Years," Addison lamented in 1712, "when upon examining the new Edition of a Classick Author, I have found above half the Volume taken up with various Readings." How often had he, instead of finding something important, discovered only that in some ancient manuscripts *and* was written *et* while in others it was written *ac*. "I have often fancied with my self how enraged an old Latin Author would be, should he see the several Absurdities in Sense and

---

[20]"I sometimes think I am in respect to Homer much like Sancho with regard to Don Quixote. I Believe upon the whole that no Mortal ever came near him for Wisdom, Learning, and all good Qualities. But sometimes there are certain Starts which I cannot tell what to make of, and am forced to own that my Master is a little out of the way, if not quite beside himself": ibid., pp. 283–84. On the whole, Pope found Homer's morality defensible but had trouble with five significant incidents: ibid., pp. 128–29.

[21]"We know far more about Homer and the past than Homer did and the effect of our knowledge has been to make the past more remote and Homer more anonymous . . . the setting, and the nature of the poems themselves, have been revealed as so far removed from our modes of experience that no attempt to recapture them can be successful": Norman Callan, "Homer and the Greek Learning of His Time," in Pope, *Works*, 6:lxxv. For a succinct expression of the "historicist" dilemma, see Adam Parry, "The Making of Homeric Verse," in *The Language of Achilles and Other Papers* (Oxford, 1989), p. 259.

Grammar, which are imputed to him by some or other of these various Readings. . . ."[22] No doubt Homer would have been astounded to see the *Iliad* in modern scholarly attire, in the edition of Joshua Barnes, say, or the one projected by Dr. Bentley. But would he have recognized himself any better in the Augustan garb of Madame Dacier or Alexander Pope?

3

It was not very likely. But it was hard to know for sure, especially if one's Greek was uncertain. Happily, for those who may have wondered, Pope speedily obliged with another venture that offered a similar set of difficulties. Hardly was the *Iliad* abroad when he undertook a further exercise in scholarship, this time an edition of an English poet, William Shakespeare. Here, for all to see, was a parallel to his treatment of Homer but without the special problems posed by translation. Pope undertook to rescue the Elizabethan from the obscurity of the past in something of the same way that he had the ancient Greek, by restoring his meaning accurately and finding ways to make him intelligible to a modern reader. And this time he was without the handicap of having to transform the original language into an exact modern equivalent. Pope failed and the story of his failure is well known. It need not therefore detain us very long except for what it adds to our tale about Pope's attitude toward scholarship and his quarrel with the pedants.[23]

Pope undertook his new task almost at once after completion of the *Iliad*. Just about the time he was beginning it, he received a letter from his friend Francis Atterbury. This was the man who had led the attack on Bentley in the quarrel over Phalaris and anticipated the Scriblerians. Lately he had been reading Shakespeare and now he complained that "in an hundred places I cannot construe him, I don't understand him." It was not, he went on to say, merely "the faults of the Edition but the Obscurity of the Writer. . . . There are Allusions in him to an hundred things, of which I knew nothing and can guess nothing. . . . I protest Aeschylus does not want a Comment to me, more than he does. . . ."[24] The problem was plain enough, even to someone as suspicious as Atter-

---

[22]*Censor* (by Lewis Theobald), Mar. 30, 1717, pp. 36–37; William Broome, "Preface being an Essay on Criticism," in *Poems on Several Occasions* (London, 1727), p. 5; *Spectator*, Aug. 29, 1712.

[23]See, besides Sherburn's *Early Career*, pp. 233–47, James R. Sutherland, "The Dull Duty of an Editor," *Modern Language Quarterly* 16 (1955): 237–46, reprinted in *Essential Articles for the Study of Alexander Pope*, ed. Maynard Mack (Hamden, Conn., 1964), pp. 675–93; and especially R. F. Jones, *Lewis Theobald* (New York, 1919).

[24]Atterbury to Pope, Aug. 2, 1721, in Pope, *Correspondence*, pp. 78–79.

bury of the methods of modern scholarship. How could one appreciate an Elizabethan writer when the texts were obviously corrupt, when the language had become obscure through time, when all contemporary allusions were lost? In a way, the problem was subtler than with Aeschylus or Homer because of the superficial connections of language and culture that disguised the gulf between the Elizabethans and the Augustans. For two centuries scholars had collaborated to restore the texts and contexts of classical literature but almost no effort had been made to do the same thing for an English writer.

Pope was obviously not the man for the job. If translation was onerous and restricted his poetical genius, mere editing was so much the worse. He had descended, he complained, "first from a pretending Poet to a Critick, then to a low Translator, lastly to a meer Publisher."[25] He despised the work, which he farmed out again as well as he could to several friends and employees. (Both Gay and Fenton were among those who were paid to help him.)[26] He was not ignorant of the requirements of the job; critical editions of the classics were too much a part of the literary atmosphere. He saw that he must try to correct the text by collating copies of the early printed editions (which here substituted for manuscripts) and several times advertised for help.[27] In the end he employed many early quartos besides the first and second folios. And in the preface to his edition, which appeared finally in March 1725, he put on a bold front. "I have discharg'd the dull duty of an Editor," he wrote in a phrase that was to echo for a long time, "to my best judgment, with more labour than I expect thanks, with a religious abhorrence of all Innovation and without any indulgence to my private sense or conjecture. . . . The various Readings are fairly put in the margin. . . . Some suspected passages which are excessively bad . . . are degraded to the bottom of the page. . . . The more obsolete or unusual words are explained." "I have never indulged my own Conjectures," he wrote to a friend, "but kept meerly to such amendments as are authorized by the old Editions in the Author's life-time."[28]

Alas, it was not true. Despite his brave assertions, Pope did not really

[25]Pope to Judith Cowper, Nov. 5, 1722, in ibid., 2:141–42.

[26]Ibid., pp. 80–81, 130; Sherburn, *Early Career*, p. 234. Arbuthnot seems also to have contributed; see Pope, *Correspondence*, 2:100–101. At one point, Pope wrote to Tonson, he resolved to spend a week in London, "purposely to get together Parties of my acquaintance ev'ry night, to collate the several Editions of Shakespeare's single Plays, five of which I have engaged to this design": *Correspondence*, 2:118.

[27]In the *Daily Post, Daily Courant,* and *London Evening Post* (1722–1724); Sherburn, *Early Career*, p. 234; Pope, *Correspondence*, p. 102n.

[28]Pope to Judith Cowper, Nov. 25, 1722, in Pope, *Correspondence*, 2:141–42; Pope to Broome, in ibid., pp. 269–70. Pope's preface, based on the 1725 and the revised 1728 versions, may be found in *The Prose Works of Alexander Pope*, ed. Rosemary Cowler (Oxford, 1986), pp. 10–40.

understand and certainly had no patience for collating texts, listing variants, or making sound emendations. He knew something of what was
expected of him, having attended that far at least to the pedants, but he
found himself entirely unable to accomplish it.[29] In fact, his method was
haphazard and careless, and while he introduced a few metrical alterations in the text which have lasted, most of his changes were decidedly
for the worst. Among other things, he found some 1,560 lines that he
thought unworthy of Shakespeare and either reduced them to the bottom
of the page or eliminated them altogether. Nor did he, as he had promised, inform the reader of what he was doing and supply the variants that
would have allowed an independent judgment. His chief criterion remained his own (Augustan) sense of poetic propriety. Since he knew
almost nothing of Elizabethan literature or history, he was frequently
misled by the apparent meaning of the text and entirely unable to offer
helpful elucidation.[30]

Unfortunately for Pope, at least one of his contemporaries saw this at
once. In 1725 Lewis Theobald was an obscure young writer with a sound
classical education and an interest in Shakespeare. He had been struggling
for some years as a miscellaneous writer, turning out poetry and plays,
pantomimes and operas, and editing a short-lived journal patterned on
the *Spectator*, which he called the *Censor*. In 1714 he translated La Motte's
discourse on the *Iliad*, and he praised Pope's translation extravagantly
when it appeared. He even began a translation of the *Odyssey*, as well as a
number of Greek tragedies. In the *Censor* he did not hesitate to satirize
pedantic learning, and even to dissent a little from Bentley's criticism of
the letters of Phalaris. Somewhere along the way, however, he fell under
the spell of that "Great Man in Critical Learning," and absorbed the
lessons of his scholarship. (He even published Bentley's only known
poem in a miscellany called *The Grove*.)[31] In Theobald's later years he

---

[29]"Pope in his edition undoubtedly did many things wrong, and left many things
undone; but let him not be defrauded of his due praise; he was the first that knew, at least
the first that told by what helps the text might be improved. If he inspected the early
editions negligently, he taught others to be more accurate": Johnson, *Lives of the Poets*,
3:139.

[30]See especially Thomas Lounsbury, *The Text of Shakespeare* (London, 1906), and
(more sympathetically) P. Dixon, "Pope's Shakespeare," *Journal of English and Germanic
Philology* 63 (1964): 191–203, and John A. Hart, "Pope as Scholar-Editor," *Studies in
Bibliography* 23 (1970): 45–59. Lounsbury was no doubt too severe on Pope but his detailed
comparisons remain indispensable, and even more sympathetic critics, such as Sutherland
and Mack, do not differ substantially from his judgments. So too Brian Vickers, Introduction to his *Shakespeare: The Critical Heritage, 1693–1733* (London, 1974), pp. 15–16.

[31]*Censor*, nos. 26, 33, 68, 91. For Bentley's poem, see James Henry Monk, *The Life of
Richard Bentley*, 2d ed., 2 vols. (London, 1833). For Theobald, see besides Jones, *Lewis
Theobald*, John Nichols, *Illustrations of the Literary History of the Eighteenth Century*, 8 vols.
(London, 1817–1858), 2:707–48. Theobald admired and praised Pope's *Iliad* in the *Censor*.

attempted the same kind of philological criticism of ancient authors as his master, including conjectural emendation, and on one occasion he tackled some Greek inscriptions that he thought had been badly transcribed by George Wheler. Although he had to retract one with some embarrassment, on the whole the results were not discreditable and proclaimed him a scholar who fully understood the methods of the new learning.[32] On other occasions, he was able to discover an error in Cuper's *Apotheosis Homeri* (a misunderstanding of Eustathius which he corrected) and several oversights in Kuster's edition of Suidas.[33]

Theobald had long had his own ideas about Shakespeare, even to writing an adaptation of *Richard II*. When he read over Pope's new version of the plays, he responded at once with a work that was calculated to win him reputation. He called it *Shakespeare Restored, or a Specimen of the many Errors as well committed as unamended by Mr Pope in his late Edition of this Poet* (1726). It was a very original work, not in its method, which was borrowed directly from classical philology, but in its subject, which was a modern vernacular author. Theobald had not Pope's resources but he saw the necessity of reading widely in Elizabethan literature, in the sources used by Shakespeare, as also in his contemporaries; he understood what collation and emendation could accomplish for the text, and he was not put off by pedantic detail, considering even punctuation to be significant for an editor.[34] His tract created a scandal and was followed by a controversy in which Pope and his friends lashed back by heaping scorn on what they called sardonically "verbal criticism." "Tibbalds will be the follower of Bentley," Pope wrote to his publisher gleefully, "and Bentley of Scriblerus." He promised to enshrine them both in his new work on dullness so that Martin would be allowed to have the last word.[35] Meanwhile, however, he had to wait nervously while Theobald set to work on his own rival edition of Shakespeare, the first attempt at a critical rendering of any modern English author.

When it appeared, Theobald's Shakespeare (1734) was a popular suc-

[32]Rather like Bentley, he had boasted that, "though I have never been in Greece nor seen the inscriptions any where [but] in his book, I think I can restore them to their true sense and numbers": Nichols, *Literary Illustrations*, 2:739. Unfortunately, he had neglected to look at Spon and so made an error over a votive tablet which he was forced to retract; a useful lesson, perhaps. See ibid., pp. 653–54; Jones, *Lewis Theobald*, pp. 199–201 and app. C.

[33]Theobald to Warburton, March–April 1730, in Nichols, *Literary Illustrations*, 2:554–56, 565, 596, 601.

[34]"This very dull and laborious man," wrote Pope's biographer, "hit upon the true and rational method of correcting and illuminating his author, that is, by reading such books (whatever trash Pope might call them) as Shakespeare read and by attending to the genius, learning, and notions of the times": Warton, *Essay on Pope*, 2:235. For Warton and his circle, see Joseph M. Levine, *Humanism and History* (Ithaca, N.Y., 1987), pp. 193–203.

[35]Pope to Tonson, Nov. 14, 1731, in Pope, *Correspondence*, 3:243–44.

cess and showed even more decisively than his earlier work the inadequacies of Pope's scholarship. Not that it was free from error or carelessness; but it was a distinct improvement and one that pointed in the right direction. Theobald's conjectures, like Bentley's, were sometimes overzealous, but he saw that neither an arbitrary alteration of the text nor a mechanical collation would do. Editorial duty was neither dull nor trivial. "Where the Authority of all Books makes the Poet commit a Blunder (whose general Character it is, not to be very exact) 'tis the Duty of an Editor to shew him as he is and to detect all fraudulent tampering [like Pope's!] to make him better."[36] He offered several hundred emendations, many still acceptable, and two hundred explanatory notes; he restored a couple of hundred faulty alterations from Pope's edition, and attended to such matters as stage directions, division into acts, and punctuation. "Shakespeare's Case," Theobald explained, "has in great Measure resembled that of a corrupt Classic; and consequently, the Method of Care was believed to bear a Resemblance."[37]

What he did not do was to offer any comment of the other kind; he made no special effort to illustrate Shakespeare's "beauties," although he recognized that also to be a legitimate function of criticism. (At the same time, he could not resist offering a few Greek emendations in the preface as a kind of tribute to Bentleian method, although even he realized they were hopelessly irrelevant and open to ridicule.) Indeed, where Pope had insisted that the aesthetic judgment was the only proper office of a critic, and the rest beneath contempt, Theobald suggested that no evaluation was possible until the text had been cleared of difficulties and the author understood.

On this ground, then, Theobald demonstrated that Pope had failed with his Shakespeare in the very same way that Dr. Bentley knew that he had with his Homer.[38] Indeed, at one point, after he had been abused by Pope, Theobald himself contemplated a new attack on the translation which he would have called "An Essay upon Mr Pope's Judgment extracted from his own Works and humbly addressed to him."[39] And with his genuine classical training, he might well have inflicted as much injury there as he did with his *Shakespeare Restor'd*. From the vantage point of

[36]Nichols, *Literary Illustrations*, 2:210.

[37]From Theobald's preface to *The Works of Shakespeare*, 7 vols. (London, 1733), 1:-xxxix; Jones, *Lewis Theobald*, p. 173.

[38]The contrast between Pope and Theobald was put by the anonymous author of *Some Remarks on the Tragedy of Hamlet* (1736): "I would not have Mr. Pope offended at what I say, for I look upon him as the greatest Genius in Poetry that has ever appear'd in England; But a province of an Editor and Commentator is quite foreign to a Poet; the Latter, by the Corrections and Excellency of his own Genius, is often tempted to give us an Author as he thinks he ought to be." He naturally preferred Theobald's text. See the edition by Clarence D. Thorpe for the Augustan Reprint Society (Los Angeles, 1947), p. 4.

[39]Theobald to Warburton, Mar. 10, 1730, in Nichols, *Literary Illustrations*, 2:551–57.

scholarship, Pope's efforts at Greek and Elizabethan English came to much the same thing. But it would be too simple to leave it at that; the values of translation and edition are not identical. We are assured by a recent writer that it *is* possible to get to the original *Iliad* through Pope's Homer (though no one has seriously suggested that we read Pope's Shakespeare for that purpose), and that in a curious way his translation is more useful to the reader who knows his Greek than to one who does not.[40] If this idea makes any sense, however, it does so *despite* Pope's deficiencies in Greek and not because of them. It is due perhaps to the fact that Pope was a great poet, and it can be argued that a great poet speaks to some extent a universal language that is not bound by merely temporal considerations. There may well be something universal in life and art in Homer's original—or in Shakespeare's—which was responsive to Pope's poetic gifts. (So, for example, Pope was able to reject the *Double Falsehood*, which Theobald accepted as genuine Shakespeare.) And indeed, if the past were completely and entirely obliterated by change, if there were no continuities whatsoever, then it is very unlikely that the historian, let alone the translator, could find any access to it; both history and translation would be impossible.[41] On the other hand, while some essential qualities of the poem and of the past may be retrievable by poetic intuition, the whole color and context and in the end the very authenticity and historical meaning of the text would seem to depend upon the more mundane and pedantic concern for details, however piddling, that Pope despised.

As usual, Pope was partly aware of this. He saw that the translator could not "omit or confound any Rites or Customs of Antiquity," and that modern terms of war or government such as platoon, companies, junto, etc., were not permissible equivalents for the institutions of Homer's world. But he was not—could not in his ignorance be—consistent. Perhaps Matthew Arnold may be allowed to have the last word. The translator of Homer, he urged, must try to satisfy the scholar as well as the ordinary reader. "A scholar may be a pedant it is true and then his judgment will be worthless; but a scholar may also have poetical feeling and then he can judge him truly; whereas all the poetical feeling in the world will not enable a man who is not a scholar to judge him truly. For the translator is to reproduce Homer, and the scholar alone has the means to knowing that it is Homer who is to be reproduced."[42] Scholarship is thus a necessary if not a sufficient condition for retrieving the past. In his heart Pope knew this; and he thought that he could satisfy Arnold's ideal

---

[40]H. A. Mason, *To Homer through Pope* (London, 1972), pp. 41–55.

[41]See the remarks of Adam Parry and his father, Milman Parry, in "Making of Homeric Verse" (n. 21 above), p. 259.

[42]Matthew Arnold, "On Translating Homer," in *Essays* (Oxford, 1914), p. 264.

readers, "those who have at once a Taste of Poetry, *and* competent Learning."[43] But he also suspected that he had not done full justice to learning,[44] a suspicion that probably accounts for his increasing asperity against the critics, some of whom, such as poor Thomas Hearne, had never once provoked him. But whether he knew it clearly or not, the critics had gotten on to something more than mere envy. They had spoken truly and, however briefly, penetrated the mask of satire and provoked the poet and his fellow wits. For that they were more than repaid; they were enshrined forever—Theobald, Dr. Bentley, Thomas Hearne, and others—in the *Dunciad*, as the very symbols of pedantic learning.

4

But there was yet another way to reply to Pope. The controversy over Homer had begun with the rival claims of the *Iliad* and the *Aeneid*, and Pope, despite some initial hesitation, had taken sides firmly with Homer against Virgil. In no place was this more evident than in the eighteenth book, where, following Boivin and the Daciers, he had reaffirmed the superiority of the shield of Achilles to the shield of Aeneas. But this was not likely to satisfy the proponents of Virgil, and it was not long before they responded. In July 1718 there appeared a new translation of the *Aeneid* with preface and notes. In confident but courteous terms it replied to Pope's claims for Homer and the shield.

The author was the first professor of poetry at Oxford, Joseph Trapp. The chair had been established in 1708 and Trapp, as a fellow of Wadham College and a practicing poet, had been a natural contender. "He is a Person of good Parts," noticed Thomas Hearne in 1706, "and has got some Reputation among the Witts for Writing a Play call'd *Abram Mule*. He has likewise some verses in the *Musae Anglicanae*." This achievement had been enough, along with "mean Circumstances," to elect him without opposition, "to the great satisfaction of the whole university." Hearne was among those gratified, but his pleasure turned to chagrin when Trapp turned out to be a follower of the hated vice chancellor. The professor of poetry was transformed at once into a craven character, "given to cringing and a great commender of the Tricks of Lancaster." Hearne never forgave him.[45]

---

[43]"Since a meer Modern Wit can like nothing that is not Modern, and a Pedant nothing that is not Greek": *Poems*, 7:23.

[44]When Pope brought out a second edition of Shakespeare (1728), he silently incorporated many of Theobald's emendations; see Sherburn, *Early Career*, p. 247.

[45]Hearne, *Remarks and Collections*, 1:212; 2:120, 122, 141.

Trapp's lectures were very successful. They were "drawn up in very elegant language, and were constantly attended by very crowded audiences." He printed a volume of the *Praelectiones poeticae* in 1711, another in 1715, and a third in 1719; eventually they were turned into English.[46] They brought him a measure of fame as a critic, although not everyone was impressed. He was praised extravagantly by Henry Felton and by Thomas Tickell,[47] but not by Thomas Hearne. If this was partly due to politics, there was also the natural distaste of the scholar for the wit. When, for example, Tickell lectured in Trapp's place upon bucolics (ancient and modern), Hearne thought it a "silly and indiscrete performance." The trouble was, apparently, that "once or twice he mentioned Criticks and spoke very disrespectfully and ignorantly of them." No doubt Tickell had treated them just as Pope had—although in fact we cannot be sure, since his lecture has disappeared. When later Mr. Dennison, the senior proctor, made a speech proclaiming the achievements of the university press, and singled out Trapp's *Praelectiones* for special praise, Hearne was astounded. With all the serious works of scholarship to its credit, it was absurd to choose that "trivial" performance. Why had he not preferred Dr. Hudson's edition of the Greek geographers (to which Mr. Dodwell had so prominently contributed), or Archdeacon Batteley's *Antiquitates Rutupinae*? "These two Books . . . are really Books of solid Learning, will last and ought to be remembered hereafter in the Annals of the University, where such Books as Trapp's ought not to have a place."[48]

Perhaps there is something to be said for Hearne's judgment, since even Trapp's translator thought the lectures (privately) "a very superficial book."[49] But the work was popular if only because it was so commonplace. Trapp drew upon the scholarly "poetics" of Vossius and of Monsieur Dacier, of Rapin and Bossu, occasionally differing but generally arguing his case within the terms dictated by those standard works. He displayed not the slightest interest in those meaner offices of criticism, philology and textual criticism. Like his models, he set his mind exclusively to loftier things, to elucidating in a general way the beauties of ancient literature. In the last and climactic chapter, he wrote about epic, enlarging (improving, he thought) upon Bossu's definition. It was "a Poem express'd in a Narration, form'd upon a Story partly real, and

[46]Joseph Trapp, *Lectures on Poetry* (London, 1742). See *Biographia Britannica*, 7 vols. (London, 1747–1766), 7:174–75.

[47]Henry Felton, *A Dissertation on Reading the Classics and Forming a Just Style* (London, 1715), pp. xv–xvii; Thomas Tickell, *Prospect of Peace* (London, 1713), p. 22.

[48]Hearne, *Remarks and Collections*, 3:111, 144–45.

[49]John Nichols, *Literary Anecdotes of the Eighteenth Century*, 9 vols. (London, 1812–1815), 2:149n. Trapp himself made no claims to scholarship; see Trapp to D'Orville, July 13, 1739, Bodleian MS. D'Orville 482, ff. 282–83.

partly feign'd, representing in a sublime and flowry style, some glorious and fortunate Action, that is distinguish'd by a Variety of great Events, to form the Morals and inflame the Mind with Love of heroic Action." Thus armed, he was ready to expound the virtues of the *Aeneid*.[50]

Trapp's translation was thus a particular example of the general precepts worked out in the *Praelectiones*. His preface and notes were meant, like Pope's, to expound the poetic merits of the original. He deliberately avoided the ponderous subjects of history, antiquities, and geography, content to refer his readers for such matters to the "common school book" edition of Ruaeus. But praise for Virgil involved him unavoidably in the comparison with Homer begun by Scaliger and Rapin. Like Pope, he attempted a moderate judgment; he had no wish to disparage Homer and thought that Scaliger had gone too far. (But so had Madame Dacier in castigating Scaliger!) And like Pope again, he used Bossu's approach to epic to organize his argument. He was thus prepared to show how in every respect, from the fable to the diction, Virgil was superior to Homer, even in those things that Pope had especially claimed for the Greek: invention, style, and vividness of description. Indeed, Virgil even surpassed Homer where he had directly copied from him, in the funeral games, for example, or in the descent into Hell, and not least, in the descriptions of the shields of the heroes. The Roman history and the temples of Augustus upon the buckler of Aeneas were thus far superior to the "merely ornamental Sculptures upon Homer's."[51] Like Pope, he left to the notes his detailed argument.

If Pope had had the advantage of Boivin and Monsieur Dacier for his defense of the shield of Achilles, Trapp also found some of his own arguments in the work of a Frenchman, Jean Regnard de Segrais. Segrais had translated the *Aeneid* many years before in a poetic version that continued in use until the nineteenth century. He had adorned it also with notes, as befitted a writer who, though he was not himself an *érudit*, numbered among his friends many who were.[52] One of his notes took up the problem presented by the shield of Aeneas. It was nothing less than the very difficulty that had presented itself in Homer: how could so many adventures—enough to fill an ample gallery—be engraved upon a single piece of armor? It was not enough for Segrais to show that this fear had also been claimed for the shields of Homer and Hesiod, Silius Italicus

[50]Trapp, *Lectures in Poetry*, p. 330. The translation was titled *The Aeneis of Virgil*, 2 vols. (London, 1718–1720). Brief notices about Trapp appear in *Modern Language Notes* 41 (1926): 158–63; *Philological Quarterly* 28 (1950): 413–16; and *Modern Language Review* 53 (1958): 81–83.

[51]Trapp, *Aeneis*, I:xxiv.

[52]Jean Regnard de Segrais, *Traduction de l'Eneide de Virgile* (Paris, 1681); see W. M. Tipping, *Jean Regnard de Segrais* (Paris, 1933), esp. pp. 153–66.

and Statius; or that sculptors had resolved similar problems in stone by using perspective and diminishing the figures. He showed that the poet, like the painter, was at liberty to invent and to suggest. As Trapp summarized Segrais's argument, "It is not necessary to suppose they were all engravers; it is enough some were; the Range of the Poet's Fancy may be allow'd to solve the Rest." But if the Frenchman was content to grant the poet this liberty, in the end Trapp was not. There was no need for it, he thought, to account for the shield; everything on it might be literally true if one only remembered first the stature of the heroes and consequently the size of their shields and secondly the lessening of the engraved figures. Everything that Virgil had described on the shield could thus easily have been engraved upon it.[53] And so regarded, it was distinctly superior to its model in the *Iliad*. Virgil was in this, as everywhere else, far above Homer; Pope had been quite wrong.[54]

It remained to do but one thing more for Virgil that Pope had already accomplished for Homer: to show exactly what the shield would have looked like. Trapp was content with the bare assertion of its possibility, but the next translator was not. Some years after Trapp's work, a group of writers issued a new edition of Virgil in Latin and English, with the *Aeneid* translated by Christopher Pitt, and a special essay devoted to "Observations on the Shield of Aeneas," contributed by William Whitehead, soon to become poet laureate.[55] Both Pitt and Whitehead were admirers of Pope and expressly indebted to his *Iliad*. While contemplating the eighth book of Virgil's poem, Whitehead says, he was struck by the vivacity of its pictures, "which put me upon considering whether it might not be possible to connect them all together in the manner of a shield, as Mr. Pope had done with regard to the shield of Achilles." Once begun, the task was so easily accomplished that he wondered only that it had not been attempted before. (Why had no Virgilian ever tried to set the Roman poet next to the Greek in this respect too?) With the help of an engraver, he designed and printed the shield exactly after the model of Pope, in two concentric circles and sixteen scenes, a fold-out plate to demonstrate his point and give concrete reality to the shield. Then, still following Pope, he explained each scene by quoting from the poem. The

[53]Trapp, *Aeneis*, 2:87, 881–82; Segrais, *Traduction*, 2:14–15.

[54]Hearne quotes the following epigram with approval:

> Keep the Commandments Trap, go no further,
> For it is written, thou shall not murther.

Remarks and Collections, 7:286; and *Biographia Britannica*, 7:174n. See also the verdicts of Swift and Dr. Johnson, *Lives of the Poets*, 1:453. And for a modern estimate, John Conington, "The English Translators of Virgil," in his *Miscellaneous Works*, 2 vols. (London, 1872), 1:137–97, esp. pp. 19–95.

[55]*The Works of Virgil in Latin and English*, 4 vols. (London, 1763), 3:457–92.

result was indeed a fitting comparison, if not a victorious rival, to the shield of Achilles. The imagination of the translator had once again recreated a lost original from the evidence of the text. But long before Whitehead wrote, Pope had already begun to chafe under the many criticisms that were, one way or another, being heaped upon his work.

5

Pope was determined to have the last word. He read each of the attacks upon him as they appeared. Some of them he had bound for him by Tonson in six volumes labeled "Curll and Company," "Libels on Swift and Pope," and so on, and they still may be seen with his underlings and annotations.[56] Pope enjoyed a quarrel but he was stung by his critics. The *Dunciad* may have had a large and exalted purpose (opinions have differed) but it was also meant simply to retaliate. Some lines seem to go back as far as 1720; by the end of 1725 a draft was on paper. It was probably Swift's visits of 1726–27 and the resumption of Scriblerian camaraderie that gave the work its last filup. The subject matter was now broadened; what had begun as a satire on bad poets was extended now to bad critics also.[57] A first version appeared tentatively in 1728; with success it was followed shortly by a more ambitious effort, the *Dunciad Variorum*. This version, Pope explained to Swift, would be printed in all pomp. "It will be attended with Proeme, Prolegomena, Testimonia Scriptorium, Indexes authorum, and Notes Variorum." If Swift wished, Pope would be pleased to have his help, "whether dry raillery; upon the stile and way of commentary of trivial Critics; or humorous, upon the authors in the poem; or historical, of persons, places, times; or explanatory; or collecting the parallel passages of the ancients."[58]

The *Dunciad Variorum* was thus intended as a characteristic Scriblerian satire and it no doubt incorporated suggestions by Swift and Arbuthnot, although as usual we cannot be sure.[59] Martin himself appears throughout, in prologue, notes, even errata. But the whole idea, a mock epic replete with ludicrous scholarly accompaniment, goes back directly to *A*

[56]In the British Library, shelf mark C 116 b 1–4, with two others in the Victoria and Albert Museum; see Pope to Tonson, n.d., in Pope, *Correspondence*, 3:399.

[57]See Sherburn, *Early Career*, pp. 303–5; James Sutherland, Introduction to *Dunciad*, in Pope, *Poems*, 5:xiii–xxiii; Nichols, *Literary Illustrations*, 2:748–68; Edna L. Steeves, Introduction to her *Art of Sinking in Poetry* (Chicago, 1952).

[58]Pope to Swift, June 28, 1728, in Pope, *Correspondence*, 2:503. In a note to the *Dunciad* (1729), Swift is said "in a sort to be Author of the Poem," inasmuch as he had snatched it from the fire and encouraged the author to proceed: Pope, *Poems*, 5:201n.

[59]Pope asked for help from Richard Savage, Thomas Sheridan, and (perhaps) Robert Walpole, besides Swift and Arbuthnot. See Robert W. Rogers, *The Major Satires of Swift* (Urbana, Ill., 1955), pp. 14–15; Pope, *Poems*, 5:xxiv–xxvii.

THE

DUNCIAD,

VARIORVM.

WITH THE

PROLEGOMENA of *SCRIBLERUS.*

LONDON.
Printed for A. DOD.1729.

The frontispiece to Alexander Pope's *Dunciad Variorum* (1729), reproduced by
permission of Princeton University Libraries

Tale of a Tub and *The Battle of the Books*, along with their progeny. The poem is a celebration of the goddess Dullness and her votaries—Pope's enemies all—and the parody is based loosely upon the *Aeneid*. The poet was not content with the stock characters of traditional satire, however, but gave to each of them a name, even a whole biography, to make his judgments perfectly explicit. Theobald, therefore, was singled out to become the hero of the *Dunciad*. "General satire in times of general vice had no force and is no punishment," Pope wrote to Arbuthnot (who seems to have needed persuasion), "people have ceased to be ashamed of it when so many are joined with them; and it is only by hunting one or two from the herd that any examples can be made." No one must be left in doubt about his victims, although Pope himself remained for a time anonymous.[60]

The *Dunciad* is not an easy work to describe, or to read. Its great fund of specific personal allusion, along with its complex apparatus, including notes to the notes, made it obscure even to some of its first readers.[61] The modern editor must add explanatory notes even to the original notes and has to conjure with the many altered editions that appeared in Pope's lifetime, containing substantial additions, contractions, and substitutions. Pope added to the confusion (deliberately) by assuming several voices in the work, attributing the prefaces, notes, and appendices to a number of authors—to Theobald, Bentley, Scriblerus, and so on— although they were almost all by himself. Although the poem had other objectives also, its chief interest to us must be its attack upon the pedants.

As we have seen, Pope hit back at the scholars in the first place through the very form of his epic. The *Dunciad* resembles a scholarly text; the poem is enshrined in a mock erudition that extends even to the errata list and index. The "remarks" and "imitations" that surround the verse set off the poem to great comic effect, and the prolegomena and appendices further exaggerate the pseudo learning of the (apparently) collective enterprise. In all this adumbration and confusion, one theme is constant: the triviality and inconsequence of all learned commentary. The very first note to the poem sets the tone. It is signed by "Theobald" and takes up the problem of the correct spelling of the title of the work.

> The *Dunciad*, *Sic* M.S. It may well be disputed whether this be a right Reading? Ought it not rather to be spelled *Dunceiad*, as the Etymology

---

[60]Pope to Arbuthnot, Aug. 2, 1734, in George Aitkin, *The Life and Works of John Arbuthnot* (Oxford, 1892), p. 150. See also "A Letter to the Publisher," in *Dunciad* (London, 1729), pp. 10–11. Theobald was usually recognized as the main provocation for the poem; see, e.g., *Mist's Journal*, June 8, 1728, and Orator Henley, *The Hyp Doctor* 29 (June 22–29, 1728), in Pope, *Poems*, 5:xii–xiii.

[61]Swift to Pope, July 16, 1728, in Pope, *Correspondence*, 2:504–5; Stratford to Harley, in *Historical Manuscript Commission Reports; Manuscripts of the Duke of Portland*, vol. 7 (London, 1901), pp. 461–62.

evidently demands? *Dunce* with an *e*, therefore *Dunceiad* with an *e*. That accurate and punctual Man of Letters, the Restorer of *Shakespere*, constantly observes the preservation of this very Letter *e*, in spelling the Name of his beloved Author, and not like his common careless Editors, with the omission of one, nay sometimes of two *ee's* (as Shak'spear) which is utterly unpardonable. Nor is the neglect of a *Single Letter* so trivial as to some it may appear; the alteration whereof in a learned language is an *Atchievement that brings honour* to the *Critick* who advances it; and Dr B will be remembered to posterity for his performances of this sort, as long as the world shall have any Esteem for the Remains of Menander and Philemon.

It is hard to say whether Pope would have been more disturbed by the world's continuing interest in Menander or in Dr. Bentley.

Yet even this much was insufficient; Pope has Scriblerus add a remark of his own (a note to the note) disputing with Theobald: "I have a just value for the Letter E," he proclaims, "and the same affection for the Name of this Poem, as the fore cited Critic for that of his Author." But in the end he finds the *Dunceiade* a Gallicism and rejects it. "Upon the whole," he concludes, "I shall follow the Manuscript, and print it without any E at all; mov'd there to by Authority, at all times with Criticks equal if not superior to Reason. In which method of proceeding, I can never enough praise my very good Friend, the exact Mr. Tho. Hearne; who if any word occur which to him and all mankind is evidently wrong, yet keeps it in the Text with due reverence, and only remarks in the Margin, *sic* M.S."[62]

Thus in a single note—the first in the work—Pope confounded the "verbal" critics, both the scholars who preferred conjectural emendation (like Theobald or Bentley) and those who preferred the authority of the manuscripts (like Hearne or Joshua Barnes). Whatever their disagreements—and they were obvious enough—the pedants shared at least one attitude toward their texts, a desire to know *exactly* what their authors had meant, and thus had in one way or the other exposed Pope's carelessness. Their learning had therefore to be confounded, if Pope's reputation was to survive. Again and again he reminded his readers of the futility of

[62]Here is Hearne's own description of his editorial methods: "I have all along followed the MSS. I have made use of. So that whenever there appears any Defect or Errour, whether in the Orthography or the Sentence, he must remember, that the same occurrs also in the MSS, it being a Principle with me not to alter MSS even where better and more proper Readings are very plain and obvious. For I have often known, that that hath prov'd to be the true reading which hath been rejected": Thomas Hearne, *Curious Discourses*, 2d ed., 2 vols. (London, 1771), 1:lxx. Hearne explained the method of his Livy to his old teacher Patrick Gordon, claiming not to have "put down any one Lection or observation but what manifestly appeared to me to be of some use." Vossius, he insisted, had been even more minute: Hearne to Gordon, June 14, 1710, Bodleian MS. Rawlinson D 1166, f. 39.

all such labor, whether conjectural criticism or the pouring over old manuscripts by Wormius, that is, Thomas Hearne.

> But who is he, in closet close y pent?
> Of sober face, with learned dust besprent?
> Right well mine eyes arede the myster wight,
> On parchment scrap y-fed, and Worms hight
> To future ages may thy dulness last
> As thou preserv'st the dulness of the past.[63]

Pope even appended an errata list, which he ascribed to Scriblerus, and continued the fun into the index, where (for example) under "Shakespeare" the hero of the *Dunciad* was again mercilessly pilloried.

And yet there was more still, the joke depending indeed upon its reiteration. Pope's ingenuity was unfailing, from the preface ("Martinus Scriblerus Of the Poem") to the appendices, which grew with each edition and came to include such delicious anti-Bentleian items as "Ricardus Aristarchus of the Hero of the Poem"[64] and even Arbuthnot's *Virgilius Restauratus*. In the poem itself—even apart from the notes—Theobald was satirized as a scholar, especially in a mock description of his library. Pope had never forgiven his rival for using Tudor literature to illustrate Shakespeare, "A Gothick Vatican! of Greece and Rome well-purg'd,"

> But high above, more solid Learning shone,
> The Classicks of an Age that heard of none;
> There Caxton slept, with Wynkin at his side,
> One clasp'd in wood, and one in strong cow-hide.

Caxton, Pope reminded his readers in a note, was an early printer whom Tibbald had quoted in *Mist's journal*, "concerning a *strange and mervaylous beaste called Sagittarye*, which he would have Shakespear to mean rather than Teucer, the Archer celebrated by Homer."[65] It seems never to have occurred to Pope that Theobald was right, that the difference was important, and that research was required for an answer. As always, he appears oblivious to the possibilities of philology—and antiquities—to the recovery of the past. "You laugh at what you don't understand," Thomas

---

[63]*Dunciad*, III, ll. 185–90, in Pope, *Poems*, 5:329.

[64]Apparently by Warburton: Joseph Spence, *Observations, Anecdotes, and Characters of Books and Men*, ed. James M. Osborn, 2 vols. (Oxford, 1966), 1:149; Pope, *Correspondence*, 4:434.

[65]See Nichols, *Literary Illustrations*, 2:203–4; Sutherland, "Dull Duty of an Editor," p. 643. Pope returns to this "discovery" several times in the *Dunciad* and includes as an appendix "A Copy of Caxton's Preface to his Translation of Virgil."

Bentley had told him.[66] And yet, behind his contempt for Wynkyn and for Theobald, so often (indeed too often) reiterated, was there not perhaps just a glimmer of recognition, the barest sign, that his critics had scored after all and that Pope had in fact been mistaken?

6

Still Pope was not satisfied. How could he be? Despite the triumphs of Dullness, scholarship continued unabated and the critics of Pope remained unabashed. Was there nothing to embarass the pedants and compel submission? Pope must try again. In 1742, not long before his death, he published his final work, the new *Dunciad*, a fourth book to complete the devastation of the first three. Here at last Pope would pillory the pedants for all time.

Not that Pope had been idle in between. On the one hand he had supported such enterprises as the *Grub Street Journal* and Mallet's poem *Verbal Criticism*, which continued to carry the attack into the enemy camp.[67] On the other hand, he scattered in his own works passages that resumed his own criticism. *The Sober Advice from Horace* continued the device—now almost stale—of satirizing the Bentleian commentary. (Pope's poetic imitation was accompanied by *Notae Bentleianae*, some of them like those in the *Dunciad*.) According to his friend Joseph Spence, he planned a second part to the *Essay on Man*, an "Essay on Education" that would have shown the limits of all scholarly knowledge.[68] In an *Epistle to the Earl of Burlington* (1731) he again made fun of the virtuoso collectors: Pembroke, Mead, Sloane, and Thomas Hearne; while in the *Epistle to Dr. Arbuthnot* (1735) we hear again of "slashing Bentley" and "pidling Tibalds,"

> Each Wight who reads not, and but scorns and spels,
> Each Word-catcher that lives on syllables.[69]

But Pope was determined to put it all together again. The new *Dunciad* began with the projected work on education; it grew finally into a

---

[66]Bentley had gone on to show Pope how his text too had been corrupted by the printer and should be emended by verbal criticism!: *A Letter to Mr. Pope*, pp. 8–9.

[67]See chap. 8 below.

[68]Spence, *Observations*, 1:134; Pope to Swift, Mar. 25, 1736, in Pope, *Correspondence*, 4:5–6.

[69]See the *Epistle to Burlington*, in Pope, *Poems*, 3, pt. ii:134–36; the *Epistle to Arbuthnot*, in ibid, 4:108; and the fourth satire, in ibid., 3:29.

complete restatement of the themes of 1728–29.[70] Its original lines are
most to our point, for they rehearse, for the last time, Pope's complaints
against the scholars. Here are specific names again (Barnes, Bentley,
Wasse, et al.), though Theobald has vanished and, in some places anyway, the satire is broader and less personal. It is Bentley who represents
the false learning of philology:

> Before them march'd that awful Aristarch;
> Plow'd was his front with many a deep Remark.

He is characterized especially by his large hat and his love of port. In
mock-heroic style he addresses the goddess:

> Mistress! dismiss that rabble from your Throne:
> Advaunt—is Aristarchus yet unknown?
> Thy mighty Scholiast, whose unweary'd pains
> Made Horace dull, and humbled Milton's strains.
> Turn what they will to Verse, their toil is vain,
> Critics like me shall make it Prose again.
> Roman and Greek Grammarians! know your Better:
> Author of Something yet more great than Letter;
> While tow'ring o'er your Alphabet, like Saul,
> Stands our Digamma, and o'er tops them all.

Pope was careful to explain Bentley's allusions in a footnote. The pedant
was referring to "the boasted restoration of the Aeolic Digamma, in the
long projected Edition of Homer."

But the great scholar had only begun: Pope continues,

> Tis true, on Words is still our whole debate,
> Disputes of *Me* or *Te*; of *aut* or *at*,
> To sound or sink in *cano*. O or A,
> Or give up Cicero to C or K.

According to Spence, Bentley's speech recalled an actual conversation
between Bentley and Lord Granville, who had long looked forward to
meeting the scholar. When at last they came together, "Mr. Pope said
that the two hours were wholly taken up by his lordship debating and
settling, how the first verse in the *Aeniad* was to be pronounced and

[70]Spence, *Observations*, 1:151; George Sherburn, "The *Dunciad*, Book IV," *Texas Studies
in Language and Literature* 24 (1944): 174–90, reprinted in Mack, *Essential Articles*, pp. 730–
46.

whether we should say Cicero or Kikero?"[71] Now, in the new *Dunciad*, Bentley is made to boast of these achievements, preferring the obscure commentaries to the originals, the ancient fragments to completed poems.

> The critic Eye, that microscope of Wit,
> Sees hairs and pores, examines bit by bit.

The scholars, Pope insists (and now he names Kuster, Burman, and Wasse), were incapable of distinguishing the good from the bad, the significant from the trivial, the whole from the parts. "Some critics," Warburton added in 1751, "having had it in their choice to comment either on Virgil or Manilius, Pliny or Solinus, have chosen the worse authors, the more freely to display their critical ability."[72] Precision and detail were incompatible with grace and proportion. What could be the point of such learning except as an end in itself? Having demonstrated the futility of all his work, Bentley is permitted to vanish.

> "Walker! our hat"—no more he deign'd to say.
> But stern as Ajax' spectre, strode away.

Nor was Pope entirely mistaken. When it came to the beauties and uses of classical learning, somehow he and his friends were indeed the experts and the scholars the amateurs. Did he not in these matters appreciate the *Iliad* better than Kuster, Barnes, or Bentley? Was it not true too that the scholars on the whole *did* prefer to work on the obscure writers and lesser poets, even the fragments, to the relative neglect of the major works? There lay the greatest challenge to their skills, the most intriguing puzzles and tantalizing obscurities. Bentley may have had as much contempt for Malelas and Manilius as Pope, but that did not deter him from giving years to their study. (It was no extenuation to say that he had spent as much time on Horace and the New Testament; the disproportion remained only too obvious.) The scholars may have set out to elucidate classical literature, but in their attention to detail in and for itself they had begun to drive a wedge between their own achievement and the very uses for which their scholarship had been invented, namely, the direct appreciation of the ancient works for their beauty and relevance to practical life. It is no accident that Bentley's heir (and the best equipped of all modern writers to appreciate him), A. E. Housman, could write to the poet Robert Bridges about his own lifelong work on

---

[71]Spence, *Observations*, 1:149–50.
[72]*Dunciad*, IV, l. 1226n., in Pope, *Poems*, 5:365.

Manilius and tell him forthrightly not to waste his time reading that dull and obscure poet. (On another occasion he wrote to a colleague, "If you prefer Aeschylus to Manilius you are no true scholar; you must be deeply tainted with literature.") Why bother, then? Because, as Housman put it elsewhere, scholarship is its own reward, knowledge justifies itself, curiosity is a motive intrinsically worthy of satisfaction.[73]

It was an argument that would not have persuaded Pope or his friends. Perhaps they were not scholars and misunderstood antiquity; nevertheless they had assimilated it somehow in their own (imperfect) fashion and transformed it into something alive and immediately valuable. Nor could it ever be said of them what Housman had pronounced of Bentley, that "the greatest scholar that England or perhaps Europe ever bred" had never developed a true appreciation of poetry.[74]

[73]See A. S. F. Gow, *A. E. Housman* (Cambridge, 1936), p. 13; *The Letters of A. E. Housman*, ed. Henry Maas (London, 1971), p. 144; Housman, Introductory Lecture (1892), in *Selected Prose*, ed. John Carter (Cambridge, 1961), pp. 16–17.

[74]Housman, *Selected Prose*, p. 12.

Chapter Eight

Bentley's Milton

I

Bentley's *Paradise Lost* remains a puzzle. Just why the great man should think of editing a modern poem, in obvious haste and against all advice, and risk his reputation as the most celebrated scholar of his time is not at all apparent. In 1730 he was almost seventy years old and locked in mortal combat with the fellows of Trinity College, his case awaiting trial in the House of Lords. He had fought his way to fame with a series of ambitious works that won him the admiration of learned Europe; but he had no obvious credentials for his new task, and in fact he blundered badly. The world of letters was scandalized, and despite an occasional attempt at exoneration, has continued to find the episode amusing. There is probably not much that can be done now to salvage Bentley's reputation in this matter, but it is undoubtedly worthwhile to look again at what he was attempting, if only because it may help to bring to a proper conclusion our story of the battle of the books. Bentley had been at or near the center of the controversy for many years, and this last peculiar work may be seen as his final contibution, and in a way a fitting climax, to the long English quarrel between the ancients and the moderns. It certainly will not do to toss it off, as some have done too easily, as the result simply of dishonesty, senility, or worse.[1]

Bentley's successes had stemmed in the first place from his wonderful

---

[1]For some useful previous discussion, see J. W. Mackail, "Bentley's Milton," in his *Studies in Humanism* (London, 1938), pp. 186–209; Robert E. Bourdette, Jr., "To Milton Lending Sense: Richard Bentley and *Paradise Lost* (1732)," *Milton Quarterly* 14 (1980): 37–49; Michael M. Cohen and Robert Bourdette, Jr., "Richard Bentley's Edition of *Paradise Lost* (1732): A Bibliography," *Milton Quarterly* 14 (1980): 49–54; John K. Hales, "Notes on Richard Bentley's Edition of *Paradise Lost*," *Milton Quarterly* 18 (1984): 46–50.

ability to restore the meaning of a classical text in Greek or Latin. This he
did with a mastery of the scholarship of centuries and a divinatory genius
that struck awe into his learned contemporaries and nearly everyone
since.[2] We have seen that restoring the ancient texts meant as a rule doing
such humdrum things as collating manuscripts, compiling dictionaries
and indexes, rescuing obscure allusions, understanding meters—in a
word, employing the whole armory of modern philology against the
good taste and better judgment of the defenders of antiquity. But it also
entailed a kind of inferential reasoning from evidence that allowed for
emendation: correcting errors and sometimes adding or subtracting from
the received versions. Here lay some of Bentley's most famous victories.
Since this reasoning was essentially circular, however, from the individual word or textual problem to the whole and back again (the famous
philological circle), it was not always easy to understand or to demonstrate to the uninitiated.[3]

And it was bound to offend conservative sentiment. When one of
Bentley's disciples, Joseph Wasse, came to visit Thomas Hearne in 1722,
he praised Bentley's conjectures on the New Testament mightily, saying
that he had restored some passages without any manuscript authority.
"He said the best way to criticize upon Places is first to correct, and then
to see how the MSS are." Hearne was especially scandalized, since he had
devoted himself to recovering and preserving every comma—and every
error—in the old manuscripts that he himself was editing.[4] Moreover,
since so much depended upon analogy, great learning was essential.
Bentley had assimilated almost the whole of classical literature in his
youth and retained an extraordinary memory in old age. (He could read
the fine print in his Greek New Testament at the age of eighty.) To
elucidate a point or remove an obscurity, he could draw effortlessly on
the accumulated learning of centuries. But not many of his readers, then
or now, were ready to follow him through the tangled paths of his
erudition.

[2]A. E. Housman thought Bentley "the greatest scholar that England or perhaps Europe
ever bred," a view recently endorsed by C. O. Brink, *English Classical Scholarship: Historical
Reflections on Bentley, Porson, and Housman* (Cambridge, 1985), pp. 78–83; see Housman,
Selected Prose, ed. John Carter (Cambridge, 1961), p. 12.

[3]"We are working in a circle, that is a fact there is no denying": A. E. Housman, "The
Application of Thought to Textual Criticism" (1921), in *Selected Prose*, p. 145. For emendation as practiced in the period, see E. J. Kenney, *The Classical Text* (Berkeley, 1984), pp.
21–75, who cites August Boeckh and Ulrich von Wilamowitz, among others, for the
circularity of the process. The idea of a philological circle goes back at least as far as
Schleiermacher; see now the very useful introduction to his *Hermeneutics*, trans. James Duke
and Jack Forstman (Atlanta, 1977).

[4]Thomas Hearne, *Remarks and Collections*, ed. C. E. Doble et al., 11 vols. (Oxford,
1885–1921), 7:378–79.

When Pope and Theobald turned to Shakespeare, they opened up, as we have seen, apparently for the first time, the very same issues that surrounded the interpretation and use of the classical authors, but this time for a modern writer. What was the best way to read and appreciate an author? By a criticism based on literary skill and experience in the world, as Temple and Pope had claimed? Or by the philological and historical scholarship of Wotton and Bentley? The battle of the books had made it hard to believe that the two could ever be reconciled. "A good Poet, and an Honest Historian," writes the Earl of Shaftesbury, "may afford Learning for a Gentleman. And such a one, whilst he reads these Authors as his Diversion, will have a truer relish of their Sense, and understand 'em better, than a Pedant with all his Labours, and the assistance of his Volumes of Commentators."[5]

In fact, one Patrick Hume had already attempted something of a commentary on *Paradise Lost* (1695) to meet the needs of scholarship. Hume was not much worried about the condition of Milton's text, however, which he accepted in its latest version, but he was prepared, as his subtitle explains, to find every biblical allusion and parallel in Homer and Virgil, to explain all the obscure passages, and rescue every old or obsolete word so that the reader could better appreciate the poem.[6] To that purpose he brought an undeniable learning, both ancient and modern, in the classical languages and Hebrew, and in the works of Gallileo, Gassendi, and the rest. Only once or twice did Hume stumble over a textual problem and try to resolve it. Surely, he thought, Milton must have meant "Universal Blot," not "Universal Blanc," a mistake of the printer which he eagerly corrected.[7] Eventually Bentley too happened upon the crux, but he accepted "blanc" and emended the next line instead, turning a "blanc of words" into a "blanc of works." The modern editor, it turns out, has no need for either; but it may have been suggestive for Hume to have put the blame on the printer rather than on Milton.[8]

When Pope attempted Shakespeare, he pretty much ignored explanation and attended rather to marking the "shining passages" in the text so

[5]Shaftesbury, *Characteristics of Men, Manners, Opinions, Times* (1711), quoted in Maynard Mack, *Alexander Pope: A Life* (New York, 1985), p. 480.

[6]Patrick Hume, *Annotations on Milton's Paradise Lost*, "Wherin the Texts of Sacred Writ, relating to the Poem are Quoted: the Parallel Places and imitations of the most excellent Homer and Virgil cited and Compared; all the Obscure Parts render'd in Phrases more Familiar; the Old and Obsolete Words, with their Originals, Explain'd and made Easie to the English Reader" (London, 1695). Hume provides only three textual notes; see Ants Oras, *Milton's Editors and Commentators from Patrick Hume to Henry John Todd* (New York, 1964), pp. 22–49.

[7]Hume, *Annotations*, III, 48 (p. 100).

[8]*Milton's Paradise Lost*, ed. Richard Bentley (London, 1732), p. 79; *The Poetical Works of John Milton*, ed. Helen Darbishire, 2 vols. (Oxford, 1952–1955), 1:293n.

that the Elizabethan playwright could be better appreciated by a contemporary audience. And he deliberately denied employing that bugaboo of modern philology, conjectural emendation, although he silently introduced many changes and removed some 1,560 lines of the text as unworthy of the author.[9] "I have never indulged my own Conjectures, but kept meerly to such amendments as are authorized by the editions in the author's life time."[10] He would not, he said, make Bentley's mistake of boasting in his Horace, that "Conjecture can cure all; conjecture whose performances are, for the most part, more certain than anything that we can exhibit from the manuscripts."[11] "Reason and the subject matter," Bentley liked to say, "are worth a hundred manuscripts."[12] It was a familiar boast of the philologists, and the modernist claim of reason over authority runs like a refrain through all of Bentley's works. Here is a characteristic statement by Bentley on the subject, a note from his edition of Horace, in a contemporary translation:

> In these our Labours upon Horace, a good deal more is owing Conjecture, than to the Assistance of Books, and if I mistake not, what arises from Conjecture is much more certain than what is founded upon the Authority of Books; for in various Readings the very Authority often imposes upon, and flatters the depraved Itch of your pitiful Emendation; whereas both Fear and Shame put us on a ground, and make us cautious against the Faith of Books, and Reason alone, the Evidence of sense, and pure necessity [should] govern us in this matter. Certainly, if you produce a reading out of one or two Books, which differ from others, you are to be condemn'd if you prefer the Testimony of one or two Witnesses to that of a hundred, unless you can strengthen it with such Arguments, as wou'd of themselves be sufficient to prove the Matter in question, almost without the aid of Books. I wou'd not have

[9]See Mack, *Alexander Pope*, p. 425; Peter Dixon, "Pope's Shakespeare," *Journal of English and Germanic Philology* 63 (1964): 191–203.

[10]Pope to Judith Cowper, Nov. 5, 1722, in Pope, *Correspondence*, ed. George Sherburn, 5 vols. (Oxford, 1956), 2:141–42; cf. Pope's preface to his Shakespeare, in *Eighteenth-Century Critical Essays*, ed. Scott Elledge (Ithaca, N.Y., 1961), 1:289–90.

[11]"In conjecturis vero contra omnium Librorum fidem proponendis et timor pudorque aurem vellunt": Preface to Horace (Amsterdam, 1728), sig. **3v. It was this passage that caused James Harris to speak, in a famous phrase, of Bentley's "rage of conjecture"; see Harris, *Works* (Oxford, 1841), p. 397.

[12]"Nobis et ratio et res ipsa centum codicibus potiores sunt": Bentley's note to Horace, *Odes*, 3.27.15, in *Q. Horatius Flaccus, ex recensione et cum notis atque emendationibus R. Bentleii* (Cambridge, 1711), p. 231. In the sixteenth century another Horatian editor, well known to Bentley, had already claimed the right to conjecture, "even though all the manuscripts contradict me": *Emendationum rationes in Ciceronis Opera Omnia* (1565–66), quoted by Anthony Grafton, *Joseph Scaliger: A Study in the History of Classical Scholarship* (Oxford, 1983), p. 270n.

you pay a blind Veneration to dealers in Books alone, but dare you to think for yourself.[13]

Of course, Bentley knew Pope's Shakespeare, and Theobald had been openly following Bentley's lead when he had criticized Pope's edition. "If want of authority in collating old copies, if want of judgment in digesting his author's own text, or want of sagacity in restoring it when it is manifestly defective, can disable any man from a title to be editor . . . Mr. Pope appears absolutely unequal to the task."[14] Was it not an obvious temptation for the old scholar to show the world how the work might be truly done, and to vindicate yet again the modern achievement?

2

Pope's quarrel had been chiefly with Theobald, but it was impossible, in so far as principle was involved, to avoid bringing Bentley in. Ever since *A Tale of a Tub*, the Scriblerians had been picking away at the great man and the pretensions of modern scholarship. But now Pope's critical methods and reputation were on the line and once again the world was being asked to choose. For a long time Bentley stood aloof, absorbed in his classical studies and college problems.

Just how and why he elected to edit *Paradise Lost* at this particular point in his life has always bothered his readers. That he took an interest in contemporary literature we know; among other things, the princess, later Queen Caroline, liked to get him into arguments about literary matters with Samuel Clarke.[15] No doubt the quarrel over Shakespeare in the 1720s piqued his interest. George Sewell, Pope's collaborator, had suggested in 1725 what was fast becoming the ordinary view. The learned world, he pointed out, had shown how to retrieve and correct the good old authors; now it was time to do justice to the great English

[13] *The Odes and Epodes of Horace in Latin and English with a Translation of Dr. Bentley's Notes, To which are added Notes upon Notes*, 2 vols. (London, 1712–1713), 1:11–13. This work, which selects only some of Bentley's notes and translates them freely, has been attributed to William Oldisworth. The satirical notes to the notes may have been by Bentley's old enemy William King, and are in his manner: see R. F. Jones, *Lewis Theobald* (New York, 1919), app. B, pp. 256–57. Bentley's methods have always provoked criticism but are ably defended by Housman (n. 2 above) and by Paul Maas, *Textual Criticism* (Oxford, 1958), p. 41. See also Kenney, *Classical Text*.

[14] *Daily Journal*, Nov. 26, 1728, quoted in Thomas R. Lounsbury, *The Text of Shakespeare* (New York, 1906), pp. 318–19.

[15] *Biographia Britannica*, 2d ed., ed. Andrew Kippis, 5 vols. (London, 1778–1793), 2:243.

writers, who deserved no less, since "they are in some degree our Classics."[16] And if there was one modern work that was certain to draw Bentley's attention, it was bound to be Milton's poem. In English literature, only *Paradise Lost* could presume to vie with the best of antiquity. Epic was universally adjudged the supreme form and Homer and Virgil had set the standard. As *Paradise Lost* won gradual recognition, it was matched again and again with the ancient poems, as in Dryden's famous epigram that adorned the 1688 edition:

> Three Poets, in three different ages born,
> Greece, Italy, and England did adorn.
> The first, in loftiness of thought surpassed;
> The next in majesty; in both the last.
> To make a third, she joined the former two.[17]

Of course, the comparison had inspired Milton himself, and it was discussed again and again in a growing critical literature by such as John Dennis, Charles Gildon, and above all, by Joseph Addison in the *Spectator* papers of 1712.[18] Week after week, Addison returned to the poem to examine it in the light of Aristotle's precepts and the examples of ancient epic. It was Addison who showed the world beyond a doubt that *Paradise Lost* was a classical poem that could be held to classical standards. His close comparison was intended to point up the beauties and the defects of Milton's poem, and when it was reedited for Jacob Tonson a few years later by Thomas Tickell (1720), it was accompanied by the *Spectator* essays. It was this beautiful edition that Bentley read and annotated.[19]

Beauties *and* defects; the closer the comparison, the more obvious it was that Milton had departed in many ways from his ancient models. The critical question that had come to divide the partisans of the ancients and the moderns was whether this practice was permissible or desirable in a work that aspired to literature. And this was a problem that must naturally have interested Bentley, as it had all the original combatants in the battle of the books. Even Addison, who rarely hesitated to promote

---

[16]Preface to Pope's *Works of Shakespear*, vol. 7 (London, 1725), in *Shakespeare: The Critical Heritage, 1693–1733*, ed. Brian Vickers (London, 1974), p. 419.

[17]Dryden's epigram appears beneath Milton's portrait in the 4th ed. of *Paradise Lost*, published by Tonson (London, 1688). See *Milton: The Critical Heritage*, ed. John T. Shawcross (New York, 1970), p. 229. For a similar view at the time of publication, see James Rosenheim, "An Early Appreciation of *Paradise Lost*," *Modern Philology* 75 (1977–78): 281.

[18]Addison's essays have been separately edited by Albert Cook, *Criticism on Paradise Lost* (1892; rpt. New York, 1968).

[19]Bentley's copy is now in the Cambridge University Library. R. G. Moyles thinks that this is not the copy text, however, but only its source; see his *Text of "Paradise Lost": A Study in Editorial Procedure* (Toronto, 1985), p. 162n.

the poem, allowed that *Paradise Lost* was in some respects inferior to Homer and Virgil. It was the "faults in the language" that bothered him the most and that came to preoccupy subsequent critics.[20]

But even on the textual level there appeared to be difficulties. In 1717 Francis Atterbury returned a copy of *Paradise Lost* to Pope with a note about problems of collation. He had found the new editions "revised and augmented" as advertised, and promised to discuss the alterations when next they met. Five years later the matter had become more urgent, and Atterbury hoped that he might obtain the manuscript of the first book, which was still in the printer's possession and which alone might solve the difficulties. "I long to see the Original Manuscript of Milton," he wrote to Pope, "but I don't know how to come at it, without your repeated assistance. I shall have superstition enough to Collate it with my printed Book if Tonson will allow me the use of it for a few days."[21] In fact, none of the previous editors had been equal to the task and the text had been steadily deteriorating. The latest effort, by Elijah Fenton (one of Pope's collaborators on the *Odyssey*) from 1725 to 1730, only further corrupted the original so that even contemporaries complained. Thus the *Gentleman's Magazine* cautioned in its first issue for the year 1731, "The restoring of the text of a valuable author to the original sense and reading, is a work of merit, if not undertaken by one unequal to such a task. The *Traveller* in this paper has pointed out a few specimens of the ignorance, want of taste, and silly officiousness of Mr. Fenton in his corrections of Milton. . . . All the various readings of this edition are either mean or trifling."[22] Had the critics known of the many *silent* corrections that Fenton and his predecessors had introduced, they might well have protested even more vigorously; as it was, the objections to Fenton's "suggested emendations" must have sounded a clarion call to the great scholar who had built a career out of just such "divination."

Bentley used Tonson's 1720 edition; by 1726 he was seriously interested in emending the text.[23] But it was only later, about 1730, or so it appears, that Bentley mentioned the matter to Queen Caroline, who at once urged him to print his views. The "command" could not have come at a better moment, since Bentley felt the need for some personal advertisement as his legal case worked its way through the House of Lords. (Just so he had hurried his Horace through the press to win the favor of

---

[20]*Spectator*, no. 297, Feb. 9, 1712; no. 417, June 28, 1712.

[21]Atterbury to Pope, Nov. 8, 1717, and June 15, 1722, in Pope, *Correspondence*, 1:451–52, 2:124–25.

[22]*Gentleman's Magazine* 1 (1732): 55.

[23]Evidence of Bentley's interest in 1726 may be found in John Byrom's journal, Jan. 2, in *Selections from the Journals and Papers of John Byrom*, ed. Henri Talon (London, 1950), p. 79; and *Biographia Britannica*, vol. 2 (London, 1748), n. R.

the new government.)[24] He was certainly at work on it in 1730, since the *Grub Street Journal*, Pope's ally against the dunces at this time, was already discussing some of his emendations in that year.[25] Bentley finished his edition in apparent haste just before the appointed deadline in 1732. (The annotations to the later books grow more and more skimpy.) The scandal was immediate and probably did not help his cause. It was a little disingenuous of him to declare in his preface that the notes were all *ex tempore*, "and put to the Press as soon as made," and yet it is undoubtedly true that most of them were composed in his usual manner pretty much as they came into his head.

The critical problem for Bentley, as for many of his contemporaries, was that he both admired and objected to *Paradise Lost*, that he thought it was a great but greatly flawed classical epic. With typical clarity of mind, he saw that from a contemporary point of view, it contained many evident mistakes and breaches of decorum. The only question was how to explain them, and it occurred to him that most of them might not be due to the author at all, but like the classical works that he so much admired and had spent his life correcting, it might well have been corrupted in transmission. "Our celebrated Author," he wrote in the preface, "when he composed this Poem, being obnoxious to the Government, poor, friendless, and worst of all, blind . . . could only dictate his Verses to be writ by another. Whence it necessarily follows, that any Errors in Spelling, Pointing, nay even Words of a like near Sound in Pronunciation, are not to be charg'd upon the Poet, but on the Amanuensis." These errors Bentley naturally wished to correct, along with the apparently faulty meter. According to the great scholar, the incompetent editor had done so badly in seeing his work through the press, "he did so vilely execute that Trust, that Paradise under his Ignorance and Audaciousness may be said to be twice lost."[26]

Nor was the problem just incompetence; Bentley believed that it was willfulness as well. He was quite convinced that the editor, Milton's supposed friend, taking advantage of the poet's blindness, had even dared to fob off his own bad verses on the text. Bentley was convinced that neither the first nor the second edition (1667, 1674) had ever been read to Milton for correction, for the poet "could not possibly let pass such gross and palpable Faults." (Bentley detected only four significant

[24]James Henry Monk, *The Life of Richard Bentley*, 2d ed., 2 vols. (London, 1833), 1:397. For the royal command, see Bentley's preface to *Paradise Lost*; and *Biographia Britannica*, ed. Kippis, 2:245.

[25]*Grub Stree Memoirs*, nos. 9, 12, 25. See James T. Hillhouse, *The Grub Street Journal* (Durham, N.C.: 1938), pp. 84–104.

[26]*Paradise Lost*, ed. Bentley, sig. a.

changes in the second edition, each one he thought for the worse.)[27] The only marvel was that *Paradise Lost* had survived all these handicaps to become a recognizable classic, rivaling if not excelling Homer and Virgil. The awe and veneration that it had inspired had, however, blinded readers for two generations to its faults. All this Bentley now hoped to set to rights.

Bentley printed the received text, using the 1720 edition, reserving his alterations for the margins and his excisions for brackets. In this regard he was more conservative than Pope, who had not hesitated to remove the offending passages in his Shakespeare and put them at the bottom of the page. (Did Bentley notice that when Pope discovered some anachronisms in *Troilus and Cressida*, he ascribed them to the printer rather than the author? Or that Shakespeare's first editors had indicted all previous versions as "stolne and surreptitious copies, maimed and deformed by the frauds and stealths of injurious impostors!"?)[28] In all, Bentley proposed more than eight hundred emendations (a few less than for his Horace) and about seventy deletions, one of as many as fifty-five lines (III, 444–98). Even the two last lines of the poem, which Addison had thought superfluous, were assigned by Bentley to the editor and duly corrected. Most of the emendations were for single words only and only a few have been generally accepted.[29]

Did Bentley really believe in his unscrupulous editor? What is clear is that he needed some kind of excuse for his elaborate exercise in correction. He was determined to improve the text of *Paradise Lost*, to bring it into line with his own predilections about classical epic, much indeed as Pope had done before him with the *Iliad*. (It was Atterbury who, even while he was calling for an improved text, urged Pope to take *Samson Agonistes* and polish and improve it. He was sure that with a little trouble it could be turned into a "perfect model and standard of tragic poetry.")[30] Nor is it surprising, therefore, that when Pope read Bentley's version, he actually admired it, penciling in the margins of his copy such frequent commendations: *recte, bene, pulchre,* and the like. "It was a satisfaction," says a later editor, "to see what so great a genius thought particularly of that edition, and he appears throughout the whole to have been a very candid reader, and to have approved of more than really merits approbation."[31] In fact, Bentley had treated the evidence for his conjectures with

---

[27]Ibid., Preface and notes to I, 505 (p. 23); V, 639 (p. 170); XI, 485 (pp. 364–65). There are others but they are less obvious.

[28]Pope cites the passage in the *First Folio*. See Mack, *Alexander Pope*, pp. 426–27.

[29]E.g., VII, 321; VII, 451; see Milton, *Poetical Works*, ed. Darbishire, 1:301–2; Moyles, *Text of "Paradise Lost,"* pp. 142–43.

[30]Atterbury to Pope, June 15, 1722, in Pope, *Correspondence*, 2:124–25.

[31]Thomas Newton, ed., Preface to *Paradise Lost*, 2d ed. (London, 1750).

something of the same disdain that Pope had shown in his commentary on Homer. His collations of the printed editions were not very complete and he never mentioned the manuscript that Atterbury had tried to borrow from Tonson and that he seems to have known.[32] Indeed, when Tonson read Bentley's Milton, he noticed several places that Bentley claimed had been altered by the printer which were "exactly true to the copy."[33] Bentley's hypothetical editor seems thus a desperate device to free him from the constraints of the received text so that he could emend its "faults" with impunity.

3

Still, in method and attitude Bentley's Milton was not much different from his Horace or from any of his other works; in the parlance of the day, they were decidedly modern. The text of the Roman poet, he saw, had been corrupted by ignorant medieval scribes who had foisted their own misreadings, sometimes deliberately, on a hapless text. His scorn for the "librarians" was exactly like his contempt for Milton's amanuensis. Bentley's avowed intention in either case was to retrieve the original as he imagined it must have been when it left the author's own hand, and he used every device of modern philology to accomplish this task.[34] And true to his modernist viewpoint, he sometimes allowed that it was Horace himself who had made the mistake—he does this again with Milton—not hesitating to offer his own improvements.[35] On one occasion, in his Horace, he admitted offering a conjecture simply as "exercise

[32]The text may be found in The Manuscript of Milton's "Paradise Lost," Book I, ed. Helen Darbishire (Oxford, 1931); and Milton's Complete Poetical Works, ed. Harris T. Fletcher, vol. 2 (Urbana, Ill., 1945). See Helen Darbishire, "Milton's Paradise Lost," in Somerville College Chapel Addresses (Oxford, 1962), p. 125; James H. Hanford, "The Manuscript of Paradise Lost," Modern Philology 25 (1927–28): 313–17.

[33]Tonson's letter is printed in full in the Introduction to Darbishire, Manuscript of "Paradise Lost." In her preface she describes the "unusual pains" that Milton took in preparing his text for publication. See also Robert M. Adams, "The Text of Paradise Lost," in his Milton and the Modern Critics (Ithaca, N.Y., 1955), pp. 60–111; John T. Shawcross, "Orthography and the Text of Paradise Lost," in Language and Style in Milton, ed. Ronald D. Emma and John T. Shawcross (New York, 1967), pp. 120–53.

[34]This is Helen Darbishire's ambition in her modern edition of Milton's poems. "My aim has been to offer a text as near as possible to that which Milton himself would have given us if he had had his sight": Poetical Works, 1:vi. There is a most helpful discussion of the issues here in G. Thomas Tanselle, "The Editorial Problem of Final Authorial Intention," in his Selected Studies in Bibliography (Charlottesville, Va., 1979), pp. 309–53, esp. 324–25.

[35]Harold R. Joliffe counted some 689 changes proposed by Bentley for Horace, 157 without manuscript support: "Bentley vs. Horace," Philological Quarterly 16 (1937): 286n. Joliffe's article is based on his dissertation, "Critical Methods and Influence of Bentley's Horace," University of Chicago, 1939.

for the reader's judgment," rather than as a serious correction.[36] Bentley may even have believed, with some of his modern admirers, that it was less the rightness or wrongness of his conclusions that really mattered than provoking critical thought.[37] In any case, he was determined to make sense of every crux and eager to try any alternative to see whether it could be solved. It was reason and decorum, syntax and meter, that were invariably sovereign, the assumption being that the poet must always have reasoned logically, wrought appropriately, and hewed always to a correct grammar and a regular metrical scheme. "Two things there are," Pope wrote sardonically in the *Dunciad*, "upon which the very Basis of all verbal Criticism is founded and supported: the first, that the Author could never fail to use the best word on every occasion: the second, that the Critick cannot chuse but know, which it is. This being granted, wherever any doth not fully content us, we take upon us to conclude, first the author never us'd it, and secondly, that he must have used that very one which we conjecture in its stead."[38] That this assumption entailed a peculiarly Augustan aesthetic did not bother Bentley, any more than it had bothered Pope in his edition of Shakespeare, though Bentley's philological learning should certainly have taught him that no single poetic standard existed for all eternity.

By the time Bentley turned to Milton, he had spent a lifetime "correcting" the poets that he read, so that his pose and method were habitual. His delight in discovering an alternative reading was either infectious or infuriating, depending on the text and the reader. Bentley's emendations to Greek authors seemed wonderful and generally convincing, perhaps because the texts were usually obscure and few readers knew enough Greek to challenge his readings. It was another matter with the New Testament and with the Latin authors. Here his findings seemed more problematical, if only because Horace and Terence, like the Bible, belonged to everyone, and ordinary schoolmasters such as John Ker and Alexander Cunningham could find fault, though no one could pretend to

---

[36]"Atque haec quidem a nobis dicta sint, magis ut lectoris judicium exerceamus, quam ut hoc ab Horatio profectum esse praestare velimus": Bentley's note in *Odes and Epodes of Horace*, I, 25, 11 (p. 64).

[37]See besides Housman and Brink (n. 2 above), Maas, *Textual Criticism*, p. 17; M. L. W. Laistner, "Richard Bentley, 1742–1942," in *The Intellectual Heritage of the Early Middle Ages* (Ithaca, N.Y., 1957), p. 252n; D. R. Shackleton Bailey, "Bentley and Horace," *Proceedings of the Leeds Philosophical and Literary Society* 9 (1959–1962): 105–16. Not everyone has been convinced; see besides Joliffe (n. 35) B. L. Ullman, "Horace and the Philologians," *Classical Journal* 31 (1935–36): 407.

[38]*Dunciad Variorum* (1729), in *The Poems of Alexander Pope*, ed. J. Butt et al., 10 vols. (New Haven, 1961–1967), 5:96. As a consequence, Pope was cautious about accepting Bentley's emendations when he set about his own Horatian imitations; see Lillian D. Bloom, "Pope as a Textual Critic: A Bibliographical Study of His Horatian Text," *Journal of English and Germanic Philology* 47 (1948): 150–55.

rival Bentley's divinatory gift or range of learning.[39] Even so, Bentley
won much applause and great respect for his efforts, not least from his
old enemy Francis Atterbury.[40] With English it was an altogether different matter, since there was hardly a literate Englishman who could not
pretend to equal skill in the language. Bentley did not take the trouble to
read widely in Milton's sources and contemporaries, and as a result could
not use his favorite method of analogy very capably.[41] He did not know
much about seventeenth-century usage and rather assumed that Milton
had employed the same grammar and syntax, the same spelling and
pronunciation as those current in his own time. (Of course, Bentley had
been born in 1662 and was thus a young contemporary of *Paradise Lost*;
but the language had been changing faster than he either knew or was
willing to allow.) He agreed with Addison that Milton was a classic, and
he treated the text with the respect that was due to an ancient work; but
he did not really use the kind of learning that he and others had devised to
establish and explicate a classical text, either because he did not think it
necessary or because he had something else in mind.

What he did do, as usual, was to examine every word and line in the
poem for its sense, consistency, propriety, and grammar; and whenever
he discovered a problem, he proposed a solution. Most of these alterations he offered with his customary assurance as corrections of the editor
or printer; but sometimes he was more tentative. "I do not disapprove
Conspicuous," he writes disarmingly at one point, "but if the Author had
thought of it, I believe he would have preferr'd this before it" (VI, 299; p.
192). One whole paragraph Bentley found so inaccurate and indistinct
that, "without criticizing it, I'll propose in my thought, what, or what
like, he would have given, could he have revis'd his Poem" (VII, 239; p.
225).[42] Sometimes, Bentley wavered between assigning blame to the
editor or the poet. "If the Author gave it thus," he remarks at one place,
"its a slip of human Inattention." He preferred to believe it "a prank of

[39]For Ker and Cunningham, see Monk, *Life of Bentley*, 1:320–21, 2:161–67; A. T.
Bartholemew, *Richard Bentley: A Bibliography* (Cambridge, 1908), pp. 48–53. Bentley's
projected New Testament involved him in bitter controversy, but Kenney thinks that it
might have been his greatest editorial achievement: *Classical Text*, pp. 100–101.

[40]Atterbury to Bentley, April 19, 1712, thanking Bentley for "that Noble present of
your new Edition of Horace." He was indebted, even though "I cannot but own to You the
Uneasiness I felt, when I found out how many things in Horace there were which, after
Thirty Years Acquaintance with him, I did not understand": *The Correspondence of Richard
Bentley*, ed. Christopher Wordsworth, 2 vols. (London, 1842), 1:430–31.

[41]To be sure, Bentley did make occasional use of Sidney and even more of Spenser, and
I have found one reference to Chaucer and another to Dryden's Virgil. But this was not
enough to save him from simple errors in usage such as those noticed by Darbishire in her
edition of *Paradise Lost*, in Milton, *Poetical Works*, 1:284, 296.

[42]See also I, 204 (p. 11); IV, 400 (p. 120).

the Editor" (II, 611; pp. 58–59). At times he seems to blame Milton directly. "'Twas hard if not impossible, in our Poet's Condition, not sometimes to forget and make his Fictions inconsistent" (II, 969; pp. 72–73).[43] "Our Author should have taken great Care, what Notions, what Points of Philosophy, he puts into the Mouth of an Archangel" (V, 415; p. 162). And more than once he castigates Milton directly: "'Tis difficult here to excuse the Poet himself; no pragmatical Editor can come here to acquit him. 'Tis credible that for Joy that he was finishing the Second Book, he relax'd his Attention, and forgot his own System." (Bentley simply removed one of the offending lines, II, 1052, p. 76.)[44] His longest excision was offered typically as a device for preserving the integrity of the poem. "I wish, for the Poet and the Poem's sake, that the Reader would be of my Opinion, that all this long Description of the outside World, the *Limbo of Vanity*, was not Milton's own, but an insertion by his Editor. There's nothing either of his Spirit or Judgment seen in it; in its several Parts it abounds with Impertinences. . . . In the Whole, 'tis a silly Interruption of the Story in the very middle" (III, 444–98; pp. 92–93).[45] In this case, Bentley thought the damage *must* belong to the editor; but on another occasion, Bentley actually dared to compose a verse of his own to improve the text. "Why may not I add one Verse to Milton, as well as the Editor who has added so many; especially since I did not do it, as he did clandestinely" (IV, 810; pp. 136–37).

In short, Bentley's notes and excisions were meant chiefly to correct editor, printer, *and* author. He had clearly formulated in his own mind an idea of the poem as he thought Milton must, or should, have intended it, and he was determined to make it so. "What native, unextinguishable Beauty," Bentley asked in his preface, "must be impress'd and instincted through the Whole, which the Defoederation of so many Parts by a bad Printer and a worse Editor could not hinder from shining forth?" His task here, as with Horace, Terence, Manilius, and so many others, was to retrieve a hidden composition and explain how it had come to be deformed. He knew that not everyone would be persuaded; that some would, as he puts it in his preface, "fancy this Persona of an Editor to be a

[43]Already at I, 169 (p. 9), Bentley was trying to make Milton more consistent. He believed the poet had "improved" his own ideas about angels by the sixth book, so "those few Passages therefore must be alter'd, to make this Poem more consistent: and 'tis pity the blind Author had so good an Excuse for not doing it himself." Bentley continued to correct Milton's mistaken views about angels, e.g., at II, 996; III, 397; V, 381.

[44]I, 342 (p. 17); for other examples of forgetfulness or inattention, see Bentley's notes at III, 556; VII, 215; VII, 251; VIII, 508; X, 601.

[45]Bentley believed that Milton excelled in his speeches but not in his descriptions, which he therefore generally ascribed to the editor; see his note at IX, 368 (p. 280). He also corrects Milton's astronomy, blaming the editor, as at VII, 366 (p. 230); VII, 381 (p. 231).

mere Fantom, a Fiction, an Artifice to screen Milton himself"—and of course this is precisely what happened. But it was as a persona of the author, Bentley pretending to be Milton, that he most offended.

What Bentley should have been trying to do in his edition of the poem, we think (as did most of his contemporaries), was to try to restore the "original purity" of the text, rather than to establish its contemporary meaning; to present *Paradise Lost* as Milton intended, rather than as Bentley or Pope wished it to be.[46] As an anonymous author insisted later, comparing Pope and Theobald, the province of an editor and commentator is very different from that of a poet. "The former endeavors to give us an Author as he is; the latter, by the Correctness and Excellency of his own Genius, is often tempted to give us an Author as he thinks he ought to be."[47] The object of philology was fundamentally different from that of criticism or fresh creation. Of course, the opposition between the two had been overt throughout the battle of the books, but apparently no one was yet ready to resolve the antinomy with an appeal to relativism or historicism.[48] As a modern and the foremost philologist of his time, Bentley certainly appreciated the differentia that separated past from present, and no one saw better than he the significance of anachronism to historical and literary criticism, the gulf that separated (for example) the culture of Homeric times from his own. But Bentley was an Augustan who heartily shared in the moral and aesthetic values of his own time and believed them to be universal, eternal in an ideal sense, the sovereign criteria for all culture, ancient and modern.

It took that good Bentleian Lewis Theobald to glimpse the confusion and urge that the English poets of the past be understood and appreciated in their own context through the use of a philological method that was divorced from contemporary criticism. Bentley had gone astray in his edition of *Paradise Lost*, just as Pope had erred in his translation of the *Iliad*.

---

[46]This was Theobald's message in *Shakespeare Restor'd* (London, 1726), p. i. See Matthew Concanen, commending Theobald in *London Journal* (1726): "Every Writer is obliged to make himself understood of the age in which he lives; but, as he cannot answer for the changes of manners and language which may happen after his death, those who receive pleasure and instruction from him are obliged . . . to endeavor to perpetuate his memory, by preserving his meaning. . . . We whose manners are so variable, and whose Language so visibly alters every century, have not one Poet . . . who has met with the good fortune of a kind hand": in John Nichols, *Literary Illustrations*, 2:189.

[47]*Some Remarks on the Tragedy of Hamlet* (1736), probably by Thomas Hamner, ed. Clarence D. Thorpe for Augustan Reprint Society (Los Angeles, 1947).

[48]Theobald may have come the closest; in his own work, however, he deliberately separated the two functions, leaving critical appreciation to others. See his preface to his Shakespeare (1733), in *Eighteenth-Century Essays on Shakespeare*, ed. D. Nichol Smith, 2d ed. (Oxford, 1963), p. 75. And he was not averse to writing of the "general absurdities of Shakespeare," and remarking on the "errors" in his plays; see ibid., pp. xviii–xix.

It is plain, it was the Intention of that Great Man [Bentley] rather to correct and pare off the Excrescencies of the *Paradise Lost*, in the manner that Tucca and Varius were employ'd to criticize the *Aeneis* of Virgil, than to restore the corrupted Passages. Hence, therefore, may be seen the Iniquity or Ignorance of his Censurers, who, from some Expressions, would make us believe, the Doctor every where gives us his Corrections as the Original Text of the Author; whereas the chief Turn of his Criticism is plainly to shew the World, that if Milton did not write as He would have him, he ought to have wrote so.[49]

For Tonson it was a simple matter: "If Bentley was in the right, *Paradise Lost* is the worst and one of the most nonsensical (to use one of his terms) poems that ever appeared in the world."[50] Thus Theobald could rightly claim that it was his version of Shakespeare—not Bentley's Milton—that was the first genuine effort to treat a modern English work as a classic and to employ all the devices of modern scholarship to understand it properly.[51] For the moment, it seemed that Bentley had forsaken his philological purpose in order to show how *Paradise Lost* could be read as (or improved into) a perfect epic poem.[52]

Unfortunately, Bentley was not much of a poet himself, no Pope certainly, and his efforts to turn *Paradise Lost* into an acceptable Augustan poem, as he believed his rival had done with the *Iliad*, were bound to be unsuccessful, and in fact convinced no one. Even his disciples winced at his effort. Theobald wrote to his friend William Warburton just before the event, "I own, I venerate him so far as a Classical Critic, that I am sorry he has now dabbl'd in a Province, where even the Ladies are prepar'd to laugh at, and confute him."[53] For Joseph Wasse, a scholar whom Bentley himself respected, the master had pointed out many faults

[49]Theobald was careful to distinguish his work from Bentley's, which he described as a "Performance of another Species": ibid., p. 75. "In shaking off the similitude betwixt our tasks," he wrote to Warburton, "I hope that neither he, nor his Friends, will come to expect any sneer. The Stating of Differences was absolutely necessary on my Side, and I think I have avoided saying anything derogatory on his": Mar. 5, 1734, in Jones, *Lewis Theobald*, pp. 323–26. Bentley seems not to have minded and subscribed to Theobald's Shakespeare.

[50]Jacob Tonson to his nephew, Feb. 5, 1731, in John Hale, "Notes on Richard Bentley's Edition of *Paradise Lost*," *Milton Quarterly* 18 (1984): 48–49.

[51]Theobald expressly acknowledged his indebtedness to the Amsterdam edition of Bentley's Horace for the form of his footnotes; see Theobald to Warburton, Nov. 18, 1731, in Nichols, *Literary Illustrations*, 2:621. Meanwhile, Thomas Bentley was assisting Theobald with his Shakespeare; see Jones, *Lewis Theobald*, p. 221.

[52]Cf. Tenney Frank on Bentley's manuscript conjectures for Virgil, which he finds similarly neoclassical and prosaic: "Comments on Virgil's *Aeneid*," *Classical Journal* 30 (1935): 466–67.

[53]Theobald to Warburton, Oct. 30, 1731, and Mar. 21, 1732, quoted in Jones, *Lewis Theobald*, pp. 277–79, 298–301. In December the *Grub Street Journal* (no. 101), reported that all of Bentley's friends were trying to dissuade him from publishing.

in the text rightly, "but not being used to English verse corrects very indifferently."[54] For an old Christ Church opponent, Dr. Robert Freind (now reconciled), the work was a mixed blessing. "His Milton is all printed off," he wrote to the Earl of Oxford, "and his preface, part of which he read to me, is sent off to the press—it will be diverting when it comes out. Though many of his corrections that he communicated to me are right, [and] the faults often acutely observed, [they are] not so often well amended, especially when he goes beyond a word or two, and gives half lines and whole lines of his own."[55]

Even Bentley's nephews tried to talk him out of the work: Richard, who was given the task of seeing it through the press, and Thomas, who got into a bitter argument about it with the old man. Typically, Bentley had suggested turning the phrase with Hesperian "fables" into "apples" (IV, 251–52). The original read, "Hesperian Fables true . . . and of delicious taste," but Bentley could make no sense of a "true fable," which seemed to him an oxymoron. On the other hand, he could show that Hesperian *apples* were famous in classical literature, and so with a stroke of the pen, he emended the error. It was for him a characteristic blunder of the editor. When, however, Thomas pointed out that Hesperian apples were always made of gold and thus unlikely to be tasted, Bentley relented, though now by excising the whole passage as a needless interpolation.[56] "I will tell you," Thomas wrote to a friend, "that I disputed with him that night about this place and some others, and indeed his whole design, till I quite put him out of humour, and till he called me Ignoramus and several other hard words. I told him I would never object again, since I saw he could not bear it, and hoped he would take the ill language to himself, if I proved in the right. So we parted, and I have not been able to talk with him since, since he can't forbear talking of Milton, and I can't forbear the nonsense and absurdities he puts on him."[57]

For Pope's friends, and for Pope himself, the edition proved a godsend, a wonderful example of the confusion caused by "verbal criticism," as in the satirical poem of that name by David Mallet, subtitled "An Epistle to Mr. Pope occasion'd by Theobald's Shakespear and Bentley's Milton" (1733). Here Bentley,

[54]Joseph Wasse to Philippe d'Orville, April 10, 1732, Bodleian MS. D'Orville 485, f. 230; and Feb. 21, 1732, ibid., ff. 228v–29.

[55]"He made some excuses for his adventurous spirit, having had some reputation for poetry in his youth": Robert Freind to the Earl of Oxford, Oct. 1731, in *Historical Manuscript Commission Reports: Manuscripts of the Duke of Portland*, vol. 6 (London, 1901), p. 41.

[56]Bentley's text, IV, 250–51 (p. 114), reads thus:

> Hung amiable, [Hesperian Fables true,
> If true, here only] and of delicious taste.

[57]For the text of the letter, transcribed by J. C. Anderson from a copy in the Trumbull Library, New Zealand, see *Times Literary Supplement*, Aug. 27, 1925; John K. Hale, "More on Bentley's Milton," *Milton Quarterly* 14 (1980): 131.

> . . . prime pattern of the captious art,
> Out tibbalding poor Tibbald, taps his part;
> Holds high the Scourge o'er each fam'd author's head,
> Nor are their graves and refuges for the dead;
> To Milton lending sense, to Horace wit,
> He makes them write what never poet writ.[58]

Besides Mallet's, several other pamphlets appeared to mock the old scholar, including one that conveniently set out all the altered passages next to the originals, entitled *Milton Restored and Bentley Deposed*. Pope waited awhile but enjoyed another parody with the *Notae Bentleiani* that he attached to his third Horatian imitation. And, of course, the popular journals had a field day.[59] Bentley had underestimated the opposition, even though he had anticipated their objections. The "awe and veneration" that had come to surround Milton had, he remembered, once protected the text from criticism. "Who durst oppose the Universal Vogue? and risque his own Character while he labour'd to exalt Milton's?" Now, forty years later, the time seemed more propitious and the risk less obvious. But Bentley was mistaken, though in a paradoxical way: it was the serious opposition, the scholarly criticism that Bentley's own work provoked, that really did him in.

There is no need perhaps to pursue all those earnest critics who set themselves to answering Bentley with Bentleian methods and so helped to establish the value of historical scholarship to modern literary studies: Zachary Pearce; the Richardsons, father and son; Thomas Newton, who created the first true Dutch variorum for the poem; and so on. Newton was determined to edit Milton "as the work of a classic author," and did exactly that, while the Richardsons supplied a whole new book of explanatory notes.[60] Pearce, who was Thomas Bentley's correspondent and had edited a classical text himself, was first in the field with a respectful (though anonymous) reply.[61] Like most of Bentley's readers, Pearce was not willing to accept a deceitful editor, and he used John Toland's life of Milton to dispute the circumstances of the work's first publication.

---

[58]David Mallet, *Of Verbal Criticism* (London, 1733), ll. 131–36.

[59]See Bartholemew, *Richard Bentley*, pp. 77–79; Hillhouse, *Grub Street Journal*, pp. 84–96; and (correcting Hillhouse) Bertrand Goldgar, "Pope and the *Grub Street Journal*," *Journal of Modern Philology* 74 (1977): 366–80. For Pope, see Mack, *Alexander Pope*, who also prints a wicked epigram still in manuscript, pp. 624 and 910. Pope denied inspiring Mallet but approved his work; see Pope to David Mallet, Nov. 7, 1732, and Pope to Jonathan Richardson, Nov. 3, 1732, in Pope, *Correspondence*, 3:326–27, 329–30.

[60]See *Paradise Lost: A New Edition* (London, 1749), Preface. The Richardsons published their work in 1734 as *Explanatory Notes and Remarks on Milton's "Paradise Lost."*

[61][Zachary Pearce], *A Review of the Text of the Twelve Books of Milton's "Paradise Lost" in which the Chief of Dr. Bentley's Emendations are Consider'd and Several other Emendations and Observations are Offer'd to the Public* (London, 1733). Pearce edited Longinus in 1724.

Certainly, he thought, Milton would have discovered the fraud by the time of the second edition. The bulk of Pearce's book was devoted to reviewing Bentley's alterations and excisions one by one and defending the original readings. He began from a point of view opposite to Bentley's, that the text of the first two editions was basically sound and needed only to be altered in extremity, though he accepted the idea that Milton's poem was not flawless.[62] With the aid of dictionaries and some contemporary works, common sense and a more liberal notion of poetic possibility, he was able to find reasons to oppose most—though not all—of Bentley's conjectures. What was true in philosophy, he saw, was not always true in poetry.[63] Milton's learning was not the same as Bentley's; nor were their poetic sensibilities identical. Even so, there was much to explain. As the elder Richardson put it immediately after reading the new edition, "Bentley has cut me out a good deal of work, not to answer Blunders, Conundrums, and Impertinences, but to read Milton with more care and attention than I have yet done. Tho' I have been an Admirer of him for above Forty Years, I discover Faults or Incorrectnesses I had rather call 'em, which I had not observ'd till Now."[64] Thus Bentley's critical perceptions—his demonstration in detail that Milton had departed from classical and contemporary usage—had the paradoxical but undoubted effect of stimulating the serious study and historical appreciation of *Paradise Lost*, even while his conclusions were being largely rejected.[65]

When all is said and done, then, it seems unlikely that Bentley truly believed in his nefarious editor, though as he warmed to his task and piled on alterations and emendations through all the twelve books, he may well have convinced himself of his fiction. On the other hand, it is just possible that he really meant his preface and commentary satirically, tongue in cheek, like a very Scriblerian. Why not? Bentley had a sense of humor and he may have learned something from his old enemies. At one point it certainly crossed Theobald's mind that it might be so and that

[62]"I should think that when the common reading may be defended, every sober Critic is bound to be a tenacious textuary": ibid., p. 177. Frequently Pearce corrects Bentley's readings by referring to the first printed texts; elsewhere he allows that Milton himself erred, though he rarely adopts Bentley's suggestions. He specifically defends Milton's "Poetical liberty of expression": ibid., p. 318.

[63]Ibid., p. 130; see also pp. 217–19, 373–74.

[64]Jonathan Richardson, Sr., to Ralph Painter, Mar. 13, 1732, in Mack, *Alexander Pope*, p. 624. Among other things, the younger Richardson corrected Bentley's view of the early editions and the circumstances of their composition: *Explanatory Notes*, pp. cxxii–cxxv. The Richardsons had assisted Pope with Shakespeare, collating in 1723; Pope in turn was pleased with their work on Milton and offered help; see Pope, *Correspondence*, 2:177n.; 3:240, 326–27, 330–31.

[65]Two copies of Bentley's Milton in the British Library, with copious notes by Benjamin Stillingfleet the Younger (C134 hi) and William Cole (641 k22), illustrate this response.

Bentley had written "maliciously to turn the Art into Ridicule."[66] If so, instead of laughing *at* Bentley for his evident fiction, we should perhaps be laughing *with* him! Either way, it is true to say that his notes are still worth attending (as with Horace and the rest), as the result of an acute and vigorous mind defending a particular view of poetry not unlike that of Pope and the wits, and in some ways anticipating the later cavils against Milton by such as Ezra Pound and T. S. Eliot, F. R. Leavis and William Empson. Had Bentley presented his idea of *Paradise Lost* directly as literary criticism, rather than masquerading as literary history, he might well have been more convincing, though that would have been much out of character and less provocative. After a lifetime of textual commentary, writing an essay like Addison or a poem like Pope was no doubt beyond him. But the conjectural emendation that had won him so much fame and notoriety, and that had always served him for so much more than mere verbal criticism, was his natural medium. If he betrayed his philological mistress here, forsaking the historical and literary context for his own Augustan taste and assuming it to be universal, was not that what his enemies had always done? And were not their satirical replies, stimulated by this new provocation, bound to betray them in the end to the grudging admission that modern historical scholarship, however lowly and pedantic, was after all indispensable to the reading of a historical text? If that is so, then Bentley's *Paradise Lost* would turn out paradoxically to be his most successful work, and it would be the formidable doctor and his modern allies who would have had the last unexpected laugh in the battle of the books.

[66]Theobald to Warburton, Mar. 21, 1732, quoted in Jones, *Lewis Theobald*, pp. 298–301. Dr. Johnson reported some gossip that Bentley "in private life allowed it to be false," and Monk doubted that Bentley ever really believed his fiction: *Life of Bentley*, 2:312–13. But R. C. Jebb was certain that he broached it in perfect good faith: *Bentley* (London, 1878), p. 185. For Thomas De Quincey "it was a fiction of modesty, at once of prudence, and not of fraud, which saved him from the necessity of applying his unmeasured abuse immediately to Milton": *Works*, ed. David Masson, 14 vols. (London, 1853–1860), 7:127.

PART TWO

HISTORY

Chapter Nine

History and Theory

I

The battle of the books had gradually narrowed the focus in the old quarrel between the ancients and the moderns to one commanding issue. Long before Bentley's career concluded in derision, it was clear that the controversy was above all about history, about how to read and understand past authors, and about how to recapture and represent past customs, institutions, and events. The struggle between rhetoric and philology, between the critical standards of the poets and men of the world on the one hand and of the scholars and antiquaries on the other, was from this perspective really an argument about the respective claims of two different and perhaps incompatible ways of doing history. And so it is not surprising that both the ancients and the moderns wrote and deliberated about history during the battle of the books, about the meaning and method of getting at the past, and about what they thought had transpired in ancient and modern times. Thus was added a further dimension to the conflict.

In the next pages, we shall take a look at some of these works in order to see how they both reflected and deepened the issues that were at stake in the quarrel. Temple had taken up history as one of the traditional humanities and defended the ancients there, as in all classical literature, for their eloquence and practical value in furnishing examples to men of affairs. Herodotus and Livy were like Homer and Virgil, supreme in their own domain, models of form and content till the end of time. The best a modern could hope to do was to imitate, that is to say, to adapt the style and shape of the ancient works to later history, though necessarily at a lower level. Wotton had of course objected. Here, as elsewhere, he paid his respects to the ancients, but he tried to diminish the supreme value of rhetoric to the writing of history, urging the relatively plain Polybius as a valid ancient model and the more discursive Sarpi as a modern who had preferred to write of secret diplomacy before the great events of politics and war. More profoundly, he made a bold claim for the new sciences of philology and antiquities, which he believed could actually correct and supplement the ancient histories—"improve" them, if you will. We have already seen some of the consequences of this disagreement for poetry; we shall discover that they were at least as profound for the theory and practice of history.

2

Temple's ideas about history were general and commonplace. They might be found in the classical authors directly, in the promoters of eloquence such as Cicero and Quintilian, or in the little *artes historicae* of Lucian and Dionysius of Halicarnassus, with their many Renaissance progeny.[1] Or they might come from France, the source of so much of English classical culture in the later seventeenth century. So, for example, it is likely that Temple knew the works of Père Rapin, the chief proponent of *ancienneté* in the reign of Louis XIV and one of the most popular critics in England for at least two generations, though it is hard to be sure, since Temple rarely acknowledged his sources. Rapin had set out his views about poetry, oratory, and moral philosophy in a series of treatises and "comparisons" that were first printed in 1671 and found their way into England soon afterward. In 1677, as though to complete his review of the humanities, he added two new works on history: a set of "instructions" for writing it and a comparison of the two best of the ancients, Thucydides and Livy, to guide the student in reading it. Like

---

[1] A good example is Edmund Bolton, *Hypercritica* (London, 1618), who specifically endorses Lucian and Dionysius as "the best for Historiography among all the Heathens." See *Critical Essays of the Seventeenth Century*, ed. Joel E. Springarn, 3 vols. (Oxford, 1908–1909), 1:99; Daniel R. Woolf, "Edmund Bolton, Francis Bacon, and the Making of the *Hypercritica*," *Huntington Library Record* 11 (1983): 162–68. Another characteristic example is John Hales, "The Method of Reading Profane History," in his *Golden Remains* (London, 1673, 1688); see John J. Murray, "John Hales on History," *Huntington Library Quarterly* 19 (1956): 231–43. For the *ars historia* in general, see Beatrice Reynolds, "Shifting Currents in Historical Criticism," *Journal of the History of Ideas* 14 (1953): 471–92; George H. Nadel, "Philosophy of History before Historicism," in *Studies in the Philosophy of History* (New York, 1965), pp. 49–73; Astrid Witschi-Bernz, "Main Trends in Historical-Method Literature: Sixteenth to Eighteenth Centuries," *History and Theory* 12 (1972). It was still possible to argue in 1746 that Lucian's precepts had not been superseded by those of any modern writer; see P. Whalley, *Essay on the Manner of Writing History*, ed. Keith Stewart, Augustan Reprint Society 80 (Los Angeles, 1960).

the rest of his works, they were soon translated into English more than once.[2]

It was Rapin's task to "abridge" what he found in the ancient authors and their modern followers, to supply a convenient summary of the commonplace wisdom on the subject. As in his art of poetry, it was Rapin's intention to reduce a somewhat disorderly body of theoretical remarks and obiter dicta to an orderly digest, to furnish guidelines, if not actual rules for the practice of history. In short, he meant to bring the Renaissance *ars historica* up to date and render it into classical French.

In both his works, Rapin explicitly accepted the classical notion that history was a branch of rhetoric which aimed at eloquence. As a result, he believed that the historian could learn his craft best by carefully and exclusively imitating ancient models, chief among them Livy. The only moderns who interested him were those who had successfully patterned themselves on the ancients, such as the Spaniard Juan de Mariana.[3] He repeats the Ciceronian notion that history deals with great things worthy of recollection; that is, high politics and war. It must always be a continuous narrative, with nothing distracting or superfluous, and in a natural rather than strictly chronological order. (Rapin clearly will have nothing to do with either medieval chronicles or antiquarian compilations.) Historical style should be elevated, decorous, pure, and simple. The principal task of the historian should be to discover and portray the motives and passions of his protagonists and to avoid at all cost wearying his readers or failing to instruct them. For this purpose, Rapin urges all the usual rhetorical embellishments of classical narrative, though always counseling moderation: rhetorical figures, descriptions, set speeches, portraits, and moral reflections. "The Historian has his Matter given to him . . . but the distribution of it is his special province, and to manage that as it ought to be, he should not so much reflect on what he says, as on the manner how he says it; for in this as in other parts of Eloquence, the manner is all in all."

It is the writing, therefore—or rather rewriting—that is the chief business of the historian; and here too Rapin takes his cues from classical precept and example. Rapin would like to distinguish the historian from

[2]René Rapin, *Instructions for History: With a Character of the Most Considerable Historians Ancient and Modern*, trans. John Davies (London, 1680); *Monsieur Rapin's Comparison of Thucydides and Livy*, trans. T. Taylor (Oxford, 1694); *The Whole Critical Works of Monsieur Rapin*, trans. Basil Kennett, 2 vols. (London, 1706). Included in Rapin's works are comparisons of Homer and Virgil, Demosthenes and Cicero, Plató and Aristotle, as well as reflections on eloquence and poetry.
[3]Rapin, *Instructions for History*, pp. 3–4, 14–19. See Juan de Mariana, *The General History of Spain*, trans. Capt. John Stevens (London, 1699); Georges Cirot, *Etudes sur l'historiographie espagnol: Mariana historien* (Bordeaux, 1905).

the poet by his commitment to truth rather than fiction. By "truth," however, he means truth of character, and he urges the historian to recover the motives that govern past actions. He accepts the advice of Lucian and Tacitus in particular to guard against partiality and prejudice, against false invention and conjecture. The truth is to be determined primarily through knowledge and experience of men and the world. "To unravel what is most mysterious in the most secret Intrigues, the Historian must above all things study Man in general." No need here, or indeed any mention, of the pedantry of exact scholarship; no instructions for unearthing or examining the documentary or archaeological record, no research of any kind. It will be difficult, Rapin admits, to penetrate the actions of the past, especially when motives are usually concealed and when historians (so often) are biased; but the clever historian who is well versed in the ways of the world can hope to detect them—as Tacitus did, for example, in discovering fury beneath the outward calm of Octavia when her brother was murdered. Rapin understood the value of eyewitness testimony and the awkwardness of its absence, but he could not offer, any more than the ancients themselves, much help about how to derive it from—or distinguish it in—the written sources. Nor did he see any significance in the fact that Thucydides (as he reports) confined himself to his own time for want of reliable earlier testimony.

It is Livy, however, who is Rapin's hero, above Tacitus and all the Greeks, including Thucydides. In the comparison that he draws between the ancients, he portrays Livy as the ideal historian:

> He had an exquisite Faculty of expressing his Thoughts nobly, an admirable Genius for Eloquence in general, that is, for the purity of Discourse, for a fineness of Speech, for the Dignity of Expression, and a certain elevation of Soul, that made him most fortunate in his Imagination. He was . . . choice in his Words, just in the order of his Discourse, great in his Sentiments, noble and proportionate in the Disposition and universal oeconomy of his Design. He was, in short, a Master of all the Rhetorick of History: for History has a peculiar Rhetorick of its own, and this Rhetorick has its Rules. . . . Perhaps there was never an Historian more engaging by the Talent he had of expressing Nature to the Life.[4]

Rapin does not seem to have minded that poetry too, according to fashionable theory (including his own), was bent on portraying character and motive, usually from the past, as well as representing nature to the

---

[4]René Rapin, *A Comparison of Thucydides and Livy*, in *Works*, 234–35. See too *Instructions for History*, pp. 38, 48.

life. But the confusion between fiction and history which was bound to result from intentions that were so similar, and that had been latent throughout the classical tradition, was beginning to resurface. In France particularly a doughty little band of "pyrrhonists" had started to train their skepticism on the ancient narratives, not least on Livy, transforming them into a kind of poetry.[5] For the moment, however, Rapin was secure in his admiration of the ancient Roman who had drawn his knowledge of the world from a familiar acquaintance with the court of Augustus and whose material was unmatched anywhere, "the most glorious Subject History ever had." No ancient, he was sure, could rival him, much less any modern, though Rapin allows a little merit to those who had rescued historical writing from medieval ignorance: Philippe de Comines, Niccolò Machiavelli, Juan de Mariana, and George Buchanan. Like most of his countrymen at this time, he seems to have known nothing whatever about the English, who were left to make up their own list of modern worthies, if indeed they could find any.

3

Of course, there were many other voices of *ancienneté*, as pure and undefiled by modern sentiment as Rapin, to add to the chorus that had been singing the praises of the ancient historians since the Renaissance. There were other Frenchmen known in England, such as François La Mothe Le Vayer, Père Le Moyne, and the abbé Vallemont, whose *Elémens de l'histoire* was translated and enlarged by Thomas Hearne as *Ductor Historicus* and reissued frequently in the eighteenth century.[6] All were agreed with Rapin about the nature, purpose, and method of history; all had drawn on pretty much the same sources and evaluated pretty much the same historians, differing only in points of detail, as, for example, in how far to employ speeches in the narrative. Father Le Moyne characteristically advocated history over philosophy, renewing the ancient commonplace that history was really philosophy teaching by example,

[5]See Joseph M. Levine, "*Et tu Brute?* History and Forgery in Eighteenth-Century England," in *Fakes and Frauds*, ed. Robin Myers and Michael Harris (Winchester, 1989), p. 71n.
[6]Pierre Le Lorrain, abbé de Vallemont, *Les Elémens de l'histoire* (Paris, 1696), trans. by W. J. as *Ductor Historicus; or, A Short System of Universal History and an Introduction to the Study of That Science* (London, 1698). Hearne's enlarged edition appeared in 2 vols. (reversed) (London, 1705, 1704). See I. G. Philip, "The genesis of Thomas Hearne's *Ductor Historicus*," *Bodleian Library Record* 7 (1966): 251–64. The fullest and best of these works may be that of Lenglet du Fresnoy, who drew on all his predecessors and received an English translation by Richard Rawlinson, *A New Method of Studying History*, 2 vols. (London, 1728).

"philosophy purified from the pedantry of the schools." History, he offered, in a definition that would have suited most, was "a continued Narration of things True, Great and Politick, writ with Spirit, Eloquence, and Judgment, for Instruction to Particulars and Princes, and the Good of Civil Society."[7] Polybius and Livy, he added, could teach more in a day than the followers of Plato and Aristotle in a month. Needless to say, the philosophers responded much like their ancient counterparts, with indifference, or as in the case of the Cartesians, with an outright hostility to the claims of history.[8]

"Since as the Wise Man says, nothing is new under the Sun, a Learned and Judicious Reader may learn to foretell by the past, and regulate what he has to do, by what has been done."[9] Classical imitation always meant deeds as well as words, although in neither case could the moderns hope to surpass their models. It was their misfortune to have been born fifteen hundred years after Livy and Tacitus! Several of the *artes* showed exactly how imitation could be expedited by collecting and classifying examples in a commonplace book. But everyone agreed with Rapin that history was a branch of literature; as Cicero had said succinctly, "History is the most important part of Oratory, *opus oratorium maxime*." A well-told narrative alone could furnish the proper examples of virtuous or successful action and at the same time move the reader to emulate them. In a way, Cicero had taught Livy how to write history, and Livy could still teach the modern student how to speak as well as act.[10]

French *ancienneté* was planted in fertile ground; for more than a hundred years the English had been teaching their young very much the same message in the schools, and many of the same sentiments could be rehearsed from English schoolbooks and gentleman's manuals, and from English editions and translations of classical authors. It is not surprising, then, that the greatest poet in England should have shared these views and aspired to be a historian: after all, history, poetry, and oratory were the kindred disciplines of the *litterae humaniores*. All his life John Dryden had been wrestling with the conflicting claims of the ancients and mod-

---

[7]Pierre Le Moyne, *Of the Art Both of Writing and Judging of History with Reflections upon Ancient as Well as Modern Historians* (London, 1695), pp. 30, 53–54, 109. See H. Chérot, *Etude sur la vie et les oeuvres du P. Le Moyne (1602–71)* (Paris, 1887), pp. 397–419.

[8]See René Descartes, *Philosophical Works*, trans. Elizabeth S. Haldane and G. T. Ross, 2 vols. (New York, 1955), 1:339; Nicolas de Malebranche, *De la recherche de la vérité*, ed. G. Rodes-Lewis, 2 vols. (Paris, 1965), 1:147–51; and for an English example, John Norris, *Reflections upon the Conduct of Human Life*, 2d ed. (London, 1691), pp. 46–50.

[9]Le Moyne, *Of the Art*, p. 45.

[10]Livy's eloquence was usually placed with Cicero's, though La Mothe Le Vayer thought that "if Cicero had attempted to write a History, he would have been inferiour to him in the performance of it": *Notitia Historicorum Selectorum; or, Animadversions upon the Ancient and Famous Greek and Latin Historians*, trans. William Davenport (Oxford, 1678), pp. 188–200.

erns with respect to poetry. His first great work of criticism, *An Essay on Dramatic Poesy* (1667), was a dialogue in which he deliberated about the claims of each. But if at first he inclined toward the modern side, arguing in both his theory and his practice for a real measure of freedom from classical precedent, it looks as though in his later years he turned more and more to antiquity, perhaps inspired by the French.[11] By the end of his life, certainly by the time of his Virgil, he had become persuaded that the classical authors were invincible, although with Dryden there was perhaps always a little inconsistency.[12] So at least it looked to Swift. In the *Tale of a Tub*, he has Dryden deliver a long harangue to Virgil, "call him Father, and . . . make it plainly appear, that they were nearly related." They agree to exchange horses, "but when it came to the Trial, Dryden was afraid, and utterly unable to mount."[13]

In 1683 John Dryden was busy with history, and he confessed that it was "always the most delightful Entertainment of my life." By then he had won the job of historiographer royal to Charles II and set about writing some history of his own as well as translating some classical authors.[14] And by then it is clear that his *ancienneté* had deepened. In the introduction that he wrote for a new version of Plutarch's *Lives* (1683), Dryden composed an apostrophe to the ancients that is as enthusiastic and unqualified as anything in Sir William Temple, and that could well have inspired Temple's "Essay upon Ancient and Modern Learning."[15]

[11]The whole question of Dryden's modernity needs further investigation; his ambiguity even in the *Essay on Dramatic Poesy* (which was reissued, incidentally, in 1684 and 1693) was noticed by Dr. Johnson, who remarked on its "successive representations of opposite possibilities": *Lives of the Poets*, ed. G. Birkbeck Hill, 3 vols. (London, 1905), 1:412. In 1674 Dryden put his modernist view in a way that might have satisfied William Wotton, combining "all due reverence to the Antients" with a denial of "that blind implicit faith in them that some ignorant Schoolmasters would impose on us, to believe in all their errrours, and owne all their crimes": "Notes and Observations on the *Empress of Morocco*," in John Dryden, *Works*, vol. 17 (Berkeley, 1971), pp. 180–84. However, with the appearance in England of the critical works of Rapin and Rymer, Boileau and Bossu, Dryden seems to have qualified even this qualified modernity. After the Revolution, Dryden's personal circumstances were such that he could not afford to enter directly into the battle of the books.

[12]James Sutherland writes of this inconsistency, "The chronic hesitation between a deep respect for the Ancients and an awareness that the modern world was very different from that of ancient Athens and Rome was shared in various degrees by most of his contemporaries": *English Literature of the Late Seventeenth Century* (Oxford, 1969), p. 396.

[13]Jonathan Swift, *A Tale of a Tub*, ed. A. C. Guthkelch and D. Nichol Smith, 2d ed. (Oxford, 1958), pp. 246–47.

[14]See Roswell Ham, "Dryden as Historiographer-Royal: The Authorship of *His Majesty's Declaration Defended*, 1681," in *Essential Articles for the Study of John Dryden*, ed. H. T. Swedenberg, Jr. (Hamden, Conn., 1966), pp. 135–53. But see Edward L. Saslow, "Dryden as Historiographer Royal and the Authorship of *His Majesty's Declaration Defended*," *Modern Philology* 75 (1978): 261–72.

[15]"Life of Plutarch," in *Plutarch's Lives Translated by Several Hands* (London, 1683), in the California edition of *The Works of John Dryden* (Berkeley, 1956–), 17:238–88, 429–40.

"How vast a difference there is betwixt the productions of those Souls
and those of ours! How much better Plato, Aristotle, and the rest of the
Philosophers understood nature; Thucydides and Herodotus adorn'd
History, Euripides and Menander advanc'd Poetry, than those Dwarfs of
Wit and Learning who succeeded them in after times!" Nor had any age
yet succeeded in equaling Plutarch.[16]

Dryden's Plutarch was a publisher's venture, a collaborative effort to
translate the *Lives*.[17] Dryden's contribution consisted of a life and evaluation of the author in his usual discursive style, with a generous passage
about the nature and purpose of history. The life, he admitted, was a
"patchwork" drawn essentially from two earlier editions of Plutarch, a
learned Greek-Latin text by Rualdus (Jean Rualt, 1624), which he
ackowledges, and an English version by Thomas North, with additions
by S. G. S. (Simon Goulart, 1603), which he does not.[18] Dryden typically rewrites, condenses, and interprets his two sources, interpolating a
few remarks of his own, as well as a few from Montaigne and St.
Evremond. In perfect accord with classical literary practice, he makes no
pretense at research and offers no citations.

Plutarch, Dryden tells us, traveled to Rome for firsthand information,
not content to sit in his study; but Plutarch, he imagines, sought out only
books from the distant past, not records or documents or archaeological
evidence. If so, he did more than Dryden himself, though much less than
modern antiquarian scholarship would have required. As for history
itself, Dryden thought it unnecessary to repeat the conventional praise,
so much rhetoric had already been expended on the subject. But he could
not resist a few commonplaces.[19] History, he agreed, was indispensable
"for instruction, for the regulation of private manners and the management of publick affairs." It was the most enjoyable school of wisdom. "It
informs the understanding by the memory: It helps us to judge of what
will happen, by shewing us the like revolutions of former times. For
mankind being the same in all ages, agitated by the same passions, and
mov'd to action by the same interests, nothing can come to pass, but
some Presedent of the like nature has already been produc'd, so that
having the causes before our eyes, we cannot easily be deceiv'd in the
effects, if we have Judgment enough to draw the parallel."

It was a view that nearly everyone shared. When Dryden's old friend
and rival Sir Robert Howard elected to write some history about this

[16]John Dryden, "To the Duke of Ormonde," in ibid., pp. 227–28.
[17]See Arthur Sherbo, "The Dryden-Cambridge Translation of Plutarch's *Lives*," *Etudes
anglaises* 32 (1979): 177–84.
[18]See Maurice Wallace, "Dryden's Knowledge of Historians, Ancient and Modern,"
Notes and Queries n.s. 6 (1959): 264–66.
[19]Dryden, *Works*, 17:270–77.

time, he too sought a parallel from the past to inform the present (though from the opposite political persuasion), since "the actions of former Ages are made Presidents to our present times." And when later in life Alexander Pope considered the matter, he too insisted on the importance of history as a practical guide to life. He told Spence that he had begun by reading it for pleasure but soon discovered its use. "I would mark down: on such an occasion the people concerned proceeded in such a manner, it was evidently wrong and had an ill effect; a statesman therefore should avoid it in a like case. Such a one did good or got an honest reputation by such an action: I would mark it down in order to imitate it where I had an opportunity." As Dryden put it conventionally, "All history is only the precepts of Moral Philosophy reduc'd into Examples."[20]

Dryden was equally commonplace and ancient-minded in his account of historical veracity. Like the rest of his literary contemporaries, he could not offer much beyond what the rhetoricians had so often said. The "laws of history" certainly included, besides clarity of expression, truth of matter. Indeed, truth was the foundation of history, all the rest was disposition and perspicuity. "One is the being, the other the well-being of it." How to establish the truth and differentiate it from fiction was another matter, particularly in the absence of critical scholarship. Dryden preferred to talk about the various forms of historical narrative. He follows Rualdus in distinguishing commentary and annals from history proper, which he says adds to the bare story a grave style and an insight into the springs and causes of great actions. Inevitably he counsels against passion and partiality. The best historians were for him Thucydides and Polybius among the Greeks, Livy and Tacitus among the Romans. (For biography as another form of history, he prefers Plutarch.) The best of the moderns were Francesco Guicciardini and Enrico Davila, and especially Philippe de Comines. "I am sorry I cannot find in our Nation . . . any Proper to be ranked with these." Only the Scot, Buchanan, draws some qualified admiration.[21]

Dryden's own contributions to history included two translations: Louis Maimbourg's *History of the League* (1684) and Père Bouhours's *Life of St. Francis Xavier* (1688). Neither is distinguished for its historiography, though Dryden, who wrote them as propaganda for the crown, defended them vigorously. Indeed, it was hard to acclaim Maimbourg's work for impartiality when it never even mentioned the Edict of Nantes and when its whole purpose was so blatantly polemical. Yet Dryden probably believed in the parallel between the troubles of sixteenth-

[20]Ibid., p. 274; Sir Robert Howard, *The History of the Reigns of Edward and Richard II Written in 1685* (London, 1690), p. 2; Joseph Spence, *Observations, Anecdotes, and Characters of Books and Men*, ed. James M. Osborn, 2 vols. (Oxford, 1966), 1:241.

[21]Dryden, *Works*, 17:273.

century France and seventeenth-century Britain. Maimbourg put on a brave face and protested his own veracity. His one criterion for historical truthfulness was fidelity to the sources, which must be scrupulously followed and cited. The historian was accountable only for what he reported, "on the credit of those from whom he had them." Eyewitness accounts were desirable when they could be obtained. The historian's method was scissors and paste, sticking together the bits and pieces of previous accounts, and "compiling out of all of them a new body of History." It was new, though it contained nothing that was not to be found in the sources. The historian's chief business was "to find out the most secret motives . . . [and] to make an exact description of the principal actions and the greatest and most signal events."[22] Whatever its claims as theory, Maimbourg's practice seems to have exceeded his protestations and he was immediately attacked for his partiality and unreliability, a judgment that has continued. As a piece of history, Bouhours's biography was little better.[23]

It was just at the beginning of the battle of the books (1693) that Dryden was asked again to write an introduction to a classical translation, this time for his favorite, Polybius, "the most sincere, the clearest, and the most instructive of historians." Dryden preferred him to Livy, "commonly esteemed the Prince of Roman History," in part because Livy still smacked of pagan superstition and in part because Livy had depended on Polybius as the most veracious and instructive of historians.[24] Here he accepted the opinion of the great scholar Isaac Casaubon, who had earlier furnished a Latin text and commentary, which was his source. Polybius "weighed the authors from whom he was forced to borrow . . . and oftentimes corrected them, either by comparing them each with another, or by the light which he had received from ancient men of known integrity. . . . Having gained permission from the senate to search the Capitol, he made himself familiar with the records."[25]

Did Wotton read these words? A year later he repeated much the same view in his *Reflections*, again choosing Polybius over Livy. For Wotton, Polybius had the obvious advantage of furnishing a running critique of previous historians and of supplying a strong caution against too much rhetoric. He was the most "scholarly" of the ancient narrators. (Nor was it unusual for the moderns to use an ancient to serve the cause of modernity!) But Dryden chose to close out his preface with a rhetorical comparison of Polybius and Tacitus in which he singled out eloquence and

---

[22]Louis Maimbourg, *History of the League*, trans. John Dryden, in Dryden, *Works*, 18:16. For Maimbourg, see ibid., pp. 439–56.

[23]See the commentary in Dryden, *Works*, 19:472.

[24]John Dryden, "Character of Polybius," in Dryden, *Works*, ed. Walter Scott, rev. George Saintsbury, 18 vols. (London, 1882–1893), 18:23–24.

[25]Ibid., p. 39.

experience of the world as the principal criteria for excellence. And it was with this in mind that he proposed the two ancients as models for everyone afterward. The implication was plain: if a modern history was to be written, it would still have to be composed according to the standards of antiquity, by someone with a real familiarity with the world and a due regard for style and form. From that point of view, the whole history of England remained to be done.

4

To much of this, even the moderns gave assent. Certainly Wotton had acknowledged the preeminence of the classical historians, though he was always more optimistic about the future than his more conservative contemporaries. John Locke, we have seen, had scrupulously avoided the quarrel but was undoubtedly on the modern side. When he was asked his views about education, he objected to what he thought was the excessive emphasis placed on classical Latin and especially Greek texts. He allowed that eloquence was a sensible objective for a man of the world but he preferred it to be in English; and he thought that histories were useful and instructive but that the moderns should be read along with the ancients. Nevertheless, even he conceded that a gentleman had to know some Latin and much ancient history, and he accepted the general notion of narrative history as essential to the man of affairs.[26] When the Countess of Peterborough asked Locke for advice about her son's education in 1697, he replied with a letter urging the boy to begin with the classical histories. He thought that a young man would need help, someone to explain the difficulties in language and to point out the felicities of style, as well as those things "relating to a man's private conduct in common life or to the turns of state in public affairs." He recommended Livy above all others as "the great repository of the Roman antiquities as well as the best history of the state." It might be necessary to explain something about Roman customs, but "other critical expositions wherewith men versed in that sort of Learning use to abound, I think that they have neither needs nor right to be trifled with. Young persons of quality should have none of their time wasted in studies which will be of no use to them as men." The only point in reading a historian such as Livy was "to give an account of the actions of men as embodied in society. History was nothing less than "the true foundation of politics."[27]

[26]John Locke, *Some Thoughts Concerning Education*, in *The Educational Writings of John Locke*, ed. James L. Axtell (Cambridge, 1968), pp. 268, 279, 282, 292–93, 307.
[27]Locke to the Countess of Peterborough (1697), in *Educational Writings*, pp. 393–94. Cf. Henry Nevile, "Whosoever sets himself to study Politicks, must do so by reading History": *Plato Redivivus* (London, 1681), p. 89.

Temple would certainly have agreed; and Locke's letter seems to echo something of what his old teacher Richard Busby and the Christ Church wits meant when they said they preferred to read a chaste and unadorned classical text. In 1697 Bentley was writing his "Dissertation" for Wotton, and Locke must certainly have heard a lot about the claims of philology and classical scholarship. But all through his life he remained obdurate against its pretensions, even though he seems to have taken some interest from time to time in criticism and even exchanged letters with continental friends on some recondite matters. In an early essay, "Of Study," he spoke out flatly against historical knowledge for its own sake. "He that can tell all the particularities of Herodotus and Plutarch, Curtius and Livy, without making other use of them may be an ignorant man with a good memory." Already Locke dismisses all those "useless, curious and difficult inquiries in antiquity . . . as the exact dimensions of the Colossus, or figures of the Capitol, the ceremonies of the Greek and Roman marriages, or who it was that first coined money."[28] "History," he wrote to his young lawyer friend Edward Clarke in 1687, "is the great mistress of prudence and civil knowledge and ought to be the proper study of a gentleman, or man of business in the world." It was helpful to know a little geography and chronology, but as to those endless controversies on small points, "all that learned Noise and Dust" could be completely disregarded.[29] In 1693 he repeated these views exactly in "Some Thoughts Concerning Reading and Study for a Gentleman." He continued to counsel reading the classical histories as a means of learning Latin and as a foundation for political wisdom, but he was willing to add to his reading list a few moderns as well: Mariana, Comines, and Thuanus, and among the English, Francis Bacon's *History of Henry VII*, Lord Herbert of Cherbury's *Life of Henry VIII*, and Gilbert Burnet's *History of the Reformation*.[30] Like Wotton, he was distrustful of too much rhetoric; but unlike Wotton, he never seems to have seen the possibilities of historical research in constructing or evaluating a narrative.

5

For more on the subject, Locke recommended the most ambitious of all the English *artes historicae*, a work that Temple is also very likely to have known. It had appeared first in the Latin of Degory Wheare in 1625,

[28]John Locke, "Of Study" (1677), in *Educational Writings*, p. 410.
[29]Locke to Clarke, July 15, 1687, in *The Correspondence of John Locke and Edward Clarke*, ed. Benjamin Rand (London, 1927), pp. 214–20.
[30]John Locke, "Some Thoughts Concerning Reading and Study for a Gentleman" (1703), in *Educational Writings*, p. 403.

enlarged in 1637, and turned into English by Edmund Bohun in 1685 as *The Method and Order of Reading Both Civil and Ecclesiastical Histories*. Wheare was the initial incumbent of a chair in history that had been set up at Oxford by William Camden, the very first of its kind in England, and he had for many years lectured dutifully on an ancient historian, as the terms of the endowment required. "He should read a civil history," Camden had explained, "and therein make such observations, as might be usefull and profitable for the younger students of the University, to direct and instruct them in the knowledge and use of history, antiquity, and times past."[31] Wheare chose Lucius Florus for his text and set about his duties manfully, although one modern reader has found his lectures "sad stuff"—not much more than a list of literary sources "punctuated by trite observations."[32] In 1632 Wheare was forced to apologize for having covered only 128 sections of his book in eight years! The only lasting consequence was the *Method and Order*, which began life as an inaugural lecture. Meanwhile, a similar effort at Cambridge did no better,[33] and both ancient chairs went swiftly into a decline that lasted until the nineteenth century. As for modern history, nothing at all was done until 1724, when two new regius professorships were founded, only to lapse almost immediately.[34] It is fair to say that neither the ancients nor the moderns won any advantage in the universities.

Wheare's *Method and Order* was organized as a bibliography of the ancient works, "an exact Series and Method of Reading all the Greek and Latin Histories," arranged in succession, with a short description and introduction for each. For Wheare, as for everyone else, "the principal end of History is Practice, and not Knowledge or Contemplation"; it was, as usual, philosophy teaching action by example.[35] His bibliography is very long but offers no surprises. Livy is still the best, "famous

[31]See H. Stuart Jones, "The Foundation and History of the Camden Chair," *Oxoniensia* 8–9 (1943–44): 169–92; William H. Allison, "The First Endowed Professorship of History and Its First Encumbent," *American Historical Review* 27 (1922): 733–37; Kevin Sharpe, "The Foundation of the Chairs of History at Oxford and Cambridge," *History of Universities* 2 (1982): 127–52.

[32]H. R. Trevor-Roper, review of Christopher Hill, *The Intellectual Foundations of the Puritan Revolution*, in *History and Theory* 5 (1966): 67. Wheare's lectures are in Bodleian MS. Auct. 5, 10–11, "Lucii Annei Flori Punica publicis praelectionibus illustrata." The last was delivered in 1645. For correspondence about the chair, see *Camdeni epistolae*, ed. Thomas Smith (London, 1691), pp. 313–51.

[33]See Norman Farmer, Jr., "Fulke Greville and Sir John Coke: An Exchange of Letters on a History Lecture and Certain Latin Verses on Sir Philip Sidney," *Huntington Library Quarterly* 33 (1969–70): 217–36.

[34]See C. H. Firth, "Modern History in Oxford, 1724–1841," *English Historical Review* 32 (1917): 1–21; Norman Sykes, *Edmund Gibson* (London, 1926), pp. 94–107.

[35]"History is nothing but Moral Philosophy, cloathed in Examples": Degory Wheare, *The Method and Order of Reading Both Civil and Ecclesiastical Histories*, trans. Edmund Bohun (London, 1685), pp. 298–99.

above all others, for his Eloquence and his Fidelity," and his style and orations are particularly commended. Wheare does have room for some modern works, but he can find no complete English history worthy of the name, although he gives some faint praise to John Speed's recent *History of Great Britain*. He is reduced to listing some shorter pieces in chronological order to make up the deficiency and parallel his classical reading list. He begins with some medieval chronicles and concludes with Thomas More's life of Richard III, Bacon's history of Henry VII, and William Camden's *Annals of Elizabeth*. Only the last was really worth comparing with the best of the ancients, a compliment to his patron and perhaps an opening wedge for the moderns. Wheare's translator, Bohun, thought that he could add Samuel Daniel's short account of medieval history, "written with great brevity and Politeness, and his Political and Moral Reflections very fine." But he had to admit that he could find no good history written after Camden's time.

Bohun's translation found a second edition in 1694, the same year as Wotton's *Reflections*, and it was then that the latest Camden professor, Henry Dodwell, was called upon to write as an introduction his "Invitation to Gentlemen to acquaint themselves with Antient History." We have already examined this curious piece with its very conventional arguments for the usefulness and superiority of classical history. Dodwell, we have seen, tried to mediate in the contest between the ancients and the moderns. Here he enlists completely with the conventional wisdom of the proponents of antiquity. "History," he writes, "is much more fitted for an active than a studious Life, and therefore much more useful for Gentlemen than scholars."[36] Later he was to engage with Bentley and write the unreadable, scholarly, and very modern *De Cyclis*. It was, of course, not unusual to find a modern agreeing with the ancients about the value of classical literature, but Dodwell's muddled mind was more than most, averse to facing, much less solving, the problem of how to reconcile the new with the old, classical narrative with classical philology. Through all his copious output, he never tried.

Among other moderns who set out their ideas about history in the period, we should not perhaps overlook Locke's friend and admirer Jean Le Clerc. Le Clerc was possibly the best-known scholarly publicist of his time, and Wotton had drawn him deliberately into the battle of the books, reporting to him blow by blow as the quarrel developed. After a little hesitation, Le Clerc pronounced decisively for the moderns with an

---

[36]"The peculiar Employment of a Gentleman, who would be eminently servicable to his Country in that Station, should be to accomplish himself in Politicks, and the Art of War": Henry Dodwell "Invitation to Gentlemen," in Wheare, *Method and Order* (London, 1694), sig. A4. "A sedentary studious course of Life," he adds, "does naturally break that vigor of mind which is requisite for Action": ibid. [sig. A6].

article in the *Nouvelles de la république des lettres* (1699).[37] Bentley's "Dissertation" was applauded there without reservation, though later rivalry with the great man may have given Le Clerc some second thoughts.[38] For the moment, however, he had no doubt; it was only a pity, he wrote, that the entire dispute had not been turned into Latin so that the whole learned world could profit from the controversy.

In the same year Le Clerc published the first volume of his own *Parrhasiana*, a little book of somewhat random reflections on the humanities in the style of those popular collections of table talk, or ana, which were then circulating. He sent a copy to Locke and was pleased to find it translated into English almost at once.[39] He began with poetry and explained that although no one had yet appeared to rival Homer and Virgil, it was simply because the moderns were too preoccupied with imitation and needed to free themselves from pedantic repetition of the classics. The shield of Achilles he accepted as too improbable for belief, despite the arguments of Monsieur Dacier. In a chapter on eloquence he praised the moderns forthrightly as superior at least in method. "'Tis an undeniable truth, that in this respect we very much surpass the Ancients, whatever the Admirers of Antiquity may pretend." Descartes, Port-Royal and Le Clerc himself are invoked to prove the point. A third chapter is devoted to history and the "Difference between the Modern and Ancient Historians."[40]

Here again, however, it is the case of a modern implicitly accepting many of the conventions of classical historiography while tempering them with some qualifications and much optimism. Le Clerc begins with an invocation to modernity. "If the thing be ill of itself, the Example of the Ancients does not make it a jot the better, and nothing ought to

[37]*Nouvelles de la république des lettres*, June 1699; see Le Clerc to Locke, June 8/18, 1699, in *The Correspondence of John Locke*, ed. E. S. de Beer, 8 vols. (Oxford, 1976–1989), 6:636–38.

[38]Bentley may have been angered by the attempt to make Le Clerc a colibrarian; this at least is what some nobleman told Joseph Wasse, who passed it on to Le Clerc many years later; see Amorie van der Hoeven, *De Joanne Clerico et Philippo a Limborch* (Amsterdam, 1843), p. 279. John Henry Monk makes some other suggestions in *The Life of Richard Bentley*, 2d ed., 2 vols. (London, 1833), 1:266–80; and Annie Barnes gives Le Clerc a sympathetic hearing in *Jean Le Clerc et la république des lettres* (Paris, 1938), pp. 220–24.

[39]Le Clerc to Locke, June 8/18, 1699, in Locke, *Correspondence*, 6:636–38. He sent the second volume, May 19/30, 1701; ibid., pp. 324–25. The first volume was translated as *Parrhasiana; or, Thoughts upon Several Subjects as Criticism, History, Morality and Politics* (London, 1700). It was reviewed in *Miscellaneous Letters, Giving an Account of the Works of the Learned*, 1:515–22. Long before, Le Clerc had published a book by his uncle David with an *Oratio in vituperium Homeri* (1687), thus anticipating the *querelle*; see Noémi Hepp, *Homère en France au XVIIe siècle* (Paris, 1968), p. 526. He set out some modernist views of his own in "Règles de critique pour l'intelligence des anciens auteurs," *Bibliothèque universelle et historique* 10 (1688): 309–78, esp. 363–78.

[40]Le Clerc, *Parrhasiana*: Shield of Achilles, p. 19; on eloquence, pp. 54–97; on history, pp. 97–165; on philology, pp. 166–91.

hinder us from doing better than they. The Republic of Letters is at last become a Country of Reason and Light, and not of Authority and implicit Faith. . . . There is no Divine or Humane Law which prohibits us to bring the Art of Writing to Perfection, as we have endeavor'd to bring to Perfection the other Arts and Sciences." For history, Le Clerc counsels truth over fiction and matter over form, but he admits the need for classical rhetoric and the value of a universal ethical and political vantage point. "'Tis ridiculous to dishearten the Reader by a barbarous style." He is opposed (with Lucian) to partiality and bias. And like all his contemporaries, he believes in a fixed and unchanging human nature, a character "imposed upon all Men, of what Condition or Quality soever, and in what place or time they are born."

Except to insist upon exact citations, Le Clerc says nothing here about scholarship. He reserves philology for his next chapter, "On the Decay of Humane Learning and the Causes of It." He thus effectively separates erudition from "history," that is, from narrative. He also qualifies his enthusiasm for scholarship; apparently one could have too much of a good thing. Le Clerc did not at all approve of the Dutch variorums or the Delphin classics, with their suffocating and frequently inept commentaries. On the other hand, he could not agree with the ancients in discarding learning altogether. With a fine impartiality he condemned the "excesses" of both the ancients and the moderns. The partisans of antiquity had claimed too much for the classical authors, who had their defects too; and the partisans of modernity had exaggerated the virtues of their scholarship. He preferred, with his correspondent Wotton, to try to join the two, "to read the ancient Authors, perfect their Knowledge by ours, and not despise those, who excel in the Modern Learning." Still, it was hard to see how Le Clerc could reconcile the conflicting claims of the two sides any better than Dodwell, especially with respect to ancient history, where the great works of narrative, like the poetry of Homer and Virgil or the prose of Thucydides and Livy, still stood largely beyond criticism, the models for all time of how the job should be done. It only remained to see whether it could be done again.

6

Of course, philology was only one part of modern historical scholarship. There was also the antiquarian enterprise which was always linked to it but which tried to retrieve the past by examining objects as well as books, things as well as words. By 1700 its method too had become articulate. In particular, interest was growing in the importance of fieldwork, in leaving the library for the actual sites, and in calling for new standards of precision and criticism. One of William Wotton's friends, the Kentish antiquary John Batteley, typically laid down some of the "laws of antiquaries." He first tells how he began his collection of ancient remains on a trip to Reculver, strictly cautioning the natives *not* to clean the rust off the old Roman coins by rubbing them with sand, "as I had seen many of the most valuable by that means quite obliterated." He urged them to sell no brass to the brasiers but to bring it to him, for he would pay a higher price; to break no urns or pots,

> and if they found them broken, and inscribed with marks or letters, to bring them to me.
>
> Let him who is curious in such researches, open barrows; let him explore encampments, trenches, and the places adjoining; let him examine the public ways; let him, without superstition and dread, open and ransack sepulchres, which are generally by the road-side; let him carefully explore the ruins of cliffs; when he finds any traces of antiquity, let him pursue them, and call in the connoisseurs; if he should discover any coins, either lying in a heap, or inclosed in an urn or pot, let him observe the latest, for they will nearly determine the time when they were buried. . . . When he meets with inscriptions, let them be accurately copied, and without envy, communicated to the world.[41]

Batteley's own efforts wound up in a Latin tract, the *Antiquitates Rutupinae* (1711), but he seems never to have considered, much less solved, the problem of turning an antiquarian compilation into a history.

Did anyone, then, see the advantage of combining classical narrative with the possibilities of philological and antiquarian scholarship? Certainly not the wits and men of the world, who continued to insist on the uses of history for practical life. Admittedly, some knowledge of antiquities, especially coins, could shed light on history or, as Joseph Addison pointed out in a popular dialogue, on ancient poetry. Indeed, collecting coins and medals had for a long time been a gentlemanly preoccupation, and their value to a classical education, like the grand tour itself, was generally recognized.[42] Addison was thus taking up a familiar subject

[41]John Nichols, *Illustrations of the Literary History of the Eighteenth Century*, 8 vols. (London, 1817–1858), 4:87n; Joseph M. Levine, *Dr. Woodward's Shield* (Berkeley, 1977), pp. 170–71. I have given many other examples of the theory and practice of antiquarian research there and in *Humanism and History* (Ithaca, N.Y., 1989), chaps. 3–4. When Wotton visited Batteley in 1704, he was delighted to look over his collection of Roman antiquities. On his return, he sent him a newly unearthed Roman urn: Nichols, *Literary Illustrations*, 4:99.

[42]For the beginning of this gentlemanly preoccupation, see Henry Peacham, *Complete Gentleman* (1634), ed. G. S. Gordon (Oxford, 1906), pp. 105ff.; Levine, *Dr. Woodward's Shield*, p. 116. There were various popular manuals for the collector; e.g., Charles Patin, *Histoire des médailles* (Paris, 1695); Louis Jobert, *Las science des médailles* (Paris, 1692), trans.

when he set out to explain the use of these old monuments, as he had recently done in his description of his own tour through Italy. In his dialogue, he lets Philander answer Cynthio's strictures against the antiquarian enterprise, although he allows far too much of the criticism to have satisfied any real scholar.[43]

In the ancient coins, Philander argues, one can see the features of classical heroes, the figures of pagan gods, and something of the art, architecture, and daily life of antiquity. Coins could be used to check the accuracy of literary sources, to furnish missing chronology, and to supply information not otherwise available. At best a medal could supply a vivid picture, a veritable epitome of history or poetry, worth a volume of words. Yet Addison was typically on guard against too serious an interest even in these helpful objects. "Should I tell you gravely," Philander says characteristically at one point, "that without the help of coins we should never have known which was the first of the Emperors that wore a beard, or rode in Stirrups, I might turn my science into ridicule."[44] Addison satirized the chronologists mercilessly and the antiquarian love of rust and ruins. Learning must always have its practical application, and like the Scriblerians, who were paying careful attention, Addison found everything else excessive and foolish. In his periodical essays he continually disapproved of the philological concern with "minute Particulars," which had no value "but because they are despised and forgotten by the rest of Mankind." "Men of Wit," he lamented, "do so much employ their thought upon fine speculations that things useful to mankind are wholly neglected and they are busy in making emendations upon some editions in a Greek author, while obvious things, that any man may have use for are overlooked." In one *Spectator* essay, he parodied the verbal critics with some learned annotations on a popular song, "My Love Was Fickle and Changing."[45] He concluded the first of

---

by Roger Gale as *The Knowledge of Medals* (London, 1697); Obadiah Walker, *The Greek and Roman History Illustrated by Coins and Medals* (London, 1692); and John Evelyn's *Numismata* (London, 1697); for which see chap. 11 below. The scholarly alternative was a massive work by Ezechiel Spanheim, *Dissertationes de praestantia et usu numismatum antiquorum* (Rome, 1664). The work was revised and enlarged and printed in London in 1706–1717.

[43]*Dialogues upon the Usefulness of Ancient Medals*, in Addison's *Works*, ed. Thomas Tickell, 4 vols. (London, 1721), 1:429–559. Addison's *Remarks on Several Parts of Italy etc. in the Years 1701, 1702, 1703* were published first in London, 1705; the grand tour is defended for its use to *ancienneté* in the *Spectator*, no. 364. The *Dialogues* were probably begun during Addison's travels; he refers to them in a letter to George Stepney in 1702; see *The Letters of Joseph Addison*, ed. Walter Graham (Oxford, 1941), pp. 35–36; Peter Smithers, *The Life of Joseph Addison*, 2d ed. (Oxford, 1968), pp. 44–88.

[44]Addison, *Works*, 1:445–46.

[45]*Tatler*, no. 18; *Guardian*, no. 77; *Spectator*, no. 470 (Aug. 29, 1712). In the *Tatler*, no. 158, Addison refers to "Editors, Commentators, Interpretors, Scholiasts, and Criticks; and in short all Men of deep Learning without common sense." See L. A. Elioseff, *The Cultural Milieu of Addison's Literary Criticism* (Austin, Tex., 1963), p. 45.

the *Dialogues upon the Usefulness of Ancient Medals* by wondering if there was anything more ridiculous than an antiquary reading the Greek or Latin poets. "He never thinks of the beauty of the thought or language but is for searching into what he calls the Erudition of an Author." Pope admired the work extravagantly and wrote a poem to Addison enthusiastically applauding its sentiments.[46] Wotton and Bentley seem not to have noticed.

History for Addison was therefore history unencumbered by pedantic learning—good classical narrative. "It is the agreeable talent of an historian," he wrote in the *Spectator*, "to be able to draw up his armies and fight his battles in proper expressions, to set before our eyes the divisions, cabals, and jealousies of great men, and to lead us into the several actions and events of his history. We love to see the subject unfolding itself by just degrees, and breaking upon us insensibly."[47] In all these ways Livy surpassed everyone, before or since. "He describes everything in so lively a manner that his whole history is an admirable picture, and touches on such proper circumstances in every story, that the reader becomes a kind of spectator." That this might endanger the literal truth of the narrative did actually cross Addison's mind, but he seems not to have been unduly alarmed or interested in prescribing a remedy. Like most of the ancients and many of the moderns, he accepted without qualms the sovereignty of classical rhetoric, and had no real patience for anything else. He must surely have agreed with the Christ Church company who quoted that great wit, St. Evremond, then living out his old age in England.

> I don't affect that sort of learned men, that rack their brains to restore a Reading, which is not mended by the Restitution. . . . As they are incapable of having nice Sentiments and Thoughts, so 'tis impossible for them to enter into the delicacy of a Sentiment or the fineness of a Thought. They may succeed well enough in expounding Grammarians . . . but they can never hit that of a polite, well bred man among the Antients, because that is diametrically opposed to it. In

---

[46]Pope's *Epistle to Addison* appeared first in *The Works of Alexander Pope*, 2 vols. (London, 1720), then in Addison's *Works*, ed. Thomas Tickell, 4 vols. (London, 1721), 1:431–33, accompanying the *Dialogues*. It is possible that the first half of the work, ll. 1–44 (minus ll. 5–10, added in 1726), was originally an independent poem on antiquities written c. 1713–1715 and adapted afterward for use with Addison's *Dialogues*; see Norman Ault, "Pope and Addison," *Review of English Studies* 17 (1941): 428–51, and *New Light on Pope* (London, 1949), pp. 121–23. For a close reading of the poem, see Howard Erskine-Hill, "The Medal against Time: A Study of Pope's *Epistle to Mr. Addison*," *Journal of the Warburg and Courtauld Institutes* 28 (1965): 274–98. The tangled relationship between Pope and Addison, at first cordial, then angry and finally cool, should not obscure the powerful influence that Addison undoubtedly had on the younger man, not least on his Homer.

[47]*Spectator*, no. 420 (July 2, 1712).

History, they never mind Men or Affairs: they lay the whole stress on Chronology, and for a date of a Consul's death, will neglect the knowledge of his Character, and of the Transactions during his Consulship.[48]

When eventually Addison wrote his own little *Discourse on Ancient and Modern Learning*—which, like the *Dialogues*, he left unpublished—he took some pains to list all the disadvantages that the moderns had in reading and appreciating the ancients. (His little work goes no further and is otherwise disappointing.)[49] He saw that the classical texts had been stripped of all those accidental circumstances that had once attended them: the secret motives of their composition, their references to people and places, their humor, colloquial speech, customs, and so on. What he did not see very clearly or care to admit was that this was just what the philologists were trying to repair with their close attention to minutiae. So, like Pope afterward, he dipped into their works for occasional help with a classical puzzle only to draw back at the size and difficulty—and perhaps the danger—of the enterprise. Addison's own scholarship was limited (like that of the Christ Church wits who were his intimates at Oxford)[50] and he never attempted to write history, so it never occurred to him to try to reconcile the conflicting claims of rhetoric and erudition.

[48]See the letter to Crécqui (1665), in St. Evremond, *Works*, trans. Pierre Desmaizeaux, 3 vols. (London, 1728), 1:203–4. The passage is also translated in Charles Boyle, *Dr. Bentley's Dissertations . . . Examin'd* (London, 1698), pp. 227–28. St. Evremond's relation to the ancients and moderns is as complicated and ambiguous as Dryden's. He too avoided the battle of the books, though resident in England, but it is possible to guess where he would have stood.

[49]It seems to have been printed first in London, 1734. The British Library copy of the 4th ed. (London, 1739) has a note signed H [Hurd?] attesting to the genuineness of the piece: "Probably it was drawn up in his younger days and not reworked, or at least finished by him." It was accepted as genuine by E. K. Broadus, "Addison's Discourse on Ancient and Modern Learning," *Modern Language Notes* 22 (1907): 1–2; and reprinted by A. C. Guthkelch in Addison's *Miscellaneous Works*, 2 vols. (London, 1914), 2:449–63. Addison's position in the *querelle* anticipates Pope's denial that either the ancients or the moderns in France were completely right; see *Spectator*, no. 327 (Mar. 15, 1712) and no. 351 (April 12, 1712). In no. 253 Addison had endorsed Boileau's view "that Wit and fine Writing doth not consist in advancing things that are new, as in giving things that are known an agreeable Turn." On the other hand, while still at Magdalen College in the 1690s, he had declared for the moderns in philosophy; his oration "Nova philosophia veteri praeferenda est" (July 7, 1693) was translated by Richard Rawlinson in *An Altar of Love* (1727) but was not included in the *Works*; see Smithers, *Life of Addison*, p. 20.

[50]Macaulay's strictures on Addison's lack of Greek and his limitation to the Roman imperial poets still seem to hold; see his *Life and Writings of Addison* (London, 1852), p. 10; modified slightly by Lillian D. Bloom, "Addison as Translator: A Problem in Neo-Classical Scholarship," *Studies in Philology* 46 (1949): 31–53. His Italian guide, the antiquary Francesco de' Ficoroni, denied that Addison knew anything more about medals than what he taught him in no more than twenty lessons; see Nathaniel Ogle, *Life of Addison* (London, 1826), p. 21.

7

In short, Addison confirms what we have found elsewhere: that there was not much possibility that a gentleman or man of the world could see much use in the drudgery of historical scholarship, and little likelihood of his undertaking it. And it was harder still to imagine—even if he should think to try—just how he would resolve that apparently intractable problem of form: how to reconcile a well-told tale with the armory of ponderous scholarship, the flow of narrative with the intrusions of learned commentary. Yet not everyone despaired. When young Thomas Hearne was asked to prepare a new edition of the popular *Ductor Historicus*, he added some passages to Vallemont which were meant to bridge the gap between the two historiographical practices. Hearne was willing to accept history as "a Narration of the most remarkable Actions and Events in general Order . . . with the Writer's Judgment upon Actions and Persons," and as the particular preoccupation of gentlemen, "exceedingly useful to them in their Conduct, not in Speculation only, but in Action, in all Conditions of Life, but especially in publick Stations."[51] But good narrative needed explanation, description of places, customs, military techniques, and so on, an inducement certainly to scholarship. And so Hearne added to his reading list of the ancient historians Basil Kennett's *Romae antiquae notitia*, which he praised extravagantly for its use in furnishing the necessary information.[52] Here was a characteristic antiquarian handbook, exactly like Potter's for the Greek antiquities, full of minute and miscellaneous detail, and arranged by topic. Even more to the point, Hearne prefixed to the second volume of his work a wholly new plea for the study of antiquities, something that had been completely ignored by Vallemont, Le Moyne, and the rest. "Because Inscriptions and Coynes are slighted by some," he wrote, "who are otherwise very much inclined to the Study of History, and esteemed to be of little Use in acquiring a compleat Skill in it, I shall take this Opportunity to show in short, how necessary an Insight therein is, for such at least, as design to be accurately acquainted with any Part of Ancient History."[53]

[51]Vallemont, *Ductor Historicus*, ed. Hearne, 1:3, 116. "History by informing us of the Actions of Mankind in former Ages, brings us the Times past into our present View, makes us as it were co-eval with the celebrated Heroes of former Times, and naturally Excites us to an Emulation with them in Glory. 'Tis a Prospect-Glass (as Mr. Dryden Expresses it) that carries our Souls to a vast distance, and takes in the farthest Objects of Antiquity. It informs the understanding by the Memory, and helps us to judge of what will happen by shewing us the like Revolutions in former Times. For Mankind being the same in all Ages . . . nothing can come to pass, but some Precedent of the like Nature has already happen'd": ibid., p. 113.

[52]Basil Kennett, *Romae antiquae notitia; or, The Antiquities of Rome* (London, 1696), with many later editions.

[53]Vallemont, *Ductor Historicus*, ed. Hearne, 2: sig. a2.

Of course, all that Hearne was doing was making explicit the need for commentary (for history, as for poetry and all ancient literature), which had given birth to classical scholarship in the first place. Unfortunately, the *Ductor* was meant only for the reader, and so had nothing much of use to offer to the writer of a history. And Hearne himself never attempted a narrative through all his copious outpouring.

A better effort to appreciate the advantages of the two modes of history was made right in the midst of the battle of the books by William Nicolson, bishop of Carlisle. Nicolson had placed himself squarely with the moderns, providing unflinching support to Wotton and Bentley throughout their travail and greeting every new advance in history and science with enthusiasm. In 1696 he issued the first part of his *English Historical Library*, a work destined to grow in subsequent editions and eventually to embrace Scotland and Ireland also. It was a survey and a critical commentary on the narrative accounts and the source materials of English history by an energetic man who had made every effort to keep abreast of his subject since the Anglo-Saxon studies of his youth and who now hoped to guide the writer as well as the reader to a better appreciation of his task. "'Tis a book very likely to take," Edmund Gibson wrote to Thomas Tanner, "and will be a good manual to inform the generality of mankind what has been done in English affairs, whether Topographical or Historical."[54]

Nicolson saw a need unfulfilled and a problem unattempted in modern English history. The need was obvious and had been widely recognized: there was as yet no single suitable general history of the kingdom. It is true that several attempts were being projected even as Nicolson wrote, but the prospects were daunting, "since the due observance of all the Rules which Lucian, Father Le Moyne, and others have laid down . . . require so many accomplishments." And if that were not enough, Nicolson wished to add to the undertaking all that vast fund of antiquarian learning that had been accumulating in England since the days of Henry VIII. To a knowledge of the world, he argued, must be added knowledge of all those peoples who had once come to conquer and to live in England: their customs, culture, religion, and politics. It was a job not for a single historian but for a "Clubb of Men of Parts and Learning, some whereof are Masters of our ancient Languages, and others of the Modern; some vers'd in the Writings of the old Britons, Romans, Saxons and Danes, and others thoroughly acquainted with the

---

[54]Gibson to Tanner, May 30, 1696, Bodleian MS. Tanner, f. 120; William Nicolson, *The English Historical Library; or, A Short View and Character of most of the Writers now extant either in Print or Manuscript which may be Serviceable to the Undertaking of a General History of this Kingdom* (London, 1696). The second part appeared in 1697, the third in 1699, and a third revised edition, including the Scots and the Irish, in 1736.

Historians since the Conquest; some that know the Geography, and others the Law of the Realm, some that have been bred at Court, and others in the Camp, etc."[55] The work of this "imaginary Fraternity" would have to include not only scouring all the records in print and manuscript but purging all previous histories of their errors. Nicolson meant the *English Historical Library* as an outline, perhaps an encouragement, for this collaborative enterprise, but he does not seem very optimistic about its actual prospects. Somehow the very definition of the task made it seem more impossible than ever. When a few years later the Society of Antiquaries was refounded in London, it undertook some of Nicolson's labor, but it never really made an effort to integrate its work into anything like a complete history. As for narrative, that was left to others, to the men of letters, not the men of learning, to attempt.

On the other hand, Nicolson appreciated the virtues of both ancient and modern historiography. He liked good writing and extolled Bacon's *Henry VII* as a particularly capable model. "He has perfectly put himself into King Henry's own Garb and Livery, giving so spritely a View of the Secrets of his Council, as if himself had been present in it. No Trivial Passages, such as are below the Notice of a Statesman are mix'd with his Sage Remarks. . . . The whole is written in such a Grave and Uniform Style, as becomes both the Subject and the Artificer."[56] Yet he saw also, as well as anyone in his time, the value of the nonliterary evidence. The third part of the *English Historical Library* (1699) consists of a survey "giving account of our Records, Law-Books and Coins from the Conquest to the end of Queen Elizabeth's Reign so far as they are serviceable to History." All this material was necessary to the "compleat" historian, and Nicolson shows exactly how it could be employed in coming to terms with the past, as well as the perils in overlooking it. For the antiquary at this time there was simply no way to avoid the responsibility of documentary evidence, the need to ground a history, as Thomas Madox insisted, on "proper Vouchers." "For my own part," Madox wrote, "I cannot look upon the History of England to be compleatly written till it shall come to be written after that manner."[57] Unfortunately, Madox never got around to saying how this might actually be done, or gave any example in his own dogged compilations. And this too remains the only disappointment in Nicolson's masterly survey: his inability to show how, or indeed whether, all this could be brought to-

---

[55]Nicolson, *English Historical Library*, sig. A, A3v.

[56]Ibid., p. 224.

[57]Thomas Madox, *The History and Antiquities of the Exchequer of the Kings of England* (London, 1711), p. v.; David Douglas, *English Scholars*, 2d ed. (London, 1951), p. 241. Cf. Thomas Tanner, *Notitia monastica; or, A Short History of the Religious Houses of England and Wales* (Oxford, 1695), Preface. For Madox, see below, chap. 11.

gether, and rhetoric reconciled with philology; how England could gain a national history worthy of its place in the world by measuring up to the standards of both the new and the old historiography. Nicolson's very grasp of the subject seems only to suggest what we have seen already: that the progress of modern scholarship had come somehow to endanger, rather than enhance, the conviction in *ancienneté*, and that the possibility of harmony was more remote than ever.

Chapter Ten

Ancients

I

It was a disgrace, therefore, universally deplored, that England had no national history to measure up to the classical precepts or ancient examples. Even William Wotton, who was unfailingly optimistic about the possibilities of modernity, could only look abroad for examples, while William Temple and the ancients, who were convinced that imitation must fail to match the originals, were nevertheless regretful that no one had really tried. At least England's rivals had made the attempt, and the classicizing histories of Mariana for Spain, Mézeray for France, and Buchanan for Scotland were well known in England in the original and in translation. Yet all that England could show were some old-fashioned chronicles such as the popular but rather jejune work of Sir Richard Baker, which kept appearing throughout the century in updated versions and was still being read (and lamented) during the battle of the books.[1] Baker's *Chronicle of the Kings of England*, it was agreed, was woefully inadequate because it followed medieval rather than classical precedent in style and form. It jumbled together in mindless and disconnected fashion a random assortment of events, both large and small, without apparent sense or discrimination. It was also inaccurate.[2] Needless to say, it could hardly be of any use to the statesman who needed to know the inner

[1]Sir Richard Baker's *Chronicle of the Kings of England* appeared first in 1643, then in various enlarged editions, the eighth by Edward Phillips in 1684. William Nicolson described it as "the best Read and liked of any hitherto publish'd. But Learned Men will be of another Opinion": *The English, Scotch and Irish Historical Libraries*, 3d ed. (London, 1736), pp. 73–74.

[2]Thomas Blount caught more than eighty errors, large and small; see his *Animadversions upon Sir Richard Baker's Chronicle and Its Continuation* (Oxford, 1672). Thomas Hearne agreed: *Remarks and Collections*, ed. C. E. Doble et al., 11 vols. (Oxford, 1885–1931), 6:131.

springs of the actions that were here only outwardly paraded and who wanted to see the design of history, not its bare chronology. But little more could be said of any of Baker's predecessors, not even the more ambitious John Speed, whose *History of Great Britain* was now almost a century old and still in print, much less the Latin chronicles that had preceded it and were further disgraced by their papist bias and hagiographical content.[3] The need for a new history of the nation, composed according to classical precept and example, was thus never more apparent than when Sir William Temple took up the cudgels for the ancients and began to consider the matter.

Temple had always been infatuated by history. He had, of course, played an important role in making some, and in his *Memoirs* he had written his own account of the great events. He liked to read history besides, not only the masterful works of antiquity but newer histories of modern times and exotic places. More than any other reading, histories reminded him of his place in the world as a gentleman and man of affairs, at home in the courts of kings and on the great stage of politics and diplomacy. He had retired, it is true, and could only relive the events in his imagination, but it was impossible to withdraw altogether. When his old friend the Prince of Orange landed in England and took up the reins of government in 1689, Temple was clearly stirred again. It is said that in the next years William visited him several times at home, and although Temple could not be moved from his retirement, he may have once again offered his counsel. And it seems to have occurred to him that he might be of service in another way. Since history as the ancients understood it was always thought to repeat itself—hence philosophy teaching by example—it could always be used to evaluate or to defend contemporary events. "I believe it will be found, at one time or other, by all who shall try, that whilst Human Nature continues what it is, the same Order in State, the same Discipline in Armies, the same Reverence for things Sacred, and Respect of Civil Institutions, the same Virtues and Dispositions of Princes and Magistrates . . . will ever have the same Effects."[4] Shortly after the Revolution, Temple took up his ready pen to write some history and apologize for the bold actions of his old friend. The result is the little work known as *An Introduction to the History of England.*

[3]Nicolson thought Speed's work still "the largest and best we have hitherto extant": *English, Scotch and Irish Historical Libraries*, p. 73. Roger L'Estrange preferred John Stow's *Annales of England*; see Hearne, *Remarks and Collections*, 7:280. Edmund Bolton thought Speed the equal of any in modern times, though he had neither Greek nor Latin skill: *Hypercritica* (London, 1618), p. 220. The condemnation of Holinshed and Speed by Laurence Echard is more typical: *The History of England* (London, 1707), Preface, sig. a.

[4]William Temple, *Observations upon the United Provinces of the Netherlands* (1672), reprinted in his *Works*, 4 vols. (London, 1814), 1:37.

As we shall see, this brief piece gradually became the basis for a much grander scheme that was meant to address the still unresolved problem of how to represent the national past.

"I have often complained," Temple began, "that so ancient and noble a Nation as ours, so renowned by the Fame of their Arms and Exploits abroad, so applauded and envied . . . should not yet have one good or approved general History of England."[5] France, Spain, even the Empire had all received theirs, but England had only "mean and vulgar Authors so tedious in their Relations, or rather Collections, so injudicious in the Choice of what was fit to be told or to let alone, with so little Order, and in so wretched a Style; that as it is a Shame to be ignorant in the Affairs of our own Country, so 'tis hardly worth the Time or Pains to be informed." To retrieve something useful for the history of England, it was necessary to read through a whole library of dreary chronicles and to forget more than what was worth remembering.

Yet all was not hopeless. Here and there, Temple pointed out, there was a piece of English history worth reading, "some Parcels or short Periods . . . left us by Persons of great Worth or Learning." There were, for example, a number of accounts of individual reigns, such as Thomas More's Richard III, Francis Bacon's Henry VII, John Hayward on Edward VI, and William Camden on Elizabeth. And there were copious materials, both ancient and modern, that could be collected, digested, and rewritten for a new structure. Once, apparently, Temple had thought of undertaking such a work himself on the model of Mézeray's abridgement of his French history (which he preferred to the larger original), but his political career had interfered and it proved impossible to enlist anyone else.[6] Now, with the hope of encouraging others, Temple had consented to publish his own introduction to the subject, a brief account of English history from the beginning to the Norman Conquest. "I have hereby beaten through all the rough and dark Ways of the Journey, the rest lies fair and easie through a plain and open Country, and I should think my self happy to see it well pursued by some abler Hand . . . with the same good Intentions, and with much better Success, than this small Endeavor of mine." There followed Temple's little work.

[5]William Temple, *An Introduction to the History of England* (London, 1695), sig. A2. (It is reprinted in *Works*, 3:67–201.) Temple singles out Juan de Serres and Mézeray for France, Mariana for Spain, and Pedro de Mexía for the Empire. The *Introduction* is briefly considered in Robert C. Steemsma, "Sir William Temple's *History of England*," *Neuphilologische Mitteilungen* 77 (1976): 95–107.

[6]François Eudes de Mézeray, *Abrégé chronologique* (Paris, 1667–68); trans. by John Buteel as *A General Chronological History of France* (London, 1683). See Wilfred H. Evans, *L'Historien Mézeray et la conception de l'histoire en France au XVIIᵉ siècle* (Paris, 1930), p. 74.

2

The *Introduction* is divided into two unequal parts: a quick prefatory survey of the first centuries of English history and a more expansive and detailed account of the conquest and reign of William I. The disproportion was swiftly noticed and easily explained. Temple's biographer Abel Boyer attributed it to the author's desire to justify William of Orange, who, like his Norman predecessor, was both a conqueror of England and a preserver of its laws. "It was the general Opinion," he reports, "that Sir William Temple, who continued to the last a true Friend to the Prince of Orange . . . published at that time his *Introduction to the History of England*; both to compliment that Prince, under the Character of the Norman Conqueror which he sets off to great Advantage."[7] If so, it is likely that the two parts were written separately and for different purposes, and indeed there is an awkward repetition where they are joined, the Conquest appearing redundantly in both parts. Even so, the work was predictably well written and (after Cicero's advice) smoothly flowing, a far cry from Baker's halting and episodic chronicle.

It is characteristic of Temple, whose sole concern was to tell a good story, to neglect to mention his sources except in the most general way. Of course, the ancient historians provided ample precedent for this practice, and it is as difficult to determine the sources of Livy and Tacitus (say) as it is those of their modern imitators. A classical scroll has no footnotes, and there are none in Temple's *Introduction*. Nor was it thought necessary to do much research when the historian's main ambition was to retell a story already well known. The chief task of classical historiography and its modern rhetorical counterpart was to write well and persuasively, to make the events of the past appear alive and meaningful, and not to quibble over unimportant or irrelevant details or to get bogged down in philological pedantry. Still, it comes as a bit of a surprise to learn that Temple was closely dependent on only one principal authority for substance and sometimes phrase, the Elizabethan historian Samuel Daniel, whom he never once mentions.[8]

It was a good choice. Daniel's work had appeared originally as the *Collection of the History of England* in 1618 and many times thereafter, most recently with an addition by John Trussell in 1685. It was a deceptively modest effort but it was much appreciated for its clarity and brevity and for the many observations on life and politics which gave it

---

[7]Abel Boyer, *Memoirs of Sir William Temple* (London, 1714), p. 413. In 1691 Temple published the second part of his *Memoirs*, where William is directly vindicated.

[8]See Homer E. Woodbridge, *Sir William Temple* (New York, 1940), pp. 254–61.

point.[9] Daniel was something of a modern for his time, outspoken in his defense of rhyme (which was unknown to antiquity) and of the vernacular, and he anticipated many of the best critical arguments of Dryden and others later. Like all the moderns, however, he had no real wish to disparage the ancients, and he imitated and borrowed from the classics with the best. Daniel began as a poet, but in an early work, the *Civil Wars* (1595), he already declared his interest in history. There he imitated Lucan, paralleling the Wars of the Roses with the ancient struggle between Caesar and Pompey; and he defended his faithfulness to the record. "I have carefully followed that truth which is delivered in the Historie, without adding to, or subtracting from, the generally receiv'd opinion of things as we finde them in our common Annalles: holding it an impietie, to violate that publicke Testimonie we have, without more evident proofe: or to introduce fiction of our owne imagination, in things of this nature." He allowed himself to invent only the speeches, as had Sallust and Livy, "though writers in Prose, yet in that kinde Poets."[10] By 1609 he was ready to forget rhyme (and speeches) altogether and write an unadorned prose history of England. Meanwhile, he had learned the dangers in writing a history that was meant to instruct the present by parallel and gotten into serious trouble with the Privy Council over a work that recalled too closely the recent rebellion of the Earl of Essex. His defense, that all times produced universal notions and like occurrences, "so that there is nothing new under the Sunne, nothing in these tymes not in bookes, nor in bookes that is not in these tymes," was of course the standard doctrine of both ancient and modern historiography. It barely sufficed to get him off.[11]

[9]So Thomas Fuller, *The History of the Worthies of England*, (London, 1662), pt. 3:28. Nicolson too found Daniel's work "penn'd in so accurate and copious a Style, that it took mightily": *English Historical Library*, p. 193. And Dryden praised it in the dedication to *Don Sebastian* (1690), in *The Works of John Dryden* (Berkeley, 1956–), 15:69.

[10]Samuel Daniel, *The First Four Bookes of the Civile Wars between the Two Houses of Lancaster and York* (1595), edited as *The Civil Wars by Samuel Daniel*, by Laurence Michel (New Haven, 1958), pp. 67–69. See George M. Logan, "Daniel's *Civil Wars* and Lucan's *Pharsalia*," *Studies in English Literature* 11 (1971): 53–68. Daniel's *Defense of Ryme* (1607) contains his boldest modern ideas. "All our understandings," he writes there, "are not to be built by the square of Greece and Italie. We are the children of nature as well as they": *The Complete Works of Samuel Daniel*, ed. Alexander B. Grosart, 5 vols. (London, 1885–1896), 4:46. For Daniel's ambiguous modernity, see Arthur B. Ferguson, "The Historical Thought of Samuel Daniel: A Study in Renaissance Ambivalence," *Journal of the History of Ideas* 32 (1971): 185–202.

[11]Daniel to Lord Cranborne (1605), quoted in Daniel, *Complete Works*, 4:liii–liv. The text of *Philotas* with Daniel's Apology has been edited by Laurence Michel (New Haven, 1949) with a useful introduction. See also H. Sellers, "A Bibliography of the Work of Samuel Daniel, 1583–1623," *Oxford Bibliographical Society Proceedings and Papers* 2 (1927–1930): 51; Cecil C. Seronsy, "The Doctrine of Eternal Recurrence and Some Related Ideas in the Works of Samuel Daniel," *Studies in the Renaissance* 54 (1957): 387–407; G. A. Wilson,

The *Collection* seems to have begun life as a preliminary sketch that was (mistakenly) published only in Temple's day under the name of Sir Walter Ralegh as *A Breviary of the History of England* (1693). In the course of its evolution to the *Collection* that Temple read, the work lost two prefaces that might have confirmed Temple's view of history. In one, Daniel argued again for the essential identity of history beneath the changing fashions of dress and language. "We shall find the same Correspondences to hold in the Actions of Men; Virtue and Vice the same, though rising and falling according to the Worth or Weakness of Governors; the Causes of the Ruins and Change of Commonwealths to be alike, and the Train of Affairs carried by the Precedent in a Course of Succession under like Figures."[12] In the second, he expatiated on the value of past history to present politics and hence his decision "to deliver only those affaires of action, that most concerne the government." He had deliberately left out all that was irrelevant in his sources in order to provide a succinct account of English history for those who had the greatest need to know but the least leisure to study it.[13]

The one preface that did survive in 1685 Temple surely read with great sympathy. "It is more than the Worke of one man," Daniel began, "to compose a possible Contexture of the whole History of England." So too it had begun to seem to Temple. "For though the inquisition of Antient times, written by others, be prepared, yet the Collection and Disposition I find most Laborious." (For the antiquary, needless to say, the problem was exactly the reverse.) Unlike Temple, Daniel listed his sources and promised marginal citations to make them plain, "so that the Reader shall be sure to be payd with no counterfeit Coyne, but such as shal have the Stampe of Antiquity." Unfortunately, he seems to have forgotten his promise. To keep the narrative smoothly flowing, he elimi-

---

"Daniel's *Philotas* and the Essex Case: A Reconsideration," *Modern Language Quarterly* 23 (1962): 233–42; Joan Rees, *Samuel Daniel* (Liverpool, 1964), pp. 98–101. Daniel's contemporary John Hayward had the same problem and pleaded the same excuse, but did not get off so lightly; see Margaret Dowling, "Sir John Hayward's Troubles over the *Life of Henry VI*," *The Library* 4th ser. 11 (1930): 212–24; Evelyn Mary Albright, "Shakespeare's *Richard II* and the Essex Conspiracy" and "Shakepeare's *Richard II*, Hayward's *Henry IV*, and the Essex Conspiracy," *PMLA* 42 (1927): 686–720, 46 (1931): 694–719. When the queen asked Bacon for legal advice as to whether there was treason in Hayward's history, he replied, "No Madam, for treason I cannot deliver opinion that there is any, but very much felony. The Queen apprehending it gladly, asked, How, and wherein? Mr. Bacon answered, Because he had stolen many of his sentences and conceits out of Cornelius Tacitus": *Apophthegms*, in *The Works of Francis Bacon*, ed. James Spedding, R. L. Ellis, and D. D. Heath, 14 vols. (London, 1857–1874), 7:133.

[12]Samuel Daniel, *An Introduction to a Breviary of the History of England* (London, 1693), pp. 4–5. See R. B. Gottfried, "The Authorship of *A Breviary of the History of England*," *Studies in Philology* 53 (1956): 172–90.

[13]Samuel Daniel, *The Collection of the History of England* (1618), Epistle Dedicatory to Robert Carr, in Daniel, *Complete Works*, 4:76.

nated the documents in his sources (letters, treaties, etc.), hoping to print them separately in an appendix, but somehow he never got the means. That Daniel should have had such scruples is noteworthy and suggests a distinctly modern sensibility; but he himself was no antiquary. He never thought to seek out the documents except as he found them in the chronicles, and his method remained still scissors and paste. "For the Worke itselfe," he concluded, "I can Challenge nothing therein but onely sewing it together, and the observations of those necessary circumstances, and references which the history naturally ministers."[14]

Thus the refashioning mattered more than the research, rhetoric more than philology. "I had rather be Master of a small piece, handsomely contrived, then of vaste roomes ill proportioned and unfurnished."[15] For Daniel's continuator, John Trussell, the objective was the same. He remembered Prince Henry complaining "that of all Nations the English were most blame-worthy: that being inferior to none for praise-worthy achievements, yet were over-passed by all, in leaving the memory of those praiseworthy actions to posterity."[16] Trussell saw the great merit of Daniel's work, which had stopped abruptly before the Wars of the Roses, and he admired Bacon's Henry VII; he thought that he might fill up the intervening period. Like Daniel, he forswore adding anything of his own to the chronicle sources, calling out the truth like an echo; and like Daniel, he determined to pare off all superfluities (coronations, marriages, jousts, pageants, floods, monsters, and the price of corn) "with which the Cacoethes of the Writers of those times have mingled matters of state." Unfortunately, Trussell did not command Daniel's style or his sententious wisdom, and the continuation was universally adjudged a failure.[17] The history of England had gotten off to a good start, perhaps, but it was still largely unwritten.

3

It is easy to see why Temple admired Daniel and borrowed from him so unreservedly. And it is understandable perhaps that he should do so without acknowledgment, since despite his protestations, Daniel had done much the same thing; that is to say, he had leaned heavily on one barely or completely unacknowledged authority (often a modern one)

[14]Eistle Dedicatory to Queen Anne, in ibid., pp. 81–83.
[15]Ibid., p. 81.
[16]John Trussell, *A Continuation of the History of England*, 5th ed. (London, 1685), "To the Courteous Reader." Trussell's *Continuation* first appeared in 1634.
[17]See Nicolson, *English Historical Library*, p. 194.

for long stretches of his narrative, only occasionally interpolating or correcting from another source.[18] Just so had the ancients done before.

Temple's *Introduction* began, like Daniel's, with Roman Britain. He was content to discard all the earlier history as fabulous. How much or whether he was conscious of a debt to the antiquaries is unclear. But of course it was the antiquaries who had exploded the traditional medieval accounts of Celtic or "British" history, from Brutus, the Trojan founder of Britain, to Arthur and the knights of the round table, as legendary.[19] As always, Temple was indifferent to their labors, and it did not embarrass him that he did not have the languages or any of the other skills that might have helped to unlock the early history of the nation. The problem was not unlike that of the *Epistles of Phalaris*, but this time Temple accepted the results of a learning he did not possess. He prefers to begin with Julius Caesar, "the best Writer, as well as the greatest Captain of his Age or perhaps any other." And after a brief account of the Romans in Britain he quickly dispatches the whole of Anglo-Saxon England in a few hurried pages. King Alfred gets a single sentence. When William Nicolson read Temple's sneer at the early sources ("the Dust and Rubbish of such barbarous Times"), he felt he had to defend the antiquaries who were trying so laboriously to decipher them. Temple might think it beneath him to refine so little gold out of so much dross, "but some other inferior People may think this is worth their Pains; since all Men are not born to be Ambassadors. . . . There is a deal of servile Drudgery requir'd to the Discovery of these Riches, and such as every body will not stoop to: for few Statesmen and Courtiers . . . care for travelling in Ireland or Wales purely to learn the Language."[20] Nicolson himself had worked hard at Celtic and Anglo-Saxon and took a keen interest in the discovery of early English antiquities, then in full progress.

It is with the appearance of the Conqueror, however, that Temple's narrative comes fully into its own. Certainly William I is portrayed vigorously alive and immediately relevant. No matter that Temple is not quite sure of the year of the Conquest: was it 1066 or 1068? What he *is* sure about is William's character and motivation, the inside of a story

[18]Thus for William I, he used a sixteenth-century compilation known as *L'Histoire et cronique de Normandie* (1581), an abridgment of a fifteenth-century work, with only one vague marginal citation to "the History of Normand." See Rudolf Gottfried, "Samuel Daniel's Method of Writing History," *Studies in the Renaissance* 3 (1956): 157–74. See also William Leigh Godshalk, "Daniel's History," *Journal of English and Germanic Philology* 63 (1964): 45–57; May McKisack, "Samuel Daniel as Historian," *Review of English Studies* 23 (1947): 226–43.

[19]Temple, *Introduction*, p. 19. The best account remains T. D. Kendrick, *British Antiquity* (London, 1950).

[20]Nicolson, *English Historical Library*, pp. 71–72, referring to Temple, *Introduction*, pp. 22, 31, 51–52.

that was usually told from without. "I have not been so particular as other Writers," he admitted, "in the Names of Places or Persons, or Distinctions of Years, because in such Antiquity of Times and Variety of Authors, I find them very hard to be ascertained." Like Daniel and Trussell, he was also happy to omit the "strange Comets, Inclemencies of Seasons, raging Diseases, or deplorable Fires, that are said to have happened in this Age and Kingdom," mere accidents of time and chance, irrelevant to his theme: "the Virtues and Vices of Princes . . . which serve for Example or Instruction to Posterity, which are the great Ends of History, and ought to be the chief Care of all Historians." Here, of course, Temple was on his own ground; here the experience of a lifetime in politics could be made to tell. "Since all great Actions in the World, and Revolutions of States, may be truly derived, from that Genius of Persons that conduct and govern them, so as by comprising both to-gether, and observing the Causes as well as Events, it may be easie to discern by what Personal Qualities and Dispositions of Princes, the happy and glorious Successes . . . are generally atchieved."[21] Unless that were done, events would have to be left to chance and all the examples of history would be useless.

William I is the hero of Temple's story and it is upon his fortunes that the bulk of the narrative turns. Temple follows Daniel in retrieving William's reputation from the malevolence of the medieval monks who had a special grudge against him. But he reconceives the events for himself, often imagining the scenes and motives more fully and vividly than his source.[22] And he could not remain completely satisfied with Daniel's interpretation of events. The fact is that for half a century the meaning of the Norman Conquest had been debated by all parties in the great political controversies of the day. From the English Civil War through the various crises of the Restoration to the Glorious Revolution, everyone had turned to history for justification, and the events of 1066 seemed pivotal. The parliamentary opposition, led by Coke and the

[21]Temple, *Introduction*, pp. 300–301.

[22]Perhaps one instance will show the difference: the two accounts of what followed immediately upon the invasion. Daniel gives a characteristically succinct analysis of the motives that he believed governed each of the classes in receiving William. Temple is more elaborate, imagining the scene more fully and vividly. "In the City of London, besides the great Numbers and Riches of the Inhabitants, were returned most of the great Nobles of the Kingdom, both the Ecclesiastical and Secular. . . . Upon Decision of the last Battel, they all consulted together with the Citizens, which was best to be advised and done for their common Interest and Safety." Temple follows Daniel in considering the motives of each class, although he reverses the order and gives his own conclusions, believing the councils of the church to have been pivotal—and wise. Echoes of 1688–89 hang over the whole story. Cf. Daniel, *Complete Works*, 4:133–83, with Temple, *Introduction*, pp. 128–34. Basil Kennett gives a flattering comparison of the two histories in his introduction to Rapin's *Whole Critical Works*, 2 vols. (London, 1706), 1: [sig. A6].

common lawyers, had tried to discredit Charles I's absolutist pretensions by finding precedents for English rights and parliamentary privileges in the earliest times. Later the radicals of the revolutionary period developed a theory of the Norman yoke, a despotic government fastened upon England by William the Conqueror which had deliberately snuffed out the liberties of free Englishmen. The royalists responded to both challenges by denying the antiquity of parliaments and the independent rights of Englishmen and proclaiming an absolutism that some said went back to the beginning of human history, to Adam himself. At the time of the Exclusion crisis (1680), all these arguments were rehearsed and elaborated with a new display of historical erudition. The "Tories" in particular found fresh inspiration from history, discovering a feudal setting for parliament and the common law which they now assigned to a particular time in the Middle Ages and made dependent on the royal will. In their hands and for the first time in England, feudalism became a genuine historical concept, in contrast to the timeless and anachronistic views of "Whigs" and radicals. Unfortunately, they left out the monarchy and so fell victim to something of the same ahistorical sense of continuity and changelessness that had characterized their enemies. In much the same way as the classicists, many medievalists of the seventeenth century were discovering change and discontinuity in one part of the past only to restrict it again in another out of a persistent conviction in certain timeless values.

Temple was very conscious of these historical arguments.[23] Had William I established his claim to rule by conquest and gone on to change the laws of the kingdom? Or had he been bound by the coronation oath to observe the laws of his predecessors and the rights of his Saxon subjects? Were the commons of England free in Saxon times and represented in the parliaments of the Saxon kings through borough and shire representatives? Was Magna Carta a reaffirmation of the rights of the commons as well as of the nobility, or merely a feudal charter applicable only to the great? On such questions the very legitimacy of the acts of Charles II, James II, and now William III had seemed to depend. Yet merely to raise these questions was to suggest a program of philological investigation and antiquarian research that was anathema to Temple. Although a mass of technical commentary had already appeared when the lawyers and their allies entered the fray, Temple would have no part of it. He did not see how reading obscure charters in a barbarous language or quarreling about the meanings of words was likely to provide what alone was truly needed: an insight into the political decisions that William had to

[23]For the immediate debate, see M. P. Thompson, "The Idea of Conquest in Controversies over the 1688 Revolution," *Journal of the History of Ideas* 38 (1977): 33–46.

make under the trying circumstances of his invasion and rule. Temple hoped to reconstruct the past by narrative, not polemic, by recapturing William's motives and intentions in a concrete and immediate situation. For this purpose present politics was a more reliable guide than pedantic scholarship.

Now it was a fact that William had claimed the crown upon his arrival without ever mentioning a conquest. And William had taken the coronation oath "to protect and defend the Church, to observe the Laws of the Realm, and to govern the People justly." It remained only to ask whether he did so out of his own prudence or as a result of the good counsel of those who had invited him to come. No doubt, Temple imagines, William understood correctly that the victory of a foreigner was not enough to ensure his rule over a brave and prosperous people; and he saw that he must satisfy his subjects. So he scrupulously avoided the name of conqueror; expressed his resolution to govern the nation as a legal prince, preserving the traditional laws and liberties; took no vengeance against the vanquished; and appropriated only the lands of the defeated barons.[24] For the royalists to deny any of this was to make nonsense of an otherwise plausible (and edifying) story and willfully to accept the biased tale of William's monkish enemies.

Thus Temple took side with the Whigs. He credited the Saxons with trial by jury and with the borough law, with the justices of the peace and most of the taxes, all of which were confirmed by William. Norman parliaments were once Saxon "gemoots," though their original composition remained still unclear and had caused much controversy. Temple was inclined to place the commons in them, "whose general good or ill Humour, Satisfaction or Discontent will ever have the most favorable Influence for the Preservation or Ruin of any Estate."[25] Even where the language and forms had evidently altered from Saxon to Norman, Temple believed that the original laws and institutions remained pretty much continuous. There was simply no way that his narrative method and political predispositions, and the implicit assumption that the essence of history was changeless, could avoid anachronism. Temple concludes with a general assessment of the Conquest, more gain than loss, and a quotation from Fortescue to the effect that English laws and institutions had been preserved through five different governments—Normans, Danes, Saxons, Romans, and Britons—"and so have continued for a longer Course of Time, than those of Rome or Venice, or any other Nation known in Story!" Temple admitted the possibility of exaggera-

[24]Temple, *Introduction*, pp. 132–39.
[25]Ibid., pp. 173–74. He would not enlarge on the early parliaments, however, "because I find no clear Evidence of the Nature and Constitution, the Times or Occasions of them": ibid., p. 297.

tion here, but he was perfectly sure about the last three periods, and that, he thought, was "sufficient to illustrate the Antiquitie of our Institutions."[26]

4

One might argue with Temple's politics; it was harder to dispute his style and skill in narrative. The *Works of the Learned* had no reservations whatever. Everyone had to agree with Temple's regret that England had not yet received its due. But was it any wonder when one considered the many qualifications that were necessary for the job? "What Nobleness, Majesty, Purity and Simplicity of Stile. . . . What Judgment for the Choice, and Order and Disposition of Subjects, so as to omit nothing worthy to be recorded to Posterity and at the same time to avoid all Trifles and common things which are not of Publick Concern. . . . What Candour and Sincerity to do equal Justice to all Parties." And so on. How few among the ancients, even fewer among the moderns, had even approached success! At least Temple had shown how the work might be done, choosing for his model Livy above Tacitus, keeping his reflections few and his digressions short. His portrait of William might be fairly placed alongside Livy's Hannibal or Sallust's Catiline, "which have always been look'd upon as the Masterpieces in that kind."[27]

The moderns, of course, were less satisfied, even when they shared his political bias, and only too aware of the shortcomings of Temple's scholarship. Wotton spotted several embarrassing errors of fact and Nicolson was deeply offended by Temple's neglect of learning throughout the early pages of his work. Yet even so, Nicolson was forced to admire Temple's description of William's character and reign, "upon all which he makes such Reflections as become a Statesman, and a Person so conversant in the Management of publick Affairs, as that Author is known to be." It was, of course, much harder for a scholar who opposed the Revolution to find any merit in the work, though even Thomas Hearne had to agree many years later that it was still popular.[28]

As for Temple himself, it seems clear that he had hoped to accomplish two different things with his little work. On the one hand, he had hoped

[26]Ibid., pp. 112, 313.

[27]*Miscellaneous Letters, Giving an Account of the Works of the Learned* 1, no. 4 (Oct. 31–Nov. 7, 1694): 59–62.

[28]"Sir Wm. Temple's Intro. to the Hist. Eng. is recommended by some. But without cause. Those who commend it are Novices": Hearne, *Remarks and Collections*, 6:252; Nicolson, *English Historical Library*, pp. 202–3. Edmund Gibson thought Nicolson had been a little too severe in criticizing Temple's history: Gibson to Thomas Tanner, Bodleian MS. Tanner 24, ff. 179–80.

to reinforce the Whig reading of the past and bolster William's claim to rule England; on the other hand, he had hoped to inspire someone to fill the gap in English history with a well-written, convenient, and practical volume that would dignify the subject and edify the reader. Whatever success he had had with the one, the other still remained to do. As he thought about it, on the eve of the battle of the books, it seems to have occurred to him that there were actually two different ways in which the gap in English history might be repaired. Either one could continue to rewrite and abridge the whole story in a single consistent work, as Daniel and now Temple had begun to do, or one could take up those several little parcels that already existed and met classical standards and connect them somehow into a whole. Either way, the *Introduction* might be employed for a much grander and more important achievement and thus help to remedy the national failure.

Just as Temple must have been wondering about the prospects, a publisher appeared on the scene eager to undertake the work. John Dunton was an old admirer of Temple's and he relished the *Introduction* particularly, with its strong Whig bias. Dunton we have met as the organizer of the Athenian Society, in those years before bankruptcy and madness, an incorrigible optimist of infinite projects. Those were the years, he recalled in his autobiography, when the world smiled on him. "I sailed with the wind and tide; and had humble servants enough among the Booksellers, Stationers, Printers, and Bookbinders."[29] Apparently, sometime in 1694, he determined to publish a new history of England and employed someone for the job. Now, encouraged by Temple's new work, he appealed to the master for advice. Temple's secretary, Thomas Swift (filling in for Jonathan), returned an answer in November. "He is of Opinion that the best and readiest way to compile a good Generall History of England will be to take in all those parts of it which have allready been written by any approved and esteemed Authours. And to write nothing new besides those Parts which have not yet been touched by any authors of name and estimation." Temple thought that the variety of authors and styles, far from disturbing the narrative, would actually make the work more agreeable to the reader than a single pen, and more likely to be accomplished. He suggested that the *Introduction* be followed by Daniel's narrative from William Rufus to Edward III. (Daniel is here acknowledged to be "an author of good Judgment and no ill Style.") He thought he remembered a good life of Richard II, well written but anonymous. (Perhaps he was thinking of the work by Robert Howard.) The period from Henry IV to Henry VI was a problem and

[29]John Dunton, *The Life and Errors of John Dunton*, ed. J. Nichols, 2 vols. (London, 1818), 1:xv.

must be freshly written. Thomas More's Edward IV and Richard III could follow, though old-fashioned in style and manner. Then there was Bacon's Henry VII and the very full accounts of Herbert of Cherbury on Henry VIII, John Hayward on Edward VI, and Camden on Elizabeth, all of which would have to be abridged. This was the best that he could offer; Temple himself had to decline the editing, altering, or correcting that would be necessary, "being not of an age or a Humour at present to engage in such a Trouble."[30]

What Temple had in mind, in other words, was a kind of anthology of humanist histories to include all those pieces that had been taken by general consent to meet the standards of classical historiography. Much earlier, Peter Heylyn had already expressed the growing view that the chronicles of Holinshed and Stow were "full of confusion and commixture of unworthy relations," and he contrasted them directly with the superior narratives of More, Bacon, Hayward, Daniel, and Camden. The canon had thus been pretty much set by Temple's day. And Temple would probably have subscribed to Heylyn's notion of a history as a "memoriall or relation of all occurents observable, happening in a Commonwealth, described by the motives, pretexts, consultations, speeches, and events, together with an especiall care had of time and place."[31]

Unfortunately, Dunton did not pursue the project; for one thing, it seems that he could not get title to all the needed pieces. As a result, he returned to something like his original plan to promote what Temple had warned might prove too difficult, a freshly written new history of England. Later he claimed that it was Temple who had suggested Sir James Tyrrell as the author, but this seems unlikely, since Temple was more than a little annoyed and embarrassed when he saw Dunton's project advertised under his name toward the end of 1694. It was to be called A General History of England, "pursuant to the Model laid down by Sir William Temple."[32] And it was to be based on the books mentioned in

[30]Thomas Swift to Dunton, Nov. 9, 1694, Osborn Collection, box 67, no. 18, Yale University. A. C. Elias has tried to sort out matters in Swift at Moor Park (Philadelphia, 1982), pp. 55–66, but with his usual animus toward Temple. He discusses the letter in app. B, pp. 314–16.

[31]Peter Heylyn, Mikrokosmos: A Little Description of the World (Oxford, 1639), pp. 23–25; quoted in F. J. Levy, "Hayward, Daniel, and the Beginnings of Politic History in England," Huntington Library Quarterly 50 (1987): 27–28.

[32]See Dunton, Life and Errors, p. 178. Elias, Swift at Moor Park, cites a first announcement in the London Gazette, Nov. 8, and another in the Athenian Mercury, Nov. 13. The Proposals for Printing a General History of England appeared Nov. 21. I have used a transcript of what seems to be a unique copy in the Houghton Library, Harvard University, prepared for me many years ago by my student John Attig, to whom I give my belated thanks. The Proposals were reprinted at the end of the index to the Present State of Europe, vol. 5, licensed Jan. 3, 1695; see Elias, p. 230n. The undertakers now included, besides Dunton, Henry Rhodes, John Salusbury, and John Harris.

the *Introduction* and in Temple's letters of advice, along with other vaguely described manuscripts and memoirs. The models were to be Thuanus, Mézeray, and Buchanan, in about four hundred sheets folio, with the first part of the work (from the Flood to William the Conqueror) promised to subscribers within six months. Tyrrell, it seems, had been preparing his materials for a long time.

Temple was furious. Dunton was disregarding both his advice and his history while continuing to use his name. Once again Temple sent Swift off with his proposals, this time to a new set of publishers; in this way he hoped to nip the *General History* in the bud and accomplish something of his original plan. Accordingly, Swift wrote a new letter to one of the team, the printer Richard Bentley, in February 1695, complaining about Dunton and asking the partners to reprint Temple's *Introduction* with the rest of his suggestions.[33] Swift thought that Temple's scheme and name virtually ensured success. On the other hand, "if you pretend to take up most of your history *de novo*, it will either take up many years doing, or will prove but a second edition of Sir Richard Baker." Swift promised many subscriptions and the use of the great man's influence. One of the undertakers was Awnsham Chiswell, who had just begun another large enterprise with a new version of Camden's *Britannia* and who may also have been thinking independently of a general English history. In April 1694 the young editor of Camden, Edmund Gibson, bought a large paper-book and began "a scheme of the English historians." But he soon came to think the project implausible. "We forsooth are to thrash among the Saxons and Danes, where the materials for a History are soe narrow and have in them soe little of connexion, that after a man had done all he could, it should look more like dry Annals than a just History. And at this rate pray where [is] either the pleasure or reputation of the Work?"[34] Gibson had actually edited the *Anglo-Saxon Chronicle* and knew far more than either Daniel or Temple about the subject, but even so, he cheerfully turned the task back to the proprietors. Undeterred, Bentley and his partners began to advertise their new scheme.

The race was on. "There's hardly a Bookseller in London," Gibson wrote to a friend, "that is not trumping up a New-History of England, of one sort or other. Even John Dunton thinks he has still soe much reputation left as to give him leave to advance his project among the rest. And happy's the man that can get first out."[35] When the new *Britannia*

[33]Thomas Swift to Richard Bentley, Feb. 14, 1695, in *Letters by Several Eminent Persons . . . Including the correspondence of John Hughes*, ed. John Duncombe, 2 vols. (London, 1772), 1:1–7. Bentley owned the rights to Camden's *Elizabeth*; see Elias, *Swift at Moor Park*, p. 233n.

[34]Edmund Gibson to Thomas Tanner, Apr. 20 and Oct. 21, 1694, Bodleian MS. Tanner 25, ff. 138, 250–51.

[35]Gibson to Charlett, Nov. 13, 1694, Bodleian MS. Ballard 5, f. 70.

appeared, Chiswell announced his scheme. "There are now in the press and will speedily be publish'd *A Compleat History of England*, written by several hands of approv'd ability: containing the Lives of all the Kings, the Effigies engraven in Copper; several Coins, Medals, Inscriptions, etc., for illustration of matter of fact . . . a Map . . . large Index's and a Glossary . . . the whole to be contain'd in two Volumes in folio, the first whereof to be publish'd in Trinity-Term 1695."[36] The *Proposals*, which appeared about the same time, promised a collection of histories very like those in Temple's plan but with a few differences, not least the substitution of John Milton's history of early England for Temple's *Introduction*.[37] What Temple thought of this we do not know.

In the event, following a further exchange of insults, Dunton's scheme won out; Tyrrell's volumes began to appear, while the *Compleat History* seems to have died stillborn—at least until it was resurrected a decade later. But Temple did not live to see either done. He died in 1699. Nevertheless, the idea of a complete new history of England, elegantly written and worthy of her reputation, lingered on to tease and inspire the next generation.

5

For the moment, Temple's original scheme was kept alive by his young secretary and literary executor, Jonathan Swift. It is likely that he had assisted Temple in the first place, preparing the *Introduction* for publication. And it may be that Swift was among those too "modest" to write the abridgment that Temple had first contemplated. He certainly started to compose something like it—we have the fragment—but he put it aside for other things and never completed it. Not surprisingly, it is just like the work of his master in outlook and intention, if somewhat different in style.

What we have in fact are two fragments and an introduction written much later.[38] The first is a brief piece that abstracts the history of En-

[36]Advertisement, after the Preface, in William Camden, *Britannia*, ed. Edmund Gibson (London, 1695). "I find in the *Gazette* (the only information of the State of Learning I have in Cambridge) that there is two projects on foot for a general history of England, the one is Chiswell, Smith, and some others of the great booksellers of St. Paul's, the other of Dunton and (I think) by Mr. Tyrril": John Archer to Edward Lhwyd, Feb. 18, 1695, Bodleian MS. Ashmole 1814, f. 85.

[37]*Proposals for Printing a Compleat History of England* [Feb. 1695], a broadside in the Houghton Library, Harvard University, described by Elias, *Swift at Moor Park*, p. 235n. The undertakers were Chiswell, Bentley, and Brabham Aylmer.

[38]For what follows, see Irwin Ehrenpreis, "Swift's History of England," *Journal of English and Germanic Philology* 51 (1952): 177–85; and *Swift: The Man, His Works, and His Age*, vol. 2 (Cambridge, Mass., 1967), pp. 59–65. The text with a valuable introduction has been edited by Herbert Davis, *Miscellaneous and Autobiographical Fragments and Marginalia*

gland from the invasion of Julius Caesar to William the Conqueror.
Although it was printed together with the larger work by Swift's later
editors, it seems not to have had any connection with it. It may have
been meant merely to summarize his reading, as Swift was inclined to
do, or perhaps even to assist Temple.[39] But by itself it is a trifle, too
slight to hold any interest.

Not so the larger piece. Here Swift wrote a narrative on the scale of
Daniel and Temple, describing the reigns of William II through Stephen,
breaking off abruptly in the middle of Henry II. It was an obvious
continuation of Temple's *Introduction*, but it too was laid aside before
completion and never published. Many years later, Swift took it out and
thought to complete it for another purpose. He prepared a dedicatory
letter to the Swedish count de Gyllenborg (1719), in which he recalled his
intentions. He had meant to write a history that would be of use to both
Englishmen and foreigners, "not a voluminous work, nor properly an
abridgment, but an exact relation of the most important affairs and
events, without regard to the rest."[40] He had been diverted both by the
difficulty of the task and by thoughts and business of another kind.
Now, like Temple earlier, he decided to publish it anyway as an encouragement to others.

Among his diversions, Swift mentioned the party faction then prevailing. Not only had he become involved in it, he had written his first
major work as a contribution to contemporary politics—though it too
was history after a fashion. He called it *A Discourse of the Contests and Dissentions in Athens and Rome* (1701).[41] Typically, it was an appeal to ancient history to draw out the eternal analogies between past and present
politics. "If you parallel the men you read of to any you have read in
Greek or Latin History," went the ordinary tutorial advice, "or to any
that now live, it will fix their characters better in your memory, and help
you to judge of men." Swift offered a set of conclusions "deduced" from
the particular events of Greece and Rome which might be employed
under the same circumstances—history, as ever, teaching by example.
(Thus the example of Aristides was pointed toward Lord Somers,
Miltiades to the Earl of Oxford, etc.)[42] And he did much the same thing

---

(Oxford, 1962). See also John Robert Moore, "Swift as Historian," *Studies in Philology* 49
(1952); James William Johnson, "Swift's Historical Outlook," *Journal of British Studies* 4
(1965): 52–77.

[39]Or perhaps as a teaching aid for Swift in tutoring Stella or one of Temple's grand-
daughters; see Elias, *Swift at Moor Park*, p. 320.

[40]Swift to Count de Gyllenborg, Nov. 2, 1719, in Swift, *Miscellaneous and Autobiographical Fragments*, pp. ix–x.

[41]For text and commentary, see the edition by Frank H. Ellis (Oxford, 1967).

[42]"Let us see from this Deduction of particular Impeachments, and general Dissentions
in Greece and Rome, what Conclusions may naturally be formed for Instruction of any

in his English history. Indeed, there is one passage on the constitution that appears almost unchanged in both works. For Swift, the mixed constitution was the ideal polity for all ages; and the proof, he was sure, lay in history, both ancient and modern, so that the same reflections could apply to both worlds. The experience of antiquity was thus exactly relevant to the English scene. We have seen Swift's contempt for scholarship, so we shall not expect to find it in his history. His purpose, like Temple's, was to retell and reinterpret what was already known. In fact, Swift had read widely in the ancient and modern historians while still at Moor Park. He owned several versions of Livy and read Clarendon at least four times![43] But his own history of England is based again largely on Samuel Daniel, although it is filled out from time to time with bits taken from published chronicles and later works. In its unfinished state it reveals its sources a little more obviously than Temple had done. As we would expect, Swift deliberately avoids the antiquaries, even on the origins of parliament, despite their great (but unavailing) pains. "To engage in the same enquiry, would neither suit my abilities nor my subject."[44]

Swift's job was selection and interpretation, and in both respects he resembles his old mentor and follows the classical standard. As ruthlessly as they, he leaves out all but the great affairs of state. He has no compunction about omitting most of Stephen's reign, "a period of much misery and confusion which affords little that is memorable for events, or useful for the instruction of posterity." He dwells on the examples that do matter, for good or for bad, and he seeks out the causes of events when he can ferret them out.[45] And always he points the contemporary moral. When liberality becomes excessive, as in the case of Henry I, the king's subjects "must all be oppressed to shew his bounty to a few flatterers, or he must sell his towns, or barely renounce his rights, by becoming pensioner to some powerful prince in the neighborhood," all of which "we have come to see performed by a late monarch in our own time and country."[46]

Swift did not think his history worth publishing, so we must not

---

other State, that may haply, upon many Points, labour under the like Circumstances": ibid., p. 222. For Temple's likely influence here, see Robert J. Allen, "Swift's Earliest Political Tract and Sir William Temple's Essays," *Harvard Studies and Notes in Philology and Literature* 19 (1937): 3–12. For some other contemporary examples, see Addison Ward, "The Tory View of Roman History," *Studies in English Literature* 4 (1964): 413–56.

[43]See Harold Williams, *Dean Swift's Library* (Cambridge, 1932), pp. 52–53.

[44]Swift, *Miscellaneous and Autobiographical Fragments*, p. 36.

[45]Ibid., pp. 49, 64. For Swift's notions about good and bad history, see his marginal comments on Herodotus, Clarendon, Burnet, and other historians in ibid., pp. 243, 266–94, 295–320.

[46]Ibid., pp. 44–45.

dwell on it. Its only interest lies perhaps in the ambition with which it was begun: to fulfill Temple's dream of rewriting English history to the classical standard. Bolingbroke thought that Swift was the best man in the kingdom for the task. But as Temple foresaw clearly, it would not be easy for any single author to accomplish, however able. By 1703 Swift had discovered other talents and ambitions more uniquely his own; in the next year appeared *A Tale of a Tub* and *The Battle of the Books*. Swift's lifelong ambition to become a historian was never fulfilled.[47]

6

It was left to the publishers to try to realize Temple's scheme, and in the first years of the eighteenth century both of his notions came to a kind of fruition, although it is doubtful that he would have been happy with either. On the one hand, James Tyrrell kept to his great task of trying to reconstruct English history from the ground up, and one by one the large volumes began to appear, although in the end even that indefatigable man had to give up and fall short of his goal. On the other hand, a new consortium of publishers picked up where the Bentley-Chiswell partnership had failed and once again attempted a complete and composite history of the realm. This time they brought it off.

The new syndicate was unexpectedly large and many of the members were prominent in the trade. But so too was the project, three enormous folio volumes. It took some 780 subscribers to launch it. Thomas Hearne was undoubtedly right when he said that it was done "merely for Gain,"[48] but the result was undeniably impressive, more certainly than Temple had anticipated. When it was done in 1706, it was called *A Complete History of England* and it was successful enough to be revised and printed again in 1719. It was meant to be a summary of the best of the new historiography, an anthology of all those pieces that had aspired to literature since the Renaissance and that might be assembled somehow into a coherent whole. And, although its subject was modern, its ambition was ancient: to turn the history of England into a form that would have satisfied a classical Roman.

For the publishers, the essential thing was to find an editor. Exactly how they went about it remains obscure. It used to be thought that their choice was White Kennett, the future bishop of Peterborough, a scholar

---

[47]Swift hoped to become historiographer royal at Rymer's death (1714); see the *Correspondence of Jonathan Swift*, ed. Harold Williams, 5 vols. (Oxford, 1963–1965), 2:2, 63, 69, 73, 82–83; Ehrenpreis, *Swift*, 2:744–48.

[48]Hearne, Aug. 2, 1706, in *Remarks and Collections*, 1:280.

and antiquary, in many ways well equipped for the job, and the work still sometimes appears under his name. But Kennett categorically denied his authorship in a letter to Thomas Hearne, admitting only to composing the last volume, on the Stuarts. Hearne printed Kennett's denial but was not perfectly convinced. He had been told by a friend that the printer Benjamin Tooke paid Kennett £200 for his work on the *Complete History*, "besides about 100 libs. that it cost him in treats." The sum seemed too large merely to assist in the work, "and yet not trouble himself, nor give his Direction, in some of the most material Parts of it." Certainly the Whig bias that persisted in the history seemed to Hearne consistent with the views of that "notorious Republican and preacher of Rebellious Doctrine." Some years later, Hearne was told again by two separate sources that Tooke had paid Kennett to do the job, and Hearne preferred to believe that he had been hired to supervise, if not to compose the whole.[49]

Nevertheless, Hearne's opinion was built on hearsay and colored by political animus, so that Kennett's denial should probably be allowed to stand. "I was not the author, publisher, or revisor of that volume, or any note or line in it, as anyone of the booksellers could have informed you."[50] The compilation of the first two volumes, from the beginning of English history through the reign of James I, was undoubtedly the work of someone else, probably John Hughes or John Oldmixon, both of whom certainly contributed something to it.

Perhaps it does not matter a great deal. The design, we have seen, was already abroad and only needed someone to carry it through. And, as Pat Rogers once suggested, the careers of Hughes and Oldmixon were so remarkably similar that they had almost identical credentials for the task.[51] Both were miscellaneous writers who dabbled in nearly every Augustan genre; neither was a conspicuous success, although Hughes was cut off somewhat prematurely at his best moment. Both came from dissenting backgrounds and had Whiggish sympathies. They even knew each other. In 1706 they both needed employment and either would have looked like a good bet for the job.

Whatever the case, it appears that Hughes wrote the preface at least to

[49]Ibid., pp. 282–84, 311, 332; 2:88, 138; 3:170, 269–70, 321, 339, 392, 424; 10:131, 134.

[50]White Kennett to Hearne, Dec. 3, 1711, and reply, Dec. 12, in *Letters Written by Eminent Persons in the Bodleian Library*, ed. John Walker (London, 1813), pp. 224–27. Hearne printed Kennett's denial in his edition of John Leland's *Itinerary*, 9 vols. (Oxford, 1710–1712), 7:xv–xvi. See too William Newton, *The Life of Dr. White Kennett* (London, 1730), p. 33.

[51]I am grateful to Pat Rogers for sending me a copy of the supplement to his Cambridge dissertation, "Oldmixon, John Hughes and the *Complete History*," in "The Whig Controversialist as Dunce: A Study in the Literary Fortunes and Misfortunes of John Oldmixon (1673–1742)" (1967).

the *Complete History* and translated some Latin annals of Mary Tudor for it. In 1706 he was twenty-nine years old and had published a number of pieces in prose and verse. He hobnobbed with the wits and poets in London, among them Congreve, Addison and Steele, Nicholas Rowe, and Godfrey Kneller, who painted his portrait. From time to time he contributed essays to the *Spectator*, the *Tatler*, and the *Guardian*. He wrote songs and libretti for Pepusch, Handel, and others; and he did a lot of translating from Latin, Italian, and French. In 1702 he turned Fontenelle's *Dialogues of the Dead* into English, adding two of his own. Later he returned to Fontenelle and translated the *Plurality of Worlds* with the famous appendix on the ancients and moderns that had so provoked Temple. He wrote one very popular play, *The Siege of Damascus*, living just long enough to see it produced before he expired in 1720. He received a nice obituary by Steele and left a sufficient reputation to have his poems and letters published posthumously and get a brief life by Samuel Johnson.

Hughes brought a conventional Augustan viewpoint to almost everything he did. His early poems were all classical imitations, Pindaric odes and Horatian paraphrases. In 1698 he wrote an essay, "Of Style," which deliberately echoes Sir William Temple.[52] Polite learning is there set against pedantry, the gentleman against the mere scholar. History and poetry are the two chief branches of polite learning, but Hughes confines himself for the moment to prose and the several attributes that he believed contribute to a correct and elegant style. Each genre has its own needs; history requires less adornment than letters or essays, since it concentrates on "matter of fact." But all prose requires propriety, perspicuity, elegance, and cadence. Temple, with one or two others, is proposed as the best model for English style.

Could there have been a better choice to write the introduction? The preface to the *Complete History* is a wonderful epitome of all that was conventional in the ancient wisdom about history and might well have been written by Temple himself. It begins with the usual commonplaces about the use and pleasure of the subject for public and private life, "for what we admire we are easily disposed to imitate." And it proceeds to expatiate on the particular value of English history for an Englishman. Unfortunately, as everyone recognized, the national past was largely disregarded, the result of works that were mean and imperfect and that no one wanted to read. Hughes believed with the ancients that this neglect was entirely due to a failure of rhetoric, a disregard for the classical models, "for tho' the Matter of History is the first thing to

---

[52]"Of Style," in John Hughes, *Poems on Several Occasions and Several Select Essays in Prose*, 2 vols. (London, 1735), 1:247–55.

recommend it, the Form, which depends wholly on the Writer, is almost of equal Consequence."[53]

The laws of history were therefore, for Hughes, like the laws of poetry for Alexander Pope, "but the Dictates of good Sense, drawn out and methodiz'd." Happily, there were many books on the subject that one could read, from Lucian to Le Moyne, Rapin, and Le Clerc. The perfect historian needed to combine many virtues with his natural genius. He needed both study and experience of the world, wide reading and direct acquaintance of courts, councils, and civic and military affairs. He must learn to adorn the appropriate materials with all the graces of a polite language. And he must show neither passion nor prejudice. Above all, he must employ "a judicious Proportion of all Parts of his Story; a beautiful Simplicity of Narration; a noble yet unaffected Stile; few and significant Epithets; Descriptions lively, but not Poetical; Reflections short and proper; and lastly . . . a good Conduct thro' the whole, and an animating Spirit that may engage the Reader in every Action as if personally concern'd." If this was difficult enough to imagine in a short compass, how much harder must it be to accomplish for a whole national history, which like an epic poem was the very summit of its genre. With Homer and Virgil, Hughes can think of matching only two historians, one ancient and one modern: Livy and Mariana.

Hughes shared Temple's view that the only things the English had so far provided to fill the gap were chronicles and antiquarian compilations, the first tedious and full of frivolous matter and private circumstances, the second "a laborious Plunder of Libraries, Manuscripts, publick Rolls and Records, tho' put together by many Years Application, in a cold and Barren Stile." Only a "Club of Men," to use Nicolson's expression, who joined together to share the burden could properly accomplish the task, although it was a most unlikely prospect. Under the circumstances, what better than to adopt Temple's notion of bringing together those smaller parcels of English history that had been well written into a whole? And, of course, this is just what the Complete History intended to do.

But even this much was not easy. For one thing, finding the briefer pieces turned out to be more troublesome and expensive than anyone had anticipated. Some were scarce, others corrupt in later editions, and fresh

---

[53] A Complete History of England, 3 vols. (London, 1706), 1: Preface (the 1719 edition is nearly identical). According to the Biographia Britannica (London, 1747), p. 2701, the Preface "certainly gives as clear, as satisfactory, and as impartial account of the Historians there collected as can be desired, and that in a stile and manner very pleasing and natural." Oldmixon shared most of Hughes's sentiments, to judge by a later work; see his Essay on Criticism (London, 1728). He tries there to steer a middle way between Perrault and Boileau, but sides completely with the rhetoricians against the philologists and antiquaries. In an early work he mocks a modern who prefers Sir Richard Blackmore to Virgil, Horace, and the Greeks; see John Oldmixon, Poems on Several Occasions (London, 1696), pp. 102–6.

translations had sometimes to be made. Annotation was required to correct and update them. Furthermore, not all the gaps could be filled in this way; some pieces had to be newly composed. The result was certainly various and uneven, but at least it could be said that it was more likely to be diverting in this form than a long work by a single author, "tho' written ever so elegantly."

Curiously, the *Complete History* began not with Temple's *Introduction* but with John Milton's *History of Britain*. Were the editors barred from using Temple's work, or did they really find it too sketchy—in Hughes's words, "not particular enough," and too much in haste to get on to the Conqueror?[54] In any case, Hughes was willing to promote Milton's history as equal to anything in antiquity. "In his Thoughts and Language, he appears with the Magestick Air of old Greece or Rome." Hughes relied on the modern Fontenelle to argue that if one steeped oneself in antiquity, it was possible to transplant the ancient genius to modern times. Paradoxically, "even the greatest Admirers of Antiquity have a particular Reason to rank him [Milton] with most of the Ancients, whom he so nearly resembles." (Like so many of the moderns, Fontenelle had given the palm of eloquence and history to the ancients, and could think of nothing superior to Cicero and Livy.) If his self-conscious *ancienneté* made Milton sound a little strange to some of his readers, it was "like the Roman Architecture heretofore when the Gothick was in Fashion." It was only to be regretted that Milton had not continued his history beyond the Norman invasion.[55]

The editors drew again on Samuel Daniel for the period after the Conquest down to the time of Edward III. "His Narration," Hughes wrote, "is smooth and clear, and carries every where an Air of good Sense and just Eloquence." Hughes admired Daniel's style especially, which seemed to him more idiomatic than Milton's, but he characteristically neglected to say anything about the contents of the work. He was disappointed with Trussell's continuation, "the stile so wretched," so that the period from Richard II to Henry IV would have to be rewritten. For Edward IV he recommended the work of Edward Habingdon, painted in lively colors but moralizing a bit too much. For Richard III

---

[54]This was certainly the opinion of the reviewer in the *Journal des Scavans*, 1708, pp. 332–33.

[55]John Milton, *The History of Britain* (London, 1670), ed. G. P. Krapp, in *The Works of John Milton*, 18 vols. (New York, 1931–1938), vol. 10; Constance Nicholas prepared an *Introduction and Notes to Milton's "History of Britain,"* Illinois Studies in Language and Literature 44 (Urbana, 1957). Still useful is C. H. Firth, "Milton as Historian," *Proceedings of the British Academy*, 1907–8, pp. 227–57; Henry Glicksman, "The Sources of Milton's *History of Britain*," University of Wisconsin Studies in Language and Literature, no. 2 (Madison, n.d.), pp. 105–44. See also J. Milton French, "Milton as an Historian," *Publications of the Modern Language Association* 50 (1935): 469–79.

there was Thomas More's little work, here newly translated from its masterly Latin. "In this Reign the Intrigues of the Protector and his Creatures against the young Princes, are related with wonderful Clearness and Judgment in the Affairs of State; the Speeches are sensible, and the Descriptions proper; that of King Richard's guilty Terrors after the Murther of his Nephews, is admirable, which is mention'd here, because 'tis certain, Description in History as well as in Poetry is a dangerous Part to manage, and the soonest betrays an affected and injudicious Writer."[56] Hughes seems blissfully unaware that there might be as much danger in successful rhetoric as in bad writing, or that More's speeches might be thorough inventions and the whole narrative suspicious. Yet the editors actually included George Buck's life of Richard also (presumably to complete More's unfinished history, though it was "too loosely writ for a History"), despite the fact that it expressly defended Richard against More's accusations.[57] And in a later piece, John Hayward's *Life and Raigne of King Edward the Sixt*, they permitted the antiquary John Strype to criticize Hayward for systematically inventing and distorting the speeches. It may have been too much to ask for consistency in a collaborative work of this kind, but it was perfectly clear that the attention of the editors—and very likely of the readers—was more upon the pleasures of the narration than upon the truthfulness of the tale.

The editors were able to conclude the first volume of their work with what was surely the best of the new histories, Francis Bacon's *History of Henry VII*, "one of the most applauded Pieces of History that has ever been writ in our own or any other Language, either Ancient or Modern."[58] Bacon had brought to the task all the virtues of a statesman, orator, and philosopher, with the result that he had outdone even his model, Tacitus, in combining clarity of style and expression with political insight and judgment. It did not matter to Hughes and his friends that Bacon had done little more than combine the few narrative sources that were equally available to them; as the antiquary Thomas Baker complained, "it is finely wrote, but wants vouchers."[59] They saw correctly that Bacon had reenacted Henry's reign in his own political imagination

[56]Nicolson held the same opinion of More, "who has sufficiently shown how a short and doleful Tale may be improv'd into a Complete History, by a Person of good Skill and Judgment": *English Historical Library*, p. 220.

[57]See George Buck, *The History of King Richard III* (1619), ed. Arthur N. Kincaid (Gloucester, 1979).

[58]Again Nicolson agreed: *English Historical Library*, p. 224.

[59]Thomas Baker to Hearne, Nov. 7, 1728, in Frans Korsten, "Thomas Baker and his Books," *Transactions of the Cambridge Bibliographical Society* 8, pt. 5 (1985): 505. The best discussion of Bacon's sources remains Wilhelm Busch, *England under the Tudors: King Henry VII*, trans. Alice M. Todd (London, 1895), pp. 391–423, esp. 418–22. But see also Daniel R. Woolf, "John Selden, John Borough, and Francis Bacon's *History of Henry VII*, 1621," *Huntington Library Quarterly* 47 (1984): 47–53.

and created an exemplary ruler with a contemporary message. Bacon, they agreed, had the knack of making every part of his story instructive without belaboring the message. Above all, "he does not content himself with a superficial Narration, but enters deeper into his Subject, and discovers the Motives of Affairs, which every where seem true Representations, and not fanciful Conjectures." It was no coincidence that the author had been among other things lord high chancellor of England.

7

For the second volume of the *Complete History* there were the works recommended by Temple: Lord Herbert of Cherbury on Henry VIII, John Hayward on Edward VI, and Camden on Elizabeth. It was thought advisable to correct Hayward's account with some notes provided by the learned John Strype, just then beginning to flood the world with his ecclesiastical histories of the Tudor period. Strype also provided annotations for several earlier reigns and for the piece on Mary Tudor, a Latin work by Francis Godwin which was excerpted and translated into English by Hughes.[60] Finally, to conclude the volume, a life of James I by Arthur Wilson was provided with notes by James Welwood.[61] Oldmixon claimed many years later (with some obvious exaggeration) that he himself had been the sole editor, writing all the notes and several of the reigns, as well as the entire index.[62] Nevertheless, even he thought the result was very uneven,[63] and it is doubtful that Temple would have

[60]The *Annals* of Francis Godwin are presented as translated by J. H. with notes by J. S.; there are also notes signed J. S. for the reigns of Edward IV and Richard III. Strype scribbled a note on a letter to him from the printer Henry Bonwicke, who asked him for assistance on "our English history," Aug. 2, 1705: "the booksellers were printing the Complete History of England, i.e. the Lives of the Kings and Queens. I added Annotations to the History of Richard III, K. Edward VI and Q. Mary": Cambridge University Library, Baumgartner Papers, I, ii, no. 270. See also Hearne, *Remarks and Collections*, 1:286; Strype to Thoresby, July 1, 1707, in *Letters of Eminent Men to Ralph Thoresby*, 2 vols. (London, 1832), 2:57; *Notes and Queries*, 2d ser. 8 (1859): 343–44; and John Strype, "Animadversions upon Sir John Hayward's Life and Reign of King Edward VI," in *Ecclesiastical Memorials, 1513–1558*, 3 vols. (London, 1721), 2:470–82.

[61]James Welwood or Wellwood was the author of, among other things, *A Vindication of the Revolution in England* (1689) and *Memoirs of the Most Material Transactions in England for the Last Hundred Years Preceeding the Revolution in 1688* (London, 1700). Four editions of the latter were issued by 1710.

[62]Oldmixon first claimed to be the sole editor in *A Review of Dr. Grey's Defence* (London, 1725), p. 57. Rogers accepted this claim as plausible. A note in Pope's *Dunciad Variorum* (London, 1729), bk. 2, l. 199, accuses Oldmixon of misediting Daniel, but Oldmixon neglects to mention Strype's annotations.

[63]"I was well acquainted with [the *Complete History*], having been the Editor; but it being a Collection of several Authors Performances, some very bad, and some very good, it could not satisfy Men of Taste and Judgment." It suffered from "want of a just Design,

approved. Certainly the final volume of contemporary history, by White Kennett, made the collection even more problematical, kicking up a storm of political controversy and wrecking the proportions of the project.

The choice of Kennett was deliberate. Just as the project was developing, there had appeared, with great fanfare and general approval, the three massive volumes of Clarendon's *History of the Civil Wars* (1702–1704). This was the work that we have seen praised extravagantly by both the ancients and the moderns, by both Temple and Wotton, as a masterpiece of historical writing. For most contemporaries, it appeared definitive in form and style and generally sensible in its moderate royalist and antipuritan sentiments. Evelyn, for example, was ready to set it above any history, ancient or modern, that he had ever read.[64] But Oldmixon remembered that the work had posed a problem by some by its overt political judgments. "Great was the Consternation the Whigs were thrown into on the formidable Appearance of that History; and the Vogue it got for its unhistorical Qualities, *study'd Periods*, and *florid Narrations*, at once insensibly took in unwary and unskilful Readers to like the Facts as well as the Stile. It had such a Torrent of Currency at first, that it bore all down before it."[65] Oldmixon was certainly exaggerating, for he wrote long afterward when his own political position had hardened (and the terms "Tory" and "Whig" had altered their meaning), but the work certainly provoked a reconsideration of the great events of mid-century.[66] Kennett, once a royalist, now turned apologist for the Glorious Revolution, seems to have been employed for the task.

---

and one Point of View regularly pursued": John Oldmixon, *Critical History of England* (London, 1739), sig. Alr. Oldmixon seems to have disliked Kennett's contribution particularly. In 1728 he still thought Daniel's *Collection* "the only English History that has the least Appearance of Uniformity and Regularity of Design": *An Essay on Criticism*, p. 17. This was still the view of P. Whalley, *An Essay on the Manner of Writing History* (1746), ed. Keith Stewart, Augustan Reprint Society 80 (Los Angeles, 1960), p. 26.

[64]See his long letter to the later Earl of Clarendon, Oct. 28, 1702, Christ Church Evelyn Letters, XV, no. 1696.

[65]John Oldmixon, *Memoirs of the Press . . . 1710 to 1740* (London, 1742), pp. 35–36. Oldmixon attacked Clarendon forthrightly in *Clarendon and Whitlock Compar'd* (London, 1727), but had to admit that "the History of the Rebellion is cloathed with Eloquence and Imagination; the Painting is glaring every where, and attracts one's Eye to much of the Lustre of the Picture, that we are heedless of the Likeness": pp. xxviii–xxix. In an appendix to his thesis (n. 51) Rogers provides a useful calendar of the Clarendon controversy, stirred up by Oldmixon's charges that some of Clarendon's work was fraudulent.

[66]James Tyrrell was not the only Whig who applauded its appearance volume by volume; see his correspondence with Locke, Aug. 7, 1701; July 18, 1702; Oct. 6, 1702, in *The Correspondence of John Locke*, ed. E. S. de Beer, 8 vols. (Oxford, 1976–1989), 8:683–85. One problem was that the work had been edited at Christ Church by Aldrich, Atterbury, et al., who were suspected of tampering with it; but even Oldmixon, who made the charges (much later), agreed that everyone admired it. When David Gregory took up the first chair of modern history at Oxford (1725), he spoke "very long, it seems, in Commendation of

It was not an enviable job and Kennett did not succeed very well. The trouble was that while he had some of the right credentials for the task—sound political principles and a solid historical training—he was much more of a scholar than a rhetorician.[67] In 1693 he drew up the life of a man he much admired, William Somner, celebrating his linguistic skills and antiquarian achievements. "His most constant delight," Kennett wrote with appreciation, "was in classic Histories, in old Manuscripts, Ledger-Books, Rolls, and Records."[68] Kennett showed his own skill in these matters by writing the first real scholarly history of a parish, his own Ambrosden (1695); and he helped also to inspire the great collaborative enterprise of George Hickes and his friends, which was then aimed at recovering the whole literature and history of Anglo-Saxon England. He knew that "there be some who slight and despise this sort of learning, and represent it to be a dry, barren, monkish study," but he insisted on its value in understanding "the state of former ages, the constitution of governments, the fundamental reasons of equity and law, the rise and succession of doctrines and opinions, the original of ancient, and the composition of modern tongues, the tenures of property, the maxims of policy, the rites of religion, the characters of virtue and vice, and indeed the *nature of mankind*."[69] It was history, not histories, that interested Kennett and his fellow scholars, but Kennett had been commissioned to write a narrative.

Yet the greatest inducement to historical scholarship at the time, particularly for a divine, was ecclesiastical controversy, and the scholar Kennett was drawn inevitably into the bitter quarrels that were then dividing the church. After 1701 he took his stand with Archbishop Wake

Lord Clarendon's History, and the Fidelity of that Historian": Hearne, *Remarks and Collections*, 8:364. In Scotland, Sir Robert Sibbald praised its style and impartiality in a letter to Robert Wodrow, Feb. 1703, in *Memoirs of the Royal College of Physicians at Edinburgh* (Edinburgh, 1837), p. 34; and in Hanover, Leibniz and the electress read it with pleasure; see Leibniz to Brunet, May 12, 1704, in *La Correspondance de Leibniz avec l'électrice Sophie de Brunswick-Lunebourg*, ed. Onno Klopp, 3 vols. (Hanover, 1874), 3:78–83. For Edmund Gibson (Nicolson's friend), "it is the most instructive and entertaining Book that I ever read": Gibson to Charlett, Aug. 18, 1702, Bodleian MS. Ballard 6, f. 78. So too John Evelyn in a letter to Pepys, Jan. 20, 1702, in *Diary and Correspondence of Samuel Pepys*, ed. Lord Braybrooke, 4 vols. (London, 1890), 4:384–85; and *The Diary of Ralph Thoresby*, ed. Joseph Hunter, 2 vols. (London, 1830), 1:467. Le Clerc abridged it and praised it extravagantly, comparing it favorably to Sallust; see *Mr. Le Clerc's Account of the Earl of Clarendon's History*, trans. J. O. (London, 1710); and it was still being praised by Defoe in 1722 as the only impartial history; see William Lee, *Daniel Defoe*, 2 vols. (London, 1869), 2:38.

[67]See G. V. Bennett, *White Kennett, 1660–1728* (London, 1957), esp. chap. 7, pp. 158–77; Newton, *Life of Dr. White Kennett*.

[68]Kennett's life of Somner appeared with Somner's posthumous *Treatise on the Roman Ports and Forts in Kent* (1693); see Joseph M. Levine, *Humanism and History* (Ithaca, N.Y., 1987), p. 96.

[69]White Kennett, *Parochial Antiquities of Ambrosden*, ed. B. Bandinel, 2 vols. (Oxford, 1818), 1:xvii.

(and William Nicolson) against Francis Atterbury in the Convocation Controversy, drawing effectively on historical precedent to meet the arguments of the opposition. And on the anniversary of Charles I's martyrdom in 1704 (always a day for Tory fanfare), Kennett delivered a celebrated sermon, *A Compassionate Inquiry into the Causes of the Civil War*. In it he analyzed the reasons for the rebellion that had overturned "the best Constitution in the World," carefully apportioning blame between a fanatical religious party and a dangerous and ill-conceived royal policy. The high-church divines replied at once and Kennett's political credentials were confirmed.[70]

It was Kennett himself who introduced the third volume of the *Complete History* by adding a note to Hughes's preface. He apologized for his anonymity there by pointing out the difficulties that faced any historian of contemporary events, of which everyone had imperfect recollections and confused notions, "Partiality to one side, and a Prejudice to another." No prudent man would set his name to a work that was bound to displease. Nevertheless, he had tried to strike a balance and mete out only truth and justice. For the period after James I, there was only one real historian worth remembering, the "inimitable" Earl of Clarendon.[71] Kennett had found him relatively impartial and elected to follow him where he could, even to including the best parts: those memorable portraits that the historian had composed so carefully from personal acquaintance.

Temple would almost certainly have been disappointed. Kennett had no real literary ambitions, and his inclusion of so much of Clarendon served only to show off the weakness of his own narrative. He chose a rigidly annalistic method and thus reverted to something like the traditional chronicle, but slowed down the story further still by including many documents.[72] He offered little description, and the political judgments were too obviously the work of a clergyman rather than a man of

---

[70]White Kennett, *A Compassionate Enquiry into the Causes of the Civil War* (London, 1704), p. 16. The five main causes of the rebellion were "a French interest . . . Apprehension and Fears of Popery . . . Jealousies of Oppression and Illegal Power . . . the Growth of Profaneness and Immorality . . . Hypocricy and Prejudice."

[71]"To the Reader," at the end of Hughes's preface to the *Complete History*, vol. 1; 3:207. White Kennett's brother, Basil, shared his admiration for Clarendon, and found him the perfect historian of Rapin's prescription: Introduction to Rapin, *Whole Critical Works*, 1: [sig. A7].

[72]Kennett remained true to his method in a later work, the *Register and Chronicle, Ecclesiastical and Civil* (London, 1728), which he described accurately enough as a "tedious and heavy Book. . . . The Scheme was laid for Conscience Sake to restore the old principle, that History should be purely Matter of Fact, and when such Matters are deliver'd upon profest authorities for them, every reader by examining and comparing, may make out a History upon his own judgment": Kennett to Thomas Baker, June 13, 1728, B.M. MS. Add. 5831, ff. 159–60.

the world. In fact, the point of view was not so far from Clarendon's, although the narrative extended much further into recent events.[73] It was no doubt Kennett's unqualified denunciation of James II that roused the high-church party and particularly his old friends the nonjurors to a frenzy of denunciation.[74]

But the calumnies of George Hickes and Hearne and their friends could neither make nor break the *Complete History*, which had set out to meet the need for a new history of England and done pretty well to accomplish the task. The three great volumes that appeared in 1706 had something magisterial to them, and they certainly included much of the best historical narrative that had so far appeared in England. But they had not quite done what Temple had once hoped to achieve: to set out in a single place a smooth-flowing and agreeable narrative of English history which might be set alongside Livy without embarrassment. Once again, it appeared, the moderns had failed to match the ancients on their own ground.

8

Meanwhile, James Tyrrell was trying the other approach, a whole new work by a single hand. Tyrrell was an English country gentleman of independent income and modest pretensions.[75] He is best known as a friend and for a time a collaborator of John Locke. In 1661 he published a work on politics by his famous grandfather Archbishop James Ussher. For the rest of his life he retained an interest in scholarship and politics, using the one to reinforce the other. In the 1680s he entered the political arena on behalf of the Whigs, answering (as Locke did also) the famous tract of Sir Robert Filmer on absolute monarchy with his own *Patriarcha non monarcha*. The historical argument, he saw, had to be met with a

[73]"I am glad you have so much justice and charity for K. James I who has really been abused and vilified beyond all measure of truth by Weldon, Osborn and Willson and the annotater on him in the II vol. of the Complete History of Eng. who I suppose was Wellwood. . . . However no one Life or Reign is so imperfect in our Histories, Qu Elizabeth had a Camden and K. CH a Clarendon but poor K James I has had I think none but paltry Scriblers": Kennett to Charlett, May 26, 1716, Bodleian MS. Ballard 7, ff. 71–72.

[74]See Bennett, *White Kennett*, pp. 172–73. He was "now stampt a Whig Writer, which was as bad as being a Republican, and a Presbyterian, which was worse than being a Papist": Newton, *Life of Dr. White Kennett*, p. 36. See Hickes to Kennett, No. 1, 1711, Bodleian MS. English History b 2, ff. 152–69. Roger North was still complaining in 1740, in *Examen, or an Enquiry into the Credit and Veracity of a Pretended Complete History* (London, 1740).

[75]See J. W. Gough, "James Tyrrell, Whig Historian and Friend of John Locke," *Historical Journal* 19 (1976): 581–610.

historical argument. After the Revolution he returned to the fray in an effort to answer the still more formidable Royalist apologies of Dr. Robert Brady, which had appeared in the interim.

For a time, during the high tide of Tory politics, Brady's views had come to dominate the historiographical scene. He was indeed a formidable opponent. In 1684 he published a large volume that reprinted several of his tracts against the Whig historians and in the next year an even larger volume that he entitled *A Compleat History of England*. It was the first part only and carried the story down to the reign of Henry III. Brady seems to have won official patronage for his work, which he had labored over for nearly a decade. All his strength was bent on answering the opponents of absolute monarchy, republicans and Whigs, those who wished to place sovereignty directly in the hands of the people and those who wanted merely to exempt their liberties from the royal dominion. He saw little to choose between the two.

Brady's *Compleat History*, like his other works, was an appeal to the record, to "matter of fact," to settle the issues.[76] Brady understood with the antiquaries that the printed chronicles were not alone sufficient to supply the information that was needed for the laws and constitution of the kingdom, and so he spent long hours poring over ancient manuscripts and legal documents, translating and copying them directly into his work.[77] Thus was born, or rejuvenated, a new form of historical narrative that combined the annalistic form of the medieval chronicle with the antiquarian compilation of sources. "I have not," Brady admitted, "laboured after an Exact and Even Style, nor can it be Expected when there is such Variety of Matter, and where Men are confined to, and limited by the Translation of other Mens Language."[78] Besides the documents, Brady included the full apparatus of modern historical scholarship: quotation, annotation, footnotes, indexes, and appendixes. He understood the importance of a philological investigation into the original use of all problematical terms.[79] He separated his own views from the

[76]Robert Brady, *A Compleat History of England* (London, 1685), sig. A3. The *Compleat History* was preceded by *An Introduction to the Old English History . . . in Three Separate Tracts* (London, 1684); see J. G. A. Pocock, "Robert Brady, 1627–1700: A Cambridge Historian of the Restoration," *Cambridge Historical Journal* 10 (1951): 186–204, and *The Ancient Constitution and the Feudal Law* (Cambridge, 1957), pp. 182–228; Connie C. Weston, "Legal Sovereignty in the Brady Controversy," *Historical Journal* 15 (1972): 409–31. Pocock has since added a postscript to the second edition of his book (Cambridge, 1987), replying to Weston and J. R. Greenberg, *Sovereigns and Subjects: The Grand Controversy over Legal Sovereignty in England* (Cambridge, 1981).

[77]"I could not be satisfied but that I must re-search now what Authors I could, both Printed and manuscripts, that I might make Publick an Authentick and well-grounded History of those Times": Brady, *Compleat History*, p. 52.

[78]"To the Reader," in ibid., n.p.

[79]When the antiquary Sir William Dugdale received a copy of the *Introduction*, he wrote, "I have diligently read it over, and do finde it to be done with much judgment as well as great paines, you having therein clearly and amply manifested what the words, *populus*,

narrative, introducing each section with something like a legal brief, and forswearing any embellishment or commentary within the text. He believed that the truth of history was best retrieved by a literal reproduction of the documents and the least intrusion by the historian.

Brady distrusted those writers who mixed the facts with their own reflections or political observations, thinking that there was no value to a history without them; they served "only to Pervert and Disguise Matter of Fact, and make History Romantic." As a result, he assembled his diverse sources rather mechanically, deliberately divesting them of their hagiographical and romantic material and removing whatever color they might once have had. The technique, says J. G. A. Pocock, was "strictly scissors and paste."[80] The narrative was necessarily dry and very dull, though enlivened from time to time by polemical essays at the beginning of each section which were full of historical insight.

It would carry us away from our purpose to linger over Brady's views of English history. Suffice it to say that he built on the outlook of his predecessor, the royalist antiquary Sir Henry Spelman, who had written earlier in an article on parliaments, "When States are departed from the Original Constitution and that original by tract of time worn out of Memory; the succeeding Ages, viewing what is past by the present, conceive the former to have been like to that they live in, and framing thereupon erroneous propositions, do like-wise make their erroneous inferences and Conclusions."[81] Exactly like the classical philologists, Spelman and Brady saw the danger of anachronism and believed that a correct understanding of the past required a systematic and critical examination of contemporary sources in the original languages. "It hath been and ever was," Brady complained, "an Act of some Men, to interpret and confound New Laws by old Practice, and Usage; and Old Laws by late Usage, and Modern Practice. When perhaps if they would endeavour to find out the History of those Laws . . . there would be found no congruity between them."[82] If the words sounded alike, it was enough; the Whigs had erred in reading back into the past those institutions that they most admired in the present. In this matter, at least, it was the Tories who were the moderns.

Fortunately for the Whigs, Brady's "historicism" had its limits too; the "substantialism" of the age infected even its most advanced historical

---

plebs, communitas, liberi tenentes, and divers others, do meane . . .": Dugdale to Robert Brady, Oct. 6, 1684, in The Life, Diary and Correspondence of Sir William Dugdale, ed. William Hamper (London, 1827), pp. 436–38.

[80] "A constellation of brilliant analyses studding a waste of annalistic narrative": Pocock, "Robert Brady," p. 201; Ancient Constitution, p. 225. See Brady, "To the Reader," in Compleat History, n.p.

[81] Reprinted in the Reliquiae Spelmannianae (Oxford, 1698), p. 57. See Pocock, "Robert Brady," p. 195.

[82] Brady, Compleat History, p. xliii.

critics. What Richard Bentley was doing for the Greeks, Brady was trying to do for the historical character of (medieval) language and literature. Even William Nicolson had to admit that Brady's application to the sources had cast much light on many "dark passages" in early English history.[83] And Brady had been able to detect many surprising frauds and forgeries among his sources. (That Temple should become the victim again is not entirely coincidental.) But still Brady was unwilling to submit his own political values to the same test. If the feudal law was nothing more than the specific creation of the monarchy at a given time, the monarchy itself was given no proper beginning, or development. "Ordinary People," he wrote in one tract, "always have been, and ever will be, Instruments of Designing Men against the Government."[84] Nor were the feudal tenures introduced by William the Conqueror allowed any adumbration afterward.[85]

It was the Glorious Revolution that gave Tyrrell both the opportunity and the incentive to answer Brady. Just about the time that Temple was writing his *Introduction*, Tyrrell decided once again to put pen to paper to trumpet the Whig cause. By the spring of 1692 he was ready with the first dialogue of an apparently endless series that, so he wrote to Locke, his printer had advised him to issue once a month.[86] In two years' time he was able to bring together thirteen pieces (with more still to come) under the title *Bibliotheca Politica; or, An Enquiry into the Ancient Constitution* (1694). In 968 pages Mr. Meanwell, a civilian, is answered and corrected by Mr. Freeman, a gentleman, and taught the fundamentals of Whig history. Tyrrell allows that the dispute was indeed about "the Signification of Words, in what sense they were used in the Age we are now treating of."[87] But he remains true to his original convictions, persuaded of the antiquity of the common law, Parliament, and the rights of free Englishmen; the importance of the coronation oath and Magna Carta, and the unimportance of the Norman Conquest.[88]

As a result, Tyrrell must have seemed the obvious choice when Dunton needed an editor in 1694 for a new *Complete History*. For Tyrrell it

---

[83]Nicolson, *English Historical Library*, 2:xxxii–iv, 3:58.
[84]Brady, *Introduction to the Old English History*, p. 378.
[85]Brady, *Complete History*, pp. 155–56; Weston, "Legal Sovereignty," p. 431.
[86]Tyrrell to Locke, Mar. 9, 1692, Locke *Correspondence*, 4:408–9.
[87]James Tyrrell, *Bibliotheca Politica*, no. 6 (1693) (London, 1694), pp. 375–78.
[88]In the sixth dialogue of the *Bibliotheca Politica*, Tyrrell answered Brady's latest, *An Historical Treatise of Cities and Burghs or Boroughs* (London, 1690). He tried to prove somehow that the Saxon boroughs must have been very like their modern counterparts in size and status. Brady had written scornfully that the Whigs treated the cities as though they were "Aeternal, or at least Coevil with the Creation, and so many ready Wrought, and Framed small Commonwealths, lifted out of the Chaos, and fixed upon the surface of the Earth, with their Walls, Gates, Town or gild-Halls, Courts, Liberties, Customs, Privileges, Freedoms, Jurisdictions, Magistrates and Orders!" (p. i). Tyrrell kept insisting that it must be so; but neither side had a very adequate notion of the Saxon social situation or a proper setting for the legal question.

was the perfect opportunity to answer Brady, not simply on controversial points but with an alternative history altogether. For the publishers it was a golden opportunity to employ a gentleman of proven interest and capacity at little cost. For Temple, as we have seen, it was very frustrating, all the more so as Tyrrell had neither the means nor the intention of fulfilling the old man's purposes and attempting a masterpiece of English prose modeled on the ancients. Nor was Tyrrell much taken by Temple's *Introduction*, which he seems quite deliberately to have ignored, except perhaps for its sympathetic Whiggish views.

Brady had shown and Temple seen how very difficult it would be to attempt the task of composition all alone. While the one had lavished his energy on collecting and transcribing materials and the other on polishing his style, neither had been able to get beyond the Norman kings. And so it was to be again for Tyrrell. Although his first volume was speedily accomplished, it only just reached the reign of William I. Three years elapsed before another volume carried the tale to Henry III, and it took four years and two volumes more to reach the reign of Richard II (1704). A promised last volume never got into print, though Thomas Hearne thought that it might have been finished.[89] Even so, in its incomplete state, the four volumes contained more than four thousand folio pages. The work was intended to be a definitive English history, and in bulk and scope it certainly outdistanced the rest. But Tyrrell not only failed to complete his complete history, he spoiled his chances of composing a definitive work by his clumsy writing and unreconstructed Whig bias. He hoped, he wrote to Locke, that "what I have already written may not prove too tedious to nice readers."[90] But though he tried to enliven his story from time to time with occasional digressions and amusing anecdotes, his method of composition doomed him to dullness no less than Brady, and the result has been fairly described as "cumbrous and ill-digested, tedious and pedantic."[91]

Tyrrell betrayed his purpose even in the preface to the first volume. There he takes up the familiar notion that England still lacked an acceptable history and he offers his own suggestions. Certainly no previous work would do. Some of the sixteenth-century chroniclers, such as

[89]Hearne, *Remarks and Collections*, 10:367; Hearne to James West, Dec. 23, 1728, B.M. MS. Lansdowne 778, f. 105. See also *Remarks and Collections*, 2:220; 4:376; 10:77, 455.

[90]Tyrrell to Locke, July 18, 1702, in Locke, *Correspondence*, 7:653–55.

[91]See "Tyrrell, James," in *Dictionary of National Biography*, and Gough, "James Tyrrell," p. 606. John Mill recommended it when it first came out as by an author he thought "the best versed in English History of any man in the Kingdom." For the most part, political opinions seem to have determined the reaction. "None I meet with but grant it to contain several good things, nor any undertake to vindicate it from a great many faults." George Fleming to Daniel Fleming, June 15, 1697, in *The Flemings in Oxford*, 3 vols., Oxford Historical Society (Oxford, 1904–1913), 2:351. Fleming also reported that the booksellers were not satisfied and that Tyrrell would have to continue publishing by himself.

Richard Grafton and Holinshed, had furnished a lot of information, "yet not only their dry and uncouth Way of Writing and dwelling so long on the exploded Fables of Geoffrey of Monmouth, but the Stuffing of their Histories with divers mean and trivial Relations unworthy of the Dignity of the Subject, have rendered their Labours tedious and in a great measure unuseful to their Readers." Their more recent successors were better. Stow and Speed had taken the trouble to seek out manuscripts, the one improving his chronology, the other employing coins; but neither had made full use of the opportunities afforded him. Tyrrell shows almost no interest in style or form or classical models. He dismisses Bacon and Daniel as too brief; Milton as only a little better. They omitted too many documents, everything about ecclesiastical affairs, and most regrettably "the Ancient Saxon Laws and Original Constitutions of this Kingdom." Brady is, of course, severely criticized; the *Compleat History* was obviously incomplete (though still in progress), indifferent to the rights of Englishmen, and generally shameful.[92]

Tyrrell's method, then, was to preserve the chronicle form and stuff it fuller than ever with useful—that is, legal, constitutional, and ecclesiastical—facts for every year and every reign. Tyrrell learned from Brady, though perhaps not so well, to appreciate the antiquarian enterprise; he valued manuscript sources and legal documents, made some efforts at collation, and understood the importance of strictly contemporary evidence. He was scrupulous to the point of pedantry in his citations and quotations. Like Brady, he wrote long introductory essays analyzing the law and the constitution, rebutting his adversaries at every step. He was, in short, in these matters exactly like his Tory foe, a modern. And with Wotton and Bentley, he thought he must be adding to a cumulative progress of knowledge by incorporating new information, though like them he risked the charge of dullness and pedantry.[93] But his modernity, like that of all the moderns, was less than appeared, if only because he held so insistently to the substantialist notion of the repetition and continuity of the past even in the face of all evidence for change.

Of the history itself little more needs to be said. In the British Library there is a copy of Tyrrell's work with his own annotations, meant perhaps for a second edition. His scissors-and-paste method of composition could hardly be plainer, for he simply adds (or occasionally subtracts) at each chronological point. There is no sense of classical proportion or coherence, and very little reconstruction or description. Tyrrell writes as though the example of the ancients did not matter, and except for a shift

---

[92]James Tyrrell, "Preface to the Reader," in *The General History of England*, 4 vols. (London, 1697–1704), 1:n.p.

[93]Tyrrell apologizes in the Preface for all those stretches not pleasant or agreeable, "since the dryness of the Matter and the barrenness of those few Authors . . . in some Periods will not always equally afford it": ibid., p. xxvii.

of emphasis—a distaste for hagiography and a predilection for the law—
his chronicle might well have been written in the Middle Ages. He uses
all kinds of documents, it is true, but rather than build his narrative out
of them, he interpolates them arbitrarily into his text. In the end, Tyrrell
himself began to despair. "That a Compleat History of England can ever
be wrote from the Records I believe no Man that understands any thing
of it, as he should do, will be so bold as to Affirm."[94] In the preface to the
second volume, he gave up the title of historian altogether. "These Collections (for I shall not presume to give them the Title of a Complete
History), being Register'd in a due and exact Order of time, may at least
deserve the name of Annals." He had never pretended to "exact or elegant Writing," he had meant only to set the record straight, to correct
and improve upon Brady. He had always preferred, he wrote to Locke,
"the Character of a true before that of a fine writer, which I do not
pretend to."[95]

Tyrrell's chief design had always been to defend the ancient constitution against its enemies.[96] And as we have seen, this objective often
betrayed him into anachronistic judgments, though he easily saw
through Brady's unhistorical absolutism. Like Temple and his Whig
predecessors, he accepted the essentially "Gothic" nature of the constitution, with the Saxon witenagemot as the forerunner of Parliament and
the basic continuity of English legal and political institutions. Among
other things, he was forced to accept some fraudulent documents, such
as The Mirror of Justices, which Brady had correctly denied. To do so
Tyrrell had to improvise arguments not unlike the Christ Church wits
defending The Epistles of Phalaris.[97] It is startling, then, to find Tyrrell
coming slowly around to the conclusion that the whole vast enterprise,
the great Whig collaboration to reconstruct the past and undo the Tory
history, was unnecessary and perhaps irrelevant. (It is possible that John
Locke had seen this from the beginning.)[98] In the introduction to his final

[94]Ibid., 3:xv.

[95]Tyrrell to Locke, July 4, 1704, in Locke, Correspondence, 8:339–40; Tyrrell, General
History, 2:xvi, xix. He had tried for a mean between "a lofty and florid Stile, which is not
proper for an Historian," and "a mean abject way of writing, below the dignity of the
Subject" (p. xxiii).

[96]"To shew the Excellency of our English Constitution [and] the danger in departing
from it": General History, Preface.

[97]"Tho' it be accounted by some of but a doubtful Authority . . . if it were taken out of
some old Saxon Monument now lost . . . this Passage [about the election of the monarch
and the original contract] may serve as a great Proof": ibid., 1:xlix–l and 308. William
Nicolson also caught the anachronisms in the Mirror; see his letter to Thomas Wood (1699)
defending his views in the English Historical Library, B.M. MS. Add. 34265, ff. 45–46.

[98]But Locke eventually recommended Tyrrell's General History; see "Some Thoughts
Concerning Reading and Study for a Gentleman (1703)," in The Educational Writings of John
Locke, ed. James L. Axtell (Cambridge, 1968), p. 400; Locke to Richard King, Aug. 25,
1703, in Locke, Correspondence, 8:56–60. And he seems to have encouraged Tyrrell to
continue; see Correspondence, 8:272–73.

volume, Tyrrell remarks that after four hundred continuous years in Parliament there was really no way of calling the rights of the commons into question, especially when the balance of property, "and consequently of Power," was now in the hands of the gentry and freeholders. In short, it no longer seemed to matter whether the commons had been represented before that (or indeed even as long as that). Tyrrell was willing now to find the whole matter "dark and profound," clouded by political bias and a lack of reliable evidence. In the meanwhile, Brady died, and his promised continuation (1700), which had carried the story through the fourteenth century, failed to address Tyrrell.[99] Curiously, the new Whigs were beginning to find some use for Brady's arguments, first during the Convocation Controversy, then later when Walpole adopted them! Somehow, Tyrrell's own effort was beginning to lose point in the new political situation, and even he began to feel "that it now seems rather a Question relating to Antiquity, than to the present Constitution of Government."[100] Tyrrell was almost prepared to detach the distant past altogether and leave it safely to the disinterested inspection of philologists and antiquaries. Only a lingering notion that it was still vital to remind the young of the defense of their ancient rights and privileges kept him to his original purpose—though, to be sure, the last volume of his work never appeared and may never have been written.

So Temple had been right after all. "If you pretend to make most of your history de novo," he had warned, "it will either take up many years doing, or you will prove but a second edition of Sir Richard Baker."[101] "We have had a Locke, a Newton, and a Dryden," wrote an anonymous author in 1742, repeating the common observation, "but we cannot boast a Livy, a Thucydides, or a Tacitus."[102] In history, as in poetry, it was still hard, if not impossible, to deny the superiority of the ancients.

[99]Robert Brady, A Continuation of the Complete History of England (London, 1700). Brady seems to have died before writing a preface or analytic essays. His work was undoubtedly slowed by loss of proximity to the documents after 1689; see Thomas Swift to Brady, July 2, 1692, Bodleian MS. Smith 59, f. 3.

[100]Tyrrell, General History, 3:i, v. For the appropriation by the Tories of the "Whig history," see Isaac Kramnick, "Augustan Politics and English Historiography: The Debate on the English Past, 1730–35," History and Theory 6 (1967): 33–56.

[101]Thomas Swift to Richard Bentley, in Letters of Several Eminent Persons, Including the Correspondence of John Hughes, ed. J. Duncombe (London, 1772), p. 7.

[102]Collection of State Letters of the First Earl of Orrery (1742), quoted in M. A. Thomson, Some Developments in English Historiography during the Eighteenth Century, University College Inaugural Lecture (London, 1957), p. 11. Lawrence Echard's History of England, 2 vols. (London, 1707–1718) was another effort at a complete history that seems to have been stimulated by Temple's scheme and relies on his Introduction. The first volume, which carried the story from Julius Caesar to James I, may even have been intended as an introduction to Kennett's volume of the Complete History, though Echard eventually completed it by himself. See Deborah Stephan, "Lawrence Echard: Whig Historian," Historical Journal 32 (1989): 843–66.

Chapter Eleven

Moderns

I

Meanwhile the moderns were hard at work. If the history of England could not be perfectly represented as narrative, then perhaps it could be reconstructed as a body of antiquities. In that case, there was a model already in place: William Camden's famous *Britannia*. It remained only to see whether that familiar work could be brought up to date as a collaborative new enterprise in scholarship. "We have the best stock of true remains of antiquity of any nation perhaps in Europe," wrote William Nicolson in 1694, "and yet our histories hitherto have been most lazily written."[1] Once again it was the publishers who led the way. Apparently the idea had already been bruited in 1690–91, perhaps encouraged by a new life of Camden by Thomas Smith, but it was the young printer Abel Swalle who seriously undertook the task a couple of years later. "Swalle is here with big words about the Britannia in English," wrote a skeptical Edward Bernard from Oxford, "promising great and accurate maps of each county: but it would be more for the honor of Mr. Cambden and the use of Scholars, to have that immortal worke represented again in the Latine and with his additions."[2] But this was to treat the *Britannia* as a

---

[1] Nicolson to Thoresby, May 7, 1694, in *Letters to Ralph Thoresby*, ed. W. T. Lancaster (Leeds, 1912), p. 162.

[2] Edward Bernard to Thomas Smith, n.d., Bodleian MS. Smith 47, f. 108. On July 9, 1690, Bernard had written to Smith that the printer Chiswell was designing a *Britannia*, but he doubted that it would ever be: ibid., f. 68. Many years later Hearne recalled that about 1691, Thomas Gale intended to reprint the *Britannia* in Oxford: Thomas Hearne, *Remarks and Collections*, ed. C. E. Doble et al., 11 vols. (Oxford, 1885–1921), 3:53; he himself thought several times of attempting a Latin version; see Hearne to Cherry, Sept. 23, 1708, Bodleian MS. Rawlinson Letters 36, f. 313; Hearne to Brokesby, Mar. 10, 1711, Rawlinson D 1170, f. 16; Charlett to Hearne, June 27, 1715, Rawlinson Letters 14, f. 348. Smith's *Gulielmi Camdeni Vita* appeared in 1691.

classic with a fixed content, and Swalle was undoubtedly right to think
of improvement and to aim at a larger audience. Still, the project proved
too ambitious for him, and he had to find a partner. In 1693 he was
joined by the very respectable Awnsham Churchill, and that seemed
enough to assure the success of the work.[3]

In 1693 Swalle and Churchill advertised their proposals and called for
contributions. The response was remarkable. Camden's original work
seems to have been known to almost everyone, either in Latin or in
English translation. Its popularity was a result of its initial success in
completing the heroic effort begun two generations earlier by Henry
VIII's antiquarian, John Leland. Leland had been the first to see the value
of canvassing all the original sources of English history, both written and
archaeological, and to take an inventory of them in a geographical fashion.[4] He taught his successors the importance of the literary documents
and the monumental remains, especially the ancient manuscripts, coins,
and inscriptions, for retrieving and understanding the past; and he saw
the need to recover the lost languages of ancient Britain, Latin of course,
but also Celtic and Anglo-Saxon. His notes were read and copied by
successive generations of English antiquaries who tried to contribute one
way or another to his project, right down to the battle of the books,
when Thomas Hearne finally edited and published most of them.
Camden was Leland's heir (some said his plagiary), and he was able to
realize Leland's ambition in a masterful survey of British antiquities systematically arranged by county. He added new information to each of
the successive editions of his book (1586–1607) and was helped by contributors throughout England, eager to celebrate and memorialize their
local monuments. In 1610 the *Britannia* received an English translation by
Philemon Holland which was reprinted in 1637.[5]

The *Britannia* was a wonderful exercise in antiquarian erudition by a

---

[3]"Mr. Swall does not perhaps in some respects deserve a better character than you have
heard of him but I believe he will perform his proposals and Mr. Churchill who is joyntly
concerned with him in the undertaking is a very honest and substantial man and there is no
question that betwixt them 'twill be well performed both for their reputation and for
Profit": John Woodward to Edward Lhwyd, July 13 [1693?], Bodleian MS. Ashmole
1817b, f. 362. Dunton draws a lively sketch of Swalle, "the owner of a good deal of wit and
learning," but whose fortunes had already fallen by 1705, in *The Life and Errors of John
Dunton*, ed. J. Nichols, 2 vols. (London, 1818), 1:299.

[4]For what follows, see Joseph M. Levine, "The Antiquarian Enterprise," in *Humanism
and History* (Ithaca, N.Y., 1987), pp. 73–106. John Leland's *Itineraries* and *Collectanea* were
published by Hearne in fifteen volumes, 1710–1715; the *Commentarii de scriptoribus Britan-
nicis* by Anthony Hall (Oxford, 1709). Leland may not have held an official post as *anti-
quarius* but he certainly aspired to the position; see Arnaldo Momigliano, "Ancient History
and the Antiquarian," in *Studies in Historiography* (New York, 1966), pp. 38–39.

[5]See Levine, *Humanism and History*, pp. 79–98, and the literature cited there, especially
F. J. Levy, "The Making of Camden's *Britannia*," *Bibliothèque d'humanisme et Renaissance* 26
(1964): 70–97; Stuart Piggott, "William Camden and the *Britannia*," *Proceedings of the British
Academy* 38 (1951): 199–217.

schoolmaster familiar with the latest and best in European scholarship. What saved it from the usual fate of serious learning was its obvious appeal to the governing classes of the nation. The *Britannia* managed to combine an overall view of the British Isles with a scrupulous attention to local detail. One could find in it for the first time a complete description of the kingdom, both topographical and historical, along with an inventory of local antiquities and much genealogy. (The original came with a complete set of county maps, almost the first such atlas produced in England.) A long preparatory essay recounted the history of Britain through the successive peoples that had come to live in the island, rather than the great deeds of state and church. One could see the island as a whole and as never before, while at the same time every country gentleman could find something of interest in his own neighborhood. As an exercise in patriotic and local sentiment, the *Britannia* could hardly be surpassed. As an exercise in ponderous modern scholarship, it could easily be forgiven.

Swalle and Churchill must have been very encouraged by the response to their advertisement and their queries for information. They received offerings from many parts of England. From Lancashire came information about the discovery of Saxon coins and a list of forgotten earls, as well as the promise of a corrected map.[6] From Chester news came of a freshly discovered Roman altar, "so authentic a piece of Antiquity, I presum'd it very proper for the present Edition of Camden." A letter from John Foxcroft told of the discovery of "the Footsteps of two Roman Stations upon the Fosse between Leicester and Lincoln, not taken notice of by Camden or any other." There were descriptions of a silver plate found near Ely, a Roman inscription in Monmouthshire, several collections of medals at Cambridge, an account of the antiquities at Bath, and so on. John Evelyn could offer little at the moment except encouragement, but he suggested consulting John Aubrey and Thomas Gale.[7] The publishers approached John Locke, who turned them over to James Tyrrell, who thought that he could make a contribution to "that usefull worke."[8] To Ralph Thoresby in Leeds the printers wrote to ask for coins and inscriptions; they promised to spare no cost or charge to make good on their proposals.[9] In reply to their queries, they also received much

[6]For what follows, see the letters collected in Bodleian MS. Dep. C 225–26.

[7]John Evelyn to Awnsham Churchill, Aug. 23, 1693, Christ Church Evelyn Letterbook, 2:171.

[8]"Tho' they are not concerning Coynes or Inscriptions . . . but what I have collected as to seates of ancient Familyes and some natural things I shall transcribe and communicate": Tyrrell to Locke, Oct. 26, 1693, in *The Correspondence of John Locke*, ed. E. S. de Beer, 8 vols. (Oxford, 1976–1989), 4:732–34.

[9]Churchill and Swalle to Thoresby, June 29, 1693, in Lancaster, *Letters to Thoresby*, pp. 26–27. By September, Churchill was asking Thoresby to take on the whole of the West Riding: D. H. Atkinson, *Ralph Thoresby, the Topographer: His Town and Times*, 2 vols. (Leeds, 1885, 1887), 1:73.

information about natural history. The proposals were spread around the coffeehouses of Norwich by Edward Barnes. "I shall doe what in me lyes to assist you in as much as I become a subscriber and labourer for my selfe as well as the publique." And there was advice even about the printing and annotation.[10] Thomas Machell was willing to send some drawings of altars and inscriptions but only on condition that the whole figures of the stones be carefully engraved, "since I designed them to be embellished to my native County, and doe rob myself of them (for they are taken out of my Antiquities of Westmorland and Cumberland)." For his labor he expected a suitable gratuity.[11]

Swalle's first editor died unexpectedly in 1693 and for a moment the project faltered. The publishers turned to that indefatigable busybody and patron of learning, the master of University College, Oxford, Arthur Charlett, who promptly recommended for the job a brilliant young student named Edmund Gibson.[12] Gibson was then only twenty-four years old, but he was already the editor of two celebrated texts, Quintilian's *Institutes* and the *Anglo-Saxon Chronicle*. Hearne thought the first carelessly done, and in fact it did not pretend to great erudition;[13] the second was more original. The *Anglo-Saxon Chronicle* had been discovered and indeed printed some years before by Abraham Wheloc as an appendix to his edition of Bede. (Here were some of the materials that Temple had ignored but that were essential to any attempt at Anglo-Saxon history.) Bishop Fell and John Mill asked William Nicolson to try again, taking advantage of some new manuscripts. Nicolson was preoccupied, however, and the job fell to his young friend, who promptly received his encouragement and criticism.[14] It was about this time also

---

[10]"If any persons send you Additions to Camden where the sence ought to be continuous, I should think it most gratefull to the Reader if they were printed in the worke it selfe but in an Italick letter and with a Starr . . . prefixed to them; as for marginal notes, they should be used where Cambden is corrected without a continuation of sense": John Beaumont to Churchill, n.d., Bodleian MS. Dep. C 226, ff. 283–84.

[11]Thomas Machell to John Houghton (intended for Swalle), Aug. 3, 1693, Bodleian MS. Dep. C 226, f. 400. For Machell, see John Rogan and Eric Birley, "Thomas Machell, the Antiquary," *Transactions of the Cumberland and Westmorland Society* n.s. 55 (1956): 132–53.

[12]For Charlett as "Abraham Froth," see *Spectator*, no. 43 (Apr. 19, 1711); according to Hearne, he was commonly call "the Oxford Gazeteer," but Hearne recognized him eventually as a genuine patron of learning; see *Remarks and Collections*, 1:214–15, 236–36; 3:153–54; 4:55. For Gibson, see Norman Sykes, *Edmund Gibson* (London, 1926). The first editor was a Mr. Harrington of Christ Church, "a gentleman of vast acquaintance and interest who had undertaken the management of most part of it": Edward Lhwyd to John Lloyd, Feb. 4, 1693, in *Archaeologia Cambrensis* 7 (1861): 32–33.

[13]Hearne, *Remarks and Collections*, 1:29. Gibson did collate three manuscripts and eight printed editions but confined his notes to variants. It was printed as *De institutione oratoria* (Oxford, 1692).

[14]"You cannot imagine what a reputation it will be to your self, your College and your Country, to engage yourself heartily in the work": Mill to Nicolson, Oct. 10, 1686,

(1693) that Gibson helped to draft a commencement address favoring Anglo-Saxon study and inveighing against those whose "hands are so delicate that they dare not handle parchments covered with dirt and dust," and whose "minds are too tender to be able to bear the more repulsive sight of Saxon, Gothic, or Runic script."[15] Unfortunately, Gibson mistook the several manuscripts of the chronicle to be different recensions of the same text, as though written by a single author rather than by different witnesses, and he conflated all without distinction. This was a natural enough error for a classicist unfamiliar with the peculiarities of medieval composition, and it left difficulties of interpretation that were not resolved until the late nineteenth century.[16] But it was a service still to have made the work available to historians (with a close Latin translation) and to have reaffirmed the importance of Anglo-Saxon studies to the history of the nation. Many years later, Gibson disclosed a new intention to make the same point. "I have a great desire to make the Saxon Chronicle a Complete Work by additions which may be had from other Manuscripts and by reducing every piece of History whatever that has been originally written in Saxon, and may be determin'd to a certain year or nearly, into one body of Saxon Annales with proper distinctions to show from whence anything is taken." Thus he would present at a single view everything of value to Anglo-Saxon history, "from which Circumstance there is no doubt but all our ancient Histories derive their

---

Bodleian MS. Add. C 217, f. 68. Gibson thanked Nicolson in the Preface; Nicolson returned his somewhat embarrassed gratitude. See Nicolson to Gibson, Sept. 22, 1692, ibid., f. 3; and Gibson to Nicolson, Aug. 23, 1692, ibid., f. 63, where Charlett is revealed as his principal patron.

[15]The address is attributed to Thomas Hooper, *Linguae avitae septentrionales postliminio recuperatae*, and was printed in *Theatri oxoniensis encaenia* (Oxford, 1693); see David Fairer, "Anglo-Saxon Studies," in *History of the University of Oxford: The Eighteenth Century*, ed. L. S. Sutherland and L. G. Mitchell (Oxford, 1986), p. 815. Gibson mentions his part in a "declamation upon the Septentrional Tongues": Gibson to Charlett, Apr. 20, 1694, Bodleian MS. Ballard 5, f. 30.

[16]See *Two of the Saxon Chronicles Parallel*, ed. Charles Plummer and John Earle (Oxford, 1899), pp. cxxviii–cxxxi; David Douglas, *English Scholars*, 2d ed. (London, 1951), pp. 69–71. Of the five manuscripts that he used (three more than Wheloc), Gibson writes, "One of them is certainly the very original Book, that formerly was kept in the church of Peterborow. . . . Yet it must be said of the other four, that each of them contains a great many things that are not in any of the rest. Soe that the method they seem to have observ'd in drawing up their Chronicles, is this, to lay before them what was agreed upon by the Councill; and to interweave with it the Histories of particular places. . . . Out of these is now published one entire *Saxon Chronicle* the method whereof is this. Whatever new matter is in one, which is wanting in the rest, that is inserted in the Text in its proper place, with notice given at the bottom of the page by a letter of Reference to which of the Copies it is owing. But where Copies agree . . . and differ only in expression, the best expression is put at the bottom. . . . The Latin Version, answering the Saxon text line for line, is almost word for word. . . . To the Book are added three Indexes": Bodleian MS. Tanner 25, f. 12; see also Gibson to Nicolson, Oct. 29, 1691, Bodleian MS. Add. C 217, f. 59. The text was printed as *Cronicon Saxonicum* (Oxford, 1692).

chief Authority."[17] Unfortunately, he never found the time to complete the work.

Gibson was ambitious, personable, and destined for high office in the Church of England, eventually as bishop of London. He had proved his skill as an editor and his interest in English antiquities with several projects still in the works.[18] Could the publishers have hit upon a better choice to edit the new *Britannia*? Yet Gibson struck a hard bargain. When he looked over the translations that had been done so far, he found them harsh and uneven, and had to persuade the undertakers that they must be done all over again, regardless of the cost. They gave him a free hand to choose the new translators and discussed raising the fees. "They have invited me, if I please, to dine constantly at one of their houses without any charge, but that I shall decline, that I may not seem to depend on them too much." To Charlett, Gibson reported that Swalle and Churchill had met nearly every one of his demands; it was agreed to submit any disputes to Charlett's arbitration.[19]

Gibson set about his work with a relish. First he had to resume contact with John Evelyn, William Nicolson, and all those who had already been asked to contribute. Then he had to find others, such as his friend Thomas Tanner, to fill out the team. Initially it was hoped to assign each county to an individual, and in fact most of the work was accomplished that way. (Nicolson, for example, took care of Northumberland; Tanner, with Aubrey's help, Wiltshire.) Edward Lhwyd was approached for several Welsh counties and eventually took on the whole.[20] In the early months of 1694, Gibson wrote letters and made the rounds. He visited, among others, Samuel Pepys, "who stoutly defended the design of our English Camden according to our model, against a certain Doctor in company that insisted upon a Latin one." While there, he wangled an invitation to dinner with Thomas Gale and Richard Bentley.[21] He called upon Obadiah Walker, who had undertaken to write the notes for the eight or nine plates of coins that were projected, forty or fifty medals to a plate. He found that "the old Gentleman relishes a Coyn as well as ever."

[17]Gibson to Charlett, Jan. 2, 1720, Bodleian MS. Ballard 6, ff. 139–40.
[18]According to White Kennett, Gibson, having completed the chronicle, "is now designing K. Alfred's Saxon Translation of St. Gregory's Pastoral. . . . He further intends a new edition of the Saxon laws imperfectly and corruptly published by Mr. Lambert, and to restore other Monuments of Antiquity of the like nature, for which he is absolutely qualified." He was also assisting in the publication of Somner's *Roman Ports and Forts*. See Kennett to Samuel Blackwell, n.d., B.M. MS. Lansdowne 1013, f. 248. All these projects were eventually completed, though not all by Gibson.
[19]Gibson to Charlett, Dec. 24, 1693, Bodleian MS. Ballard 5, f. 13; Gibson to Thomas Tanner, Jan. 25, 1694, Bodleian MS. Tanner 25, ff. 114–15.
[20]See Gwynn Walters and Frank Emery, "Edward Lhwyd, Edmund Gibson, and the Printing of Camden's *Britannia*, 1695," *The Library* 5th ser. 32 (1977): 109–36.
[21]Gibson to Charlett, May 12 and 19, 1694, Bodleian MS. Ballard 5, ff. 14, 35.

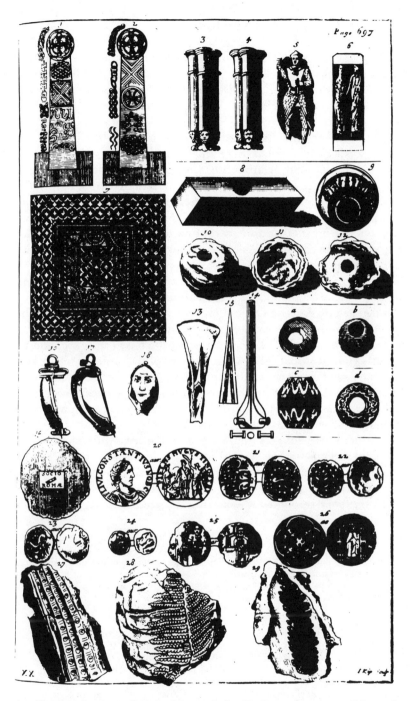

An illustrated page of antiquities and fossils from the new edition of Camden's *Britannia*, ed. Edmund Gibson (1695), reproduced by permission of Princeton University Libraries

Arrangements were made for Robert Morden to do the maps and for the naturalist John Ray to supply a catalogue of plants for each county, and thus to "secure us the Botanists and Natural Philosophers.[22] What between herbs, camps, highways, families, etc.," Gibson exulted, "we shall have meat for all palats!"[23]

Gibson urged the contributors to send him the new material undigested, so that he could write up the additions in a uniform style. Unlike Temple and the editor of the *Complete History*, he believed that an "inequalitie of stile and composition . . . must needs prove a great deformitie in the whole." This required great tact, especially since it meant incorporating and also excising information sent by many different contributors. He hoped that proper acknowledgments in the preface and the text would obviate the problem.[24] As a principle of selection, Gibson thought to include everything that Camden himself would have used had he known of it; as for corrections, there would be nothing to disparage the great man "more than a bare correction of the slips."[25] "If Mr. Camden had liv'd to this day," Gibson wrote in the preface, "he had been still adding and altering; and had (no doubt) left his *Britannia* much more complete." By April 1694 the publishers had chosen the paper and Gibson was confident that there was no danger of the project's miscarrying. Only an unexpected frost that winter held up the binding and delayed publication. "I have often observed," his friend Tanner wrote to him with satisfaction, "that there are no men so ready to communicate, and do mutual offices of kindness one to another, as Antiquaries."[26]

Gibson's indebtedness to antiquarian generosity is duly acknowledged throughout the *Britannia*. Almost every English scholar of consequence seems to have contributed. The preface singles out Pepys and Evelyn, Tanner and Thoresby, Kennett and Nicolson, among many others; while scattered through the text are the names of many more.[27] For

[22]"I told them that I had indeed by me some Observations made in my Simpling voyages . . . if they thought it might be acceptable to the Readers or advantageous to the sale of the Book, I would collect and send them with Catalogues of the locall Plants in each County": Ray to Lhwyd, June 1, 1694, in Ray, *Further Correspondence*, ed. R. T. Gunther (London, 1928), pp. 244–47. Walker (1616–1699) was a Catholic fallen upon hard times, the author of, among other things, *The Greek and Roman History Illustrated by Coins and Medals* (London, 1692). For the *Britannia*, Walker was given help by Ralph Thoresby; see Lancaster, *Letters to Thoresby*, pp. 31–32.

[23]Gibson to Charlett, Mar. 19, 1694, Bodleian MS. Ballard 5, f. 14.

[24]Gibson to Charlett, Feb. 1, 1694, Bodleian MS. Ballard 5, ff. 21–22.

[25]Gibson to Charlett, Mar. 31, 1694, Bodleian MS. Ballard 5, ff. 23–24; May 31, 1694, in *Original Letters of Eminent Literary Men*, ed. Henry Ellis for Camden Society (London, 1843), pp. 221–22.

[26]*London Gazette*, Feb. 7–11, 1695; Tanner to Gibson, scribbled on the back of a letter, Gibson to Tanner, Jan. 30, 1694, Bodleian MS. Tanner 25, f. 117v.

[27]*Camden's Britannia, Newly Translated into English: With Large Additions and Improvements*, ed. Edmund Gibson (London, 1695), "The Preface to the Reader." See also the enumeration in Bodleian MS. Dep. C 225.

Scotland there was Sir Robert Sibbald, and for Wales, we have seen,
Gibson had the special help of Edward Lhwyd. Lhwyd was then keeper
of the Ashmolean Museum, a brilliant young Welshman who combined
an interest in antiquities with natural history. He had just been helping
William Nicolson with the Celtic place names for his projected history of
Northumbria when he was approached by Swalle to do two or three
counties in North Wales. There was the usual haggling over payment,
but Lhwyd eventually agreed to take on the whole province. Unfortunately, the undertakers would not pay him to take a trip through the
country, "their business being only to procure subscribers, the which
they have allready done to their satisfaction . . . and in order to make a
great noyse, but not to extend their purses much." But then booksellers
were always "back friends to learning."[28] Lhwyd was reduced to asking
for help from his Welsh friends, who responded generously, and to
circulating queries. Most agreed that it was "a very needfull, as well as
usefull, undertaking."[29] Although one of his correspondents "railed"
against Camden for his errors, Lhwyd was convinced that the great
scholar had done his work very well and that he should be treated civilly.
"But as to what we can adde or correct, I make no question were he
alive, but he would be thankfull for it; for he seems to have been a man of
very candid temper."[30] It was intrinsic to the antiquarian enterprise to
believe in scholarly progress.

When Gibson took over, he told Lhwyd that the additions would have
to be brief and uniform, "contrary to the agreement we made at first
with the printers." One friend advised Lhwyd to quit, and he learned
that Kennett was giving up on Oxfordshire for that very reason, but in
the end he submitted. His own plans for something grander were already
forming. "If I gain any credit by this its not unlikely but our own gentry
may be hereafter willing to encourage something more considerable." In
the end (with Nicolson's advice), Gibson treated him very favorably,
printing all that he sent and engraving all the figures. When it appeared,
Thomas Hearne thought that it was the best part of the Britannia. If
Lhwyd could not pretend yet to have made "any curious search into the

[28]Lhwyd to Richard Mostyn, Jan. 11, 1695, in Nesta Lloyd, "The Correspondence of
Edward Lhuyd and Richard Mostyn," Flintshire Historical Society Publications 25 (1971–72):
51–52. See also Lhwyd to Swalle, n.d., Bodleian MS. Dep. C 225, f. 92v.

[29]Nicholas Roberts to Lhwyd, Aug. 21, 1693, in F. V. Emery, "A New Reply to
Lhwyd's Parochial Queries," National Library of Wales Journal 10 (1957–58): 397–99.

[30]The unidentified quotations in this paragraph are from letters of May 16, May 23,
Aug. 4, Oct. 9, and Oct. 10, 1693, in R. T. Gunther, Life and Letters of Edward Lhwyd, Early
Science in Oxford 14 (Oxford, 1945), pp. 191–93, 197–203, 207–8. A copy of Lhwyd's
queries for the Britannia is in the Penros Collection, Bangor University Library, 4:929. (My
thanks to Clyve Jones for the transcript.) It was obviously the inspiration for the queries
used later by Lhwyd for his own Archaeologia; see A Design of a British Dictionary Historical
and Geographical; with an Essay entitled "Archaeologia Britannica" and a Natural History of Wales
(1695), in Gunther, pp. 13–16. The Parochial Queries (1696) follow.

monuments of his Country," he had at least mapped out what was to become his life's work.[31]

Among the many contributors, it looks as though only Thomas Smith failed to get his due for furnishing the materials for Gibson's life of Camden.[32] Charlett was acknowledged as the general benefactor and foremost promoter, and the work was dedicated with careful deliberation to John Lord Somers, lord keeper of the Great Seal and a known friend to learning. The *Britannia* was thus in nearly every respect the perfect embodiment of the modernist commitment to the collaborative advancement of learning. Naturally, it was still imperfect; for the moderns the future always promised improvement. "Rome was not built in a day," wrote Abraham de la Pryme in his diary, " . . . every age sees something more than another and every Year almost some Monuments are digg'd up out of the Earth some where or other that was not discover'd before." Or as Thomas Tanner put it with satisfaction in 1695, "The Advances that all fruits of Learning have within these few Years made in England are very obvious; but the progress is visible in nothing more than in the illustrations of our own History and Antiquities."[33] The Augustans may well have despaired at matching the ancients in modern narrative; in antiquities they had not the slightest hesitation in setting the new Camden, like the old one, against the examples of Strabo and Pausanias. Even Locke thought that every English gentleman should own a copy. Nor is it surprising that Gibson was soon at work again on a new enlarged version of the *Britannia*; and that almost a century later, it should be attempted yet another time.[34]

2

The popularity of the *Britannia* shows that the gap between learning and polite literature was not absolute; and indeed, it was generally be-

[31]See Lhwyd to John Lloyd, St. David's Day, 1694, *Archaeologia Cambrensis* 3d ser. 5 (1859): 161–62; Gunther, *Life and Letters of Lhwyd*, pp. 227–28; Lhwyd to Richard Mostyn, Mar. 8, 1694; to Martin Lister, Nov. 13, 1694; and to Mostyn, Nov. 29, 1694, all in Gunther, pp. 230–32, 253–55. The printer's copy with Gibson's instructions survives and is analyzed by Walters and Emery (n. 20 above).

[32]See Hearne, *Remarks and Collections*, 3:65.

[33]*The Diary of Abraham de la Pryme* (1695), ed. Charles Jackson, Surtees Society Publications 54 (Durham, 1869), p. 60; Thomas Tanner, *Notitia monastica* (Oxford, 1695), Preface.

[34]John Locke, "Some Thoughts Concerning Reading and Study," in *The Works of John Locke*, 10 vols. (London, 1824), 10:409. For the comparison of Camden with Strabo and Pausanias, see Gibson's "Life of Mr. Camden," in *Camden's Britannia*, n.p. Gibson had actually completed a new edition by 1710, though it did not appear until 1722, in two folio volumes; see Gibson to Thoresby, Mar. 4, 1710, in *Letters of Eminent Men to Ralph Thoresby*, 2 vols. (London, 1832), 2:229; "Eight Letters from Edmund Gibson to Bishop Humphreys, 1707–1709," *National Library of Wales Journal* 10 (1957–58): 365–74; Gibson to Charlett, Oct. 30, 1718, in Ellis, *Original Letters*, p. 237. Richard Gough retranslated and enlarged the work in 1789 in three folio volumes and again in 1806 in four.

lieved that a little of antiquities, like a little philology, could well suit the man of affairs, as long as it was not overdone. From the time that Henry Peacham added a chapter on the subject to his *Complete Gentleman* (1634), it was customary to assume that the young aspirant to worldly station should begin to acquaint himself early with—perhaps even to collect— some of the antique statues, inscriptions, and coins that he was likely to encounter in his travels. The custom of furnishing a "cabinet" with these curiosities became almost universal, especially after the institution of the grand tour. Even the schools began to supplement their exclusive diet of classical texts with some reading in antiquities.[35] Nor was it forgotten that "those old memorials tend to the illustration of Historie, and of the antiquitie of divers matters, places, and cities, which otherwise would be obscure, if not altogether unknowne to us."[36] Of course, one could have too much of a good thing, and the satirists were kept busy throughout the century poking fun at pedantry and the antiquarian preference for rust. An "antiquary," it was said in 1699, is a "curious Critick in old Coins, Stones and Inscriptions, in Worm-eaten Records and ancient Manuscripts; also one that affects and blindly doats, on Relicks, Ruins, old Customs, Phrases and Fashions."[37]

Inevitably scholarship outran the need for a smattering of antiquities. Baron Ezechiel Spanheim was one of the greatest scholars of the age; he was also Brandenburg's ambassador to France and eventually to England, where he lived out the last years of a long and productive life. In 1664 he published a monumental treatise on coins which summarized the accumulated learning of two centuries: the *Dissertationes de praestantia et usu numismatum antiquorum*. He spent his old age enlarging the work, until he was able to publish a new volume in London in 1706, and another that appeared posthumously in 1717. It was a massive Latin treatise for scholars to read and appreciate; but it was a far cry from Addison's light dialogue or even Obadiah Walker's little handbook.

Walker had been the choice of Camden's editors, no doubt because of his recent work. He had spent a long life as a tutor and as master of University College, Oxford, writing some well-known if rather conventional textbooks on education, until his disgrace as a Catholic at the time of the Glorious Revolution. In 1692 he published his work, which he called *The Greek and Roman History Illustrated by Coins and Medals repre-*

---

[35]Thomas Godwin's text, for the use of the Abingdon School (1622), went through sixteen editions by 1696: *Romanae historiae anthologia: An Exposition of the Roman Antiquities wherein Roman and English Offices are parallel'd and divers obscure Phrases are explained* (Oxford, 1638). In general, see Joseph M. Levine, *Dr. Woodward's Shield:* (Berkeley, 1977), pp. 114–18, 127–29, and *Humanism and History* (Ithaca, N.Y., 1987), pp. 82–87.

[36]Henry Peacham, *Complete Gentleman*, ed. G. S. Gordon (Oxford, 1906), pp. 105–24.

[37]*A New Dictionary of the Terms Ancient and Modern of the Canting Crew* (London, 1699), quoted in Stuart Piggott, "Antiquarian Studies," in *History of Oxford: The Eighteenth Century*, ed. L. S. Sutherland and L. G. Mitchell (Oxford, 1986), p. 757.

senting their Religion, Rites, Manners, Customs, Games, Feasts, Arts and Sciences . . . Necessary for the Introduction of Youth into All the Useful Knowledge of Antiquity. It did not pretend to originality, but sufficed as a handbook to guide anyone who was "minded to furnish a Cabinet." Even its pedagogical purpose was obscured a little by its emphasis on connoisseurship. "Medals are esteemed," he writes, "1. for their Antiquity, 2. for the goodness of their Matter, 3. for their well-conservation, cleanness, and beauty, 4. for their greatness, 5. for their Erudition, 6. for their rarity, 7. to make up a series." Walker furnished some long lists of coins culled from various writers but no illustrations. Nicolson recommended it to Thoresby, but even on a popular level there was room for something better.[38]

It was John Evelyn who seized the opportunity, encouraged by Wotton and assisted by Richard Bentley. He had begun his own work on coins, he says, as an offshoot of his interest in how to furnish a library.[39] When he learned that Walker intended to write on the subject, he halted his own tract, only to resume it when he saw that improvement was still a possibility; "there being abondance of writers on this subject in all other polite European languages and but one very short and partial one in ours."[40] Even so, Evelyn did not claim to be much of a scholar (not like the "incomparably learned Spanheim")[41] and so he turned to Bentley for help. In this enterprise, as in everything else he did, Evelyn remained an amateur—a "virtuoso," in contemporary parlance—more interested in patronizing modern learning and science than actually going about it directly. Nevertheless, he did good service to modernity here as elsewhere, and his book met an obvious need. "The Reader," he hoped, "will yet find something New and Entertaining, and I hope not unusefull in this Essay."[42]

Evelyn's design for the *Numismata* is already clear in a letter he wrote

[38]Nicolson to Thoresby, July 9, 1692, in *Letters Addressed to Ralph Thoresby,* ed. W. T. Lancaster (Leeds, 1912), p. 24.

[39]Evelyn to Dr. Godolphin, Feb. 8, 1698, in *Seven Letters of John Evelyn Written between 1665–1703* (Oxford, 1914), pp. 15–16; John Evelyn, *Diary and Correspondence,* ed. William Bray, rev. Henry B. Wheatley, 4 vols. (London, 1906), 4:15–18. See also Evelyn to Henshaw, Mar. 1, 1698, in *Seven Letters,* pp. 17–19. Evelyn had translated Gabriel Naudé, *Instructions Concerning Erecting a Library* (London, 1661); by 1689 he seems to have been contemplating a reprint with some observations on coins.

[40]Evelyn to Tooke, June 2, 1694, in Evelyn, *Diary and Correspondence* 3:478–79.

[41]Evelyn to Godolphin, in *Seven Letters,* pp. 15–16. Evelyn makes another deferential reference to Spanheim in a letter to the Archbishop of Canterbury, Feb. 20, 1697, Christ Church Evelyn Letter-book, 2:231.

[42]"To the Reader," in John Evelyn, *Numismata: A Discourse of Medals* (London, 1697). In the same year a French treatise by Louis Jobert was translated by Roger Gale as *The Knowledge of Medals; or, Instructions for Those Who Apply Themselves to the Study of Medals Both Ancient and Modern* (London, 1697). It too chooses the popular ground and defers to Spanheim; see p. 61.

to Pepys in 1689. Pepys had asked for some advice about how to decorate his library with pictures of men "illustrious for their parts and Erudition," and this request led Evelyn to a typically garrulous reply. He considers portrait paintings at some length and then turns to medals. "Men curious of Books and Antiquities have ever had Medalls in such estimation, and rendered them a most necessary furniture to their Libraries: because by them we are not onely inform'd whose Image and Superscription they beare, but have discover'd in the Reverses, what heroic Exploits they perform'd, what famous Temples, Thermae, Amphitheaters, Triumphal Arches, Bridges, Aqueducts, Circus's, Naumachiae, and other pompous structures were rendered by them, which have been greatly Assistant to the Recovery of the Antient and magnificent Architecture." For the moment, Evelyn allows his interest in contemporary building to carry him away. But he returns to the subject eventually and to the peculiar value of medals in portraying legislators, poetic heroes, philosophers, and others; in helping to understand the ancient weights and measures and the value of money; and in showing the effigies of emperors and popes in chronological series. For the moment he passes over the tricky problem of authenticating coins and medals, "the filing, sharpnesse and due extancy, Politure, Varnish and other markes critically necessary to be skill'd in, to prevent being impos'd on by Copies for Originals," and he refers Pepys instead to the large literature on the subject, "above all, the most learned Spanhemius." He offers some practical advice about buying and some information about English collections, before going on to other matters.[43]

In June 1694 Evelyn sent his printer some copy and some medals from his old friends the Earl of Clarendon and Robert Plot for engraving.[44] He was contributing now to the *Britannia* and beginning to support his two new friends, Wotton and Bentley, in their defense of modern learning. He had managed to get Bentley appointed the first Boyle lecturer and he tried (unsuccessfully) to get Wotton appointed as his successor. In return, Bentley offered to help him with the *Numismata*, and Wotton with his new edition of *Sylva*.

Bentley's contribution was to edit Evelyn's text and see it through the press. In January 1695 he called upon the publisher, Tooke, for the first time and took home two copies of the first sheets, "one to write my Alterations in, which I have done with so much freedom and simplicity;

---

[43]I quote from Evelyn to Pepys, Aug. 26, 1689, in *The Carl Pforzheimer Library: English Literature, 1475–1700*, 3 vols. (New York, 1940), 3:1216–26; there is a variant dated August 12, 1689, in Evelyn, *Diary and Correspondence* 3:434–56.

[44]Evelyn to Tooke, June 2, 1694, in Evelyn, *Diary and Correspondence*, 3:478–79. A series of letters from Tooke to Evelyn, 1694–1697, chronicling the slow progress of the printing, is in Christ Church Correspondence, Evelyn XI, nos. 1253–62.

such seeming fastidiousness and Hypercritic (though most free from all
Livor and dens caninus), that I should fear to send them, but that I am
convinced of the excellent candour and honesty of Mr. Evelyn's temper.
The other I send you with a blank margent, to excerpt what you like out
of my Writing, and make a sheet for the Press according to your own
mind." He hoped Evelyn would exercise the same freedom in changing
or rejecting his suggestions that he had taken in offering them.[45] Progress
was slow and the corrections were many: some typographical, some
stylistic, some substantive. Bentley's philological learning was especially
helpful in saving Evelyn from errors. Once at least he offered two whole
paragraphs, "one about the Greek money, and another about reducing
the Ancient money to our modern Computation." And another time he
had a rare medal drawn for Evelyn's use.[46] Evelyn was grateful, though
he despaired that his work would become an antiquity itself before it
appeared. The need to engrave a hundred plates did not help. In the end,
he was so exasperated by the printers' errors that he added to the preface
a line about their work which had to be excised: "Finding it so miserably
deformed through the confident Undertakers." Tooke objected and
Bentley thought it might hinder the sale of the book.[47] Evelyn agreed
and the tract finally appeared in 1697, just as Bentley was publishing his
own dissertation on Phalaris and using the evidence of ancient coins to
make his case.

Evelyn's *Numismata* was subtitled *A Discourse of Medals Ancient and
Modern*; and as this suggests, he neglected common coins and ordinary
money to concentrate on those particular pieces that were struck to
commemorate special occasions, "such Medals as relate purely to something historical."[48] On the whole, he follows the scheme laid down in his
letter to Pepys. He writes in his usual discursive fashion about the use of
medals and their classification, about their portraits, reverses, and inscriptions; and he adds some instructions about how to collect, authenticate, and arrange a collection. Another chapter, which Bentley agreed
should be the last, treats physiognomy, leaving the reader (Bentley added tactfully) "with an appetite and a wish that the Book were longer."[49]
Perhaps the most valuable feature of the work was its copious illustrations.

Evelyn intended his treatise for a gentleman, not a scholar, but he had

[45]Bentley to Evelyn, in *The Correspondence of Richard Bentley*, ed. Christopher Wordsworth, 2 vols. (London, 1842), 1:92–95.

[46]Bentley to Evelyn, Feb. 15 and Feb. 22, 1695, in ibid., pp. 94, 114.

[47]Bentley to Evelyn, Oct. 23, 1697, in ibid., pp. 153–54.

[48]Evelyn to Robert Plot, Aug. 27, 1693, in Evelyn, *Diary and Correspondence*, 3:473. For
the moderns, he was inspired by the recent *Histoire métalique* by Jacques de Bie and M. Bizot
for France and Holland; see Evelyn to Godolphin, June 16, 1696, in ibid., 4:3–8.

[49]Bentley to Evelyn, Feb. 15, 1695, in *Correspondence of Bentley*, 3:95–96.

a genuine appreciation for the uses of modern learning. Medals were for him the "Vocal monuments of Antiquity," and they, like all other remains of the past, needed classification, explication, and criticism. They had the great advantage that they had "outlasted the most ancient Records, and transmitted to us the knowledge of a thousand things of twice a thousand years past." He applauded the uses that divines, historians, critics, and other learned men had made of them, and he listed the great scholars at home and aboad who had depended on them, from Scaliger and Lipsius to Camden, Selden, Marsham, and Greaves. He singles out especially Cuypers's *Apotheosis of Homer* and Spanheim's *Dissertationes* as *instar omnium*. He is especially insistent on the value of the reverses as indispensable aids to history, chronology, and ancient geography. He chooses a recent edition of Pliny by the Jesuit Jean Hardouin to show how that scholar was able, from the reverses of medals alone, to recover and illustrate "the true Names of diverse Regions, Rivers, Mountains, Ways, Limits and Boundaries . . . Colonies, Cities, Metropolis, their Founders, Privileges and Immunities, the Value of Moneys and Weights; the Annual *Fasti, Acta Caesarum, Aera's, Epochas*, etc. In computation of Time and Years," he concludes, "where several famous and memorable things happen'd and were perform'd, others that had been quite forgotten . . . Medals alone have preserv'd the Names of, and other Circumstances of great use in History." The labors of antiquaries had shown how "all that was heroical and great, peculiar and eminent, and properly regarding antient History, its Circumstances and Accessories, is, we see, fetcht out of Medals and their Reverses." Not only were medals "vouchers to history," they actually verified books and authors, rather than the reverse. Evelyn understood (from Spanheim) that the skeptics could be answered by these antiquities "with far more certainty than from any other perishable Records whatever."[50]

Evelyn saw that it was not only ancient history that could be served by medals, but that English history could be improved by them also. He was easily able to imagine a complete series of coins that would furnish "an Historical Discourse with a chain of Remarkable Instances, and Matters of Fact, without Fiction or Vain Hyperboles."[51] Indeed, anyone who took the trouble to read Evelyn's work, or any of the other manuals then appearing in Europe, or who bothered to leaf through the plates of the new *Britannia*, could easily see that antiquities might be used for historical purposes. But neither Evelyn nor any of the contributors to the *Britannia* had shown just how this could actually be done, how this

[50]Evelyn, *Numismata*, pp. 2–3, 51, 64, 72. For the reply of antiquaries to Pyrrhonists, see Momigliano, "Ancient History and the Antiquarian" (n. 4 above), pp. 1–39.
[51]Evelyn, *Numismata*, p. 157.

information could be joined to eloquence or employed in writing a narrative. When Evelyn received a copy of Nicolson's *English Historical Library*, with a polite notice of his own work there, he replied with a fulsome tribute to the value of history in the curriculum. "'Tis pity young gentlemen should meet with so little of this in the course of their academic studies, at least if it continues as in my time, when they were brought up to dispute on dry questions which nauseate generous spirits." An education in history "would not only grace and furnish the bar with excellent lawyers, but the nation with able persons fit for any honourable employment, to serve and speak in Parliaments and in councils; give us good magistrates and justices for reference at home and abroad; in a word, qualified patriots and pillars of state, in which this age, does not, I fear, abound."[52] Yet Evelyn's practical advice in the *Numismata* was restricted to organizing a cabinet, and he did not try to show there how any of this learning could be used for any of these purposes, except as ornament. "Mr. Evelyn has not answered my hopes upon the subject," Nicolson wrote frankly to William Wotton, "though there is a great deal of fine and gentleman like learning in his book." And Evelyn himself did not make great claims for his "rash adventure."[53] But Nicolson, who promptly added a section on English coins to his own work,[54] did little better, although the wish was certainly there. Thus even in this matter, the ancients and the moderns remained separated in the way they chose to restore and represent the past, even among those generous spirits who would have liked to forge some sort of rapprochement.

3

To all this Wotton was an interested spectator. When he received a copy of the *Numismata* from Evelyn, he wrote at once to acknowledge the gift and the mention there of his own small contribution to the subject. It seems that an old friend, Sir Philip Skippon, who had owned a fine cabinet of medals, had once sent him an account of some Saxon coins found in Suffolk, which Wotton then printed in the *Philosophical Transactions* in 1687, under their joint initials. Unfortunately, the new editors of Camden took no notice of it, "tho' I gave 'em warning and tho' there were some there which are not in their Collection." Evelyn, however,

[52]Evelyn to Nicolson, Nov. 10, 1699, in *Letters to and from William Nicolson*, ed. J. Nichols, 2 vols. (London, 1809), 1:137–45.
[53]Nicolson to Wotton, May 7, 1698; and Evelyn to Nicolson, Nov. 10, 1699, in ibid., pp. 106–8, 137–45.
[54]William Nicolson, "Of the English Medals and Coins from the Conquest to the end of Queen Elizabeth's Reign," in *The English Historical Library*, pt. 3 (London, 1699), chap. 7.

had mentioned them in the *Numismata*, and Wotton was grateful. Evelyn was equally happy with Wotton's contribution to his *Sylva*, and eager to encourage the young man's projected life of Boyle. Meanwhile, Wotton was pleased to report that he had found confirmation for one of his arguments against Temple, that the ancient place had been called Delphi, not Delphos, in a coin that was published by Hardouin.[55]

In general, Wotton's prospects must have looked pleasing at the end of 1697. It is true that it was just about then that he chose to print the second edition of his *Reflections*, and the storm that broke over Bentley's disser-tations caused him some anxiety; but the stalwart support of Evelyn, Nicolson, and others brought much comfort. The next year Gilbert Burnet, bishop of Salisbury, turned to Wotton for help with a new task. Burnet had been asked by the king to undertake the education of Princess Anne's young son, the Duke of Gloucester. From the first the little boy had been well attended, with special attention to history. From the age of four he had heard from his first tutor stories of Alexander and Caesar, Pompey, Hannibal and Scipio, Solon, Croesus, and so on.[56] When Bur-net took over, he supervised his reading in religion and virtue, history, geography, politics, and government. He too emphasized the ancient sto-ries, though from a very different point of view. "I make Xenophon's *Cyropedia* my text-book, and have already twice read that book through with him. I shall also endeavor to make the names of Alexander, falsely styled the Great, and of Julius Caesar, ever odious in his eyes. Their [example] even from the cradle infects nearly all princes with distorted principles. I ever set before him the incompatibility of true piety with superstition and cruelty."[57] It was perhaps natural for Burnet to turn to his brilliant young protégé for help. And it was as a result of this col-laboration that Wotton came to write a piece of history of his own. Although its composition was occasional—in the event, almost acci-dental—it reflects a view of history that was exactly appropriate to this champion of the moderns, who always preserved a true respect for antiq-uity and an express desire to mediate between the two.[58]

[55]Wotton to Evelyn, Jan. 20, 1698, in Evelyn, *Diary and Correspondence*, 4:19–21. Bentley had defended Wotton's usage; see the *Dissertation's upon the Epistles of Phalaris*, ed. Wilhelm Wagner (London, 1883), pp. 56–58.

[56]See Jenkin Lewis, *Memoirs of Prince William Henry, Duke of Gloucester* (London, 1789), p. 9.

[57]T. E. S. Clarke and H. C. Foxcroft, *A Life of Gilbert Burnet* (Cambridge, 1907), p. 355; Gilbert Burnet, *History of His Own Time*, 6 vols. (Oxford, 1823), 1:233, 305; 4:376–77. There are some "Directions for the Education of the Duke of Gloucester," by Edward Bernard, in Bodleian MS. Smith 4, f. 37.

[58]Richard Bentley was also drawn into the project to educate the young prince. Oxford was asked to contribute some editions of classical authors for the purpose (as had been done for the dauphin across the Channel), and Bentley advised about the Virgil; see the account of Bentley in *Biographia Britannica*, 2d ed., ed. Andrew Kippis, vol. 1 (London, 1778).

At Burnet's request, Wotton drew up some papers to help in the instruction of the young prince. They consisted of two pairs of lives of Roman emperors: Marcus Aurelius and Commodus, Elagabalus and Severus Alexander. Burnet had selected them for their moral instruction, "as the properest Examples in the whole Roman History, to Instruct a Prince how much more Glorious and Safe it is, and Happier both for Himself and for his People, to govern well than ill." To instruct a prince by the example of the ancients was of course one of the oldest and most persistent of humanist purposes. The need to reply to the expediency and immorality of Machiavellian teaching (which also depended upon the use of ancient example) had never seemed more pressing. The two pairs of imperial lives that were proposed each included a good and a bad prince; Wotton agreed that they were "the properest Instances to set Virtue and Vice, and the Consequences of them both, in a clear and full Light."[59]

So far, the exercise was ordinary enough, although the choice of these late emperors, well beyond the classical period, was a little unusual. Unfortunately, the boy died before Wotton's work could be completed and Wotton was left to try to make something of the fragments. He decided that the best thing to do would be to take the four biographies and connect them with a narrative that would supply the missing emperors and twenty-six years. That would turn his work into a continuous history and make it more intelligible. It would also make it more original, because it was not an ordinary thing to attempt to write, or rewrite, ancient history. For the party of the ancients it seemed folly to compete with the ancients on their own ground. For the moderns such a rivalry was conceivable, though not nearly so tempting as modern history. Perhaps the choice of late imperial history, a period that had produced no outstanding classical works, made the risk seem less apparent.

In fact, ancient history had been attempted only once in England since the Renaissance, and that only recently by a young man working for the booksellers, named Laurence Echard. In the preface to his *Roman History* he excused his venture on the ground that there was not one single classical work extant that told the whole story. His anxiety about his undertaking is evident in the need that he felt to find some fault with the ancients even while praising them for being "very extraordinary in their kind, and for the most part an excellent Pattern to imitate, if it be done with judgment." He recounted the flaws that the critics alleged in each of the greatest classical historians of Rome, from Dionysius Halicarnassus to Livy (a great man but too verbose and circumstantial). He himself did

---

[59]William Wotton, *The History of Rome from the Death of Antoninus Pius to the Death of Severus Alexander* (London, 1701), Preface. Wotton explains Burnet's role in the dedication, sig. A2.

not aim very high, addressing his work to students and young gentlemen in a plain and unadorned style. He hoped to provide some insight into Roman institutions such as a narrative could supply but could not be learned easily from books of "mere antiquities."[60] It was thus not enough to describe or list the tribunes of the people without furnishing a history of their creation and subsequent activities. Echard finished the first two volumes from 1695 to 1698; three more followed anonymously.[61] The second volume included the period covered by Wotton and was also addressed to the young Duke of Gloucester, who is said to have read the first volume with delight. It supplied, Echard claimed, "such variety of extraordinary Examples, proper for the instruction of Princes, such Miracles of Virtue as well as Prodigies of Vice, and such amazing Consequences of both, as are scarcely to be found in any other History." Wotton must have read the book but he does not mention it.

He seems to have had a much larger ambition. He meant to write a narrative with the usual intention of showing "the causes and springs of every Emperor's Actions,"[62] but he intended also to employ a wide range of literary and nonliterary sources to reconstruct the events and at the same time to display and criticize them as he went. Here Wotton's philological and antiquarian training were to be given full play. He admitted relying on the recent continental works of Tillemont and Dacier, who had already employed most of the ancient sources, but he was not content simply to copy them and he often disagreed, checking them carefully against the originals.[63] In addition, he intended to employ the evidence of the ancient coins throughout his work. "I have all along payd a great Deference to the Authority of Medals, in illustrating the History of every Emperor, and in fixing the Times of their greatest Actions. That is a Field which has not been so thoroughly cultivated as most others have been; and it is only lately that Learned men have had such general recourse to those undisputed Monuments of Antiquity to explain many things which the Historians do very lamely tell us. . . . There is scarce any part of Antiquity that Learned Men do not explain at every turn by

[60]Laurence Echard, *The Roman History* (London, 1695). Echard could find only four predecessors, but three of them—Ralegh, Ross, and Howell—had dealt with universal history, and the fourth, Pedro de Mexía, only with imperial history. The work was very popular, judging by the number of editions that were quickly printed.

[61]According to John Tomlinson, the work was not usually applauded, although the first two volumes were thought better than the rest; he had heard that Dryden corrected the first "which made it excellent": "The Diary of the Rev. John Tomlinson," in *Six North Country Diaries*, ed. J. C. Hodgson, Surtees Society Publications 118 (Durham, 1910), p. 130.

[62]Wotton, *History of Rome*, Preface.

[63]André Dacier wrote a life of Marcus Aurelius which was prefixed to the Daciers' translation of the *Meditations*; it was turned into English and appended to a translation of the *Meditations* by Meric Casaubon (London, 1692); and again by Jeremy Collier (London, 1702). For Tillemont, see n. 67 below.

Ancient medals." The authority of Spanheim is inevitably recalled and four pages of plates follow.[64] Wotton promised to give causes only as they appeared in his authorities; when he had to conjecture, he would justify his guesses with a full explanation in the notes. As for style, Wotton repeated the indifference he had urged in his *Reflections*. "Affectation of Eloquence becomes History the least of anything, especially such a History as this, which like Mosaic Work must be made up and interwoven with the Thought and Sentences of other Men, and where to add to, or diminish from ones Authors, may be of ill consequence." He meant to strive for simplicity and clarity, above all for accuracy, rather than for rhetorical effect.

Wotton's *History of Rome from the Death of Antoninus Pius to the Death of Severus Alexander* appeared in 1701. Although Wotton had modestly eschewed eloquence, he had in fact made an honest attempt to marry classical narrative with modern scholarship. He wanted his history to teach moral and practical lessons of statecraft and at the same time to satisfy the critical standards of the new historiography for accuracy of detail. He tells a story, but he is not embarrassed to intrude into it the evidence of antiquarian scholarship and to append onto it the criticism of modern philology. His style is plain but it is clear; his citations are full and his notes are copious. The *History* is no indiscriminate collection of information but an exercise in selection. If the result is something of a compromise, and thus bound to disappoint both extremes in the battle of the books, it was yet something of a milestone in contemporary historiography, pointing the way to what might one day be a much grander effort at collaboration between the rival parties.

In some respects, Wotton and Temple had to face similar problems. Both took up a subject that had been treated by earlier historians and that had generated an elaborate controversial literature. Both found the original sources abstruse and difficult. But Wotton was undismayed by the problems that he found and was prepared to tackle them with all the ingenuity of the new scholarship. Unlike Temple, he could read the documents in the original languages; and he was quite prepared to use all the new techniques of chronology, epigraphy, and numismatics, as well as his beloved philology, to help out. He sought out aid wherever he could find it, even calling upon Henry Dodwell for assistance with chronologi-

---

[64]"They are chiefly taken from the Collections of Angeloni, Morelli, and Vaillant, who are justly esteemed amongst the greatest and most skilful Antiquaries of this last Age. And Mr. Gribelin the Engraver, who has copied them from the Originals, has performed his part with so much Skill and Fidelity, that it will be no difficult matter from these Medals to form a distinct and just Idea of the Persons of all those Princes and Princesses who have any share in the ensuing History": Wotton, *History of Rome*, Preface.

cal problems.[65] He also felt an obligation to inform his readers at each step of the way about his use of materials. It is much easier therefore to reconstruct his history than Temple's, and readers can usually make up their own minds on disputed points with all the evidence set before them. Of course, all this evidence required Wotton to interrupt the narrative from time to time and place a full commentary in the notes, which, however, he put deliberately at the end of each section. If this device was an undoubted sacrifice to the grace and easy flow of a narrative like Temple's, at least Wotton resisted the temptation to tell everything he knew about every related subject. The bottom of the page and wide margins might well serve the classical commentary (to the disgust of the wits) but it hardly suited a decent narrative.

It is to Wotton's notes, then, that we must turn to see him at work. No one realized better than this young man the collaborative and cumulative character of modern erudition. To a common stock of knowledge wrung from the contemporary sources, Wotton saw that each scholar must add his own contribution: new evidence, new criticism, new insight. The footnote commentary was thus no idle parade of empty learning, but the essential groundwork of the narrative, the underpinning that established its credit and allowed each new student to improve upon his predecessor. An example is the note on the Roman wall in the north of Britain. Temple had offered a few casual conjectures about its construction without indicating his sources; Wotton systematically reviews both the ancient evidence and the modern accounts, recommending in particular "the Notes of my very Learned Friend, Mr. Nicolson, Arch-Deacon of Carlisle, upon Camden's Discourse concerning the Picts Wall."[66] Although he too was unable to solve the puzzle, he saw that a combination of literary and archaeological evidence was necessary for its resolution, and he would have welcomed, as surely as Temple would have derided, the astonishing antiquarian labors of John Horsley in the next generation.

Wotton was lucky that the indefatigable Frenchman Le Nain de Tillemont had gone before him. Here he found one of the most impressive achievements of modern scholarship, a painstaking annalistic account of imperial history, which made no pretense to literature but in which every

---

[65]Wotton sent Dodwell the chronology of Marcus Aurelius's life, with some criticisms of Pagi and some questions about the so-called Thundering Legion, Feb. 4, 1700, Bodleian MS. English Letter C 28, ff. 43–44; he was still asking for a reply just before publication. "I long for your thoughts of the scheme I sent you and of the following only because on those times you are the greatest master living and corrections (could I meet with approbations!) from you without hypocricy would be great ornaments to my work": May 28, 1701, ibid., ff. 54–55.

[66]William Temple, *An Introduction to the History of England*, in his *Works*, 4 vols. (London, 1814), 3:88–89; Wotton, *History of Rome*, pp. 369–70.

literary source was sifted and every date established. "In my Opinion," Wotton wrote later, Tillemont had "set a Pattern of Exactness and Judgment to all that will come after him, and has greatly outdone all that have gone before."[67] But Wotton was unwilling to accept any authority without question, eager to test Tillemont's history at every point and correct his account against the coins and inscriptions and the early Latin and Greek works for the period: Dio, Herodian, and the *Historia Augusta*.[68] All these accounts Wotton knew in their several editions and with their learned commentaries. With characteristic modern effrontery, he did not hesitate to correct both the ancient sources with the use of antiquities and the modern scholars, including Scaliger and Casaubon, with his own philological skills. One very long note is devoted to proving that Sir Thomas Elyot's *Image of Governance* (1540), which pretended to treat the acts of Alexander Severus, was not the translation of a genuine Greek work but a modern forgery, although it had fooled even Selden and Tillemont.[69] When he had to decide on the names of the emperors, whether Elegabolus or Heliogabalus, Severus Alexander or Alexander Severus, he sided with the modern antiquaries over the ancient historians, using the evidence of coins over the authority of the *Historia Augusta*. He understood that medals had problems too, but when they agreed in such matters, their testimony was decisive. They were, he insisted, "the truest Monuments of Antiquity."[70]

Of course, there were limits to Wotton's criticism too. The literary testimony for this period is particularly difficult and unreliable. Wotton

---

[67]William Wotton, *Some Thoughts Concerning a Proper Method of Studying Divinity* (London, 1734), p. 35. Tillemont said that he wrote without style or ornament. "The author never entertained the thought of writing a history [as being] . . . far beyond his talents and capacities"; he meant only to prepare the way for some future work. See David P. Jordan, "Le Nain de Tillemont: Gibbon's Surefooted Mule," *Church History* 39 (1970): 493. Tillemont's *Histoire des empereurs . . . durant les six premiers siècles* (Paris, 1690–1738) was accompanied by *Mémoires pour servir à l'histoire ecclésiastique des six premiers siècles* (Paris, 1693–1712), 22 vols. altogether. See, besides Jordan, Bruno Neveu, *Un Historien à l'école de Port-Royal: Sébastien Le Nain de Tillemont, 1637–1698* (The Hague, 1966).

[68]See, for example, *History of Rome*, pp. 156, n. t; 166, n. e; 171, n. w; 367, n. l; 531, n. b; 548, n. i.

[69]Ibid. pp. 533–40. Elyot's work was titled *The Image of Governance, Compiled of the Actes and Sentences Notable of the Moste Noble Emperor Alexander Severus, late Translated out of the Greke into Englyshe* (London, 1541). Elyot claimed to have translated from a Greek manuscript by Alexander's secretary, Eucolpius (transformed by him into Encolpius), lent to him by a Neapolitan gentleman. For modern discussion, see H. H. S. Croft, Introduction to Thomas Elyot, *The Boke Called the Governour*, 2 vols. (London, 1883), 1:cxlv–clxiv; Mary Lascelles, "Sir Thomas Elyot and the Legend of Alexander Severus," *Review of English Studies* n.s. 2 (1951): 305–18; Robert C. Pinckert, "Sir Thomas Elyot's 'The Image of Governance' (1541)" (Ph.D. dissertation, Columbia University, 1964), p. xlviiiff.

[70]Wotton, *History of Rome*, pp. vii, 377–78. On occasion Wotton was willing to question the genuineness of medals, as one for Occo; see ibid., p. 370, n. s; and p. 423, n. e, where he discusses the difficulty of dating them.

knew all the sources that are available to us today, and he understood that they required careful scrutiny. The *Historia Augusta*, for example, involves so many problems, still unresolved, that a whole library of subsequent literature about them could easily be assembled.[71] Wotton saw something of the problems of date and authorship which needed to be answered before the work could be employed, but he misunderstood the critical task. Rather like Gibson with the *Anglo-Saxon Chronicle*, he thought that the main problem was simply to "reconcile" the various accounts there, to dovetail them where possible, and to choose one or another, if necessary.[72] In this task he was ingenious and painstaking, certainly beyond the comprehension or patience of someone like Temple, who did not wish to bother at all. Wotton did not ask of this composite work, or any of his other sources, what exactly it was and what it was meant to accomplish. Although he sometimes verged on the question when he discovered discrepancies in the testimony, he was neither persistent nor systematic in pursuing them. But to have done so would have been to anticipate the nineteenth century and the next great step in modern historical criticism.

If, therefore, Wotton was a modern in 1701, he was not entirely modern in our sense. His willingness to question sources, to collect and employ contemporary texts, and to use nonliterary evidence was new and helpful. Had Temple thought to do any of these things when he wrote the history of early England, he would have discovered a very different past. But Wotton's criticism was still too much a matter of matching authorities, too little an investigation of the point and purpose of past testimony. Even so, Wotton's history is separated from us by an even greater gap, for he still subscribed to the prevailing *ancienneté* of the period by accepting the traditional didactic and apologetic purposes of narrative: history teaching by example. Although Wotton possessed a much more developed historical sense than Temple, there is still an

[71]See, for example, Harold Mattingly, "Appendix on Sources," *Cambridge Modern History*, vol. 12 (Cambridge, 1939), pp. 598–99, 710, 730; André Chastagnol, "Le Problème de l'histoire Auguste: Etat de la question," *Historia-Augusta-Colloquium* (Bonn, 1963), pp. 43–72; and Ronald Syme's skeptical account in *Emperors and Biography* (Oxford, 1971), a sequel to his earlier *Ammianus Marcellinus and the Historia Augusta* (Oxford, 1968); and his reply to Arnaldo Momigliano's review (*English Historical Review* 84 [1969]), *The Historia Augusta: A Call to Clarity* (Bonn, 1971).

[72]Typical is his skepticism about the stories related by Capitolinus, one of the alleged authors of the *Historia*, on the cruelty of Macrinus, "because they are not so much hinted at by Herodian and Dio Cassius, who lived in and about that time, and speak of him and his Failings with great impartiality. . . . Elagabalus after Macrinus's death, employ'd Writers to blacken him and his Son; and after them Capitolinus seems to have taken this account": Wotton, *History of Rome*, p. 345. Unfortunately, Wotton is not consistent, and the authorship and motives of the *Historia* are much more complicated than he allows. A little later he follows Lampridius (another of the alleged authors) in preference to Herodian, despite chronological discrepancies; see ibid., pp. 445, 488–89; 531, n. a; 544, n. g; 548–49.

element of timelessness in the moral judgments that he lavished on his subject. No doubt he found them already in his sources, for they were already characteristic of classical and especially imperial historiography. But he found them perfectly congenial and, as we have seen, the original inspiration for writing his history in the first place. Wotton's history, then, is the history not of the empire but of its emperors; it is really a series of exemplary lives. If he introduced into the text and notes some information about contemporary institutions, thus drawing upon the learning of the antiquaries, he used it primarily as background to his story. We are never allowed to forget that this is the tale of "a very Bad prince who immediately succeeded a very Good one; and a most Extraordinary Prince, who came after one of the most Profligate of men."

The work was well received abroad—by Leibniz, anyway, who was grateful for receiving a copy, and by the *Acta Eruditorum*, which gave it a good review.[73] Leibniz recommended it to the elector of Hanover (the future George I), "and it was the first piece of Roman History which he read in our Language."[74] At home it was little noticed, although the *Works of the Learned* gave it a full summary.[75] Naturally, Evelyn and Nicolson were pleased with it and sent their gratitude.[76] And it did eventually receive a proper appreciation and a hearty endorsement from Thomas Hearne in the new *Ductor Historicus*. There it was described as "a Book that ought to be universally Read, as containing not only a most exact History of that Time justified with Critical Notes, and written in a manly Polite Style; but also very Judicious Observations upon the Actions of two most Virtuous and two most Vicious Princes. This he does in a manner that sets Virtue and Vice in their true Lights, as they ought to be shewn to a young Prince, the purpose the Work was undertaken for, in the Days of that illustrious Youth, whose Loss we can never enough Deplore."[77]

But for all its virtues, and despite its originality, Wotton's work was really less successful than Temple's. It was probably too much of a

[73]Leibniz to Wotton, April 25, 1702, in *Der Briefwechsel des Gottfried Wilhelm Leibniz*, ed. Eduard Bodemann (1895; rpt. Hildesheim, 1966), p. 396; *Acta Eruditorum* (Leipzig, 1702), pp. 486–90. See also Cuperus to Antonio Magliabecchi, n.d., in *Clarorum Belgarum ad Ant. Magliabechium Epistolae*, vol. 1 (Florence, 1745), pp. 101–2.

[74]"Life of Wotton," B.M. MS. Add. 4224, f. 158.

[75]*Miscellaneous Letters, Giving an Account of the Works of the Learned*, December–January 1701–2, pp. 749ff, 37ff.

[76]"The Choice you have made in this Collection is so admirably suited to the purpose of which it was designed that it may be reckon'd amongst the best Institutions not of a Prince only, but of all other persons. . . . This I say you have done, and established with so much learning as shews you a Master of consummate erudition": Evelyn to Wotton, October 1701, Christ Church MSS., Evelyn Letters, T–W. See also Nicolson to Wodrow, Sept. 8, 1701, in the Wodrow MSS., Advocates Library, Edinburgh.

[77]Pierre Le Lorrain, abbé de Vallemont, *Ductor Historicus*, ed. Thomas Hearne, vol. 1 (London, 1705), p. 189. This praise was all the more remarkable because Hearne disliked Wotton, and did not normally restrain his feelings.

compromise between conflicting intentions. Had it been better written, it might have been more popular; had it incorporated all the antiquarian lore for the period, it might have been more useful to scholars. Still, one cannot help regretting that the *History* was not better known, for if nothing else, it pointed the way to a solution of the still unresolved problem of contemporary historiography: how to reconcile the different modes of the ancients and the moderns. As it was, it was not ignored, although it seems to have brought Wotton little reward. Some years later a greater scholar, and certainly a much better writer, read it with profit. But with the appearance of *Decline and Fall of the Roman Empire*, it passed finally into oblivion.[78]

4

It seems to have been Wotton's destiny to do yeoman service for all parts of modern learning and then to be forgotten. Perhaps that was inevitable for one who believed so firmly in the progress of knowledge. No doubt it was also a result of his purpose, which, as in the *Reflections*, was more generally to popularize the work of others than to attempt anything new. His next project in these years was the life and works of Robert Boyle, encouraged by his aging patron, John Evelyn, and the fellows of the Royal Society, but it seems to have faltered after the death of that worthy man.[79] Meanwhile, he was busy seeing a new translation of Louis Ellies Du Pin's ecclesiastical history through the press, at the same time that he was bringing out the third and last edition of the *Reflections on Ancient and Modern Learning*.[80] He began and may have finished a Latin translation of two of John Greaves's antiquarian tracts, his *Pyramidographia* and his *Discourse on the Roman Foot and Denarius*.[81] And he continued to hope for advancement in the church, though in the

[78]For Gibbon's familiarity with Wotton, see Joseph M. Levine, "Edward Gibbon and the Quarrel between the Ancients and the Moderns," in *Humanism and History* (Ithaca, N.Y., 1987), pp. 183–85, 188.

[79]According to Clarke, who had seen some *adversaria* on the subject, Wotton's papers were either lost or destroyed and he had not had the heart to begin again; "Life of Wotton," pp. 165–66. But Wotton was still apologizing to Sir Hans Sloane in 1709 for his slowness and the difficulty of the task: Wotton to Sloane, April 23, 1709, B.M. MS. Sloane 4041, f. 317. See also Hearne (May 2, 1706), *Remarks and Collections*, 1:239.

[80]See Wotton to the Bishop of Norwich, Sept. 5, 1706, B.M. MS. Add. 29747, f. 50, referring to Du Pin's *New Ecclesiastical History of the Sixteenth Century . . . revised and collected by a learned divine of England*, 2 vols. (London, 1703–1706). In Du Pin's *New History of Ecclesiastical Writers*, 2d ed. (London, 1703), the advertisement credits Wotton for revision, "after the several Translators had finished their Parts." Wotton's contributions to these two works are reported in *Works of the Learned* 7 (October 1706): 625.

[81]Thomas Smith to Hearne, Sept. 13, 1705, in Hearne, *Remarks and Collections*, 1:44. Hearne reports an unsatisfactory conversation with Wotton on the subject, Sept. 22, in ibid., p. 47. Greaves's works appeared originally in 1646–47.

meantime he had to settle for employment as chaplain to the Earl of Nottingham, rector of Middleton Keynes, and eventually tutor to Nottingham's son.[82]

Wotton shared the growing enthusiasm for English history and of course he read Temple's *Introduction* when it appeared. Needless to say, he was not impressed. It contained too many "strange Mistakes," such as Temple's double error of attributing the mission of St. Augustine to Pope Boniface and setting Athelbert on the South Saxon throne, "tho' every body knows that Athelbert was only King of Kent, and that it was Gregory the Great who sent Augustine into England."[83] Exactness in detail was admittedly not one of Temple's strengths. What Wotton thought of his style he does not say, but style, we have seen, meant little to him in comparison with substance. Classical scholars, unlike classical gentlemen, were willing to bear with the most awkward and difficult works as long as they contributed to the progress of knowledge. Much later, Wotton wrote an apology for that very learned but notoriously difficult antiquary John Selden. His "Way of Writing is obscure and intricate, and his Digressions long and many," he agreed, "but the uncommon Variety of things worth knowing compensates for the Trouble."[84]

Wotton's contribution to the history of England was neither as original nor ambitious as his Roman work, but it was perfectly in character with his modernist skills and prejudices. He had, after all, spent much of his life with kindred spirits such as Nicolson and Evelyn, who readily communicated their passion for the English past. "Last Night I was with Mr. Wotton (who writ the Essay on Ancient and Modern Learning)," wrote Thomas Hearne in 1705, "at the Tavern, together with Mr. Thwaites and Mr. Willis." The talk was of English antiquities and Hearne was clearly envious of Wotton's friendship with both of these men.[85] Edward Thwaites had just helped to complete one of the greatest antiquarian enterprises of all time, and Wotton was characteristically prepared to help to publicize its achievement. In his *Defense of the Reflections*, he singles out Isaac Newton's *Optics* and George Hickes's *Thesaurus of the Northern*

---

[82]Tancred Robinson to Lhwyd, Dec. 10, 1696, and Nicolson to Lhwyd, May 25, 1706, Bodleian MS. Ashmole 1816, f. 549. In 1705 Wotton was made prebendary of Sarum, "he being, it seems, a Whigg, or any thing else, as he finds 'twill be for his Interest": Hearne, *Remarks and Collections*, 1:71.

[83]William Wotton, *A Defense of the Reflections upon Ancient and Modern Learning* (London, 1705), p. 18. Temple corrected the first of the two errors in the 2d. ed. of his *Introduction to the History of England* (London, 1699), p. 67.

[84]William Wotton, *Some Thoughts Concerning a Proper Method of Studying Divinity* (London, 1734), p. 7. The work was published posthumously.

[85]"Mr. Wotton is a Person of general Learning, a great Talker and Braggadocio, but of little Judgment in any one particular science": Sept. 22, 1705, in Hearne, *Remarks and Collections*, 1:47. Hearne's antipathy was probably a result of political prejudice as well as a touch of envy.

Tongues as the two latest performances to advance the moderns above antiquity. Thanks to the latter, "we may reasonably expect in the next Age to see the Learning of our Northern Ancestors better known to us, than it ever was to them in any single Age in which any of them lived."[86] Here Wotton echoes what he had already boasted about modern classical philology.

Two years later Wotton published a brief Latin epitome of Hickes's work. Just how he got involved in the project does not appear, though he is likely to have known about it all through its long gestation. Like most of the divines in this period, Hickes believed in ecclesiastical history as the chief authorization for contemporary religious practice, and he made himself a master of patristics and a student of Hebrew so that he could defend the Church of England equally against Catholics and Dissenters.[87] In the 1680s he became interested in Anglo-Saxon, a new historical discipline already flourishing at Oxford, and for much the same reason. Already in 1679 William Nicolson had become the first college lecturer on the subject, and he kept his interest very much alive after he went north to Carlisle; ten years later Edward Thwaites entered Queens College and helped to create a veritable "nest of Saxonists." One of these young men was Edmund Gibson, whose edition of the *Anglo-Saxon Chronicle* appeared in 1692. In 1689 Hickes published an Anglo-Saxon grammar in Latin which drew self-consciously upon his predecessors and in which he explained the value of that early language to the history and literature of the nation, as well as to theology, jurisprudence, philology, and eloquence.[88] He was very conscious of continental example; as he later explained, "I undertook the work at first purely out of zeale to make known the language, customes, laws, and manners of our ancestors, and so to set our English antiquities in a good light."[89] But this was only the first step toward a vast and original work that came to exemplify all the virtues—and defects—of the new historiography.

At the Revolution, Hickes refused to take the oaths, resisted his removal, and had to go into hiding. He became the leading nonjuror of the period, and was surreptitiously appointed bishop. In these trying circumstances, and with an integrity that is still astonishing, Hickes continued his Saxon studies. He was at once and continuously encouraged

---

[86]Wotton, *Defense of the Reflections*, pp. 36–39.

[87]For information about Hickes I am grateful to Richard Harris, who has supplied me with transcripts of letters, the biography of Hickes by Hilkiah Bedford in Bodleian MS. Eng. Misc. e 4, and much else of value; see his article "George Hickes, White Kennett and the Inception of the *Thesaurus Linguarum Septentrionalium*," *Bodleian Library Record* 11 (1983): 169–86; and David Douglas, *English Scholars*, 2d ed. (London, 1951), pp. 77–97.

[88]George Hickes, *Institutiones grammaticae Anglo-Saxonicae* (Oxford, 1689), Preface *ad lectorem*.

[89]Hickes to Thomas Parker, June 1, 1704, B.M. MS. Stowe 750, ff. 2–3.

by Gibson and Nicolson and Arthur Charlett, even after political differences separated them. His first ambition was simply to enlarge and expand the Saxon grammar to include, among other things, old high German (or "Francick"), and he appealed to Nicolson (by way of Gibson) for help. Nicolson had been to Germany as a young man and the two scholars soon entered into friendly debate over the dates of Ulphila's Gothic and the early Runic inscriptions in Denmark and Sweden.[90] Over the years Nicolson sent what information he could, as well as each of the parts of his *English Historical Library* as he completed them, welcoming but sometimes disputing Hickes's criticisms.[91] When Nicolson was attacked by that "pert Gentleman of Christ Church," Francis Atterbury, he was assured that it would be folly to persist against the combined might of the college. "And what an irrecoverable Loss would the Learned World have," he wrote to Hickes, "if all my Saxon should perish in the same pit of Destruction with Dr. Bentley's Greek!"[92]

Unfortunately, Hickes does not seem to have declared himself in the battle of the books. But the implication of Nicolson's letter is clear enough: Anglo-Saxon scholarship, like classical scholarship, was a "modern" subject, whatever its political or religious purposes. Hickes was profoundly conservative in sentiment, even reactionary, but he did not feel compelled to abide by past authority simply because it was ancient. Late in life Hickes applauded his friend John Kettlewell, who "was no Slave or Bigot to the Opinions of Philosophers upon the Account of their Authority or Name; but a Friend to Truth wheresoever he found it, whether in Aristotle or des Cartes, or in any other Writer of Ancient or Modern Fame, Foreign or Domestick."[93] And there is not much doubt where he stood with respect to our quarrel. Philology was an indisputably modern subject, and Hickes believed forthrightly in the advancement of modern learning. (One of his many projects at this time was an improved version of Degory Wheare's *Method and Order of Reading Both Civil and Ecclesiastical Histories*.)[94] Indeed, in this matter he seems to have been more progressive than Gibson, who certainly wavered during the battle of the books. In a letter to Charlett, Gibson regrets that

[90]See the letters in Bodleian MS. Add. C 217, ff. 55, 59, 65. Besides Harris and Douglas (n. 87 above), see J. A. W. Bennett, "Hickes' *Thesaurus:* A Study in Oxford Book Production," *English Studies* 1 (1948): 28–45.

[91]See Nicolson to Hickes, Sept. 11, 1697, B.M. MS. Add. 34265, f. 23v.

[92]Nicolson to Hickes, April 11, 1700, B.M. MS. Add. 34265, f. 68v. For Hickes's indedtedness to Nicolson, see Nicolson to Hickes, April 25, 1699, in *Letters to and from Nicolson*, 1:119–21.

[93]George Hickes, *Memoirs of the Life of Mr. John Kettlewell* (London, 1718), pp. 37–38.

[94]See Hickes's letters to Charlett, Nov. 24, Jan. 19 and 28, and Mar. 15, 1694–95, Bodleian MS. Ballard 12, ff. 97–99, 60. Hickes seems to have hoped that Kennett might undertake the project; it foundered when the former editor, Bohun, refused his permission.

Bentley seemed to be going too far in his resentment against Boyle; meanwhile, "Dr H---s has given us a glorious character of their [Anglo-Saxon] poetry, and will hardly allow the Ancients to take place of them in that particular. I have read some of it formerly, but could never meet with any thing that relish'd half soe well as Homer or Virgil."[95] It was not easy for the Saxonists to justify their interest in the Middle Ages against the prevailing *ancienneté*, and the discovery that Anglo-Saxon poetry had merits of its own may have been the most original (as it proved to be one of the more controversial) of Hickes's discoveries. Even Mrs. Hickes seems to have been prejudiced against "the uncourtly Gothic and Saxon."[96]

It seems likely that it was while he was hiding out in the household of White Kennett (in 1696) that Hickes enlarged his ambitions and began to turn the Anglo-Saxon grammars into a full-scale antiquarian survey of Anglo-Saxon England, although he continued to refer to it for some time as a "second edition."[97] This was well before the *Complete History*, when Kennett was still a country vicar and local antiquary. Kennett invited him to stay, at the request of his patron, Francis Cherry, and looked after him at some personal risk. He also read over Hickes's work and began to learn Anglo-Saxon, encouraging his mentor to his great work, by mail and in person, buying books, and developing a scheme of his own for a "universal English Glossary or a *Thesaurus Linguae Anglicanae* by which our Mother Language may be as much indebted to your judgment and my Labour as the Greek one to Stephens and the Latine to another."[98] Some evidence remains of their mutual work, and Hickes remembered to thank Kennett in a preface to the *Thesaurus* for having especially urged him to his work and as its chief begetter, although they argued about it later.[99]

Despite the friendship of Cherry and Kennett, it was not easy for Hickes to carry on serious scholarship, or for that matter ordinary life.

[95]Gibson to Charlett, Jan. 10, 1695?, Bodleian MS. Ballard 5, ff. 84–85.

[96]R. T. to Hickes, June 4, 1691, Bodleian MS. Eng. hist. b 2, f. 263.

[97]"Dr. Hickes saies he has been hard at labour (this winter) in reviewing his Grammar, and providing for a second Edition": Nicolson to Thwaites, May 7, 1698, in Eleanor N. Adams, *Old English Scholarship in England* (New Haven, 1917), app. 1, pp. 124–25. See also Hickes to Nicolson, April 25, 1699, Bodleian MS. Don. d 88, ff. 309–10.

[98]Kennett to Hickes, Nov. 2, 1696, Christ Church MSS., Upcott Collection, II, no. 43.

[99]Preface to Adam Ottley, in George Hickes, *Linguarum Vett. Septentrionalium Thesaurus Grammatico-Criticus et Archaeologicus*, 2 vols. (Oxford, 1703, 1705), I:iv; William Newton, *The Life of Dr. White Kennett* (London, 1730), p. 12; Douglas, *English Scholars*, p. 95. "I believe I have glossed for him a thousand old, and topicall English words": Hickes to Charlett, July 7, 1696, Bodleian MS. Ballard 12, ff. 121–22. Something of their collaboration can be seen in B.M. MS. Lansdowne 1033. Their later reminiscences are colored by political acrimony but confirm Hickes's indebtedness; see Kennett in B.M. MS. Lansdowne 1034, ff. 6–7; Hickes in Bodleian MS. Eng. hist. b 2, ff. 152–53.

Thomas Hearne remembered how Hickes, who was then living disguised and under the name of Smith, was discovered one night at Cherry's house by the authorities, "but he got out at a back door, passed through the Gardens in the Church Yard and escaped to Bagshot to Collonel Grymes's, and his wife followed."[100] Fortunately, there was always someone to befriend him, and the work went steadily forward, particularly after his retreat into Herefordshire and the household of William Brome, who also contributed to the enterprise.[101] After a while, thanks to the intercession of Lord Somers, who issued a *nolle persequi* in 1699, Hickes was free to return to London and complete his work, although he continued to labor in the services of his outlawed church.

It was in these years then, between 1696 and 1699, that the grammars turned into the *Thesaurus*. One by one Hickes collected his collaborators and put them to work. He had decided now to include every scrap of available evidence for Saxon England, not merely its language but its antiquities also. This meant discovering and describing all the literary and nonliterary materials that were still extant: manuscripts, inscriptions, and coins. For the literary materials he was fortunate to discover a brilliant young man named Humfrey Wanley, who had begun life as apprentice to a draper, been discovered by William Lloyd, and sent to Oxford, where "by a strange bent of nature" he gave himself up to the study of antiquities, especially ancient manuscripts and Anglo-Saxon.[102] He had been inspired to his passion (he said) by reading Pierre Gassendi's life of the famous virtuoso Peiresc, which he read in an English version dedicated to John Evelyn.[103] For a time he lived with Arthur Charlett and looked after the

[100]Hearne, *Remarks and Collections*, 10:237.

[101]The year with Brome, Hickes "lookt upon as the best part of his Life": ibid., 8:211. Hickes to Smith, Dec. 10, 1696, Bodleian MS. Smith 50, f. 101, retails his progress then. He has done little, he writes, but add one new chapter, de dialecto Dano-Saxonica, but that has occasioned him to add another, de dialecto poetica, and that will produce a third, de dialecto Normanno-Saxoxonica, in which he may treat de dialecto Semisaxonica—to all of which he hopes to add a de prosodia or poetica! Meanwhile, he longs to see the manuscripts in the Cotton collection under Smith's care: characters and diplomas, calendars and menologies, poems, hymns, and verses, chronicles and epistles, coronation oaths, histories and laws, councils, rituals, and ecclesiastical offices, homilies, penitentials, and glossaries. The work was obviously well on its way.

[102]Pepys to Thomas Smith, April 15, 1695, in Samuel Pepys, *Diary and Correspondence*, ed. Lord Braybrooke, 4 vols. (London, 1890), 4:320–21. Wanley never finished his degree. For Wanley, see Douglas, *English Scholars*, pp. 98–118; Kenneth Sisam, "Humfrey Wanley," in *Studies in the History of Old English Literature* (Oxford, 1953), pp. 259–77.

[103]Wanley recalled that Tanner had been won to these studies by reading the life of Somner, "perhaps as Piereskius his life did the same to me": Wanley to Thomas Tanner, Oct. 15, 1694, Bodleian MS. Tanner 25, f. 243. See Pierre Gassendi, *The Mirrour of True Nobility and Gentility*, trans. W. Rand (London, 1657). Apparently he used Somner's dictionary; see his abbreviation with a note dated May 3, 1692, B.M. MS. Harl. 3317, f. 30. He continued to work hard at the language and for his efforts received Tanner's praise in 1695. With the help of Pepys he visited the Cotton library to look at some manuscripts not mentioned in Hickes's grammar; see Wanley to Tanner, April 16 and 19, 1695, Bodleian, MS. Tanner 24, ff. 1–2, 4.

A Saxon manuscript illustration of St. Dunstan from Hickes's *Thesaurus* (1703–1705), reproduced by permission of Princeton University Libraries

coins and manuscripts in the Bodleian Library. According to Ralph
Thoresby, "he designs and draws admirably well; having besides an unac-
countable skill in imitating any hand whatever."[104] Moreover, he had a
colossal ambition, which he never quite fulfilled but on which he worked
for many years. "My intent," he wrote in 1697, "is to trace the Greek and
Latin letters from the oldest monuments of antiquity now extant, as the
marbles and medals, to the MSS and so down to the present age. When any
other language derives from these as the Coptic or Russian from the
Greek; the Francic, Irish, Saxon, etc., from the Latin; I shall consider them
in their several times, but the Saxon I would especially bring down from
the oldest charters to the present English hands. The Charters I believe
may be older than the Books and may determine the age of all the Saxon
MSS." He thought that it would take many years, but he hoped also to add
a second volume, *De re Anglorum diplomatica*.[105]

The reference was to Jean Mabillon's *De re diplomatica* (1681), which had
in effect established the new science of diplomatics and taught Europe how
to evaluate and authenticate medieval manuscripts. The work and the man
were well known in England, particularly in the learned circle of Thomas
Smith, Thomas Gale, and Edward Bernard, and it was probably through
Bernard that Wanley made its acquaintance.[106] It was just about this time
(1696) that Bernard completed his last service to learning with a catalogue
of British manuscripts and called upon Wanley for help. (Apparently

---

[104]Thoresby to Gibson, Oct. 26, 1697, in *Letters of Eminent Men to Thoresby*, 1:304–6;
Charlett to Pepys, Nov. 17, 1696, in Samuel Pepys, *Private Correspondence*, ed. J. R. Tanner
(London, 1926), pp. 130–32. It was Charlett who brought Wanley to Hickes's notice; see
Hickes to Charlett, Oct. 17, 1695, and Feb. 14, 1696, Bodleian MS. Ballard 12, ff. 107, 68.

[105]Wanley to Thomas Smith, June 20, 1697, in *Letters Written to Eminent Persons from the
Bodleian Library*, 2 vols. (London, 1813), 1:80–81; Douglas, *English Scholars*, p. 110. Later
Wanley hoped to travel abroad to compile a book of specimens. "I intend to consider the
original and progress of writing and letters, and deduce the severall hands especially Greek
and Latin from the oldest Monuments to this age. As to the alterations of hands, I must
begin with the Marbles and Medals as being older than any books now extant. These
Inscriptions and Coins as well as MSS I must view with my own eyes," etc. The design was
approved by Dodwell, Charlett, Pepys, and Aldrich, among others; but Wanley never did
get away. See B.M. MS. Harl. 5911, ff. 1–2; B.M. MS. Loan 29/259; and "Mr. Pepys
Report Touching Mr. Wanley's Proposition," June 18, 1700, in Pepys, *Private Correspondence*, pp. 366–67.

[106]For correspondence between Bernard and Mabillon, see Bodleian MSS. Smith 9, f.
13; Smith 45, ff. 107, 177; Smith 47, ff. 34, 37, 39. "The best rules for distinguishing the
dates of MSS are to be had in F. Mabillon's learned treatise *De re Diplomatica*. If you have
that book, you need no further help": Nicolson to Thoresby, July 17, 1699, in Lancaster,
Letters to Thoresby, pp. 75–76. See also Gilbert Burnet to Thoresby with the same advice,
Aug. 29, 1699, in *Letters of Eminent Men to Thoresby*, 1:385–86. A good description of the
work is in L. Levillain, "Le *De re diplomatica*," *Mélanges et documents publiées à l'occasion du 2ᵉ
centenaire de la mort de Mabillon* (Paris, 1908), pp. 193–252. See also Henri Le Clercq,
Mabillon, 2 vols. (Paris, 1953), 1:154–80; David Knowles, "Jean Mabillon," in *The Historian
and Character and Other Essays* (Cambridge, 1963), pp. 213–39. According to Sisam, Wanley
first learned to copy by imitating the hands in Mabillon: "Humfrey Wanley," p. 263.

Wanley contributed the description of Coventry manuscripts and the index.)[107] He was soon compiling a "book of Alphabets," which Hickes found very useful in deciphering the language of his materials.[108] Wanley hoped to look at all the major collections of medieval manuscripts, "and then when I have the whole Treasure of England in that kind by me, to be seen at one view, I would endeavour to see if one could prove another to be true or false, and how the Hands of England (Latin and Saxon), have gradually altered from the time of Athelbert King of Kent to that of King Stephen; and take Specimens of them accordingly."[109] Only when the manuscripts were dated correctly could their authenticity be established and their material used; and here Wanley was ready to correct even the great Dr. Bentley.[110] He understood the peculiar importance of charters for this kind of work and the need for meticulous comparison. "Paleography," it has been said, is for medieval studies "what epigraphy is to the classical historian—a principal means of precision."[111] The work for Bernard and Wanley's passion for paleography were perfect preparation for his collaboration with Hickes: a critical and historical catalogue of all the extant Anglo-Saxon manuscripts in England.

Wanley's scheme was typically ambitious. He intended to account for all the books he could find in Anglo-Saxon and compare the various manuscripts of each.

I have further described all manner of Epistles, Wills, Covenants, Notes, Charms, Verses, Catalogues, etc., that I foresee may be of use. . . . In one word, if Dr. Hickes will accept from me a Catalogue of all the Saxon MSS that I know in England, I will do my endeavour to restore many to their proper Authors; will specifie particularly whatever has been printed and what not; with a multitude of Remarks and Observations. . . . With this Catalogue I shall annex the Specimen of Characters of the most considerable MSS of the Languages of the Northern Nations, as

[107]Edward Bernard, *Catologi librorum manuscriptorum Angliae et Hiberniae in unum collecti cum Indice*, 2 vols. (Oxford, 1697). Bernard had been working on it since 1692; he died in . 1696.

[108]See, for example, Hickes to Wanley, Jan. 28, 1699, B.M. MS. Harl. 3779, ff. 81–82.

[109]Wanley to Hickes, May 28, 1697, Bodleian MS. Eng. Hist. c 6, f. 16. "I have already the chief Alterations in the Greek Latin Character (as used in Books) for near 1300 years; with the derivations of the Coptic, Russian, Gothic, Runic, Francic, Saxon, and Irish Letters from them, in a Dissertation in the Catalogues of MSS": ibid, Feb. 18, 1698, ff. 17–20.

[110]See Wanley on the Alexandrian Bible, after visiting Bentley: Wanley to Charlett, May 30, 1698, in *Letters from the Bodleian*, pp. 89–92. Eventually Wanley tried (unsuccessfully) to become Bentley's assistant in the Royal Library upon Hickes's recommendation: n.d., Bodleian MS. Eng. hist. b 2, f. 172.

[111]Sisam, "Humfrey Wanley," p. 271. For a wonderful example of Wanley at work (over the Anglo-Saxon Bede), see Wanley to Smith, Aug. 28, 1703, Bodleian MS. Eng. hist. c 6, ff. 40–41.

the Gothic, Francic, Langobardic and Icelandic, besides the Saxon, with Specimens of MSS in Welsh, Cornish, Scotch and Irish.[112]

Hickes later decided to add an account of the Scandinavian manuscripts also, thanks to the help of several foreign correspondents.

In the end Hickes was delighted with Wanley's scheme, although it meant delay and expense. "Nothing is more acceptable to me than your desire to finish my Catalogue," Hickes wrote in 1699. "It makes me sleep easy."[113] They agreed on exactly how it should be done,[114] but Wanley had to be coaxed sometimes and coddled. When he wrote early in their acquaintance about a toothache, Hickes warned him about the danger of libraries, "and in particular, the Bodleian hath killed many brave men, as Dr. Langbaine, and Mr. Clerk the learned Squire-bedell, and God grant it may not kill you. The Cottonian is paved all with cold marbell and therefore when you go thither be sure to carry the mss out of it into the next room, as learned men usually do, and for want of doing of which Dr. Marshall once got such a cold, as had like to have killed him."[115] It was not easy to get permission for Wanley to use the Cotton library, since the keeper, Thomas Smith, had his own designs on the ancient manuscripts, and Hickes had to use all his influence to procure admission.[116] Eventually Wanley's help was required for all parts of the *Thesaurus*. "I have learnt more from you," Hickes wrote gratefully in 1698, "than ever I did from any other man, and living or dying, I will make my acknowledgment more wayes than one." Wanley had become, so Hickes believed, "one of the greatest judges of hands, and ages of MSS and authority of MSS that now is or perhaps ever was." About this time, Wanley wrote a brilliant piece that was later printed by the Royal Society laying out the rules of diplomatic criticism. His only weakness was a barbarous Latin style, fortunately not very noticable in a catalogue.[117]

---

[112]Wanley to Charlett, Oct. 19, 1699, in Ellis, *Original Letters*, pp. 290–93.

[113]Hickes to Wanley, Nov. 21, 1699, B.M. MS. Harley 3779, f. 111.

[114]"We have consulted together much about it, and agreed upon certain rules in making of it." Among the rules was one "to compare MSS that have the same, or the like titles to see whether they are the same, or different . . . to see which is the ancienter, the perfecter, the nobler . . . the differences of hand in which they are written and . . . to add the specimen of all the English hands both in the Saxon and latin MSS from the ancientest that occurs to the times of Henry II": Hickes to Charlett, April 26, 1700, Bodleian MS. Ballard 12, ff. 139–40.

[115]Hickes to Wanley, Feb. 24, 1696, Bodleian MS. Ballard 12, ff. 125–26.

[116]"He over and over desired me not to rival him in his undertakings, for he had resolved to publish some of the Saxon Charters, with the old Saxon Letters, and would by no means be prevented": Wanley to Charlett, April 30, 1698, Bodleian MS. Ballard 13, f. 61.

[117]Hickes to Wanley, Mar. 14, 1698, B.M. MS. Harl, 3779, quoted in C. E. Wright, "Humfrey Wanley: Saxonist and Library Keeper," *Proceedings of the British Academy* 46 (1960): 104n. See also Hickes's recommendation cited above, n. 110. "Coming by chance at

William Nicolson too, off in Carlisle, was ready to defer to the young man, "your knowledge in every thing (even within what I thought my own Sphere) having already outgone."[118] But Edward Thwaites, who had begun to steer the work through the press in 1698, thought that Wanley was sluggish, and that he lagged because he was afraid of robbing himself. "I doe not expect he will give us all he has for he fears he shall diminish the glorie of his owne book." Wanley naturally felt that the work he was doing for Hickes was interfering with his own career, which had still not gotten off the ground.[119] It took much tact and real leadership to hold the team together. Not the least of difficulties was how to pay the cost of printing when no publisher would risk the venture; and when subscriptions proved insufficient, Hickes was forced into debt.

Meanwhile, Hickes needed help for the Saxon antiquities also. It was Thwaites who introduced him to Sir Andrew Fountaine, a virtuoso collector of paintings, coins, and other objets d'art. He was no scholar but a man of the world who had in fact been educated among the wits at Westminster and Christ Church and who later became intimate with Swift. Wealth and foreign travel encouraged his collector's instincts, and he became quickly known as a discerning connoisseur. "Sir Andrew," Thomas Hearne remembered, "was look'd upon as one of the hopefullest young Gentlemen in England. He travelled when very young, and hath been a great Traveller since. . . . His skill in Coyns is unquestionable, tho' not so much in the learned Part, as in the intrinsick Value of them,

---

Oxford," Hickes continues, "to discern his great and singular talents, I persuaded him to leave the university and come to London." When Wanley tried to go abroad, Hickes dissuaded him, loath to lose him for England—and (no doubt) himself. "He hath hitherto lived meanly and precariously writeing as an hireling." Wanley's piece for the Royal Society was printed in the *Philosophical Transactions*, no. 300 (June 1705), pp. 1993–2008. Gibson complained about Wanley's Latin preface, "which soe abounds with Anglicisms, and is wrot in a style so much different from the genius of the Latin, that I fear it will doe noe kindness to the work either at home or abroad": Gibson to Charlett, n.d., in Adams, *Old English Scholarship*, p. 131.

[118]Nicolson to Wanley, n.d., Bodleian MS. Harl. 3780, f. 255. In 1702 Nicolson was still encouraging Wanley to go on with *De re diplomatica*. "You cannot do a more acceptable service to the Commonwealth of Antiquaries. And, without flattering, you are the best qualify'd for the Undertaking": July 23, 1702, ibid., f. 261.

[119]Thwaites to Hickes, Jan. 14, 1699, Bodleian MS. Eng. Hist. C 6, f. 96. "I have my hands full of business, and Dr. Hickes Catalogus is a great Hindrance to the Augmenting my Fortunes. However I hope in time to get over it": Wanley to Charlett, April 5, 1701, Bodleian MS. Ballard 13, f. 99. Nevertheless, it was Hickes who introduced Wanley to Robert Harley in 1701, and the meeting led eventually to his life's employment as Harley's librarian; see Cyril E. Wright, Introduction to *Fontes Harleiani* (London, 1972); and his Introduction to *The Diary of Humfrey Wanley, 1715–1726* (London, 1966). Thwaites too had other business, as he explained in his letter of Jan. 14—fifteen or sixteen students to tutor in his "class of young Saxons." His hostility to Wanley continued; see Wright, "Humphrey Wanley," p. 105.

and in distinguishing what are rare and what not."[120] Nevertheless, he was able to supply a collection of Saxon coins for engraving from his own collection and from such willing helpers as Ralph Thoresby, and (with the aid of Hickes and William Elstob, one of Thwaites's students) he produced a learned dissertation on them to help fill out the *Thesaurus*. Much later, despite his friendship with Swift, he was satirized by Alexander Pope for his various virtuoso activities.[121]

Of all Hickes's helpers, Thwaites may have been the most important. It was to Thwaites that Hickes entrusted the printing of the *Thesaurus*. In 1698 Hickes was still incognito and needed a hand in Oxford. Thwaites was teaching at Queens College, where he had become an able Saxonist in his own right, eventually "Anglo-Saxon preceptor" of his college. "He was," Brome remembered, "a north country man of good Family, beautifull in his personage, pleasant in conversation, great vivacity, and of a most agreeable natural Behaviour. The best septentrionalist next the Dean of his Age, was great master of the learned languages and well skill'd in the modern ones, he was of invincible courage. . . . Besides these excellencies he wrote the finest hand I ever saw."[122] In 1698 he published an Anglo-Saxon edition of Aelfric's *Heptateuch*, which he dedicated to Hickes, while his pupils Christopher Rawlinson and Thomas Benson were making other valuable texts available. "Mr Thwaites skill, care, and diligence make it needlesse for me to be there," wrote Hickes to Charlett, "and the book will be better for passing through his hands." It was a great comfort, Nicolson concluded in 1698, to see "our English Antiquities in so fair a way of being restor'd to us . . . and that chiefly by the Members of our own College." Gibson too was pleased to hear of the work, and encouraging.[123]

[120]Hearne, *Remarks and Collections*, 6:220. "He is a very honest Gentleman, one that has spent much of his time upon coyns and pictures and understands them well and has a good collection of both, especially of Italian prints": Thwaites to Hickes (under the pseudonym "Potter"), Jan. 19, 1699, Bodleian MS. Eng. Hist. C 6, f. 102, For Fountaine as a collector, see Brinsley Ford, "Sir Andrew Fountaine: One of the Best Virtuosi of the Age," *Apollo* 122 (November 1985): 352–58.

[121]It was Hickes who got Thoresby to help Fountaine; see Hickes to Thoresby, Oct. 30, 1703, in Atkinson, *Thoresby*, 2:100–101; Fountaine to Thoresby, Dec. 11, 1703, Yorkshire Archaeological Society MS. 7. Thoresby described Fountaine's collection in his diary, Jan. 24, 1709; see *The Diary of Ralph Thoresby*, ed. Joseph Hunter (London, 1850), 2:28–29, 34. For Pope's satire, see the "Epistle to Burlington" (1731), ll. 7–11, in *The Poems of Alexander Pope*, ed. F. W. Bateson, pt. 2 (London, 1951), pp. 130–32.

[122]Brome to Rawlins, Oct. 25, 1735, Bodleian MS. Ballard 19, ff. 48–49; John Nichols, *Literary Anecdotes of the Eighteenth Century*, 9 vols. (London, 1812–1815), 4:148–49. When Hickes needed a transcription of a sheet of Greek in Saxon letters, he thought at once of Thwaites, one of very few who could understand both languages: Hickes to Thwaites, June 23, 1702, Bodleian MS. Rawlinson D 377, f. 38.

[123]Nicolson to Thwaites, May 7, 1698; Gibson to Thwaites, May 20 and July 22, 1697, Bodleian MS. Rawlinson D 377, ff. 110–11, 116, 122 (some of this correspondence is printed in Nichols, *Literary Anecdotes*, 4:141–49); Hickes to Charlett, Jan. 5, 1699, Bodleian

Thwaites acted for Hickes in many matters, receiving information, translating, raising subscriptions, and supervising the printing. The work was slow and the subscribers grew restless. Already in 1699 Nicolson was writing to complain about the "clamours" of some of the contributors, who had begun "to want patience," and he suspected that the addition of a table of coins would delay the book further. But he himself kept on sending new information, including news about Saxon coins and the Runic inscriptions at Ruthwell and Bewcastle, first mentioned in *Camden's Britannia*.[124] It was not easy to coordinate and print a book when fresh information, some of it from abroad, kept arriving daily and when so many pieces were being independently written. Wanley's catalogue was especially tardy, and he was often scolded for dawdling (a little unfairly) by Hickes and Thwaites.[125] Even procuring the famous Junian types in which the work was set proved an ordeal. The matrices and punchions that Francis Junius had left to the university had

---

MS. Ballard 12, ff. 134–35. See also Thwaites to Nicolson, Nov. 5, 1697, B.M. MS. Add. 4276, f. 149. Rawlinson edited King Alfred's Boethius (1699), Benson a reviewed edition of Somner's *Anglo-Saxon Dictionary* (1701). A specimen of the latter was already in print in 1698; see Bodleian MS. Rawlinson D 377, ff. 80–81. According to Hearne, the work was really by Thwaites with the help of several of his students: *Remarks and Collections*, 1:248. See Douglas, *English Scholars*, pp. 56–57, 66–70.

[124]Nicolson to Thwaites, July 10 and Sept. 13, 1699, Bodleian MS. Rawlinson D 377, ff. 46–47, 63–64; Nicolson to Thoresby, Sept. 17, 1699, in Lancaster, *Letters to Thoresby*, pp. 77–78. For the importance of this work, see J. A. W. Bennett, "The Beginnings of Runic Studies in England," in *Viking Society for Northern Research Saga-Book* 13, pt. 4 (London, 1950–51), pp. 269–83. See also Albert S. Cook, "Notes on the Ruthwell Cross," *Publications of the Modern Language Association* 17 (1902): 267–90, and *Some Accounts of the Bewcastle Cross, 1607–1861*, Yale Studies in English 50 (New Haven, 1914); Eric Mercer, "The Ruthwell and Bewcastle Crosses," *Antiquity* 38 (1964): 268–76. Nicolson's contribution appeared in *Camden's Britannia*, p. 841, and emended in the Icelandic Grammar of the *Thesaurus*, plate II.

[125]"As to the Continuall Clamour I had from Mr. Hickes and Mr. Thwaites for more Copy, more Copy, I observe, (1) they seldom, if ever, were at such a Stand for want of Copy as was pretended. (2) Mr. Thwaytes sent not up the Sheets of the Catalogue, as they were printed off, which he promised to do. This Neglect disabled me from making the Reference necessary in many places. A Defect easily visible in the Catalogue. (3) Although my Copie was own'd to have been written as fairly and distinctly, as any Copies that ever came to the Theater-press, they have printed my Catalogue very incorrectly; indeed with Thousands of Faults of their own making. I wrote therefore for my Copie, in order to giving the Errata . . . but after above forty several Demands could not receive so much as one line. Afterwards I heard that it was all destroyed." There was also trouble placing the index. And "after all the Out-cry against me by Dr. Hickes that I was the sole Hinderer of his Book seeing the Light . . . his book was actually published, in above three years after." Wanley says that he was promised £3 a sheet, but received only £65 altogether, plus three copies of the work, although he had paid all his own expenses. He complains also that Hickes used his transcripts and citations throughout the work, "with an Air of Confidence, just as if he had seen or used the Originals Himself," and that he often "trump'd up my Notions as his own." All this is in a reply (which he may not have sent) to a letter, June 1703, of Thwaites to Wanley asking for more copy: B.M. MS. Loan 29/257. Hickes eventually repaid Wanley by procuring him his job.

quite vanished until Wanley discovered them in a hole in the keeper's study.[126] By August 1698 a few sheets were already in the press; twelve months later, there were fifty-five; but it was to take several more years and two mighty folio volumes before the work finally saw the light and satisfied the impatient subscribers.

5

Meanwhile, the price had gone up and had to be extenuated, as Thwaites's advertisement explained in 1704. "The Work having grown upon the Author beyond expectation, and he being encouraged by learned Men, to make it as compleat as conveniently he could . . . it is encreased to twice as many Sheets as were at first devised, with a great number of costly Plates."[127] At last it appeared under the title *Linguarum Vett. Septentrionalium Thesaurus Grammatico-Criticus et Archaeologicus* (Oxford, 1703, 1705). When Thomas Hearne bought a copy, he found it no small burden to his purse.[128] There were nearly four hundred subcribers, including Bentley and Atterbury, Pepys, Evelyn, and Wotton, as well as many cathedral chapters and most of the colleges at Oxford and Cambridge. Still, Hickes was left with many copies and a heavy debt; and it was in these circumstances that he seems to have turned to Wotton for help. He thought of himself as a man "who hath spent nine yeares in hard labour, and broken his constitution in bringing the antiquities of his countrey out of dust and darknesse to light, and risqued his utter ruin to do it."[129]

Hickes turned to Wotton, the acknowledged spokesman for modern learning, to promote the book. "I am printing in Latin a *Notitia*," he wrote to Wanley in 1707, "of my, or as I should say to you, of our book. It is drawn up by a Learned Man, who is of opinion, that it will help the sale of the copies, which lye in great numbers upon my hands unsold."[130] Wotton was naturally interested in the new linguistic worlds opened up by the works of Hickes and Lhwyd, and Nicolson found the Welshman busily engaged on his "Comparative Etymology" when he called on him

---

[126]The keeper, Dr. Thomas Hyde, thought they were Ethiopian, till Thwaites identified them as Gothic; see Tanner to Charlett, Aug. 10, 1697, in Adams, *Old English Scholarship*, pp. 162–68.

[127]The advertisement is dated Nov. 27, 1704, and signed by Thwaites.

[128]Hearne to Smith, Jan. 11, 1709, in Hearne, *Remarks and Collections*, 2:163. It was Hickes who first urged Hearne to edit medieval manuscripts, and Thomas Smith who urged him to learn Anglo-Saxon from the *Thesaurus* and devote himself to medieval history rather than edit the classics, which had been so well done already; see ibid., pp. 248–49.

[129]Hickes to Rev. Jonathan Kimberly, June 19, 1705, Bodleian MS. Autograph D 21, f. 8. He was then £800 in debt.

[130]Hickes to Wanley, Sept. 25, 1707, B.M. MS. Harley 3779, f. 249.

in 1706. "He is a person of extraordinary sagacity," Nicolson wrote
Lhwyd, "and at the present is greedily bent on the study of the Northern
Languages, these being all that he's not yet perfectly acquainted with."[131]
To Wotton it was clear that "the Learned World never yet saw anything
like [the *Thesaurus*] or comparable in this Kind of Literature." It was "the
Arcana of remotest Antiquity . . . A Treasure." In due course he produced his *Conspectus brevis* (London, 1708), which proved useful enough
to find an English translator many years later. Wotton's son-in-law explained afterward that Hickes himself had taken care of the impression and
written all the notes except those on coins, which were by Thwaites. "This
Dr. Hickes had no mind to have known, that it might not look too much
like puffing." Apparently Wotton added nothing of his own. "It was
carefully examined by the author of the *Thesaurus*, and made such as he
would have it, a little sketch of his design, to raise the curiosity of the
readers to farther enquiries or (as you would say in the Trade) to call in
customers." Sir Andrew Fountaine got Leibniz's consent to print a letter
that he had written to Wotton on the subject. And Hickes was able to add
two unpublished Saxon wills and a charter from King Edgar from
Harley's library to add further interest.[132]

Wotton's summary was convenient, but it was not easily accomplished. Hickes's work was a treasure, to be sure, but it was sprawling
and badly organized. One could learn from Wotton what it was about
and use it as a rough table of contents to its hidden riches. But its genius
lay in its massive detail, and that was what had to be sacrificed. The first
volume contained Hickes's original grammar enlarged, with the addition
of the Frankish (thanks to Nicolson) and Icelandic, stuffed with all kinds
of philological erudition and many documents. For that purpose, Hickes
and his colleagues had surveyed practically every Teutonic manuscript in
northern Europe. There were two chapters of Saxon poetry, "which of
themselves would make a compleat Volume." A preface to a friend
enlarged upon "the Dignity of Grammatical Studies" and the need to
distinguish spurious documents. The second volume contained two long
essays, including the crown of the work, an immense dissertation by

---

[131]Nicolson to Lhwyd, May 25, 1706, Bodleian MS. Ashmole 1816, f. 549.

[132]Fountaine to Leibniz, Dec. 7, 1706, Niedersachsische Landesbibliothek MS. Leibniz's
letter to Wotton duly appeared in the *Conspectus*, dated July 10, 1705. In it he sends his
thanks for news about Lhwyd's work and waits impatiently for the *Thesaurus*. In the
meanwhile, he has sent Fountaine some Anglo-Saxon coins from Count Swartzenburg's
library, "exactly taken in water-glue." See also Hickes to Harley, Feb. 10, 1708, in *Historical
Manuscript Commission Reports: Manuscripts of the Duke of Portland*, vol. 4 (London, 1898), p.
477; Clarke in Nichols, *Literary Anecdotes*, 2:110n.; Smith to Hearne, Feb. 21, 1708, in
Hearne, *Remarks and Collections*, 2:96. The work was translated by Maurice Shelton as
*Wotton's Short View of George Hickes's Grammatico-critical and Archaeological Treasure of the
Ancient Northern Languages* (London, 1735).

Hickes, dedicated to Sir Bartholomew Shower, as well as another on
Fountaine's coins. The dissertation dealt with a whole variety of things
beginning with the Anglo-Saxon laws, including the origin of juries
(unknown before William I's time), and going on to wills, donations,
homilies, and many other miscellaneous matters. Here Hickes discoursed
on the use and meaning of charters, and demonstrated, by discovering
their anachronisms, that the long series in the Croyland Abbey Chronicle
were forgeries. (Thomas Smith had already pointed this out to Wanley in
a long letter in 1697 and John Smith a little later.)[133] As Wotton put it,
"From arguments of this kind, our Author pronounces almost all the
Anglo-Saxon Charters in the History of Ingulf of Croyland forged, since
many Words and Expressions occur in them that favor of the Norman
Times, or of those Ages at least that were of later date than those Kings,
whose Names they bear." Unfortunately, Hickes's demonstration did
not settle the issue, and the false charters continued to bedevil medieval
history until late in the nineteenth century.[134] Still, even the great
Mabillon was impressed by Hickes's skills, although his own work had
been criticized in the book.[135]

[133]See Thomas Smith to Wanley, July 18, 1697, B.M. MS. Harl. 3781, ff. 84–85; also
Aug. 24, f. 86; John Smith to Harley, July 6, 1703, BM. MS. Harley 7526, ff. 148–49. In
1695 Henry Wharton had already suspected the authenticity of the documents supposedly
collected by Ingulf of Croyland; see Douglas, *English Scholars*, p. 173. For background, see
H. A. Cronne, "The Study and Use of Charters by English Scholars in the Seventeenth
Century: Sir Henry Spelman and Sir William Dugdale," in *English Historical Scholarship in
the Sixteenth and Seventeenth Centuries*, ed. Levi Fox for Dugdale Society (Stratford-upon-
Avon, 1956), pp. 73–92. Ingulf's *Chronicle* had been recently edited without suspicion by
William Fulman in Thomas Gale's *Rerum Anglicarum scriptores* (Oxford, 1684). Hickes and
Smith agreed about a false charter attributed to King Kenwulf; see the letter, Aug. 7, 1699,
Bodleian MS. Smith 50, f. 117; and more discussion about forged charters, "which Mr.
T[yrell?] has so horribly misapplyed and perverted," in ibid., April 24, 1702, Bodleian MS.
Smith 63, ff. 19–21.

[134]"Thus, for Instance, when in a Charter of Aethelbald King of the Mercians, written,
as is said, in the 716th Year of Grace we meet with *Leucae, Librae, Leglis Monetae*, and other
Norman Words and Phrases, and mention in it made of Black Monks, even before St.
Benet's Rule was ever received in England (who had not that Name till St. Ronald's Time,
a Monk of Cassinus in the Year of our Lord 1070), we must warrant that Charter forged":
Wotton's Short View, p. 37. W. G. Searle enumerates all those who used the chronicle
without suspicion to his own time in "Ingulf and the *Historia Croylandensis*," in *Cambridge
Antiquarian Society Transactions* 27 (1894): 149–51. See also Henry Thomas Riley, "The
History and Charters of Ingulphus Considered," *Archaeological Journal* 19 (1862): 32–49,
114–33.

[135]Mabillon praised him as one in ten thousand, who had plumbed his subject to the
bottom; see Elizabeth Elstob, *An Apology for the Study of Northern Antiquities* (1715), ed.
Charles Peake, Augustan Reprint Society 61 (Los Angeles, 1956), p. xxxiv; Douglas,
English Scholars, p. 94. Thomas Smith thought that the *Thesaurus* "would not be Disagreeable or Ungratefull to the French Antiquaryes; no, not to P. Mabillon, tho' he may find
there some of his assertions and opinions examined and censured. This can do not prejudice
to his incomparable worke, *De re Diplomatica* which I heare, hee is reviewing and reprinting
with several enlargements": Smith to Redmayne, April 17, 1705, Bodleian MS. Smith 65,
f. 187. For the controversy that ensued, see the *Nouveau Traité de diplomatique*, by the

Wotton defends Hickes's methods in much the same way that he had stood by Bentley. Hickes had used the sign of the cross to date official documents. "But those things, how frivolous and minute soever they may seem to those who are not curious, and make but light of Charters, are nevertheless of no little moment, since by the form of the Cross we are able to determine now and then the age of the Charter, provided it be an Original. For the Anglo-Saxons made a different Cross from the Normans." He does not forget to notice the examples of Du Cange and Mabillon. When he comes to Fountaine's contribution, ten copperplates of coins and a learned commentary, many published for the first time, he again points out the use of such matter to the study of history. He concludes with a description of Wanley's catalogue and a sample of its wares. Needless to say, so brief a summary was not likely to satisfy everyone; Thwaites felt it necessary to supply an epitome of his own for the grammatical part. But the fact is that Wotton's *Conspectus* had the full authority of the author himself, and it served an undoubted use in both the original Latin and the subsequent English editions.[136] It may even have helped to sell a few more copies of the *Thesaurus*, though not nearly enough to take care of the original impression.

6

In many ways, Hickes's work was the capstone of the antiquarian enterprise, the most remarkable work of modern scholarship in its time, but it was by no means alone. In these same years the advancement of scholarly learning seemed to progress on nearly every front, despite the misgivings of many, and the moderns produced a series of massive works that are still astonishing for their erudition and methodological sophistication. It would be pointless to try to describe or even to list them all here, but it may be well to conclude with a word about one modest and retiring scholar who lived out and articulated the antiquarian ideal better perhaps than anyone else. For David Douglas, he was "the first of the moderns," the true climax to this greatest age of medieval

---

monks of St-Maur [Charles François Toustain and René Tassin], 4 vols. (Paris, 1750–1759), 1:18–20; 4:200–205.

[136]Hearne found it typically a "trivial, mean Performance," but he thought somehow that Wotton's new addiction to "Middle Age Antiquity" might correct his disrespectful views about the classical authors in the *Reflections*; see Hearne, *Remarks and Collections*, 2:92. Thwaites's work, the *Grammatica Anglo-Saxonica ex Hickesiano Thesauro excerpta* (Oxford, 1711), was meant to be joined to Wotton's *Conspectus*. Nevertheless, the Saxonist Edward Lye still found Wotton's summary stimulating in 1735: Lye to Maurice Shelton, June 12, 1735, B.M. MS. Add. 28167, f. 47. He hoped Shelton would go on to translate Hickes's dissertation.

scholarship, although he was less appreciated (perhaps for that very reason) by his contemporaries.[137] We know almost nothing about Thomas Madox except that he attended the Middle Temple but not the university, never practiced law but got a job eventually as a clerk in the Court of Augmentations, and began to write some amazing antiquarian works. He was rewarded eventually by being elected to the new Society of Antiquaries and was made historiographer royal in 1714 instead of Jonathan Swift. For the most part, he seems to have kept to himself and left little behind except his published works and ninety-four volumes of transcripts now in the British Library.

It was his job in the Office of Augmentations that got him started on his lifework. He quickly saw the immense value of the official legal records of the kingdom in recovering its history and set to work rescuing them. Although he was the least contentious of men and tried to suppress his polemical purpose, it is clear that he hoped to throw light on that most controversial of historical problems, the origin and course of the English common law. And he seems to have felt that the principal value of history was to engender a reverence for the past as a check on precipitous action. He felt deeply that all previous students of the subject, from Sir Edward Coke and Sir Henry Spelman to his contemporaries (whom he tactfully leaves nameless), had failed to ground their histories in the proper documents and had tended to read the present back into the past. He recognized the usefulness of the medieval chronicles and church registers, especially those that recorded contemporary events, but he believed firmly that "the publick records of the crown and kingdom are the most important and authentic of all." These were the best foundations of history, the only "proper vouchers" to test the rest. Madox had no hesitation in recalling his readers from his text to the "testimonies couched in the margin: for they are in my opinion, the most valuable part of the work; and by consequence, the most worthy to be read."[138]

Madox's first work appeared in 1702 as the *Formulare Anglicanum*, "a collection of ancient Charters and Instruments of Divers Kinds, taken from Originals, placed under several Heads, and deduced (in a Series according to Order of Time) from the Norman Conquest to the end of the Reign of Henry the VIII." It was another exercise in diplomatics, this time for a later medieval period, and Madox, like Hickes and Wanley, whom he knew, had read his Mabillon. He edited some 783 charters

---

[137]He seems to have been rediscovered by J. H. Round, F. W. Maitland, and others at the end of the nineteenth century; see Douglas, *English Scholars*, pp. 234–43; and before him Harold D. Hazeltine, "Thomas Madox as Constitutional and Legal Historian," *Law Quarterly Review* 32 (1916): 268–89, 352–72.

[138]Thomas Madox, *The History and Antiquities of the Exchequer of the King of England* (London, 1711), p. ix.

from the vast stores in his care, and his work (according to Douglas) has never been superseded. In his preface he declared the value of these documents in throwing light on the manners and customs of the past and in settling questions about feudal law and institutions. "One may justly wonder that Feudal learning (if I may so call it) should be so little known or regarded as it seems to be by the Students (I ask their pardon) of the Common Law of England." Was he thinking of Brady and Tyrrell? "Considerable use may I conceive be made of Them in History; and some in Chronology." The antiquaries at least understood; Hearne praised the book extravagantly and Nicolson thought it would prove "of unspeakable Service to our Students in Law and Antiquities."[139]

But the *Formulare* was not itself history; merely preparation for it. Later Madox seems to have disavowed this kind of work, "miscellaneous uncemented Collections," as little more than manual labor, "not up to the character of an Historian." It was more important, he thought, to collect and digest the materials into a historical discourse by explaining, comparing, and illustrating them. "He will do a thing useful to the Publick, if out of Them he can extract a True history, if out of Them he can supply what is wanting in other Histories, amend what is erroneous or fallacious, illustrate what is obscure, reconcile what seemeth discordant, in a word discover and in some measure establish truth or certainty."[140] And this is what Madox set out to do in his next and greatest work, *The History and Antiquities of the Exchequer of the Kings of England* (1711). He seems to have begun it by 1697 and labored unstintingly on it for the next fourteen years. The labor and expense, he complains, of visiting distant repositories, of annotating and copying countless documents, "of perusing a vast number of things for a Few comparatively that one actually collects"—only one who has attempted the task can fully appreciate. But indeed, that was just the beginning, for the documents had to be sifted for their truth and arranged to tell a story. Madox thought the pursuit of historical truth "some sort of religious act," and he employed every means he could think of to ensure the veracity of his work.[141]

In an epistle to Lord Somers at the beginning of the *Exchequer*, Madox described his method and set out the antiquarian ideal. The first thing he did (he says) was to collect the documents as fully as possible. Then he organized them in several books and drew up a general design. "When I

[139]Hearne, *Remarks and Collections*, 1:46; William Nicolson, *The English Historical Library* (London, 1736), p. 240.

[140]Thomas Madox, *Firma Burgi; or, An Historical Essay concerning the Cities Towns and Buroughs of England* (London, 1726), p. ix.

[141]"It imports Solemnity and Sacredness: and ought to be undertaken with Purity and Rectitude of Mind": Madox, *History of the Exchequer*, p. vii.

had pitched upon Chapters or Heads of Discourse, I took the Materials out of the Stock provided, and digested them in proper places under the chapters or heads assumed." The arrangement was systematic and analytical rather than narrative.[142] At each point he scrupulously reported the respective records or testimonies that he employed. His chief rule was "to give such an account of things as might be elicited and drawn out of the memorials cited from time to time; and not to cite memorials and vouchers for establishing of any private opinions preconceived in my own mind." He seems to have had in mind a notion of "scientific" objectivity (perhaps borrowed from Francis Bacon and natural history) for which he was later much appreciated.[143] His main sources were the Great Rolls of the Pipe, the Memoranda of the Exchequer, and other rolls in the Tower of London, "all which Records having been written by Publick officers and by publick authority at the time when the things recorded therein were Done carry in them a full and undoubted Credit." It is here that he proclaims the superiority of documents over written narratives and calls attention to his margins over his text.

The *History of the Exchequer* described the financial administration of medieval England from the Norman Conquest to the end of the reign of Edward II. It is organized chronologically under separate headings according to the different functions of the court. It concludes with the text of the *Dialogus de Scaccario*, a twelfth-century dialogue on the Exchequer, which Madox based on a careful collation of the manuscripts. The author was as proud of the novelty of his subject as of his method, "the Path I take, being hitherto, in Effect, untrodden." He preferred to use unpublished manuscripts in every case before printed books, "that the Reader may be entertained with something new," though this was not hard to do "because my Subject is in a Manner new and untouched."[144] In his scrupulous attention to matters of fact, Madox was perfectly aware that his discourse must turn out "the more dry and undiverting." He at least was happy to sacrifice literary artifice for accuracy and dispassion. In a way, the more useful he made his work for scholars, the less interesting it must be for the general reader. And he knew that that would lead

---

[142]For this procedure as the distinguishing mark of the antiquary, see Momigliano, "Ancient History and the Antiquarian" (n. 4 above), pp. 1–39.

[143]See Douglas, *English Scholars*, p. 243. I have examined the relationship between natural science and antiquities in "Natural History and the New Philosophy," in *Humanism and History*, pp. 123–54, and in *Dr. Woodward's Shield* (Berkeley, 1977), pp. 18–47. The notion of beginning with the documents and sifting and arranging them in natural categories for systematic use looks back to Bacon on the one hand and forward to the positivism of such as Charles Victor Langlois and Charles Seignobos on the other. Their very popular textbook, *Introduction aux études historiques* (1898), went through many editions in English and French.

[144]Madox, *History of the Exchequer*, p. vi.

to criticism. In his first work he had already tried to anticipate his critics. The reader must not expect to find any "curious or refined Learning" in his book, since the subject matter, he admitted, was low. "If any one shall endeavour to bring a disvalue upon these or other monuments of antiquity that may be offered to the publique, by calling them obsolete antiquated things, or musty records, or by such like terms: I shall leave such person to enjoy freely his own sentiments in the case." He begins to sound exactly like Richard Bentley in a similar position. "All men have not a like genius, or a disposition to the same kind of studies. However, we need not go about to undervalue all other studies besides those to which we are bent; or seek to advance the value of that sort of learning which we profess to know, by depressing the value of that of other kinds."[145] If Madox seems just a little disingenuous here, it is no doubt because he had a strong conviction of the particular value of his subject and was hardly ready to allow a choice where the truth about the past was in question.

In the Epistle to Somers, Madox addressed himself directly to anyone who wanted to know, "Of what use are these old antiquated things?" The problem was that some people saw no need to return to the distant past for present purposes. But no rational being Madox was sure, would deny the value of history altogether, and he had no trouble showing how modern history made more sense in a larger context, as part of a whole past, than on its own. Even if one preferred modern history as better adapted to present use, it was still "of greater Advantage to have Things presented in their full extent, than only in Parts." And he noticed that many of those gentlemen who were complaining had nevertheless put themselves to great trouble to learn about the culture of ancient Greece and Rome. Their instructors had persuaded them properly "that by attentive Study and conversing in well-chosen Books, Men whose Minds are capable of just Improvements, learn that Experience and Wisdom of past Ages, and acquire such a Ripeness of Judgment and Comprehension in Affairs, as qualifieth them to serve their Country." This was certainly true. "But do the political Constitution, Laws and Manners of ancient Greece or Rome bear a nearer Affinity or Resemblance to those of Britain at this Day, than the ancient Constitutions, Laws and Manners of Britain to those of Britain in the modern or present Times?" Was it more sensible to learn about the manners and customs of a more ancient and alien culture to the neglect of one's own ancestors? It is true, Madox was forced to admit, that some foreign histories, especially the classics, were more valuable than the English, "considered simply in themselves; the former being better written." But that was simply an inducement to

[145]Thomas Madox, *Formulare Anglicanum* (London, 1702), pp. viii–ix.

Englishmen to improve their histories, "to imitate the noble Patterns of this Kind which the Greeks and Romans have set."[146] Thus this profoundly conservative man took sides unequivocally with the moderns, although he never passed judgment directly on the battle of the books.

Of course, Madox (like many of the antiquaries) had missed the point. It was precisely the argument of the ancients that the Greeks and Romans were (or ought to be) much closer to the moderns than anything in that dark and barbarous time between. It was much easier for an English gentleman to imagine himself comfortably in ancient Rome than among the Saxons or Normans. Even Madox was forced to admit that an Englishman returning to the British past was "like one newly landed in a strange Country. He finds himself in another Climate. He observeth many Things strange and uncouth in Language, Laws, Customs, and Manners."[147] Yet the English gentleman brought up on the Latin classics, setting foot in Rome and the Campania, could only feel a shock of recognition. Moreover, Madox was unable to say, and certainly not to show, how one might actually write an English history on the model of the ancients while accepting the (admittedly new) demands of antiquarian scholarship for precision and truth. It would have to be a rare gentleman who could think of reading one of Madox's massive volumes through, much less recognize in it any of the traditional virtues of a narrative history. Under these circumstances, Swift might well think that he had fallen victim to a lesser man.

Needless to say, to the modern medievalist, who still employs Madox, the situation looks very different, and an album of praise might be gathered for his achievement and its evident anticipation of modern historiography.[148] In truth, the work was wonderfully done (given its premises), and it was followed by two more that seem also to have been part of a single great project to write the history of feudal England.[149] If so, Douglas remarks, it was surely one of the great unwritten books of English scholarship. Yet it must remain doubtful that Madox or any other single scholar could ever have accomplished the work according to his specifications. Madox himself was able to finish only some "parts" of an imagined whole. "My Ambition," he said, "was to form this History in such a manner that it may be a Pattern for the Antiquaries to follow, if they please. . . . For I think it is to be wished that the Histories of a Countrey so well furnished with Records and manuscripts as Ours is should be grounded throughout as far as it is practicable on proper

---

[146]Madox, *History of the Exchequer*, pp. xiii–xiv.

[147]Ibid., p. xii.

[148]See the plaudits by Maitland, R. L. Poole, and others in Hazeltine, "Madox as Constitutional and Legal Historian," pp. 370–72; Douglas, *English Scholars*, pp. 237–43.

[149]*Firma Burgi* (1726) and the posthumous *Baronia Anglica* (1736).

Vouchers." But even Madox with all his industry had touched on only a fraction of the available records. "For my own part," Madox confessed with a wish that sounds like William Nicolson's, "I cannot look upon the History of England to be compleatly written till it shall come to be written after that manner."[150] Unhappily, Madox's work, like that of all the great antiquaries, and however much we may admire it, only made the prospects for success seem less likely.

[150]Madox, *History of the Exchequer*, p. ix.

Chapter Twelve

Ancients and Moderns

I

With the appearance of the *Thesaurus*, the rehabilitation of medieval English history reached its apogee. Unfortunately, Thwaites died tragically young in 1711, and Hickes, worn out, in 1715. Thwaites had further ambitions but Hickes was pretty much done with the "septentrional" enterprise and returned to his earlier mission of defending the primitive purity of the Episcopal church against all comers. The Anglo-Saxon cause was left in the hands of a few students, who tried to carry on, but the odds were against them. The fact is that the powerful partisan motives that had first given birth to the enterprise, the political and religious quarrels that had turned men back upon the national past in the seventeenth century, were beginning to wane in the more stable conditions of the new century. It became much less pressing to feel, as Nicolson had done when he wrote to Wanley in 1705, that "next to what concerns the preservation of our Established Religion and Government, peace here and salvation hereafter, I know nothing that hath greater share in my thoughts and desires than the promotion of Septentrional Learning."[1] Meanwhile, the gathering forces of *ancienneté* were making it more and more difficult to sustain an enthusiasm for erudition of any kind, but especially for medieval learning. The quarrel between the Saxonists and the classicists which resulted was thus another episode in the battle of the books.

Of course the tension had been there all along. Hickes himself had felt the need to defend his Saxon interests against the scoffing of the wits

[1]Nicolson to Wanley, Aug. 20, 1705, in *Letters to and from William Nicolson*, ed. J. Nichols, 2 vols. (London, 1809), 2:650–52.

throughout his long labor, but he never gave any indication how or whether classical rhetoric (which he admired) could be reconciled with modern scholarship (which he employed) for a medieval subject about which he was ambivalent, or to put it more directly, just how the Saxon antiquities could be incorporated into a narrative history. Neither Samuel Daniel, Milton, nor Temple had ever made the slightest effort in that direction, and now even the publication of the *Thesaurus* had little effect. In 1706 an anonymous compilation appeared which was briefly and mistakenly attributed to Hickes, but which failed again to address the problem, although the author was certainly familiar with both the early narratives and recent scholarship.

In fact the compiler was an elderly rector from Mepsal in Bedfordshire named Thomas Salmon, who had become famous for some controversial modern views on musical theory for which he won the support of John Wallis and the Royal Society. Now he thought it necessary to come to the rescue of church and state with a work he called *Historical Collections Relating the Originals, and Revolutions of the Inhabitants of Great Britain to the Norman Conquest.*[2] Here was yet another attempt to recount the early history of England by compilation using only original sources as far as they allowed. The author meant it to be a work of Anglican apologetics, and he believed that the best way to make his case (as Hickes had done in the *Thesaurus*) was to set the evidence directly before the reader, this time the narrative sources exclusively. Salmon's work therefore consisted almost entirely of extracts from Caesar and Tacitus, Bede and the Saxon Chronicle, with a few snippets from latter chronicles at the time of the Norman Conquest. "There is no Way of coming nearer to this," he insisted, "than by viewing the Originals from whence our Modern Accounts are taken. . . . It is not possible the Judgment should be satisfied without drinking at the Fountain; which is free from all those Tinctures that the Streams receive from every different Soil through which they pass." Yet Salmon saw that it would be foolish to ignore altogether "the great Improvements, which the Learned in the last Age have made," and so he decided to add some extracts from the best modern scholars from William Camden to William Lloyd—but not Hickes, whose work may have appeared too late. These writers helped to "set Antiquity in a clear

---

[2]The best evidence for Salmon's authorship is a letter to Hans Sloane offering him a presentation copy: Salmon to Sloane, Dec. 4, 1705, B.M. MS. Sloane 4040, f. 104. Many years later Thomas Salmon, Jr., reprinted the work and claimed it for his father: *The History of Great Britain and Ireland*, 2d ed. (London, 1725). A note in the British Library copy (598 e 2) assigns it mistakenly to Hickes. For Salmon's role in the lively controversy between the ancients and the moderns over music, see Doris Silbert, "The C Clef in the Seventeenth Century," *Monthly Musical Record* 67 (1937): 169–72. The best general account of the musical quarrel remains Charles Burney, *A General History of Music*, 4 vols. (London, 1776–1789).

Light, brush off the Dust, and remove the Rubbish. Which is very necessary to be done for those of the Middle Age, when Sense and Learning
were at a very low Ebb."[3] Salmon understood the necessity of modern
scholarship for his obscure subject but not quite how to integrate it into
his story.

Needless to say, Salmon saw no need to rewrite or improve the classical authors, who remained beyond criticism, though he had no such
illusions about the intrinsic value of medieval literature or learning.
"None can relate the Transactions of Caesar in Britain with a more Pure
and Fluent Stile than he himself has done; nor is it possible to exceed the
Judgement of Tacitus." But it was otherwise with the "Ages of Ignorance" that followed, when much was lost or corrupted. "We have no
great Reason to admire the Authors of the middle age, but we must make
use of them, or we cannot come at the Knowledge of the Times. All that
we can hope for from them is Honesty and Plainness, a true Representation of Matter of Fact, and the Sense of Affairs in their proper order." In
this respect, Bede and the Saxon chronicles (for which he praised Gibson's edition and offered an English translation) were indispensable, despite their clinging to superstition. Now with the help of modern scholars who had ransacked antiquities "the Light of Learning would prevail."
Yet when Salmon came at last to the Normans, he offered his extracts
and commentary, only to conclude surprisingly with a long section
drawn from that most exemplary of all the ancients—Sir William Temple! "It may be very well suppos'd that the Reader should be pretty much
tir'd with so many dry Quotations of Authors of the Middle Age, who
wrote neither with Intrigue nor Ornament, and therefore by way of
Refinement here shall be added Sir William Temple's Account of the
Norman Revolution, who with great Elegance of Stile, and Freedom of
Thought, makes every thing he writes extremely entertaining."[4] Not for
the first time do we find a modern paying his respects to the classical
rhetoric of the other side.

2

The ancients were less generous. To the end they continued to despise, and to fear, the kind of painstaking erudition that the Saxon scholars, like their classical forebears, seemed to represent. Just after publish-

[3][Thomas Salmon], *Historical Collections Relating to the Originals, and Revolutions of the Inhabitants of Great Britain to the Norman Conquest* (London, 1706), Preface, sig. A2–4.
[4]Ibid., p. 413.

ing a new edition of *A Tale of a Tub,* Jonathan Swift conceived a new project. It was probably meant to serve his ambition to become historiographer royal.[5] In any case, he drew up a brief tract in the form of a letter to Robert Harley, *A Proposal for Correcting, Improving and Ascertaining the English Tongue,* and he published it in 1712. The partisan political tone of the letter has puzzled historians, and it provoked an immediate response from the Whigs. But Swift's point was larger than the moment, for the letter embodied some of the most cherished opinions of the ancients about language. In it he called for the establishment of an academy on the style of the French, which would reform and fix the English language once and for all. The notion had come up before in the Royal Society with John Evelyn as a leading advocate, and it had been renewed by Dryden and others, most recently by Swift himself in the *Tatler* and by Addison in the *Spectator.*[6] It reflected the common assumption that language, like literature, had certain timeless virtues that could be perfected, as the Greeks had once done, and the Romans in Augustan times. English had improved itself recently on the model of the classical tongues, but it was in danger of corruption, as Latin had once been corrupted under the influence of the barbarians of the Middle Ages. Immediate action was necessary to arrest decline.

Swift's description of the history of the classical and modern languages did not take much cognizance of modern philology. He repeats the view that Bentley had been at such pains to refute, that classical Greek had been perfected before Homer and lasted without change for more than a thousand years, and he believed that most of the modern languages had not altered much in the past few hundred years. English, he thought, had peaked in the reign of Charles I (or perhaps with the translators of the Bible) and showed dangerous symptoms of decay. The trouble was that the English were not naturally polite, and had "a tendency to lapse into the barbarity of those Northern Nations from whom we are descended, and whose Languages Labour all under the same defect." One bad sign was the recent fashion of abbreviating words and reducing English to its original monosyllabic character, "so very in-

[5]See Henry W. Sams, "Jonathan Swift's *Proposals Concerning the English Language:* A Reconsideration," in *Essays in English Literature of the Classical Period Presented to Dougald Macmillan,* ed. Daniel W. Patterson and Albrecht B. Strauss, *Studies in Philology,* extra ser. 4 (1967): 76–87. The text is in Swift's *Prose Works,* ed. Herbert Davis, 16 vols. (Oxford, 1939–1974), 4:1–21, with an introduction, pp. xi–xv. See also Irvin Ehrenpreis, *Swift: The Man, His Works, and His Age,* 3 vols. (Cambridge, Mass., 1962–1983), 2:542–49.

[6]See Oliver F. Emerson, "John Dryden and the British Academy," in *Essential Articles for the Study of John Dryden,* ed. H. T. Swedenberg (Hamden, Conn., 1966), pp. 263–80; Carl Niemeyer, "The Earl of Roscommon's Academy," *Modern Language Notes* 49 (1934): 432–37.

judiciously, as to form unharmonious Sounds, that none but a Northerner could endure."[7] Just so the Latin authors had been allowed to degenerate in the Middle Ages, until they could not be understood, "unless by Antiquaries, who make it their study to expound them." If modern English was permitted to continue changing, the modern historian must suffer to see his work antiquated: "he will be only considered as a tedious Relater of Facts, and perhaps consulted in his Turn, among other neglected Authors, to furnish Materials for some further Collector."[8]

For the poor Saxonists who were laboring so hard to recover the language and customs of their forebears, this was too much. Once again, by an odd chance it was a lady who took the field to answer the challenge. Elizabeth Elstob, like Madame Dacier, had become a scholar against all odds. She had learned Anglo-Saxon (along with Latin and Greek) from her brother and with the encouragement of Hickes and Wanley.[9] William Elstob held a living in London which supported the two; eventually he became chaplain to William Nicolson. He contributed in various small ways to the world of modern scholarship, both Latin and Anglo-Saxon. For Hickes and the *Thesaurus* he translated an Anglo-Saxon homily, among other services; for Fountaine, he helped with his commentary on the coins; he seems to have copied for Wanley; and for Wotton's *Conspectus brevis*, he offered a transcription (done by Elizabeth) in Anglo-Saxon of St. Athanasius's creed. He also picked up Gibson's idea of a collection of Anglo-Saxon laws but did but live to see it through.[10] Meanwhile, at the instigation of Hickes, Elizabeth determined to edit a work of her own, and in 1709 she published *An Anglo-Saxon Homily on the Birthday of St. Gregory*.[11] She intended to follow it with a complete edition of the Homilies of Aelfric, and printed proposals. Hickes was impressed. "I suppose you have seen Mrs. Elstob," he wrote to Charlett in 1712, "and the MSS she hath brought to be printed in your presse. The publication of the MSS she hath brought (the most

[7]"We are full of monosyllables, and those clogged with consonants . . . all of which are enemies to a sounding language": John Dryden, dedication to *Troilus and Cressida* (1679), in Emerson, "Dryden and the British Academy," p. 276.

[8]Swift, *Prose Works*, 4:18.

[9]See the series of letters, beginning 1707, from Mrs. Elstob to Wanley, in B.M. MS. Loan 29/254. For the Elstobs, see John Nichols, *Literary Anecdotes of the Eighteenth Century*, 9 vols. (London, 1812–1815), 4:122–40; for Elizabeth, see Myra Reynolds, *The Learned Lady in England, 1650–1760* (Boston, 1920), pp. 169–85; Margaret Ashdown, "Elizabeth Elstob, the Learned Saxonist," *Modern Language Review* 20 (1925): 125–46.

[10]It was completed in 1721 by David Wilkins with much help from William Nicolson; see *Letters to and from Nicolson*, pp. 447–48, 456–57, 461–66, 469–71, 476–80, 482–88, 490, 492, 505–7, 539–40; David Douglas, *English Scholars*, 2d ed. (London, 1951), p. 69.

[11]Hearne did not approve the long introduction and large apparatus: Thomas Hearne, *Remarks and Collections*, ed. C. E. Doble et al., 11 vols. (Oxford, 1885–1921), 2:289–90.

correct I ever saw or read) will be of great advantage to the Church of
England against the Papists . . . and the credit of our country, to which
Mrs. Elstob will be counted abroad, as great an ornament in her way as
Madame Dacier is to France."[12] It was about this time that she read Swift
and decided to answer. Someone had to speak up for the Saxon studies to
which she and her brother had pledged their scholarly lives.

In her first work Mrs. Elstob had already spoken out against those
who fancied themselves polite exponents of foreign learning but who
were ignorant of the religion and customs of their own forebears.[13] Now
she published a more elaborate defense of her subject, an "Apology for
the Study of Northern Antiquities," which she prefixed to her *Rudiments
of Grammar for the Anglo-Saxon Tongue* (1715). It was addressed to
Hickes. In this essay she meant "to do some Justice to the Study of
Antiquities, and even to our Language itself, against the severe Censures
of both."[14] Swift had decried Anglo-Saxon as a primitive monosyllabic
tongue. Mrs. Elstob replied by arguing that it was not simply monosyllabic, and that in any case simplicity and plainness were virtues that
should be prized. She appealed first to patriotism, for an attack on the
language seemed to her an attack on the nation. And she insisted that it
was only ignorance that could create such a presumption against a language "which in variety of Numbers" was thought by those who knew
to be "scarce inferior to the Greek itself." Much of her little tract was
taken up thereafter by a remarkable series of quotations from Greek and
Latin, and from Chaucer to Dryden, Pope, and Swift himself, to show
the use and beauty of monosyllabic expression in poetry. If it were
desirable to determine the propriety of the language (and Mrs. Elstob
made no objection), it was essential first to understand the origin and
etymology of its words; and Swift and his friends would have to be
excluded by their ignorance.

Mrs. Elstob was particularly exercised by Swift's dismissive remarks
about the antiquaries. "Methinks it very hard, that those who labour and

---

[12]Hickes to Charlett, Dec. 23, 1712, Bodleian MS. Ballard 12, f. 29; *Letters Written by
Eminent Persons in the Bodleian Library*, ed. John Walker (London, 1815), pp. 243–46. See
also Hickes to Dr. Turner, Dec. 24, 1712, Bodleian MS. Rawlinson Letters 92, f. 541;
Hickes to Bishop of Bristol, May 22 and 29, 1714, in *Historical Manuscript Commission
Reports: Manuscripts of the Duke of Portland*, vol. 5 (London, 1899), pp. 445–46, 451. A copy
of Mrs. Elstob's proposals is in B.M. MS. Loan 29/260; see also Elizabeth Elstob to Harley,
1713, B.M. MS. Birch 4253, ff. 62–63v.

[13]Elizabeth Elstob, *An Anglo-Saxon Homily on the Birthday of St. Gregory* (London,
1709), p. vi.

[14]The text has been edited by Charles Peake for the Augustan Reprint Society, 61 (Los
Angeles, 1956). S. F. D. Hughes identifies another target of Mrs. Elstob's displeasure in
Charles Gildon and William Brightland, *A Grammar of the English Tongue* (London, 1711,
etc.); see "Mrs. Elstob's Defense of Antiquarian Learning in Her *Rudiments of Grammar for
the Anglo-Saxon Tongue* (1715)," *Harvard Library Bulletin* 27 (1979): 172–91.

take so many pains to furnish others with Materials, either for Writing, or for Discourse, who have not Leisure, Skill, or Industry enough to serve themselves, shou'd be allow'd no other Instances of gratitude, than the reproachful Title of Men of Low Genius." ("I know, my Lord," the antiquary Thomas Madox had written a year or two before, "that Lovers of Antiquities are commonly looked upon to be men of low unpolite genius fit only for the Rough and Barbarick part of Learning.")[15] But that was not the worst of the charge, according to Mrs. Elstob, "for they are not allow'd to have common Sense, or to know how to express their Minds intelligibly." It was insupportable that some people should think that Hickes had employed so much time to so little purpose. Mrs. Elstob had just been reading that perfect statement of Christ Church ancienneté, Henry Felton's Dissertation on Reading the Classics (1713), in which the author remembered a friend who was familiar with both polite learning and antiquities and who was pleased to refer to the students of the latter as "Your Antiquaries; being very ready to disclaim an Acquaintance with all such Wits, and who told me the Antiquaries, were the Men in all the World who most contemn'd Your Men of Sufficiency and Self-Conceit." Mrs. Elstob replied with the examples of half a dozen polite English writers (praised by Felton) who had in fact cherished the study, including Sprat, Atterbury, Lhwyd, Nicolson, Hickes, and Gibson.[16]

It was a good plainspoken effort, and Swift at least was reduced to silence—or nearly so. Some years later he wrote out a little spoof that he left in manuscript, entitled "A Discourse to Prove the Antiquity of the English Tongue: Shewing from various Instances that Hebrew, Greek, and Latin, were derived from English." Here the mock-philologist shows how the name Aristotle, for example, really derives from English. It seems that the peripatetic philosopher used to teach while walking, so that when his pupils arrived he would *arise to tell* them what he wanted them to know. As a result he was called *arise to tell*, "but succeeding ages, who understood not this etymology, have by an absurd change, made it *Aristotle!*" Perhaps it is as well that Swift left his piece unpublished, although the modern philologist has naturally resurrected it.[17] In any case, Mrs. Elstob's plea was hardly enough to dispel the prejudice of

[15]Thomas Madox, *The History and Antiquities of the Exchequer of the Kings of England* (London, 1711), p. ii.

[16]Elizabeth Elstob, "Apology for the Study of Northern Antiquities," in her *Rudiments of Grammar for the Anglo-Saxon Tongue* (London, 1715), pp. xxix–xxxiii. Hearne vigorously approved her criticism of Felton in a warm letter to Hickes, July 31, 1715: *Remarks and Collections,* 4:83.

[17]Swift, *Prose Works,* 4:231–39. The work was first printed in 1765; it may have been meant for the *Intelligencer,* and was probably written after 1727.

Protestants and classicists, not to say enlightened philosophers, against the culture of the Middle Ages and the misplaced pedantry of erudition.[18] Twenty-five years later the Saxonist George Ballard was still defending the same cause, although he thought "that the bad success Dean Swift had met with in this affair from the incomparably learned and ingenious Mrs. Elstob, would have deterred all others."[19]

William Elstob died in 1715, leaving Elizabeth to shift for herself, and she quickly disappeared into oblivion, forgotten by an ungrateful society both as a scholar and a woman. Of the great band of Saxonists who had rallied to Hickes at the turn of the century and been celebrated by Wotton, only Humfrey Wanley was left, and he had other fish to fry. In much the same way, the remarkable effort of Edward Lhwyd to do for Celtic Britain just what Hickes was attempting for the Saxons—that is to say, collect everything that remained of the language and culture of primitive Britain—halted abruptly with his untimely death, and with only a "dry" Celtic dictionary accomplished.[20] Nevertheless, when Hickes received his copy of Lhwyd's *Archaeologia Britannica*, he was ecic and thought that it would please anyone with "a genius for antiquity." Like John Byrom, he agreed "that the Saxon must go to School to the Briton, and learn his language"; the ancient Welsh were the true aborigines, and knowledge of their tongue was essential. Hickes only wished

[18]"I wish that some have not made their Study of this kind of Antiquity seviceable to the reviving and recommending Popish superstition. This is certain, that they bring to light those Writings which contain corrupt the Doctrines, Rites and Usages of the Church of Rome. One of their Catalogues [Wanley's] consists mostly of Popish Missals, Prayers to Saints, Homilies on the Festival days of Saints, Exorcises, Reliques, Legends, Fables, etc., savouring of Superstition": John Edwards, *Some New Discoveries of the Uncertainty, Deficiency, and Corruptions of Human Knowledge and Learning* (London, 1714), pp. 43–44. Edwards also refers explicitly to Mrs. Elstob's homilies. For the "philosophical" contempt of learning and the Middle Ages, see Bolingbroke's *Letters on the Study and Use of History*, dated 1735, published in his *Works* (London, 1754), 2:261–62, 360. Bolingbroke is, of course, famous for advocating history teaching by example.

[19]George Ballard to Joseph Ames, June 29, 1737, in Nichols, *Literary Anecdotes*, 4:211–12.

[20]W. Foulkes, admittedly "no antiquary," had hoped to get Lhwyd to alter his method for the next volume, "from a dry Dictionary way into continu'd Discourses which would be more palatable and entertaining and yet equally instructive," but to no avail; Foulkes to Browne Willis, n.d., Bodleian MS. Willis 42, ff. 164–65. Lhwyd hoped that his work would "be useful to Criticks and Historians in General," and thought that it should probably be employed, "in Conjunction with the Late Exquisite Performance of Dr. Hicks, [to] encourage the Antiquaries throughout Britain and Ireland to a Narrower Inspection into our oldest Languages, Inscriptions and Manuscripts": Edward Lhwyd, *Archaeologia Britannica* (Oxford, 1707), Dedication. The work was ready for the press in 1703 but was held up by the *Thesaurus*; see Lhwyd to Foulkes, July 28, 1705, *Archaeologia Cambrensis*, 3d ser. 5 (1859): 250–52. At first Lhwyd thought that it sold surprisingly well, for "a book so foreign"; see Lhwyd to Foulkes, Aug. 8, 1707, *Archaeologia Cambrensis*, 3d ser., 6 (1860): 14–15.

that Lhwyd's treatise had been published twenty years before, so that he could have used it in his own work.[21]

3

Edmund Gibson felt much the same. "There is but one true way," he wrote to Lhwyd, "to find out the originall of Nations very ancient and concerning which no certain Records remain; and that way you have taken, and by your very useful labours have enabled future Ages to make a just judgment upon the Antiquity . . . of these Islands." How the editor of Camden would have profited from this work! "And if it be not valued by the wits of this Age it is because nothing is valued by them but what affords some present Entertainment to fill up the Vacancies of an idle unthinking Life."[22] Nicolson too saw its value to the early history of Britain. But Lhwyd was too modest to accept the praise; friends, after all, were overly generous. Anyway, he knew that "an Account of such Antiquated Languages is in the vulgar Opinion but very jejune stuff."[23] So too it seemed to William Wotton, who had early subscribed to the work. He welcomed the *Archaeologia Britannica* as a valuable addition to the commonwealth of learning, "tho' like other jewels it can be usefull but to a very few members of the republick." Indeed, most of the subscribers probably hoped that the next volume would be "more entertaining."[24] If anything, the audience for modern scholarship appeared to be shrinking.

Of course, a triumphant *ancienneté* could only make things harder and

[21]John Byrom to Thomas Tanner, Feb. 19, 1694, Bodleian MS. Tanner 25, ff. 124–25; Hickes to Lhwyd, June 2, 1707, B.M. MS. Ashmole 1815, f. 188, quoted in R. T. Gunther, *Life and Letters of Edward Lhwyd*, Early Science in Oxford 14 (Oxford, 1945), pp. 43–44. In 1696 Hickes had written to Charlett, "I would write to Mr Loyd encouraging him to study the Northern languages but that I am so utterly a stranger to him": Bodleian MS. Ballard 12, f. 68. For Nicolson, who naturally supported the undertaking from the beginning, Lhwyd was "the greatest man (at Antiquities and Natural Philosophy together) that I have ever had the happiness to converse with": Nicolson to Thoresby, in *Letters of Eminent Men to Ralph Thoresby*, 2 vols. (London, 1832), 1:206–7.

[22]Gibson to Lhwyd, Bodleian MS. Ashmole 1815, f. 89.

[23]Nicolson to Thoresby, Nov. 3, 1707, in *Letters to Ralph Thoresby*, ed. W. T. Lancaster (Leeds, 1912), pp. 166–68; Lhwyd to Sir Hans Sloane, July 26, 1707, B.M. MS. Sloane 4041, f. 3; Lhwyd to Richard Mostyn, June 22, 1707, *Archaeologia Cambrensis*, 3d ser. 2 (1847): 94. Moreover, Lhwyd discovered, "some leading men" were taking private occasions to speak slightingly of the *Archaeologia Britannica* while it was still in press, "which has done it no small prejudice": Lhwyd to Mostyn, Nov. 2, 1707, *Archaeologia Cambrensis*, 3d ser. 6 (1860): 15–16.

[24]Wotton to James Brydges, in C. H. Collins Baker and Muriel I. Baker, *The Life and Circumstances of James Brydges, First Duke of Chandos* (Oxford, 1949), p. 66. Lord Weymouth hoped (like Foulkes, n. 19 above) that "Mr. Lloyd's next Volume would bee more entertaining, for this is but drye, to old men who pretend not to learned Languages, though they are very usefull Books for Libraries": Hearne, *Remarks and Collections*, p. 444.

helped no doubt to arrest both the Anglo-Saxon and Celtic revivals. Yet it was less successful in halting the rest of the antiquarian enterprise. The fact is that some of the same humanist motives that had helped to launch modern scholarship in the first place continued to operate in the eighteenth century with undiminished force and continued to encourage it. In particular, curiosity about the Roman world, in which ancient Britain had of course played its part, continued to grow, sending English gentlemen to Rome itself in larger and larger numbers, increasing their cabinets with more and more objects and their libraries with prints and drawings, as well as rare editions of the classics. So, while the hunt for medieval antiquities began to flag (except perhaps for the indomitable Thomas Hearne), the enthusiasm for classical antiquities, especially Roman, persisted and led to some exciting discoveries and much serious scholarship. A Roman shield discovered in an ironmonger's shop in London or a Roman pavement dug up in Oxford could stir the whole learned world and attract international attention, despite the amusement of the wits. A single new Roman inscription discovered near Bath in 1708 led typically to a flurry of conjectures and publications by Hearne, Roger Gale, William Musgrave, Henry Dodwell, and others.[25] Meanwhile, work on Camden's revised *Britannia* proceeded fitfully, culminating at last with two volumes in 1722. And in 1707 Humphrey Wanley and a few friends revived the idea of a Society of Antiquaries.

Since the idea of cooperation was intrinsic to modern scholarship from the beginning there were ample precedents for formal exchange. In William Camden's day there had been a Society of Antiquaries that was not forgotten, and Thomas Hearne soon thought of editing its remains. Across the Channel, Louis XIV established an Academy of Inscriptions, and its journal was well known in England. Informally, the antiquaries often met to talk in the taverns and coffeehouses that served for clubs in Augustan England, or in their homes, where they proudly displayed their cabinets. Both Nicolson and Thoresby kept diaries of their visits to London and we can follow them closely as they made their rounds and discovered what was happening in the lively world of scholars and collectors, where everyone seemed to know everyone else. After Nicolson became bishop of Carlisle in 1702, he went to London regularly, and paid his respects to the Saxonists: Hickes, Wanley, Fountaine, and Elstob; and to all those who shared an interest in antiquities: Thomas Tanner and Edmund Gibson, Thomas Rymer and Thomas Madox, James Tyrrell, Dr. Woodward, and of course his old friends Wotton and Bentley, as well as the great collectors, the Archbishop of York and the Earl of

---

[25]See my *Dr. Woodward's Shield* (Berkeley, 1977) and the chapter on the Stonesfield Pavement in my *Humanism and History* (Ithaca, N.Y., 1987), pp. 107–22; and for the Bath inscription, *Humanism and History*, pp. 218–19.

Pembroke. While it would be wrong to seal off this community from
that other convivial society of wits and gentlemen which was congregat-
ing simultaneously, it is hard to find any evidence of their intersection.
For the most part, the wits and the scholars kept separate company and
talked about very different things. [26]

Needless to say, cooperative ventures such as *Camden's Britannia* and
Hickes's *Thesaurus* brought many scholars together and showed the value of exchanging information. [27] We have already seen Nicolson advocating a "club of antiquaries" as the only way to advance the discipline. "All
the great improvements in learning," he pointed out to Thoresby in
1694, "are carried out in France and Italy by societies of persons proper
for such undertakings. I know no reason why history and antiquities
should not be this way cultivated." [28] In some respects, the Royal Society, though pledged to natural science, had already paved the way.
Many of its members were antiquaries or collectors, and it was generally
open to learning about new discoveries and publishing them in the *Philosophical Transactions*. Nicolson had printed two important papers there in
1685, describing the Bewcastle Cross and Bridekirk Font with their runic
inscriptions. [29] Hickes contributed a letter on Saxon antiquities in 1700
and another on Etruscan inscriptions in 1705; and Wanley published a
number of things, including a remarkable essay on "judging of the Age
of MSS." The society took a keen interest in the progress of Hickes's
Thesaurus and Lhwyd's *Archaeologia*. [30] Even its more "philosophical"

[26]On Jan. 2, 1706, Nicolson took a coach to visit Hickes and found him in his study, pen
in hand. "Our Discourse was chiefly on the genuine Caedmon and Mr. Wanley's Specimen
of it out of the Bishop of Norwich's Manuscript which (being much Danish) ought not to
be believ'd (I think) to have been penn'd in Northunberland before the Danes came over; of
the Swedish Laws, whereof Sir Tho Parker and Dr. Sloan have procur'd Copies; of the
Hetruscan Inscriptions in the Arundel Library, and of the Dr's (much abused) Letter
thereon in the Transactions." A few days later he had "the agreeable company of Mr.
Wotton and Mr. Wanley . . . wherein the former better half persuaded to enter on the
translation of Junius's Caedmon, as the latter to resume his thoughts of publishing all the
Fragments of the Old Testament in Saxon." And so on. See *The London Diaries of William
Nicolson*, ed. Clyve Jones and Geoffrey Holmes (Oxford, 1985).
[27]"Having received some Northern Querys from Sir Robert Sibbald, transmitted to me
by my Lord Bishop of Carlisle, I had yesterday at dinner a set of Gothick Antiquarys, all
your humble servants, viz, Dr. Hickes, Dr. Gregory, Mr. Lloyd, Mr. Thwaites and Mr.
Elstob, to consider them. I could have wished Mr. Jackson and Mr. Wanley had been of the
same number": Charlett to Pepys, Sept. 3, 1702, in Samuel Pepys, *Diary and Correspondence*, ed. Lord Braybrooke, 4 vols. (London, 1890), 4:374–75.
[28]Nicolson to Thoresby, May 7, 1694, in *Letters of Eminent Men to Thoresby*, 1:162.
[29]*Philosophical Transactions* 15 (1685): 1287–95; the first was addressed to Obadiah Walker, the second to Sir William Dugdale.
[30]On July 28, 1703, Lhwyd's proposals for printing his *Archaeologia Britannica* were
read, his design was approved, and many present promised to subscribe; see Royal Society
Journal Book, 10:44. There is an account of some ancient inscriptions found in Scotland and
Ireland by Lhwyd in *Philosophical Transactions* 22, no. 269 (1700): 768. Hickes's letter
advertising the *Thesaurus*, and Wanley's letter (dated July 11, 1701) appeared in *Philosophical
Transactions* 22, no. 260 (1700), and 24 (1705): 1993–2011, respectively.

members made contributions of an antiquarian kind; Edmund Halley, for instance, sent a Roman inscription from Chester, read several papers on the *Antonine Itinerary*, and printed another on the time and place of Julius Caesar's landing in Britain.[31] Ralph Thoresby typically sent a whole series of reports on Roman discoveries in Yorkshire, as well as on Saxon and Norman coins, and there were many other similar descriptions to enliven the journal. In 1697 Thoresby became a fellow and a few years later paid his first visit to the society. "After the meeting was over, I had the opportunity of taking a more particular view of the curiosities in the publick museum, to which were added some Roman Plasticks I had brought from York. . . . I was invited by many eminent persons to see theirs in particular." He saw Dr. Woodward's assemblage of natural history, but also his "curious collection of Roman antiquities, not only of urns, but gems, signets, rings, keys, stylus Scriptorius, res turpiculae, etc." Evelyn, Hooke, and Sloane all showed him curiosities of various kinds, and Christopher Wren's son let him see his father's "valuable collection of Grecian medals." Later he met Baron Spanheim, who asked to borrow the manuscript catalogue of his coins. Unfortunately, "disuse had made me very unfit to hold a continued disourse in Latin, so that when Dr. Gale was not with us, we had a sad broken mixture of Latin, Dutch, and English."[32]

The time was ripe for something more substantial. In 1702 Wanley got the job that he had been holding informally, as assistant secretary to the Royal Society, and continued to regale its members regularly with descriptions of rare manuscripts in many languages, coins, and of course his own book of specimens. When Wren showed an ancient seal from Winchester to the society, Wanley dated it about the time of Edward I.[33] In 1706 he was himself made a fellow and joined Hickes and Nicolson there among other antiquaries. Soon he was working full time for Robert Harley, building the greatest historical library in England. (In a few years, we are told, it already contained more than 6,000 manuscripts and about 13,000 charters and rolls!)[34] It became a natural center of anti-

[31]Edmund Halley, *Correspondence and Papers*, ed. Eugene F. MacPike (London, 1937), pp. 98–99, 221, 227, 236, app. 19.

[32]Ralph Thoresby, *Diary*, ed. Joseph Hunter, 2 vols. (London, 1830), 2:37; D. H. Atkinson, *Ralph Thoresby, the Topographer*, 2 vols. (Leeds, 1885), 1:411–12, 415.

[33]Wanley was first given permission to attend a meeting on April 16, 1701; he had come to the library to search for Saxon remains for Hickes. While there he showed an ancient Greek manuscript and his book of specimens. On Nov. 25, 1702, he was given £30 for his attendance at meetings and copying of the letter books and journals of the society. (His salary continued thereafter at £15 a year.) See the journal books of the Society of Antiquaries, vol. 9 and 10.

[34]At Harley's death it contained some 40,000 to 50,000 books, about 350,000 pamphlets, and the 7,639 manuscript volumes that make up the present Harleian collection in the British Library. See A. S. Turberville, *A History of Welbeck Abbey* (London, 1937), 1:361–62; Douglas, *English Scholars*, p. 263.

quarian activity, in much the same way that the library of Sir Robert Cotton had served for the Elizabethans. Harley set up a small governing committee and Wanley wrote out the rules; this brief venture very likely suggested the idea of a society of his own.[35]

Wanley was a convivial soul, and it was at the Bear Tavern in the Strand that he and two friends, John Talmon and John Bagford, hatched their plan. At their second meeting it was agreed that the society should limit itself to the history and antiquities of Britain before the reign of James I.[36] Later it was proposed that its chief business should be to resolve doubts about old books and charters and to report any observations about antiquities that might be of use. Several new members were proposed, including William Elstob and Thomas Madox. A constitution was soon drawn up (in Wanley's hand) which was intended to call for a royal charter, but it looks as though Harley's fall from power and Queen Anne's death a few years later interrupted the scheme. The preamble pointed out that the last age had cultivated Greek and Roman antiquities with wonderful success, and that much had been done abroad by modern academies, but that a great deal remained to be done for Britain. "But as this must be a work of great Charge and Constant Application, and far too great for one purse, 'tis to be wish'd that a Society of Antiquaries might be sett up, from whose united endeavours, the world might receive compleat volumes Relating to Our Native Countrey, to Our Kings, Our Church, and Our People, with others of a Miscellaneous nature." Wanley supplied a long list of projects for the society, including an effort to preserve all the old monumental inscriptions in Britain and to "explain not only most of the Obscure places in our Historians and other Writers, but others in the Roman and Greek Authors, and consider of their other Antiquities."[37] For these purposes he imagined a foreign correspondence and much travel by persons fit to inspect old books and rarities, to draw ancient monuments of every kind, and to purchase useful pieces for the society's collection.

That much of this vision finally came to pass was due to Wanley's persistence and a felt need. One way or another, the antiquaries kept up their contacts and their schemes.[38] When the society resumed in 1717 at the Mitre Tavern, it had many new members, a new secretary (William Stukeley), and a sound organization. Its numbers grew swiftly and also

[35]It was 1707 and Hickes was involved: B.M. MS. Lansdowne 825, f. 77; see Joan Evans, *A History of the Society of Antiquaries* (Oxford, 1956), p. 35.

[36]See the minutes beginning Dec. 5, 1707, B.M. MS. Harl, 7055.

[37]The draft is given in Evans, *Society of Antiquaries*, pp. 40–44.

[38]Joan Evans adds two accounts of how the society resumed in these years; one by Maurice Johnson (from Nichols, *Literary Anecdotes*, 6:144), the other by George Vertue (from Bodleian MS. Top. Lond. C 2, f. 144): *Society of Antiquaries*, pp. 49–50. Both emphasize the collaborative use of the public records.

its conviviality, so that some "give us their company more for the convenience of spending two or three hours over a glass of wine than for any
love or value they have for the study of Antiquities."[39] Eventually, however, the society found a more sober meeting place and a place to secure
its own collections. But the wits did not miss the opportunity, and even
as the reconstituted society was meeting for the first time, someone
thought to revive Shakerley Marmion's old satire *The Antiquary* for the
occasion, so that the polite world could be reminded once again of the
uselessness of pedantic learning. It ran, so Samuel Gale remembered, for
two nights.[40]

4

The minute books and registers of the society tell much about the
story of antiquarian activity for the rest of the century. What is clear is
that although the antiquaries had pledged themselves to all of British
antiquity and continued to take an interest in the whole course of the
national past, it was the Romans who inspired them the most. Both the
ancients and the moderns were agreed, as Sir John Clerk put it while
defending the society, that "the heroes of antiquity [are] but so many
models by which we may square our lives and actions." It was only a
question as to how, or whether, antiquarian activity could be employed
to serve the purpose, and here Clerk typically avoided the issue, although
he saw that it would "be hard persuading a courtier that there is anything
in the study of antiquitys above other trifling studys."[41] Needless to say,
this "astonishing domination of Rome" among the antiquaries[42] was due
in large measure to the persistence of the ancients in the battle of the
books, or at least to those circumstances that made *ancienneté* plausible at
this time. The hunt for medieval and preclassical antiquities continued to
raise some interest, but it provoked at least as much distrust, even within
the ranks of the antiquaries. When one of their number, the Scot Alexander Gordon, pressed the claims of the ancient Caledonians too far
against the Romans, Clerk, who was also a Scot, was characteristically
offended. He thought a that true love of country, liberty, and glory

[39]Roger Gale to Sir John Clerk, April 22, 1726, in Nichols, *Literary Anecdotes*, 4:343–45.
It was forbidden to talk of politics or any other controversial subject. For members, see the
account in *Archaeologia* 1 (1770): xxxiii–xxxvi.
[40]Marmion's *Antiquity* was published originally in 1641; it is reprinted in *The Dramatic
Works of Shackerley Marmion* (Edinburgh, 1875), pp. 197–295; see p. 199n.
[41]Clerk to Gale, June 2, 1726, in *The Family Memoirs of the Reverend William Stukeley*, 3
vols., Surtees Society (Durham, 1882–1887), 1:183–86.
[42]Evans, *Society of Antiquaries*, p. 93. T. A. Birrell has said what is possible for the later
Saxonists in his article "The Society of Antiquaries and the Taste for Old English, 1705–
1840," *Neophilologus* 50 (1966): 107–17.

could be better instilled by the valiant actions of the Greeks and Romans than by the barbarism of the Celts. (Clerk was willing, however, to overlook Gordon's interpretation for his useful information; "his busynesse as an antiquarian rather than as an historian will attone for all.")[43] He was quickly reassured by his friend Roger Gale, the learned son of a learned antiquary, and one of the founders of the Antiquarian Society. "I cannot think it not a scandall for any nation to have been conquered by the Romans, but a great misfortune not to have submitted to their arms, since their conquests were so far from enslaving those they vanquisht, that they tended onely to the civilizing and improving their manners, reducing them under the Roman laws and government from their wild and savage way of life, instructing them in the arts and sciences, and looking upon them as fellow-citizens and freemen of Rome. . . ." The two friends probably spoke for the majority, although Clerk was still railing against the medievalists ten years later. There was no stemming the barbarians, for "Goths will always have a Gothick taste."[44]

He needn't have worried. It is true that a taste for Gothic did develop in time, but it remained thoroughly encapsulated within a classical framework and it is doubtful that anyone was ready for a very long while to reverse the traditional precedence of Greeks and Romans.[45] Meanwhile, in the 1720s some of the members of the society, including Gale, Gordon, and Clerk, organized themselves into another little group for the particular study of Roman Britain. They called themselves (only a little facetiously) the Society of Roman Knights, and took fanciful Romano-British names. In 1722 William Stukeley, the secretary of the Society of Antiquaries and a leading spirit among the knights, addressed them at a gathering in the Fountain Tavern. He began like Gibbon half a century later, looking down on the ruins of the city of Rome. "With what grief have these eyes seen the havoc, the desolation, the fate of Roman works, owing to the delusion and abominable superstition of cloyster'd nuns and fryars. What the fury of wars could not demolish, their inglorious hands have destroyed." Then he exhorts his colleagues.

[43]Gordon provoked the outburst with "An Essay to shew how far the Assertion of the Scottish Nation is just, that they were never conquered by the Romans," in *Itinerarium septentrionale* (London, 1726), pp. 135–45. Clerk thought Gordon had relied unwisely on Tacitus, who was "conforming to a liberty usuall among historians" (ibid.). Later, Clerk wrote, Caledonian glory received its honor from the great pains the Romans had to take to conquer the Scots. See "Sir John Clerk's Trip from Duncrief to Carlyle in September 1734," ed. W. A. J. Prevost, *Transactions of the Cumberland and Westmorland Society* n.s. 62 (1962): 255.

[44]Roger Gale to Clerk, June 24, 1726, in *Family Memoirs of Stukeley*, 3:86–91; Gale to Clerk, May 12, 1736, in Stuart Piggott, *William Stukeley: An Eighteenth-Century Antiquary*, 2d ed. (London, 1985), p. 56. Piggott points out that the last line had already been used by Clerk in an unpublished poem, "The Country Seat," in 1727.

[45]See the chapter "Eighteenth-Century Historicism and the First Gothic Revival," in my *Humanism and History*, pp. 190–213.

"Whilst others therefore are busying themselves to restore the Gothick Remnants, the glory is reserved for you to adorn and preserve the truly noble monuments of the Romans in Britain." It was up to the new society to search out the Roman remains and make them known. "We are to encounter time, Goths, and barbarians . . . we are to be the Secretarys, the interpretators and preservers of the memorials of our ancestors." Unfortunately, the society did not last very long, though it carried on informally among the friends who had organized it. Even Stukeley remained faithful to his Roman mission for the time being, although the Druids were eventually able to carry him off, much to the dismay of many of his old friends.[46]

Indeed, it was these men who helped to prepare the way for what was one of the most astonishing antiquarian productions of the time: John Horsley's *Britannia Romana*. For some time interest in Roman things had been growing in the north of England, stimulated especially by that greatest of ancient British monuments: the Roman, or, as it was generally known, the Picts Wall. As early as 1702–3 Christopher Hunter of Durham contributed several pieces to the *Philosophical Transactions*, describing names and sites there and using inscriptions. (He seems to have been the first to attribute the wall to Hadrian.) A little later Robert Smith, who was a close friend of William Nicolson's, took up the quest and made some "very curious observations" on the wall (1709), which were eventually published in the new edition of Camden (1722). In 1716 the surveyor John Warburton printed a new map of Northumberland from a fresh survey, taking notice of the Roman sites, which he later claimed was the cause of the Antiquarian Society's reestablishment.[47] He was a great (though somewhat unscrupulous) collector and we find him in the next year unsuccessfully trying to sell an altar dug up near the wall to Humfrey Wanley for Harley's collection. (On another occasion he took Wanley to a tavern, "thinking to muddle me and so gain upon me with selling his MSS. But the contrary happened.")[48] In the 1720s ac-

---

[46]Piggott, *William Stukeley*, p. 55. The minutes appear in Bodleian MS. Eng. misc. C 401. Piggott gives a list of the sixteen original members as well as others who joined later, including two women, the Duchess of Hertford and Mrs. Stukeley.

[47]See John Rogan, "Christopher Hunter: Antiquary," *Archaeologia Aeliana*, 4th ser. 32 (1954): 116–25; R. C. Bosanquet, "Robert Smith and the 'Observations upon the Picts Wall,'" *Transactions of the Cumberland and Westmorland Society*, n.s. 55 (1956): 154–71; C. H. Hunter Blair, "The Armorial Bearings upon a New Map of the County of Northumberland (John Warburton, 1716)," *Archaeologia Aeliana*, 4th ser. 34 (1956), pp. 27–56. Smith's "Observations" appear in *Camden's Britannia*, ed. Edmund Gibson, 2d ed., 2 vols. (London, 1722), 2:1051–60; Nicolson's diary for 1709–10 shows their close association and common interests: *London Diaries of Nicolson*.

[48]Kenneth Sisam, "Humfrey Wanley," in *Studies in the History of Old English Literature* (Oxford, 1953), p. 269. The altar was "the most beautifullest and most entire I have ever seen . . . but we could not agree about the price": Warburton to Gale, Nov. 21, 1717, Society of Antiquaries MS. Guardbook 222, pp. 386–90. For Warburton's habit of breaking up the stones, see John Horsley, *Britannia Romana* (London, 1732), p. 182.

tivity came to a boil with the works of Alexander Gordon and William Stukeley, and the visits of Clerk and Roger Gale. They scoured the countryside, shared their Roman interests and discoveries, and eventually came into contact with Horsley, an obscure northern schoolteacher who had set out on his own to encompass the field.

It was in 1729 that Horsley called upon Clerk, who promptly described him in a letter to Roger Gale.

> He was, it seems, very well known to some of our university professors some years ago, and acquired a great reputation for the mathematics, and his knowledge in all parts of philosophy. In discoursing with him I find him to be much acquainted with the Greek and Roman learning, and very ready in his notions about inscriptions and the Roman stations. He told me his design was to print an entire collection of the Roman British antiquitys, and I hear from some of our masters in the university that he is just now setting about it in London. I shall wonder if he has not made the acquaintance with some of your Society. He affects now and then a singularity in his readings and opinions, but this I did not wonder at, for the poor man writes for bread, and must surely have something new to entertain his readers. He liv'd at Morpeth for many years, and taught there in a private academy, with the benefitt of a meeting-house for his support.[49]

Clerk had passed through Morpeth in 1724 without meeting Horsley, so it looks as though the young man was then still unknown. The baron was on his way to the Roman wall, which he inspected with Gordon about that time. "Nothing," he remembered, "gave me a more magnificent idea of the Romans than this wall and the towers and castles belonging therto." Gordon memorialized the journey in his *Itinerarium septentrionale* (1726), in which he tried to account for all the Roman monuments in Scotland and northern England. He also promised there to engrave "a Compleat View of the Walls of Roman Britain," fourteen feet long, but never produced it.[50] At almost the same time, Stukeley and Roger Gale were making pretty much the same journey. When they looked upon the wall, Stukeley remembered, "we tired ourselves day by day in copying and drawing inscriptions, altars, milliary columns, basso

---

[49]Clerk to Gale, Feb. 15, 1729, in *Family Memoirs of Stukeley*, pp. 390–91. The meetinghouse was Presbyterian. Horsley taught a course in physics, for which a guide was printed; see John Hodgson, *A History of Northumberland*, 3 vols. (Newcastle, 1832), pt. 2, vol. 2, p. 448.

[50]Prevost, "Clerk's Trip from Duncrief," p. 255. See Daniel Wilson and David Laing, "An Account of Alexander Gordon," *Proceedings of the Society of Antiquaries of Scotland* 10, pt. 2 (1885): 363–82.

relievos, plans of forts, etc." Stukeley hoped that describing it again would "revive the Roman glory among us."[51]

Horsley had probably been working away for what he calls "my own amusement and pleasure," like many another local antiquary. He seems to have encountered Warburton while he was drafting his map of Northumberland, and he certainly met Gordon when he was compiling the *Itinerarium septentrionale*. Rivalry was probably inevitable, and for a time Horsley tried to conceal his activities.[52] By 1727 he was systematically trying to finish his book, and by the following year his reputation had reached London, where he was called upon to describe one of the inscriptions in Dr. Woodward's museum and received praise as "a scholar and profound student of British antiquities," as well as a good advertisement for his project.[53] Shortly afterward he met Clerk and Gale and Stukeley, all of whom vigorously supported his undertaking. He had help from northern friends as well, Christopher Hunter of Durham and especially Robert Cay of Newcastle. His assistant at school, George Mark, did his surveying and helped him in his travels. In 1729 he was ready to advertise the publication of his book, as well as a course of lectures in natural philosophy to be delivered at Morpeth.[54]

Horsley finished his preface to the *Britannia Romana* on January 2, 1732; he died unexpectedly less than two weeks later. He was about forty-six years old. He had sent his work to London (by way of Robert Cay in Newcastle) to be printed by John Ward, the professor of rhetoric at Gresham College and a good classicist. Cay had assisted at every stage; now Ward read the manuscript through and was given carte blanche by Horsley to make corrections; he also contributed many observations and a long piece of his own.[55] Printing began in 1728 and was in "good forwardness" the following year. It was being revised and enlarged even

[51]*Family Memoirs of Stukeley*, 3:143. "Worthily may we propose them for examples of virtue and public spirit": "Iter Boriale", in William Stukeley, *Itinerarium curiosum* (London, 1724), 2:56, 67, 77.

[52]Horsley urged his friend Robert Cay, June 1, 1727, not to tell anybody "and particularly not Mr. Gordon of my being busy about anything of this nature": Northumberland Record Office, Newcastle, MS. ZAN M15/A53.

[53]The Benwell slab with a dedication to Victory was bought by Dr. Cay and given to Woodward; it is commemorated in the published catalogue of the museum by Robert Ainsworth (1728); see Horsley's *Britannia Romana*, pp. 211–12; and Sir George MacDonald, "John Horsley: Scholar and Gentleman," *Archaeologia Aeliana*, 4th ser. 10 (1933): 17–18.

[54]Horsley to Cay, Sept. 18, 1729, Northumberland Record Office, MS. ZAN M13/19; Stukeley to Gale, Feb. 4, 1728, ibid., ZAN M15/A53.

[55]"Mr. Ward intends a Letter to me by way of Review of all the Observations, and there is a proper space left for that Letter . . . at the end of the Observations in the second book": Horsley to Gale, Jan. 22, 1731, Society of Antiquaries MS. 222 (1), pp. 413–14. On May 1, 1729, Horsley thanked Gale for his offer of sending a draft to Ward: ibid., pp. 48–49. For Cay's invaluable help, see the correspondence in the Northumberland Record Office, MS. ZAN M13/19.

as it passed through the press.[56] There was no subscription and Horsley complains that the cost and labor to the bookseller and himself were more than three times what they had expected. It is doubtful that he would have made any money from his work, except perhaps through the generosity of such friends as Clerk and Cay and Robert Harley. As it happened, he did not live long enough to derive from it either fame or profit.

When the large folio volume did finally appear, it was divided into three parts. In the first, Horsley wrote the history of the Romans in Britain; in the second, he collected the inscriptions; and in the last, he located the places. Throughout he provided maps, plates, and tables, and at the end several remarkable indexes. It was the second part that probably generated the enterprise and cost Horsley the greatest labor. "Several thousand miles were travelled on this account, to visit antient monuments, and re-examine them, when there was any doubt or difficulty." He went to the original sites throughout England and pored over the collections that had been assembled by the antiquaries and virtuosi: by Cotton and Camden at Conington, by Warburton and Hunter in Durham, by Clerk at Penicuik, and so on. Sometimes he had to rely on the drafts and descriptions of such friends as Stukeley and Clerk, but only by default and with great care. It had not taken him long to discover how many inscriptions were still unknown and how inaccurately the rest had been published. "And therefore I omitted no care nor pains, that was necessary to copy these with the greatest exactness, which was the principal design of the work."[57] Although he had limited means, he made a good collection of his own. Once he went to considerable expense to carry an altar to Morpeth so that he could put two broken pieces together and make out the inscription.[58] While in London, he called on the president of the Society of Antiquaries, Lord Hertford, to examine an altar and see the famous cup found at Rudge in Wiltshire. (He accepted Gale's conjecture that it was a patera used in libations but was more skeptical about Clerk's view that it had afterward been thrown into the well where it was found—wells having then been esteemed sacred.)[59] He went all the way to Aberdeen to see an inscription in the Marischal College which the owner had had gilded, but he doubted whether "our present anti-

---

[56]See Horsley to Gale, Jan. 22, 1731, in William Hutchinson, *A View of Northumberland* (Newcastle, 1778), 1:205–6.

[57]Horsley, *Britannia Romana*, Introduction to bk. 2, pp. 177–78. Of an inscription in *Camden's Britannia* he writes, "This representation . . . is another instance of the disadvantages the greatest men labour under, who have no opportunity of seeing the originals": ibid., p. 207.

[58]Horsley to Gale, Dec. 10, 1730, Society of Antiquaries MS. 222 (1), pp. 393–94; Horsley, *Britannia Romana*, pp. 294–95.

[59]Horsley, *Britannia Romana*, pp. 329–30.

quaries would scarce thank the noble Lord for this expression of his value and zeal for antiquity."[60] He intended a general "thesaurus": "a compleat collection of all the Roman inscriptions and sculptures in Britain," as he put it to Harley, "cut on copper plates with the readings at large set under each inscription."[61] In the event, he included even minor pieces and fragments, all as complete and accurate as possible (with two in Greek, expertly deciphered).[62] Even so, this very modern scholar, like Wotton and Bentley, held on to the critical (if not the scholarly) standards of the ancients. "I think the later and cruder performances . . . should be made publick, as well as those that are more antient and elegant; because it is a curiosity to observe the difference, and see the degeneracy."[63] His model was the collection that Janus Gruter had made for Europe, recently re-edited by Bentley's friend J. G. Graevius in four large volumes (1707).[64] Eventually he published about 340 inscriptions, almost half of them for the first time.

Throughout the work Horsley used both originals and copies, scrupulously reproducing the first and criticizing the second, but employing the one where necessary to help to decipher the other. (The originals had often suffered damage and wear.) He saw the need to present all the evidence: the size and shape of the stone and the relative scale of the letters and figures, criticizing his predecessors for their omissions and carelessness.[65] Again and again he went back to the original to correct the copies of Camden, Warburton, Gordon, and the rest. Everywhere he tried to emend the texts on the stones, which were often unclear or corrupt. His conjectures were, of course, exactly like the emendations of the modern philologist working with a manuscript, and he was careful

[60]Ibid., p. 204.
[61]Horsley to Harley, Feb. 11, 1731, in John Bosanquet, "John Horsley and His Times," *Archaeologia Aeliana*, 4th ser. 10 (1933), pp. 74–75.
[62]See Horsley to Gale, April 7, 1729, Society of Antiquaries MS. 222 (1), pp. 377–78; Gale to Horsley, Apr. 19, 1729, ibid., p. 141.
[63]Horsley to Gale, April 7, 1729, ibid., p. 285. Alexander Gordon knew better than Horsley, who had not been abroad, that the Roman monuments in Britain were not of the "exquisite Taste" of classical Rome. Nevertheless, he continued to prize them for their historical value, and he exhorted the Society of Antiquaries to revive an admiration for antiquity, "to the total Extirpation of Gothicism, Ignorance, and bad Taste": *Itinerarium septentrionale*, Preface.
[64]Janus Gruter, *Inscriptiones antiquae totius orbis Romani* (Amsterdam, 1707); Horsley, *Britannia Romana*, Introduction to bk. 2, pp. 177–79. Horsley points out that Gruter had used only inscriptions supplied by Camden and Cotton for Britain, and even those with some egregious mistakes, which he illustrates here.
[65]"The implication and proper cut of the letters, which is neglected by Camden, I have endeavored to supply from the original": Horsley, *Britannia Romana*, pt. 2, p. 243. "The principal defect was their being expressed only in Roman capitals, and no description of the stones": ibid., p. 254. "This instance alone is sufficient to show the expediency of keeping to the same scale in proportion through the whole of a work of this nature": ibid., p. 276.

always to distinguish the bare reading from the guess. He understood the
various new means of dating inscriptions and coins by their form and
content, including the new paleography. (Among other helps, Horsley
offered two tables for the various shapes of letters, points, and legatures
that were used in inscriptions.) He drew on the new iconography to
interpret figures. (Here again he offered a table showing some of the
sacrificing instruments and vessels frequently found on altars.)[66] And he
knew how easy it was to be misled by ornaments or flourishes in the
stone caused by accident or plow, not to say the wishful imagination of
the antiquary.[67] At least the inscriptions themselves were likely to be
genuine. "The high prices of curious Roman coins have produced a great
many forgeries contrived very artfully; but the little regard that has been
had for monuments of stone, renders us more secure of their being
altogether genuine."[68] It would certainly have been hard to fool this
expert! Like Alexander Gordon before him (and like antiquaries everywhere), he saw that archaeological evidence could be used "to prove
demonstrably those facts which are asserted in History," either to confirm or to condemn the narrative accounts.[69] Horsley's work, we are told
on competent authority, has been superseded only in recent times.

The last part of the book was not planned at first but was probably
added at the insistence of his new London friends. Here again Horsley
returned to Camden for inspiration; for the mapping of Roman Britain
had been the inspiration of that great work and of many others before
and since. Where exactly were the Roman towns and forts and roads? It
was no easy job to locate these places from the scant literary and archaeological evidence. When Nathaniel Salmon decided to write a popular
abridgement of Camden, *A New Survey of England* (1730), he quickly got
lost in that "dark affair" and had to turn to Horsley to help him out,
though he stubbornly resisted some of Horsley's suggestions.[70] Several
generations of antiquaries had attacked the problem by combining the

[66]The tables follow pp. 188 and 190 in ibid. Horsley frequently calls upon Montfaucon's
Antiquité expliquée for comparative material and to identify images. There is a good exam-
ple of a learned emendation employing Caesar, inscriptions in Reinecius and Camden,
Montfaucon, Stephanus, Gruter, Horace, and Virgil, at pp. 209–10.

[67]"But I will not say that my eyesight was no way assisted by my imagination": ibid., p.
312. He criticizes Prideaux for reproducing one of the Arundel Marbles "better than it ever
was in the original": ibid., p. 331.

[68]Ibid., p. 293.

[69]"Archaeology" is defined by Gordon as consisting of "Monuments, or rather Inscriptions, still subsisting," which help to distinguish true history from falsehood and imposture: *Itinerarium septentrionale*, Preface, sig. B.

[70]"I saw him much at a loss, and found it out of my power to retrieve him according to
the scheme he was embarked on": Horsley to Gale, quoted in Bosanquet, "Horsley and His
times," p. 73. Nevertheless, Salmon thanked the "Gentleman of Northumberland," whose
"ocular inspection" promised to settle the matter, and hoped to see his work in print soon.

NORTHUMBERLAND

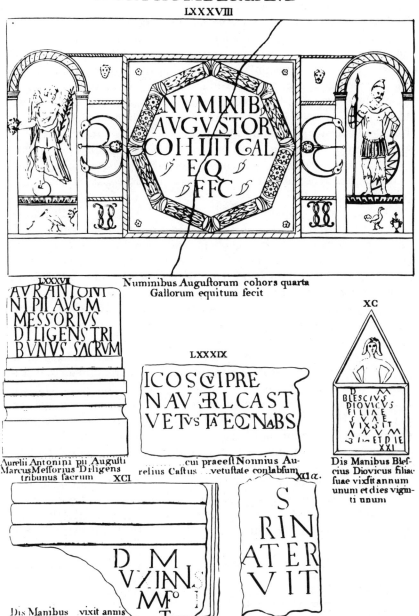

Some Roman inscriptions in Horsley's *Britannia Romana* (1731)

sparse accounts of the ancient geographers with the evidence of antiquities and etymologies, and made a slow but steady progress. In particular, they had labored over the *Antonine Itineraries* and the still scrappier
evidence in Ptolemy, the *Notitia Imperii*, and other ancient sources, in the
hope of finding the clues to the present sites. Now Horsley decided to
print them all, even though he was aware that they "are often confused
and obscure, and sometimes inconsistent with one another which may
lessen their authority; but yet they are in many cases our best guides."
Each of the five main literary sources was given in the original Greek or
Latin, several in translation, and all with a commentary that tried to
establish their authorship, date, and use. Once again Horsley was compelled to offer corrections and emendations throughout, which he does
with his usual skill and good manners—and the dependable assistance of
John Ward.[71]

One of Horsley's predecessors was his new friend Roger Gale, whose
father had worked on the *Antonine Itineraries* and who had continued to
pursue the Roman ways throughout Britain. John Warburton had corresponded with him about the problem, along with many others whose
work was known to Horsley.[72] To Gale and Horsley and their friends,
these ancient monuments, so awkward to make out and identify, were
nevertheless among the most remarkable reminders of Roman grandeur.
As John Ward put it in on the last page of the *Britannia Romana*, "When
we survey the Roman military ways, and consider the number, nature,
and vast extent of them, with the stations every where erected upon
them at proper distances, they seem to be much more difficult and surprising works, than even their porticos, temples, amphitheaters, triumphal arches, or any public buildings, tho' they be not so polite and
elegant."[73] Horsley saw the need for a reliable map that would settle
things, with "a faithfull and impartiall account of matter of fact, where
there are stations and military ways, and where there are none," and he
supplied several to accompany the texts. (Here his closest collaborator
seems to have been Robert Cay.) He explained to Gale that his method of
"ocular demonstration" was to be combined with a careful comparison
of the *Itineraries* and *Notitia*. He believed that by traveling to the sites,
where there were visible remains and other proofs of settlement, he had

---

[71]He also used the help of his friend Colin McLaurin, professor of mathematics at
Edinburgh, to explain the error in Ptolemy about the position of Scotland: Horsley, *Britannia Romana*, p. 361. Horsley offers advice about how to emend at p. 387.

[72]There are extracts of some letters 1717–18 in Hutchinson, *View of Northumberland*,
1:114. "When you come into these parts, pray bring along with you Mr. Gale's *Itinerarium
Antonini*, that I may know where I am placed according to the Roman geography, which
may put me into the road of hunting for some antiquities, which I have overlooked in my
neighborhood": Rev. Robert Dannye to Stukeley, Feb. 23, 1725, in *Family Memoirs of
Stukeley*, 3:309–10.

[73]Horsley, *Britannia Romana*, p. 520.

succeeded beyond expectation in reconciling the difficulties in the literary sources and determining the locations.[74] Even a negative result was an advance in knowledge. Stukeley, who met him just about this time, agreed.[75] And the modern scholar once again remains awed by his achievement.

Apparently it was Robert Cay who persuaded Horsley to put the historical part of the work first, with its long account of the Roman wall.[76] Here, in a way, was the nub of the matter, for of what use was this great compilation of material unless it could somehow be made into history? Horsley had accomplished the last two parts in the field, where he had shown himself to be one of the most gifted observers of all time. On the other hand, the first part, he says, "cost me much labour and time in my study." The trouble was "to draw out an history of transactions, through so many ages, and at such a distance from our own times, wherin a great part of the memorials relating to them are lost, and those which remain are so very short and imperfect."[77] Once again Camden had preceded him, and it was up to Horsley to see whether he could improve the account there with the additional knowledge now available to him. Unfortunately, the problem of integrating traditional narrative with antiquities, which no one had yet figured out how to resolve, was compounded in this case by the meagerness of both kinds of sources, and so Horsley was bound in a way to fail.

Horsley had no trouble rejecting the entire legendary history of early Britain which had been successfully undermined since the *Britannia*. "To enter into the fabulous accounts of the monkish historians would be lost time and labour. Their narratives relating to the affairs of Britain are in many instances contradictory to the Roman historians, and very often to one another."[78] Bede was exceptional, but too late to be of any use for

[74]Horsley to Gale, Mar. 24, 1729, in *Family Memoirs of Stukeley*, 3:94–95.

[75]Stukeley to Gale, Feb. 4, 1729, in ibid., 2:71. "My curiosity led me at once to search for a station at Old Radnor, and a military way to and from it. I will not say that I only got my labour for my pains; because I received a fuller conviction, that without personal view and enquiry I probably should have done, that there was no appearance or evidence of any Roman station or military way thereabout": Horsley, *Britannia Romana*, p. 390. Horsley analyzes the various kinds of evidence that can demonstrate a site—Roman monuments, place names, geographical situation, coins, Saxon rebuilding, etc.—at p. 393.

[76]Horsley to Cay, n.d., in Hodgson, *History of Northumberland* (n. 48 above), pt. 2, vol. 2, p. 445n. The letters here and the originals in the Northumberland Record office (ZAN M13/D19) show Cay assisting Horsley in many others ways also, checking inscriptions against the originals, editing the manuscript, adding learned references, and collaborating on the maps. In 1728 Horsley sent Cay some additional remarks. "If a proper place for inserting them occur to you, please to polish 'em a little and add them where you see fit if you think them worthy of notice." He was given full authority besides to correct both text and maps.

[77]Horsley, *Britannia Romana*, Preface, p. i.

[78]Ibid., bk. 1, p. 1. For the rejection of the legendary history of ancient Britain from Brutus to Arthur, see T. D. Kendrick, *British Antiquity* (London, 1950).

Roman Britain. Horsley was unwilling to depend on any modern account, even the later Roman historians, but here as elsewhere was determined to seek out and present the original sources only. He begins, therefore, with Caesar and Tacitus (both characteristically taken to be inimitable), and he adds passages from other ancient narratives, such as Dio Cassius and the *Historia Augusta*, as he advances. These are confirmed or illustrated from time to time by medals and inscriptions. He divides the period of Roman rule into stages, and for each discusses the authorities before attempting the story. For the first he depends almost entirely on Caesar, and he attempts the difficult job of rewriting the master, something that had so far daunted both the ancients and the moderns. His own contribution is to discuss various critical questions along the way, such as how many soldiers there were in a legion, or when and where Caesar had first landed. While the antiquarian matter was thus meant (as always) to illuminate the narrative, it was awkward to integrate and sometimes at cross-purposes. In describing the numbers in Caesar's transports, Horsley apologizes for having to add a paragraph, "not so much for the sake of the history, as from a thought, that it might give some light to the number of men contain'd in a legion." Halley's surmises about Caesar's landing are quoted at length from the *Philosophical Transactions* but at the cost of slowing the already stammering story. Needless to say, Horsley has some interesting things to say about Caesar's route within Britain, derived from Camden, Gale's *Antonine Itinerary*, and so on, and he weighs up all the various judgments about Caesar's success. But it is fair to say that Horsley never really intended to write the kind of rhetorical narrative that the classical partisans were still demanding, although he did make an occasional concession, such as telling an admittedly fabulous story from Plutarch.[79]

To be fair, the sources for classical narrative were simply inadequate for the purpose, particularly after Caesar and Tacitus, and Horsley's interest even here lay elsewhere. What he had wanted to relate, and was content to discover, were the times and places of the Roman occupation; he had less interest in the motives and intentions of the rulers—or the ruled. (The subject Celts are entirely ignored as though they, and Edward Lhwyd, never existed.) In general, he preferred to analyze rather than represent. And so it is the last four chapters of the first book that are the most interesting: on the Roman legions and ancillaries, and especially on the Roman wall and its stations. And for these matters it was the archaeological evidence and the work of previous antiquaries that mattered most. Close inspection and careful measurement, along with a keen judgment and imagination, led Horsley to work out the layout and

[79]Horsley, *Britannia Romana*, p. 20.

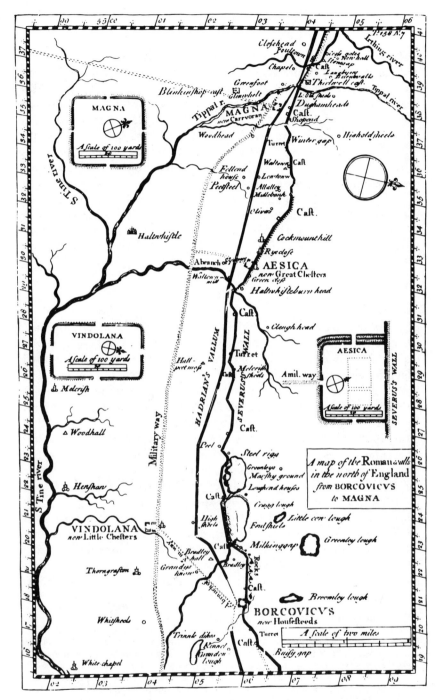

A map of the Roman wall from Horsley's *Britannia Romana* (1731)

makeup of the wall, the names of the stations, the "milecastle system," and the existence of turrets, among many other things; and although he made mistakes (such as attributing the wall to Severus rather than Hadrian), his conjectures about the problems of location and use were exactly in accordance with the evidence then available, before anything like systematic excavation was known. And his description of the visible remains was believed until recently to be the best in existence. According to R. G. Collingwood, who knew more about Roman Britain and historical method than most, "Whether you look at his field-work or at his theoretical thinking, Horsley's work on the Wall is the best that has ever been done."[80] This was all the more remarkable because Horsley seems to have written these chapters at great speed and under considerable pressure.

5

"I know there are People to be found," wrote Alexander Gordon in 1726, "and it is to be regretted, some of them of Birth and Fortune, who expose their own Ignorance, in discountenancing this Kind of Knowledge, giving out that Antiquity, and such like branches of Learning, are but the Chimeras of the Virtuosi, dry and unpleasant Searches."[81] Horsley certainly recognized the problem as he drew up the preface to his finished work. He thought that it would be worth addressing the common objection that seemed so plausible on the surface but that threatened all serious learning. "What signifies that knowledge, say some, which brings no real advantage to mankind? And what is it to any one, whether the Roman Walls pass'd this way or that? or whether such a Roman inscription is to be read this way or another?"[82]

Horsley's answer was that in the first place the search for truth was intrinsically good; it afforded, like the theorems of physics or mathematics, a "cultivation of the mind," irrespective of any practical application. "There is that beauty and agreeableness in truth, even supposing it to be merely speculative, as always affords . . . real pleasure to a well-turned

[80]Collingwood may have exaggerated Horsley's originality, since he appears to owe more to Gordon than either he or George MacDonald allowed; see Eric Birley, "John Horsley and John Hodgson," *Archaeologia Aeliana*, 4th ser. 36 (1958): 1–46; criticizing Collingwood, "John Horsley and Hadrian's Wall," ibid., pp. 1–42. We have seen that there was a rivalry between the antiquaries; MacDonald quotes from the letter of Horsley to Cay, June 1, 1727, and from another, Horsley to Stukeley, Mar. 15, 1729, pledging to act generously to Gordon and Richard Goodman, but without being bullied by either: MacDonald, "John Horsley," p. 38.

[81]Gordon, *Itinerarium septentrionale*, Preface.

[82]Horsley, *Britannia Romana*, Preface, p. ii.

mind." Furthermore, it was important to see that even the most spe-
cialized corners of knowledge were essential to the whole. It was not
possible to ignore the little things, though when considered by themselves in abstract, they might look worthless. "A minute inquiry into
particular circumstances of time and place, separately considered, may be
looked on as a matter of no great moment; and yet what is all chronology
and geography but a collection of these, digested into a regular body?"
Circumstances of time and place had always been recognized as rendering the facts more entertaining and useful. "Why then should it be
thought a trivial matter to trace them from antient monuments, when
they contribute so much to the light and pleasure of history?" Any
narrative of events could be improved by an exact knowledge of the
circumstances; and the monuments often added information about the
actions themselves, as well as the rites and customs of the past.

Of course, someone might still argue that history itself was unimportant, but he would be singular indeed, Horsley thought, who would deny
the history of his own country. In his first book he had offered the first
history of Britain that could be relied on. "I may venture to call it the
original foundation of the true history of our island." Clearing up the
chronology and geography (as in his last book) and describing the fortifications had seemed to him essential to the undertaking. As for the
second book, Horsley had there supplied much of the evidence, "together
with the pagan theology and diverse other customs," a task he thought
neither trifling nor useless. On that point he believed that even the party of
the ancients would have to agree. "The youth in every polite nation are
generally imployed in acquiring some skill in the Roman language, antiquities and customs; and an acquaintance with these is suppos'd to be
essentially necessary to a learned education."

Horsley was right. As long as the English continued to believe in the
pedagogical value of classical Latin and the virtues of ancient Rome,
there would be a place for classical antiquities, even among men of the
world. (He had dedicated his book gracefully to Sir Richard Ellys, with
the hope that he would find "some traces of that elegance of life, which
you, sir, so happily enjoy.") Horsley himself saw no need to repeat all
the commonplaces about the virtues of classical imitation, except to add a
word about the value of history in teaching the vanity of earthly works.
"It is certainly more commendable for gentlemen of estates, and persons
of quality," he concludes, "to spend their time in the prosecution of such
entertaining knowledge, than either in idleness or vicious pleasures. And
it is the glory and felicity of the present age, that we have a Hertford, a
Pembroke, an Oxford, with other persons of high rank and dignity, who
have both apply'd themselves with industry and success to these polite
and agreeable studies, and have generously encouraged them in others."

Lord Oxford we know took three copies of the *Britannia Romana*, but it was not a popular success. Horsley had made the best case he could for antiquarian study, but it did not—could not—meet the objections of those who, like Swift and Pope, saw in it dangers and difficulties unsuspected by the northern schoolmaster. Nor had he been able to reconcile in his own work the alternative advantages of polite literature and learning. What he had done was in its own right magnificent, but the great folio work that he produced was not a readable book, not even a unified and coherent account of the Romans in Britain, although it remained for a long time "the best and most scholarly account of any Roman province that had been written anywhere in Europe."[83] It was a monument to modern scholarship, as formidable in its own way as Bentley's dissertation, and it was destined to serve not the great gentlemen who sometimes bought it to adorn their cabinets but the scholars who came afterward and needed to use it in order to try to do the same thing better. But for the time being, the inhibitions of eighteenth-century philosophy and *ancienneté* retarded its progress, as they did all the other great works of Augustan erudition, and it is hard to find anyone who made much use of it for a long while except perhaps for an occasional northern antiquary. In 1763 the Society of Antiquaries was offered the plates of the *Britannia Romana* but declined to buy them, there being "but little likelyhood of a speedy Demand by the Publick of a new Impression of it." (Horsley's children, it was said, never received any reward from the work.)[84] The antiquary Richard Gough, who took the trouble in the next year to copy out the manuscript notes in John Ward's copy, agreed. When John Hodgson went to look for Horsley's grave a hundred years later, he could find neither stone nor parish register to tell where the great scholar was buried. "What a lesson to a mind that riots on posthumous fame!"[85]

6

Meanwhile William Wotton, the great proponent of modern learning, was also retreating into obscurity, although not entirely for the same

[83]F. G. Haverfield, *Roman Occupation of Britain* (1924), p. 75, quoted in MacDonald, "John Horsley," p. 2. MacDonald adds, "if a student of Roman Britain chooses to ignore Horsley, he will do so at his peril."

[84]Dec. 8, 1763, Society of Antiquaries Minute Book 9:150–51.

[85]Hodgson, *History of Northumberland*, pp. 447n, 448. Horsley had begun to write a history of Northumberland, for which some materials survive, and he finished a thirty-page "Essay on Barrows and Other Tumuli," which remains in manuscript; see Northumberland Record Office, MS. ZAN M13/D19; MacDonald, "John Horsley," pp. 28–30.

reasons. In the first years of the new century he was busy preaching and teaching, writing history and translating it, and helping in defense of the Anglican church. In particular, he took up the cause of the bishops against the deists on the one hand and against the "high-flyers" on the other.[86] And, of course, he continued to defend the cause of modern learning with a new edition of the *Reflections*. He was still youthful, his career had been fairly launched, and he had powerful friends in church and state. One reward was to be made doctor of divinity by the Archbishop of Canterbury. Another was to be given a good living and the care of Nottingham's son. There it was that Nicolson found him in 1706, "greedily bent on the study of the Northern Languages, those being all that he's not yet perfectly acquainted with."[87] But soon the brilliant young scholar ran into trouble, and his hopes (as we shall find) were quickly shattered.

In the meanwhile, however, he had to endure some more ridicule. Swift had not sat idly by under criticism, and in 1710 he resumed the attack on Wotton and modern learning with a new version of *A Tale of a Tub*. By carefully excerpting passages from Wotton's "Defense of the Reflections" and putting them among his footnotes, he was able to transform them into a paradoxically helpful commentary. (The device was not lost on Pope, who used it later for the *Dunciad*.) Swift allowed that Wotton had given some "very fair Conjectures towards clearing up some difficult Passages," but he had overstepped (as such men usually did), pretending to point out the beauties and faults, "which is no part of their Trade." The *Tale*, Swift insisted on the other hand, had been written only for "Men of Wit and Tast."[88] The advertisement for a later edition hoped that Richard Bentley's notes for the *Tale* would also turn up. "I am told this is a Masterpiece of modern Criticism, and that this Prince of Pedants has, with a vast deal of laborious learning, shewn that he can interpret almost nine passages of Antient Authors, in a sense different from that which our Author has given them." In 1710 the printer Edmund Curll produced a key to the *Tale* further criticizing Wotton, and Swift's annotations were soon collected and printed separately with his

[86]William Wotton, *A Letter to Eusebia* (London, 1704), was aimed against John Toland; *A Defense of the Rights of the Clergy in the Christian Church Asserted* (London, 1706) and *A Second Defense* (London, 1709) were directed against Matthew Tindal. In 1711 Wotton issued two more tracts in the Convocation controversy: *The Rights of the Christian Church Adjusted* and *The Case of the Present Convocation Consider'd*. For the circumstances of the *Defense of the Rights of the Clergy*, see Wotton to Bishop of Norwich, Sept. 5, 1706, B.M. MS. Add. 29747, ff. 49–50.

[87]Nicolson to Lhwyd, May 25, 1706, Bodleian MS. Ashmole 1816, f. 549.

[88]William Wotton, "A Defence of the Reflections," in Jonathan Swift, *A Tale of a Tub* (London, 1710), pp. 15, 20.

Apology for the Tale of a Tub.[89] Wotton must have relished the chance that turned up that year to reply to Swift's *Examiner*, with a sharp little tract defending the bishops.[90] Like his earlier attack on the religious orthodoxy of the *Tale*, it could only help his chances of preferment. But there must not have seemed much point in continuing the argument about learning. "When Men are jested upon for what is it self praiseworthy," Wotton had written, "the World will do them Justice; on the other hand, if they deserve it, they ought to sit quietly under it. Our Cause therefore we shall leave to the Public very willingly."[91]

It was in that same year, however (1710), that the eccentric young antiquary Browne Willis told Thomas Hearne that Wotton "was a very debauch'd Man and that by his Folly he is like to be undone." And about that time the Archdeacon of Bedford had to intercede for Wotton with his old friend the Archbishop of Canterbury "to prevent the ruin of his family." By 1714 Wotton's other great patron, the Earl of Nottingham, was forced to replace him at Milton Keynes.[92] According to a later account:

> The Doctor's morals indeed were as bad as his Facts were excellent: having no regard to common Decency in Respect to Wine and Women, both equally his Passion: it being no unusual Sight for his Parishioners to find him drunk under a Hedge and fallen from his Horse, and to know that he was 2 or 3 nights together at Houses where he could have no other business than to defraud Mrs. Wotton of her due Benevolence. His Debts . . . grew so enormous that he was obliged to quit his preferment in Buckinghamshire and retire to the House of Mr. Clarke who had married his Daughter and was Rector of Bucksted in Sussex. . . . I have heard Mr. Browne Willis say . . . so that he had his Bottle and other Amusements among which his Books and Studies had an equal Share, he little regarded how the world went on.[93]

[89]The advertisement appeared with the *Tale* in *Miscellaneous Works Comical and Diverting* (1720), p. 293; *A Complete Key to the Tale of a Tub* (London, 1710) appears also in *Miscellaneous Works*, pp. 329–48; and for *An Apology for the Tale of a Tub with Explanatory Notes* (London, 1711), see pp. lxviii–lxx.

[90]William Wotton, *The Case of the Present Convocation Consider'd; in Answer to the Examiner's Unfair Representations of It, and Unjust Reflections upon It* (London, 1711), directed against *Examiner*, no. 22 (Dec. 28, 1710).

[91]Wotton, "Defence of the Reflections," in *Memoirs of Martinus Scriblerus*, ed. Charles Kerby-Miller (New Haven, 1950), pp. 316–17. Wotton confined his criticism there to Swift's alleged irreligion.

[92]Hearne, Sept. 26, 1711, in *Remarks and Collections*, 3:236; Archdeacon Frank to William Wake, Nov. 17, 1711, with Wake's advice to Wotton, in Norman Sykes, *William Wake*, 2 vols. (Cambridge, 1957), 1:196–99; Nottingham to Wake, July 20, 1714, Wake MSS., Christ Church, Oxford, Arch. W. Epist. 3, f. 72.

[93]William Cole, B.M. MS. Add. 5841, ff. 18–19.

Sussex proved only a temporary refuge, however, and Wotton was soon forced to flee from his debtors into Wales, where for a long time he lived incognito.

It is all the more remarkable, then, that Wotton continued his studies and services to the world of modern scholarship without slackening. He had begun life with an extraordinary education in languages and he had always understood the value of philology to history. Now he added Hebrew and Welsh with the deliberate intention of opening up new vistas on the past, and he soon commanded an astonishing proficiency in both. In December 1715 he wrote to inquire of his old friends at St. John's College: "If any Body has the curiosity to know how I spend my time, you may tell him it is in Maimonides on the Misna, and that I hope in due time *reddere Rationem Otii mei*." Some years later he was still hoping to free himself from his troubles; meanwhile, he added, "god has blessed me wonderfully in this Place." Indeed, he learned Welsh well enough to give a sermon in the language, the only Englishman (we are told) who had ever done so.[94]

Wotton's Hebrew studies may have been stimulated, as they certainly were encouraged, by an old friend, Simon Ockley, with whom he stayed in close contact. Ockley had started out at Cambridge as a precocious Orientalist, but poverty, a large family, and some sort of indiscretion, possibly like Wotton's, inhibited his career. At seventeen, in 1693, he was appointed Hebrew lecturer in his Cambridge college, and by 1702 he seemed to Hearne the most accomplished Arabist in England. "He is a man of very great Industry and ought to be incourag'd, which I do not question but he will if he lives to see Learning once more incourag'd in England, which at present it is not."[95] In 1706 he published an *Introductio ad linguas orientales* in a small edition, and two years later the first volume of his *History of the Saracens*, which eventually made his fame. He continued to work unremittingly at his subject until his early death in 1720. Friendship with Wotton probably began early; by the spring of 1715 the two were exchanging manuscripts. "How many curious things have you taught me!" Wotton wrote gratefully.[96]

[94]Wotton to Dr. Walker, Dec. 7, 1715, B.M. MS. Add. 5831, f. 124; Jacque-Georges de Chauffepié, "Wotton," in *Nouveau Dictionnaire historique et critique*, 4 vols. (Amsterdam, 1750–1756), 4:764–68, from notes supplied by William Clarke, Wotton's son-in-law. Cole quotes a letter from Wake to Browne Willis, Mar. 10, 1716: "I have lately corresponded with your Neighbor [Wotton] and am pleased with all proofs of his diligence. Could he but approve his Morals, as well as his Parts, and be as good a Man, as he is good natured, I should not know a more valuable Clergyman in England. I believe he is much better in all Respects than he has been: and yet young enough, by God's grace, to make an eminent Figure in the Church": B.M. MS. Add. 5841, ff. 18–9.

[95]Hearne, *Remarks and Collections*, 1:246.

[96]Wotton to Simon Ockley, Mar. 7, 1715, B.M. MS. Harley 6941, ff. 230–31.

In fact, Wotton was working on three projects for which he desired
Ockley's help. One was "De ratione studii theologici," which seems to
have been ready in 1716 but saw the light only after Wotton's death as
Some Thoughts Concerning a Proper Method of Studying Divinity (London,
1734). It is a characteristically helpful and impressive reading list, digested into categories. The second was an edition of two ancient Talmudic texts on the Sabbath, in Hebrew and English with a commentary.
And the last was a learned treatise "concerning the Dispersion of Peoples
and the Formation of Languages at Babel," which seems to have derived
from a difference of opinion between Wotton and a Dutch scholar from
Utrecht, Hadrianus Relandus. Apparently William Nicolson of Carlisle
had also intervened.[97]

Wotton's Talmudic pieces appeared at length in 1718 with a support-
ing letter from Ockley as *Miscellaneous Discourses Relating to the Traditions
and Uses of the Scribes and Pharisees in the Blessed Saviour Jesus Christ's
Time.* The work was dedicated to William Wake, archbishop of Canterbury. It was in two volumes with a long apologetic introduction in the
first and the two Hebrew texts and translations in the second. The immediate purpose was to throw some light on recent sabbatarian disputes.
Protestant observance depended on biblical sanction and the uses of the
early church. For Wotton the problem was essentially historical and
needed to be solved by historical scholarship. In particular, the New
Testament had to be read and interpreted like any other ancient document, with the help of collateral evidence and the method of philology.
In this case, there was the testimony of contemporary Jews to help. But
since there were some who denied the usefulness of this kind of evidence,
Wotton's first task was to plead for the value of Hebrew learning for the
purpose. Here he invokes the great English scholar John Lightfoot,
among others, and defends him against the strictures of Isaac Vossius,
who in order to uphold the authority of the Greek Septuagint had insisted that Hebrew had lapsed altogether in Hellenistic times, even
among the Jews, and could not claim to report an oral tradition. Wotton
prefers the views of Richard Simon, who in a series of influential books
that had recently resumed the Erasmian tradition of biblical criticism
"stands up for the Integrity of the Hebrew." (Among other things, Wotton offers the example of the Welsh, who had very successfully preserved
their language in the face of several foreign conquests.) He must then try
to show the fidelity and exactness of the Talmud by examining the
circumstances of its composition, which he does with some care, de-

[97]Wotton to Walker, n.d., B.M. MS. Add. 5831, f. 122; Wotton to Ockley, Oct. 3,
1713, Cambridge MS. Add. 7113, no. 33.

scribing its authorship, time, and purpose. He has to meet the argument that the Talmud appears to contradict some other early authorities, including the Jews Philo and Josephus. (And to do so he has to correct Edward Bernard, among others, who had recently published a scholarly version of Josephus.)[98] This task leads Wotton to distinguish the Mishnah, or original body of law as it existed in Christ's time, from the Gemara, or later commentary of the rabbis, which carries for him less force. Even so, Wotton recognizes some value in it and also the peculiar authority of Maimonides as a commentator, although his work was written still later.

In almost all these matters he had the support of Ockley, who wrote him an obliging letter that Wotton affixed to his introduction. The Jews, according to Ockley, understand the New Testament better than most Christians. "They are largely acquainted with all the Forms of Speech, and all the Allusions, which (because they occur but rarely) are obscure to us, tho' in common use, and very familiar to them." It would be absurd to deny their value.[99]

It appears that the book was seen through the press by David Wilkins, a German scholar then attending the archbishop and a friend of William Nicolson's. (He was competent, we are told, in Hebrew, Arabic, Chaldaic, Coptic, Armenian, and Anglo-Saxon!)[100] The printer was satisfied with five hundred copies and so was Wotton, or so he told Ockley. "The Truth of it is, it is but an out-of-the-way Subject." At least the printer had done a good job, using types from Holland, "and I believe you will think the Hebrew is tolerably correct." He had hoped that the variety and novelty of the work would gain it acceptance, "notwithstanding any Prejudices against the Author." "I do not know whether the Jews will thank me," he wrote to Ockley in 1718, "but I have taken a pretty deal of Pains to reserve them from the Charge of Stupidity and Inconsistency under which they have laboured." In the end, Wotton was not unhappy with the book's reception, though it never found many readers.[101] Somehow or other that seemed to be the fate of most modern scholarship.

[98]Josephus, *Antiquitatum Judaicarum*, ed. Edward Bernard (Oxford, 1700), It was published after Bernard's death, unfinished.

[99]Ockley to Wotton, Mar. 15, 1717, following p. li of Introduction to William Wotton, *Miscellaneous Discourses Relating to the Traditions and Uses of the Scribes and Pharisees in the Blessed Saviour Jesus Christ's Time* (London, 1718).

[100]"A width of erudition purchased by a certain want of accuracy": *Dictionary of National Biography*. David Wilkins was already working on his edition of the Saxon laws; for which see his correspondence with Nicolson, in *Letters to and from Nicolson*.

[101]Wotton to Ockley, n.d. (1718) and July 19, 1720, Cambridge MS. Add. 7113, nos. 45 and 48; Wotton to Walker, May 31, 1716, B.M. MS. Add. 5831, ff. 125–26.

7

It may have been his work in Hebrew that got Wotton to thinking about the original languages. A few years earlier, however, he had been asked by his friend John Chamberlayne to help him to secure some materials for a collection of the Lord's Prayer in all the known languages, and that apparently was the immediate occasion.[102] Chamberlayne had been working away since 1710 at least on his project, enlisting the help of Thoresby and Nicolson among many others, and when his work finally appeared in Amsterdam in 1715, it had an apologetic preface by Nicolson that was vigorously applauded by Hickes.[103] A fuller English version appeared only much later, in 1730. By 1713 anyway, Wotton had formulated his views on the matter, and they saw the light in Chamberlayne's Latin edition.[104] In a long letter to Ockley that year Wotton argued that the only way to account for the differences among languages was to accept the biblical account that God had miraculously created several new tongues at Babel that were unknown before. That there were fundamental differences between Hebrew and Greek, especially in their grammars but also in the formulation of nouns and verbs, he was confident. One had only to compare the Greek of Homer and the Latin before Plautus with the Hebrew of the Mishnah to see them. Since there was but one original language, the only way to explain these alterations in a world just 6,000 years old was by a miracle. If this could be proved, Wotton thought it would be a useful service to religion.[105]

The main question that Wotton intended to solve was whether God had created new languages at Babel by a miracle or whether he had merely forced it inhabitants into a quarrel, leaving the tower unfinished and the languages to develop afterward. In other words, Wotton was trying to interpret the meaning of a biblical passage (Gen. 11:1–9) using purely historical means. This meant that he must review all that was then known about the development and alteration of the world's languages in the hope that this would throw light on the problem. What he does essentially is to divide the languages into basic sets, Eastern and Western,

---

[102]Wotton to John Anstis, July 18, 1710, Trinity College, Cambridge, MS. 665.

[103]For Hickes's praise, see his note in Chamberlayne to Nicolson, May 1, 1712, in *Letters to and from Nicolson*, 2:413–15. David Wilkins translated Nicolson's English for the occasion: ibid., pp. 426–29. For Thoresby, see D. H. Atkinson, *Ralph Thoresby, the Topographer: His Town and Times*, 2 vols. (Leeds, 1885, 1887), 2:245.

[104]*Oratio Domenica in diversas omnium fere gentium linguae versa . . . una cum dissertationibus nonnullis de linguarum origine*, ed. J. Chamberlayne (Amsterdam, 1715); William Wotton, *A Discourse Concerning the Confusion of Languages at Babel* (London, 1730). The latter is dedicated to Chamberlayne and signed Nov. 25, 1713. The manuscript life of Wotton says the Latin version was printed without Wotton's notice and "barbarously translated": B.M. MS. Add. 4224, p. 165. I have not been able to compare the two.

[105]Wotton to Ockley, Cambridge MS. Add 7113, no. 33.

to show that most of the modern tongues are related, but that some are divided in essential ways that cannot be merely derivative. There was simply not enough time in history to allow for such differences to have developed naturally, since Babel was built at the latest 1,757 years after the Creation, and the age of the world was about 6,000 years altogether. (The analogue with natural history, which was just then struggling toward the same formulations and under the same biblical-temporal constraints, is clear.)[106] There was hardly enough time even for common changes. "To form Dialects is a Work of Ages, even now when Trade and Business, and War have introduced greater Correspondences."[107] Wotton's correspondent Relandus was wrong then to find a basic (i.e., formal) similarity between Greek and Hebrew. Wotton traces the "Japhetic" line from Japheth, the son of Noah, through Greek to Gothic and Latin, but shows that Hebrew, like Finnish, "Sclavonic," and Hungarian, have no real affinity to it. He omits the American languages, Chinese, and others far afield, but he uses Hickes's description of the Teutonic languages and Lhwyd's "comparative etymology" for the various British tongues to show their family relationships.[108] He does not believe that the first language was Hebrew; but rather that it too was a product of the miraculous event. How many of these fundamental original tongues were then created he does not pretend to know.

Wotton must have taken particular satisfaction in the thought that he was combining his philological passion with his duties as a churchman and theologian, his Christian and his classical learning.[109] Needless to say, this too was controversial ground, and modern philology had had to quarrel with traditional theology ever since Lorenzo Valla and Erasmus began to employ it on the text of Scripture. Lately Spinoza and Father Richard Simon had stirred a hornet's nest of opposition with their attempts to explain the Bible as a written historical document, subject to some of the same investigations as classical literature. When the Christ Church wits assaulted Bentley for his exposure of Phalaris, they saw the danger here too. "Does he not know Whose this Sort of Proof is," they asked, "and to what ill Purposes it has been employed?"

It is famous for being made use of by Spinoza, and others, to ruine the Authority of Moses's Writings; which they would prove not to be his

[106]See Levine, *Dr. Woodward's Shield*, chaps. 2–4.

[107]Wotton, *Discourse Concerning the Confusion of Languages*, p. 38.

[108]Wotton conceded his special indebtedness to Stiernhielmius (Georg Stjernhjelm), *Discourse on the Origin and Progress of Tongues*, prefixed to Junius's edition of the Gothic Gospels (1671), a favorite text for the Saxonists. Stiernhielmius (p. 28) could find no way of reconciling the American Indian languages with those of Noah.

[109]Wotton applauded the examples of Eusebius and St. Augustine to that effect in *Some Thoughts Concerning a Proper Method of Studying Divinity* (London, 1734), p. 12.

(just as our Chronologer does here) from Places being mention'd in 'em, more Modern than He. Ought the Dr. in a Doubting Age to have employ'd such an Argument, without the utmost Caution and Guard? . . . Is he so Eager to prove Phalaris Spurious, that he cares not whether the Authority of the Sacred Writings sink with him?[110]

Wotton repeated the Erasmian answer. Philology could be employed to explain and restore the true sense of Scripture and thus to reinforce Christian conviction. He argued that the theological learning of the moderns was undoubtedly superior to that of the fathers, precisely because it employed modern scholarship to understand the meaning of the Bible. Scarcely any one of the fathers had understood Hebrew, much less Syriac, Chaldee, Samaritan, and Arabic, "not to mention the Writings of the Rabbins and Talmudists, to which the Ancients were utter Strangers." Nor had they been able to unravel the chronology of the Old Testament, like Ussher and Marsham; the meaning of the ceremonial law, like Spenser; or the geography and natural history, like Bochart. Even the New Testament, which might seem more accessible, required looking into the manners and fashions of that age and time, which the later fathers had already lost.[111] Modern theology was therefore dependent to a large extent on modern philology, and both were superior to anything known in antiquity. Now Wotton was able to offer a concrete demonstration of this conviction just as indeed his old friend Richard Bentley was doing in his own way, at about this same time, with his brilliant scholarly demolition of the deist Anthony Collins.[112]

Yet Wotton knew well enough that modern scholarship was being questioned as much for its irrelevancies as for its dangers to modern life, and so he begins his discourse on Babel with some "melancholy reflections" about a world that was likely to remain indifferent to its claims. The trouble was that "the Bulk of Men . . . measure learning by the immediate and visible Utility which it brings along with it." The chronologer takes infinite pains to fix the era of a Syrian city or a kingdom in Thrace or Pontus, "and when he has done, scarce a hundred men perhaps in Europe will read what he has writ." Geographers labor to discover the situation of an ancient city or country, though barely mentioned by a classical author,

[110]Charles Boyle, *Dr. Bentley's Dissertations . . . Examin'd* (London, 1698), pp. 120–21.
[111]William Wotton, *Reflections upon Ancient and Modern Learning*, 3d ed. (London, 1705), pp. 363–68.
[112]Richard Bentley, *Remarks upon a Late Discourse of Free-Thinking* (London, 1713).

and when he has done it, how few care whether there was ever such a city, or such an Author that mentions it? . . . And the Critic, because he sets up for a better Judgment, or at least for using it to better Purpose than other Men, in determining the true Reading, or explaining the Difficulties which are to be met with in any Passage of an ancient Author, must expect to be censured (if not derided) by the Generality of his Readers, who are invariably angry that he should pretend to see farther than themselves in the Sense and Elegancy of the Books they read.

To these men Wotton replied forthrightly that he was willing to pledge himself to one rule only: "that Truth, as such, without any View to the immediate Application, is worth knowing."[113]

8

Indeed, Wotton kept hard at work, despite his isolation in Wales, his burden of debt, and increasing gout. For his old friend Browne Willis and his book on the "mitred abbeys" he wrote two surveys of Welsh cathedrals, St. David's (1717) and Llandaff (1719).[114] For his new friend David Wilkins, who was planning to complete the edition of the Saxon laws first broached by Gibson and attempted by William Elstob, Wotton hoped to add a companion volume on the old Welsh laws. "Now I have got quit of my Talmudic Doctors," he wrote to Ockley in 1717, "I am put upon by a very great man who has a right to dispose of my Time, to prepare an Edition of the great Welsh Lawgiver Howell Dha's Laws."[115] (According to his son-in-law, Wotton had first been exhorted to the task by William Wake.)[116] Wilkins's book was finished in 1720, but Wotton

---

[113]Wotton, *Discourse Concerning the Confusion of Languages*, pp. 2–4.

[114]Browne Willis, *A History of the Mitred Parliamentary Abbeys and Conventional Cathedral Chapters*, 2 vols. (London, 1718, 1719). See the letters from Wotton to Willis sending information and correcting proofs (1716–1717), in Bodleian MSS. Willis 38 and 42. Willis acknowledged the help in a note: "Letters from Will. Wotton BD who has absconded himself out of Bucks and lived in Wales at Carmarthen with Mr. Lord and took the name of Dr. Edwards"; see George G. Francis, "On the Proposed Removal of the See of Llandaff in 1717–18," *Archaeologia Cambrensis* 1 (1846): 269. Wotton later sent Willis an account of his old parish in 1723 and in return received a list of its rectors; see B.M. MS. Add. 5836, ff. 121–25. For Willis, see J. G. Jenkins, *The Dragon of Whaddon: The Life and Work of Browne Willis* (High Wycombe, 1953).

[115]Wotton to Ockley, July 22, 1717, Cambridge MS. Add. 7113, no. 41. Wotton asked if he might borrow a half-dozen manuscripts from Oxford on security.

[116]He was already gathering material in 1713 or 1714; see Maurice Johnson to William Bowyer, June 30, 1744, in *Bibliotheca Topographica Britannica*, vol. 3 (London, 1790), pp. 96–97.

found the work harder than he had anticipated. It was not easy to recover the meaning of old legal terms and phrases that had lapsed for centuries. "My Welsh Laws go on apace, but it proves another Manner of Work than I at first imagined. The Ground which I cultivate proves to be entirely new. The Helps that I have had (and I have had what the Nation affords) are in Comparison very little." He hoped his shattered health would let him finish. "Dr. Wotton, at Carmarthen," Wilkins was able to report to Nicolson, "goes on bravely with his Hoel Ddha; and hopes to be able to print Proposals and a Specimen, in four months time. The poor man has sadly been afflicted with gout the greatest part of last Summer, which has hindered him in prosecuting his noble design with that usual vigour which is natural to him."[117]

Alas, it was not to be. When Wotton died in 1727 the work was still not done. Fortunately, the Welsh antiquary Moses Williams, who had worked for Edward Lhwyd, had been asked by Wotton to help him and was left to ready the manuscript for publication. The *Leges Wallicae* of Hywel Dha appeared finally in the name of Wotton's son-in-law, William Clarke, in 1730, with Welsh and Latin texts, commentary, an appendix of original charters, a glossarium, and an index.[118] It was a fitting last contribution to the modern learning to which Wotton had pledged his life.

Thomas Hearne had never liked Wotton, no doubt for his politics as much as anything else. In March 1727 he wrote his epitaph. "He was a man of great natural parts, and might have proved a great man, had he stuck to any particular sort of Learning. But being of a rambling genius, he dealt in many things, and in his latter time applied himself to the Brittish Language, and got a great deal of knowledge of it." His son-in-law appreciated him better. "His knowledge (to use an Expression of one of his Patrons in giving the Character of another) was all in ready cash, which he was able to produce at Sight upon any Question; his great Memory made him have little occasion for these resources, which are so necessary to those whose treasures of learning often lye by them as a dead

---

[117]Wotton to Walker, Feb. 27, 1721, Cambridge MS. Add. 5831, ff. 123–24; Wilkins to Nicolson, Dec. 24, 1720, in *Letters to and from Nicolson*, pp. 532–35. Wotton reports his circumstances to Willis in Bodleian MS. Willis 38, ff. 353–55, 367–69 and 42, f. 210.

[118]William Clarke, *Cyfreithjeu Hywel Dda . . . or Leges Wallicae Ecclesiasticae e Civiles Hoeli Boni* (London, 1730). It includes a long list of subscribes, a preface by Clarke, and a notice of the many manuscripts employed. Hywel Dda was a tenth-century Welsh king under whom the customary laws were collected and copied. For a modern version, see *The Laws of Hywel Dda*, ed. Melville Richards (Liverpool, 1954). Humphrey Wanley noted that Moses Williams had come to borrow some manuscripts for Wotton's book, June 12, 1722: *The Diary of Humfrey Wanley, 1715–1726*, ed. Cyril E. Wright (London, 1966), p. 150; his assistance in copying manuscripts is acknowledged in the life of Wotton by Birch, B.M. MS. Add. 4224, p. 163. Wotton also received help from W. Foulkes; see his letter to Willis, April 18, 1719, Bodleian MS. Willis 42, f. 170.

stock. . . . But above all he had great Humanity and Friendliness of Temper." "His Time and Abilities," he concluded, "were at the service of any Person who was making Advances in Modern Learning."[119] If his fame and his works were soon forgotten, perhaps Wotton would have accepted that as the fate of all true scholarship, destined always to be subsumed and replaced by something better.

[119]Hearne, Mar. 14, 1727, in *Remarks and Collections*, 9:286; "Life of Wotton," B.M. MS. Add. 4224, pp. 166–67. Clarke points out that he had no narrow party spirit, and was "as zealous in recommending Hickes's great work, as if it had been his own."

Conclusion

Despite the best efforts of both sides, the battle of the books ended in a draw. The ancients had given some ground, it is true, particularly in the sciences and philosophy, but they had held fast to literature and the arts. The great struggle over history had left the field divided, the ancients still throughly in command of narrative, but the moderns having won the advantage in philology and antiquities. Those who were inclined to resolve the differences found it still hard to join the two parties in a common endeavor. This fundamental fissure in Augustan culture remained pretty much constant for the rest of the century; even when the battle of the books began to recede in memory, the issues that it had raised refused to disappear or find an easy resolution.

It might be possible to trace the echoes of this conflict throughout the century, but it would not be easy and it would not advance our story very far. The trouble was that there was little to add to the arguments on either side. Of course scientific and material advancement went on apace, opening many new vistas to modernity, and the idea of progress began to take firm hold, though it was usually confined to those areas where reason and experiment reigned. The French, as often, led the way, but even Fontenelle's heir, Turgot, who was proud to proclaim the "successive advances of the human mind," exempted poetry, painting, and music from the march of progress. And Voltaire, who was actually drawn into the battle of the books when he visited England (1726–1729), came away with much the same view.[1] It was left to the apocalyptic visions of the French Revolution, to the aristocratic Condorcet awaiting the guillotine, to imagine the perfectibility of all nature and culture in a

---

[1] *Turgot on Progress, Sociology and Economics*, ed. and trans. Ronald J. Meek (Cambridge, 1973), p. 52; for Voltaire and the quarrel, see my *Humanism and History* (Ithaca, N.Y., 1987), 179–80.

heavenly city on earth. For the while, even the most complacent and optimistic of Europeans continued to look back upon the golden age of antiquity for their models of polite culture, while they took much pride in modern science and full advantage of modern comfort.

Meanwhile modern scholarship continued to threaten to undermine the whole neoclassical edifice that it had been invented to serve, but each time it faltered before the pressure of an unreconstructed *ancienneté*. For a while it appeared that the Gothic revival in England might furnish the coup de grace to the unique authority of Greece and Rome, but it too was confined and restricted, sometimes assimilated, by the ancients long before it had run its eighteenth-century course.[2] The Greek revival caused a temporary rift in the classical ranks and a brief battle between Greece and Rome, but hardly to the advantage of modernity. For the rhetoricians and essayists of the late eighteenth century, for popular writers such as Hugh Blair and Vicesimus Knox, the commonplaces of the battle of the books kept all their original meaning and were easily accepted by their audience.[3] The age of Johnson was in this respect an easy successor to the age of Pope.

Of course, the idea of accommodation remained alive too. The possibility of joining the best in ancient culture with the best in modern life had always appealed to some, not least to William Wotton, who usually insisted that he had taken a middle ground. Perhaps the best example of a later attempt at rapprochement was the life and work of Edward Gibbon. Somehow Gibbon managed to achieve the unlikely conjuncture of a scholarly career and the life of a gentleman, and he always resisted the conventional divorce between the two.[4] Admittedly it was not easy, and it could be argued that the odd little man with the peculiar voice and embarrassing goiter, the captain who never saw war, and the politician who had not once dared to raise his voice in Parliament was something of a failure in that polite world to which he aspired. Moreover, Gibbon himself admitted to something less than a true commitment to the activities of philological and antiquarian scholarship, which he alternately played at and borrowed from, without ever seriously undertaking for himself. Yet Gibbon honestly appreciated both of these normally antithetical worlds and deliberately tried to copy their achievements in the great work that made his name.

[2]See my chapter "Eighteenth-Century History Historicism and the First Gothic Revival," in *Humanism and History*, pp. 190–213.

[3]See Hugh Blair, *Lectures on Rhetoric and Belles Lettres*, 2 vols. (London, 1783) (ten English editions were issued by 1806, eight American editions by 1819, and many afterward); and Vicesimus Knox, *Essays Moral and Literary*, 2 vols. (London, 1782), esp. vol. 1, nos. 3, 47, 73–74; vol. 2, nos. 169, 174 (there was a seventeenth edition in 1815).

[4]For what follows see my chapter "Edward Gibbon and the Quarrel between the Ancients and the Moderns," in *Humanism and History*, pp. 178–189.

The *Decline and Fall of the Roman Empire* can perhaps best be understood as a self-conscious effort to combine the narrative of classical rhetoric with the scholarship of classical erudition for a subject—the Middle Ages—that was understood to bridge (and thus to explain) the great gap between antiquity and modernity. Gibbon knew and appreciated Wotton's work, not only the *Reflections on Ancient and Modern Learning* but the *History of Rome*, which helped to serve him as a model. He was well read in the French *querelle*, and his first work (in French) was an effort from the vantage point of literature to preserve the value of philology. He had studied with the *érudits* in Paris and laboriously mastered for himself much of the vast corpus of antiquarian learning that had accumulated over the centuries. In time he created an English style that was sui generis yet deliberately modeled on the classics, which were always his guide in matters of expression. He tried even to turn his learned footnotes into literature. And of course he was successful; his work was read at once and for a long time by both the scholars and the gentlemen of Europe and America.

The time was ripe for reconciliation but the moment was not to last. Others, it is true, were attempting something of the same thing, some in Gibbon's own circle, such as Thomas Warton for the history of English literature and Charles Burney for the history of music. But an ultimate reconciliation between ancients and moderns was impossible, and for two reasons. On the one hand, the march of scholarly progress was destined to resume, and with it the increasing demands of a specialist historiography. Already in Germany there were sounds of dissent and Gibbon's work was found wanting in method. After all, he had written his history entirely within the walls of his own library![5] On the other hand, Gibbon's "philosophical" point of view, so resolutely centered on the values of his own time and place—which he took unreservedly to be universal—was also beginning to seem old-fashioned. Again in Germany the dissenting voice of historicism was beginning to be heard: each historical culture was to be seen somehow individually and from its own perspective, and its values were to be accepted as relative. There was of course much life still left in the classics, but the new worlds that were being discovered before Greece and after Rome, as well as around the globe, were undoing that happy confidence in antiquity which the ancients had taught Europe from the beginning of the Italian Renaissance. No longer could the old authors and especially the old histories be allowed to guide the present by the immediate example of the past; the

---

[5]See *Göttingische gelehrte Anzeigen* (1788), cited in Arnaldo Momigliano, "Gibbon's Contribution to Historical Method," in his *Studies in Historiography* (New York, 1966), p. 40; Geoffrey Keynes, *The Library of Edward Gibbon*, 2d ed. (n.p., 1980).

classics were turning academic and history was becoming philosophical. In short, the arguments of both the ancients and the moderns were finally transformed in such a way that the old quarrel disappeared and with it those few heroic attempts at reconciliation that had tried to preserve the values and methods of both sides. But that, needless to say, is another story, perhaps for another time.

Index

Library of Congress Cataloging-in-Publication Data

Levine, Joseph M.
    The battle of the books : history and literature in the Augustan
Age / Joseph M. Levine.
        p.   cm.
    Includes bibliographical references and index.
    ISBN 0-8014-2537-9 (alk. paper)
    1. Great Britain—Intellectual life—18th century.   2. Ancients
and moderns, Quarrel of.   3. Historiography—Great Britain—
History—18th century.   4. English literature—18th century—
History and criticism.   5. Classical literature—History and
criticism—Theory, etc.   6. Classical literature—Appreciation—
Great Britain.   7. Criticism—Great Britain—History—18th century.
8. Literature, Comparative—Classical and modern.   9. Literature,
Comparative—Modern and classical.   10. Classicism—Great Britain.
I. Title.
DA485.L48   1991
907'.2042—dc20   90-55735